FAITHF

THE STORY OF THE DURHAM LIGHT INFANTRY

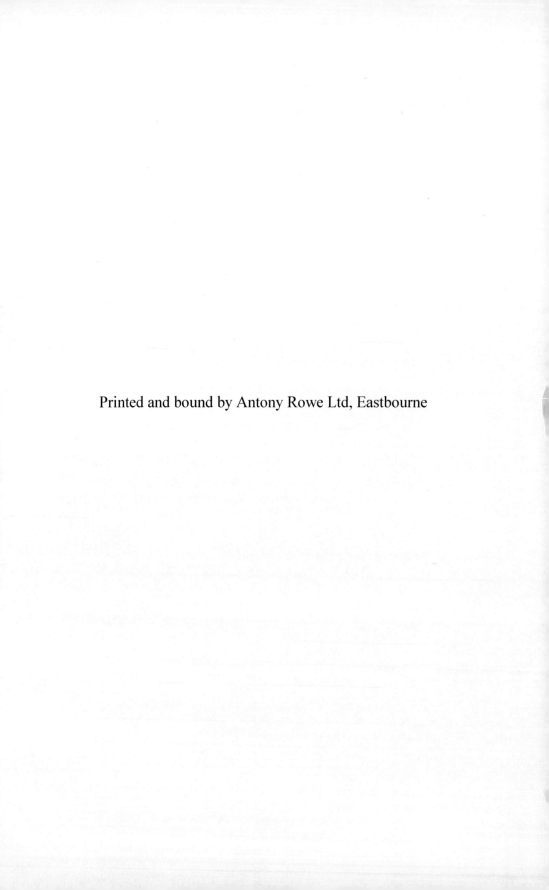

Printed and bound by Antony Rowe Ltd, Eastbourne

ACKNOWLEDGMENTS

I wish first to record my indebtedness to those who have already written of the Regiment. There was never any intention on my part to *supersede* earlier regimental and battalion histories, and indeed it was impossible, even in the generous space I was allowed, to do more than re-present and bring together the two hundred years of the Regiment's past. Those readers who need further detail may rely implicitly upon the facts given in: Colonel the Hon. W. L. Vane's *Durham Light Infantry* (1914); Captain Wilfrid Miles's *Durham Forces in the Field* (1914-1918), 1920; Major A. L. Raimes's History of the 5th Battalion (1931); Major E. H. Veitch's of the 8th (1926); Captain R. B. Ainsworth's of the 6th (1915-1918), 1919; Colonel W. I. Watson's *Short History of the 6th* (1939); Lieut.-Col. W. D. Lowe's *War History of the 18th (S) Battalion* 1920; Major L. E. Stringer's *History of the 16th Battalion* (1940-1946), 1946; P. J. Lewis and I. R. English's *History of the 8th Battalion* (1939-1945); and Mr David Rissik's *The D.L.I. at War*, 1952.

I should like to thank also all those who have so uncomplainingly supplied me with information and sometimes hospitality, and those whom I have plagued with questions and correspondence and in other ways: Lieut.-Col. R. J. Appleby, M.B.E., Mr C. T. Atkinson, Lieut.-Col. R. G. Atkinson, O.B.E., M.C., the Rt. Hon. Lord Barnard, C.M.G., O.B.E., M.C., T.D., Mr Samuel Bastow, Lieut.-Col. C. R. Battiscombe, Major-General Geoffrey Brooke, C.B., D.S.O., M.C., the late Brigadier H. Bullock, C.I.E., O.B.E., the late Colonel Sir Patrick Cadell, C.S.I., C.I.E., V.D., Brigadier J. Sorel Cameron, C.B.E., D.S.O., A.D.C., Lieut.-Col. R. B. Crosse, Mr J. J. A. Dale, Major N. P. Dawnay, M.A., Professor Alfiero Di Mambro of Castelforte, Mr Maurice Donovan, Sir John Ferguson, C.B.E., D.L., Mrs D. G. Finch Hatton, Mr H. R. Fisher, Major A. F. Flatow, Major L. L. Fleming,

M.B.E., M.C., Brigadier J. M. Hanmer, D.S.O., O.B.E., Mr F. J. Hills, I.S.M., the late Lieut.-Col. A. Howe, Brigadier P. J. Jeffreys, D.S.O., O.B.E., Mrs Gordon Jones, Mrs A. R. Laughton, the Trustees of the Linlithgow Trust, Mr J. Littlefair, Lieut.-Col. W. H. Lowe, O.B.E., D.L., Brigadier E. H. L. Lysaght-Griffin, C.B.E., D.S.O., Lieut.-Col. H. McBain, O.B.E., M.C., Herr Hans Mahrenholtz, of Hannover-Kirchrode, Colonel C. L. Matthews, D.S.O., the late Captain Wilfrid Miles, Mrs H. H. S. Morant, Lieut.-Col. H. B. Morkill, Mrs Dorothy M. Newson, Lieut.-Col. H. K. Percy-Smith, Herr Dr. J. Plath, of the Niedersächsisches Heimatmuseum, Miss C. M. M. Poland, Mrs F. A. Pumphrey, Dr William Rankin, M.B., F.R.F.P.S.G., Major-General A. H. G. Ricketts, C.B.E., D.S.O., Mr J. B. Rosher, D.S.O., M.C., M.A., LL.B., Mr Leonard Russell, Sir Malcolm Sargent, Brigadier J. Stephenson, O.B.E. and the staff of the Royal United Service Institution, Major L. E. Stringer, T.D., J.P., Mr S. C. Sutton, C.B.E., Colonel Hugh L. Swinburne, T.D., D.L., J.P., the late Lady Thompson, Mr G. C. Tompson, Lieut.-Col. R. V. Turner, D.S.O., Major G. Tylden, E.D., Mr W.M.F. Vane, T.D., M.P., Brigadier J. H. Whalley-Kelly, C.B.E., and my family: Mr and Mrs J. A. Tatam, Miss P. M. Ward, Mr and Mrs S. B. Ward, and my wife, Hilary.

From the Regiment I have received not only a complete latitude but consistent help and encouragement, and I should like to thank particularly those members of it with whom my correspondence by now fills a bulky file: the Colonel, General Sir Nigel Poett, K.C.B., D.S.O., the Deputy Colonel, Brigadier P. H. M. May, D.S.O., O.B.E., M.C., Major E. Browne, M.B.E., Colonel W. I. Watson, T.D., D.L., and Colonel F. H. Simpson.

Lastly, I wish to acknowledge my appreciation of the cordial relationship I have had with those who have so ably conducted the production of the History: Mr C. D. Hamilton, D.S.O., Mr J. C. Baines, and Mr Nicolas Bentley; and with Mr George Mansell, who drew the sketch-maps.

S.G.P.W.

Kensington,
October, 1962

CONTENTS

MAPS

FOREWORD

by General Sir Nigel Poett, K.C.B., D.S.O.
Colonel of the Regiment

This is the story of the first two hundred years of The Durham Light Infantry.

These two hundred years, 1758 to 1958, take in Wellington's Peninsula campaign, the Crimean War, the campaigns in Persia, in New Zealand and in South Africa, and the two Great Wars of our own century. The story traces the life of the soldier in the Regiment and his deeds throughout this fascinating period of social revolution in the military sciences. This is a story of the service which has brought fame to the Durham Light Infantry and honour to the whole County of Durham.

The story of our Regiment has been brilliantly and excitingly told by Mr S. G. P. Ward, a distinguished historian who had no previous connection with the Regiment or the County. He was able to delve into our past from an independent angle, looking for the truth and unrestricted by sentiment. We are proud of the story that has emerged, and we are grateful to him for the way in which he has brought our past to life.

The story shows how the Regiment has evolved in character, and even in name, since Colonel John Lambton of Durham raised it in 1758. During those years the Regiment thrived under the changes imposed on it and from the influx of new blood which the 106th Bombay Light Infantry brought to it. In going forward the Regiment became more and more an integral part of County Durham. Looking ahead, the tempo and the nature of our evolution to keep pace with the world changes of tomorrow will surely be even greater. As the Regiment of County Durham, and with the loyal and affectionate support we have throughout the County, we can be assured of continuing to contribute our full share to the Army and to the future.

Readers of these pages will sense the links we have with County Durham. Few families of the County were not represented in the ranks of our many battalions during the wars of this century. Thus the people of Durham will share with us soldiers the pride in the achievements of our Regiment. It is the people of County Durham who have made the story of The Durham Light Infantry.

Nigel Poett

CHAPTER I

AN INTRODUCTION TO THE HISTORY
OF THE REGIMENT

THREE kinds of soldier have combined to make the Durham Light Infantry what it is: the militiaman, the volunteer and the professional soldier. They differ widely in origin and history. The militiaman and the volunteer have always come from County Durham. The professional soldier, however, has only recently come to have any but a nominal connection with it. Indeed, when the standing army was small and the prejudice against it strong, it was idle to expect a single county to maintain a regiment consistently for any length of time. It is only by a series of chances that the 68th has become identified with the County, and the peculiar history of the professional soldier needs explanation before anything further is said.

I. Neither society nor the constitution in this country has readily assimilated the notion of a mercenary army in its midst. In Prussia, until 1914, it could almost be said society was centred upon the army; in France, from Louis XIV onwards the army enjoyed such a position in society that a Dreyfus affair could start a revolution in social and political loyalties that has hardly even now subsided; and in the old Austrian Empire it was the army that latterly gave cohesion to the whole unwieldy structure. Here, on the other hand, though we had had a professional army for as long as the others, it enjoyed for generations a curious outpost position, hedged about with checks and counterchecks, its needs attended to by a multitude of small government offices, itself purposely deprived of and diffident of assuming any corporate part in society. "It is," said the Duke of Wellington in 1829, "an exotic in England, unknown to the old constitution of the country."

Why? Because within itself it had its own, as it were, masonic observances drawn, as modern gypsies' are, from an international fund of experience. The Oxford lad who joined the 68th on the first day of its existence found himself, as we shall see, in a community with customs utterly strange to him. Moreover, it exacts utter obedience from its members, and consequently rouses the jealousy of a people that are traditionally argumentative, even turbulent. It is cut off from society. Yet it is not out of sight. There were few large barracks in England until early in the last century, and soldiers were quartered upon innkeepers. There was less formality between soldiers on duty and the populace—Boswell speaks of conversing with a sentry at the Horse Guards—and many soldiers eked out their pay with tradesmen's work. But there were far fewer soldiers to be seen: who will know the 68th is at Newcastle when there are only six or eight men in each company? And when the magistrates have it moved out at election times?

Officers perhaps make themselves more felt: some are in Parliament, many have connections with the great in the land. But till late in the eighteenth century all officers off duty are quite naturally addressed as "Mr." and it is rare to find soldiers occupying a seat on the local bench until after the Napoleonic Wars, or being considered qualified for one by virtue of their military rank.

The man who enlisted in the line was done for. Of this there is clear evidence from the end of Queen Anne's wars to the Boer War. "Never despise the soldier lad though his station be but low." Perhaps it is the inherent idleness in the military life that sticks in the civil gullet: Dryden's "mouths without hands, maintained at vast expense: in peace a charge, in war a weak defence". Perhaps it is the soldier's brutish habits, which so offended moralists like Hogarth— his "March to Finchley"—and the Puritan element in the national character. It was this sort of sentiment that lay behind the clause embodied in the Petition of Right (1628) which forbade the billeting of soldiers in private houses, and it was similar sentiments, harboured in the more sensitive and highly tempered breasts of New England and ignored, that touched off the riots in Boston, and contributed to the American Rebellion. Frank Richards, who enlisted in the Royal Welch Fusiliers in 1901, says that among the miners and tin-plate workers of Blaina "it was commonly believed that any young man who joined the army did so either because he was too lazy to work or else because he had got a girl in the family way. Hardly anybody had a good word for a soldier, and mothers taught their daughters to beware of them."[1] At much the same time soldiers were not admitted to theatres and music halls. Of course, in moments of popular enthu-

[1] Private Frank Richards, *Old-Soldier Sahib* (Faber, 1936), p. 19.

siasm and war the sentiment changes and then the theme is "We are the boys that fears no noise when the thundering cannons roar," and "Soldiers of the Queen". But generally speaking the red coat was a stigma rather than a recommendation.

There was certainly, and perhaps still is, a latent mistrust of the army as a body. Colonel Blimp is as much a figure of fun as an expression of the distaste, even apprehension, with which military officers as a body are regarded in certain quarters. To some extent it is a legacy of the Civil Wars and the military government of the Protectorate. It also owes its origin to the use of the army as police until the 1830s and 1840s and even later. In recent years its employment in this manner at home has not been frequent; but throughout its history this aspect of the professional army has been looked upon with suspicion, while its obvious function, the defence of the realm against the foreigner, has ever been treated with proper respect.

One result of the prejudice has been that, at any rate since the mid-eighteenth century, the soldier's pay was kept at the lowest level. The pay of the New Model Army, when they got it, was good, but only seldom until fairly recent years has army pay kept pace with the rise of wages in other trades. This, by its attracting a large proportion of "hard cases" into the ranks, has operated to emphasize and prolong the prejudice.

Bad pay, however, need not of itself discourage a man of spirit, and in times of stress it never has. As with men so with officers, and it is a singular fact that at no period have there been wanting men willing to come forward to take commissions. The whole system of Purchase, which survived until 1871, depended, ultimately, upon the existence of a demand for commissions in excess of the vacancies. The lowness of the pay was not of itself a consideration to such men, nor has it deterred men of means to whom the pay was no consideration at all from offering themselves. In certain regiments at different times it was even essential for an officer to possess an independent income. Such a situation is exceptional, but it is broadly true to say that, though the regimental officer's pay has been enough for him to live on, the pay has not been the principal attraction. The very fact that the pay was low kept away the pure mercenary and permitted, if it did not encourage, the entry of men belonging to or closely connected with the property-owning classes. Purchase, which involved laying hands on a fairly substantial capital sum, reinforced the connection established.

The nation had thus every reason to be satisfied with the results of its parsimony. It never cared for Cromwell's "plain russet-coated captain" once the war was over and he became the heavy-handed instrument of the Parliamentary tyranny; and it sent home Dutch William's Blue Guards. Through a combination of circumstances for which it was only partly responsible, it possessed an army officered by men who largely financed their own pensions by means of the purchase system, who, for the same reason, were pledged to good conduct, and were identifiable with those whose property gave them an interest in the welfare of the country. Purchase was as much a national safeguard as an officer's vested interest. It was not abolished until both were satisfied it could be safely abandoned.

This peculiar history of the mercenary soldier in this country has led to the peculiar terms on which the constitution and society will tolerate him. No one will be compelled to join the army. It must be maintained financially year by year, and replenished and recruited as best it may be. It is no good expecting localities habitually to sustain any part of it. Regiments must find their officers and recruits wherever they show themselves. Their success is mainly their own concern, and when they are stationed at home their men tend to come from wherever they rest. As it moves from one locality to another so it takes on the colour of the station in which it is quartered. When the 68th is in the Midlands it is a Midland regiment; when it has been in Ireland some time it is predominantly Irish.

It is, it must be repeated, only by a series of historical chances that the 68th, which once and once only received a fair proportion of Durham men in its ranks, should have become the regiment of the County. The first was the appointment as its first colonel of John Lambton, a member of an old and prominent family of the County. The second was the fact of Lambton's surviving until 1782, the year in which an attempt was made to give line regiments an at least nominal "territorial" connection. If Lambton had died before, as all the colonels of his date had, or if he had been indifferent, as many colonels were, it might have received any other title conceivable. The third was the fact of its being selected, on grounds purely of administrative expediency, for formation into a light infantry corps in 1808. The fourth that in the Cardwell reforms of the 1870s it should receive as a partner a battalion with no common traditions, no connection whatever with the County—nothing but the fortuitous fact of its being light infantry. The fifth and final one, that in the radical reforms of 1881, when line regiments were for the first time assigned a locality from which to recruit and when many lost their traditional connections, it should have preserved the one which Lambton had asked for a hundred years before.

The nominal connection it assumed in 1782 was, like the attempts made unsuccessfully by Colonels of other regiments earlier in the century, an aspiration, not a recognition of its Durham quality. When it was at Tynemouth and Morpeth in 1760-1761 it had absorbed quite a number (about 200) from Northumberland, but the title of Durham conferred no prescriptive rights upon the population of Durham, nor upon the militia, although it nearly always kept a recruiting party in the County. Only once, between 1806 and 1809, did it receive a material accession from the Durham Militia, when out of the 925 men volunteering from the militia 165 came from the Durham. Even at the time of the Crimean War, when regimental *esprit-de-corps* was fostered with greater assiduity than at the beginning of the century and the demand for men was no less acute, it was from the West Riding Militia principally that the 68th found their volunteers, none at all from the Durham. Even in the early 1890s, when the "territorial system" was running strong, recruits came, not from the County at large, but from Tyneside and also Bradford.

If the bonds connecting the rank and file of the 68th to the County are tenuous, those connecting the officers are as gossamer in comparison. Apart from Lambton himself, only a handful can be said with certainty to have had any. Richard Ridley (1756-1761), son of a mayor of Newcastle; William Ironside (1788-1801), whose father was chaplain of the Regiment from 1775 to 1787, and came from a family owning land at Houghton-le-Spring for several hundred years; the five officers who joined from the Durham Militia in 1809; Arthur Surtees (1830-1832), of the Dinsdale branch of the great Durham family; and George Witham (1827-1842), of the family of Silvertop, of Minsteracres. Surgeon W. K. Greenwell (1806-1812) possibly came from a branch of the Lanchester family of that name; and there are doubtless others. But neither Ridley, who came from the 23rd and was more properly a Northumberland man, nor Witham nor Surtees, who very soon left to enter the 14th Light Dragoons, joined out of sense of county loyalty; and Ironside, one feels, came in from a sense of obligation to Lambton rather than the County. It is not that the gentry of Durham were backward in making arms their profession. On the contrary, they are to be found in every one of the King's regiments. It just is that there is no recognition of a bond with the County.

Indeed, before the County connection was deliberately cultivated in the 1880s and 1890s, it is an anachronism to expect anything of that kind. Things were not ordered so in our old line regiments. There was a regimental loyalty transmitted from father to son, but this only emphasises what has already been said, that the professional army was turned in on itself and lived an existence apart from the nation at large. It asked for and needed no outside loyalties to sustain it except that to the Crown.

II. The force which the constitution tolerated and admitted in its midst was the militia. The word is an Elizabethan one, borrowed from the French to distinguish the new professional forces then in fashion on the continent from the old traditional force upon which the country had depended for its defence from time immemorial. Service in an armed force in the event of invasion is a duty so much taken for granted that the exact nature of the service is nowhere stated in the earliest documents with any precision. Before the Conquest such service was performed with the *fyrd*, and there is a fairly clear continuous tradition linking the *fyrd* of the Anglo-Saxon kings with Pitt's militia of 1757, which, like its predecessors, was levied upon the shires and the counties. It was a "national" force in the sense that in civil conflict it broke down and made way for the *ad hoc* forces raised by the parties: whereas, for instance, it played a notable part in the defence of the realm in Elizabeth's reign, it was of little account in the war between Crown and Parliament, when either side raised its own professional army. Nevertheless, despite all the social changes which transformed it in the thousand-odd years of its existence, despite the emergence of the professional army, and despite its own very indifferent performance during the Forty-five, it retained sufficient vitality to receive an eighteenth-century front-age with Pitt's Militia Act of 1757.

The conception of the militia at the time was that of a body of solid citizens drawn from the mass of the respectable population and officered by the local gentry. A property qualification was required of anyone holding a commission. A lieutenant-colonel, for instance, was required to have an estate of £600 a year or the reversion to one of £1200; a lieutenant to have real estate of £50 a year, a personal estate of £1000 value, or a combined real and personal estate of £2000, or else to be the son of a person in possession of estate of double those values. In an emergency the property qualifications of captains and below could be waived, but the intentions of the legislature are sufficiently clear. The men were supplied by a ballot in each parish, the County having a fixed quota of men it was required to furnish whenever the militia should be embodied. Durham's quota, for instance, was 400, which, with that of the East Riding and Bedford, was the smallest of any English county with the exceptions of Cumberland, Huntingdon, Monmouth, Rutland and Westmorland. The command of the militia was, at it had long been, in the hands of the lords lieutenant, and its administration characteristically remained until 1872 with the Home Department, not with the military offices.

In the last fifty years of its existence the militia, by dispensing with the ballot and the property qualification, lost much of its respectability. Even in Gibbon's time a type of man who may be described as a professional militiaman was common, as well as a rather disreputable kind of half-pay officer who had been found wanting in the regular army. Nevertheless, in its prime the militia was a fairly representative body of the population at large; fat and thin, tall and short, slightly ridiculous when first embodied, yet a useful body of men after a year or two and, what is hardly less important, possessing the good will of the community as a whole and sharing its prejudices. Contrast, for example these two consecutive entries in Wesley's Journal for 1779; that of 9th May, when he preached in Darlington market place and "all the congregation behaved well but a party of the Queen's Dragoons," and that of 10th May, when he preached at Barnard Castle "and saw a quite different behaviour in the Durham Militia, the handsomest body of soldiers I ever saw except in Ireland. The next evening they all come, both officers and soldiers, and were a pattern to the whole congregation."[2]

III. In the ballot, however, there was an element of compulsion no matter how much it may have been softened by substitution and exemption, and an Englishman prefers his services to come undemanded. Countless generations of experience have taught him that what his government takes from him as of right will persistently be undervalued. How willingly he came forward in 1914 when no one but his conscience drove him, how dull his response in 1939 when the grey hand of compulsion was suspended above him, and how enthusiastic his reception of the call for Local Defence Volunteers in 1940, when he felt his own energies were being placed in the scales. Hence his like of volunteering, which he has shown whenever the country has been threatened: in 1779, when the great "Combined", the Franco-Spanish Fleet, lay off the Channel ports, in the Revolutionary and Napoleonic Wars, and in 1859, when a second Napoleon seemed to threaten invasion. The fencibles, yeomanry, volunteer associations, local militia and rifle volunteers of those years were the direct antecedents of the Territorial Force of 1908, when the word "territorial", reserved in military jargon for thirty years for regular regiments recruited on a county basis, was transferred to the volunteers. The Local Defence Volunteers of 1940 and the Home Guard, which stood in relation to one another much as the volunteers and local militia of 1808-1814, belong to the same strain.

[2]John Wesley, *Journals* (ed. N. Curnock), Vol. 6 (1915), pp. 233-234.

The history of the Regiment, therefore, is composed of three strands: the central strand of the militia, the only one with a long traditional connection with the County as a whole; the volunteer strand, made up of many smaller and shorter components, yet all of them possessing an even stronger Durham quality than the militia; and the exotic professional strand, late in possessing a county connection yet the only one continuously in service.

§

"Durham", says a road-book of 1720, "is a county palatine; the royalty whereof belonging to the Bishop, therefore it is called the Bishopric of Durham. . . . The air is sharp, the soil diverse, the south rich, the west rocky and moorish. 'Tis very rich in coalpits, hath some lead and iron mines, not without silver in the west part. 'Tis a county richly furnished with corn, cattle, fruits and fish but its chief commodities are coal, lead, iron, etc."[3] Such was the aspect of the county for many hundreds of years before the Industrial Revolution distorted its features early in the last century.

Its situation exposed it to the depredations of war in the countless conflicts with Scotland, and the medieval forebears of its militia played a principal part in the decisive defeat of David II's invasion of 1346 at the battle of Neville's Cross, within sight of Durham Castle. From the union of the two crowns in 1603 the services of the militia are hardly to be remarked. In 1745 it was embodied, but so belatedly as to be forestalled by a volunteer association of cavalry.[4] As revivified by Pitt's Act it was embodied again in 1759 at Barnard Castle, and remained active until 1763. The strength was 369 men, furnished by the wards in the following proportions: Chester, 105; Darlington, 131; Easington, 59; Stockton, 45; Norhamshire, 11; Islandshire, 18.[5] A member of the band, and subsequently bandmaster, was William Herschel, afterwards a famous astronomer and father of another famous astronomer. He had been an oboist in the Hanoverian Guards and had come to this country after the defeat at Hastenbeck in 1757, when he was noticed by the Earl of Darlington, Colonel of the Durham Militia, who gave him his new situation. Many came to hear him when he performed in the square at Pontefract. A tangible survival of this period of its embodiment is a grena-

[3]Emmanuel Bowen, *Britannia Depicta* . . . (London, 1720), p. 268.
[4]Carson I. A. Ritchie, "The Durham Association Regiment," in Journal for the Society for Army Historical Research (*cit.* hereafter as "J.S.A.H.R."), Vol. 34 (1956), pp. 106-119.
[5]These last two detached districts, in the north of Northumberland, were not severed from the County of Durham until 1844.

dier's fur cap, one of the few specimens of mid-eighteenth century militia uniform remaining. It bears the motto *"Nec temere nec timere"* and the letters D.M. in raised embroidery in the form of a "plate", and may be the one worn by Lieutenant Crosier Surtees in the portrait owned by his descendant, Major Henry S. Surtees, of Redworth Hall. Crosier Surtees, a man of large stature and an officer of grenadiers, obtained his commission at the age of 20 in 1759.[6]

The militia was again embodied on 26th March 1778, the year in which the American Rebellion became a European war, until 1783. It was embodied again from 1st December 1792 until May 1802; from March 1803 to 14th August 1814; and for six months from 14th July 1815 to 28th February 1816. In 1852 the quota was raised to 1,096 to correspond with the substantial increase in population which had taken place in the interval, and the regiment was on 3rd May 1853 divided into three: the South Durham, the North Durham and a corps of artillery, an organisation which subsisted unchanged— except for the conversion of the 1st or South Durham regiment into fusiliers in 1868—until the radical reform of 1881.

The single battalion had always maintained its headquarters at Barnard Castle by reason of the constant lead given by the Vanes, earls of Darlington and dukes of Cleveland, living at Raby nearby, who were its colonels from 1759 to 1860 (a remarkable tradition of public service); and the 1st Durhams continued there after the division of 1853, even after the amalgamation of 1881, until the out-break of war in 1914. The 2nd, or North, Durham Militia's head-quarters were fixed at Durham; that of the artillery at Bishop Auckland, later at Hartlepool. All were embodied in the Crimean War, the 1st from December 1854 to May 1856, the 2nd from March 1855 to May 1856.

Such was the antiquity of the origins of the militia that when, in the embodiment of the Seven Years War, questions were raised as to the precedence of the militia battalions, the matter was settled by a yearly draw of lots. In 1778 the Durham Militia drew 44; in 1779, 30; in 1780, 35; in 1781, 32; in 1782, 44. In 1793 they drew 10 for the whole period of their embodiment—a measure of economy, doubtless, inasmuch as the numbers appeared on their appointments —until 1802; and in 1803 they drew 25, which they kept until 1816. In 1833 precedence was "finally and permanently" settled by a ballot drawn at St. James's Palace on 28th February, at which the 47 regiments raised before the Peace of 1763 were placed in front of those raised from 1763 to 1783 and those (mostly Scottish and Irish)

[6]The cap is now in Darlington Museum. See C. C. P. Lawson, *A History of the Uniforms of the British Army* (Peter Davis, 1941), Vol. 2, pp. 217-218.

raised in the Revolutionary War. Durham, one of the 47, drew 3, a precedence they preserved until 1855, when a board was assembled at Aldershot to determine that of the new units raised in the augmentation. The 1st Durhams continued as the 3rd, while the new 2nd Durhams received 43, being for some reason inserted after the Dorset and before the Glamorgan Militia, which both belonged to the old 47 of 1833. The artillery militia corps were at the same time numbered in alphabetical order, the Durham receiving the number 10. This order of precedence remained unaltered until 1881.[7]

The facings of the militia appear to have changed with each embodiment. In the Seven Years War there is reason to believe that the Durham had green, the same colour as that which Colonel Lambton at the same time chose for his new regiment of the line—a coincidence that should not be overlooked. In the American War they were purple. In the Revolutionary War they were buff or pale yellow. In the embodiment of 1803 they were white, and both the North and South Durham Militia wore white after the division of 1853.

Two further Durham Militia regiments were raised in the exigencies of the moment in 1797: the *Durham Supplementary Militia* and the *Durham Provisional Cavalry*. The first was the County's response to the imposition of the ballot for raising 60,000 additional men authorised by the Act of Parliament of 1796. The second was the County's response to the levy imposed at the same time requiring owners of horses, in the proportion of one trooper and one horse for every ten houses, to come forward. Both were short-lived and deserve no more than bare mention: they have neither antecedents nor descendants.

The history of the *Durham Militia*, in spite of its length, is not exciting. It consists for the most part of marches from one station in the kingdom to another, of guarding prisoners of war, and, unfortunately, of supplying reinforcements for the line—unfortunately, because this led to its undoing. The immunity from invasion which the country has enjoyed necessarily deprived of any fighting a force intended for home defence. In its later years the militia degenerated into a draft-finding force, and in 1908 it received the title of "Special Reserve" in the dismal jargon of the Adjutant-General's Office. The legislature, however, did not originally intend it to be merely a reserve, and "volunteering for the line," that useful resource of the standing army which supplied it with some of its best recruits, was, even in the most critical years, hotly debated and stoutly resisted. In 1796 and 1798 volunteering was for the first time permitted, and

[7]W. Y. Baldry, "Order of Precedence of Militia Regiments," in J.S.A.H.R., Vol. 15 (1936), pp. 5-16.

it continued at intervals thereafter, much to the detriment of the regiments. The Durham Militia, for instance, which was about 1,200 strong in 1798 (after the accession of the Supplementary Militia), was reduced to 439 at the end of 1799 by volunteering.

An inspection report of 2nd June 1807, when it lay at Woodbridge, Suffolk, reveals a very good regiment. Direct command had never, apparently, been exercised by the Colonel, the 3rd Earl of Darlington (afterwards 1st Duke of Cleveland), and they were commanded by Lieut.-Colonel James O'Callaghan, an old regular, formerly on the half-pay of the 88th, disbanded in 1783. "He is an exceedingly good officer," says General Whetham, who would recognise a good man when he saw one. "He is very clear in the field and very attentive to the observation of His Majesty's regulations in the field-exercise and manœuvres and equally so in the general discipline and interior economy of the regiment. Major Byers [a young man of 28] is also an attentive good officer. The regiment is perfect in field-exercises and manœuvres. The captains and subalterns are properly instructed and attentive. The non-commissioned officers are equally so. The men are well behaved, their appearance uniform and soldier-like. They are a good body of men, stout and active, from 20 to 35 or 40 years of age. Their clothing is well fitted and good." Of the 567 n.c.o.s and men 560 were English, and those, to judge from the volunteers the 68th received from them over the next two years, all from the County.[8]

A curious reminder of the old Durham Militia survives in Auchtermuchty, Fife, where it was stationed in 1813. It founded there a Scottish Masonic lodge, No. 320, (later 249) consecrated on 24th June as the "St. Cuthbert Durham Militia Lodge," and the descendants of the militiamen are to this day known as "Durhams".[9]

§

Of the *volunteers* raised in Durham those with far away the most outstanding record are the Loyal Durham Regiment of Fencible Infantry. Fencibles were distinguishable from professional soldiers only in the terms of their service, which limited them to service in the kingdom. (Wags called them the "Sensibles" because, while receiving their pay, they waited for their enemy to come to them.) They are properly considered under this head by virtue of their

[8] W.O. 27/91 Part I.
[9] Col. the Hon. W. L. Vane, *The Durham Light Infantry* (London, 1914) (*cit.* hereafter as "Vane"), p. 271, and information kindly supplied by Mr. J. Littlefair.

being raised in the County and to a large extent officered by Durham men.

Durham raised two fencible regiments in the Revolutionary War. The first, raised in May 1794, was one of cavalry. It was at first known as the *Durham Fencible Cavalry* and later, after the marriage of the Prince of Wales on 8th April 1795, as *the Princess of Wales's Fencible Cavalry* or *the Princess of Wales's Regiment of Light Dragoons*, an expression of loyalty not so theatrical in those years of republicanism and jacobinism as might appear. Its first lieut.-colonel-commandant was the same 3rd Earl of Darlington who was Colonel of the county militia. Its first commanding officer was Major Daniel Ord, a regular army officer born at Longridge in Norhamshire in the County—a property to which he later succeeded—and mayor of Berwick in 1786. There are some other familiar Durham names amongst the officers, such as Wilkinson, Milbanke, Clavering and others. The regiment, which maintained an average strength of about 250, was sent to Ireland in June 1798 after three years in Scotland, and there was engaged in the operations against the rebels on the Boyne under Major-General Meyrick. A request made by Lord Darlington for the return of the regiment to England, which was opposed by Major Ord and all the officers, resulted in Lord Darlington's resignation in May 1799 and his replacement by Banastre Tarleton, famous for his exploits in the American War. The regiment was disbanded at Clonmel on 22nd September 1800, and its horses distributed between the 6th Dragoon Guards and the 21st and 22nd Light Dragoons.

The second was a regiment of fencible infantry raised in December 1795 by Colonel Barrington Price, a regular cavalry officer in retirement, a nephew of Shute Barrington, Bishop of Durham. Fewster Johnson, the first lieut-colonel and second colonel, another retired cavalry officer, was also a Durham man, owning a property at Ebchester in the County, but the Loyal Durham Fencibles are principally indebted for their good name to the officer who succeeded him on his death in January 1798, Colonel John Skerrett. Skerrett came of an Irish family that had given a good many of its sons to the army. He himself had served with the 19th and the 48th, and had lately been colonel of one of the short-lived corps of those days, a corps of cavalry and infantry raised for service in the West Indies, called "Lieut.-Colonel Skerrett's Regiment," which was "broke" at the end of 1796. At the time of his appointment the Durham Fencibles had been six months at Downpatrick after a spell of fifteen months (February 1796 to May 1797) in Guernsey.

It was still in Ulster when the rebellion broke out in County

Wexford. The rebellion was a mere spark compared with the great revolution originally contemplated but it was a formidable enough affair. By the time reinforcements—mostly Irish militia and yeomanry—could be moved south, the rebels, led with religious fanaticism and an utter disregard for life and property by Father John and Father Michael Murphy, two Roman Catholic priests, had established themselves very judiciously in a central camp on Vinegar Hill. They had sacked and occupied Wexford, and were planning an advance northward upon Dublin. One column was directed upon New Ross, where it was to force the passage of the Barrow and raise Kilkenny and Waterford; the second was ordered up the Slaney to seize Newtownbarry, and moving by Carlow and Kildare, threaten Dublin from the west; the third, commanded by the Fathers Murphy themselves, was to march due north, take Gorey and Arklow, and join the county levies which awaited them at Wicklow. The first column was held at New Ross on 5th June after a savage battle lasting eleven hours and costing the rebels some 2000 killed. The second encountered two small government forces sent to recover Wexford, and, in a fight at Ballymore Hill near Ferns on 3rd June, dispersed them in the direction of Gorey and Arklow, so demoralising them that they even deserted Arklow and retired to Wicklow. If Arklow were not re-garrisoned the path of the third rebel column would be clear to Dublin.

So formidable was the reputation acquired by the Durham Fencibles in Ulster, and so conscious the rebels of its value, that when it was called south to Dublin they prepared an ambush of 7000 men at Balbriggan to intercept and destroy it. "It was," says Froude, who repeats contemporary accounts ,"the most distinguished regiment in Ireland." From Dublin a wing 315 strong was hurried south in carriages impressed by the quartermaster, Mr. Wallington, which arrived at Arklow in the nick of time at 1 o'clock on 9th June, just two hours after the approach of the rebels had been signalled.

Arklow stands at the mouth of the Avoca, on the south side of the river, which is crossed by one bridge.[10] An attempt to defend it against a force from the south placed the garrison in the classically unenviable military position, with a river in its immediate rear. Major-General Needham, however, who commanded there since the 6th, had marked out a fair position, following the line of the trees and hedges that covered his front, and had manned it with his force, which before Skerrett's arrival amounted to less than 1000 militia and

[10]The topography of the battlefield has much changed since 1798. See G. A. Hayes-McCoy, "the Topography of a Battlefield: Arklow, 1798" in the *Irish Sword*, Vol. I (1949), pp. 51-56.

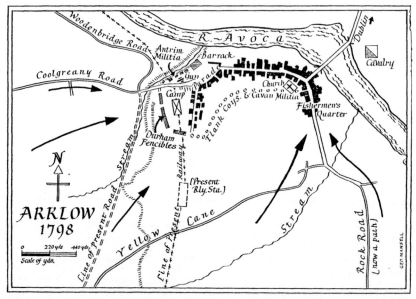

1. The Battle of Arklow, 9th June, 1798

fencible infantry, 150 cavalry and 250 yeomanry. The accession of the Durham Fencibles (which brought him also a fiery and resolute second-in-command), made his infantry up to about 1350 all ranks. The rebels, flushed with success, were estimated at anything between 19,000 and 31,000—odds of 10 if not 20 to 1.

The rebels delivered their attack at about 4 o'clock, in a long wavering semi-circular line, their hats on the ends of their pikes, shouting, screaming and howling, dashing forward under the small green banners embellished with yellow harps which they had made for themselves, and led on by their priests. The first flank of Needham's line which they struck was in the lower part of the town by the fishermen's houses, which was so stoutly defended that they never passed the barricade erected in the street although their attacks lasted over two and a half hours. The principal attack, however, was made at the upper end of the town and was led by Father Michael Murphy himself, who carried in his pocket a handful of musket balls to show to his benighted followers as evidence of his invulnerability. Here on the left of the road, behind a hedge, were posted the Durham Fencibles with their two battalion-guns, and, behind a barricade in the street, a detachment of the Antrim Militia. The fight at this point was long stubbornly contested. Charge after charge was thrown back, many of their chiefs were killed within a few yards of the guns. But at last, at about sunset, Murphy was struck by a cannon-shot from one of the Durham guns a few paces from the barricade, and the rebels drew off in a confused mass up the Cool-greany road. One thousand are said to have been killed. The King's troops lost sixty or seventy in killed and wounded.

In most accounts it is said that at one point Needham in despair was for ordering a retreat, but that Skerrett, appreciating the disaster that would follow when a handful of troops, some of whom had known defeat at Ballymore Hill, retired from such a position before quite ten times their number, refused to abandon his position. "The gallantry of the Durham Fencibles," says one account, "was unbounded. Thrice the rebels came forward in immense force against the wing of this noble regiment, and as often a destructive volley from their musketry, with grape from the battalion-guns, obliged the assailants to recede from a fire they found intolerable." Without Skerrett and the Durham Fencibles there can be little doubt the battle of Arklow would have been lost, and the fate of Dublin placed in the utmost jeopardy. It was an action of which the County may be proud.

It was, however, the first and only in which the Loyal Durham Fencibles were engaged. Needham's force arrived too late to fight at Vinegar Hill, where the rebel "army" was defeated and dispersed on 21st June, and on 2nd August Skerrett left them for an appointment in Newfoundland. Bainbridge, the lieut.-colonel, a Westmorland man, allowed the discipline to relax during his long absences in England, and though it continued in Ireland until March or April 1802, it was a changed regiment that was finally disbanded at Liverpool on 22nd May that year with a strength of 470 men.[11]

Though the fencibles were volunteers (if mercenaries as well) and have strong county connections, they have neither antecedents nor descendants; while the County volunteer corps, though living an ephemeral existence, have in common with the volunteers which became our territorial battalions at least many of the same families and the same conditions of service. They are volunteers who don their uniform in an emergency and drill together for certain periods in the week and year.

The earliest volunteer corps raised in Durham was the *Durham Association Regiment*, already mentioned, which was organised in 1745 at the instigation of Mr. George Bowes, of Streatlam and Gibside, Member for the County, entirely because the proper authorities were tardy in setting the militia mechanism in motion. It was a

[11]Col. the Hon. W. L. Vane, *The Durham Fencibles* (1912); J. A. Froude, *The English in Ireland*, Vol. 3, p. 478; Maxwell's *History of the Rebellion*, p. 131; and Musgrave's *History*, Vol. 1, pp. 540 *ff.*; W.O. 13/3837-3840.

cavalry regiment of six troops, each of 20 or 25 men, the troop commanders belonging all to the County families: Lambton, Ellison, Carr, Liddell, Clavering and Vane. It mustered on Framwellgate Moor. The money for the men's pay was raised by subscription among the "providers". It did a certain amount of patrolling to inhibit the movements of Papists and Non-jurors, but Bowes's zeal was considered excessive by the proper authorities, whose jealousy was aroused, and it was disbanded in November 1745, less than two months after it was raised.[12]

If there were volunteer associations organised in the County in the American War their names did not appear in the Gazette, and the next crop of volunteer corps dates from the perilous years of the Revolutionary War. The earliest was the *Sunderland Loyal Volunteers* or *Loyal Sunderland Volunteers*, which was raised in 1794 by Robert Hayton, a wealthy coal-fitter, "for the purpose of manning and defending the batteries at the entrance of Sunderland harbour". It consisted of three companies of 100 men, its officers and subscribers Sunderland merchants and attorneys, and landed gentry such as the Edens, and William Wilson, nephew of William Russell, the wealthy owner of Brancepeth Castle, "the richest commoner in the kingdom." Later becoming infantry in whole or in part, it was disbanded on West Pann Field, Bishop Wearmouth, on 2nd December 1802. A great number of the men were keelmen, wearing blue as opposed to white pantaloons, who were prudently kept apart from the rest except once, on the occasion of a sham fight, when the keelmen were given the task of retreating before an advance of the others. Disdaining to be conquered even in appearance, however, they refused to budge, and fired their muskets at such close range that their opponents bore the blue marks of the powder on their faces for the rest of their lives. The corps was reconstituted in August 1803.

Five other infantry volunteer battalions were raised rather later:

The *Darlington Volunteer Infantry* (1799-1802), raised at his own expense by John Trotter, later major-commandant, and re-raised in 1803;

The *City of Durham Loyal Volunteers*, or *Loyal Durham Volunteer Infantry* (1798-1802), under Howden Philipson Rowe as commandant, and William Thomas Greenwell. It did not survive the Peace of Amiens.

The *Gateshead Volunteer Infantry* (1798-1802), under Robert Shafto Hawks, captain-commandant, reconstituted in 1803;

[12]Carson I. A. Ritchie, *cit. sup.*

The *South Shields Volunteer Infantry* (1797-1802), under Sir Cuthbert Heron as captain-commandant, reconstituted in 1803;

The *Stockton Volunteer Infantry* (1799-1802), under John Allison, a wealthy Stockton merchant, as major-commandant, reconstituted in 1803.

Besides these the County also raised four regiments of volunteer cavalry and two of volunteer artillery:

The *Easington Ward Gentlemen and Yeomanry Cavalry* (1798-1802), raised in the north-east part of the County by Rowland Burdon of Castle Eden, one who from his wealth, enterprise and influence was one of the most powerful men in the north at that time.

The *North Durham Gentlemen and Yeomanry*, a small unit of some fifty men raised in Norhamshire and Islandshire by Sir Carnaby Haggerston, Bart., in 1798, and having a continuous history until 1810;

The *Staindrop Gentlemen and Yeomanry*, raised by John Ingram, of Staindrop, in 1798, with John Bourne, of Walker Hall, Newsham, as lieutenant, John Hawdon, of Wackerfield, as cornet, and Luke Seymour, of Newsham, as quartermaster, had a continuous history until 1815, when it was absorbed into the Durham Yeomanry. Its only war casualty was Pte. George Blenkinsop, who in 1805 "had his foot taken off by a thrashing machine";

The *Usworth Gentlemen and Yeomanry Cavalry*, raised in 1798 by Thomas Wade, of Scotch House and Usworth Place, and reconstituted as a "Legion" of cavalry and infantry in 1803;

The *Sunderland Artillery Volunteers* (1798-1802), raised, presumably as an offshoot of the Sunderland Volunteers when they were formed as infantry, by Thomas Scarth as captain-commandant, and reconstituted in 1803;

The *Hartlepool Volunteer Artillery* (1798-1802), raised by Charles Spearman as major-commandant and reconstituted in 1803.

The County's response to Pitt's invitation to the country at large to form "Armed Associations" in defence of the parish, uniformed only if they chose to be and confined (unless they voted otherwise) to the parish, resulted in the formation of a further four cavalry corps and two infantry, three of which survived to serve after 1803:

The *Bishop Wearmouth Volunteers* (1798-1802), organised by John Goodchild, junr., as captain, and Robert Biss as lieutenant (who in 1805 gave his services to the Sunderland Volunteers);

The Gibside Volunteer Associated Troops of Cavalry, organised in 1799 by John, 10th Earl of Strathmore (the son of the unfortunate countess who in her widowhood married the adventurer, Andrew Robinson Stoney). It was reconstituted in 1804 as the *Gibside Troop of Cavalry of the Derwent Legion* and in 1815 was absorbed into the Durham Yeomanry;

The *Durham Light Horse Association*, or the *Associated Troop of Light Horse in the City of Durham*, organised in 1798 by Henry Methold (who on his death was succeeded by Ralph Lambton), and dissolved in 1802;

The *Loyal Axwell Volunteer Association*, formed by Sir Thomas Clavering, Bart., in 1798 in the Ryton, Whickham, Lanchester and Tanfield area. It merged into the *Axwell Yeomanry Cavalry* of 1803, which was commanded by William Lockey of Axwell Park, and at some date between 23rd July and 3rd September 1814 was absorbed into the South Tyne Yeomanry Cavalry as "Clavering's Troop";

The *Durham Volunteer Association*, an infantry corps, organised by John Ralph Fenwick in 1798 and containing two members of the Salvin family, dissolved in 1802, but reconstituted in 1804 as the Durham Volunteers, with John Ralph Fenwick as lieut.-colonel-commandant, and Lieutenants Griffith, Woodifield, Orton, Liddell and Hoar from among the old "associators";

The *Stockton Volunteer Association* (1798-1799), organised by Rowland Webster, merged into the above-mentioned Stockton Volunteers, raised by John Allison, who was a first-lieutenant in Webster's formation.

The war was resumed in 1803 with a threat of invasion more real than any hitherto experienced, which was answered by so many offers of service from volunteer corps all over the country that the government offices were hardly able to deal with them. The County of Durham alone raised seven corps of volunteer cavalry, ten corps of volunteer infantry and three of artillery. Most of the cavalry corps became merged into the Durham Yeomanry, and led an existence protracted well beyond the peace following Waterloo, as a kind of mounted police to keep order during the troubled post-war years. Some of the infantry merged into the "local militia", not a spontaneous "popular" creation as the volunteers had been, but a government notion designed to absorb the infantry volunteers into a more economical and manageable body. Durham found two Local Militia battalions, one in 1809, the other in 1812; both were disbanded with the rest in 1816. The continuity, however, of the history of some of these corps is obscured by the prevailing fashion of raising "legions". They were combined corps of infantry and cavalry, inspired by the classical reading of the gentlemen who formed them, and made popular in America during the Rebellion. These may be conveniently mentioned first.

The *Darlington Legion* was formed in September 1803 by the same John Trotter, of Haughton Hall, who raised the Darlington Volunteer Infantry of 1799 which had consisted of, at most, two companies. The Legion consisted of six, with William Wetenhall as lieut.-colonel, Damer Wilson as major, and Michael Basnett, the former adjutant, as adjutant, together with two troops of cavalry, commanded by L. W. Hartley, of Middleton Lodge on the Yorkshire side of the Tees. The two split in the course of 1806, the infantry leading an independent existence as the *Darlington Volunteer Infantry* until June 1809, when, with a strength of 283 out of an establishment of 376, it was disbanded to form the 1st Durham Local Militia, while the cavalry, as the *Darlington Cavalry*, commanded by George Hartley, of Middleton Lodge, merged in 1815 into the *Darlington Independent Yeomanry*, which survived at least until February 1817.

The *Derwent Legion* was formed by the 10th Earl of Strathmore from an infantry battalion of six companies, commanded by Lieut.-Colonel Sir T. H. Liddell, Bart., (organised in about September 1803 and officered by men among whom Fenwicks and Greenwells figure prominently),which was combined in October 1804 with the Earl's old Gibside Troop, commanded by Ralph Fenwick, of Marley Hill, and occasionally referred to as the "Whickham, &c. Cavalry". The bond between the two components consisted principally in the Earl's lieut.-colonel-commandantship. They do not appear to have exercised together, and while the Battalion ceased to exist at the end of March 1813, the Troop, still commanded by Fenwick, was incorporated into the Durham Yeomanry and was employed on permanent duty in Durham City from 31st August to 7th September 1817.

The third was the *Loyal Usworth Legion* or *Usworth Cavalry and Infantry Volunteers*. It was formed on 15th August 1803 by Thomas Wade as lieut.-colonel-commandant, with Jennens Peareth as lieut.-colonel, of a squadron of four troops of cavalry and four companies of infantry, the former a reincarnation of the Usworth Gentlemen and Yeomanry of 1798, the latter a new formation. Early in 1807 the command was taken over by Thomas Burdon of West Jesmond, a distant kinsman of the Rowland Burdon who raised the Easington Ward Cavalry, and on 19th March 1808 the infantry battalion received the title of *South Tyne Volunteer Infantry*, while the squadron became known as the *South Tyne Yeomanry Cavalry* or (occasionally) as the Cavalry of the *South Tyne Volunteer Legion*. Like the Earl of Strathmore, Thomas Burdon continued to command the two at least until 1812, but the bond was slender. The infantry eventually became, with some changes, the 2nd Durham Local Militia in 1812:

the cavalry, having absorbed the Axwell Yeomanry, continued at least until 1817. They were assembled at Gateshead and Newcastle in December 1815 to quell some disturbances among the seamen, and five troops (Losh's, Lockey's, Thompson's, Hoggett's and Wilson's) were on duty at Newcastle in August 1817.

Apart from the Legions there were four corps of yeomanry and seven infantry corps:

The *Axwell Yeomanry Cavalry*, already mentioned, derived from the Axwell Association and absorbed into the South Tyne Yeomanry in 1814;

The *Durham Volunteer Cavalry*, a new formation of 1801, raised by Arthur Mowbray of Sherburn, as major-commandant, and augmented to three troops in April 1804. It absorbed in 1815 the Gibside and Staindrop Yeomanry and, latterly commanded by Lieut.-Colonel Henry Tower, of Seaham, it was generally known as the *Durham Yeomanry;*

The *North Durham Troop of Volunteer Cavalry*, derived from the North Durham Gentlemen and Yeomanry of 1798. It continued under Sir Carnaby Haggerston until disbanded in 1810;

The *Staindrop Troop of Volunteer Cavalry*, derived from Ingram's Gentlemen and Yeomanry of 1798. In 1815, commanded by Bourne, one of Ingram's old lieutenants, it was absorbed into the Durham Yeomanry;

The *Chester-le-Street Volunteer Artillery and Infantry*, a new formation raised by Luke Colling in May 1803, consisting of three companies, of which Colling's is described as "the first and artillery company". The command was taken over in 1809 by Major Samuel Cooke, of Ayton Lodge, who continued until the dissolution of the corps at the end of 1811.

The *Gateshead Volunteer Infantry*, derived from Hawks's Gateshead Volunteers of 1798, which was reconstituted in 1803 into a battalion of eight companies by Cuthbert Ellison, of Hebburn Hall, as lieut.-colonel-commandant. Hawks, who was the major, supplied from his ironworks the muskets for two companies, which were commanded by members of his family. The pay-lists of the corps cease at 24th March 1813.

The *1st South Shields Volunteers*, derived from Sir Cuthbert Heron's corps of 1797 and reconstituted by him in 1803; and

The *2nd South Shields Volunteers*, derived from the same source with Joseph Bulmer as lieut.-colonel-commandant. The 1st was dissolved in 1813, the 2nd in 1812.

The *Sunderland Volunteer Infantry*, raised in August 1803 under the lieut.-colonel-commandantship of Sir Ralph Milbanke, of Seaham

Hall, Lady Byron's father, was a re-formation of Hayton's volunteers of 1794. It was commanded by Christopher Cay, a Sunderland merchant. Its favourite march was "The swine com' jinglin' doon Pelton Lonin' ", a popular north country air. It was dissolved in 1813, many men joining the 2nd Durham Local Militia.

The *Durham Volunteer Infantry*, (1804-1813), already mentioned as the reconstituted Durham Volunteer Association of 1798, dissolved in 1813.

The *Stockton Volunteer Infantry* (1803-1813), the Stockton Volunteers of 1799 reconstituted in 1803 with many of the same officers by John Allison as lieut.-colonel-commandant, and dissolved in 1813. Characteristic of the patriotic sentiment behind the whole volunteer movement was the provision made on the dissolution of this corps, entitling the n.c.o.s and privates, their wives, widows and lineal descendants, to preferential treatment at the Stockton Dispensary, a charitable institution that gave medical and surgical assistance to the poor.

Lastly, two corps of artillery volunteers from Sunderland and one from Hartlepool.

These volunteer corps differed greatly in size. Those with captain-commandants numbered hardly more than two or three score; those with lieut.-colonel-commandants anything between 250 and 500. In 1808, for instance, the Chester-le-Street Infantry had 8 officers and 210 privates, while the Gateshead Infantry had 25 officers and 458 privates. Their uniforms approximated fairly closely to those of the line, the cavalry and infantry in red coats, the artillery in blue, but distinguished by the lace and the facings. The Derwent Legion Infantry had black facings, the 1st South Shields Infantry green, the 2nd black, the Durham Infantry white, and so on.[13]

Lastly, we come to the two battalions of Durham Local Militia. It is not to be confused with the militia, being no more than a body of government-sponsored volunteers into which, it was hoped, all county volunteer corps would eventually merge by means of the subtle pressure of withdrawing financial support for those that did not.

The *1st Durham Local Militia* was organised in June 1809 by John Trotter, of Haughton Hall, from the infantry of the Darlington

[13]The returns of the Durham Volunteer corps are in W.O. 13/3993 and 13/4307-4314. See also the *Gazettes* of the period and James Patterson, *The Volunteer Movement in Sunderland in the time of the Napoleonic Wars* (Sunderland, n.d.) The uniforms, facings, etc., are given by the Marquess of Cambridge, "The Volunteer Army of Great Britain, 1806 " in J.S.A.H.R., Vol. 31 (1953), p. 119. See also W. Fordyce, *History and Antiquities of the County Palatine of Durham* (1855), Vol. 2, p. 600 n.

Legion, from which most of the officers were obtained: William Wetenhall as lieut.-colonel, Michael Basnett as adjutant, and several company commanders. Its headquarters were in Darlington and it did 22 days training in the year in the neighbourhood of Darlington on land belonging to William Tutin and Michael Basnett. No drills were carried out after 1814 and it was disbanded in 1816.

The *2nd Durham Local Militia* was organised in about February 1812 by Thomas Burdon, of West Jesmond, principally from the infantry of the South Tyne Legion, from whom among others came the adjutant, Robert Matthew Parke. Its headquarters were in Gateshead, in competition, one might suppose, with Cuthbert Ellison's Gateshead Volunteers, who led an independent existence until 1813. It was exercised under sergeants lent by the Forfar Militia at Sunderland, and maintained a strength of close on 700. With all the other battalions of Local Militia it was disbanded in 1816.[14]

In fact nothing remained of all these yeomanry and volunteer corps after 1818; none saw any service—unless one excepts a false alarm of invasion in February 1804 created by the burning of some gorse on the Lammermuir Hills, which called out the Gateshead Volunteers, the Usworth Legion, the Derwent Legion and the Durham Yeomanry—; and they would not be worth mentioning had not the County, in common with the rest of the nation, experienced in 1859 an upsurge of military ardour of the same sort, which gave birth, as we shall see, to battalions that are still in existence after adding honours to those of the Durham Light Infantry. There is no continuity in the history of, say, the Darlington Legion and the 6th Battalion of the Durham Light Infantry; but there is a strong family tie that connects the two, and it is upon the families that served in all these corps that interest should be principally directed. From them derives that powerful urge to give military service which, harnessed to an ordinary line regiment and a county militia of great antiquity. makes a Durham regiment out of the Durham Light Infantry.

[14]The returns of the two Durham Local Militia battalions are in W.O. 13/3468 3469.

CHAPTER II

THE RAISING OF THE 68TH AND ITS FIRST CAMPAIGN

THE 68th was one of the twenty line infantry battalions that survived from the prodigious number raised in the Seven Years War. Some idea of the immensity of the effort exerted by this country in that great life and death struggle with France, fought to the kill in America, in India and in Europe, may be gained when it is said that the numbered line regiments alone rose from No. 50 to No. 124, representing an increase of over eighty battalions. The process of raising began during the period of tension in North America which preceded any formal declaration of war. First came the raising, late in 1754, of two new American battalions, the 50th and 51st, usually known as Shirley's and Pepperell's. Next, in October 1755, came the augmentation of each battalion in the army by a ninth and tenth company. Next, in January 1756, came the raising of ten new battalions, numbered from 52 to 61, to which twenty of the additional companies were drafted to provide a nucleus. Then, in March of the same year, another new American regiment, of forty companies, 62nd in order of precedence, was raised. Soon after the declaration of war that followed the Duc de Richelieu's successful attack on Port Mahon in Minorca, a Beating Order was issued, on 20th September 1756, for the raising of a second battalion of ten companies to each of fifteen old regiments. The Beating Order was made in implementation of a Royal Sign Manual Warrant authorising the establishment of the new battalions, dated at Kensington on 29th September but made effective from 25th August 1756.

One of the fifteen regiments receiving the order was a respectable old corps recently part of the garrison of Port Mahon, a garrison which had put up such a stubborn resistance to Richelieu's attack that it was allowed the honours of war. It was known as Huske's in the fashion, gradually disappearing, of calling a regiment after its Colonel; it was the 23rd in the new fashion, by order of precedence; but it preferred its own title of Royal Welch Fusiliers. Like the other three regiments of the garrison, which had equally received orders to form a second battalion (the 4th, 24th and 34th), the 23rd were at Gibraltar at the time, whence, however, they were soon brought back to this country to recruit, being stationed in and around Leicester in December 1756.

The recruiting of the Second Battalion had apparently proceeded during its absence, for in October there was enough of it to be mentioned as being quartered at Leicester and Loughborough. Sixteen men drawn from three dragoon guards regiments were transferred to provide a nucleus of non-commissioned officers, and in November all the men impressed in Northamptonshire and Leicestershire under the recent act for the impressment of vagrants were directed to it. It was not, however, large enough to receive separate mention when the First Battalion was concentrated at Leicester to be inspected by the Earl of Ancrum on 16th February 1757.

We shall now see how regiments were proliferated in the eighteenth century, and in the face of what obstacles that intangible sentiment we call *esprit de corps* was implanted in them. The authorities do not concern themselves with anything but good-sized bodies of men, with the due number of officers, non-commissioned officers, drummers and private men, dressed, armed and equipped according to His Majesty's Regulations, and performing the regulation exercises. Men are obtained from the workshops and the plough-tail, and in times of war they are not usually very difficult to procure. They are, moreover, subject to that bane of the military existence known as drafting, by which any man may be moved from one corps to another without his consent wherever the exigencies of the moment may demand. Sergeants and drummers are usually exempt. Officers are obtained from the service at large, every augmentation in time of war being hailed with delight as an opportunity for promotion out of turn, and young men like Tony Lumpkin come forward to take the vacant ensigncies as their predecessors move up.

The establishment of the new 2/23rd was: nine battalion companies each of a captain, a lieutenant, an ensign, three sergeants, three corporals, two drummers, and seventy private men; one grenadier company of a captain, two lieutenants, three sergeants, three corporals, two drummers, and seventy private men; and a staff of one major (commanding), an adjutant, a quartermaster, and two surgeon's mates—a total of 34 officers and 780 n.c.o.s and privates. Most of the men appear to have been raw recruits, unconnected in any way with any regiment. Some of the n.c.o.s were old soldiers, some the above-mentioned troopers from the dragoon guards, some, one may surmise, from the 1/23rd.

The officers have a diversity of origins. The major commanding was Major Thomas Marlay, senior captain of the 23rd. Captain William Rowley, an Irishman, came from the 78th Company of Marines. Captain William Fowler was a "new" captain in one of the recent additional companies of the 27th; so was Captain George Bingham. Captain John Fox was the captain-lieutenant of the 23rd, that is to say he was the subaltern who commanded the company belonging to the Colonel of the Regiment. Captain William Dundas was the captain-lieutenant of the new 61st. Captain Peter Hewitt, an Irishman of 51, was a lieutenant and a former n.c.o. of the 1/23rd; so was Captain Richard Lloyd. Captain Tristram Revell was a lieutenant of the 9th. Captain John Blaquiere was a cornet in the 11th Dragoons. Captain Robert Ridley was an ensign in the 1st Guards. All these were commissioned as captains in the 23rd on successive days from 25th August 1756, and it will be seen how materially the augmentation had improved their previous standing.

The two senior first-lieutenants,[1] Charles Reynell and Joseph Patterson, were both "new" lieutenants from the additional companies of the 27th. Lieutenant James Sutherland came (probably) from the Scots regiment in the Dutch service called Drumlanrig's, which was "broke" in 1752. Lieutenant Arthur Barber was an ensign and adjutant of the 30th; Philip Mercier quartermaster of the 14th Dragoons. Lieutenant Arthur Hawthorne, an Irishman, was formerly quartermaster in the 1/23rd. Lieutenant Lewis Bellew was a sergeant in the 18th, Lieutenants Robert Young and Porter sergeants in the 1/23rd, Lieutenants Edward Evans and John Haswell non-commissioned officers from the 1st Troop of the Royal Horse Guards. Like the captains these first-lieutenants were commissioned in the 23rd on successive days from 25th August, and they too will be seen to have materially profited from the augmentation. Two only of the second-lieutenants, George Orpen and William Blakeney, two Irishmen, "new" ensigns from the additional companies of the 27th, had served previously. The other seven were freshly commissioned.

Before the 2/23rd went on service many changes took place in the commissioned ranks, and in the non-commissioned ranks drafting made such inroads as to delay the growth of any corporate spirit. Eighty men from the 23rd as a whole were drafted with 900 men from the other fourteen regiments to reinforce the depleted battalions

[1]Fusilier regiments had first-lieutenants and second-lieutenants as opposed to the lieutenants and ensigns of foot regiments.

in North America on 6th August 1757. The following month the establishment of the fifteen regiments was reduced from twenty to eighteen companies of 100 men each, the youngest company in each battalion being "incorporated" into its own battalion and the youngest captain (Ridley in the 2/23rd) acting as supernumerary captain with the eldest company. On 12th November 1757 the youngest company of the 2/23rd, together with those of nine others of the fifteen, were taken away to form a new regiment for service in India, known as Draper's or the 64th. Little wonder that a Beating Order for the completion (that is to say, making up to establishment) of the 2/23rd should have been issued on 13th May 1758. The worst blow to the new battalion, however, fell after it had seen its first fighting and done its first tour of duty as an independent regiment, when in February 1760 it found a draft of 600 men for the battalions in the West Indies. From a fine body of 705 men it was reduced at one stroke to a weak skeleton of 58.

The formation in 1756 of new battalions under the ægis of old regiments was a new departure. One reason, certainly, was economy. The new battalion was a major's command, and, in contrast to a whole new regiment, dispensed with the appointment of a colonel, a lieut.-colonel and a chaplain. Such a saving, multiplied fifteen times, was no doubt a consideration of importance. Yet it is difficult to regard it as the only consideration. It may well have been that the dilution of the army was felt to have gone far enough with the creation of seventeen new battalions from nothing, and that any further creations would benefit from the kind of parental relationship prescribed for the latest fifteen, whether the relationship lasted for ever or only until the new battalion had found its feet.

If that is so one would expect a substantial contribution from the 1/23rd to the 2/23rd, and of that there is, unfortunately, only scanty evidence. On the one hand it is clear that in the initial stages the presence of the parent regiment was not necessary. On the other, there is the evidence of the first inspection report of the Second Battalion, which was reviewed by Lord George Sackville at Chatham Camp on 24th September 1757. Its strength at that time was 679 n.c.o.s and men. Over 60 *per cent.* of these men had no more than a year's service, as compared with 17 *per cent.* in the First Battalion. Eighteen *per cent.* however, 121 men, had two years' service, and 94 men had between three and thirty years' service, and these it is surely proper to assume came mostly from the old 23rd, of whom well over half were mature soldiers of over five years' service. Some shuffling of men between the battalions took place before they finally separated; the officers in the same period seem also to have been transferred from one to the other as though it were one large regiment; and there is consequently much room for speculation on the exact amount of assistance given by the Royal Welch Fusiliers to their off-spring. It is, however, safe to assume that they contributed quite 100 seasoned men towards its formation. In officers the contribution was necessarily of a different kind, since they came from the service at large. But its first two commanding officers (Marley and Adey) came from the 1/23rd, which also gave six or seven junior officers (includ-ing Humphrey Hopper, formerly sergeant-major) in exchange for the newcomers from outside. The inference may be drawn that in officers as well as men the old regiment contributed fairly substan-tially to the new.[2]

The period of "parenthood", whether intended as a temporary or a permanent expedient, was shortlived. Various dates may be given for its termination. The earliest is 22nd April 1758, the day on which the battalion's first Colonel was appointed. The latest is 25th June, a quarter-day, the day on which it was officially brought onto the establishment. A more real date is 13th May 1758, the day on which the new colonel was given his Letter of Service, authorising him to complete his regiment by beat of drum in any part of the kingdom. The decision to separate the new battalions from their "parents" seems to have actually been taken at the beginning of May. On 2nd May the new battalions are still referred to as, say, "the 1st Battalion of the 37th," but on the 6th the new battalions are being called by their Colonel's name, such as the 2/34th, which is styled on that day "Colonel Browne's Regiment of Foot (late the 2nd Battalion of the 34th Regiment)"; and from June onwards they are referred to simply by their new numbers of precedence. Both the 22nd April and the 25th June are "dates of convenience", the former to satisfy the rules of precedence, the latter to satisfy the complicated fiscal rules of the Treasury and, as it was said, "to prevent confusion to the accounts from which the said battalions were separated," the discrepancy between the two dates being reconciled by the award of back-pay to the colonel from his appointment to 25th June. The 13th May represents more truly the birthday of the new regiment, and from the account of a recruit who joined at that time it is clear that by the 19th, although the battalions were neighbours in camp, the separa-tion was regarded as having in fact taken place.[3]

[2]The Beating Order for the raising of the 2/23rd is to be found in W.O.26/23, p. 108-109; the Warrant for its Establishment is in W.O.24/325; the Inspection Reports are in W.O.27/4 and 27/5. See also A. D. L. Cary and S. McCance, *Regimental Records of the Royal Welch Fusiliers* (1921), Vol. 1, pp. 122-123.

[3]The Warrants and Beating Orders are in W.O.26/23, pp. 398, 423-427.

The officer appointed to the colonelcy of the new regiment was Lieut.-Colonel John Lambton, the senior captain of the Coldstream Guards and, by virtue of the privilege of double rank granted to captains and lieutenants of Guards regiments, lieut.-colonel in the army. Lambton, fourth and youngest son of Ralph Lambton by his wife, Dorothy, daughter and co-heir of John Hedworth, of Harraton, County Durham, belonged to one of the oldest families of Durham, who have owned the property whose name they bear at least from the twelfth century. At the age of 22, in 1732, he had entered the Coldstream, had acted as quartermaster from 1742 to 1745 and received his company on 24th January 1745/6 (O.S.). He was present with his regiment at the battle of Fontenoy. His elder brother, Hedworth, who had risen to be the Coldstream's lieut.-colonel, had already been given a regiment, the new 54th, and there can be little doubt that, in view of the way things were done in those days, John also had made his ambitions known. Indeed, one wonders whether the pressure from the younger generation of deserving officers applying for the rank of colonel was not perhaps one of the reasons for making the "new fifteen" into separate regiments. John Lambton must have been regarded as one of the up and coming officers: a better known contemporary of his, James Wolfe, was gratified with a colonelcy at the same time and given the new battalion immediately senior to his; and though the reasons for Lambton's appointment are not obvious, we shall be much mistaken if we ascribe it to influence rather than to a show of promise comparable to Wolfe's.

"Lambton's Regiment of Foot" was the 68th in order of precedence. Shirley's and Pepperell's, the 51st and 52nd, were drafted and disbanded after the losses they suffered at the capture of Oswego in 1756, so that all those junior to them went up two, Hedworth's 54th becoming the 52nd, and the 62nd Americans obtaining their well known number of 60th. Although four battalions had been raised between September 1756 and May 1758 and had already been numbered 61 to 64, the "new fifteen" were inserted in their proper places as 61st to 75th, the former 61st to 64th dropping to 76th to 79th. Lambton's, by reason of its derivation from the 23rd, which was the eighth senior of the "fifteen", became the 68th. The next regiment raised, Gage's, on 17th June 1758, became the 80th.

There is a faint tradition, repeated in Lambton's notice in the *Dictionary of National Biography*, that the 2/23rd had "been chiefly recruited in Durham," but there is no contemporary evidence to support it. Until 12th May 1757 it was quartered and recruited in Leicester, and in view of the impressment order already mentioned, directing to it the impressed men from Northamptonshire and Leicestershire, it must be regarded as being composed largely of midlanders, from whom it continued to draw the greater part of its recruits even after its return from abroad in 1760, when the London, Biggleswade, Leicester and Aylesbury recruiting-parties picked up forty recruits to every one in Durham. On 12th May 1757 it was ordered south to Reading and Wokingham, marching parallel with the First Battalion; and on 21st June the two moved south to the "lines encompassing the Dock at Chatham," where they remained from 7th July to 29th September. From 2nd October to 15th April 1758 they were stationed at Dover and Folkestone, until they were moved into camp in the Isle of Wight in preparation for embarkation. From its stations it is almost certainly wrong to deduce a Durham connection until after Lambton's appointment, which took place while they were making ready for service, and after that there is no mention of a recruiting-party in Durham until April 1760, and no mention of a Durham recruit until September of that year. The point to remark, however, is that the Regiment should have had a Durham recruiting-party at all.[4]

Lambton very laudably proceeded to take personal command of his new regiment although the new establishment included a lieut.-colonelcy, which was given to William Adey, formerly major in the 23rd, aged 32, with 12 years' service including Fontenoy, Val (or Laffelt), where he was wounded, and Minorca.

The impression given by Sackville's report of the previous September is that he took over a battalion that was shaping well. It was 94 *per cent.* English, 4 Scottish and 2 Irish. It was over establishment. Yet 32 *per cent.* of the men were under 5ft 6ins. in height, 13 *per cent.* only being over 5ft. 9ins. and allotted to the grenadier company. The officers are described as "ready in their exercise". Their uniforms were "only frocks," faced with the blue of the 23rd, and bound with a narrow gold lace. The men were deficient in white gaiters, but the brown were "complete in number and tolerably good". The men's uniform was "red, lapelled and faced with blue, with a red, blue, yellow and white-striped worsted lace". In appearance they were "a low body of men, very few old, indifferently clean under arms". Their accoutrements were "good, indifferently put on, the caps good in general, but too big". Sackville summed up by saying they were "a low body of men," but added, what was most important, that "they were well appointed, ready in their exercise and fit for service". The old regiment at the same time was called "a tall,

[4]W.O.5/44, pp. 373, 302, 357; W.O.5/45, p. 10. For recruiting see W.O.17/189.

strong body of men, very well appointed ready in their exercise and very fit for service," a comparison in which the new battalion does not suffer unduly.[5]

Such is the official view of the 68th. For a more human representation of it there is, by good chance, a description by a young lad of 15, a native of Oxford, who enlisted there or thereabouts in April 1758. On his march from Kingston to the Isle of Wight with his fellow recruits he was quartered on the publicans, but on reaching the "canvas town" in the King's Forest, between Cowes and Newport, " 'our ground' as the old soldiers styled it, we found several small boughs stuck in the earth as a mark where to fix our tents. Everyone was presently employed in setting up their little houses, and in less than half-an-hour the whole encampment, containing lodgings for a thousand men, was completed. The next thing was to fetch straw for our beds and faggots of wood to dress our provisions, which caused a great bustle among the inferior officers—or sergeants, corporals and lance-corporals—who were to see that the men did their duty in this respect." He found that six men were allotted a tent, and that besides an allowance of straw there were two blankets between them, "which, to prevent one man's having a greater share than another, are sewed together at the ends". He found too that "the usual manner of laying is head and feet, three one way and three the other, which, according to the cleanliness and health of your comrades, is more or less disagreeable. It is a settled rule that the oldest soldier lies at the further end of the tent and the youngest next the door, which is not a very desirable situation, as everyone who goes out or comes in is likely to tread on you, and, what is still worse, as some of the men at night might not go beyond the tent door you often suffer from their evacuations, as was the case with me." The soldiers, he says, sleep without shirts both in camp and quarters because in the former the straw wears them out, and in the latter because men avoid catching "any distemper" thereby and also make them last longer by not washing them, so quickly do they wear out. For long he could not understand why he, the newcomer, always received the worst piece of meat in the stew, since outwardly the way of distributing it seemed so fair. When each mess had received its stewpot from the kitchens in the rear of the "ground," one member of it was chosen to stand with his back to it. Another man stood by the pot picking out the pieces of meat, calling out as he did so "Who shall have this?" while the first man answered by naming the mess-mates one by one. He then discovered that the worst piece was always reserved for the man whose name was prefaced by the question "*And* who shall have

[5] W.O.27/5.

this?" and that man, as he says, was invariably "Jonas", which is apparently eighteenth century language for "muggins".

Their third day in camp, that is to say, on the 19th or 20th May, the recruits for the two battalions "who were not fixed to any particular company" were ordered to be drawn for. "In the first place we were taken to the doctors of the Regiment, who examined us separately to see if we were in no way disabled or ruptured. Next we were drawn up in rank like so many horses at a fair, and every officer in the Regiment had the pleasure of looking at us and making what enquiries they thought proper. Then tickets were put into a hat and the two majors drew for us. It happened to be my chance to be drawn for the Second Battalion, which was the 68th Regiment. Next we were drawn for again into separate companies. And then I was provided with everything styled necessary to make me a gentleman soldier, such as a red coat, a laced hat, a cap, gun, sword, &c.; in which garb and implements doubtless at first I looked very awkwardly. The next day I was taken out to *learn to walk*, but as our stay was not to be long here I was soon dismissed from the school of walking, and was put to learn the use of the firelock in order to face the *monsieurs*."

It is a new battalion the young man has joined, but it is an old society. The stew-pot custom, for instance, was noticed by a traveller as being used by the Janissaries of the Sultan's army in the early sixteenth century, and it was still observed both in the Spanish Army at the time of the Peninsular War and occasionally our own. He gives the impression, moreover, that there were more old hands among the two battalions than the returns suggest, though that may be a natural impression upon a newcomer.[6]

§

In May 1758 the war was passing through a critical phase. The war had started as a colonial struggle with France. But France was a continental military power, in a position, as we had learned in the previous war, to influence the colonial struggle by pressure upon those two regions of Europe where we were particularly sensitive: Hanover, for dynastic reasons, and the Low Countries, for reasons which have traditionally dominated our foreign policy. By diplomatic means outside our concern our principal ally became Frederick of Prussia, who, though himself a general of genius as well as the

[6] *A Soldier's Journal, containing a particular description of the several descents* . . . (London, 1770), pp. 3 ff. The author must unfortunately remain anonymous. He was one of the draft of 600 who were transferred to battalions in the West Indies, and though the names of those are known, the musters of the 65th, which he joined, are missing until 1768, by which date he was discharged.

autocrat of the most militaristic state in Europe, was faced by a combination of three military powers each possessing resources far exceeding his own, the Empire, Russia and France. Since he had joined in the war he had, as well as requesting British forces on the Continent, repeatedly urged the British government to profit by sea-power to make descents upon the Breton and Norman coasts with a view to detaining within their frontiers the French regiments destined for the invasion of Westphalia. Such a motive had been behind the expedition to Rochefort of September 1757, which, though usually considered a failure, nevertheless diverted a considerable number of French troops even if it failed to influence events in Hanover to our advantage. In the spring of 1758 circumstances more than ever favoured this form of diversion, and in April, Frederick, receding from his previous insistence on direct assistance in men, agreed to a subsidy in money while the British government undertook to make a descent on the coasts of France. "It was therefore of the utmost importance, as a guarantee of good faith, that an oversea expedition should be undertaken immediately. Four days after the treaty had been signed sixteen battalions were warned for foreign service and ordered to assemble at a camp in the Isle of Wight by 23rd May." The routes were timed for the battalions to arrive every day from the 11th to the 23rd. It was this movement the 23rd and 68th shared in, and the camp the one in which "Jonas" took his first military steps.

The plans for the descent were laid by Pitt in consultation with the Admiralty and Ligonier (who till recently has received scant credit for his part as a chief-of-staff). Saint-Malo, an active privateer port situated at the tip of a promontory, connected to the mainland by a long causeway, was selected as an objective. The military force, a strong one of hardly less than 14,000 men, was entrusted to the Duke of Marlborough, a competent if undistinguished grandson of Duke John, with Lord George Sackville as second-in-command. The naval arrangements were placed in the energetic hands of Hawke. The Army consisted of the light troops from nine dragoon regiments, a powerful siege-train, and five brigades of infantry:

> *Guards Brigade* (Major-General Dury): First Regiment, Third Regiment, Coldstream;
> *1st Foot Brigade* (Major-General Mostyn): 5th, 36th, 25th;
> *2nd Foot Brigade* (Major-General Waldegrave): 20th, 67th, 30th;
> *3rd Foot Brigade* (Major-General Boscawen): 23rd; 68th, 33rd;
> *4th Foot Brigade* (Major-General Eliott): 24th, 72nd, 34th.

It will be observed Lambton's Regiment was brigaded with its parent; but this brigading was modified before the Expedition sailed on the 29th by the organisation of two battalions each of five companies of grenadiers in accordance with a practice that was customary until late in the century. The grenadier companies were completed to 100 men each and placed with the 5th Regiment under the command of Major-General Mostyn in the following manner, apparently:

> *1st Battalion:* grenadier companies 20th, 25th, 33rd, 36th, 67th;
> *2nd Battalion:* grenadier companies 23rd, 24th, 30th, 34th, 68th.

The command of the grenadier battalions was not permanently given to any particular officer, but Lambton himself was appointed field-officer for the two, while Lieut.-Colonel Beckwith and Major Goodrick started by commanding the first, Lieut.-Colonel Adey (68th) and Major Ramsay the second.[7]

The embarkation was effected during the 25th, 26th and 27th May, the 3rd Brigade embarking at Cowes on the 26th. The 68th were crowded into the *Mary* transport, 383 tons, and the *Constant James*, 279 tons, not a liberal allowance of tonnage for a battalion 650 strong with women, but the "short-voyage rate" allowed for no more than a ton a man as compared with the usual 1½ tons. On 1st June the Expedition made sail in a strong gale. "Jonas" describes his first night at sea vividly: the lurching and tossing, the near panic in the overcrowded vessel as it was buffeted by the heavy seas. In the dark below decks he lost one shoe and by mistake picked up a woman's, which, however, he threw overboard when he found someone had been sick in it.

The fleet stood in and anchored in the Bay of Cancale on the 5th. The specially designed flat-bottomed boats were immediately hoisted out from those ships that carried them, the grenadiers were embarked, and after assembling at the headquarter ship, the *Essex*, were rowed ashore to La Houle under a heavy bombardment from the fleet which effectively silenced the shore-batteries. The grenadiers of the 23rd got on shore first. Advancing rapidly, they and the other

---

[7]For the descents on the French coast generally see: Sir Julian S. Corbett, *England in the Seven Years' War* (Longmans, Green, 1907), Vol. 1, *caps.* XI and XII; and more particularly, Rex Whitworth's valuable *Field Marshal Lord Ligonier* (Clarendon Press, 1958), *cap.* XII. For contemporary accounts, apart from *A Soldier's Journal* see: *A Journal . . . of the late Expeditions on the Coast of France . . .* (B.M., 102. d.43) (London, 1758); *An Impartial Narrative . . .* (B.M. E.2050); and, for the Saint-Malo Expedition, the account of Sergeant John Porter, 23rd, in the *Journal of the Royal United Service Institution* (*cit.* hereafter as "J.R.U.S.I."), Vol. 58 (1914), pp. 755-763.

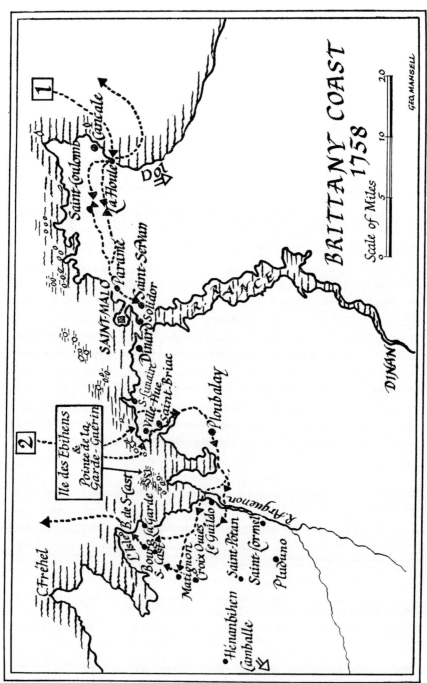

2. The two descents on Saint-Malo, June and September 1758

companies, followed later by the Guards battalions, overcame the resistance put up by the *gardes-côtes* near a windmill above the village, and took up a position on the slopes above the beach to cover the landing of the remainder. Four and a half battalions were landed that day until darkness interrupted the process. The next day, the 6th, while the grenadiers and Guards moved up through Cancale, the rest of the Army was put on shore. The battalion companies of the 68th were among the last, and it was nearly 11 o'clock at night before they could encamp. The sun, "extremly hot and scorching," had blazed down all day on the men, who had been on deck the whole night as well in expectation of being called to the boats.

On the 7th the Army was assembled and marched off towards Saint-Malo in two columns, that comprising the grenadier battalion with the 68th's men taking the high road nearest the sea. The 23rd and 68th, of Boscawen's Brigade, however, were left behind near the deserted village of Cancale with the task of throwing up works to secure the Army's retreat. These consisted of two square redoubts (called Fort Marlborough and Fort Sackville), a hornwork (called Fort Ancrum), two batteries and an entrenchment enclosing 1130 paces of ground. The labour, it is not surprising to learn, occupied the two battalions from 3 in the morning until late at night. The only men of the battalion companies in the forefront of events were those ordered forward on convoy duties.

Meanwhile, after the grenadiers had taken possession of Paramé late on the 7th, Saint-Servan was entered by parties of dragoons, and the harbour, crowded with shipping and stores, was fired. Four King's ships were burned, together with 60 merchantmen, several privateers, and great quantities of naval stores. Another detachment carried out a similar destruction at Solidor. Saint-Malo was summoned on the 8th but without success. Since the battering-train was necessary to reduce the place and the only road practicable for the heavy guns passed through Dol, several miles inland, a retreat was determined upon, a resolution confirmed by reports of a French concentration of regular troops received from a flank guard that had been sent out to Dol.

The retreat started at about 11 o'clock on 10th June with the 2nd Brigade, the Guards and the 1st Grenadier Battalion. The 2nd Grenadier Battalion and the two other brigades were detained waiting for a detachment of grenadiers under Colonel Lambton, which did not return until about 3. They reached their old ground at Cancale at 10 at night, having done five million livres' worth of damage at the cost of 30 men, mostly stragglers. The 3rd Brigade went on board first on the 11th in heavy rain, the other three foot brigades, the Guards and grenadiers following on the 12th. The last troops to embark were by that time knee-deep in mud.

Bad weather kept the fleet in Cancale Bay until 21st June. A descent on Granville was threatened, another at Havre, and a third at Cherbourg was actually started until bad weather caused it to be abandoned. After a fourth attempt at the mouth of the Orne the fleet returned to St. Helens, and on 6th July the Army landed and marched to its old ground in the Isle of Wight.

Pitt's policy had been somewhat modified in the interval. He was now persuaded direct military assistance in North Germany was essential, and, though he intended to continue with his policy of "amphibious warfare" upon the French coast, he dispatched a considerable force of cavalry to Prince Ferdinand of Brunswick as well as six battalions of infantry. Among the latter were three from the Army in the Isle of Wight, one of them the 23rd, who were thus separated from the 68th for the first time since their creation.

It now was all the fashion to go a-campaigning in Germany and get away from the accursed transports. The Duke of Marlborough, Lord George Sackville and most of the staff succeeded in getting themselves transferred to the new theatre of war. The change in command that resulted was not for the better. Though Howe was given the naval command the command of the Army in the Isle of Wight fell to a veteran of over 70, Lieut.-General Thomas Bligh, who assumed it unwillingly. It is usual to visualise Pitt as having supreme authority over our military concerns, and choosing with a sure and almost clairvoyant eye the instruments of his policy. The truth seems to lie elsewhere. Certainly at this juncture his position was far from unassailable, his arrangements liable to be disrupted by intrigue in London, particularly by the faction of Frederick, Prince of Wales ("poor Fred, who was alive and is dead"); and in the choice of Bligh it must be acknowledged both he and Ligonier were, like Homer, nodding.

The subtraction of the three battalions involved a further reorganisation. The Guards remained as they were before, but the line infantry brigades were made up as follows:

> *1st Brigade* (Major-General Mostyn): 5th, 67th, 33rd;
> *2nd Brigade* (Major-General Boscawen): 24th, 68th, 34th;
> *3rd Brigade* (Major-General Eliott): 30th, 72nd, 36th.

The grenadiers were at the same time organised into a "Corps" composed of thirteen companies (though there were but twelve battalions in the Army and three of them Guards), and placed under the command, initially, of Lieut.-Colonel Gansil and Major Preston.

Bligh's instructions ordered him to capture Cherbourg and, sub-sequently or alternatively, launch attacks on the French coast at any points he and Howe considered practicable between Morlaix and the easternmost part of Normandy. The Army was reimbarked. The 68th were put on board the *Friend's Goodwill* on the 23rd July, leaving behind many who had been taken ill in the overcrowded conditions of the previous passage, and sailed on 1st August. On the 7th the fleet anchored two leagues to the west of Cherbourg, in Marais Bay. "There is," says "Jonas", "beyond the forts on three rocky pro-montories, a succession of three bays: a sandy one, at the end of which is a promontory crowned by the fort of Querqueville, then another sandy bay, and west again a 'foul' bay, rocky." The French had thrown up lines in the two sandy bays manned by five to six thousand militia, and Cherbourg itself was garrisoned by the Irish Regiment of Clare. Howe, having reconnoitred the bays on the 8th, selected the "foul" one as that least expected. The troops were landed under cover of a bombardment from the ships, and advanced on the town, driving before them the militia and the Regiment of Clare, who retreated "after making one or two very faint fires." Cherbourg was entered the next day, the 9th, the destruction of the defences and what little shipping there was in the harbour promptly taken in hand, and burning and pillaging went on until the 15th and 16th, when the troops reimbarked unmolested by a French force which had gathered at Valognes. They had performed a useful service, even if it was marked by acts of indiscipline which contrasted strongly with the behaviour of the same Army under Marlborough. Marlborough, even his enemies confessed, had acted in the most regular manner, punishing, as "Jonas" remarks, several who plundered at Cancale— among them a man of Revell's Company of the name of Hopwood who was sentenced to be hanged but was later pardoned.

The success at Cherbourg, which was the occasion of a victory march in London and coincided with news both of Marlborough's junction with Prince Ferdinand in Germany and of Frederick of Prussia's victory at Küstrin, encouraged Pitt to order the Expedition to sea again. Bligh sailed from Portland on 31st August under the same instructions he had received before Cherbourg. These gave him, as we have seen, a fair discretion, and during his fortnight in England Lord Shelburne and the the Prince of Wales's Leicester House faction had persuaded him to make a further attempt at Saint-Malo, which was, from its situation, a suitable place to hold fast onto "until the peace". Howe was persuaded to swallow the plan under the impression that he could ship the troops across the Rance direct into Saint-Malo. There was nothing against Saint-Malo as an objective, on the contrary, it was a perfectly proper one; but, coming as a plan of the Prince's advisers, it would, if successful, redound to the exclusive credit of the faction. It was in this manner that "the Expedition set off to capture an objective unknown both to Pitt and Ligonier but selected by a Leicester House cabal".[8]

Some recovered men had reached the 68th when at sea, but they hardly replaced the casualties in deaths and sick caused by the over-crowding, the heats and colds of the alternate camps and transports, and the vermin of the previous voyages, which made Pitt's "amphi-bious policy" so unpopular in the Army. Twenty-five officers out of 37, and 534 n.c.o.s and men out of 811 embarked for Cherbourg, and the battalion cannot have numbered much more than a round 500 in the second Saint-Malo venture. The other battalions were no better off. Indeed, after the deduction of the three battalions sent to Germany and the sick, the remaining twelve together with the four squadrons of dragoons and the artillery amounted to hardly 7000 men. Though weak and reduced, the Army was nevertheless larger than any the French could bring against it for some days, and it is implicitly clear from "Jonas's" narrative that they were all practised soldiers by now, determined to give a good account of themselves and full of self-confidence even if there was some want of confidence in their commander.

The fleet anchored off Saint-Lunaire in the evening of 3rd September between the Ile des Ebihens and the Ile Agot; and the next morning, Monday the 4th, the Army disembarked in a cove near the Tertre de la Garde-Guérin, encamping near the villages of La Chapelle, Ville-Hue, Le Mesnil and La Fosse without throwing up works. The broad estuary of the Rance lay between them and their objective, which had been reinforced since June by a regiment of regular infantry. After a reconnaissance on the 5th Howe assured the General that he could not cover the crossing or safely bombard the harbour of Saint-Malo from his ships; and, since the bank of the Rance seemed too strongly held either to attempt a crossing or to carry the Army across the first bridge (Dinan), it was decided at a council of war to give up the design on Saint-Malo. Five companies of grenadiers were sent that day into Saint-Briac, where, though finding only 13 ships of the 300 they expected, they burned them.

That was the sum of the profitable destruction carried out, for the

---

[8]Whitworth, *op. cit.*, p. 265. For the Saint-Cast disaster Mr C. T. Atkinson kindly brought my attention to (and lent me) the rare and important *Saint-Cast: Recueil de pièces officielles et de documents contemporains relatifs au Combat du 11 Septembre* 1758 (Saint-Brieuc, 1858). See also *Hist. Mss. Comm.* (Stopford-Sackville), Vol. 1, pp. 296-301.

next day the weather deteriorated and compelled Howe to remove the ships to the Bay of Saint-Cast, whither the Army had perforce to follow it.

It marched at 7 o'clock on the 8th, and moving by the Château de Pontbriand and Ploubalay, it encamped on the near bank of the Arguenon after a difficult march in which it was harassed by small parties of the enemy posted in the hedges and woods. The grenadier companies in advance had run into stiff opposition at Le Guildo (which overlooks the crossing of the river on the far bank) but would have forced the passage that evening had not Bligh's Quartermaster-General persuaded the General to wait until the tide was lower. The fact is that Bligh was in no hurry to re-embark. He had a mind to take up a position near Matignon, where, supporting himself from the countryside, he could wait until a fair-sized French force was diverted against him. Competently managed, such a design was in keeping with Pitt's strategic conception, and after the failure at Saint-Malo it was, in the abstract, quite proper. But Bligh was not a competent manager, and he seems to have been unaware until the last moment of the enemy concentration moving in his direction.

More fighting at Le Guildo was spared to the Army by the arrival of a gentleman of Saint-Lormel of the name of Grumellon (whose old uncle, ironically enough, had been killed by some marauding foragers from the Army), who offered to show them the easiest pass-age across the Arguenon estuary. Early on Sunday the 9th, one column crossed at Le Guildo itself; a second at Ville Gicquel; a third at the ford of Quatre-Vaux, well into the flats covered at high water. The Army waited at Croix-Ouies, and there encamped for the night. The next day, the 10th, it moved on to a position near Matignon, where the grenadiers were deployed in a sharp fight with regular dragoons and infantry in the enclosures, and suffered some casualties.

The Governor of Brittany, the Duc d'Aiguillon, was near Brest on the 5th when he was informed of the landing, but lost no time in directing all available regular troops upon Lamballe. These were at some distance, but by forced marches four regiments (Bourbon, de Brissac, de Bresse and de Quercy) and some dragoons were concentrated and moving on Hénanbihen to sever Bligh's communication with his ships in Saint-Cast Bay. Two other battalions were moving on Bligh's flank at Saint-Pôtan and Pluduno, and the regular battalion from Saint-Malo followed in the rear. It was the vanguard of the Lamballe force Bligh's grenadiers had encountered at Matignon, and the position of the British Army at once became precarious.

Lieut.-Colonel Clark, the Quartermaster-General, who discounted reports of the enemy concentration, proposed the foolhardy course of

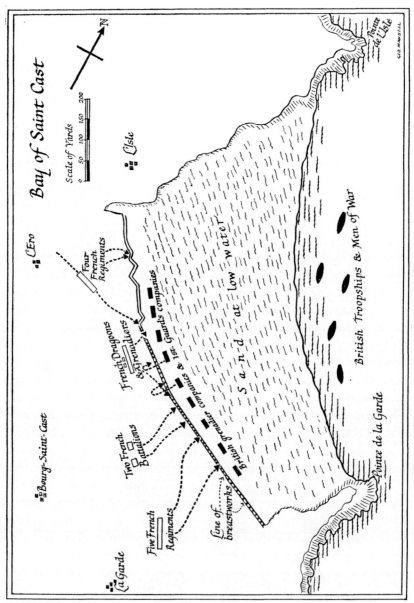

3. The Action on the Beach of Saint-Cast, 11th September, 1758

landing the artillery still on board and advancing to the attack. But a council of war rejected it and recommended an immediate embarkation. It would have been possible, though not simple, to slip away in the dark by making use of the usual *ruses de guerre*. But Bligh advertised his intentions by beating, before moving off, both the General and, half-an-hour after, the Assembly, which were customarily dispensed with in a retreat. Then, when time was of the essence, instead of taking up an advantageous position such as the Duke of Marlborough had prepared at Cancale, he proceeded to embark cattle, horses and the cumbrous ordnance while the infantry waited their turn on the beach.

Such was the situation of the Army when, at about 9 o'clock in the morning of 11th September, the Duc d'Aiguillon's van found them in the Bay of Saint-Cast (now a popular bathing-beach). The last regiment of the youngest brigade was just embarking, which we may presume to be the 30th of Eliott's Brigade. The rearguard, composed of the grenadier companies under Lieut.-Colonel Sir William Boothby and Major Griffin, were holding a line across the head of the beach. They had had no time to prepare any works, but they were protected by a dyke or breastwork some three foot in depth dug by the *gardes-côtes* some years before and only hurriedly repaired. Where exactly Captain Revell's grenadiers of the 68th were posted it is impossible to say, but being one of the youngest companies they were no doubt in the centre. At first the grenadiers bore the brunt of the French advance, but later three, perhaps four, companies of the First Guards, who, as senior, were the last for embarkation, were taken to their assistance by the brigadier, General Dury, who then took command of the whole. These stout troops, whose appearance and demeanour made a deep impression on their adversaries as being "for the most part soldiers of 5ft 6 or 8ins[9] and *faits au tour*," held out gallantly for some hours, while thirteen French battalions deployed into line against them and artillery opened on them from the surrounding heights.

The embarkation meanwhile went on in some confusion at first but, as it proceeded, with greater speed and with praiseworthy determination on the part of the boats' crews. The battalion companies of the 68th followed the 30th. There was no time to take the men to their transports, each boat making for the nearest vessel. "Jonas" remembers that he was taken to a bomb-ketch which loosed off a 13in. mortar just as he came alongside, the shell of which he saw fall in the middle of a large troop of French horse. The warships maintained throughout a destructive fire upon the enemy bat-

[9]The French *pied* was rather longer than our foot.

talions, and caused many casualties among them. Indeed, for some time it seemed that between the warships' guns and their own exertions the grenadiers and 1st Guards' companies might succeed.

The turning point came when Dury ordered a counter-attack towards Bourg-Saint-Cast from the centre. It was temporarily successful, but it masked the fire from the ships and the French were allowed to close. They swarmed over the breastwork, and after a short struggle the gallant defenders were driven back towards the sea. Some sought a rock on their left, where a hundred or so made a stand until their ammunition was exhausted and then surrendered at discretion. Some were killed as they fled. The French soldiers continued with the slaughter so long as the frigates continued firing. But when Howe ordered the guns to cease they showed great humanity. Some managed to get to the boats—Boothby was picked up after two hours in the water. Most, however, did not. "A dreadful scene it was," says "Jonas", "to see so many brave fellows lose their lives and we not able to give them any manner of assistance."

Hardly any of the Guards escaped and "every grenadier company is about cut in two," as one of the survivors reported. The Duc d'Aiguillon claimed 900 dead and 600 prisoners, including those wounded, from a rearguard which cannot have numbered much more than the sum of the two together. The losses were sufficient to put the Army in the sulky humour which is reflected in "Jonas's" comment: "Thus several hundred brave fellows' lives were lost by the temerity or misconduct of somebody, the private men not seeing the necessity of risking one of the many lives which were lost. But horses, sheep, dogs and cows," he says, adverting to the plunder taken on board in the first hours, "are more valuable to some men than the lives of eight hundred brave grenadiers." Of the 68th's grenadiers both Revell, commanding the company, and Lieutenant Grant, who had exchanged from the 23rd only a month before, were taken. The killed and wounded are impossible to establish, but the exchanged prisoners from the Regiment numbered, besides the two officers, 31 private men from a company which had been brought up to strength only on the 6th. Nearly 70 must therefore have been killed or died of wounds in captivity, the heaviest casualties of all save those of the 34th and the 1st Guards.[10]

The failure caused dismay at home. Bligh was cut by the King in public and deprived of his appointments; Ligonier, who had certainly displayed "inattention" (Pitt's word), came in for much criticism; and the "amphibious policy" was discredited and aban-

[10]W.O.4/57, p. 528, a return of prisoners exchanged, 27th April 1759.

doned before it was properly exploited. The camp in the Isle of Wight was broken up, and the Regiment, which had been landed at Cowes on 19th September was in October sent to Finsbury and to Rochester to do duty in Chatham Lines, sustaining a deduction of 173 men drafted to the 61st. The prisoners of war from Saint-Cast were exchanged and returned to the Regiment in two detachments, one in December 1758 the second in January 1759, and the recruiting-parties were partially successful in filling the ranks. In March 1759 the Regiment was marched to Southampton and Gosport, and embarked the next month to relieve the 11th in Jersey.

After an uneventful period of duty under Lieut.-Colonel Adey they returned to England in February 1760. The strength in July 1759 had been 33 officers and 785 n.c.o.s and men and it had risen to 840 by the time they disembarked at Southampton. But while there they received orders to find a draft of 600 men for regiments serving in the West Indies, which reduced them to a mere skeleton of 58 rank and file. It took them four years to recruit up to establishment, and it would have taken longer but for the introduction of the peace establishment of nine companies of 50 men (as compared with 100). That draft of February 1760 effectively broke the Regiment for the remainder of the war, and although a party appear to have served on board H.M.S. *Nassau* as marines in the summer of that year, it saw no further active service after Saint-Cast.

CHAPTER III

THE THREE TOURS OF DUTY IN THE WEST INDIES, 1764-1773, 1794-1796, 1801-1806

EVERY regiment has its day, but the 68th's was an unconscionable time a-coming. The next fifty years of the Regiment's history make disappointing, even frustrating, reading. It was never in the forefront of great events, and it shared in nothing worthy of the name of campaign: just three tours of duty in the West Indies, in which it lost in sickness men equivalent to four peacetime battalions, interspersed with periods of recruiting and reorganisation, sometimes such radical reorganisation that it is hard to discern a strong thread of continuity. There is nothing strange or disreputable in all this. Regiments were expected to be "shattered"—that is the word used—on service, and indeed they were kept on their stations until they were. We shall now see this monotonous process repeated three times.

The 68th was moved to Leeds in April 1760, to Newcastle in May, and in July of that year it was accommodated at Tynemouth in one of the few barracks in England. Lambton himself was in command. Its strength was very low. Only about 150 private men were "present fit", companies counted no more than 7, 8, or 9 men, except for Revell's, the grenadier company, which had 34, and it was 600 or 700 below establishment at this period. In February 1761 it lost 95 men drafted to the 70th Regiment. In June 1761 it was moved to Morpeth, when it succeeded in bringing up its strength to 211 privates "present fit". It moved to Berwick in January 1762, and then to Fort George, where it remained until July 1763. On 11th July 1763 it was transferred to the Irish Establishment with a strength of 29 officers and 278 n.c.o.s and privates. It was stationed at Dungannon (with companies detached in the neighbourhood) until April 1764, when it was moved to Cork for embarkation to the West Indies. With the

Peace in 1763 the establishment of the nine companies was reduced to 50, so that its disembarkation state of 448, attained by recruiting during its year in Ireland, showed only 2 "wanting to complete".

It was hardly recognisable as the 68th of Saint-Cast. Besides losing almost the whole of its strength drafted, it had changed its clothing on becoming a separate regiment. The new distinctions chosen by Lambton, which were promulgated in a Warrant of November 1758 but probably did not become effective until a year or so later, consisted of facings, linings and drummers' coats of deep green, and a new pattern lace. This is described as "white, with two yellow and one black stripe"; but the pattern deposited in 1768, which was discovered in the Windsor Archives by the Hon. Sir John Fortescue and presented to the Regiment in September 1918, is 9/16ths inches wide and made up of five stripes: three white (the two outside ones and the centre) one yellow and one black.[1]

Most of the original officers, moreover, had gone. Lieut.-Colonel Adey, for instance, resigned in 1762, Captain Revell transferred to the 24th in 1761. Indeed, few remained. Of the original captains only Dundas was still serving, of the lieutenants only Patriarche, a foreigner, Armstrong and George Munro, a Scot, one of the officers from the 23rd, who was adjutant from 1758 to 1762. Henry Hopper and James Munro, the quartermaster, survived also. The only other survivor, Charles William Este, deserves special mention. He continued to serve with the Regiment from January 1758, when he was transferred from the 23rd, until 1795, when he was appointed D.A.G. on the staff of the Commander-in-Chief in the West Indies. It is clear he enjoyed the patronage of Lambton himself, for not only did he occupy the situation of adjutant from 1767 to 1776 and of recruiting officer at Durham, but he named a son (Charles Lambton Este) after him. He was not, so far as one can say, a Durham man: his family most probably came from London, some of that name appearing in the entries to Westminster School. His career is one of the few links that make for continuity in the vicissitudes of the Regiment in those years, and indeed a continuous service of nearly 37 years in one regiment is remarkable. He was only 19 when he joined: he was 73 when he died in Duke Street, Portland Place, on 13th February 1812.

Such consistent service with the Regiment at that moment in its history was rare. The reductions following the Peace left the Regiment third "youngest" in the army, a position in the line in which it stayed for about fifteen years. Commissions in regiments so near the border-line were considered too exposed to the wind of economy to

[1]W.O.30/13A; Col. Vane's Papers at the Regimental Depot.

3

be comfortable. Young officers tended to join only for the sake of getting the rank (for the "over-regulation" above the purchase price of the tariff was usually low, even negligible), and then moved on to a more secure place. Wise colonels got themselves appointed to regiments higher up the list when they could. Most of the newcomers in the 68th in the early 1760s are young Irishmen who hardly stay longer than a year or two, or else officers from reduced regiments who are "passing through" on their way up. Even Lieut.-Colonel David Wedderburn, the extraordinary young man who commanded the battalion from September 1762 and took it to the West Indies, was an officer of this description. First commissioned in 1757 at the age of 17 and having distinguished himself in Germany, he had been given the lieut.-colonel-commandantship of the new 102nd Regiment until it was disbanded. He transferred to the 22nd a few months after the 68th landed in Antigua.[2]

In these circumstances it says much for Lambton that he stayed by the 68th until his death in 1794, despite the many other opportunities that beckoned. Though he ceased to exercise personal command, and though his marriage and his entry into Parliament as a Member for the County preoccupied him from 1761 onwards, his interest in the Regiment and, we may presume, his affection for it remained undiminished. Several turns in its fortunes are directly attributable to him. Unlike so many of his contemporaries he did not look upon it as a stepping-stone to further promotion. He did not raise the 68th, but he was in every other sense its fond father.

The 68th relieved the 38th in Antigua and landed on 31st May 1764. Its stay in the Island was for four years uneventful, and the only occasion on which it became news was in January 1766 when Governor Sir George Thomas's daughter eloped with a member of the Council, and the commanding officer, Lieut.-Colonel Josiah Martin,[3] who had succeeded Wedderburn in September 1764, was appointed to take the offending member's place.

So much did the Regiment become absorbed into the life of the colony that when it was moved in 1772 a gentleman of Antigua refers to it as "our regiment". Several commissions were taken by

[2]Later appointed to command the whole Bombay Army, he was killed during the siege of Broach, 14th November 1772, at the age of 32 years and eight months, while holding the rank of brigadier-general. He was a younger son of Peter Wedderburn of Chesterhall, Co. Haddington, a Lord of Session under the title of Lord Chesterhall.

[3]Josiah Martin (1737-1786), son of Lieut.-Col. Samuel Martin of Antigua (one of twenty-three children), after selling out from the 68th in 1767 was appointed Governor of North Carolina in 1771. The last royal governor of the province, he fled from New Bern in May 1775.

Antiguans. Martin himself had property in the island. James Stewart, an officer to whom the Regiment is as much indebted as Este for his loyalty to it, who came in from the 17th as a captain in June 1768 after serving at Ticonderoga, Crown Point, the capture of Martinique and Havana, also had propery in the islands. John Simon Farley, another loyal officer who took all his promotions in the Regiment from the moment he was first commissioned in April 1768 until he commanded it before it embarked for Walcheren, was born in the island. Joshua Crump, commissioned ensign in July 1766, Byam Crump, commissioned in August 1770, William Byam, commissioned in April 1773, and Rowland Otto-Baijer, commissioned in December 1770, were also natives of the island. There may be others: but even seven is enough to account for the island's proprietary sentiments towards the 68th.

The time was to come when the prospect of West Indian service stirred the most melancholy forebodings in those under orders, and regiments sailed there with resignation and reluctance. In the 1760s and 1770s the Caribbean was not an unpopular station. "Jonas", who dilates at length on the beauties of Guadeloupe, even re-enlisted to have a second taste of the delights. It was quite common for men considered too infirm for European service to volunteer into the regiments that relieved theirs and to serve on for some years usefully, after becoming inured to the climate. At the same time death from yellow fever was never very far away, and the 68th's first experience of it, though mild compared with its second and third encounters, caused casualties higher than any it suffered at the hands of a human enemy for many years to come.

The yellow fever, which from first to last killed over 2000 of the 68th, more than all those killed in action from its raising until 1914, is caused by a virus in the blood. A man infected with it suffers, three to six days after infection, from severe headaches, aches in the bones and a sudden fever in which his skin becomes dry and his face swells. The fever subsides after three or four days. There is a period of calm, but it is usually accompanied by the development of jaundice and often a "black vomit" of blood and bile. The mortality was high. The virus was found (but not until 1900) to be usually transmitted by the mosquito *Aedes ægypti*. Originally a mosquito breeding in tree-holes, *Aedes ægypti* is now, says Dr. Asa C. Chandler, "a 'pet' mosquito, as domestic as a rat or a cockroach". It is now hardly ever found more than a few hundred feet from human habitations, and it feeds readily on human blood. "Long familiarity with man has made it an elusive pest. Its stealthy attack from behind or under tables and desks; the suppression of its song; its habit of hiding behind pictures or under furniture; the wariness of its larva"—which, when disturbed, swim to the bottom of the water in which they hatch—"all these are lessons learned from long and close association with man. It is a diurnal mosquito, biting principally in the morning and late afternoon, with a siesta in the middle of the day, but it will bite at night when hungry . . . . It still prefers wood walls, such as those of barrels, but it is also partial to earthenware or stone containers." It carries the virus in its blood, and transmits it as it bites. All this of course was unknown to our eighteenth century ancestors, who recognised that marshes and stagnant water had something to do with the fever, but failed to connect it with their mosquito bites.[4]

The fever did not reach the proportions of an epidemic during the 68th's first West Indian service, but it killed 144 men and the undue number of 21 officers. Of the old hands the quartermaster, James Munro, died in November 1764, and the captain-lieutenant, Thomas Armstrong, a survivor from the 2/23rd, died the next month.[5] The sickness caused a steady drain on the strength. By March 1768 the 68th was 126 men below establishment, and the shortage of officers was still embarrassing in 1773.

It was considerably below establishment when in April 1768 a detachment under Captain Dixon, of two subalterns and 58 n.c.o.s and men, was sent at the request of the Governor of the Leeward Islands to Montserrat to suppress an insurrection of negroes. There was no fighting involving casualties in this episode, and half returned to Antigua in August, the remaining 26 men in November.[6]

After that things improved. Two reductions in the establishment and an accession of recruits during the early part of 1771 brought the deficiency on the strength down to 16 in May that year. A more important addition to the establishment, of which more will be said later, was that of a tenth company consisting of light troops, an innovation sanctioned to battalions on the American establishment by a Royal Warrant of 25th December 1770. In June 1771 this light

[4]Asa C. Chandler, *Introduction to Parasitology* (John Wesley & Sons, Inc., New York, and Chapman & Hall, London, 1955), *sb*. Yellow Fever.

[5]Apart from James Munro and Thomas Armstrong, Ensign Sutton and Lieutenant Stafford died in July 1764; Captain Perrin, Lieutenant Melvill and Ensign Brush in August; Captain Somerville in December; Lieutenant Lloyd on 4th April 1765, Lieutenant Goddard on 7th June, Lieutenant Duncan Monro on 17th December; Lieutenant Charles Parke on 20th May 1766, Captain Argyle Dalrymple on 14th June, Lieutenant Green at some time during that year; Lieutenant Kirkby on 5th July, 1767, Ensign Joshua Crump on 29th September, Lieutenant Turnbull on 5th October; Lieutenant Walsh died in the course of 1768; Ensign Byam Crump on 15th January 1771; Lieutenants O'Hara and Jones in January 1772.

[6]Royal Mil. Cal. (1815), *sb*. Dixon.

company, which took its place on parade on the left flank of the battalion, reached Antigua 42 strong. It was commanded by Captain Robert Tymperley, a half-pay officer 48 years of age who had seen much West Indian service, having commanded a company of free negroes raised for the expedition to Havana in 1762. In July 1771 the 68th had 307 men "present fit", only 3 below establishment. It maintained its strength until August 1772, when it went on the first active service it had seen since Saint-Cast.

In July 1772, six companies were sent to St. Vincent to assist in the suppression of a rebellion of the so-called Black Caribs. The situation in St. Vincent had been deteriorating for some months. When the island was ceded by France to Great Britain under the Treaty of 1763, it was occupied by "a few French interlopers", by some original Indians called Red Caribs, and by about two thousand descendants of African negroes who had escaped from an African slave-ship wrecked on the coast of Bequia, nearby, towards the close of the seventeenth century. The British government had at first intended removing the free negroes (who, though not Caribs at all, were known as Black Caribs), and transporting them to the African Coast or some other island. But in 1768, yielding to representations that they might remain in St. Vincent without prejudice to the Colony, the government instructed the Commissioners "to appropriate and regulate their settlement in some quarter of the island adequate to their comfort and wants but deemed least suitable for forming plantations". Whatever appearance of submission the Black Caribs had shown, they quickly abandoned it, and adopted, as the islanders of English descent later claimed, "a disposition little worthy of Royal favour or of sovereign protection by withdrawing their allegiance and attacking the King's troops who attended the surveyors then marking out the public lands". The British settlers who had obtained concessions since the Peace were not unnaturally alarmed, particularly since these free negroes, at that time an unnatural phenomenon in the Caribbean, avowed they were determined to resist any attempt made by the Crown to assert its sovereignty. In April two battalions were ordered to St. Vincent from North America as well as those troops that could be spared in the "Ceded Islands". Gage, at New York, sent the 14th from Castle William in Boston Bay, and the 31st from St. Augustine, Florida; but, so slow were communications, they did not arrive at Kingston, St. Vincent, until late in September and early October. By that time the 70th had been brought from Grenada (another of the "Ceded Islands"), and the six companies of the 68th and four of the 32nd from Dominica had been landed about 31st July. More were on the way.

The command of this small force, the equivalent of four weak battalions, was placed by Governor Leybourne in the hands of Lieut.-Colonel William Dalrymple, 14th, a genial and capable officer who afterwards was nicknamed "Agamemnon", or "Steel-Breeches", from his wearing the same pair of buckskin breeches for thirty years or more. He married an heiress, invested all his money with the Raja of Tanjore, and lost it when the East India Company seized it early in the next century. In St. Vincent he had an unenviable task. Apart from its being the worst season of the year, the Black Caribs occupied a heavily wooded region in the east of the island, where they could carry out a war of ambuscade against troops ill-fitted for this kind of fighting. It indeed called, as the Governor said, for "the utmost diligence and perseverance". But, alas, there is very little information concerning the campaign that followed.

Allowing a certain time to elapse for "the savages to take their resolution," Dalrymple started eastwards on 26th September. By 3rd October he had, as he said, "forced a passage, though attended with some loss". During November a detachment of the 31st was sent by sea to Grande Sable, in rear of the negroes' position, and during that month and December the remainder of the force closed in upon it from different directions, establishing posts, fourteen in all, as it progressed until it reached Masiraca, the utmost extent of the road formerly marked out by the King's surveyors, on 26th December.

The part taken by the 68th in all this cannot be established with any pretence at completeness. All we know is that Ensign Mackay was killed in a skirmish on 30th November, and that at one time or another, "in attacks upon the revolters and in pursuits through the woods," 9 men were killed and one sergeant and 11 rank and file were wounded in the period between 26th September 1772 and 20th February 1773. The four remaining companies, which included Captain Stewart, Lieutenants Dunbar, Schaw and Whiston, were brought over from Antigua and landed on 20th December. But the sickness of the previous years had so reduced the officers that Major Dundas, who commanded, complained from Macaricau that he had but two captains, five lieutenants and two ensigns to do regimental duty, of whom one was Lieutenant Farley, who was Dalrymple's Military Secretary, another Dunbar, who was left sick at Kingston, and Whiston, who exchanged with Lieutenant Taylor, 6th. We know also that Captain James Stewart, at one point in the operations early in 1773, when commanding "a large party that penetrated through the woods, got in rear of the enemy and made them disperse, which was the means of facilitating their submission and for which he was honoured with the thanks of the commander, General

Dalrymple". This, however, represents the sum total of our knowledge of the 68th's share in the Carib War, which, indeed, is one of the worst documented of any fought by the British army.

The war roused the most heated protests in Parliament from those who felt the free negroes were being unjustly deprived of their lands for the benefit of those few who received grants at the time of the cession. From the moment hostilities started the Government was subjected to strong pressure to stop them. Those who did not argue the injustice done to the Black Caribs urged the climate, the bad season of the year and the certainty that Dalrymple's force would be destroyed. It was some time before the effects of the opposition at home could be felt in St. Vincent. By that time Dalrymple had been reinforced by the 6th and the 50th, who joined in the campaign on Christmas Day 1772, and the 2/60th from North America, which arrived on 15th January 1773. These reinforcements raised Dalrymple's force from a little over 1000 to a little under 2000 effectives, and before orders reached him to make the best terms he could, he reported on 22nd February, "the total reduction and submission of the Caribs." A treaty was concluded between him and their leaders on 27th February by which the north-eastern portion of the island, comprising the most fertile lands, were ceded to the Caribs in perpetuity in return for an acknowledgment of the supremacy of the Crown.

He lost no time in getting his troops into quarters. Leaving the 6th, part of the 2/60th and the 70th as a garrison, he embarked the remainder. The casualties were not as bad as the pessimists in London had foretold, but the sick were very numerous, amounting to 636, roughly a quarter of the force employed. Four officers and 68 n.c.o.s and men were killed; two officers and 108 men died; two officers and 81 n.c.o.s and men were wounded. Of these the 68th lost, apart from the losses in killed and wounded already mentioned, 2 sergeants and 16 men died, and 3 deserters. Sixty-three men were still in hospital in February 1773.[7]

The Legislative Assembly of St. Vincent voted silver medals in commemoration of the campaign, not, however, to H.M. Forces but to those gentlemen of the island who had volunteered into a corps of rangers officered to a large extent by officers from the army. Medals were not favoured generally in the service at that time, being, like epaulettes, shunned as a form of ostentation. It is not surprising, therefore, that the 68th should have carried away, apart from a

[7]For the Black Carib War see corresp. in W.O.1/57, which also contains some strength returns; C.O.235/3 and 5/90; and a memorial in W.O.1/84, p. 327. See also *Caribbeana*, Vol. 2, p. 323; Royal Mil. Cal., *sb*. Gen. James Stewart.

heavy sick-list, no official memorial of their services in the war, in which, with four other regiments, it had shared from the beginning. There is a strong regimental tradition, however, which was written down about 1811—that is to say not very long after—that they obtained the name or title "Faithful" they now bear from their honourable part in the campaign. Exactly how it came to be bestowed is not known, but it derives most probably from a letter or an address delivered by the government either of St. Vincent or Antigua, and it was inscribed upon the colours, which ("of deep green mantua silk") were supplied and presented in 1772. The tradition goes on to say that when the 68th was in Ireland "on Dublin duty with several other corps, disputes frequently arose on the subject of titles, which was said to be the cause of the word 'Faithful' not being placed on the next pair of colours that was supplied, as on the old ones. It consequently died away." The 68th was in Dublin for a year from July 1776 to July 1777. When the next colours were supplied it is not possible to say. The tradition, however, is no doubt on the whole reliable and deserves respect.[8]

Orders had already been dispatched in October 1772 for the relief of the 68th at Antigua by the 2/60th. Leaving behind some 60 men either sick or volunteering for West Indian service, they embarked in March 1773 and landed in Portsmouth early in April under the command of Lieut.-Colonel Lawrence Reynolds, an officer of 34 who had come in from the 9th as a major and, after the retirement of Lieut.-Colonel Josiah Martin in May 1767, had shared the command on and off with Major Dundas. It was weak in numbers, being 112 under establishment and having only 216 men "present fit". It was still predominantly English (56 *per cent.*), but it still retained a number of Scottish men probably recruited ten years before (25 *per cent.*), and a small number of Irishmen from its years in Ireland (17 *per cent.*).

When it was inspected at Farnham in June 1773 by Lieut-General Irwine, who had campaigned with it in Brittany, there is no disguising the fact that it had suffered much from its West Indian service. He found the n.c.o.s attentive to their duty but "of bad appearance", the men a "bad corps and low-sized", (a true enough observation, as 52 *per cent.* were 5ft. 6ins. and under.) Its movements were correct but too slow; its manual exercise well performed but too quick. The clothing, received in June 1772, before the service in St. Vincent, was (understandably) much worn, and the hats were neither properly cocked nor of the regulation size. "This Regiment," General Irwine concluded, "is at present not fit for service, being

[8]Digest.

composed in general of very indifferent men, their number very small, and 46 are ordered to be discharged." The officers, he said, were "expert at their duty;" but clearly the Regiment needed drawing together after their tour of duty besides a replenishment of the ranks.[9]

§

This is a convenient moment to discuss one of the oldest articles in its possession, the leather cap now in the Regimental Museum known as the "Lambton Cap," which must date from this period of the Regiment's history. It is a combed brown leather cap, of a "Roman" type generally similar to those known to have been worn by light infantry companies of other regiments, with a pierced brass frontlet formed of the monogram "J.L." in a decorative design, surmounted by the crest of a ram or lamb and bearing on a scroll below the motto "Faithful". It was once in the possession of Brigadier-General Sir H. Conyers Surtees, of Mainsforth Hall, who presented it in 1919 to the 4th (Militia) Battalion. Its previous history is not known, but there is no reason to doubt its authenticity or its antiquity, and the only questions that have arisen are as to its military or civil use; and if military, whether it was in wear by the light company of the 68th and at what date.

The peculiarities that have puzzled those best qualified to judge are the fact of its bearing the monogram "J.L." and the crest, presumably the distinctions of the Colonel, when by a Royal Warrant of 1751 Colonels were forbidden to place their arms or parts of their arms upon the equipment of their regiments. If, therefore, we assume the Warrant to have been obeyed, the frontlet dates from a period seven years before light companies were employed on service, twenty years before they were admitted into the establishment of any marching regiment, and quite seven years before John Lambton could have placed his monogram upon his regiment's appointments. This difficulty has led one competent judge to doubt its being military at all, and to suggest that it was intended for some peer's or gentleman's *fourrier* or groom, who, there is ample evidence, wore caps of a similar description. This, however, is to overlook both the crest, which is Lambton's (a "ram cabossed"), and the motto "Faithful", which have yet to be shown to have been the device of any *armiger* with a surname beginning with L. It is surely easier to assume, taking into account its provenance from an old Durham family, that the monogram, the crest and motto are those of Lamb-

[9]W.O.27/28.

ton's regiment, the crest being of the punning variety favoured at one time, and the motto that recently assumed by the 68th on its colours after its return from St. Vincent.[10]

If that is so the date of the cap is one subsequent to 1773, a year in which, it is also to be observed, the Regiment was inspected not only by Lieut.-General Irwine, who made no remark on such an irregularity, but the King himself at Portsmouth on 22nd June. It is not the first time or the last that a sumptuary law has been disregarded, and the very fact that the rule relating to Colonels' arms and devices was repeated in a Warrant of 1768 suggests that the Warrant of 1751 was not universally complied with. Though not safe we are not positively unsafe in taking the Warrant to have been disregarded. But we must place the date of the cap after the Regiment's departure from the Argus eyes of the King, or else guess that the caps were prudently left in quarters on 22nd June 1773.

The cap used to be called a grenadier cap. Its similarity to the type of cap known from well authenticated examples to have been worn by the light companies in the 1770s and 1780s is too striking for it to be considered as anything else. Sime, the second edition of whose *Military Guide for Young Officers* appeared just as the light companies were sanctioned, said he was informed light infantrymen were to wear "black leather caps with three chains round them and a piece of plate upon the centre of the crown: in the front 'G.R.', a crown and the number of the regiment". Neither of the caps that have survived accords exactly with this description, and they differ from each other in several particulars. The Colonel and the manufacturer seem to have consulted their own fancies, and while one, for instance, has a horse-hair crest, the other has no crest or comb at all. There is consequently nothing surprising in the fact that the "Lambton Cap" should show further variations.

A tailor's account of March 1776 quoted in Vane's *History* contains items such as "one hat, cap, made with a comb, 3s. 6d.," "6 caps and combs at 10½d. each, 5s. 3d.," and "altering 60 hats into caps, 15s." The critic who doubted the military use of the cap very justifiably doubts the possibility of making up such as the "Lambton Cap" for such sums as these. According to a statement of losses of accoutrements sustained in St. Vincent, the cost of a light infantry cap was 13s.[11] The account must therefore refer to some repairs or modifica-

[10]For a statement of some of the difficulties see on the one hand Major H. P. E. Pereira's note in J.S.A.H.R., Vol. 34 (1956), p. 80, and on the other W. Y. Carman (*ibid.*, Vol. 36 (1958), p. 41), who doubts its military origin. Cf. W. Y. Carman's article on a cap of the 5th regiment (*ibid.*, Vol. 32 (1954), pp. 119-122, and Lawson, *op. cit.*, Vol. 3 (1961), p. 75).

[11]Memorial of General Lambton, 6th March 1775 (W.O.4/93, pp. 229-230).

tions, not to the complete cap. It is useful, however, as confirming that a cap with a comb was in wear by the 68th at March 1776. That is an important contribution towards the general indication that in the "Lambton Cap" we are looking at a genuine part of the uniform worn by the 68th at about the time of its tour of duty in Ireland in the 1770s.

§

From Farnham the Regiment was moved by easy stages north-wards. At Chelmsford, in July 1773, Lieut.-Colonel Reynolds was left sick, and was succeeded temporarily in the command by Captain Dixon, second senior captain and commander of the grenadier company. In August it was at Yarmouth, in September at Norwich, with detachments at Burnham, Fakenham, and Walsingham. Late in October it moved to Newcastle, leaving in its progress, sick at Peterborough, Lieutenant James Hackman, a newly joined officer, who put his convalescence to good use by making the acquaintance at Hinchingbrooke of Miss Martha Ray, the beautiful and talented actress who was the mistress of Lord Sandwich. In December head-quarters moved to Tynemouth, where four companies had already been detached, though four companies remained in Newcastle. In July 1774 it was moved to Fort George, where it remained over a year, and then, to complete the similarity with its tour ten years before, it was brought onto the Irish Establishment and quartered at Donaghadee in December 1775. In January 1776 it was at Armagh, with detached companies at Drogheda, Hamilton's Bawn, Fews and Charlemont. In July 1776 it was brought in to do Dublin duty, where it remained until July 1777.

It was very slow in recruiting its strength. While at Farnham it was 112 men under strength, at Norwich it was 175, and only 114 were with the colours, so many were then discharged. In the north recruiting started to improve, and Major-General Evelyn, who in-spected the Regiment at Newcastle on 16th May 1774, reported favourably. "The Regiment," he said, "promises to be a very good one when recruited." Many joined in Scotland. When it passed through Belfast on 8th December 1775, on its march from Portpatrick on disembarkation, the local paper noticed that its companies were "near full, but the men mostly young and many of them recruits". Through the exertions of the recruiting parties the strength had risen by May 1777 to 470 men, 132 below establishment, a creditable achievement in view of the war, which had not only raised the

establishment to ten companies of 56 privates but also made competition for recruits correspondingly severe.[12]

Nevertheless, there was not the improvement that was to have
been expected; the sick-rate and the desertions were abnormally
high; and Lord Cavan in his inspection report of 28th May 1777,
put his finger upon several shortcomings.

> "This regiment", he said, "seemed to require great care and
> attention. A dissolute spirit somewhere prevailed in it, for there were
> at the time of my review confined in prison no less than eight men,
> besides one under sentence of death for different robberies. There
> seemed also a want of due inspection, for the Regiment had been and
> still continued so disproportionately sickly to the other regiments as
> not to be able to furnish the ordinary number of men for duty. And
> it has likewise been no less irregular from a daily loss of men by deser-
> tion. And as to its discipline [drill] it required amendment in some
> points. A proper silence was not observed, there being every moment
> a buzz of voices heard. The files were extremely open, and in so great
> a degree that, when the three ranks came to fire together standing,
> the weight of fire was reduced to—or no better [than]—that of a
> single rank of men placed at proper distances from each other. The
> men in general levelled but very indifferently. And when the Regi-
> ment came to move off its ground in line, the files either closed too
> much or flew so wide from each other as to leave immense intervals.
> And the operations in general were performed in so great a hurry
> and with so little preparation as to cause some confusion and
> disorder.
>
> "To account in some measure for these effects [sic] particular
> circumstances are to be explained. Lieut.-Colonel Reynolds is in a
> bad state of health, for the recovery of which he is obliged to be absent
> from the Regiment at different times, and, when present, I think he
> has not sufficient activity for due inspection; but as he seems to be on
> the mending hand, I do not doubt but more care will be taken. The
> late major, Dundas [one of the original officers of 1756, he was
> promoted into the 1st Regiment in October 1776], was an easy
> gentleman. The present major, Munro [another officer from the
> 23rd], lately appointed, is a very sensible intelligent gentleman and
> a good officer, but I fear much, from his time of life [48], he will
> soon want the necessary activity. And withal, the Regiment has been
> for a long time without an adjutant. Lieut.-Colonel Reynolds has
> lately acquainted me that he had given in the memorial of Captain
> Este for permission to resign his adjutancy in favour of Lieutenant
> Potts, who is recommended for the same.
>
> "The men", he went on, "were in general young and active and
> well made and of a good size [36 *per cent.* were 5ft. 6ins. and under]
> and none but what were serviceable. The men were clean and well
> dressed except as to the wear of their caps and hats, which were rather

[12]W.O.27/30; extr. *Belfast News Letter*, Dec. 1775, *cit.* in *Regimental Review* (1925),
p. 9.

laid upon the top of their heads than well pressed down on their foreheads, and occasioned the men to appear to great disadvantage."[13]

In July 1777 the 66th, 67th and 68th were relieved from Dublin
duty by the 11th, 30th and 32nd, and the 68th moved north to
Belfast, with detachments at Armagh and elsewhere. But it was back
in Dublin in July 1778, and from the inspection report of Lieut.-
General Lancelot Baugh, who reviewed it on 21st May 1779, it
appears that the shortcomings had been largely repaired. Reynolds
still commanded—he was but 40, though he had had 26 years'
service—but Munro had been replaced by James Stewart as major,
and Potts was adjutant. The establishment had meanwhile risen to
81 privates to the company, but in spite of that the strength had risen
to 685, only 125 short. Several ensigncies were granted to men
bringing a quota of recruits, a fact which is apparent both from the
number of young Irishmen (Dillon, Lynch, Coane, Smith, Breviter,
Sir Richard Cox, Kelly, Hill, Montgomery) whose names make a
brief appearance as ensigns, and from the number of recruits (378)
obtained in the intervening two years, which would have strengthened the Regiment still further if it had not been immediately
depleted by drafts. General Baugh reported well of the officers and
n.c.o.s, and of the men he said they were "of a tolerable good size
[though 45 *per cent.* were 5ft. 6ins. and under] young and well made
clean under arms, well dressed, steady and attentive, hats well
cocked, black spatterdashes according to order". Of the Regiment
generally he observed it was "a good regiment, and very fit for
service. It has suffered much by desertion and has not yet recovered
[from] the drafts that have been made from it". The Earl of Ross,
when he inspected it in October of the next year at Limerick, was
not so enthusiastic, vouchsafing only that it "made a pretty good
appearance, but not equal to the 36th". But its strength was then
up to 787 effectives (n.c.o.s and privates), and clearly it had recovered its form. It still contained a fair proportion (13 *per cent.*) of
the Scots recruited at Fort George and Aberdeen, but the Irish
element (51 *per cent.*) now well outnumbered the English (36 *per
cent.*)[14]

Interesting in view of the later history of light infantry was the
detachment of the light company under Captain John Brydges
Schaw and Lieutenants Lynch and Coane, to a camp of light infantry organised, presumably, in imitation of the similar camp at
Coxheath in Kent. In 1778 it was at Kinsale, in 1779 at Carrigaline,

[13]W.O.27/37.
[14]W.O.27/44; papers at the Regimental Depot.

south of Cork, where, with the light infantry of the 3rd, 11th, 19th, 30th, 32nd, 36th, 66th and 67th, it was formed into a battalion under the command of Lieut.-Colonel Alexander Stewart (Buffs).

Moved from Dublin in July 1779 to Waterford, the Regiment was at Rathkeale in October, at Galway in April 1780, Limerick in October, where it remained (with detachments) until October 1781, when it was brought down to Cork. It embarked there for Portsmouth on 8th September 1782, and while at Hilsea in December received drafts from the newly formed 75th to complete it to an establishment of 847 all ranks in preparation for service in Jamaica.

The war which, starting as a revolt in the American Colonies, had developed into a naval war and a struggle for the West Indian islands, was approaching its conclusion. Indeed, the Peace was signed at Versailles on 20th January 1783 while the 68th were in transports at Spithead. The prospect of the West Indies had caused dismay among the new regiments under orders, particularly amongst those men, of whom the 68th contained a fair proportion, who had enlisted on a "three years or the duration" engagement. Riots broke out amongst the seamen in almost every south-coast port. The 77th Highlanders and the 81st at Portsmouth and the 83rd in Guernsey refused to embark. The 68th caught the contagion on hearing that the 77th had gained their demands, and one shipload, of about 300, compelled the master to bring his vessel so close to the shore that they could disembark. The whole Regiment was then put on shore, and because the General Officer Commanding at Portsmouth refused them quarters in the town, they were returned to Hilsea Barracks. The military authorities had not been overscrupulous in observing their side of the bargain during the war, and the mutinous combination of the soldiers at Portsmouth was a timely if regrettable reminder of their obligations. In the midst of the riots which followed the disbanding of regiments and the paying off of ships' companies in every part of the kingdom in an age, moreover, when men showed their exasperation in violence, it was one small incident among many score.

In March 1783 the Regiment was moved to Winchester on prisoner-of-war duty, but it returned to Hilsea in October, when it was embarked for Guernsey and Jersey. There it remained under the command of Lieut.-Colonel James Stewart and Major Schaw until October 1785. The next nine uneventful years were spent in garrison at Gibraltar. From an inspection made by the eccentric, amiable and shrewd Governor, Major-General the Hon. Charles O'Hara, on 30th May 1788, it appears to have reverted to a more normal peacetime appearance. The establishment had been reduced to ten companies of 40 rank-and-file, and with 382 effectives it was fairly well up to strength. There was not a man of a year's service and under: over 70 *per cent.* were mature soldiers of four years' service and upwards. Only 37 *per cent.* were 5ft. 6ins. tall and below, while Captain Daniel O'Meara's grenadier company contained several men of over 6ft 1in. Most of the Irish taken on in the war had gone, and the Irish element numbered but 60 (16 *per cent.*) as against the English 264 (69 *per cent.*) and the Scottish 54 (14 *per cent.*) The men, said O'Hara, were "upon the whole slight, but young, clean and attentive. The general appearance of this regiment is good, and upon the whole would in a little time be fit for any service as the men are improving." This was praise from such a one as O'Hara and compared well with the blistering remarks he devoted to some of the others in garrison, though not, perhaps, so commendatory as his report on the 2/1st, and the 18th and the 50th. It was clearly a good regiment that was sent late in 1794 to be "shattered" again in the West Indies.[15]

Two important turns in the Regiment's fortunes were made during the last pre-Revolutionary decade, in both of which the hand of Lambton may be traced. The first in importance (the second chronologically) occurred in 1784. The reductions following the Peace were made in a curious manner. Instead of disbanding all regiments above a certain number, as it had in 1763, the government disbanded down to No. 70 but retained six high-numbered regiments that had been raised for or were serving in India: the 73rd, the 78th, the 98th, the 100th, the 101st and the 102nd. Originally, it appears, it was the intention to disband at least as far as the 67th for on 7th June 1784 the Secretary at War wrote to Lambton and the other Colonels informing them of the proposed reduction. The lively protests the letters provoked must, however, have been sufficient to cause a change of mind at the Horse Guards, for it was the 98th, the 100th the 101st and 102nd that went and the old Seven Years War regiments that were preserved.

The second, which occurred in 1782, gave the Regiment its county connection. Some Colonels had made attempts at establishing a connection with certain counties to stimulate recruiting for their regiments much earlier in the century, even before the War of the Austrian Succession. The idea was close to the heart of that vigorous and sensible administrator the old Duke of Cumberland, who had first-hand knowledge of what county patriotism could achieve in the Forty-Five, when the militia organisation so signally failed and the

[15]W.O.27/62.

county "Association Regiments" had tried to take its place. Each county, he was said to have proposed, should have one or more regiments of its own. A Colonel of the Buffs said in a debate in the House of Commons on the subject in 1780 that he had always recruited out of Somersetshire, and that there were other regiments generally known in the service as "the Yorkshire Regiment", the "Lancashire Regiment", "the Edinburgh Regiment", and so on from their attachment to localities. No doubt it was the increasing difficulty, experienced at that critical juncture of the American War, in obtaining men that provoked ventilation of an idea which had never been practicable for long and, indeed, was never practicable until the State assumed reponsibility for recruiting and provided the necessary machinery for its realisation. At all events, in May 1782 the Adjutant-General wrote to the agents of infantry corps up to 70 inclusive, except those in Ireland, requiring them to ask the Colonels they acted for if they wished their regiments to have "any particular connection or attachment to a particular county", and if so which. Shortly after the Colonels themselves were approached directly by the Adjutant-General, who asked them the same question. Some did not bother to reply; others, like the Colonel of the 4th Kings Own, indignantly repudiated the idea of "forfeiting the respectable name the regiment now bears"; others answered slowly and only after consulting the officers of the regiment. Lambton's reply, however, was quick and unequivocal in favour of Durham. He wrote on 6th August; and on 15th the Commander-in-Chief, Conway, having sorted out any claims that competed—there were no others for Durham—gave Lambton for his Regiment the county title of "Durham", with a view, as he said, of "cultivating and improving that connection so as to create a mutual attachment between the County and the Regiment that may at all times be useful towards recruiting the Regiment". It was not, as we have seen, an attachment that in normal times counted for much in the composition of the Regiment. But the 68th almost invariably kept a recruiting-party in Durham, and from that year until 1808 it was officially known as the "68th or Durham Regiment of Foot".[16]

The reductions of 1784 once again brought the Regiment near the left of the line, where it was exposed all too openly to be considered a safe situation for an ambitious officer. It was less, however, a home for "birds of passage" than it had been before the war. Officers were beginning to bring their sons into it. The first was Lieut.-Colonel

[16]G. H. Cleare, "County Names for Regiments in 1782" (J.S.A.H.R., Vol. 36 (1958), pp. 34-38); W. Y. Baldry, "County Titles and Infantry Regiments" (*Ibid.*, Vol. 14 (1935), pp. 223-225).

James Stewart, whose eldest son Gilbert, placed on the list at the age of 8, was second senior lieutenant at the age of 20 in 1788 when all but one of his juniors were older than he, and he was soon followed by two younger brothers, James and Isaac.

It is a pretty good test of a concern when fathers put their sons into it and the sons stay on; and there were other signs to indicate that the 68th had developed a personality of its own and was attracting a better type of officer. Stewart, Schaw, Farley and Este, survivors from the first tour of duty in the West Indies, were still serving, and some good officers came in from the disbanded regiments in 1783 and 1784, notably Captains Daniel O'Meara (from the 98th) and Norman Maclean (from the 73rd). Lieutenant Henry Charles Sirr, who came of a good Irish family, served from 1778 until retiring in 1791 when the Regiment was still in Gibraltar. He is better known as the Town-Major of Dublin during the Rebellion in 1798, when he was the chief agent for the Castle authorities and arrested one of the prime conspirators, Lord Edward FitzGerald, the Duke of Leinster's son, who, curiously enough, had been a brother officer in the 68th for a year in 1782. It is still, however, impossible to generalise upon the type of officer that entered the Regiment. Lieutenant Hackman, for instance, whose unhappy love-affair with Martha Ray led him to retire from the army, enter the Church, and then shoot the unfortunate lady outside Drury Lane Theatre, was the son of a Gosport tradesman who had come up in the world on obtaining a commission in the Hampshire Militia.[17] Lieutenant Adolphus Lewis Hinuber (1770-1840), who joined in 1788 and was to prove himself an enterprising regimental officer and, later, an able staff-officer, was the son of Karl Heinrich von Hinüber, of an old Hanoverian family, Hanoverian Minister in London.[18] William Ironside, who joined at the same time, has already been mentioned as one of the few Durham-born officers in the Regiment. Captain Alexander Mark Ker Hamilton (1767-1842), who distinguished himself in the West Indies, was the son of an old officer of the 31st who had taken up residence in the Colony of New York. In short, they come from no particular part of the country, nor, apparently, from any particular class. They do, however, tend to stay longer than their predecessors of the early days.

§

[17]Neville Williams, *Knaves and Fools* (Barrie & Rockliff, 1959), pp. 103-109, gives a good account of this famous little tragedy.
[18]Information kindly supplied to me by Herr Hans Mahrenholtz, of Hanover.

When war broke out between this country and republican France at the beginning of 1793, our military effort was devoted to four objects. The first was the time-honoured policy of preserving the free navigation of the Scheldt. Though the most obvious theatre of war in a struggle between the nations, when our alliances comprised Prussia, Holland, the Empire (which at that time governed the Low Countries), and Spain, the Low Countries were the one which absorbed, initially at least, the smallest proportion of British troops. The second object was direct assistance to the Royalist party in France. This policy took the form of a descent on Toulon and threatened attacks upon the French coast, and either occupied or kept in animation several brigades including a part of the garrison of Gibraltar. The third was directed towards subsidising the military levies of our allies. Always a very material part of our military policy, it reached enormous proportions after 1795, when the First Coalition collapsed and our army no longer had a foothold on the Continent. The fourth was aimed at the destruction of French influence in the West Indian islands, in those days not only the principal source of sugar for the whole of Europe but the seat of a wealthy and powerful interest which was disproportionately represented in Parliament.

This was the policy closest to the heart of Dundas, Secretary of State for War and Colonies, and claimed in the first years of the war by far the largest proportion of British troops. Because of sickness and mismanagement it was destined to succeed at such a cost that the nation counted it as a failure. It created havoc in the army—indeed it went near to destroying the small army of 40,000-odd we possessed in 1793. But, viewed as our ancestors viewed it, it was not so senseless a policy as some historians would have it. Dundas's view was that "it is as much the duty of those entrusted with the conduct of a British war to cut off the colonial resources of the enemy as it would be that of a general to destroy the magazines of his opponent". This is an adaptation of what passed as the most advanced contemporary thought in France, where it was being said the object in war was the destruction of the enemy's magazines: destroy rather the elements of military power than men, who are nothing without their stores.

The realisation of Dundas's intentions started with the powerful West Indies expeditionary force commanded by Sir Charles Grey and Sir John Jervis, a combination of military and naval talent and energy hard to match. It reduced Martinique in March 1794. In April it captured St. Lucia. And in the same month Grey went on to capture Guadeloupe. There, however, the Army stuck. Garrisons, operations and an unwontedly sickly season reduced Grey's force, and at the same time the French received reinforcements which made a stalemate of the situation. Operations entered upon a second and more bitter phase. The first had been carried on in a recognisable form. The arrival of reinforcements and with them some fanatical commissioners of irrepressible ardour in the republican cause (among them Victor Hugues, a mulatto jacobin already responsible for the reign of terror in Rochefort) introduced a new element into the struggle: the rising and arming of the black population, the nightmare of planter society for generations. The British force at first parried the blows aimed at it; but Grey and Jervis went home; the troops in Guadeloupe at last succumbed in January 1795; and thereafter, for a year, as Hugues and his satellites spread alarm and revolution into the other islands, the British commander anxiously waited each new blow, threw in the reinforcements as they arrived piecemeal from Europe and watched them evaporate, asked for more, and hoped. The third phase begins with the arrival of Sir Ralph Abercromby's Army in April 1796, which more than redressed the balance in our favour. But by that time the 68th, which had arrived as a reinforcement in December 1794, had almost ceased to exist.

In December 1794 Lieut.-General Sir John Vaughan, who had succeeded to the command on Grey's departure, was in a precarious situation. Berville Camp, in Guadeloupe, had been forced to surrender with the best of the troops, and on the 10th Fort Matilda, the last British-held point on the island, gave in also. This left him with about 1200 fit men to defend ten islands. His sick numbered as many as his fit and he needed, he estimated, a reinforcement of 7500 men. He was told he could expect six battalions, three from England and three from Gibraltar. Only the Gibraltar troops (the 46th, 61st and 68th), however, were at full strength, as those from England had already lost their flank companies (the grenadiers and light companies) in the surrender at Berville. A reinforcement of 3500 was therefore the most he could expect.

The Gibraltar convoy arrived on 21st December, and the 68th was almost immediately dispatched to St. Lucia to share the duty there with the 9th. The Regiment was only 64 below establishment, having 498 privates "present fit" and 22 officers. The 9th, though itself much reduced, had received drafts from the 6th and was somewhat stronger. The revolution among the negroes had already started. As the regimental digest puts it, "a great body of runaway negroes and others of colour assembled in the wood, procured arms and became a daring enemy. They were called Brigands and said to be about 7000 men." That was the situation in St. Lucia at its simplest.

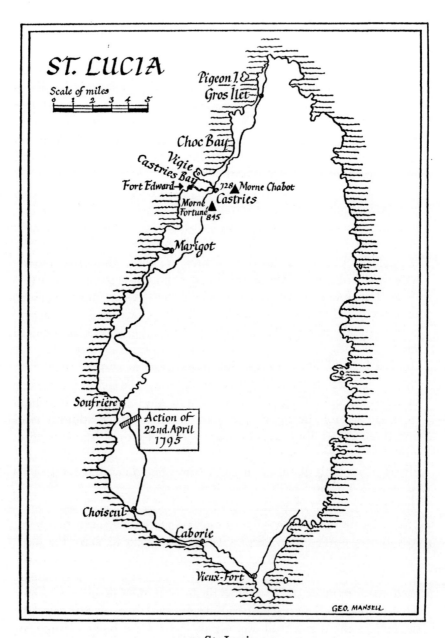

4. St. Lucia

At first the white garrison of St. Lucia, which was commanded by Lieut.-Colonel Stewart, 68th, (who had received the local rank of Brigadier-General on 25th December 1794), succeeded in keeping the "revolted negroes" in check. With the assistance of a useful negro corps, (usually referred to as "Malcolm's Corps" though it eventually became the 1st West India Regiment) he scattered them whenever they assembled. However, in March, 1795, a bloody revolution broke out both in St. Vincent and Grenada, which compelled Vaughan to detach to Grenada 140 men from the 9th and 68th—we shall say more of this later. In April the Brigands in St. Lucia received reinforcements from Guadeloupe which gradually forced back the garrison until it held only the Morne Fortuné, the height regarded as the key point in the island, and the town of Castries, the principal harbour, below it. To reinforce Brigadier-General Stewart Vaughan sent, from what may perhaps grandiloquently described as his strategic reserve in Martinique, the 34th and the 61st.

Stewart was thus enabled to resume the pressure on the Brigands' camps and also to undertake an offensive against Vieux-Fort, at the southern extremity of the island, their principal rendezvous and the place where they received most of their supplies. Having embarked a force consisting of the flank companies of the 9th, the 61st, the flank companies of the 68th, a detachment of Malcolm's Corps commanded by the enterprising Malcolm himself, and another black corps originally recruited from free negroes in South Carolina in the American War and known as the Carolina Corps, he landed near Vieux-Fort on 15th April. In the afternoon he sent Malcolm's Corps, the 9th's detachment and the light company of the 68th with an amuzet to make a circuit of the hill that commands the town, and the next morning, having reconnoitred under the protection of the grenadiers of the 68th, he advanced 50 men of the 61st and two field-pieces by one way, while by the right, along the shore, he brought forward the grenadier and light companies of the 61st. The encircling movement was completely successful. The enemy retreated precipitately, most, however, escaping to another defended position of theirs at Soufrière.

Vieux-Fort recovered, Stewart followed along the coast to take Soufrière. On the 18th he reached Laborie. On the 19th he arrived at Choiseul. Although his force was much exhausted by the march, he sent ahead two small bodies of men: one a detachment of the 9th and Malcolm's Corps, which was posted on a height three miles to the front; the other, consisting of the light company of the 61st and the flank companies of the 68th, was posted on a height to the left of the first. The next day, the 20th, receiving reports that the enemy were near Malcolm's position, he prepared to attack him. He sent

Malcolm's Corps and the two companies of the 9th to act on the enemy's left, while he, with the light company of the 61st and the flankers of the 68th, advanced straight to the front. The distance to the enemy, however, proved greater than expected, and Stewart, having only advanced half-way and hearing firing from Malcolm's direction, ordered his force to Malcolm's support. He arrived to find Malcolm had beaten off a sharp enemy attack, but at the cost of Malcolm (who could ill be spared), who had received a wound in the leg.

On the 21st, on the arrival of the guns Stewart moved forward again. In the afternoon he found them in great numbers in a strong position a mile short of Soufrière. Under cover of a cannonade he so disposed his force that a column under Major O'Meara, 68th, of the 68th's grenadiers and a detachment of Malcolm's Corps, should move from the left; a column under Captain Riddell, 61st, of the light companies of the 61st and 68th and the rest of Malcolm's Corps, should move from the right; while the main body, protected from the rear by a small force under Major Barlow, 61st, advanced up the road with the artillery. The preliminaries were not, however, completed before dark, and the force had to lie on its arms in the dirty road and pass "a disagreeable squally night with heavy showers and repeated false alarms". At day-break on the 22nd the attack started. Riddell, advancing on the enemy hill through some cotton-fields, gained the summit almost immediately, driving the Brigands before him with his light troops. This cut them off from Soufrière. But they retired to another strong position, entrenched and improved by a breastwork, behind a deep and impassable morass, their right covered by a "high mountain", their left by a hill.

At about noon Stewart attacked them again. Sending Captain Waugh, 68th, who, attached to Malcolm's Corps, had succeeded to the command on Malcolm's disablement, to ascend the "mountain" with the blacks and turn the enemy's right flank, while the light company of the 68th under Lieutenant Hamilton tried to do the same lower down, he ordered Major O'Meara, with the detachment of the 9th, the light company of the 61st and the grenadiers of the 68th, round the morass. He himself remained with a company of the 61st protecting the guns on the road. The attack immediately provoked a heavy fire from the enemy behind the breastworks, which was replied to so vigorously by Waugh's men that they soon ran out of ammunition. Much to everyone's surprise the Brigands behaved with "the greatest coolness and intrepidity", coming out of their trenches twice and charging the guns on the road. These counter-attacks were broken up by the light companies of the 61st and 68th under Lieutenants Hamilton and Stewart (the Brigadier's son, acting as his a.d.c.), who chased them back behind their works. But Stewart's attack was effectively spoilt, and though the stubborn action lasted until 7 in the evening Stewart's men could make no impression. O'Meara's detour past the morass proved impracticable; each man had spent his 60 rounds of ammunition; casualties were mounting and many left the ranks to accompany the wounded to the rear; the men had thrown away their rations; and it was impossible for them to remain in such a position ten miles from their ammunition and supplies at Choiseul. There was nothing left for it but to retreat.

Stewart started back that evening, his retirement covered by the flank companies of the 68th and the 61st Regiment. He reached Choiseul exhausted in the morning of the 23rd. He had not enough men to garrison Choiseul and Laborie, so he went on to Vieux-Fort, and there embarked for Castries. His casualties had been quite heavy. Waugh, with the Rangers (or Malcolm's), had been killed early on in the action. Lieutenant Malet, 68th, "a spirited and brave officer", was wounded in the knee-cap and had to suffer amputation, from which he succumbed soon after. Altogether Stewart lost one officer and 29 men killed and eight officers and 144 men wounded, of whom the 68th flank companies lost, apart from Waugh and Malet, one man killed and fourteen wounded, including three men wounded on the 15th.

This was the last blow struck by the attenuated garrison of St. Lucia. After Stewart's return to Castries and the Morne Fortuné the situation deteriorated steadily. St. Lucia was always considered an unhealthy island and the sick-list and the death-rate rose alarmingly. In January the 68th had a total of only 34 sick: by June this had risen to 130, not counting those in Grenada, and 40 died in May. The whole garrison numbered some 1200 rank and file of whom 600 were sick. The Brigands, on the other hand, multiplied with success. Sir John Vaughan, who made a tour of inspection round the three unhappy islands early in June, estimated them at 6000 in St. Lucia, and was himself contemplating evacuation. As the days went by they closed in on the Carénage of Castries. On 6th June they launched a powerful attack on Gros Ilet and Pigeon Island. Unfortunately the report of this episode is missing. But it appears that Pigeon Island was garrisoned by detachments from different regiments under Major Barlow, 61st, Captain Dodsworth, 34th, and Captain Vernor, 61st, and Gros Ilet by four sergeants and 42 rank and file. Some men behaved ill and refused to advance. Vaughan surmised that "this backwardness was too general," though both Dodsworth and Vernor were "not boys but experienced officers". The communication between Fort Charlotte on the Morne, though not cut, nevertheless became precarious. On the night of the 17th the Vigie was attacked under a powerful bombardment. It was defended by a party of marines and seamen who were "depressed and worn out with fatigue" and daily diminishing by death. The result was not long in doubt.

On the loss of the Vigie Stewart summoned a council of war, which met the next morning. They all considered that it would be improper to await an assault and unanimously agreed evacuation was necessary. The same evening, 18th June, the troops marched down from the Morne to a bay close by Fort Edward on the south side of the entrance to the Carénage, and there embarked without loss. 53 combatant officers and 740 n.c.o.s and men were taken off, together with 625 sick. Except for the 34th, which Vaughan dispatched to St. Vincent, all were carried back to Martinique.

The part of the 68th in the loss of St. Lucia is not very easy to establish. From a return of 18th June it appears that, together with 15 officers and 38 sergeants, they had 104 men in garrison on the Morne, 49 on the Morne Garnie, 4 at Fort Edward and 108 sick, and all of them (318 all ranks) were brought off. On the other hand it appears from the monthly returns of July (June's, the important one, is missing) that the Regiment had lost in "missing and prisoners of war" 61 rank and file and Lieutenant Ironside "prisoner with the enemy". The only occasions on which these casualties can have been suffered were the actions of 6th and 17th June. Since that of the 17th at the Vigie was fought by seamen and marines, the most probable explanation is that Ironside and 60 men were sent up to reinforce Barlow at Pigeon Island and were lost with Dodsworth and Vernor and 24 of the 34th and 41 of the 61st in that morning's melancholy work. Certainly a reinforcement of some kind was sent up, and one must assume that Stewart lost 126 men when the garrisons laid down their arms. Since we also know from another source that the books and records of the Regiment were "lost in the Island of St. Lucia in the year 1795", we must also conclude that the evacuation, though effected without loss of life, was carried out in an atmosphere of hurry and confusion. It is a matter on which Stewart's reports are less than candid, concealing as they probably do a dismal picture of frustration and depression all too clear to Vaughan when the garrison was landed in Martinique.[19]

Meanwhile the situation in Grenada was hardly less precarious. An insurrection more bloody than that in St. Lucia had broken out

[19]For a detailed account of operations in St Lucia see the corresp. in W.O.1/83. The monthly returns are in W.O.17/2486.

in March. It was, says a shrewd soldier, inspired by the effect of French intrigue on the restless French inhabitants—Grenada was one of the "Ceded Islands" of 1763. The French whites treated the blacks under the conviction that the whites were superior and would prevail. But the blacks were too numerous and hardy. Their condition was so abject that they willingly took advantage of French political offers to overthrow a constitution which they had no interest in maintaining. Quick to appreciate how essential they were to the revolutionary white, they found they could exact their own terms of freedom and idleness from their new employers. The conspirators assembled at La Baye (now Grenville) in the night of 2nd March, butchered all the white English planters who fell into their hands, and then moved on to Gouyave and did the same there. The negroes on the plantations, seeing what was happening, either joined the rebels or fled. After their first delirium had subsided the conspirators assembled on the estate of a mulatto planter named Julien Fédon. "This new leader had never been distinguished for his enterprising or ambitious behaviour, but had generally been remarked by the English as a man of a distant and reserved but civil and prudent deportment." His estate was admirably calculated for the purposes of the rebels, being situated in the centre of the mountains that occupy the whole length of the island. The few approaches to it were capable of defence by many narrow and woody defiles. To this estate, Belvidere, below Mount Qua Qua (now Morne Fédon), the rebels drove all they had plundered from the plantations and a number of English hostages, including Mr. Ninian Home, the lieutenant-governor, whom they had captured.

In 1793 the garrison had consisted of two British battalions and the Carolina Black Corps, but these had been so reduced by successive demands that barely 200 men remained. The militia had been much neglected and comprised, moreover, a number of the conspirators. What there were, however, succeeded in wresting Gouyave from the rebels and repelling two attacks.

The only reinforcements Vaughan at first could spare were 140 men of the 9th and 68th, which he dispatched from St. Lucia in the *Beaulieu* frigate on 13th March under Lieut.-Colonel Schaw, 68th, while Brigadier-General Lindsay was ordered to assume command of operations. The 68th detachment consisted of 82 rank-and-file under Lieut.-Colonels Schaw and Este, Major Maclean, Lieutenant Hinuber, and Ensigns Leigh and Carr. On 15th March Lindsay marched from St. George's for Gouyave with all the troops and militia safely available with the intention of driving the rebels from Fédon's estate, where, on the slopes above, three camps had been

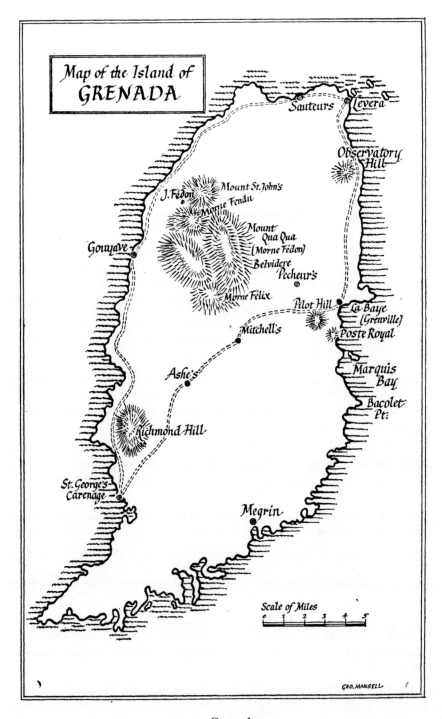

5. Grenada

constructed, named "Camp la Liberté," "Camp l'Egalité" and "Camp la Mort". Lindsay's men got as far as the plantation of Jean Fédon, Mount St. John, and dispersed the rebels opposing them. He pursued; some of his best troops got caught in an ambuscade; and heavy rains stopped any further movement. Fatigue and anxiety then overcame Lindsay, and in the morning of 22nd March he put an end to his existence.

The command in Grenada fell to Mr. Mackenzie, the President of the Council, who was, as Vaughan said, "respectable as a gentleman but totally unqualified for the conduct of a military operation". A convoy of troops from Europe opportunely arrived that moment at Martinique, which enabled him to send two whole battalions, the 1/25th and the 1/29th. The first was commanded by a fine officer of immense proportions who was to show himself one of the first soldiers of the day, Lieut.-Colonel the Hon. John Hope, but he was junior to Lieut.-Colonel Archibald Campbell, 29th, who on 2nd April took over from Schaw the unenviable task of coaching Mackenzie.

Neither Schaw nor Campbell was able to prevent the President from indulging in his favourite notions of detachments sent in every conceivable direction without regard to the force at his disposal. To avoid confusion it is well to say at the outset that as a result of this policy there were three "fronts", in only two of which the 68th were concerned:

(a) a force of 150 sent under Captain Gurdon, 58th, to seize Pilot Hill above La Baye, which landed at Levera, found Pilot Hill strongly occupied, and retreated to Observatory Hill. Though reinforced by a party under Major Wright, 25th, they were attacked at Mirabeau while drying their clothes, and failed to get beyond Pilot Hill for some weeks.

(b) a force of 200 sent on 3rd April under Major Mallory, 29th, from St. George's up the main La Baye road to occupy Michell's. Mallory, however was attacked at Ashe's and wounded, and Lieut.-Colonel Este was sent up to form a post there, which remained the limit of our advance in that direction for some weeks.

(c) the force on the Gouyave side, in which the 68th detachment was most actively engaged. On 7th April Mackenzie got Campbell against his better judgment to launch an attack on Fédon's camp. Dividing his force into three columns (that containing the 68th detachment under Major Maclean being commanded by Lieut.-Colonel Hope and attacking on the right flank), he started at 4 in the morning of the 8th. Neither Hope's nor the other flanking column succeeded in reaching the rebels' breastworks on the slippery hillside, and the enemy proved twice as numerous as Campbell expected; so he retired, having lost 3 officers and 20 men killed and 50 wounded. This reverse was the signal for Fédon to bring out his hostages and murder them in the most revolting circumstances. But it also prompted Vaughan to send over a more senior commander, Brigadier-General Oliver Nicolls, who arrived at St. George's on 14th April.

Nicolls, a true soldier, active and buoyant, succeeded, by landing a reinforcement in Marquis Bay on 29th April, in capturing Pilot Hill on the 30th. La Baye fell into our hands as well. On the side of Gouyave, however, which was the key to any approach into enemy country from the west, the situation remained much the same for months, a war of patrols and outposts. Major Maclean, 68th, is mentioned as having, early in May, established a post close to the enemy from which he sent out a detachment under Lieutenant Hinuber, who surprised a party of 50 rebels in a house, killing six and wounding several. Though, as Nicolls acknowledged, this sort of thing was in no way decisive, it "gives our people confidence and depresses the enemy". Later, in June, a party protecting masterless negroes searching for plantains (similar to bananas) was attacked and lost several men before beating them off; and a picked force, said to be under Fédon himself, came down and fired on a party under Hinuber, but fled when twenty yards away on hearing Hinuber giving the order to charge.

Otherwise throughout the summer the situation became stationary. Nicolls maintained his positions: Gouyave on the west, and the hill above it; Ashe's; Mégrin; La Baye and Pilot Hill under Colonel Hope; Observatory Hill; and Sauteurs, as a protection for the harbour of Levera. Fédon, on the other hand, maintained posts at: the Morne Fendu, between the Morne Félix and Mount St. John's; at his house at Belvidere; the camps on Mount Qua Qua; at Ashe's; Michell's; and Pécheur's.

More active operations came to a standstill with the onset of the yellow fever, which struck at all, but most particularly the 25th and 29th. On 7th July the Grenada garrison numbered 1280 regulars and 168 sick, and in that month the 29th alone lost 80 dead. The 68th detachment in the island was 7 officers and 129 rank and file strong, stronger than the detachment in Martinique, which numbered only 72 rank and file with 155 sick. It was not work for European soldiers. Though Vaughan and Nicolls pressed for powers to raise fresh corps of negroes, who are for some reason not so susceptible to the fever, the planters were reluctant to part with their slave property, and the authorities at home were slow to grant permission. Vaughan and Nicholls however, anticipated the permission. While most of the commissions were given to French gentlemen, some of the more enterprising officers left the regular battalions to take up service in what eventually became West India Regiments, among them Major Daniel O'Meara of the 68th. The rebels, on the other hand, were never short of men and numbered, according to Vaughan's estimate, 10,000.

In August the sickness in the La Baye garrison was so bad that the 68th detachment was transferred temporarily to that front; and on 1st September Nicolls received the remainder of the Regiment, under Lieut.-Colonel Schaw, from Martinique. In point of men it was not much of a reinforcement. The deaths in the Regiment were running at about 40 a month. Only 15 combatant officers and 238 n.c.o.s and men fit were left. (Colonel Este was now in charge of the Adjutant-General's department at Headquarters in Martinique, Stewart, with his son James as his brigade-major, were in St. Vincent). Some were in the works on Richmond Hill, two miles from St. George's, thrown up in the American War; most, however, were at Gouyave, the healthiest station, and in the posts on the hill above.

In October the situation changed suddenly for the worse. The arrival of a brig from St. Lucia carrying 150 French reinforcements encouraged Fédon to make an attack on the position at Gouyave. Gouyave and the posts around were held by a garrison consisting of 3 gunners, a company of the Loyal Black Rangers under Captain Augier (3 officers and 56 n.c.o.s and men), a company of Grenada negroes of Colonel Webster's Corps (3 officers and 66 n.c.o.s and men) and a detachment of the 68th of 9 officers and 134 n.c.o.s and men, a total of 17 officers and 268 n.c.o.s and men, all under the command of Lieut.-Colonel Schaw, 68th. As it was a healthy station the sick from some of the others had been brought there for convalescence, and amounted to 5 subalterns and 133 men.

The hill above the town had been occupied by us since 27th April. On three sides it is steep and difficult of access, and though on the side of the mountains towards Qua Qua not so much so, the ridge is narrow and had been strengthened by an entrenchment and an abattis. A breastwork had been thrown round the top of the hill and a picquet-house built within. Colonel Webster had recently offered to bring up from his estate the materials for a blockhouse in which the whole garrison might have been accommodated; parts of it were already on the hill ready for erection. As it was, the picquet of about 40 was placed in the picquet-house, and the remainder of the garrison was quartered in some houses and negro huts about half-way down the hill towards Gouyave. It was an imperfect arrangement, for it took some time to collect and bring the main body to the assistance of the picquet, and in bad weather this could not possibly be accomplished in time to repel a sudden attack on the picquet. Though a deserter from Fédon's men in Colonel Webster's Corps reported to Schaw on the 14th or 15th October that seven enemy companies were assembled at Morne Félix with the intention of surrounding the town and attacking the hill "at the crowing of the first cock," apparently Schaw failed to alter his dispositions.

The night of the 15th was dark and rainy. Captain Hamilton took over the picquet—one sergeant, one corporal and 38 men, of whom 11 were blacks—after dark.

> "I then," he says "detached one corporal and three British soldiers to a path pointed out by Captain Hinuber to Colonel Schaw with orders that, should the enemy approach that way, to give them their fire and then retire to the huts and alarm the men there and immediately to join Colonel Schaw at [Gouyave] House, it being impossible for them to rejoin me from the nature of the ground. This left me with one sergeant, one corporal and 35 men including the blacks. I then fell them in round the breastwork in order that each man should know his post in case of alarm, on doing which I found that I was obliged to leave a space of two yards and better between each man to enable me to occupy the whole of the ground within the breastwork; and, as the night was extremely dark, I thought it necessary to put thirteen sentries.

> "At a little after 11 o'clock Lieutenant Carr (who was my subaltern) visited the sentries, and on his return informed me he had found them perfectly alert. In about five minutes after which we heard one of them fire, on which we immediately turned out and had time to fire from four to five rounds per man previous to the enemy's getting upon the breastwork; after which we disputed it with our bayonets until overwhelmed by numbers. Some confusion took place among the gunners which prevented them from firing the field-piece (the only gun we had) immediately on the attack; and on the enemy's getting near the breastwork it was impossible to fire without endangering our own men; and, indeed, it would have been of little avail as we were attacked on all sides.

> "With respect to our loss or that of the enemy I cannot take it upon me to say what it may have been, as the night was so dark as to prevent me from seeing. Neither can I attempt to say what was their strength. Before Lieutenant Carr and I quitted the post there appeared to be at least 100 of the enemy within the breastwork, and from the noise without, they appeared to be advancing in great force. I am inclined to think that their loss must have been considerable, as our fire appeared to be well directed and our men disputed the breastwork bravely with their bayonets, besides which they, the enemy, fired on each other for some time after we had been obliged to quit the post. Lieutenant Carr remained with me within the works, though wounded, until we found that our men were all driven out. After which we retired. The man who bayoneted him attacked me, when I fortunately shot him, by which I escaped."

Schaw, considering his force insufficient to attempt to recover the hill, and the situation of the main body being untenable, retired to St. George's, twelve miles away, where he arrived at 9 in the morning of 16th October. He left behind in the enemy's hands two sergeants and 34 men of the 68th and all the sick there save one subaltern and 16 men who were able to march. Nicolls recognised that Hamilton's picquet did all in its limited power, but the loss of Gouyave was a grievous blow for which he blamed Schaw's inadequate precautions. The Commander-in-Chief expressed in public orders his strongest disapprobation of his conduct, and when the news reached London the Secretary of State gave orders for him to be tried by court-martial. The proceedings of his trial have not survived, but the unhappy man, who had many years of service in the Regiment, retired on 30th August 1797.

This was the last active service the 68th performed in the campaign. They were brought into garrison at Fort George, on one of the promontories that formed the Carénage. Only 86 were "present fit" on 1st November, a figure which dropped steadily until July 1796, when there were but 61. They had been the strongest battalion but two in January 1795: by June 1796 they were the weakest of any.[20]

Meanwhile, after the loss of Gouyave the situation in the island continued to deteriorate. The rebels "quit their mountain fortresses" and appeared before every British-held post. On 18th December they invested Pilot Hill, and even threatened St. George's itself. The regulars fit for duty dwindled to 566 rank-and-file. On 29th February 1796 Major Wright was compelled to evacuate Pilot Hill and La Baye after an honourable defence of over two months, but succeeded in bringing away his men by making a circuit to Sauteurs.

This, however, was the lowest ebb of the Grenada garrison's misfortunes. A few days later Nicolls received 700 reinforcements from Barbados, and a further 600 arrived under Lieut.-Colonel Dawson, 8th, in the middle of March, 1796. With these he succeeded, after landing at Bacolet, in re-establishing himself at Pilot Hill and Poste Royal on 28th March. Moreover, the "Great Reinforcement", under Sir Ralph Abercromby, which had been forming in Britain for many months and expected for as many in the Caribbean, eventually arrived in May. It reconquered St. Lucia first; then, in

[20]For operations in Grenada see: corresp. in W.O.1/84 and 1/85; C.O.318/17, p.170; the letters of Lieut.-Col. the Hon. John Hope (later 4th Earl of Hopetoun) to Gen. Nicolls (Hopetoun House, Linlithgow Mss., Box 1) and a narrative by him (*ibid.,* Box 1, fos. 252*ff.*); and the returns in W.O.17/2486-2487.

June, it went on to Grenada; and Nicolls was at last able to finish his gallant campaign with the reduction of Fédon's camp on 21st June 1796. The rebels murdered more hostages before they were taken. Fédon himself disappeared, drowned, some say, in attempting to escape from the island.

It is pretty clear from Nicolls's reports that the 68th, certainly as a regiment, played no part in these last operations, and it would not be worth examining the possibility that it did had not Sir James McGrigor, then surgeon of the 88th, stated that he remembered a soldier of the 68th, during the fighting for Pilot Hill, sparing the life of a French drummer who fell on his knees to beg for mercy when overtaken. Though writing at fifty years' distance from the events, McGrigor is in other respects remarkably reliable, and anything he states categorically is worthy of attention. The returns of the force Nicolls took with him to Poste Royal just admit the possibility of his taking a small detachment of the 68th and they do not exclude the chance of the odd man of the 68th accompanying the force. But it is equally certain that the bulk of the Regiment, by now the weakest battalion in the island, was retained in garrison near St. George's.[21]

The process of attrition is now almost over. Eighteen months hard service has broken a battalion of over 500. In July 1796, with 14 other battalions, it drafted its fit men and came home. The 68th's drafts went to the 63rd in St. Vincent. It arrived in England a skeleton: 3 captains, 5 lieutenants, 1 ensign, 13 sergeants and 7 drummers landed at Portsmouth under the command of Captain Henry Darling on 22nd September, and 1 officer, 5 n.c.o.s and 2 privates at Chatham at about the same date—a total of 10 officers and 27 n.c.o.s and men. Some officers and n.c.o.s came back later from the West Indies. But it had lost 10 officers killed and died from fever and wounds, and at least 334 men from the same causes.

§

The reconstruction of the Regiment took some years. At first ordinary methods of recruitment were tried. In October 1796 it was moved north under the command, it is said, of a sergeant, Sergeant William Preston, to Leeds; in November it came south to Colchester; and in March 1797 it was marched to Liverpool for embarkation to Ireland, where it was quartered for a year at Malahide, and then at Boyle. The English establishment at this critical moment in the war

[21]Sir James McGrigor, *Autobiography and Services*,(London, 1861), p. 63; return of 27th May 1796 (Linlithgow Mss., Box 1, fos. 119-120); W.O.17/2487.

had risen to ten companies of 100 men each, and, though the Irish establishment was somewhat smaller, the 68th was one of six regiments allowed an additional two companies as recruiting-companies. Some recruits had been obtained by them in the Regiment's absence; but most, if not all, appear to have been assembled with recruits obtained by other regiments abroad and embarked on board H.M.S *Asia* for duty as marines in an uneventful cruise under Admiral Duncan, and never to have reached the 68th.[22] In November 1796 no less than thirteen recruiting-parties were out in all parts of the Midlands and the south ; notwithstanding their efforts the strength in March 1797 was 955 below establishment. When called upon to do Dublin duty at the time of the Rebellion, when the whole of Dublin garrison was called out—and when the Durham Fencibles were proudly marching south to Arklow—the 68th could count no more than 36 firelocks. In other words ordinary recruiting had failed, and it was not until the Irish militia were allowed to volunteer for the line early in 1800 that the ranks were filled again.

Not many of the officers of Grenada days stayed on. Lieut.-Colonel Stewart had been promoted onto the English staff as major-general, and his son, James, remained as his a.d.c. Schaw retired. Farley, who did not join until August 1795, was detained as a prisoner of war (in what circumstances we do not know) for some time, though he returned to command from June 1800 onwards. O'Meara raised a corps of negroes and remained in the West Indies; so did Hamilton temporarily (he eventually became Colonel of the 5th West India Regiment). Hinuber stayed on the staff in the Caribbean as inspector-general of the foreign corps. Potts, formerly adjutant, was promoted in the 10th in Grenada. Maclean had died in Grenada; and the commission of the major, Malby Brabazon, who died in Grenada also, was given by Abercromby to his Deputy Q.M.G., Major Picton, a distinguished soldier on the threshold of a promising career but not an effective officer in the Regiment. Of the old hands only Farley (eventually), Captains Lucas and Ironside, Lieutenants Richard Thompson, Leigh, Cox, Winniett and Reed and the quartermaster, David Aird, stayed to carry on the old traditions of the 68th.

In the ranks the continuity was hardly less slender. Of the 500 privates who sailed from Gibraltar in December 1794 only 29 were still serving as privates in March 1797, and 17 of these were discharged unfit as soon as they returned from furlough. The 12 survivors' names are: John Berry, Richard Bull, Thomas Bulger, John Connor, William Gathen, Thomas Hannon, Joseph Healey, Law-

[22]W.O.4/159, p. 170.

4

rence McDaniel, Henry McGee, John Morris, Samuel Reynolds and John Roser. Of the corporals two only survived. Of the sergeants seven survived from the sergeants of 1794: Sergeant-Major William Hanbury (who had lost his corporal's stripes in September 1791 but had risen to sergeant in November 1793), Quartermaster-Sergeant Robert Gall, Sergeants James Cooney, William Preston, Thomas Perkins, John Swain, and Thomas Waggitt; fourteen were men who had been privates or corporals or fifers in 1794; the rest were men recently appointed from new levies such as Talbot's Corps, the Dublin Volunteers, the 90th, 93rd, 99th and 121st. In all there were 42 men to present the old 68th to the new: not very many.[23]

Ordinary recruiting in England having for some time failed partly as a result of the unprecedented mortality in the West Indies, volunteering from the English militia had been allowed in 1798. There had been much opposition to any active employment of the Irish militia, however, and the desire to volunteer in Ireland had arisen out of the larger desire for union with Britain which, strange as it may seem nowadays, was an aspiration ardently nurtured in Irish bosoms and received with some embarrassment in this country. After the suppression of the Rebellion, in which some Irish militia regiments had shown praiseworthy devotion, the dearth of recruits overcame opposition. In January 1799 the Irish parliament, assembled especially for the purpose of debating the measure of allowing the militia to volunteer, passed three resolutions, by which volunteers were admitted to a number not exceeding 10,041. Bounties were granted to those coming forward and ensigncies in the line given to those militia officers who brought 40 or more recruits.

The military authorities were quick to take advantage of this bounteous source during the month (27th January to 28th February 1800) in which it was permitted to flow. Regiments short on the establishment, regiments raising third battalions, regiments not even in Ireland, all were hurried across to catch the drops before the pump dried up.

Five battalions in Ireland that were particularly low in strength were selected for preferential treatment. These were: the 1/1st at Newry (471 strong), the 13th at Charlesfort (271 strong), the 54th at Limerick (422 strong) the 64th at Belfast (318 strong) and the 68th, the lowest of all (199 strong), which was Trim, Navan and Kells. They were to recruit only volunteers for life service, but they could be recruited "to any extent". Arms were to be issued on arrival in England. The recruits were to be marched, clothed up to 1799 but

[23]W.O.12/7625.

without arms or accoutrements, to the stations of the regiments they chose.

The response was extraordinary. By 28th February nearly 6000 had volunteered, and the satiated battalions were dragged away to allow others to have a turn. For some reason the 68th was far and away the most popular with the Irish militia, which gave it the unprecedented number of 1777 volunteers in the month, and more following them after they had embarked for England. Nearly all the volunteers given by the Dublin County, the Kildare, the Leitrim and Meath regiments went into the 68th. The proportions may be seen in the table below. The table also shows the ensigncies in the 68th that were granted. They number 48, more than all the officers in the Regiment

	Quota allowed	Vols. to 68th	Vols. to others	Total	Ensigncies in 68th
Antrim	344	112	214	326	3
Carlow	215	88	90	178	2
Clare . .	174	44	60	104	1
Cork County, North .	232	22	5	27	
Cork County, South .	232	87	2	89	2
Donegal	290	14	116	130	
Dublin County . .	258	203	7	210	6
Dublin City . .	232	39	56	95	1
Fermanagh . .	258	10	82	92	
Kildare	215	188	12	200	3
Kilkenny . . .	232	5	137	142	
Leitrim . .	258	189	9	198	3
Limerick County . .	232	1	110	111	
Londonderry . .	290	28	238	266	1
Longford . .	258	41	36	77	1
Mayo, South . .	301	38	109	147	3
Meath . . .	344	213	1	214	8
Monaghan . .	344	145	56	201	3
Queen's County . .	258	27	137	164	2
Roscommon . .	312	10	186	196	1
Sligo . . .	258	136	26	162	3
Tipperary . . .	430	51	346	397	1
Tyrone . . .	430	1	330	331	
Westmeath . .	234	16	123	139	
Wicklow . . .	174	69	8	77	2
Armagh . . .	232				1
Louth . . .	387				1
		1777	4056	5763	48

in 1795. (Before two years were out there was not one left: twenty-five had died, and the remainder either transferred or went on half-pay.)[24]

When it was nearly 2000 strong the 68th was moved to Newry and embarked for Liverpool. It arrived in Sunderland at the end of March, and there during the course of May was organised into two battalions.

[24]For the volunteers from the Irish militia see: H.O.100/90; Sir Henry McAnally, *The Irish Militia, 1793-1816: a social and military study* (Dublin and London, Eyre & Spottiswoode, 1949).

The officers of the First Battalion (on paper at least) remained substantially those of the old 68th. They were, as we have seen, comparative newcomers. Lieut.-Colonel George Airey, father of the Crimean Army's Q.M.G., whom Abercromby had brought in from the 48th to take Picton's commission, commanded from about December 1796, but he did not stay long, nor did many of the newcomers, who were on the whole "birds of passage". Some were hardly more than paper appointments. Eight lieutenancies, for instance, were filled from ensigns in a recruiting levy known as Podmore's, which had been raised in August 1795 by Major John Podmore, 124th, and drafted into old corps the following 25th September, the officers remaining unattached until vacancies could be found for them. Only one stayed in the 68th longer than a year, Lieutenant Summers, who survived to die of Walcheren fever in 1809. Some useful officers, however, joined during those years. One was William Gough, a younger son of a country gentleman of Limerick who was lieut.-colonel of the Limerick Militia. He joined in June 1799 and served until being drowned at sea in 1822. (His younger brother Hugh received a viscountcy for his military services.) Another was John Reed, for whom his father bought an ensigncy in March of the same year. His father had been sergeant-major of the 68th and was at that time adjutant. He went on half-pay with the reductions in 1803; but the son took all his promotions in the Regiment, he was adjutant for some years from 1805, and he rose to command the battalion thirty years after his first commission in circumstances which shall be described in due course.

The officers of the Second Battalion (again at least on paper) were quite different. They were obtained by Lord Cornwallis, Lord-Lieutenant and Commander-in-Chief of Ireland, by bringing together all those holding commissions of the rank of major and below in the five weak battalions, the 1/1st, the 13th, 54th, 64th and 68th, and selecting from them the "eldest" of each rank. The list was then made up as follows:[25]

> Major (Bvt.-lieut.-col.) J. S. Farley, 68th, became 1st lieut.-colonel, 2/68th.
> Major Francis Mannooch, 1/1st, became 2nd lieut.-colonel, 2/68th.
> Captain George Scott, 64th, became 1st major, 2/68th.
> Captain William Wright, 54th, became 2nd major, 2/68th.
> Captain Charles Irvine, h.p., 30th, became 1st captain, 2/68th.
> Capt.-Lieutenant Henry Clay, 64th, became 2nd captain, 2/68th.
> Capt.-Lieutenant Richard Thompson, 68th, became 3rd captain, 2/68th.

[25]H.O.100/90, p. 120.

Capt.-Lieutenant William Williams, 54th, became 4th captain, 2 /68th.

Capt.-Lieutenant Mossom Soden, 13th, became 5th captain, 2 /68th.

Lieutenant Edward Galway, 64th, became 6th Captain, 2 /68th.

Lieutenant Samuel Blakeney, 6th, became 7th captain, 2 /68th.

Lieutenant H. R. Arnot, 1 /1st, became capt-lieutenant, 2 /68th.

Broadly, therefore, it is true to say that while the ranks of the two battalions were composed principally of new men, albeit partially trained soldiers of a good stamp, and while the subalterns of both were composed of militia officers, the First Battalion senior officers were largely former officers of the 68th and the Second Battalion senior officers a mixture from the 1st, the 13th, 54th and 64th. On paper, that is. In fact the battalions were much more closely assimilated. For instance, Lieut.-Colonel J. R. Napier, who had come into the 1 /68th from the 60th, commanded—at least for a time—the 2 /68th; and Farley, who was properly first lieut.-colonel of the 2 /68th, commanded the 1 /68th from June 1800 onwards. Similarly the returns of 1801 show that the 2 /68th contained a fair proportion of old 68th officers: Hinuber, Leigh, Lucas, Armstrong, James Stewart, Winniett and Summers.

This is a far cry from the 68th of Lambton's day. It had ceased to be a personal affair: it had become, for a time at least until it shook down, a military bureaucrat's creation. It was well the old gentleman was spared the spectacle. He had died at the age of 84 on 22nd April 1794, to be succeeded by four Colonels in quick succession until the appointment, on 25th March 1795, of Lieut.-General Thomas Trigge, a capable and amiable soldier, if from all accounts, rather over-fond of his emoluments, but judicious, straightforward and generous. On the organisation of the Second Battalion the Colonelcy was shared with a Colonel-Commandant, Lieut.-General Charles Eustace, formerly of the 33rd, an Irishman, who, on his death in June 1801, was succeeded by Lord Cavan, the son of the general who inspected the 68th in 1777, a man of wide interests whose principal claim on our gratitude is his attempt to move Cleopatra's Needle from Alexandria. Indeed the Colonel's powers were slowly whittled away in these years of emergency, which called for measures more far-reaching than any within the resources of a single individual however powerful.

Gone, for instance, was the regimental chaplain. He had usually been a personal appointment of the Colonel's, seldom accompanied the regiment on its travels, and remained comfortably in his vicarage at home. The 68th's chaplain had never served abroad: Lewis Boisdaune (1758-1766), Claud Criggan (1766-1771), Charles Roberts

(1771-1772), Crispus Green (1772-1775), William Ironside (1775-1787), father of Captain William Ironside, perpetual curate of St. Helen's, Bishop Auckland, William Nesfield (1787-1794), John Lindow (1794-1796) are never shown as "present" in the returns. In 1796, "from the nearly universal want of personal attendance among the chaplains of regiments, and of care in providing proper deputies", they were gradually discontinued. Because they had purchased they were offered the option of joining before 25th December 1796 or of retiring on 4s. per day; and because Colonels had received the benefit of the purchase-money it was arranged that all infantry Colonels in whose lifetime any chaplain died, whether on full or retired pay, should receive £500 by the sale of one or more ensigncies. Army chaplaincies were from that period staff-appointments supplied by a military sub-department. It is a small indication of the beginning of a new, post-Revolutionary type of public morality.[26]

It was hardly to be expected that a heterogeneous mass like the 1/68th and 2/68th should immediately become efficient units. When they were brought south by sea in June to the new camp of exercise at Swinley, on the Ascot side of Bagshot Heath, where about 35,000 men—including a new thing called the "Experimental Rifle Corps" —were assembled for training, all the infantry was found to have improved "except the 68th, which," wrote no less a person than the King, "I fear must have many officers changed and a more strict discipline before any good can be effected".[27] No drastic changes that can be ascribed to this cause can be traced, however, and after two months at Canterbury (with some companies detached as far apart as Weymouth, Godalming and Guildford), both battalions were considered fit enough to be embarked for the West Indies. They sailed from Portsmouth in December 1800.

§

The 1/68th was sent to Martinique, where it arrived under the command of Lieut.-Colonel Farley at the end of January 1801, 205 men below establishment, with a strength of 45 officers and 790 n.c.o.s and men "present fit". The first two years were, if sickness is excepted, comparatively uneventful. In March it contributed a detachment of 177 men under the command of Major Johnston and eight officers to the expedition sent to take possession of the Danish

[26]W.O.4/166, p. 372.
[27]Letter George III to Frederick Duke of York, Weymouth, 14th Aug 1800 (papers at the National Army Museum, Sandhurst, kindly communicated to me by Major N. P. Dawnay, M.A.)

and Swedish islands of St Bartholomew, St Martin, St Thomas, St John, Saint-Croix and St Eustatia after hostilities with the Baltic powers had begun and, to all intents and purposes, terminated with Nelson's action at Copenhagen. The detachment returned late in April; but two more detachments were sent to Montserrat and St Kitt's, the first of which remained until the end of the year. Headquarters were moved to Barbados in July, though almost half the Battalion, under Major Johnston, stayed on at Saint-Pierre, Martinique, until the island was handed back to the French in September 1802.

The 2/68th had a more adventurous career during its two years' existence. The main body arrived at St. Anne's Braracks, Barbados, between 24th January and 3rd February 1801, with 40 officers and 729 n.c.o.s and men. But the *Devon* transport carrying two companies (7 officers and 178) men parted off Madeira, and for the time being they were returned as "not since heard of". They eventually turned up in the *Bryan* and *Sally* transports in the first week of March, by which time a detachment of four companies under Major A. M. K. Hamilton (19 officers and about 320 men) had been detached to the Saints to relieve the 45th. In March headquarters and the other companies were moved from Barbados to Martinique and in April to Dominica, where they were stationed on the Morne Bruce under the command of Lieut.-Colonel Francis Mannooch. Hamilton's detachment remained in the Saints until the end of the year: the main body of the Battalion remained in Dominica until its dissolution in September 1802.[28]

The Commander-in-Chief of the Windward and Leeward Islands at that time was the Colonel of the Regiment, Sir Thomas Trigge. The Governor of Dominica was Brigadier-General Andrew Cochrane Johnstone, tenth son of the 8th Earl of Dundonald, who after marrying a daughter of the 2nd Earl of Hopetoun had assumed the additional name of Johnstone. He was a man without scruples, one whom even the sober *Dictionary of National Biography* characterises as "adventurer". After the events of which we shall speak he was involved in several disreputable transactions, which culminated in 1814 in his famous Stock Exchange fraud when with his nephew, Lord Cochrane (who mitigated his unscrupulousness with the talents of a brilliant seaman), he spread the false news of Bonaparte's death and netted many thousands of pounds. He rose to his respectable rank and situation in the army in the great days of commission-trafficking of the 1790s, and had somehow obtained not only a lucrative West Indian government but the colonelcy of the 8th West India Regi-

[28]W.O.17/2492; 4/341, p. 71.

ment. This regiment, stationed in Dominica, was a comparatively new levy, and, though partly composed of "Dominican Creoles," consisted for the most part of "New Negroes" or negroes recently imported from Africa, a duller and less electric type of man than the native negro. His rule in Dominica, it is said, "was marked by tyranny, extortion and vice. He drove a brisk and profitable trade in negroes and kept a harem".

Trigge and his predecessors, in view of the heavy rate of sickness, had urged the clearing and draining by military labour of some marshland near St. Rupert's, a necessary work whether viewed in the light of our own or the contemporary knowledge of yellow fever. This was entirely after Cochrane's heart. He was not interested in the marsh: he was interested in the higher land surrounding it, eminently suitable for profitable exploitation as a sugar-cane plantation; which he proceeded, under the cover of a syndicate, to buy. Trigge, knowing his Cochrane Johnstone, forbade him to use the negroes of his own regiment on the work unless he paid them the customary 9d. per day that was allowed to British troops, "in order to preserve the feeling of superiority over the generality of negroes" that he had always striven to foster. Cochrane Johnstone turned a deaf ear. There was too much money in the business. The result was almost inevitable. The scheme blew up in his face with the mutiny of his regiment.

The men, after they had been working in the swamp every afternoon for a fortnight, came to believe that they were not to be kept as soldiers but divided among the estates and returned to slavery. The arrival of a small party of the 68th in the evening of 9th April 1802 alarmed the African negroes, who thought the soldiers were come to carry them off to the plantations while they were at work. Cunningly deceiving their officers, they rose that night at Fort Shirley, killing three of their own officers and the white sergeant-major, the assistant-commissary Mr. Laing, Sergeant McKay, 68th, who was attached to the office at St. Ruperts, Mrs. McKay, and several others.

Cochrane Johnstone was at Roseau when he received the news early on 10th April. Sending to Trigge for every assistance "for God's sake," he ordered from Morne Bruce five companies of the 2/68th under Major Hamilton, who had commanded the picquet at Gouyave six years before, and Major George Scott, together with two companies of militia and a detachment of artillery. They went by sea and landed on the evening of the 11th, and were joined by a detachment of marines, some staunch men of the 8th under Major Gordon and a detachment of the 1/1st (Royals) from the Saints. Posting Hamilton with 200 militia and marines across the swamp road to prevent escape in that direction, Cochrane Johnstone advanced early next morning, the 12th. He refused the mutineers' terms, and under a flag of truce announced that he would march into their barracks at one o'clock in the afternoon.

The main body of his force, of which the 2/68th under Hamilton and Scott formed the principal part, arrived on the parade-ground shortly after two. They found the 8th West India Regiment drawn up in line, and were formed up in line facing them, the 2/68th in front, the Royals and the marines in rear. They then advanced until fifteen paces separated them from the mutineers, who gave a general salute, which they returned. Cochrane Johnstone ordered the mutineers to ground arms. All except the grenadiers did so. He then ordered them to take three paces to the front. At this, however, they stood still, and one grenadier ran along the line urging them to take up their arms, firing his own musket as he did so. The firing immediately became general, and at the same moment some mutineers opened up from the battery on the Inner Cabrit, the hill immediately overlooking the barracks. Many fell on both sides. But there was no withstanding the one and only charge which the 2/68th gave in the whole of its existence. Hamilton and Scott's men pursued the broken mutineers to the Outer Cabrit, where they were exposed to the fire from H.M.S. *Magnificent*, while Major Gordon, with the blacks who remained loyal, attacked the Inner. In half an hour it was all over.

Cochrane Johnstone estimated the mutineers' loss at over 100 killed and wounded. His own force lost 3 men killed and 15 wounded from the 2/68th, and 1 man killed and 9 wounded in the 1/1st, marines and militia, besides himself and Lieutenant Home of the navy, who were touched. The Regimental *Digest* adds that several other men of the Battalion were killed and injured when some ammunition that was kept under the guard bed blew up as a result of one of the guard lighting his pipe.

Seven mutineers were condemned to death at the Court-Martial, of which Major Scott was president, and the 8th West India Regiment, about 300 men, was brought to Martinique to be disbanded. They were sent to Barbados, where those that were not implicated (mostly the "Creoles") were distributed among other regiments, and those that were were branded and made pioneers. That was the end of the 8th West India Regiment. It was also the end of Cochrane Johnstone's career in the Antilles. His government was taken from him, and he carried his shady transactions to Europe until he eventually disappeared, no one knows how or when or where.[29]

[29]For the suppression of the mutiny see C.O.318/19.

Meanwhile the Treaty of Amiens had been signed that ushered in eighteen months of uneasy peace. Large scale reductions in the army inevitably followed. The companies of the foot guards were reduced to 100 men, cavalry regiments to 10 troops of 60 men; 16 regiments of fencibles, among them the Durham and Princess Charlotte of Wales's, were disbanded; regiments with third battalions drafted them into their second, and twelve infantry battalions with second battalions drafted them into the first.

One of the twelve to go was the 2/68th. Those that had survived the attention of *Aedes ægypti* were drafted into the 1/68th to make a single battalion. The fever had played havoc with both battalions since their first arrival in the West Indies. Up to the end of December 1801 the First Battalion had lost 326 men, the Second Battalion 393, and during the nine months of its existence in 1802 the Second Battalion had lost a further 30, in all 423 men, most in the late summer of 1801, when 140 went in one month. No wonder the guide-books inform us that Morne Bruce is haunted and that on dark nights there may be heard the tramp of phantom troops and the sound of bugle-calls. Thirty-two officers of both battalions had also died, twenty-five of them the former officers of the Irish militia. In September the effective strength of the First Battalion in Barbados and Martinique was 570 rank and file, that of the Second Battalion in Dominica 487.

The drafting, which took place in Barbados on 24th September 1802, created a single battalion of 1014 effectives. The reduction in officers was effected by reducing to half-pay the "youngest" officers of each rank, and since, as has been said, the Second Battalion was by no means exclusively composed of the "youngest", it led to many disappointments and, it may be surmised, to some disorganisation. Major Hamilton, for instance, being the junior of the four majors, went, though he managed to return after giving evidence at Cochrane Johnstone's court-martial. Captains Stewart and Cox went, as well as the junior captain-lieutenant, John Reed, father of Lieutenant Reed, who, however, was "above the line". Away too went all the survivors from the Irish militia, who transferred to the full-pay of other regiments in the Caribbean, most to the 3rd, the 11th and the 37th. The colonel-commandantship naturally lapsed.[30]

§

In the summer of 1802 Sir Thomas Trigge went, and was succeeded as Commander-in-Chief by Lieut.-General William Grin-

[30]W.O.1/624, p. 221; 4/341, pp. 344-346.

field, who arrived in Barbados on 16th August. Grinfield was an enormous Guardsman, who had run his battalion like a machine and now ran his headquarters and his new command like a battalion. After his arrival there was no sitting over dinner, but constant parades and inspections. Very prudently as it turned out, his first act was to inspect the islands that were to be returned to the French under the Treaty, and he made his capable young Adjutant-General, Lieut.-Colonel George Murray, draw up plans for their attack.

On 5th June 1803 he was warned that discussions in Paris were breaking down. He immediately summoned Commodore Hood and his Q.M.G. to a council of war where it was decided that if war broke out Tobago and St. Lucia could almost certainly be captured with ease, and that St. Lucia, having the best harbours and from its situation commanding to some extent Martinique, the most important French possession, should be attacked first. Transport was hired and stores embarked immediately for a force of 3300 consisting of:

artillery, artificers, pioneers	290
1 / 1st	670
64th	670
68th	670
3rd West India Regiment (reinforced by drafts from the "broken" 11th)	600
7th West India Regiment (made up from the "broken" 9th and 12th	400

Grinfield, therefore, was ready to go the moment he received instructions. These arrived on 14th June. They ordered him to take possession of Martinique, St. Lucia and Tobago, but Martinique only if there was reasonable chance of success. Hood arrived late on the 17th, the troops were embarked on the 19th; and, despite some delay in shipping the stores, the expedition sailed on the 20th.

Murray's plan recommended that any landing in St. Lucia should take place in Choc Bay, and certainly to the north of the Morne Fortuné. Though Murray was not present to see it executed, his plan worked with complete success. The troops landed in Choc Bay on 21st June, and by half-past five in the evening the French outposts were driven in and Castries entered. The governor, General Noguès, refused to surrender until the Morne Fortuné was attacked. This Grinfield carried out at four the next morning, 22nd June, in half an hour, by two assault columns respectively under Brigadier-Generals Prevost and Brereton. The 68th acted as a reserve under Brigadier-General Picton (who had been suspended from the government of Trinidad and accompanied Grinfield as a volunteer) and were not engaged. The garrison of rather over 600 officers and men then surrendered after inflicting casualties of 20 men killed and 110 officers and men wounded.

When Grinfield sailed on to take Tobago in an equally brisk fashion, the 68th, with three companies of 3rd West India Regiment, remained under General Brereton to garrison St. Lucia. According to the monthly returns the strength of the Regiment on 1st July was 736 rank and file "present fit" and 24 officers, so that unless some were left temporarily in Barbados, Grinfield's estimate of 670 was on the conservative side.[31]

Thus for a second time in less than ten years the beautiful island of St. Lucia became the grave of the 68th. The sickness had not been unduly heavy in Barbados in 1802. But St. Lucia had a bad reputation for fever, and the barracks on the Morne Fortuné, where the 68th were quartered for nearly two years, was the unhealthiest place on the island. On 11th January 1805 the unhappy state of the Regiment was the subject of a special report from the Chief Engineer, as well as of a special report from Lieut.-General Myers (who had succeeded to the chief command on the death of Grinfield from yellow fever) to the Secretary of State. This corps, they observed, "has been nearly annihilated". Between 22nd June 1803 and 31st December 1804, 5 officers and 524 n.c.o.s and men had died and 7 officers and 171 n.c.o.s and men were invalided to Europe. In February 1805, when there were only 216 men "present fit" and the battalion was 436 below establishment, Myers withdrew it to St. Vincent. Even that, however, failed to arrest the progress of the fever, and in April it was moved to Antigua. There the strength recovered somewhat: and in May 1806, the last return before its embarkation, the strength was 18 officers and 309 n.c.o.s and men fit, and the sick had dropped from about 100 to about 50.[32]

John Green, who enlisted in the 68th in 1807 after its return home, says it had gone out to the West Indies 2500 strong and lost 2000 men in sickness. He is not far wrong in the aggregate. He is wrong in saying it went out 2500 strong: the most that can be made out of the sum of the two battalions in February is 1830. But there was a steady stream of recruits reaching the 68th which may have amounted to 2 or 300; the Regiment received some drafts from other battalions, notably the 2/60th in March 1805, when it received 50 men; and there were besides a number of so-called "culprits", mostly former Irish rebels of '98 who were condemned to perpetual service in the

[31]C.O.318/21; 318/22.
[32]C.O.318/27, pp. 65, 99, 115; W.O. 17/2493-2497.

West Indies and passed from one regiment to another as it was sent home and relieved. It is difficult to say how many of this type the 68th received altogether. Seventy joined the First Battalion in January 1802, newly arrived from New Geneva, near Waterford, and in October 1802 out of a total of 1290 in the Windward and Leeward Islands 104 were serving in the 68th. Many were men of excellent character and some were valuable n.c.o.s. When the 68th was drafted in June 1806, 1 sergeant, 3 drummers and 63 rank and file were of this description. It is therefore, perhaps fair to say that possibly 500 men joined and Green's 2500 is not gross exaggeration. What can, however, be said with some degree of accuracy is that thirty-eight officers (including Hanbury, formerly sergeant-major, commissioned quartermaster in 1799) and about 1520 n.c.o.s and men died during those five and a half years. Over 200 were invalided.[33]

In May 1806 the Regiment was ordered home. Having drafted, besides the 67 "culprits", 131 men who volunteered to remain in the West Indies—most went to the 70th (64) and the 96th (121)—it embarked on 9th and 12th June for England with a strength of 23 officers, 39 sergeants, 15 drummers and 109 rank and file. It landed at Portsmouth on 16th August under the command of Lieut.-Colonel Farley.

[33]W.O.1 /624 (letter and encls. of 3rd Dec 1802); C.O. 318/27, p. 339. Between January 1801 and May 1806 the First Battalion lost 1071 corporals and men, the Second Battalion, between January 1801 and August 1802, 423, a total of 1494.

CHAPTER IV

WALCHEREN AND THE PENINSULA

THE 68th is the third regiment to have been converted into light infantry; and since we have arrived at the point in its history when the conversion took place, this is the moment to pause to consider what was meant by light infantry in 1808.

It was far from being a new "invention". Even in the early eighteenth century, when there appears to have been more emphasis laid upon form than power, it is a mistake to visualise fighting as consisting merely of two long lines of infantry dressed impeccably at forty or fifty yards distance, firing volleys until one or the other gave way. That is a true picture of a battle like Fontenoy, and in such a battle it is admittedly hard to exaggerate the rigidity, the precision and the formality of the movements. But battles occurred hardly more than once, perhaps twice, in a campaign. Sometimes they did not occur at all. Campaigns consisted principally in sieges, outpost affairs at the fringe of the encampments and cantonments, foraging-parties and ambuscades, which might perhaps reach the proportions of an "affair" but seldom those of a battle in which the full might of the line infantry was invoked. The ordinary military existence was composed of these incidents, and they were properly undertaken by fast moving, lightly armed troops who could strike hard and get away quickly. When the recruits of most European armies came from townsmen and country lads in whom whatever capacities they might have had for this kind of fighting had been extinguished on the parade ground, the man best suited for it was the "irregular" from central Europe whose peacetime avocations were not far removed. Hence arose the ironical situation in which the Austrian Nether-lands, where peculiar circumstances favoured warfare at its most formal, became the theatre in which the irregular from the Austro-

Ottoman frontier, the *Grenzgebiet*, was allowed full play. It is impossible to read of any campaign in the Low Countries without finding mention on almost any page of the activities of outlandish-looking gentlemen with long black moustaches, their hair in plaits and sometimes riding small, hardy ponies: "Pandours", "Croats", "Hussars", "Hulans", "Lycanians" (Liccaner), and *"compagnies franches"*. The employment of these provoked the employment of similar people on the part of their enemies. The French had their own *"compagnies franches"* and the "Corps de Fischer" (1743-1792) and the "Grassins" (1744-1749).

In our own service we were on the whole content to profit by the irregulars and light troops of our allies. But in the Seven Years' War on the continent we were tending in that direction when we raised a special light troop in every cavalry regiment; and at the same time in America, after Braddock's defeat, there was not much that was recognisable as line infantry and cavalry. Several British infantry regiments were made "light" by the 3rd Viscount Howe before he fell at Ticonderoga in 1758; the 60th became, by virtue of their recruitment among the Swiss and German settlers in the Colonies, a light regiment; and Gage's 80th and Morgan's 90th were specially raised as such. From that time something of a light infantry tradition became embedded in our own service.

It might seem as though every successive war creates a fresh demand for light troops and that every war becomes progressively less "regular". On closer inspection it does not appear so simple a progression. In peace in every service there is a tendency to standard-ise, a polarity towards the line; and the irregulars of one war tend to become the regulars of the next. Fischer's Corps, for instance, becomes the Saxe-Hussards; the Liccaner are almost assimilated into the Austrian line as the 60th; and in our own service our High-landers are subjected to a similar process. With every new war the business of creating light troops starts all over again.[1]

It was therefore a refreshing and important innovation to create in 1770 those light companies which have already been mentioned as having been added to every infantry battalion. A *corps d'élite* like the grenadiers, they were composed of the most agile and intelligent men of the regiment. It was usual to detach them from their parent regiment, form them with other grenadier and light companies into

---

[1]It may be rather far-fetched, but it should be noticed that when mounted infantry were organised in the 1880s, 1890s and 1900s, there was never any question of re-forming the dragoon regiments to play the part for which they had been originally raised. "Cavalry" they had become and "cavalry" they remained, and the M.I. were extemporised from the infantry.

"flank battalions" or "grenadier" and "light" battalions, and train them and employ them separately—a practice which lasted for over thirty years and was common form throughout the American War. That war, however, exercised not only our light companies but our whole army in light infantry tactics for six solid years, from which it emerged as the best light infantry army of any European power. The decisive superiority of these troops was demonstrated in St Lucia in 1778, when five light companies of colony-trained men under Colonel Medows beat off an attack of two battalions of European-trained French infantry after inflicting in three hours a loss of 400 killed at a cost to themselves of only 13.

It is melancholy to relate that this vast accumulation of experience was dissipated in the years of peace. Many of the light troops were American loyalists and German *jäger* mercenaries who naturally left our service when the war was over. But what was properly our own evaporated under the influence of the so-called German school, which enjoyed especial favour here in those vital ten years. The German school, formed on the model of Frederick of Prussia's camps of instruction, was formalism itself. It is not perhaps true that Prussian sergeant-majors carried astrolabes in their halberds to preserve mathematical alignment and perfection of direction in their elaborate manœuvres, but it is not an unfair exaggeration. The leading light in our army was Colonel David Dundas, who, despite extensive experience in the continental campaigns of the Seven Years' War, had seen no service in America and was bewitched and beguiled by Prussian military writers like Saldern. We consequently entered the war in 1793 with nothing to show for our American experience.

This was particularly unfortunate because even warfare in the Low Countries no longer favoured formal evolutions, even on the battlefield. The country was no longer starred with fortresses—most had been dismantled; it was no longer the rolling arable of Marlborough's day—enclosure had transformed this as it had transformed the English landscape; and the French army of the Republic no longer consisted of the well drilled and docile regiments of the monarchy, but of swarms of aggressive and self-reliant *tirailleurs* and *voltigeurs* who, using ground intelligently, worked up to the line with impunity and peppered it until the large masses in the rear came up to deliver the *coup de grâce*. At first our lack of light infantry in this theatre was not embarrassing. We could still rely on the Pandours and Croats of our Austrian allies, and more particularly on the *émigré* and other foreign regiments in our pay, who performed these functions for us without any exertion on our part. But after the

Coalition had dissolved and we had been forced back on our own resources and were threatened, if somewhat remotely through Ireland, with invasion, we became acutely aware of the lack. Howe, Cornwallis, Grey, Moira, Tarleton and other officers of the old American school were still at hand to lend their experience, and the "school" was large enough to form a sympathetic body of opinion; but the men who had made up the old American infantry had long since disappeared—seventeen years is a long time for them; and the only formed body of men ready to hand was the remnants of the foreign corps that continued in our pay.

Their quality varied greatly, but some were very good indeed. The best, notably the Royal York Fusiliers, Latour's Royal Foreigners, Hompesch's Chasseurs-à-pied, Ramsay's York Rangers and Waldstein's, which were incorporated into the 2nd, 3rd and 4th Battalions of the 60th, and Hompesch's Light Infantry and Löwenstein's Fusiliers and Chasseurs (or Jäger), which between them entirely composed the new 5/60th, were taken into our own service. The cold-blooded professionalism of the last-named in the West Indies, as they phlegmatically shot down the bandits without taking their long pipes from their mouths, had been an eye-opener to our people, who therefore listened, perhaps over-attentively, to all they had to say. The most articulate among their officers was Lieut.-Colonel Franz von Rothenburg, of Hompesch's Light Infantry, who in 1797 published a manual of light infantry drill which with the full support of the Duke of York was translated and approved as official doctrine on the controversial subject.

Rottenburg (to give the usual English form of his name) was by origin a Danziger. He had entered the French service as a young lieutenant of 25 in the regiment of La Mark-allemand in 1782, and having assisted the Swiss general Antoine de Salis-Marschlins in the reorganisation of the Neapolitan army and having quitted the French army at the Revolution, had joined Kosciuszko's Polish Patriot Army which was crushed by Suvórov in 1794. He had then joined one of the Hompesch brothers' levies in British pay, Hompesch's Hussars, in which he was given a majority. He afterwards transferred to another, Hompesch's Light Infantry, the one that was incorporated so firmly into the 5/60th that the battalion and, later, the whole 60th took over their green clothing and, it is said, the black Maltese cross of Hompesch as its badge. As might be expected from one of such wide experience, Rottenburg's manual was more than a mere drill book. It taught indeed the movements to the sound of the bugle, the use of the rifle and the order of skirmishing, but it also prescribed a new morality for the soldier acting independently and urged humane treatment on the part of his officers. The first tangible result was the formation of an "Experimental Rifle Corps" which was exercised at Swinley under the King's eye in 1800. This corps, which attracted the adventurous element among officers and recruits alike (including a dozen from the Loyal Durham Fencibles), survived as the 95th or Rifle Brigade, and with the 5/60th, which remained preponderantly German until 1816, represented the army's response to the challenge of the *tirailleur*.

With the resumption of the war in 1803, which, starting with a threat of invasion more immediate than any for over a hundred years, appeared to favour the formation of light troops from among the Volunteers, the discussion became more widespread. Carried on both inside and outside the army, it ranged over a multitude of aspects, most with a view to raising the standard of intelligence of the recruit. Here the old American school, hitherto silent, became more vocal. Cornwallis, for instance, and other, younger, men, who had been attached to the Austrian Armies in the great campaigns, pronounced themselves unfavourable to rifle corps. They conceded the accuracy of the weapon, but they had seen whole bodies of Tyrolese *jäger* overrun in the open while struggling to load it, and they preferred to see light troops armed with a modification of the regulation flintlock. There were those who said it was vain to expect accurate musketry. "How is it, Colonel," an Irish officer was asked who had come through the whole war unharmed, "that you were never wounded?" "Faith," he said, "and wasn't it because they aimed at me? Sure and I always rode a white horse on purpose." No doubt the discussion would have continued without finality had not a brigadier, commanding one of the most "exposed" brigades on the Kent coast, making use of Rottenburg's manual and inspiring it with his own magnetic personality, created out of the 95th and two very ordinary marching battalions a model light infantry force.

In Moore and his Shorncliffe brigade the two strains of the "American" and the "foreign" schools may be said to have merged in a compromise. Moore abandoned neither the regulation drill nor the regulation musket. Yet he taught his men also to skirmish in open order and form again. Above all, exercising a very strict selection in the choice of his officers and animating them with a very good tone, he produced not only a drill but a discipline—in its widest sense— that remained unimpaired long after his death, even when handled by commanders the very antithesis of himself, and spread throughout the army at large (and even beyond it into the police force). The 68th nas been doubly fortunate: it came directly under Rottenburg, and it later came under one of the best of Moore's officers.[2]

Moore's intention had been, as he later confided, not so much to form regiments differing from those of the rest of the army as to introduce into the British infantry in general a system that gave it greater promptitude and elasticity than that copied from the Prussians by Dundas. His Shorncliffe brigade was only the beginning of a vaster project. In any case, when the regular army numbered 160 battalions—or even the 60 or 70 at home available for immediate service—a brigade of light infantry was not a formidable proportion. When in 1808 the Spanish rising offered an opportunity of really extensive operations, an augmentation of the light battalions was plainly needed. The order was issued on 10th September 1808, at a moment when the pick of the service battalions available were either in, or under orders for, the Peninsula.

> "His Majesty," it says, "having taken into consideration that the proportion of light troops was much too small for the extended scale of the British army, and that the utility of this description of force had been most eminently displayed on every occasion when they have been employed, and the whole of that army being at this moment embarked or employed upon foreign service, I have to acquaint you that His Majesty has been pleased to command that two more battalions of the Line should be formed into light troops with all practicable dispatch, and that the 68th and 85th regiments should be allotted for this purpose and assimilated with regard to their clothing, arming and discipline to the 43rd and 52nd regiments, and that, in consequence thereof, an additional lieutenant, sergeant and corporal per company be borne on the establishment of the 68th and 85th Regiments."[3]

The 68th, which was at Hull when these orders were issued, was immediately marched south to the shingle barracks at Brabourne Lees, near Ashford in Kent, to train as light infantry with the 85th. Their instruction was entrusted to none other than Rottenburg himself, who had been training some light infantry on the Curragh of Kildare. Six months later, in March 1809, the two battalions of the 71st were added to the brigade.

Why was the 68th chosen? In the absence of any definite information only conjecture can be made. If past performance was a consideration, the Regiment had not, in all fairness, shown any particu-

[2]The best books on light infantry are still Maj.-General J. F. C. Fuller's *Sir John Moore's System of Training* (1924) and *British Light Infantry in the Eighteenth Century* (1925), which need, however, some modification now.
[3]W.O.40/29; 3/96, p. 157.

lar aptitude. Nor had the 85th—nor indeed had the 43rd or the 52nd. It does not appear either that the commanding officers or any group of officers had given proof of any special qualification. Lieut.-Colonel Cuyler, of the 85th, had not; Lieut.-Colonel Pack, of the 71st, though a very capable officer with a distinguished career before him, had not either. In the 68th itself Colonel Farley, 57, with 41 years' service, more than most commanding officers had, though highly respected and much beloved of his men, was so "very old" that Rottenburg had him tactfully removed from the command. Lieut.-Colonel William Johnston, his successor, was 37 with 19 years' service. As a subaltern in the 18th he had known the 68th in the garrison of Gibraltar in 1793 and had accompanied his regiment to Toulon. For a short period from 1795 to 1797 he had held a captaincy in a Corsican levy known as "Major Smith's Union Regiment", and had served in an expedition sent from Corsica to Tuscany under Colonel D. D. Wemyss. The Union Regiment is not, however, to be confused with Hudson Lowe's Corsican levy which so impressed Sir John Moore with its light infantry movements. According to Green, Johnston was "an officer that loved his men and by whom he was respected in return," but nothing in his career marked him out as a light infantry commander. Major Richard Thompson, the second-in-command, who in Green's book appears as a first-class officer of great humanity and in the inspection reports as an able commanding officer, was outwardly no better qualified. It seems mistaken therefore to seek a reason in the special aptitudes or training of the officers.

The most likely reason for the choice would appear to be the unexciting one that it was filled by young recruits, and adaptable on that ground. The 85th, which had returned from the West Indies in 1806 also, was in a similar situation. There is some confirmation for this view in the fact that Rottenburg considered the 1/71st, which reached Brabourne Lees after hard service in the retreat to Corunna, a more difficult battalion to train for that reason. And when we come to speak of the 2nd Bombay Europeans we shall see that its very newness constituted a ground for making it light infantry.[4]

On its return from the Caribbean the 68th had been moved from Portsmouth to Staines, from Staines to Leeds, where it remained until November 1806, and thence to Ripon, where it stayed for a year. John Green, a young lad apprenticed to a carpet-weaver in his native town of Louth, Lincolnshire, who enlisted at Leeds in October 1806, was the fourth recruit to join since its return from

[4]W.O.40/7; 27/94; pp. 213-215 inf.

abroad, and one of the four deserted immediately after. There were only 90 rank and file present fit at that moment, and the numbers only gradually improved over the next months. In November 1806 there were no less than fifteen recruiting-parties out: at Limerick, Durham (Captain Hawthorne), Sheffield, Edinburgh, Tullamore, Wolverhampton, Crieff, Dublin, Mullingar, Lisburn, Glasgow, Preston, Doncaster, Blandford and Belfast. But recruiting did not markedly increase until October and November 1807, when the Regiment moved to Doncaster. There started then a steady stream of volunteers from the militia which continued until June 1809. It moved from Doncaster to Malton and Pickering in February 1808, and in March to York, and thence in July to Hull. It reached Brabourne Lees by way of London (where Sir Thomas Trigge offered it hospitality) on the 18th October, by which time it was 436 rank and file strong.[5]

The bare facts conceal one that is apparent only in retrospect, namely that a new and brighter era is opening for it. In the first place it has in these years some claim to being a Durham regiment. During the period from September 1806 to June 1809 it received 925 recuits, of whom 521 were from the militia. Fair quantities came from the Dumfries, the South Lincolnshire and West Riding Regiments, but far and away the largest single contributor was the Durham Militia, which, though not stationed in the 68th's vicinity, gave 168 during those years. There were further some recruits brought by the Durham party, so that it may be said when the Regiment embarked for Walcheren in July 1809 it was nearly one-quarter composed of Durham men. A good many were lost in the expedition, however, and by the time it embarked for the Peninsula in June 1811 the proportion had fallen to a bare one-seventh. The fate of these men may be summarised from the pay-rolls as listed on the following page.[6]

These men brought a calm and unemotional quality into the Regiment which one associates, rightly or wrongly, with men of the County. People in Barnard Castle long remembered old Willie Robinson, one of the 58 survivors, who volunteered in April or May 1809 and served in No. 4 Company. "He used to speak in a quiet reserved style without a particle of animation as if all that his regiment had performed were a mere matter of course, the superiority of the British soldier being so well known and universally acknowledged that it was not worth while saying anything to prove it."

[5]W.O.12/7632; John Green, *Vicissitudes of a Soldier's Life* ... (Louth, 1827), pp. 14-20 (*cit.* hereafter as "Green").
[6]Compiled from the pay-rolls in W.O.12/7632-7635.

At the same time five officers of Colonel O'Callaghan's fine regiment received ensigncies in the 68th, presumably on terms similar to
those on which the Irish militia officers received theirs in 1800: James
Nixon, who died in Walcheren; Henry Stapylton, who died of
wounds received at Œyregave in February 1814; Roger Stopford,
who was killed at the Nivelle, November 1813; William Loftus, who
resigned in 1811; and David Skene, who after being wounded at
Vitoria and Lesaca stayed with the Regiment until 1823. Small

Volunteered from the Durham Militia, 1807-1809		168
Brought by the Durham recruiting-party . .		9
		177
Less: Deserted or claimed as deserters . . .	12	
Died at home	6	
Discharged	10	
Killed and died of wounds in Walcheren .	2	
Died in Walcheren or soon after . . .	46	
	—	76
		101
Volunteered from the Durham Militia, May 1811 .		15
Available for service in the Peninsula, July 1811 .		116
Less: Killed and died of wounds, 1811-1814 . .	10	
Died in the Peninsula or soon after . .	38	
Prisoners of war	3	
Deserted	3	
Transferred to Veteran Battalions or invalided home and discharged	6	
	—	60
		56
Prisoners of war repatriated		2
Remaining on the books, December 1814 . .		58

though the proportion of Durham men may appear, it is the first
occasion since the nominal county connection was established on
which the Regiment contained a proportion worth mentioning and,
indeed, the only one until the last decade of the century, when the
connection was deliberately cultivated.

Secondly, it appears for the first time in British military history
equipped and clothed as a regiment of light infantry. According to
Green it was issued with "japanned muskets with double sights," a
statement which seems to confirm the impression that British light
infantry were armed with the short, 39in. barrel, smoothbore

flintlock of the "New Land Service Pattern". Whereas line infantry ordered on service carried the "Indian Pattern" flintlock, whose barrel was polished as bright as hands could make it, with a foresight only, the light infantry musket barrel was habitually "browned," had a backsight and was provided with the pistol-grip trigger-guard which is its most distinguishing feature. In calibre and other respects, however, it differed little from the musket of the line. At Christmas the 68th was issued with the new clothing. Instead of shoulder-knots the new coatees carried wings, and the shakos, instead of white tufts, had green, and bugles in place of the large stamped brass plate.[7]

The Regiment's assimilation of light infantry drill was not so quickly accomplished, and indeed was not complete before it went on service. Socially and to outward appearances it was a most like-able regiment. An officer from another regiment who knew it at that time wrote that its officers, "more steady, perhaps, from being more experienced than their brother flankers of the 85th, were a remark-ably pleasant set of men, many of whom bore the appearance of having seen some hard service". In its training Rottenburg reported on 3rd May 1809 that it had improved since inspected in October 1808, that the volunteers it had received were "particularly good and more adapted to the light service than the old men of the bat-talion," and that it had made "considerable progress" in light infantry movements. But "the officers," he says, "require a great deal of instruction yet, the recruiting service having much impeded the same"—20 officers were absent from this cause. "My instructions relative to target-firing"—evidently particularly exacting, involving a scale of ammunition expenditure equivalent to that of the 95th—"having been duly attended to has produced a considerable number of good shots." He goes on to say (what is proof that the light infantry was cast in a double role) that "it had not yet attained in its field exercise and movements when acting as troops of the line any great degree of precision, its whole time having been taken up with light infantry movements". Colonel Farley, he says, "being a very old man, appears not well qualified for the command of a light infantry regiment. The first major, Brevet-Lieut.-Colonel Johnston, is a very active and excellent officer. The second major, Major Thompson, is also a willing officer and attends to his duty particu-larly." The upshot of this was the removal of its very popular com-manding officer, who, though low on the colonels' list, was promoted to a brigadier's command in Jamaica. He was replaced by Colonel

[7]Green, pp. 22-23; R. Scurfield, "British Military Smoothbore Firearms" (J.S.A.H.R., Vol. 33 (1955), pp. 147*ff.*)

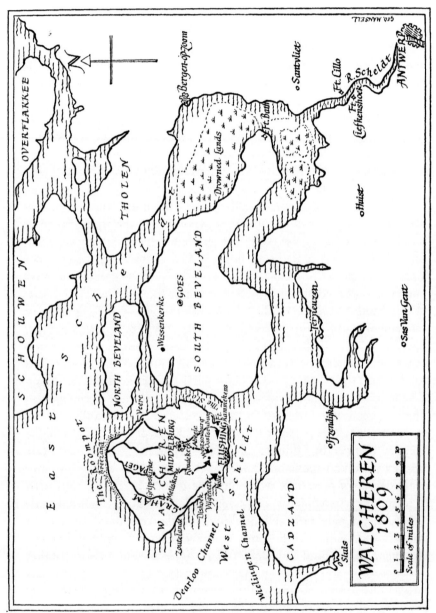

6. Walcheren, August-September 1809

Johnston, who commanded the 68th with only short intervals throughout its service in Walcheren and the Peninsula. It was some years before the battalion showed the effects of Johnston's grip, but clearly its record in the Peninsula owes much to him. Green, who is quite candid on the subject of his officers, always speaks of him with liking and respect, and it was a happy thought which eventually gave him the Colonelcy.[8]

Thirdly, for the first time in its history, the 68th took part in a campaign in the very forefront of the military history of the nation. The Walcheren Expedition turned out unhappily, but at its outset it represented the whole military effort of the country, a service to which the pick of the army was allocated, and an opportunity on which all general, staff and regimental officers from the Horse Guards downwards set their hearts.

§

It had been projected for some time. We are accustomed nowadays to regard Trafalgar as putting an end to the threat of invasion. Our ancestors did not. Napoleon's endeavours to increase his navy had led to our Copenhagen Expedition of 1807 and to the Portuguese campaign of 1808, which effectively disposed of his attempt to seize the Danish and Portuguese fleets. But the ship-building resources of his Empire were still considerable, and when an important French squadron under Admiral Missiessy lay in the Scheldt at Flushing, a "conjoint" expedition that would destroy both it as well as the great shipyards at Antwerp presented an attractive appearance. Some military diversion in favour of the Austrians, who were locked in a mortal struggle outside their capital, was clearly desirable while Napoleon's best troops were committed and, so to speak, his back was turned. After the Berlin Decrees some outlet for our manufactures into the continent was not only desirable but necessary for our economy; and Walcheren and Flushing promised to be a useful "emporium". The conjoint expedition destined for the accomplishment of the design was entrusted to a force of eight divisions, 32,000 men, under Lord Chatham, and a powerful naval armament of warships and transports under Sir Richard Strachan. Having regard to the means available at the time, it was the largest combined operation undertaken by this country before 6th June 1944.

The original plan (which circumstances altered even before the

[8]Major John Patterson, *Adventures, 1807-1821* (London, 1837), p. 123; W.O. 27/94.

whole army was assembled in the Downs) comprised, first, a landing at Cadzand and an advance along the south bank of the West Scheldt upon the Tête-de-Flandre, immediately opposite Antwerp; and, second, a landing on one or other of the islands in the East Scheldt and an advance into Beveland in the general direction of Antwerp. For this purpose the Army was divided into two wings, a right and a left, to each of which was given a formation of light troops. The Right Wing had three brigades of them, one of cavalry, two of infantry; the Left Wing had but a regiment of cavalry and the so-called 13th Brigade commanded by Rottenburg (who took Captain Winniett as his Brigade Major), consisting of:

68th (Lieut.-Colonel Johnston)	.	.	.	773
1/71st (Lieut.-Colonel Pack)	.	.	.	955
85th (Lieut.-Colonel Cuyler)	.	.	.	571
2/95th, 2 companies	.	.	.	199
				—— 2498

In the event this organisation was modified, Rottenburg's Brigade forming the light infantry brigade of a corps commanded by Lord Paget which landed in Walcheren.

The Regiment, well above establishment, embarked in the warship *Cæsar* at Spithead on 16th July 1809, at 6 o'clock in the morning. They sailed for the Downs on the 25th and anchored there on the 27th while the great fleet assembled. They weighed the next day. At 5 in the afternoon of the 30th the *Cæsar* moored off the Breezand on the north coast of Walcheren. An advance party of seamen went ashore, and the disembarkation of the 68th, which was carried out in flat-bottomed boats, was completed in two hours between 6.30 and 8.30 the same evening. They lay all that night and the morning of the 31st on the sand in light marching order, with haversacks, canteens and rolled greatcoats but without knapsacks. Two companies, Reed's and Hawkins's, were detached to accompany Graham's Brigade, forming the extreme right of the Army, while the other eight companies remained with Rottenburg's Brigade, which, with Browne's, formed the centre under Lord Paget.[9]

The fort of Veere, which blocked the advance on Middelburg and Flushing, was masked on the 31st. Graham's column moved forward that afternoon to Meliskerke, Paget to Grijpskerke, the enemy retiring before them. On 1st August the advance was resumed. Graham, moving along the south-west coast through Zoutelande, Dishoek and Vijgeneter, came under the fortifications of Flushing in

[9]Royal United Service Institution, Long Papers (MM 219 G); *Cæsar's* Log (Ad. 51/2255); letters of Gen. Brownrigg (Q.M.G.) in Gen. Sir Willoughby Gordon's Papers (B.M., Add. Mss. 49500).

the evening. There the 68th fought its first engagement as light infantry. The garrison prepared to resist, and the companies of the 68th and 95th were ordered forward to dislodge them. Green, who was with them, says the first onset "very much terrified" him but that he quickly became calm and deliberate. The small skirmish, which cost the 68th a few wounded, was successful in pressing the enemy back to their works, and Graham bivouacked that night with Nolle on his right and Westsouburg on his left. Meanwhile Paget in the centre, moving by Koudekerke, reached Westsouburg at about the same time. Like Graham's men they found the enemy drawn up to resist them, but these were soon dispersed by the 68th's eight companies and the 85th under Rottenburg, who advanced in the most gallant style. They pursued too far, however, right up to the gates of Flushing, and although they took 200 prisoners they paid for their rashness with fairly heavy casualties. Eleven n.c.o.s and men were killed and three officers and about twenty men wounded. Paget's column bivouacked that night near Westsouburg, in a position they continued to occupy for the next fortnight.

Meanwhile the remainder of the troops disembarked in Walcheren converged on Flushing, and the investment of the place was completed by the end of the day. Operations, however, were not confined to the island of Walcheren. A powerful division under Sir John Hope landed in South Beveland, pressed on and captured the fort of Bath (or Batz) on the 2nd, where it threatened a descent on the mainland, either on Liefkenshoek or Lillo, the forts behind which Missiessy had taken refuge. The descent on Cadzand, which was an essential component of the original plan, had to be abandoned owing to contrary winds; and, what was worse than its abandonment, the enemy was enabled to pass the troops assembled to meet it across the estuary to reinforce the garrison of Flushing. Hope was unable to proceed further without naval assistance; naval assistance was not forthcoming until Veere, Rammekens and Flushing were reduced; and thus events waited upon the outcome of the siege of Flushing.

The siege was begun with some deliberation—excessive deliberation in Chatham's opinion, who relieved the chief Engineer, Colonel D'Arcy, replacing him by Colonel Fyers—and the garrison showed astonishing enterprise considering the quality of the troops available. During the preparation of the works the 68th lost further casualties in small actions on the 3rd and 5th August, and their discomfort in camp was increased on the 11th when the enemy cut the dyke and inundated the ground in front of the town, which was "a clear flat of low meadows". More troops than were at first considered necessary were diverted to the siege, and only two divisions, Hope's and

Huntly's, could be spared for other objects. However, the batteries were ready on 12th August and opened at half-past one on the 13th. The ships of the fleet stood in to force the passage of the Scheldt and joined in the bombardment on the 14th at a range of 1400 to 1800 yards. The place was soon in flames and within a hour the enemy ceased to return the fire. At 4 o'clock the garrison commander was summoned but he refused. At midnight he asked for 48 hours in which to prepare a capitulation. That was refused. At half-past two in the morning of the 15th he sent a second flag declaring his readiness to surrender, and the garrison of rather over 4300 men marched out with the honours of war on the 17th, the day after British troops occupied the gates of the town.

The reduction of Flushing cost the Army about 750 killed, wounded and missing, of whom the 68th lost in the affairs of the 1st, 3rd and 5th August eight officers wounded (Major R. Thompson, Captains Crespigny and Soden, Lieutenants Menzies, Macdonald, Hinds, and Smyth, and Ensign Thomson), 15 n.c.o.s and men killed, and 43 wounded. Major Thompson, a Scotsman whose services went back to Grenada days, who lost his right arm from a bomb thrown from the fortress during the erection of the batteries, was a serious loss to the Regiment. He did not retire for some years, but his disability deprived the Regiment of his services in the Peninsula. Green was his servant for a time. He bears witness to his humanity and kindness in teaching him to read and write, and parted from him, in tears, only when the Regiment sailed for Portugal.

The Scheldt was now clear. Lord Chatham moved the Army into South Beveland with a view to "try what can be done towards Antwerp". There was no plan. There was a suggestion of advancing a light corps towards the Tête-de-Flandre to destroy the shipping in the Antwerp yards by howitzer shells while the main body made a demonstration on the right bank opposite. But the enemy, who in spite of warnings had at first been surprised at the magnitude of the Armament, had been given time to recover, and profited by it. Everyone in Chatham's Army was convinced before Flushing fell that no attempt could be made on Antwerp; but Chatham himself, very properly determining to be the last to relinquish all hope, deferred deciding whether or not to persevere until his whole disposable force was assembled. That was not accomplished until 24th August. By that time the enemy was reckoned to have 35,000 men as well as a substantial garrison in Bergen-op-Zoom. Unless the Army was maintained by land transport the co-operation of the navy was essential, and to have that it was necessary to reduce Lillo and Liefkenshoek and invest Antwerp on both banks. Bergen-op-Zoom would need masking, requiring a detachment of 12,000 troops; a garrison of 2000 was necessary in South Beveland; and that left only 14,000 for the sieges of Lillo, Liefkenshoek and Antwerp.

Someone less firm than Lord Chatham (who was kept badly informed of naval proceedings by Strachan) might have hazarded his Army on the risky undertaking. Instead he summoned a council of war, which unanimously voted against going on; and on 27th August the evacuation of all but the island of Walcheren, which was to be held as an "emporium" by seven brigades, was decided upon.

Walcheren is a curious shape, much resembling a saucer. Only the rim is above sea-level; the rest lies below, intersected by dykes of standing water which offer an admirable breeding-ground for the mosquito *anopheles* which carries malaria. The islanders were well acquainted with the fever, and French occupying forces had suffered from it in the past. It was already beginning to take its toll before the decision to abandon the Antwerp enterprise. "There is," wrote Brownrigg, the Q.M.G., from Middelburg on 8th September, "as much anxiety shown to get away from this island as if it had been a second St. Domingo." By then the sick list had risen to 6000, and those that returned home considered themselves lucky.

The 68th had been carried across on 21st August to South Beveland, where they were quartered in Wissenkerke near Goes. The whole of Rottenburg's Brigade having been selected to form part of the Walcheren garrison, it returned to Veere on 4th September, where it remained for the next three months. Already at Wissenkerke they had 117 sick, and clearly they were not in good shape. "Some extraordinary exertion," Brownrigg wrote to the Military Secretary on 12th September, "should be used to place officers at the head of the 68th and 85th regiments capable of putting them in order. I think they are among the worst corps I have ever seen, nor is Rottenburg . . . calculated to make them any better. He is indolent and does not know how to exercise command over British troops, or, in other words, has not the art of making commanding officers do their duty." Here speaks one perhaps unduly prejudiced against the foreign light infantry school, for the Military Secretary took no steps to replace Johnston. But there is no disguising the Regiment's unhappy situation. On 25th September 537 men were sick and the strength was reduced to 99 men "present fit", a figure which dropped to 76 on 25th October. Captain Summers, Lieutenant Nixon, and Ensigns Reid, Jenkins and Todd had died, and by December no fewer than 21 officers and 599 men had been sent home sick. 103 men died in the island itself, and that was not the full extent of the calamity, for the deaths continued after their return to Brabourne Lees and even for a time rose. The Regimental record gives the total figure of deaths due to Walcheren fever as 384. The monthly returns give a total of 218 over the period from 25th August 1809 to 25th October 1810, the first date at which no deaths are returned. This figure, when compared with the mortality of the Durham men, seems the more probable.[10]

It was proving a somewhat expensive way of keeping an emporium, and in response to the representations of General Don, who succeeded Chatham in command, it was decided to evacuate the garrison. By that time only 4500 were fit for duty and not a third of those capable of marching five miles. The 68th, consisting of 89 men, was brought home in the *Nile* in December, and was back in Brabourne Lees in January 1810.

So ended the Walcheren Expedition, the mightiest enterprise of its kind undertaken by any nation since the Armada, in failure, anticlimax, and recrimination. Like all the others the 68th was reduced to impotence. It was something well known in the army in those years, a "Walcheren regiment", one, that is, that will have half its men in hospital after any exertion. It was not fit for service for another eighteen months, and it did not walk off the Walcheren fever until the summer of 1812.

If only numbers are considered the Regiment recovered surprisingly quickly. Although the establishment was raised in January 1810 to 76 men per company, it was only 150 men short that month and 289 men were "present fit". This figure rose steadily as the months went by until in November it stood at 558, and the sick correspondingly dropped from 297 to 62. In May 1811 it had 37 officers, 74 n.c.o.s and 560 drummers and privates fit for service.

The inspection reports, however, reveal a more difficult convalescence. When it was inspected by its former commander, General Oliver Nicolls, at Hythe on 16th May 1810, he reported that it could do no more than receive him and march past in review order, "which they did well", and could carry out no field exercises "from the effects of the Walcheren fever". The debility of the sufferer from the malaria parasite, which attacks the red blood corpuscles, brings on anæmia and in this instance affected, as it can do, the intestinal tract, giving rise to symptoms resembling cholera or dysentery, is plainly discernible. The paroxysms experienced by one attacked by the commonest parasite normally die down after two weeks; they remain quiescent for six to fourteen months, they recur at intervals of a month or two, but can be revived by such physical shocks as exhaustion. The sufferer's vitality is progressively lowered, his spleen becomes en-

[10]B.M., Add. Mss., 49500; Digest; W.O.12/7633; 25/1976.

larged, and he "finally reaches a chronic run-down condition". The symptoms may be watched in the words of Green as he describes their progress. The whole 68th at this period may be regarded as a malaria patient. When it was inspected by Major-General John Murray at Hythe on 16th October 1810 Lieut.-Colonel Johnston told him the Regiment had been barely in a state to parade for several months.

In October 1810, however, Murray reckoned he was inspecting a regiment that "has become healthy". "Although," he said, "I cannot give this regiment the same unqualified approbation I have given to the 2/52nd, I have much pleasure in stating that it is very rapidly improving in discipline [i.e. drill]. I do not know in what state it was previous to the Walcheren Expedition, but certainly some months ago it appeared to have been much neglected in its field movements. ... But since, . . . the parades and drills have become regular and the improvement great. Lieut.-Colonel Johnston, who has commanded the Regiment during the greatest part of the period, appears a zealous officer; and Major Thompson [who commanded from October to 24th December] carries out the duty in a way that to me is highly satisfactory. It is indeed under the latter officer that I have remarked the most rapid steps to improvement." The soldiers, a third of whom had done less than two years' service, he found were "a good serviceable body of young men. Their behaviour, in common with the other regiments composing the garrison at Hythe, was some time ago rather disorderly, but in this point as in all others they are much improved."

In March 1810 the Regiment had been moved from Brabourne Lees to Hythe, and in the beginning of December 1810 to Littlehampton. In February 1811 they were moved to Lewes as a result of an undignified fracas between three officers and some townsmen who had insulted them, which ended with Lieutenant Robert Jackson and William Smyth as "prisoners with the civil power".

Their convalescence may be said to have been completed. Many of the other Walcheren regiments had been sent off again, and Green records that rumours of foreign service were circulating in November. On 31st May 1811 they received their final inspection from Major-General James Erskine, whose report was satisfactory. "Lieut.-Colonel Johnston," he said, "is clear in the field and appears to be perfectly acquainted with every duty of the Regiment." The drill in formation was "very satisfactory, the light infantry movements were performed with celerity and precision, and the men are perfectly acquainted with the sounds of the bugle. The officers are generally acquainted with the names of the men of their respective companies. The men are of a middle size, young, and of healthy good appearance but not particularly well set up. The recruits and volunteers are extremely good. . . . The Regiment made generally a very good appearance, was steady under arms, and with the exception of a very few trifling instances was very correct in their movements." It still had nine recruiting-parties out (Bath, Maghera, Dublin (2), Armagh, Leeds, Ipswich, Omagh and Musselburgh). Ireland was still a fairly bounteous source of recruits, and the 68th that sailed for the Peninsula was 42 *per cent.* Irish, 47 *per cent.* English and 11 *per cent.* Scottish. There were still serving 89 men of those who had joined in 1800. All but 250 had served in Walcheren, that is to say a full two-thirds of the Regiment were mature soldiers.[11]

Leaving the colours with the depot at Lewes—an arrangement not unusual in light infantry—it embarked[12] at Portsmouth on board the *Melpomene* on 7th June 1811, and although the ship did not sail until the 18th it arrived off Lisbon after an astonishingly short passage of ten days. It was disembarked on 28th June. While awaiting orders from Headquarters it was accommodated for a week or so in the Convent of St. Domingos near the Rossio. The Army being at that time in the Alentejo, the 68th joined by a normal route towards Elvas, which consisted of a short passage by boats up the Tagus as far as Valada followed by a nine-day march by way of Santarém, Golegão and Abrantes across the gently rolling heath and downland of southern Portugal to Portalegre, where the commander of the 5th Division had instructions to forward it to the 7th Division at Arronches. It reached Arronches on 17th July. By General Orders of 19th July it was placed in Brigadier-General Sontag's Brigade, which was composed of the 51st (which had been converted to light infantry in May 1809), the Chasseurs Britanniques, who were to be its constant companions for the rest of the war, and their old acquaintances the 85th, who, however, were sent home soon after.

The 7th Division, at that time commanded by Major-General Houstoun, had not yet established a reputation or acquired a personality. The other divisions had, and were being given the nicknames they bore for the next three years—old hands who said, "they

---

[11]Asa C. Chandler, *op. cit.*, pp. 180ff.; W.O.27/98; 27/100; 27/102 (Part II).

[12]The officers embarking for the Peninsula were: Lieut.-Col. William Johnston, commanding: Bvt.-Lieut.-Col. Adolphus Hinuber; Captains James Winniett, William Gough, J. P. Hawkins, John Reed, G. C. Crespigny, Nathaniel Gledstanes, William North; Bvt.-Major James Miller; Captain Henry Anderson; Lieuts. William Mackay, J. U. M. Leith, Robert Melville, George Macdonald, George Archbold, H. B. Mends (attached to the Commissariat), Honeyman Mackay, James Sloane, Patrick Grant, William Bolton, James Thomson; Ensigns F. Finucane, R. Clarke, William Loftus, James Carson, David Dawes, William Gibson, J. H. Parvin, James Mitchell, William Mendham, Henry Forbes; Paymaster John Wood; Adjutant John Hinds; Quartermaster John Wilson; Surgeon John Cole; Asst.-Surgeons George Rudsdell and W. K. Greenwell.—W.O.17/189 (4).

tell us there is a seventh division but we have never seen them". The 7th was formed bit by bit from reinforcements sent out in the spring, who joined in the pursuit of Masséna from the Lines of Tôrres-Vedras as they arrived. At first the 51st and 85th, both Walcheren regiments, were the only native British in it: the remainder were Portuguese, *émigré* regiments like the "C.B.s", the Chasseurs Britanniques (once good but now recruited too much from deserters, who were inclined to desert again), two excellent light Hanoverian battalions from the King's German Legion, and the Brunswick-Oels Light Infantry, nicknamed the "Broomsticks". The Division was aptly called "the Mongrels". The command changed too quickly for it to derive any character from its general officers. It had done well and suffered severely in the recently abandoned siege of Badajoz; but it was not really until the latter half of 1812 that it established itself as a fighting formation, and not until the battles of the Pyrenees in July 1813 that it gained a reputation. The conduct of the 68th contributed materially to the result.

§

Though not apparent at the time, in July 1811 the crisis in the Peninsular War had come and, by 17th July it had already passed. Two French armies had assembled to enter Portugal for a fourth time; Wellington had concentrated his forces to meet them; and in the great unfought battle of the Caia he had silently willed them to withdraw. Before that moment, Wellington, outnumbered, had adapted his movements to his opponents': after it the initiative passed insensibly to him.

To explain Wellington's break-out into Spain it must be said that the eastern frontier of Portugal, though on casual inspection incapable of defence, has in fact but three military entries, and two only of importance. That in the north lies to the south of the great gorge of the muddy yellow Douro, which, with its limpid Spanish tributary, the Agueda, effectually protects the frontier southward to the level of Almeida. This entry is guarded on the Portuguese side by the fortress of Almeida and on the Spanish by the fortified town of Ciudad Rodrigo. To the south rises a chain of mountains which, running roughly east and west and crossing the frontier under various names—the Serra da Estrêla, the Serra de Malcata, the Jalama, the Sierra de Gata and the Sierra de Francia—form an effective barrier almost as far south as the barren rocky gorge in which the Tagus flows. The principal entry in the south, and the one by which almost every Spanish army has entered Portugal, lies at the point where the sluggish Guadiana turns south to form the frontier between the two

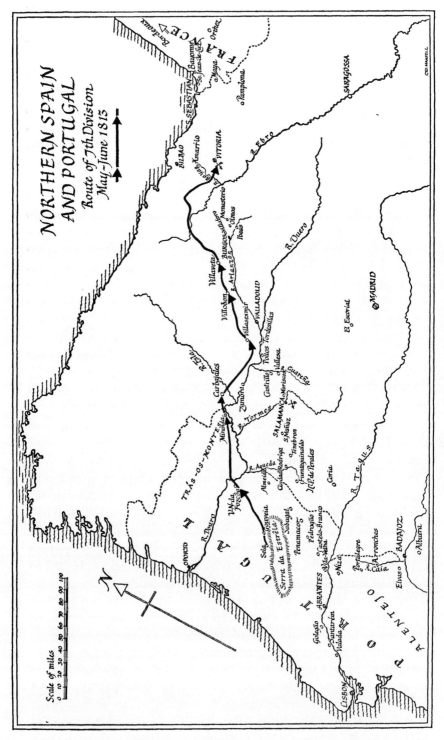

7. General Map of Portugal and Northern Spain

countries. On the Spanish side it is backed by a fertile plain which provided an admirable victualling ground and concentration area: the Portuguese landscape opposite is an endless succession of gentle undulations presenting none of the natural obstacles that hinder an army entering by Almeida. This entry is guarded by the Portuguese fortified town of Elvas and the Spanish fortified city of Badajoz. The third entry lies to the north of the Tagus gorge. The country on both Spanish and Portuguese sides is wild and inhospitable, however, and no fortresses of any magnitude guard the passage. It had not been used for many years until Junot càme that way in 1807, and except that it is practicable it would not be worth mentioning.

Any army protecting Portugal or entering Spain from this direction could only use the Almeida and Elvas "doors". But it could also use both at once. It had been Wellington's worst fear in 1810 that Masséna would do so and, but for the period in the winter of 1810-1811 when he had his whole Army near Lisbon, he always kept a proportion of it at both. They are widely separated by difficult country; but the "lateral communications"—on the Portuguese side the road by Vila-Velha, Castelo-Branco, Penamacor and Sabugal, on the Spanish side the road through Coria and the Pass of Perales— were deeply marked by the boots of French and British soldiers as the threat from one receded and the other was reinforced.

Such a stage had been reached in the summer of 1811. The French armies of Soult and Marmont had dispersed without fighting. On 18th July Wellington, "most anxious not to allow this moment of the enemy's comparative weakness to pass by," considered the courses open to him. He would not for the time being attempt forcing an entry by Badajoz; he would not attempt to relieve Cadiz. That left the entry by Ciudad Rodrigo, which, he said, "upon the whole promises best". The Army therefore, with the exception of a corps of observation under Hill, which remained in the Alentejo, was put in motion for the north, and all Wellington's endeavours until January 1812 were concentrated upon the preparations for the reduction of Ciudad Rodrigo.

The 68th had barely arrived before it was on the march again. On 23rd July it was at Niza, and marching with the rest of the 7th Division by the bridge of boats at Vila-Velha (31st July), through Sarnadas (1st August), Castelo-Branco (2nd), Escalos-de-Cima (3rd), S. Miguel-d'Ache (4th), Pedrógão, Penamacor, Sabugal (8th) and Alfaiates, it arrived at Vilar-Maior on 9th August. It was a "neat village," Green says, "delightfully pleasant," lying somewhat to the south of the great swath of devastation left by Masséna's Army in its retreat in the spring, in a country that is wild and hilly but handsome. Cantoned in the same village were the 51st and the head-quarters of the Division, for some days now commanded by the senior brigadier, Sontag, a punctilious German officer, something of a martinet, who had entered the British service thirty years before. His career had been principally on the staff and on secret missions on the continent. Nobody, however, looked less like a spy. He had a prominent purple nose which hung on his cheeks "like two red mogul plums". He usually wore a strange civil combination of a cocked hat and jacket, tight blue pantaloons and brown top hunting boots.

In this village they lay comfortably for nearly six weeks while the forward divisions of the Army kept a close observation on Ciudad Rodrigo almost amounting to investment—so close in fact that when Marmont, in late September, introduced a convoy of provisions into the place the movement of his whole force was involved. Against the possibility of such a movement Wellington had prepared a forward position at Fuenteguinaldo, and a rear position, stronger and more compact than that of Buçaco, in the high ground between Rendo and Souto. At the outset of the operations he brought the Army out of its cantonments. The 7th Division was moved down to a central reserve position at Alamedilla early on 23rd September, the 68th being quartered in Aldeia-da-Ribeira. It moved on the 26th back to Albergueria, on the left of the Fuenteguinaldo position, to conform with the rearward movement of the forward divisions, and early on the 27th it continued the retirement to the heights between Alfaiates and Nave. On the 28th the whole Army was brought back to the strong position prepared for it. The 7th, marching by Nave, was placed at Ozendo in the second line to the 3rd at Cardeal. There was some fighting on the 4th Division front at Aldeia-da-Ponte on 28th September, but nothing in which the 7th, always in reserve, was involved. In the night of the 28th/29th Marmont, finding the position impregnable, drew back northwards and the British Army resumed its watch on Ciudad Rodrigo in a manner that allowed it to settle in its winter cantonments. For this purpose the 7th was brought farther back, and moving by Sabugal to Urgeira on 29th September reached Penamacor, its destination, on the 30th.

The 68th, however, moved one march farther south to Pedrógão (without orders, it appears) some time during November. It could expect to remain there until the beginning of the campaigning season in March or April. Its exertions had reduced its strength appreciably, as was to be expected in a Walcheren regiment and one new to the country. On the first march it made with the Army its stragglers were so many and its pace so slow that it received a stern but not unkindly rebuke in General Orders. The march even from Lisbon into the Alentejo raised the sick-list to 85, and on 25th October it had 367 sick and only 323 rank-and-file "present fit". (No wonder Wellington speaks of his men at this period as an "army of invalids".) The sick dropped to 264 in December, but until February 1812 25 men died every month. In March 1812 the strength (rank-and-file) dropped to below 300, and although the deaths by sickness dropped to an average of 6 or 8 a month and although 106 reinforcements reached the Regiment during the course of the year, there were only two months in 1812 when the strength rose above 270 "present fit". Paymaster Wood, an old soldier who had come in from the 25th as Quartermaster in the bleak days of 1797, died in Lisbon on 31st March, and Captain Mossom Soden, one of the officers brought in on the augmentation of 1800, died at Elvas on 24th April.

Nine officers came out from England in the course of the year: Lieutenants Smyth, Leith and Sorlie, Ensigns Skene, Ball, Stretton, Kortwright and Fowke, and Major Crespigny. Crespigny, whose name is often spelt "Cripney", arrived in December 1812 having left the Regiment for the 89th and then purchased a majority in the 68th. Serving with the Regiment at this time was an old acquaintance, Brevet-Lieut.-Colonel Hinuber, who had so distinguished himself in Grenada. He had held several appointments in the Adjutant-General's Department—in the Mediterranean under Stuart, in the Windward and Leeward Islands, at the Horse Guards, and with Wellesley's Army in the campaigns of 1809—and had rejoined the Regiment in August 1811. He returned home, however, in September 1812 and sold his majority to Crespigny, a transaction which, if Green reflects regimental opinion, was not to the Regiment's advantage.

The campaign of 1812 opened unexpectedly early in the first week of January while the snow still lay on the ground. Wellington, concentrating the Army suddenly when Marmont's forces were dispersed, make a quick advance on Ciudad Rodrigo, invested it, besieged it and stormed it in a remarkably rapid operation that was over in a fortnight and gave him the northern entry into Spain. His attention then turned south. Secretly marching his Army inside the Portuguese frontier division by division, he invested Badajoz. The siege was tedious and expensive, and the place was barely stormed before the French came to its assistance. But the thing was just accomplished, and Wellington had secured the southern entry into Spain by the first week in April. His intention then was to march upon Seville and "relieve the Andalusias from the enemy". But an attempt of Marmont's to blockade Ciudad Rodrigo brought him north again, and placed him in a position to strike a blow at the French communications running through Castile, a blow which would of itself bring about the evacuation of Andalusia. His object was secured by the battle of Salamanca on 22nd July.

The first moves of the 1812 campaign involved the 7th Division in nothing more serious than hard marching. During the siege of Ciudad Rodrigo it lay in a covering position near Fuenteguinaldo. During the siege of Badajoz it formed part of a covering force of three divisions under Graham, which twice unsuccessfully attempted to flush some outlying French brigades in Estremadura. On 25th April it was back in the Beira hills, the 68th at Sto. Estevão.

It was inspected on 12th May in its cantonments at Castelo-Branco by Brigadier-General von Bernewitz, a little Brunswicker of fifty, who had taken over the brigade at Christmas. His remarks are illuminating. There was, he reports, "no striking unanimity between the commanding officer and the officers," and "the junior officers do not possess that activity and intelligence which is required of a light infantry officer". The privates, he says, were "not so clean or healthy as could be wished"; they were "not well set up " and they had committed several serious excesses—five men were court-martialled at this period, but it was the first and last occasion on which anything so serious occurred. Over half the Regiment were men of more than four years' service: only 48 had seen less than a year's. Of the 34 officers, 34 sergeants, 29 corporals, 18 buglers and 527 privates in the country over 300 privates were sick and only about 220 "present fit". It is not a very flattering picture. As to the Regiment's health it is clear that the long sick-list was partly the price paid by Wellington for disregarding (advisedly and for good reason) the convention of the day in fighting his Army in winter. By 25th May the sick had dropped to 223 and the strength had risen to 320. Though Bernewitz cannot have known, the Regiment had emerged from its last serious bout of Walcheren fever.

The Army started to move out of its cantonments in the last days of May, and after concentrating behind Ciudad Rodrigo it crossed the Agueda in three large columns on 13th June, advancing by easy marches along the parallel roads that lead to Salamanca. The 7th Division, which had been commanded since early May by Lieut.-General John Hope, an elderly, gouty officer who had started his career in the Scots Dutch regiment of Houstoun, was again placed under Graham with the 1st and 6th Divisions, and marched on the right of the Army by Tenebrón and Villalba de los Llanos.

Salamanca is a handsome city built, like Rodrigo, of the golden-coloured stone of the country but one of a ruddier tinge. It has two cathedrals standing side by side, many convents, and a university whose colleges closely resemble in appearance those of Oxford and Cambridge. It stands proudly on a slight eminence on the north bank of the Tormes and the fine tower of the new cathedral dominates the landscape for many miles in most directions. The country is open and almost treeless except near the banks of the rivers, whose courses may be traced by the dark line of the willows bordering them. It undulates gently like Salisbury Plain, but unlike the Plain the land is arable and in June is under wheat ripe for the harvest. Altogether in summer Salamanca and the country round are scorched and baked into a terracotta-like appearance under a pitiless sun.

Marmont had withdrawn on Wellington's approach, but he had left a small garrison in some forts improvised in the colleges in the south-west corner of the city to guard the Tormes bridge. The investment of these was entrusted to two brigades of the 6th Division while the main body of the Army, 40,000 strong, was carried forward a few miles to a low but clearly defined ridge to the north-east known as the heights of S. Cristóbal. This was the ground onto which Wellington had chosen to draw his opponent. For two days all was quiet. But in the afternoon of the 20th June Marmont came forward with all the divisions he had managed to assemble, about 20,000 men. They looked as if they meant business, and Wellington, much satisfied, assumed his battle formation. It ran from S. Cristóbal de la Cuesta on the left to Cabrerizos on the north bank of the Tormes, and was occupied by five strong divisions: Pack's and Bradford's Portuguese Brigades on the left, then the 3rd Division (Pakenham), the Light (Charles Alten), the 4th (Colville), the 7th (Hope), and on the extreme right the 1st (Graham). The reserve consisted of the 5th (Leith), Hulse's Brigade of the 6th and D. Carlos de España's Spanish Division.

Just before dusk the French, moving with great deliberation, entered the village of Castellanos de Moriscos in front of the British right centre, and pushed on to Moriscos, which lay at the foot of Wellington's position. The 68th, with some Brunswickers in support, had shortly before been moved down to occupy Moriscos as an advanced post, and the French movement gave these untried troops an opportunity of showing their mettle.

Green says he had got permission to fall out a few minutes before, and that before he had time to rejoin Moriscos was under attack.

> "Colonel Johnston ordered one company to the principal entrance of the village and small detachments to each of the lanes. Being thus placed, a most desperate firing commenced, the enemy advancing up the main street in great force. The Colonel ordered two companies

to charge, but finding they were not sufficiently strong he commanded the whole forward. At this time my right-hand front-rank man, a corporal of Captain Gough's company, was killed on the spot, not giving a single struggle. We charged the enemy to the end of the street and were so near to them that the Colonel pulled one of the French soldiers into our column. It now became so dark that we could scarcely see each other.

"The companies that were stationed at the end of the streets were sharply engaged, and my comrades now began to fall in all directions. At length an aide-de-camp arrived from General Graham with orders for our retreat to the top of the hill. But before we retreated the Colonel made an excellent speech, professing his regard for every man under his command and at the same time declaring he could keep the town until morning, and if he had not received orders from his superior in command he would keep possession in spite of the enemy. He added, 'We will not retreat without taking every man that is wounded along with us.'

"We reached the end of the village in close column and then called in our detachments, and sent from the column a number of skir-mishers about ten paces in front, who kept up a constant fire on the enemy, who was not more than thirty or forty yards from us. In this position we retreated to the top of the hill. When any man fell the column halted to ascertain the event, and if only wounded we carried him along with us. We at last arrived at the top of the hill in good order and there made a stand. The enemy returned into the town and made a number of fires and only left a line of sentries to look out for us."

This spirited defence cost the Regiment two sergeants and four men killed, two officers and about 20 men wounded, and one officer and one man captured. Captain Hawkins was wounded, and Lieu-tenant W. Mackay received no less than twenty-two bayonet wounds but recovered and continued to serve. Lieutenant George Mac-donald and Private John Moore were taken. Macdonald, a native of Arisaig, Inverness, was released in September but remained on parole in Lisbon until joining the Commissariat Department as a deputy-assistant from August 1813 until the end of the war, and rejoined only then; Moore died in captivity.[13]

The Army slept that night in full expectation of an attack on the morrow. In that, however, Wellington was disappointed. He was then for attacking himself. But those around him counselled caution, and he demurred. On the 22nd he did no more than test Marmont's intentions with a partial offensive movement on the 7th Division front. The Hanoverian Brigade, covered by their skirmishers, moved down early that day to Moriscos, and soon after Bernewitz's Brigade was advanced to attack a knoll immediately above the village.

[13]Green, pp. 89-90; W.O.17/189; 25/1977.

"They carried it in an instant," an observer noted. The 68th had been a mile in rear, and the wood and watering parties were out when the alarm sounded. It formed immediately and ran up the hill under a sharp fire of musketry. When they got to the summit, from which the enemy had withdrawn, the 68th and the Chasseurs Britanniques formed square; and while the 51st, twenty yards away to the right, drew up in line firing kneeling, they together repelled the counter-attacks that ensued. The 68th remained just below the brow of the hill till afternoon, when they retired to cook their dinner. "Our troops," says Wellington, "conducted themselves remarkably well in this affair, which took place in the sight of every man of both armies."

The Regiment, being sheltered by the brow of the knoll, suffered but lightly. One man only was killed and about eight wounded. The two brigades as a whole suffered proportionately more. But they had shown what the Mongrels could do when put to it.[14]

Marmont withdrew next morning to Aldearrubia and attemped nothing further on that front. In fact these were but the opening moves of a long fencing-match between two wary and highly skilled opponents that lasted for over a month and ranged over the whole plain between the Tormes and the Douro. On the 27th the last of the Salamanca forts fell to the 6th Division. Marmont gave up any attempt to relieve the place and retreated behind the Douro. Wellington followed and, placing his left at Pollos and his right opposite Tordesillas with a reserve of two divisions (the 1st and 7th) at the important road-junction of Medina del Campo, waited.

There followed that exciting sequence of events that has found its way into almost every military text-book. Marmont, reinforced, took the offensive. Feinting towards Toro and deceiving Wellington into drawing off his reserves and his right to the west of the Guareña and the Trabancos, he counter-marched during the night of 16th/17th July and crossed in force at Tordesillas. By dusk on the 17th the French Army was concentrated at Nava del Rey. When Wellington found he had been humbugged he turned his main body to face eastwards along the Guareña between Castrillo and Vallesa, the 1st and 7th Divisions forming the right flank. On the 19th and succeeding days Marmont edged southwards feeling for Wellington's right flank. The Armies marched parallel with each other, sometimes no more than a mile apart, as often in sight of one another as the ground permitted. No one who saw it has failed to describe the magnificent spectacle. "It was an extraordinary and grand sight," says Green,

[14]Lieut.-Col. W. Tomkinson, *Diary of a Cavalry officer . . . 1809-1815* (London, 1895), p. 168; Wellington, *Disp.* (1852 edn.), Vol. 5, p. 721; Green, p. 91.

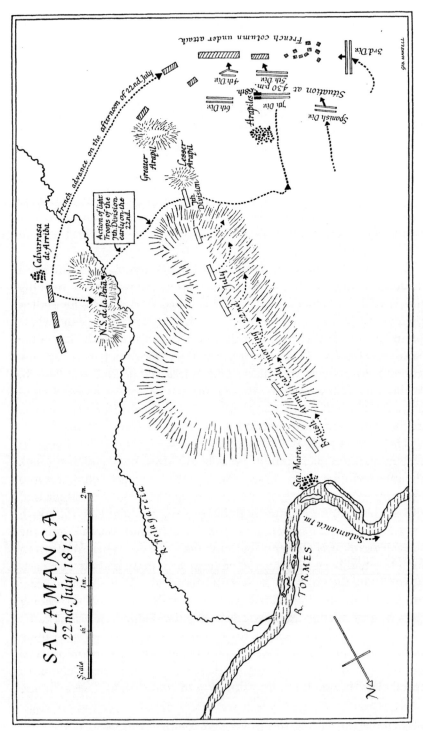

8. Salamanca, 22nd July, 1812

"to see two armies drawn up ready for battle and manœuvring during a whole day without fighting." Nor does anyone omit to describe the fatigue of the marches under the hot sun across the treeless Castilian plain, and the anxiety.

On the 21st Wellington's Army was covering Salamanca in the S. Cristóbal position, while Marmont, who appeared to be winning the race, was preparing to cross to the south of the Tormes. This he proceeded to do in the afternoon by the fords of Huerta. Wellington conformed. Passing all but one division across the river by the fords of Santa Marta, he brought his Army into line on the raised plateau facing south-east over the Pelagarcia stream. The 7th Division was on the extreme right flank in one of the few woods in that country-side, almost opposite the hill on which stands the chapel of Nuestra Señora de la Peña.

July 22nd started like any of the preceding days. It had become almost a habit for Marmont to feel for Wellington's right. All he could see was the troops of the 7th Division: the rest were invisible behind the crest, except for some of the baggage-train, which was filing off towards the Tenebrón road to Rodrigo. The British Army would presumably follow. He was tempted meanwhile to provoke a skirmish with the only troops visible, and he threw out the tirailleurs of Foy's Division across to the 7th Division's heights. Wellington, not wishing his position to be so closely examined, sent out a powerful screen of two whole light battalions, the 68th from Bernewitz's Brigade and the 2nd Caçadores from the Portuguese Brigade of the Division, to push them back. A man in the 51st saw the 68th go in. He lost sight of them in the trees but heard them engaged, "and from the great number of wounded brought to the rear in waggons it was clear they had dropped in for a hot breakfast". Between them the two battalions pressed the French back to the top of the hill and, reinforced by a squadron of light dragoons sent up by General Hope, maintained the ground they had won despite the fire from a battery brought up to play on them. Brevet-Major Miller was wounded in this skirmish, which cost the 68th a few men wounded besides. They remained there without taking off their accoutrements till the early afternoon, when they were relieved by the 95th from the Light Division, which had taken the 7th's position in the line.

The whole action had meanwhile become general as Marmont, extending his left westwards to cut off Wellington's communication with Ciudad Rodrigo, pressed on the British right, which Wellington extended correspondingly. By the time the 68th was relieved the 7th Division was two miles to the west near the village of Arapiles in second line to the 5th, Bernewitz's Brigade on its left (or eastern) flank. Wellington had suffered the probing long enough. He had taken the 3rd Division from across the Tormes and had launched it at the head of Marmont's column, which crumbled before one of the fiercest onslaughts of the whole war. The 4th and 5th Divisions, supported by the 6th and 7th, then advanced against the columns opposite them.

Green's account suggests that the Regiment suffered more heavily on its march to join the Division than in the morning's engagement, and adds that Lieutenant Finucane, a promising young officer from the staff of the Military College at Marlow, was killed at this stage as well as Sergeant Dunn, whose wife marched with the Regiment. By 4 o'clock it was in position on the left of Bernewitz's Brigade, on the extreme left flank of the Division and next to the 6th, and at half-past four, Green says, Wellington came to the front of the 7th and pulled off his hat. The men gave three cheers and, without firing, advanced into the mass of three French divisions, which, though partially broken, nevertheless put up a desperate resistance. When the firing did start Green says it was "like the long roll of a hundred drums without an interval". But this was the last stand the French made as they were forced back into the woods, and darkness put an end to the destruction.

The 68th, which was about 300 strong in the morning, lost during the battle two officers and seven men killed or mortally wounded, and one officer (Captain North) and ten men wounded. Brevet-Major Miller died of his wounds at Ciudad Rodrigo on 13th August.[15]

The pursuit after the battle at first took the direction of the Douro, but the 7th was one of the divisions turned off in the direction of Madrid, which was reached almost unopposed on 12th August. It was the first division to enter, and the 68th and the 51st were the first regiments to march through the excited crowds. "The bells of the different churches rang," says Green, "the ladies waved their handkerchiefs from the windows, and every countenance beamed with joy welcoming their deliverers."

That evening Madrid was illuminated, but for the 68th there was work to do. When the French Army of the Centre retired on Aranjuez a small French garrison had been left in the fortified depot and magazine in the Retiro and the china factory within it. It consisted of some 2000 men, who, it was feared, might profit by the confusion to make a sally. 300 men from the 3rd Division were told off to break into the Park wall on the north near the bullring, while 300 from the 51st, 68th and Chasseurs Britanniques attacked the south-west angle

[15]Green, pp. 98-102; *The Letters of Private Wheeler* [51st], ed. Capt. B. H. Liddell Hart (London, Michael Joseph, 1951), p. 87 (*cit.* hereafter as "Wheeler").

of the works, which was formed by the wall of the Botanical Garden. This party moved after dark, got clear of the houses, and quickly entered the outer line near the Prado after the 68th's main party had found and broken open a postern. They waited under the protection of the inner works until dawn. The noise made in breaching the wall provoked a heavy musket-fire from the garrison, which, however, did little harm; and in the morning, while they were still making ready to assault the inner works and the improvised fort of the china factory, the garrison ceased fire and surrendered. Wheeler of the 51st says "the 68th was fortunate enough to fall in with the clothing, and well stocked themselves with new shirts, stockings and shoes," and then enjoyed themselves eating fruit from the trees and catching—and eating—the goldfish in the Retiro gardens.[16]

The Regiment remained quartered in a convent in Madrid for a fortnight. Colonel Johnston having been appointed Commandant of the city the command fell for the time being to Captain Winniett, who although he had obtained his ensigncy in the Regiment as far back as 1795 had shown a greater aptitude for the staff than for regimental duty. He had been Brereton's Military Secretary in St. Lucia, Rottenburg's Brigade-Major in Walcheren, and he was Brigade-Major to the other British brigade of the 7th Division in February 1813. Green did not care for him. "I have often trembled," he says, "when I have had to be inspected by him, although I always passed his severe scrutiny," and compares him unfavourably with Johnston.[17]

Late in August Wellington moved north to the Douro to complete the destruction of the army defeated at Salamanca. The 7th Division, which had already been moved out to the Escorial, started on 1st September. The Army reached Valladolid on the 7th and continued without meeting any serious opposition until a few miles short of Burgos on the 16th, when the French retired through the town leaving a strong garrison in the castle. While the 1st Division undertook its investment, the remainder marched up the Vitoria road to take up a covering position across it near Rubena with picquets at Monasterio de Rodilla. The 68th was bivouacked with the rest of the brigade near Olmos (Green says "Villatormes", that is Villatoro, which seems too far away) "under a few scattered oaktrees" on the south of the high-road. The rains started soon after their arrival, and the "wigwams" they constructed gave but scant protection. The strength was down to 245 rank and file "present fit," and eight officers were in hospital through wounds or sickness.

[16]Green, pp. 107-108; Wheeler, p. 94.
[17]Green, p. 111.

. The investment of Burgos Castle, which was to have been no more than an incident, proved a tedious operation; and when on 13th October the French showed signs of coming forward Wellington was still a long way from success. A powerful enemy force drove in the picquets at Monasterio that morning, and Bernewitz's Brigade was moved up in support. It mounted strong guards every day and the rest were employed in constructing a work across the valley. In the evening of the 18th an advanced guard descended on the picquet-line at Sta. Olalla, held by some Brunswickers, who were taken. The position at Monasterio being now untenable, Wellington withdrew the covering force to a line running from Ibeas de Juarros on the Arlanzon, through Rubena, to Sotopalacios on the left. The 7th Division were on the right, the 68th near Olmos, where the brigade sustained a sharp attack from a reconnoitring force, which, hotly disputed by the Chasseurs Britanniques, was brought to a conclusion by a movement of Wellington's with his left. Continued pressure, however, on this front, combined with his failure at Burgos and news of a movement against his force at Madrid, convinced Wellington the game was up. On 21st October he decided on retreat.

Green's memories of the skirmishes around Olmos are not unnaturally confused. Both he and Wheeler vividly describe the three battalions being herded together in a church for two nights, sleeping with their muskets between their legs, and the near-panic that ensued when one man awoke from a nightmare crying out the French were on them, which was calmed only when Hinds, adjutant of the 68th, the only officer present, passed round the word it was no more than a scare. Wheeler says the church was at Olmos; Green at Monasterio. In the brisk skirmishing near Olmos on the 20th the 68th were engaged without loss, but the Regiment had to leave ten sick men behind when they retreated.

The retreat from Burgos needs no description. As far as Salamanca it was a fighting retreat; the days were fine if the nights were "uncommonly cold". Thereafter it deteriorated into a disagreeable march in rain and mud. Four men of the 68th were captured in this distressing period, one on 7th November near Pitiegua, the others on the 17th or 18th, when the 7th Division was drawn up in the final engagement of the campaign to dispute the line of the Huebra at S. Muñoz. When the return was made out on 25th November at Alamedilla the strength was 235 rank and file "present fit" and 247 sick.

So ended the campaign of 1812. It had been a year of wonderful achievements. Maps had been brought out that had lain folded in portmanteaux for four years, and the Army had marched as conquerors into places unmentioned since the innocent days of 1808. But the campaign ended, alas, geographically at any rate, where it had started.

The Army was dispersed widely in its winter cantonments. The 7th was brought back into the centre of Portugal, in the northern foothills of the Estrêla overlooking the principal road from Lisbon to Almeida. In December the 68th was quartered in the twin villages of Paços-de-Baixo and Paços-de-Cima, whence in February 1813 they moved a few miles away to S. Martinho. The strength of the Regiment was so low—it was, it must be remembered, a single battalion regiment, without a second battalion to provide reinforcements—that for a time Wellington contemplated doing what he did with several other weak battalions, combining them in pairs to form "Provisional Battalions"; and at one moment there was a rumour that the 51st and 68th were to be transferred to the Light Division in the august company of the 43rd and 52nd.[18]

Neither of these changes took place; but the 7th Division, since October commanded by Lord Dalhousie, underwent a thorough reorganisation. The Hanoverian Light Battalions, forming the 1st Brigade, were transferred to the 1st Division, and a new first Brigade was formed consisting of the 1/6th, the 3rd Provisional Battalion (2/24th and 2/58th), and nine companies of the "Broomsticks." The 1/82nd, which had come up from Cadiz to Madrid, was introduced into the 2nd Brigade as a fourth battalion with the 51st, 68th and Chasseurs Britanniques. "Little" Bernewitz left during the winter, and although Inglis, of "Diehard" fame at Albuera, eventually took command, the Brigade was commanded until July 1813 by the senior battalion commander, Colonel Grant, 82nd, described by Colonel Roberts of the 51st as a "worthy veteran". The divisional Portuguese Brigade (Lecor's), consisting of the 2nd Caçadores and the 7th and 19th Line, remained unchanged. Reorganised in this manner the 7th Division of 1813 and 1814 bears a less "mongrel" appearance. The two British brigades were to prove themselves second to none, and the whole formation had a reputation to sustain and some hardened soldiers with which to improve it.

The 68th shared in the remarkable transformation that the Army underwent that winter. Good quarters, light duty, regular rations, new clothing and reinforcements from the depot wrought a radical change in their appearance. Colonel Johnston, who after returning to command in September had retired sick to Lisbon in December, took over the command from Major Hawkins in April. Captain

[18]*Disp.*, Vol. 6, pp. 200-201; Capt. Baring to Lieut.-Col. Mercer, 13th Dec 1812 (Scot. Reg. House, Edinburgh, Fordell Papers, Bundle 14).

Nathaniel Gledstanes, who had been serving in the Q.M.G.'s Department since December 1811, returned to regimental duty after falling under the Q.M.G.'s displeasure for an episode in the retreat in which he had entrusted to a servant a letter particularly confided to him. A nephew of General Albert Gledstanes, whose a.d.c. he had been, he was an amiable officer with 12 years' service in the Regiment. The strength of the 68th on 25th April 1813 was 439 rank and file "present fit", the highest since its arrival in the Peninsula, and the sick numbered only 97. It had been inspected at S. Martinho on 9th February by Bernewitz, who in his report officially recognised the improvement in its appearance by saying that it was "particularly well drilled in light manœuvres" and that the private soldiers were "much improved in health, cleanliness and conduct".

When exactly Wellington formed in his mind the grand project which took the Army in one bound from the centre of Portugal to the foot of the Pyrenees it is impossible to say. It was, however, worked out in detail between 21st and 24th April. Beside it the advance in the summer of 1812 looks like an amateurish improvisation. The main body of the infantry, instead of facing north-eastward and crossing the Douro in the face of opposition at the obvious places around Toro and Tordesillas, was faced north and crossed the Douro in the peace and quiet of Portugal. Hill's Corps, the habitual guardians of the Elvas entry, having been allowed by the previous year's operations to canton in the passes of Perales and Baños, could be moved alongside due north as the right flank without uncovering its communications. The whole would swing east only after it had reached the headwaters of the Ebro, and Burgos of unhappy memory was left well to the right. The whole conception was magnificent in its sweep and comprehensiveness, and was crowned with the success it deserved.

There were no bridges over the Douro below Zamora; but by concentrating ferry-boats at the important crossing-places of Régua, Vilarinho and Pocinho, Wellington was able to bring the five infantry divisions and four cavalry brigades quartered in Portugal into the Trás-os-Montes and array them on the north-eastern frontier by routes hitherto unused and at a "door" hitherto unsuspected. The second obstacle was the Esla. It had saved Moore's Army, but now it was likely to be guarded by the enemy's picquets. There were, however, fords, and if his luck held Wellington could fairly rely on low water.

The farthest formations started their march in the first week of May. The 6th and 7th Divisions, being quartered near each other near Gouveia and Seia, were directed upon the ferry at Pocinho, below Vila-Nova-da-Fozcôa, and started on the 15th and 14th respectively. The 7th crossed without mishap punctually on the 18th, reaching the "concentration area" between Malhadas and Miranda-do-Douro on the 23rd. On the 28th they moved forward to the Esla by Constantim, Fonfría and Carbajales, where they arrived on the 29th.

Unfortunately, on the 31st the river was in spate, and although the left and centre columns of this wing of the Army succeeded in crossing at the ford of Montamarta, the right, consisting of the Hussar Brigade, the 7th, 6th and 4th Divisions (in that order), which had been allotted the ford of Almendra, could not. The leading battalion of the 7th, the 51st, got over, but only just and at the cost of several men drowned. The 68th, the next, who were standing on the bank, waiting their turn with their pouches on top of their knapsacks and not relishing the prospect, were marched off with the remainder to the pontoon-bridge, which had just been laid for the wheeled traffic. The enemy picquets proved less of an obstacle than the Esla: they were caught off their guard and either taken or dispersed.

The march was then resumed. The 6th and 7th Divisions were brought across to the right of the whole Army and placed next to Hill's Corps as the "Right Centre Column". On the way they were inspected by Wellington near Morales de Toro. Then, marching by Villasexmir (4th June), Peñaflor (5th), Villalba del Alcor (6th), Villalobón (8th), Támara (9th), Itero de la Vega (10th), Villaveta (12th), Sasamón (13th), and Villanueva de la Puerta (14th), they left the torrid Castilian plain and penetrated into the cool foothills of the Cantabrian Mountains, gradually swinging east towards Vitoria on the high-road to France. Few soldiers have anything to say of the unfamiliar Portuguese marches; a few remark on the beauties of the mountainous landscape they were entering; all, however, remark on the changes in their habits caused by the tents they carried with them for the first time, and on the canvas towns that suddenly sprang up as if by magic on reaching the end of a march; and all, from about 10th June, speak of hunger. Wheeler of the 51st speaks rather apologetically of taking some loaves of bread off a shepherd. Green says that in the twelve days before the battle of Vitoria he believes he did not get more than three pounds of bread or biscuit, and remembers that when placed as a sentry over a commissariat magazine he was approached by an officer who actually stole a loaf under his eyes. "I reproved him for his conduct, but such was his reply that I let him go with what he had obtained." He says it was a common practice to catch the blood when the bullocks were slaughtered and boil it till it was "sad," when it served as a substitute for bread. Four months of exertion on the part of the Commissariat had kept the Army going for three weeks: after that the pace of the march was too much for it.[19]

From the crossing of the Ebro things began to reach a crisis. The French armies had been outflanked from every successive position they had taken up and, as a British general said, they were being "walked out of Spain". By the 19th Wellington's Army lay along the River Bayas, and the British commander was contemplating a new outflanking movement with his left which would cut the road to France in rear of the French armies concentrating round Vitoria. On that day, however, when it became plain that the French would stand and fight, the five Allied columns were given a south-easterly turn. Hill, on the extreme right at Poves, was directed on La Puebla de Arganzón and the heights above it; the Right Centre Column (4th and Light Divisions) at Subijana and Morillas were directed on Nanclares; the Left Centre Column (3rd and 7th Divisions) which had come up from Villalba de Losa by Berberana over mountainous roads through Sta. Eulália and Jocano to Apricano, were directed over the Sierra de Badaya through Hueto towards Mendoza; the Left Column (1st and 5th Divisions), making a wide circling movement through Marguía, was directed on Gamarra Mayor and Avechuco; and Giron's Galicians, in the left rear, moved by Arciniega and Amurrio to Orduña.

The French had been plainly visible from British headquarters occupying a position covering Vitoria, protected by the winding course of the Zadorra. Their left (opposite Hill) rested on the heights of La Puebla. Their centre lay on a high ridge behind a bend in the river called Jundiz, or Inglesmendi, which is traditionally the ground occupied by an advanced guard of English knights destroyed in a gallant fight in 1367. Their right acted as a *tête-de-pont* on the north bank of the river in Aranguiz, Avechuco and Gamarra Mayor.

Wellington's attack on this formidable position on 21st June was begun by Hill's men, who swarmed up the heights of La Puebla and pressed forward despite heavy counter-attacks. The next phase started when it was discovered that none of the eleven bridges had been destroyed, and a brigade of the Light Division, crossing unopposed at Trespuentes, moved forward against Jundiz. The advance of the Right Centre should have been followed by that of the Left Centre composed of the 7th and 3rd Divisions. But its command had been entrusted for reasons of seniority not to Picton, who was in fighting form that day, but to Lord Dalhousie, who, though an able soldier when he exerted himself, had left his heart in his Scottish estates and had in any case little experience of high command. His

[19]Green, pp. 154, 155.

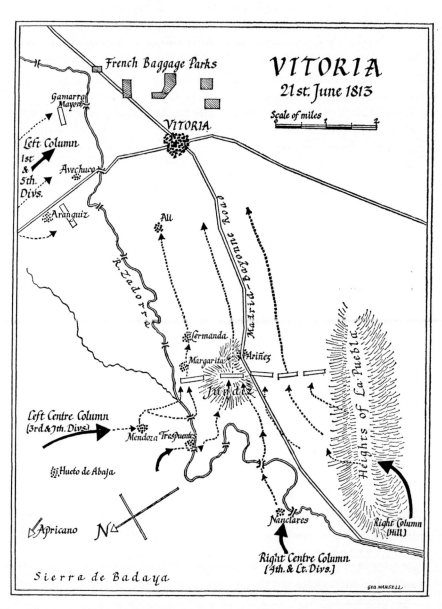

French Baggage Parks

VITORIA
21st. June 1813

Scale of miles

Gamarra Mayor

VITORIA

Left Column
1st
&
5th.
Divs.

Avechuco

Aranquiz

R. Zadorra

Ali

Madrid–Bayonne Road

Germanda

Margarita

Ariñez

Juaidiz

Heights of La Puebla

Left Centre Column
(3rd.&7th. Divs.)

Mendoza Trespuentes

Hueto de Abaja

N

Apricano

Nanclares

Right Column
(Hill)

Right Centre Column
(4th. & Lt. Divs.)

Sierra de Badaya

GEO. MANSELL

9. Vitoria, 21st June, 1813

movements through the Sierra de Badaya were so slow that Picton had been waiting near the bridge of Mendoza for some time before he came up, and even then he arrived with but one, Grant's, of his three brigades. By then Graham with the Left Column had descended on the French *tête-de-pont* at Aranguiz and Avechuco and was fighting a desperate battle for the river crossings in that sector.

Picton refused to wait. Seeing Kempt's Brigade of the Light Division lying unsupported under Jundiz, he launched his three brigades at the height across the Mendoza bridge and a ford, and Grant's Brigade followed. The French had drawn off some troops from this front to assist in the struggle for the Puebla heights; they were already under a frontal attack by this time from the direction of Víllodas and Nanclares by the Light and 4th Divisions; and the four brigades from Mendoza completed their discomfiture. They withdrew to a line farther east running south from Margarita and Lermanda, where a stubborn conflict ensued. For a time Grant's Brigade, led by the Colonel himself riding a white horse, his cocked hat in the old-fashioned style square to the front, supported Picton's left brigade nearest the river. But when this was withdrawn after suffering heavy casualties, Grant's was brought up into the first line to take its place, and suffered in its turn in the bitterly contested struggle for Margarita and Lermanda.

"I don't know," says Green, "that I ever saw the 68th Regiment march better in line than they did in the battle of Vitoria: every man was as steady as possible". For 300 yards they advanced under a very heavy artillery and musket fire, so heavy that Green thought "if it had lasted much longer there would not have been a man left to relate the circumstance". They were at length compelled to take shelter in a deep ditch about 200 yards from the French guns around Lermanda, while one company, Reed's, was sent forward to skirmish with them. For a time there was deadlock, and Dalhousie hesitated. But Vandeleur's Brigade came up from the rear to resolve Dalhousie's doubts for him, and together the two brigades sprang over the ditch, gave three cheers and charged, each vying with the other for the honour of its division. The German defenders of Lermanda could not resist the impetus of the charge and reeled back in disorder leaving 250 prisoners.

The whole then advanced in one splendid line on Vitoria— Grant's Brigade, the 3rd and 2nd Divisions—which beat back the enemy through Ali and beyond the town itself. The 68th encamped that night two miles beyond, among the tumbrils of the great convoy of plunder King Joseph's Army carried with it from Spain. It was spectacular evidence of the decisive victory the Regiment had shared in, and the men were not slow to take full advantage of it. According to Green, when the men were searched for plunder some days after the battle, an average of £32.10.8¾d. was found on them.

It had, however, suffered heavily. It had gone into action with 25 officers and 358 n.c.o.s. and men. Of these, two officers (Captain Anderson and Lieutenant Parvin) and 24 n.c.o.s and men were killed or mortally wounded; ten officers (Johnston himself, Captains Gough and Reed, Lieutenants Honeyman Mackay and Sorlie, and Ensigns Ball, Fowke, Stretton, Skene and Adjutant Hinds) and 90 n.c.o.s and men wounded. The Chasseurs Britanniques were the worst hit in the brigade, but the 68th lost more in proportion. Johnston did not return to the regiment until December, the command in the interval being exercised by Major Hawkins.[20]

When the French armies retired into France they left several garrisons in Spain, notably in S. Sebastian and Pamplona. Wellington, unwilling to invade France both for military and political reasons, took up a position in the Pyrenees with S. Sebastian behind his left and Pamplona behind his right. S. Sebastian was besieged, Pamplona invested, while the main body of the Army was brought up into the majestic mountains that divide the two countries. It was not a very satisfactory position from the British point of view. The force besieging S. Sebastian lay only two miles behind the troops covering it; and as for Pamplona, though it lay more than twenty miles behind the front, there were no positions in the interval in which the Army could stand and fight, and only very poor and very few lateral communications by which any threatened part of the line could be reinforced. Hence an otherwise insignificant penetration of the mountain screen was liable to carry serious consequences.

The situation was, however, dictated by the intractable facts of geography, a geography, moreover, that is embellished with outlandish Basque place-names which any student of the following operations may be pardoned for confusing. There were no passages over the Pyrenees for many miles east of those leading from Saint-Jean-Pied-de-Port to Pamplona. The Pass of Roncesvalles, or Roncevaux, was consequently the easternmost point which Wellington's Army had need to guard. Between that and the lower Bidassoa at Béhobie, where the Spanish high-road crossed, there was one important pass, that of Maya, and several smaller ones: Vera, Echalar and Les Aldudes. On the French side, where the country is not unlike parts of Montgomeryshire, roads are fairly numerous, and the French general could choose his points of concentration freely and at the same time mask his movements from his opponent. On

[20]Green, pp. 162-164, 170; W.O.25/1977; 12/7635.

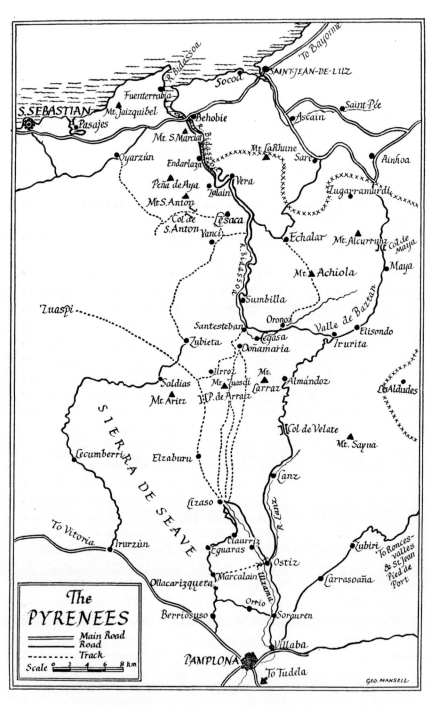

10. The Battles in the Pyrenees, July and August, 1813

the Spanish side, where vast green mountains separated by deep valleys spread south for thirty miles and more, there were but three fair north-and-south roads, and nothing but tracks running parallel to the front, the first east-west road being that from Vitoria to Pamplona. The necessities of the moment disclosed more, some even passable for artillery; but they struck dismay even in those accustomed to Portuguese roads, and they made movements slow and difficult. If, say, Wellington's flank at Roncesvalles was energetically thrust out of place, it could not be quickly succoured unless the whole Army was brought back near the Pamplona road, and even then operations would be embarrassed by the presence of the enemy garrison in the town. If the position was simultaneously assaulted either at Maya or Béhobie as well, the situation rapidly became critical.

For the time being these apprehensions were overlaid with optimism. The French armies had suffered such a beating at Vitoria that it was as victors and not as defenders that the Allied Army assumed its lofty Pyrenean positions, from which the fair French countryside could plainly be seen as far as Bayonne. The 7th Division, after sharing for a few days in the blockade of Pamplona, was taken, against slight resistance, into the hills to the left of the Col de Maya, whose defence was entrusted to Hill's Corps under the general supervision of Hill. On 4th July it reached Lizaso by Berriosuso, Marcalain and Eguaras; on the 5th it was at Santesteban; and on the 7th it was marched by a track up the great mountain, shown as Achiola on old maps, from Bertiz to a point where a track from Elizondo to Echalar crossed it. The 1st Brigade and the 1/82nd of the 2nd were moved to the right to a position near Monte Alcurrunz to support Hill's men stationed in the Pass. The Portuguese and the 2nd, which, since Grant was wounded at Vitoria, had come under the very able and energetic command of Inglis, were encamped on the forward slopes of the mountain nearer Echalar.

The defeated French armies had meanwhile been placed under Soult. He succeeded in the remarkably short space of a fortnight in reorganising them and re-establishing their morale. He then launched an offensive for the relief of Pamplona, which, though not unexpected, coincided with the failure of Wellington's first attempt to storm S. Sebastian. The offensive took the form of a powerful attack by one corps under d'Erlon on Hill's position at the Maya, and another of six divisions under Reille and Clausel on Cole's position at Roncesvalles. This double attack took place on the 25th July. The 7th Division's brigade at Alcurrunz was able to bring timely and effective assistance to the hard-pressed 2nd Division in the Pass of

Maya, and d'Erlon made only a slight advance beyond. But Cole, and with him Picton, who had been on Cole's left rear at Zubiri, retreated and did not stop till just short of Pamplona; and Hill and Dalhousie had perforce to conform with a rearward movement in case Soult cut in between. On the 27th, however, Picton and Cole stood to fight on a strong height in front of Pamplona near Villaba. Here, on the 28th, their divisions fought a hard but successful delaying action until the divisions on their left came up to reinforce them and give them the victory.

On the 26th the 7th Division (less the four battalions under Barnes, which marched with Hill) was brought off their mountain and moved down to Sumbilla. On the 27th it was ordered back to Lizaso through the Puerto de Arraiz by the track (running parallel with the main road in the Lanz valley) which they had used coming up. They marched all the afternoon and all through the night in the midst of a violent thunderstorm and torrents of rain. They reached Lizaso at midday on the 28th drenched to the skin and exhausted. But Welling-ton ordered them on to Ollacarizqueta, and after a six hours' halt they went on again by the Marcalain road towards Sorauren and the right flank of Soult's army, which by then had received its decisive check. They bivouacked late at night between Marcalain and Eguaras. The next morning they got to Orrio, two miles from Sorauren. But they arrived too late to take part in the battle, and they had hardly arrived before they were ordered back again.

Soult, who had failed to beat Wellington even when his concentra-tion was half complete, refused to admit defeat. Rather than retire at once before Wellington had gathered his reinforcements for a powerful counterstroke, he attempted a rash move to the west to join with d'Erlon (who had got no farther than Lanz) and make a penetration around Irurzún between Wellington's divisions and S. Sebastian. It involved a flank march across Wellington's front, and the risk he ran needs no emphasis.

Wellington's measures for dealing with the new movements were put into execution in the morning of 30th July. The part allotted to the 7th Division was to advance to the heights west of Ulzama and take in flank the French columns marching in the valley below. While Cole, Picton and the 6th Division fell on the French rearguard, Inglis's Brigade made for the steep heights above Ostiz. There, at about 8.30 a.m., they fell on the two battalions of Clausel's flank guard and drove them headlong into the valley. The skirmishing party, led by Hawkins, encountered serious opposition, and every officer but himself was either killed or wounded. There was close fighting with the bayonet at the bottom, "a small level covered with small bushes of underwood"; but the French gave way and retreated up the main road closely followed by Inglis's men. Green remembered this engagement, the first excitement in a series of arduous marches, by the fact that when the Regiment was collected and everyone began as usual to ask who was killed and who was wounded, "the first person mentioned was our second major [Major Crespigny]. He had received a ball in his neck, or rather in his windpipe, which killed him instantly. As soon as this was generally known amongst us joy was seen in every countenance, and I verily thought we should have had three cheers, for several of the men began to cry 'hip! hip!' which was always the signal for cheering. He was a cruel man to us and his death was considered as a happy release."[21]

At Ostiz a road leads off to join that by which the division had moved south, and where d'Erlon was pressing Hill at Lizaso; but Clausel preferred the main road over the Col de Velate. His men had been roughly handled in the fight at Ostiz and they had little thought but to put the Pyrenees between them and their pursuers.

On the 31st Dalhousie was directed towards the Puerto de Arraiz on Hill's right flank at Venta de Urroz. Soult attempted to pass Reille's and Clausel's Corps behind d'Erlon in the direction of Echalar. This took him across the front of Hill, who with his depleted battalions had been involved the day before in a desperate fight. But Hill brought his men upon the retreating French, and while they were engaged in a somewhat unequal struggle, Inglis's Brigade came up on their right to lend a hand by attacking a strong body of d'Erlon's Corps posted on a high hill. The regiments had to climb up a steep slope which was covered with trees, but the men, pulling themselves up by the branches, were not to be denied and closed in, the 68th on one side, the 51st on another, and the 82nd and the Chasseurs Britanniques on a third. The enemy's volleys cut down the branches above their heads, and a good many men had fallen before the 82nd fired their first volley. "We then," says Wheeler of the 51st, "slapped a volley into them that seemed to say 'Well done 82nd.' Before the noise was well subsided, bang goes the 68th, which spoke as plain as possible 'Well done the whole.' Now fifty buglers were sounding the charge, and the drums of the 82nd and C.B.s were beating time to the music. A general rush was made

[21]Green, p. 181. Lest the poor man's reputation should go down to posterity on one man's evidence, I should add I have seen a letter written within two months of Crespigny's death by a common acquaintance, who said a braver young man never existed and that every officer and man of the 68th he had spoken to lamented his loss.

by the whole brigade, accompanied by three tremendous British cheers." D'Erlon's men retreated precipitately down the hillside. The brigade followed—an action for which it received a lecture from the Brigadier on its return to the top; but, says Wheeler, "the General is a good old soul, and although he endeavoured to look mighty angry we could see he was not so much displeased as he pretended". The Donamaria Passes were cleared, and Hill advanced into the Baztan valley by Almándoz, leaving Dalhousie to pursue Soult's main body towards Echalar.[22]

Soult's position at Santesteban was now most uncomfortable. The 4th Division was at Elizondo to block his retreat by the Maya; the 7th Division was pressing him in rear; and his only route lay through Echalar. Wellington, however, had no clear picture of his difficulties, and his orders for 1st August envisaged nothing more than a continuation of the pursuit; the 4th Division along the north bank of the Bidassoa towards Santesteban, the 7th on the south, but without forcing the enemy from positions, merely "keeping up a perpetual skirmish". Part of the Light Division from Lecumberri managed to reach Yanci and there surprised some of the French rearguard; but Dalhousie, late in starting, was too far in the rear to exert effective pressure. It was a disappointing day, which, for the 7th Division, finished at Sumbilla.

The next morning Soult arrayed the remains of his army, 25,000 men, on the heights forming the frontier behind Echalar. Though Wellington had only three divisions up, he attacked. Dalhousie happened, more by good luck than judgment, to be opposite a weak point in the centre of the French position. Barnes's Brigade delivered such a devastating assault that Inglis's men, directed on Echalar, were deprived of a chance of getting properly to grips. Soult, his centre broken and his flanks threatened, drew back, part to Sare, part to Aïnhoa. There was no pursuit. Everyone was tired out.

On 2nd August the 7th Division was ordered to resume on the 3rd "the position it held before the late movement of the Army upon Pamplona"—a way, certainly, but a singularly tame and colourless one, of describing the immense exertions that earned all concerned the battle honour of the *Pyrenees*. The French lost 12,500 in killed, wounded and missing: the Allied Army about 6400. The 68th's losses in the actions of the 30th at Ostiz and the 31st at Urroz[23] were

[22]Wheeler, p. 122.

[23]In old regimental returns (W.O.25/798) this action is called Zara. It arises almost certainly from some mistaken identification. Few of these affairs were given any name at the time, being lumped together under the general name of "Pyre-

one officer (Major Crespigny) and fifteen n.c.o.s and men killed and mortally wounded; three officers (Captain Irwine, Lieutenant Leith and Ensign Connell[24]) and about 34 n.c.o.s and men wounded; and two men captured. They are not severe losses, but they are a fair proportion in a battalion that went into action with a strength of 229 rank and file. Nor do they give a fair indication of what these men performed. Anyone who has seen the country these actions were fought in cannot fail to exclaim in surprise that such hills and mountains, so imposing and magnificent as a backcloth, were not only climbed but fought for, day after day for a week, by men laden with heavy packs, muskets and ammunition pouches, in rain and sun, and heat and cold. If Gibbon had known he would not have spoken of "the delicacy of the modern soldier".

There was naturally less optimism in the month that followed, the Army narrowly watching every move the enemy made to see whether this or that sector was being reinforced. Soult did nothing until the eve of the great assault on S. Sebastian, and then he struck at the left of the line in one further effort to relieve the place before it fell. The principal attack across the Bidassoa was aimed at the heights of S. Marcial, opposite Béhobie, which were held by Spanish divisions. But it was accompanied by a subsidiary offensive, across the Bidassoa fords at Endarlaza, Zalain and Vera, designed to pass behind the Peña de Aya and take the S. Marcial position in rear. The bridge at Vera was guarded by the Light Division, the fords by the 4th, Zalain and Endarlaza by the Portuguese Brigade of that division. On 30th August, in response to obvious indications of an attack on the left, Dalhousie was ordered to make a diversion on the Echalar front, which he accordingly did by detaching his Portuguese Brigade (Lecor's) to demonstrate in front of Zugarramurdi; but later that day the whole division was ordered immediately to Lesaca to reinforce the Zalain position. Inglis's Brigade, the nearest, having taken no part in the Zugarramurdi demonstration, marched that evening (Barnes, who was in support of Lecor, could not follow till next day); and it arrived on the hills above Zalain as the haze was clearing in the morning of the 31st to disclose the 4th Division's Portuguese Brigade (Miller's) already under attack by two French divisions that had crossed near Endarlaza.

The Portuguese were retiring up the slope near the forge of S. Anton before the advancing mass. Inglis took command of Miller's

nees". This one, which took place somewhere between Urroz and the Donamaria Passes, is nowadays usually called Venta de Urroz.

[24]The *Gazette* says Ensign Connell, but the returns do not include Connell's name until after the action near Lesaca on 31st August.

Brigade, and made his dispositions. The 68th was drawn up in extended order across the front of the 82nd four hundred yards from the summit. They opened fire when the French were about two hundred yards off, and retreated firing until the summit was reached, when they fired another volley, cheered, and charged. The enemy were driven back for a time, but, reinforced, they came on again, and Inglis, finding they were getting round his left flank, withdrew his men to the height in rear near Lesaca. This was accomplished, with difficulty and some loss, under the cover of the 68th and the Brigade's assembled light companies. These kept up a constant fire until forming behind the 51st, 82nd and Chasseurs Britanniques, which had been drawn up in two lines on a spur near the foot of the hill. A severe struggle then took place. Every inch of ground was gallantly disputed. But Inglis's men, outnumbered, were gradually forced back.

At midday, however, after the fight had been going on about two hours, the French divisions were called off. They had reached half-way up the slope opposite the Col de S. Anton, over which the track to Oyarzún and S. Sebastian runs; but Soult's attack on S. Marcial had failed, and Clausel's supplementary offensive on the upper Bidassoa had ceased to serve a purpose. Clausel is said to have exclaimed "*Mais que veut donc le Maréchal ? L'opération est à moitié faite!*" A blinding rainstorm came down at that moment, the river rose, and, harried by Inglis's attenuated brigades, the two French divisions with much difficulty recrossed at dusk.

The action at Lesaca is one of which the Regiment may be justly proud. Sir George Murray, the Quartermaster-General, who was an eye-witness of the affair, "expressed his entire approbation," and the conduct of the 68th was praised in Wellington's dispatch. The Brigade as a whole suffered almost as heavily as at Vitoria. The 68th was fortunate to come off with the loss of 25 n.c.o.s and men killed and mortally wounded, and three officers (Lieutenant Skene and Ensigns Gibson and Connell) and about 45 n.c.o.s and men wounded. Amongst the wounded was John Green, who unfortunately speaks no more. When struck, he was left to take care of himself, so hot was the fire; but he called out to Captain Gledstanes who was near, saying "Sir, am I to be left in this condition, to be killed or taken by the enemy?" "No my man," he says Gledstanes replied, "I will assist you," and seizing him by his right arm and giving him a stick in his left hand, he led him out of the fire. "I can never think of Captain Gledstanes but with pleasure," he adds.[25]

The fall of S. Sebastian on 8th September and the receipt of news

[25]Green, pp. 186-191; copy memorandum by Gen. Inglis (10th Mar 1830) in Digest; Wheeler, pp. 125-126; W.O.25/1977; 12/7635.

that the armistice in Central Europe had been denounced removed two of Wellington's principal reasons for declining to enter France. On 7th October he launched the great forward movement known as the battle of the Bidassoa which carried his Army across the frontier. The 7th Division was hardly engaged, and the 68th remained near Echalar. But on 10th November, on the fall of Pamplona, Wellington, who could survey the whole of Soult's position from the dominating mountain of Larrun, or La Rhune, made a fresh advance in the long-matured offensive movement known as the battle of the Nivelle. Soult had spent the intervening months preparing an elaborate position strengthened by a network of redoubts and other fieldworks, all closed at the rear, and many mounting field-pieces. It was a kind of Lines of Tôrres-Vedras, sited in depth and running from the sea near Socoa (opposite Saint-Jean-de-Luz) to about Aïnhoa. Its ruined redoubts may still be seen. To attack it seemed a formidable proposition, but Wellington had his own ideas on its strength. "Those fellows think themselves invulnerable," he said one day to a Light Division brigadier, "but I will beat them out, and with great ease." "That we shall beat them," said the brigadier, "when your Lordship attacks I have no doubt, but as for the ease—" "Ah, Colborne," replied Wellington, "with your local knowledge only you are perfectly right. It appears difficult, but the enemy have not men to man the works and lines they occupy. They dare not concentrate a sufficient body to resist the attacks I shall make upon them. I can pour a greater force on certain points than they can concentrate to resist me."

That was the essence of the battle that followed. The whole Army was closed up to the left and squeezed in opposite the line from Socoa to Urdax, Hill's Corps from Roncesvalles being brought round to Urdax and launched at the extreme French left. The 7th (temporarily commanded by the Portuguese General Lecor) was directed from roughly where it stood about the Pass of Echalar upon the redoubts of Grenade, and then upon a long line of works protecting the village of Sare.

Inglis's Brigade carried the two redoubts of Grenade at the first rush, the 68th entering the left-hand of the two before the garrison could fire more than a few rounds from their cannon, and with such surprising ease that, instead of allowing Barnes's Brigade to leap-frog past them, they raced on across the Harane rivulet to Sare. On their left the Redoute Sainte-Barbe fell to the 4th Division, and on their right the 3rd were making progress. Outflanked, the works in front of Sare scarcely resisted, and the Brigade passed on to the large Redoute Louis XIV on the hill behind the village. This was manned

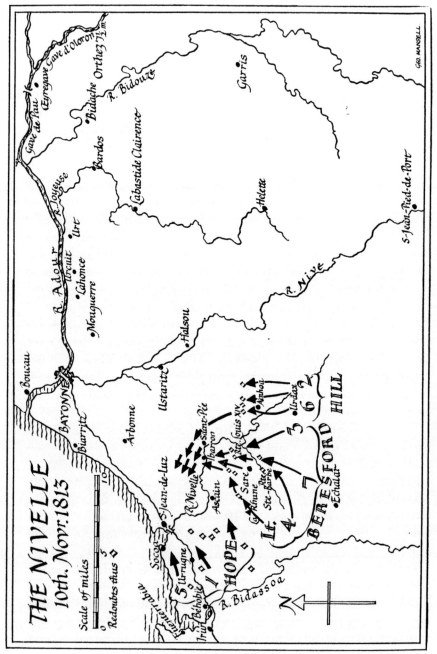

11. The Nivelle, 10th November, 1813, and Bayonne

by troops hitherto unengaged. Inglis's triumphant course was checked, but Barnes's Brigade was brought up and the 4th Division was approaching on the left. For a time the struggle was bitter. But together they fought their way in, beat off a counter-attack, and the 7th pursued the enemy in the direction of Saint-Pée, well beyond the fortified area. Beresford, commanding the three divisions, halted the 7th for a time before Saint-Pée, but then unleashed it, across the Nivelle at and around Ibarron, at the heights of Habancenborda behind it. "The 68th," says Inglis, "made the attack with its usual vivacity." Supported by the 82nd and the Chasseurs Britanniques, without whose assistance it could not have maintained itself, it carried the heights and held them.

This formidable attack established the Army in the rear of the French right. Given another hour of daylight Wellington would have caught Soult's men before they got back to the entrenched camp of Bayonne. As it was darkness came down to put an end to a brilliant operation in which the Regiment and the Brigade had played a decisive part and had shown what it could accomplish under first-class leadership.

The 68th bought its distinction at a moderate cost. Two officers (Captain Irwine and Lieutenant Stopford) and fourteen n.c.o.s and men were killed or mortally wounded; five officers (Captain Gledstanes, Lieutenants Archbold, Clarke and Mendham, and Ensign Browning—a volunteer who had been commissioned after the fight at Lesaca) and about 26 n.c.o.s and men were wounded. Such casualties reduced its strength to its lowest since Vitoria, 197 rank and file "present fit".[26]

After the Nivelle Wellington placed his Army in winter cantonments in front of Bayonne. An awkward combination of circumstances deprived it of mobility until early January; and although Wellington extended the cantonments across the Nive early in December (a move which provoked an attempt of Soult's to cut off the corps that had crossed), the 7th Division, which was in a central position in reserve, was involved in a certain amount of marching but no fighting. The 68th moved with Inglis's Brigade from Saint-Pée to Arbonne on 19th November, and to the banks of the Nive at Ustaritz after Soult's attack had been handsomely beaten off by Hill on 13th December. At Christmas it was moved to Halsou, a few miles farther up the river, where it remained until the resumption of operations in February 1814.

Its strength improved slightly over the months: from 197 in

[26]Digest; Vidal de la Blache, *L'Evacuation de l'Espagne et l'Invasion du Midi* (Paris, 1914), Vol. 1, pp. 556, 564.

November, to 219 in December, 223 in January, and 258 in February.
Johnston returned to command in December, Hawkins departing
for England on leave; and though Lieutenant Pennefather died on
board ship in Bilbao harbour on 19th December, Lieutenants
Stapylton and Connell returned from hospital. The sick-list dropped
from 199 to 126. It was, however, one of the eighteen battalions with
less than 350 rank and file fit for duty which, consisting of veterans,
Wellington favoured retaining contrary to the wishes of the Duke of
York. It was in a particularly unfavourable position inasmuch as the
Depot at Hythe contained no more than 24 recruits. If the war had
not ended when it did no doubt the Duke of York would have insisted on its being drafted and sent home.[27]

The new year's offensive started on 13th February. Wellington's
design was to draw Soult's reserves to the extreme left of his line on
the Joyeuse, so that, while Soult's attention was diverted, the left
British divisions could be carried across the Adour estuary to the
north bank by an enormous pontoon-bridge to complete the investment of Bayonne. Hill's Corps was moved south-eastwards towards
Helette. The 7th Division was moved across the Nive to occupy the
position evacuated by Hill around Lahonce, Urt, Urcuit and
Mouguerre, thus becoming the left of the mobile army. The rivers
flowing parallel north-westwards from the Pyrenees formed serious
obstacles in the path of an advance. It was Wellington's intention
to use his right, under Hill, with which to cross the shallower upper
reaches and outflank every successive position, while his left, under
Beresford, contained the French on the lower reaches.

Hill reached Garris on the 16th and at the same time Beresford
seized the crossing of the Joyeuse at Labastide-Clairence with the
7th Division. In the next few days, while Hill went on towards
Sauveterre on the Gave d'Oloron, Beresford moved by Bardos and
Bidache to complete the occupation of the line of the Bidouze. On
the 19th Wellington, having succeeded in drawing the enemy from
Bayonne, returned to Saint-Jean-de-Luz to prepare for the crossing
of the Adour. The weather, however, was against him, so he turned
back to continue the operations to the east. On 23rd February he
moved Beresford forward in a demonstration against the lower
Gave de Pau with a view to distract Soult from his movements higher
up. This involved the 68th in a successful attempt on the enemy
tête-de-pont at Œyregave, in which Captain Leith, Lieutenant
Stapylton and two men were killed or died of wounds, and seven
n.c.o.s and men were wounded.[28]

[27]Wellington, *Suppl. Disp.*, Vol. 8, pp. 495-498.
[28]W.O.12/7635.

The crossing of the Adour was at last effected at the same time by Sir John Hope at Le Boucau. Soult, forced back farther and faster than he wished, abandoned touch with Bayonne and concentrated his army behind the Gave de Pau around Orthez. Hill's Corps, crossing the Gave d'Oloron between Viellenave and Navarrenx, was moved up to Magret by Loubieng, while Beresford's Corps (3rd, 4th and 7th Divisions) came up by Labastide-Villefranche to Bérenx, where it forced a crossing. On 27th February Soult, his line violated, stood and fought to the west of Orthez.

Wellington's attack on his position was made in four columns: there was a crossing by Hill above Orthez; an advance by the 4th Division, supported by the 7th, up the spur leading to Saint-Boès on which Soult's right rested; an attack by the 3rd Division, along a more southerly spur on the French centre; and an attack by the Light Division, supported by the 6th, between the two former. The battle began with the assault of the 4th Division on Saint-Boès. Soult's was an ideal defensive position, and although the 4th carried the village itself it received a sharp check at the heights behind, which were swept by artillery fire, and was forced to fall back. This was unusual; and furthermore, Picton's diversionary attack was held for a time also. The British brigades of the 7th Division (under Walker since December) were then brought in to redress the situation around Saint-Boès. Detaching the Brunswickers and the Provisional Battalion to the left, and the 6th to cover the formation of Inglis's Brigade, Walker delivered his main assault with the 68th, 82nd and Chasseurs Britanniques. They charged along the narrow neck on which the road runs, down the dip beyond, up the steep slope of the heights beyond where the 4th Division's attack had been broken, and carried them. The French fell back fighting, but the position was won. Inglis's Brigade, perhaps a thousand men strong, had, by Walker's able dispositions, defeated a whole division.

The other attacks simultaneously made progress, and Soult drew off north-eastwards in some disorder. He had lost 4000 men, double Wellington's casualties, which, considering the savagery of some of the fighting, were remarkably light. In the 68th six men were killed or mortally wounded, and two officers (Captain Archdall and Ensign Sheddon) and 25 men wounded.[29]

The battle of Orthez was the 7th Division's last. After the Army had assembled in the neighbourhood of Saint-Sever Beresford was detached on 8th March with the 4th and 7th Divisions to seize Bordeaux. Marching by Roquefort, Captieux and Bazas, Beresford took possession of the city without fighting on 12th March. Here

[29] *Suppl. Disp.*, Vol. 8, pp. 611-612; W.O.12/7635.

6

Dalhousie resumed command—Walker had been wounded at Orthez—and, indeed, assumed command of the whole British force when Beresford and the 4th Division were ordered back to the Army on the 15th. There was a body of French troops around Marmande, but it did nothing; and although Inglis's Brigade was placed at Langon and, later (24th March) at La Réole, to keep it at arm's length, the 68th was unmolested even when Dalhousie took out the other brigades to the north of the Gironde to fight a small action at Étauliers. There was an affair on 28th March, but one of such insignificance as to receive no mention in Dalhousie's reports.

When news reached the Army of Napoleon's abdication, Hope's divisions were investing Bayonne, Dalhousie was in and around Bordeaux, and Wellington, having defeated Soult in the bloody battle of Toulouse on 10th April, was nearing Castelnaudary and going hard towards Carcassonne. It was naturally some time before this wonderful fighting machine, dispersed over such a wide area and composed of Spanish and Portuguese as well as British, could be withdrawn, reassembled and embarked for new destinations. The 68th, ragged in its 1813 clothing until May, remained at La Réole until early in June, when it was marched (422 all ranks) to a large camp at Blanquefort on the Gironde. They were brought to the embarkation camp at Pauillac on 2nd July, and embarked for Cove on the 8th. They reached Belfast on 22nd September.

The Regiment had been on service for just over three years. It was a weak battalion, and though its losses—9 officers and 100 men killed or died of wounds, 3 officers and perhaps 350 men died of disease, 23 officers and 266 men wounded—were not heavy compared with others', they were losses it could ill afford. It had, however, won a name for itself. Its conduct at Lesaca, at the Nivelle and at Orthez had been worthy of the best traditions of the British service. For Inglis to have spoken of its "usual vivacity" on one of those occasions shows that it had acquired a stamp and a character on which its leaders could rely. "The 68th has always been a good regiment," the Duke of Wellington said in 1844, when he had not seen it since he had commanded it and experienced its worth. The battle honour *Peninsula*, the Regiment's first, was granted on 6th April 1815; those of *Salamanca, Vitoria, Pyrenees, Nivelle*, and *Orthez* were added on 20th June 1823. At last, after over fifty years frustrating service, it had achieved something and shared in glory.

CHAPTER V

THE FORTY YEARS PEACE
AND THE CRIMEA, 1814-1856

DURING the next forty years, between Orthez and the Alma, the 68th never fired a shot in anger, but moved peaceably from one station to another.

The age that followed Waterloo is difficult to characterise. On the one hand it is an age of immense wealth accumulated during the war, an age of ostentation and sometimes vulgarity. On the other it is an age of recurrent economic difficulties, an age of retrenchment in public expenditure in the face of increased liabilities. And it is besides an age of growing public conscience, of a rapidly increasing population, involving problems too vast to solve except on a national scale. There is an increasing pressure on "the Government" to undertake responsibilities hitherto undertaken by private persons and concerns; there is a readiness on the part of the departments to assume them; but there is a reluctance to provide them with the money and the powers to do so.

The effects on the army are correspondingly contradictory. The ostentatious spirit prevailing gave the British soldier, whose baggy, ill-fitting clothing had been the joke of the French caricaturists, the bell-topped shako and a host of elaborate and starchy embellishments that transformed his uniform from something comfortable into something very uncomfortable. The spirit of retrenchment disbanded a large number of battalions and reduced the establishments of those that remained, at a moment when the colonial possessions acquired in the war enlarged the army's commitments. The result was to keep infantry battalions abroad much longer than was good for them. Three years in hot countries such as the West Indies or India was considered enough to "shatter" them: a tour of ten years, on the other hand, was nothing exceptional, and in those forty years the

68th served no more than two years in England. At the same time the military government of the army emerged from the war with powers immensely enhanced, and exercised control to a degree unheard of in 1793. The temper of the times being generally liberal (whatever social historians may say), the standard it exacted was both consistent and high. Regiments are not only given a rigorous inspection but are required besides to furnish all kinds of information unthought of in old days. How many Catholics and Presbyterians do they contain? How many nights in bed in the week do the soldiers get? How many Bibles are there? Do the girls of the regiment learn stitching and knitting? (Yes, apparently they do). Does the band use the pitch of the Ancient Philharmonic Concerts? (No, on the whole they use one rather sharper). Soldiers' complaints are listened to by inspecting officers, not for the good old reason which brought an inferior before his superior as man to man, but to satisfy some hypothetical question raised by a Radical member in Parliament. The Inspection Reports ceased to be merely a description of the bargain the Crown had struck; they became an instrument of the military inquisition, a kind of torch of enlightenment. At the same time, while the increased power of the Horse Guards tended towards standardisation, they were used also for fostering *esprit-de-corps* to an extent of which most Colonels of former days had been incapable.

In other words, though these years are usually described as an age of reaction, they are in fact years of tension, of immense forces pulling in opposite directions. Economy sends the infantry abroad and drives it to drink; the increased powers of government lead at one and the same time to standardisation and to regimental distinctions; and the searching beam of public conscience both highlights the shortcomings (for which its thrift is responsible) and makes "abuses" out of what was formerly ordinary human aberration or neglect. The defects of the Crimean Army have been sufficiently emphasised over the years. Yet, when all is said, it was a larger and more efficient army than the one with which we entered the war in 1793. It had been shorn of many necessary auxiliary services, a deficiency which the inadequacies of the theatre of war quickly exposed. The fault, however, lies as much in the choice of the theatre as in the army. It is characteristic of that cantankerous time that it should deprive the army for two generations of the wherewithal, send it to fight where it can hardly exist, complain when it runs into difficulties and exaggerate its misfortunes. That, however, is the age which the 68th is entering.

After spending four years in Ireland, it embarked under the command of Colonel Johnston for the Canadas (as they were called) in May 1818. From Quebec it was moved in June 1819 into the English-speaking province of Upper Canada, (west of the Ottawa River) where it was placed with headquarters at Fort George, Niagara, and detachments as far distant as York (now Toronto) and Amherstburg. In May 1820 it was brought to Kingston. In May 1823 it was moved to Quebec again, where in 1825 it was inspected by its old divisional commander Lord Dalhousie. In October it returned to Kingston, and in July 1827 to Toronto. In May 1829 it was brought back into the French-speaking Lower province, and in preparation for its embarkation for home it was stationed at Montreal and then at Quebec. In November 1829 it was at Fermoy; in June 1830 at Athlone.

On its return it is revealed as a curiously inbred concern. Colonel Johnston had handed over to Lieut.-Colonel Hawkins in 1825, and although, at the time the Regiment was inspected at Fermoy by Major-General Sir George Bingham, Hawkins was still nominally commanding, the command in fact was exercised by the Major Reed who has been several times mentioned already. Neither Hawkins, Reed nor any of the senior officers showed themselves capable of ruling with a tight hand a regiment that had somewhat run to fat. "They have never had a commanding officer who has introduced any system, and lately Lieut-Colonel Hawkins, who had never been brought up in a good school, has been labouring under monomania to that degree as to be totally unfit to be allowed at large, much less to have been continued in command of the Regiment. Major Reed is active, zealous and intelligent, but labours under the disadvantage of never having been in any other regiment (for I shall certainly call it so). He was born in it; his father, having risen from the ranks, was adjutant. He is so connected with the corps that he would never purge it of the old and useless, and although I consider him fully equal to command a regiment of the line he is not the person I would wish to see continue in this regiment of light infantry. Major Menzies has just purchased the rank he holds, is not young, and anything but active or, as far as my observation goes, intelligent. A volunteer from a regiment of Scotch militia [the Royal Perth], he labours under the disadvantage of having been eleven years recruiting in Scotland (as I am informed) whilst his regiment was on service at Flushing and in the Peninsula."[1]

The Peninsula officers were past their prime. "The officers are many of them old and worn out and encumbered with large families, so that to expect to make them effective as light infantry is quite out

[1]This is not quite true. Menzies did serve in Walcheren. He was wounded in the chest before Flushing on 3rd Aug., and was brought home on 23rd September.

of the question. Two or three of them are upwards of fifty years of age and are supposed to be older than is given in against their names." Captain Jackson—the Jackson who had had the brush with the Littlehampton magistrates—was one. Born in Limerick in 1789, he had served at Flushing and in the last six months of the Peninsular War without, however, being engaged. He is described as being "of an immense size and of unwieldy proportions, and being in advanced life, would never make an eligible major in this corps". Captains Gledstanes (43), North (47), Kennedy (56) and G. Macdonald (48) were also "from age" unfit for light infantry service. The Quartermaster, George Macbeath, was another. A highlander, born at Wick, Caithness, in 1777, he had enlisted in the 94th on its raising in 1793 and risen to the rank of quartermaster-sergeant in 1806, having fought at Malavelly, Seringapatam, Fort Jalna, Assaye, Asirgarh, Argaum, the siege of Gawilgarh and Chandore, and had been twice wounded. He had been promoted Quartermaster of the 62nd and had seen the latter months of the Peninsular War before his appointment to the 68th. He had a son in the 68th, an ensign of a year's service. He was considered by Bingham "a very old man" and "past the time of life to be able to take the field". There was besides an odd skeleton in the regimental cupboard, Lieutenant Houghton Madely, born at Horncastle in 1806, who, though having served five years and received a lieutenancy, had hardly done a day's duty. "He is totally unfit for any military duty from the consequences of a paralytic stroke when a child, and of so nervous a temperament from taking quantities of laudanum that some doubt might have been entertained as to the soundness of his intellect. Yet this person has been continued and even recommended for promotion with a sort of understanding that he should retire after it, and kept on the outposts of Canada, perhaps to prevent his being seen at the half-yearly inspections. Major Reed very properly intimated to him, on his having for the first time commanded the corps, that 'he had better make arrangements for retiring from the active part of the service' "— which he did on 25th November 1830.

The n.c.o.s, whom it had become the practice in the Regiment (as it had in some others)[2] to promote by seniority, were "from weight, size and appearance quite unfit for light infantry". Thirteen sergeants had upwards of 21 years' service (two, Joseph Harewood and William Aird, were survivors of the Durham Militia volunteers of 1807 and 1809; one, Gilbert Hinds, had enlisted in 1797). The men were described as having improved in the field exercise and move-

[2]*Cf. The Diary of Colour-Sergeant George Calladine, 19th, 1793-1837*, ed. Major M. L. Ferrar (London, 1922), p. 97.

ments but to have "no idea of outpost duty" and only a "very slight" knowledge of light infantry movements, "the practice of which I have not encouraged, as the first principles were most essential". And in addition Sir George Bingham observed a "curious anomaly" by which the facings of the men were green while those of the officers were "nearly black and not at all corresponding".

Old regiments are not like new levies; the evils were not deep-seated; and the measures enforced by the Horse Guards on receiving Bingham's adverse report, together with the effects of deaths and retirements, combined to remedy the defects in a short space of time. Hawkins, Reed and Menzies retired in the course of the year; North, Kennedy, Jackson and Macdonald retired soon after; Gledstanes died at Athlone of apoplexy in October 1830; Quartermaster Macbeath died at Devonport in July 1835. Another loss was Lieutenant and Adjutant James Duff, who died at Kingston, Jamaica, in April 1840 at the age of 53. He had enlisted in the Regiment in October 1807, had served in all the actions, had been wounded at Flushing and the Nivelle, had risen to the rank of sergeant-major in January 1814, and was promoted ensign and adjutant in 1823. Paymaster Henry Read, formerly a subaltern in the 51st, deserted. Thus within a few years the Regiment passed from the hands of the old "Peninsulars" to a younger generation.[3]

The matter of the command could not, however, in the absence of any suitable candidate within the Regiment be settled so easily. Acting in some manner that is not clear, the Horse Guards promoted to the vacancy left by Hawkins the second major of the 52nd, which was still Moore's nursery of light infantrymen. He was John Cross, born in 1787 of the good Irish family of Cross of Dartan, County Armagh. He had entered the 52nd from the Armagh Militia in Moore's day and had served throughout the Peninsular War (in which he was three times wounded) and at Waterloo. He was not only a very experienced but a very able and energetic officer, a zealot for light infantry, on which he had published a drill-book in 1823, as well as being a man of humanity and understanding. After his assumption of the command on 1st April 1831, the improvement of the Regiment becomes immediately noticeable in the inspection reports.[4]

But apart from that Cross's appointment has a wider significance. He brought into the Regiment his nephew William Cross (he

[3]Bingham's Inspection Report is in W.O.27/198; see also W.O.3/127, pp. 77-78; 27/203; 3/127, pp. 197-198. For the officers' services see 25/798.
[4]Details of Cross's family kindly communicated to me by Lieut.-Col. R. B. Crosse.

himself was a bachelor), who became a very efficient adjutant in 1840. William Cross, after retiring from the 68th in 1847, was introduced into the Armagh Militia as commanding officer in 1854, and he made such an impression upon them that when volunteers were called for to fill the ranks of the line battalions in the Crimea no less than 225 came forward and 207 of those for the 68th. The 68th was already nearly half Irish, and it became even more so until the Cardwell reforms established the Durham connection.

In the second place John Cross brought with him the best of the Moore tradition, in which he had himself grown up and lived for twenty-six years—the Moore tradition, that is, as distinct from the light infantry one. In 1830 the old light infantry frenzy was almost moribund. Light infantry movements were still practised, and military theorists still kept up a faint echo of the controversy. But it is plain from the inspection reports that in this country light infantry and line were slowly becoming assimilated. Rottenburg's influence had hardly persisted to the end of the war. Wellington's use of light infantry regiments in his campaigns had not distinguished any save two from the line, and anything Wellington did or did not do was sacrosanct for two generations. Likewise the peace, so far from favouring the assembly of battalions into formations in which light infantry could make their peculiar contribution to a permanent organisation, required them to be scattered over the face of the globe and take their turn in the roster with other infantry. In 1830 therefore light infantry regiments, apart from some not very material distinctions in internal organisation (such as having no grenadier or light companies) and their clothing and appointments, differed from the line in little but name. On the other hand with Cross there was introduced into the 68th not only a distillation of Moore's light infantry drill, but that peculiar relationship between superior and subordinate that permeated all regiments that Moore touched. Cross introduced a "system" to fill the lack which Bingham had drawn attention to, in the form of a code of orders which, written down later by an Irish officer of the name of Huey, developed into the *Standing Orders* of the Durham Light Infantry. Huey's version is barely recognisable in the modern editions, but an officer of the 52nd who has seen the earlier ones observes that they contained "sentences too closely resembling sentences in that regimental bible to which I have been reared to leave any doubt as to their origin".

Cross held the command for ten years. He took the Regiment from Ireland to Edinburgh in 1833, from Edinburgh to Gibraltar in 1834, and from Gibraltar to Jamaica in June 1838. He did not retire until 1843, but he ceased to exercise effective command in June 1841, when he remained in Jamaica as Deputy-Governor while the Regiment moved to Canada under Major Huey. The inspection reports are eloquent testimony of the beneficial effects of his command. "The 68th," says Lieut.-General Sir Lionel Smith, the unpopular Commander in Jamaica on its first arrival, "is a plain unaffected, active yet steady regiment. Lieut.-Colonel Cross is a soldier-like, efficient commanding officer. I am very well satisfied with the Regiment, and the men are not too young for the tropics, which is a common objection to newly arrived regiments. This regiment came from Gibraltar and has as yet been very healthy; but then we have had a remarkably healthy season. They drank to excess on first coming, and the usual evils occurred from rum delirium. It is over; and the Regiment is behaving well, and I would not desire to have a more serviceable regiment under me." "The state of discipline of the 68th," says Lieut-General Sir William Gomm, Smith's successor, in the autumn of 1840, "appears to me very deserving of commendation. The trials for drunkenness, however, are frequent in the corps, almost exclusively confined to that portion of it quartered in the town of Falmouth. This detachment has, however, conducted itself creditably and with great steadiness under the direction of Major Huey on the occasion of a riot in the town of Falmouth. Lieut.-Colonel Cross's unremitting attention to improving the station of Maroon Town, enlarging the parade-ground, constructing durable roads, &c., cannot be too pointedly brought under the notice of the General Officer Commanding in Chief." The Regiment had not earned such consistently golden opinions in the whole of its existence, and an inspection in those days was no mere formality: those old generals were tigers.[5]

Its luck was in. After an eighteen months interval in which it came under the competent but not, apparently, very inspiring command of Major Huey, it passed to an officer as distinguished as Colonel Cross, and one certainly to whom it has even greater reason to be grateful: one for whom the Regiment was close to his heart, who gave it the weight of his interest and influence for over fifty years after he had ceased to command it actively.

Lord William Paulet, born in 1804, the fourth son of the 13th Marquess of Winchester, came of a family that, until his generation, had given few of its sons to the services, though a seventeenth-century ancestor had held Basing House for the King in the Civil War. He was first commissioned in the 85th in 1821, and he had served in several regiments before transferring to the 68th as a major in 1833. He had commanded a detachment which had helped to suppress

[5]W.O.27/213, 27/279, 27/293.

some riots in Glasgow that year; he had been second-in-command of the battalion in Jamaica in 1838 when Cross was Deputy-Governor; he had then returned home to take over the command of the depot-companies at Chester from Major Huey in 1840; and he again relieved Huey, when, at the age of 38, he took command of the service-companies in Canada on 30th September 1842. Huey had had the mis-fortune of commanding a widely dispersed battalion. The Regiment had been moved to Canada at the height of the so-called Maine Boundary dispute (that interesting episode in our relations with the United States, which originated with the loss of the map that accompanied the Peace Treaty of 1783 and brought us to the verge of war until two marked maps were discovered: one by the British Government, which was found to support the American claims, the other by the American Government, which was found to support the British). The battalion had been distributed over the disputed area (Fort Ingall, Madawaska, Rivière du Loup and Dégelé); and Huey had had only three officers and the staff with which to command the half-battalion stationed at the headquarters at Sorel. When Paulet took command the Ashburton Treaty had been signed, and the 68th was concentrated at Quebec.

The inspection reports describe the progress of the improvement in an already good battalion. "I have every reason," says the first, of March 1843, "to be satisfied with the state and appearance of the 68th Regiment. Lord William Paulet is well qualified for being com-manding officer, and drunkenness and crimes in general not more frequent than can be expected from the cheapness and facility of getting liquor." "The state of the 68th," says the second, of August 1843, "is in all respects highly creditable to the commanding officer, officers, n.c.o.s and men. Since the Regiment has been together in Quebec great attention has been paid to the drill of the men. A number of cases of ophthalmia has existed, and the Regiment has been encamped on the Plains of Abraham to enable the Jesuits' Barracks and the hospital to be thoroughly cleansed and purified." "The 68th Light Infantry," says the report of October 1847, just after Paulet had handed over to Huey on the Regiment's return to Ireland, "is in the highest order both as regards discipline and interior economy." The average height of the men was 5ft. 8¼ins.; they were, the report adds, "particularly well drilled, very steady under arms, *obedient* and *respectful*." The series ends with the inspection at Mullingar on 26th May 1848: "The 68th Light Infantry are in the highest order not only at the headquarters of the corps but throughout all the detached stations. Field movements, includ-ing light infantry, admirably performed. Conduct praiseworthy.

In fact I cannot say too much in praise of this beautiful regiment."[6]

Lord William Paulet ceased to command on 11th October 1847: in five years he had brought the Regiment to the highest pitch of efficiency. And what is as remarkable is that under successive commanding officers it never relapsed. By some means or other he had discovered the secret of securing for it a high state of discipline long after he gave up active command. There was to be no repetition of the lamentable state of affairs of 1830. Part of his secret lies in his careful selection of officers. It is an interesting fact that, before his coming, the Regiment had not received a single officer from Eton, but that from 1833 onwards a small but steady stream of young men came forward from a school that, so far as it supplied the army, favoured the cavalry, the foot guards or the rifle regiments. Henry Smyth, who commanded throughout the Crimea, and H. A. K. Proctor were commissioned in 1833; T. S. Beale in 1834; H. G. Wynne a very good officer, killed at Inkerman, in 1836; the Hon. H. L. Noel, a son of Lord Gainsborough, in 1842; P. A. F. C. Stuart in 1843; E. S. Savage in 1846; Henry White in 1850; H. L. Battiscombe in 1853; C. E. B. Pownall in 1855. In 1859, the Fourth of June was celebrated in Burma by a four-oared boat race between "Eton" and "the Regiment," in which "Eton" was represented by Major Savage, Captains White (cox) and Sparke, Lieutenant Pownall and an officer of the 69th of the name of Brace. The 68th of pre-Paulet days would not have worried about the Fourth of June.

It is not that Eton was or is the sole repository of the military virtues, of wealth and influence; nor is it that the Regiment drew a majority of its officers from that source. What is true is that whereas, for instance, in Peninsula days it is not easy to discover the origins of the officers, in Crimea days it is very clear that many, if not most, were sons of substantial landowners and well connected families. Colonel Henry Smyth was the son of a Yorkshire squire and a daughter of the Duke of Grafton, (Lieut.-Colonel Harry Smyth was no relation); Major Blount was the son of a Worcestershire baronet; Wynne came from the landed family of Wynne of Voelas, Denbighshire; Greer was the son of a gentleman of County Tyrone; Finch was the younger son of the 5th Earl of Aylesford; Morant came of a Hampshire family that had owned a large estate in Jamaica; Captain C. C. FitzRoy, a kinsman of Colonel Henry Smyth, was the son of Lord Charles FitzRoy, and a grandson of the Duke of Grafton; Captain R. L. Edwards, who was killed before Sevastopol, was heir

[6] W.O.27/329, 27/334, 27/372.

to a property said to be worth £12,000 a year at Nanhoron, Car-narvon; Sheffield Grace was the son of an Irish baronet; Lieutenant F. G. Barker, killed at Inkerman, was the son of a Berkshire country gentleman; John Cator, the son of a Suffolk gentleman; Hamilton, adjutant in the Crimea, the son of a County Meath gentleman; Vaughan, Hamilton's successor, was the son of a Cardiganshire gentleman. The list may be extended considerably. It could not have been before Paulet's time. In other words Paulet had made the 68th in some degree fashionable; and while a regiment remains fashionable it may pick and choose from among the applicants, and its reputation is fairly secure. If its officers are good, the rest—such is the British soldier—may safely take care of itself.

How much of all this was Paulet's doing? In the absence of any definite evidence the impression must remain that he was ultimately responsible. It is not a process in which all regiments of the line, or light infantry for that matter, shared at the same time. It starts too suddenly with Paulet's connection with the Regiment for his part in it to be taken lightly, and it lasts too long. Though he ceased to command at the end of 1847, the Regiment came under his eye in the Crimea and he was its Colonel from 1864 until his death in 1893. "The welfare of his regiment," says Colonel Vane, "was its Colonel's first thoughts, and he was always ready to use his influence for the benefit of all ranks." His impact on the 68th was no less decisive than Lambton's, and the Regiment's debt to him no less great. Very fitting and very proper was its response at his death. He was buried in the family vault at Amport, near Andover; the descendants of the old 68th, the 1st Battalion Durham Light Infantry, were then at Aldershot. Permission to attend the funeral was given on the condition that the public was put to no expense. The officers sub-scribed; and on 13th May 1893 the whole battalion, about 750 strong, marched from Aldershot to Farnborough, entrained in a special for Andover Junction, marched to Amport, where they were entertained by the Marquess of Winchester, Lord William's nephew, and inspected and addressed by the Commander-in-Chief; and travelled back to Aldershot in one day. Surely no more remarkable and touching farewell tribute was ever paid by a regiment to its Colonel.

There is more therefore than meets the eye in the painting now in the Regiment's possession which shows Lord William Paulet, his adjutant, Captain Cross, and a number of his n.c.o.s and men in the clothing and appointments in wear in the late 'forties. It is the 68th of Paulet's creation at the peak of its efficiency; it is the "beautiful regiment" which Sir Guy Campbell spoke of at Mullingar. There seems every reason to suppose it was painted to the order of Lord William Paulet himself. Traditionally it was painted at Weedon in 1846 by an artist of the name of Scanlan, but more recent inquiry inclines to the opinion that it is the work of a Hampshire artist, D. Cunliffe, who was interested in military subjects and was responsible for a number of similar regimental groups. If so it is likely to have been executed when the Regiment was at Portsmouth between 29th July 1845 and 27th January 1846. The men are portraits and their names are recorded. None served in the Crimea.[7]

The history of the Regiment during the forty years of peace was otherwise uneventful, and followed the pattern of any other infantry battalion of the period. It was kept fairly well up to the establishments prescribed for it, which varied between 56 and 74 rank and file per company. There was some sickness during its tour in Jamaica (1838-1841), but the mortality (104 n.c.o.s and men) did not approach the catastrophic proportions reached in the earlier tours. Nor did it fall below establishment to the extent it did in the peaceful years before the American War. In 1843 it was over establishment.

Recruiting, "nationalised" during the Napoleonic Wars, had reverted to being a regimental concern at the Peace, but the introduction of the depot-company system after the war kept regiments up to strength better than the haphazard methods used before. The regiment was composed of ten companies, which were kept together so long as the battalion was in Britain or Ireland, but separated into six "service-companies" and four "depot-companies" on the embarkation of the former for duty abroad. The depot-companies of two or more regiments, though moving from one part of the country to another, were commonly grouped into "depot-battalions" until the service-companies' return, when they were detached to rejoin the parent battalion. While the 68th was on its first tour in Canada (1818-1829), its depot-companies were at Devonport and Buttevant; they were at Portsmouth and in southern Ireland during the Regiment's tour of duty in Gibraltar and Jamaica (1834-1841); and at Chester Castle from 1840 to 1843, and at Perth and Stirling until the return of the Regiment from Canada in June 1844. The long sojourn in Ireland of both depot and service-companies naturally maintained the Irish element in the ranks, which in 1842 stood at 38

[7]On a suggestion that the painter was not Scanlan but Cunliffe see Major H. P. E. Pereira, ".... Some Observations on D. Cunliffe..." in J.S.A.H.R., Vol. 33 (1955), pp. 144-145.

per cent. (as against 62 *per cent.* English); in 1844 at 43 *per cent.* (as against 56 *per cent.* English). But curiously enough, in 1847, although the Regiment had been a year in Ireland, the Irish proportion had dropped to 34 *per cent.* (as against 64 *per cent.* English, many of whom appear to have come from the West Riding.) In 1854, on the eve of its departure for the Crimea, the proportions were very similar.

The 68th remained in Ireland under Huey's command until 1851. In 1846 it was in Dublin. In October 1847 it moved to Mullingar. In September 1848 it was at Galway; and in April 1850 at Limerick. It embarked at Cork for Malta in February 1851. Quartered at first in Lower St. Elmo Barracks, it was moved in October 1852 to Isola; in April 1853 to Floriana Barracks; and in October to Strada Forre Barracks; in July 1854 to Fort Ricasoli.

Lord Arthur Lennox, from the half-pay of the 6th, relieved Huey on 14th September 1852. But on 30th December 1853 the command reverted to an officer of the Regiment, Lieut.-Colonel Henry Smyth, who commanded it throughout the Crimean War. At 37 he was a remarkably young commanding officer for those days. He was one of Paulet's Etonians who, commissioned in 1833, had bought his way up, passing in the process his namesake the first major, Harry Smyth, who had started ten years his senior. He was, indeed, one of the youngest battalion commanders in the Crimea, one of the five in the Crimean Army who commanded a battalion from first to last. His letters reveal him as a gentle and resilient soldier, and he was a firm and able commander of men.

"This regiment," says Lieut.-General Sir James Fergusson, who inspected it in Malta on the eve of its embarkation for the East, "is in the highest state of discipline and in the same excellent order as at my last report." This was saying something, as the Malta garrison had a reputation for smartness. Its stay in Malta was uneventful, but it had made a name for itself at cricket.[8]

§

The war that followed is usually known as the Crimean War; and it is written off as an episode of small account in which our army showed itself to poor advantage. No one would guess that it was in fact a war of titans: France, Great Britain and the Ottoman Empire ranged against the Russian Empire. Wars with Russia have always been bloody and usually unsuccessful. But this was one in which after gigantic exertions we achieved our object. The fighting was not confined to the Crimean theatre: there were engagements in the

[8] W.O.27/441; *D.L.I. Gazette* (1859).

Baltic, in the Balkans and the Caucasus as well as on the Russian Black Sea coast. Our ancestors—and, curiously enough, the Russians called it the "War in the East"; some the "Russian War". Certainly "Crimean War" gives no suggestion of the immensity of the forces that were brought into play.

Its immediate causes hardly concern us. We had long been apprehensive of Russian expansion. In the far east it had been the underlying reason for the Afghanistan Expedition (and incidentally the occasion of the raising of the 68th's future partner); and Russian expansion in the Balkans had aroused periodical and increasing anxiety the more it became apparent the Turkish Empire was too weak to arrest it. In 1853 a Russian army occupied the Turkish provinces of Moldavia and Wallachia (now in Romania), and a Russian fleet destroyed the Turkish fleet at Sinope. The aggression provided a convenient pretext for the Great Powers to combine in their Russophobia. A Franco-British naval and military force was assembled to support the Turks in the Black Sea. Although by the time it was ready to act the Russians had retreated from Moldavia and Wallachia, our blood was up, and nothing would do but the destruction of the Russian Black Sea Fleet and its base at Sevastopol.

In the absence of any such military reserve in Britain as there had been in the Napoleonic Wars, all the troops available for the east were drawn from home stations or the nearest foreign garrisons. In view of the danger from the Black Sea Fleet it was imprudent to denude the Mediterranean garrisons unduly, and at first only three battalions from the Malta garrison, the 41st, 47th and 49th, could be spared. By June 1854, however, sufficient troops were assembled at Varna, in the Turkish province of Bulgaria, to form two cavalry brigades and four infantry divisions. It was July before it was decided a further reduction in the Mediterranean could be risked. This released the 68th for operations; and at the same time reinforcements from home made possible the formation of a fifth infantry division on the eve of the Expedition to the Crimea. The organisation of this (the 4th Division) remained incomplete for some months. Two of its battalions were missing at the battle of the Alma on 20th September; the last companies of one brigade did not arrive until after Inkerman; and whereas the four senior divisions (the Light, the 1st, 2nd and 3rd) had been issued with the new hard-hitting muzzle-loading Minié rifle when at Scutari in May and June, the 4th was still carrying the old percussion musket at Inkerman on 5th November.

It was therefore some time before the war made its impact on the

68th. Its establishment, like that of most battalions, was raised to 810 rank and file in February 1854 and to 1140 in June; but it lost 96 men who were transferred to the 41st, 47th and 49th when volunteers were called for in April to fill their ranks; and for that and other reasons the strength of "present fit" was down to 389 rank and file in May. By August, however, the figure had risen to 678, partly from a draft of 124 from the Depot (which moved from Belfast to Fermoy in July), partly from volunteers from the 3rd (Buffs), 9th, 14th and 62nd. "We are made up to strength," said Colonel Smyth, "very hastily of odds and ends and young recruits, who I am afraid will at first be very troublesome." It embarked at Malta in the *Cambria* in the evening of 7th August with a strength of 29 officers and staff[9] and 843 n.c.o.s and men.[10]

Destined originally for the 3rd Division, it disembarked for a few days at Beikos in the Bosporus, where it shared a camp with the 1 / Rifle Brigade, the 20th and the 63rd. But on disembarkation at Varna on 1st September it was posted to the new 4th Division, which was formed on the arrival of Lieut.-General the Hon. Sir George Cathcart on 3rd September, and consisted provisionally of the following:

1st (Right) Brigade (Colonel Horn, 20th): 20th, 21st, 68th, 4 companies 1/Rifle Brigade;
2nd (Left) Brigade (Brigadier-General A. W. Torrens): 2 companies 46th, 63rd, 4 companies 1/Rifle Brigade.

Its late arrival deprived the Regiment of no promising opportunities. Rumours had reached it even as early as the 18th August and as far distant as Beikos that it was to go to the Crimea; but although the destination of the Army was loudly proclaimed in the press and elsewhere and embarkation orders had already been issued, the Expedition did not in fact sail until 7th September. On the contrary, its lateness was a merciful dispensation. 1853 and 1854 were years in which the Asiatic cholera entered Europe from India,

[9]Lieut.-Cols. Henry Smyth (commanding) and Harry Smyth; Major H. G. Wynne; Captains George Macbeath, Herbert Blount, J. E. Lewis, T. H. Somerville, H. H. Morant, the Hon. D. G. Finch, E. S. Savage, and Stephen Croft; Lieuts. John Cassidy, C. U. Shuttleworth, W. H. Seymour, C. C. FitzRoy, F. G. Barker, Herbert Vaughan, R. L. Edwards, John Cator, H. E. Smyth, H. L. Battiscombe, C. B. Wilkinson, H. S. Light; Ensigns A. H. Tucker, J. Marshall; Adjutant T. de C. Hamilton; Quartermaster Thomas Tunks; Surgeon J. S. Graves and Asst.-Surgeon J. F. O'Leary. Paymaster William Hadley was left sick in Malta.
[10]W.O.12/7667, 17/661, 17/670. The quotations from the letters of Lieut.-General Sir Henry Smyth are from ms. copies kindly lent to me by his descendant, Miss C. M. Poland.

and the plague, whose origin was as yet unknown, had already attacked the troops in Bulgaria and continued to strike at the Army until the onset of the cold weather in November. The 68th received its fair share of sickness, but it was at least spared the demoralising effects of the cholera until it landed in the Crimea.

The invasion of the Crimea and the destruction of Sevastopol was a hazardous undertaking, more hazardous than the Walcheren Expedition. Though it was said the native population, which was Tartar—the Crimea was wrested from the Turks only in 1783—was apathetic or even hostile to the Russian government, there was no positive intelligence as to the resources of the country, the fortifications guarding Sevastopol, or the enemy strength. Most of the intelligence possessed by the Allied command had been gleaned from reconnaissances made from the sea, which indicated that the Russians had at least 45,000 troops in the peninsula in addition to the sailors of the fleet, and that there were some naturally strong positions at their disposal between Evpatoria and Sevastopol. Except for a large new fort on the north side of the harbour it did not appear that the landward defences above the town to the south were very formidable. But the very lack of positive information increased all the risks inherent in landing 60,000 troops in a hostile country under the eyes of a powerful army and an undefeated navy. There had been no secrecy: the whole enterprise had been canvassed by everyone for weeks. Lord Raglan, commanding the British contingent, whose beautiful manners, high sense of duty and immense prestige gave him an unassailable ascendancy, even if he lacked decided military views and presided rather as a chairman of a committee than as a commander, disliked the idea from the moment it was first agitated in May. Neither he, however, nor Saint-Arnaud the French commander was prepared to resign. Both felt it unworthy not to attempt something with their fine armies; and on the assumption that they were undertaking a *coup-de-main*, not a prolonged campaign, they acquiesced in its execution. They were soldiers enough to recognise that "war is in its nature hazardous and an option of difficulties".

In the event they were justified. The Franco-British Army (56,000 strong) was carried across and landed safely in Kalamita Bay, about 25 miles north of Sevastopol, without meeting any more trouble than if they had been a party of day-trippers on an outing to Boulogne.

The business of landing occupied four days, from 14th to 18th September. On the 19th the combined Army, though not equipped with the transport for long marches, moved forward. Pushing back a small Russian force posted on the River Bulganak, they arrived on he 20th before the position on the River Alma where Prince Menshikov had chosen to dispute the advance with an army of 40,000 men. The French, their right on the coast, were faced by a range of high and sometimes precipitous hills overlooking the Allies' bank of the river: the British, inland, faced a glacis-like slope which had been strengthened by two large fieldworks or redoubts mounting cannon. The French troops on the extreme right scaled their heights with alacrity and made towards Menshikov's left. The British and the two French divisions in the centre attacked frontally across the river, and met with determined opposition.

The 4th Division under Cathcart, much against its fiery commander's inclination, played but a small part in the battle. Being barely half complete, it had followed in the rear of the Army. Horn's Right Brigade had suffered on landing the detachment of two companies of the 68th (Captain Macbeath's and Captain Blount's), under Captain Macbeath, to serve as Lord Raglan's guard at Headquarters; and Torrens's Left Brigade, only 14 companies strong, was no more than a few miles from the point of disembarkation on the morning of the action. While the Light Division and the Guards Brigade of the 1st Division delivered their gallant attacks upon the formidable Russian position, the 4th lay on their left rear behind the Highland Brigade of the 1st Division. The 68th, Colonel Smyth wrote, were on the extreme left of the Army. The Alma was hardly an obstacle at this part of the front; and while the heavy bludgeon-work was proceeding in the centre, the Highland Brigade and Cathcart's men were able to approach it and cross it near Tarkhanlar opposed only by a large force of cavalry protecting the enemy right, which was kept in check by Cathcart's skirmishers until retiring with the rest of the Army when the Russian centre gave way. The Regiment sustained no casualties in its advance, though at one juncture it came under artillery fire.

The Russian retreat, at first orderly, developed into a rout and finally a panic, as Menshikov led his defeated army (which was to have held the Alma for three weeks) back into Sevastopol. If the Allies had advanced on their heels as Raglan intended, there was a fair chance of seizing the town without much loss. Saint-Arnaud, however, a dying man, lacked the necessary resolution, and the Army did not resume its advance until the 23rd. The 68th was kept on the battlefield for two days, "two horrible days," collecting the wounded and burying the dead. By that time Menshikov had determined on evacuating Sevastopol, which was left to be guarded by sailors and marines, and took the field army into the interior. Meanwhile the Allied commanders, unaware of their opponent's movements, took the risky course of a flank march towards the south side of the town. They ran into the rear of Menshikov's army as it disappeared north-eastwards. But neither seemed to care for the other. Each went his way: the Russians to Bakchisaray, the British to Balaklava, the French to Kamysh, where the two Allies respectively resumed contact with their shipping and established their bases.

The 4th Division, moving by Balaklava, did not reach the position in front of Sevastopol until the 28th. Cathcart, who carried in his pocket a dormant commission appointing him Raglan's successor in the event of any accident, proposed storming the town that day with his own division, by then strengthened by the arrival of the 57th. But the proposal, much to Cathcart's chagrin, was not accepted. "Though we must have done it," wrote Colonel Smyth, "the loss would have been very great." (This, it may be said, is one of the great "ifs" of military history.) Instead, the landing of the siege-train was begun; and the long, tedious and expensive Siege of Sevastopol started.

The siege differed in many respects from the classical sieges of previous generations. Indeed, in retrospect, it much more resembles the trench warfare of 1914-1918, to which it may be regarded as an introduction. Whereas previous sieges had been undertaken by a proportion only of an army, this was undertaken by the whole. Whereas investment had been an essential preliminary, here the garrison, so far from being isolated, was in perpetual contact with the main field army and received reinforcements and everything else from outside throughout. In earlier sieges it had not been unusual to throw up "lines of contravallation" to protect the rear of the besiegers, but it seldom happened as it did at Sevastopol that the field army should approach within assaulting distance of the besiegers and remain there for months on end in equal and, more often, superior numbers, and able, if it had exerted itself, to cut the besiegers' communication with their bases. From November 1854 to February 1855 it was hard to say who was besieging whom. Originally conceived as a short, sharp stroke, the capture of Sevastopol developed into a long test of obstinacy.

The geography of Sevastopol needs some explaining. The town itself lies at the foot of the high table-land of which this corner of the Crimea consists. Known to the ancients as the Heracleotic Chersonese, it is roughly the shape of a shield. Two of its sides are formed by the sea and the estuary of the Chernaya; the third is formed by a ridge, the Sapun Ridge. From here eastward the ground falls sharply in an escarpment to the country below, which, though covered by undulations and even hills, is nevertheless a plain in

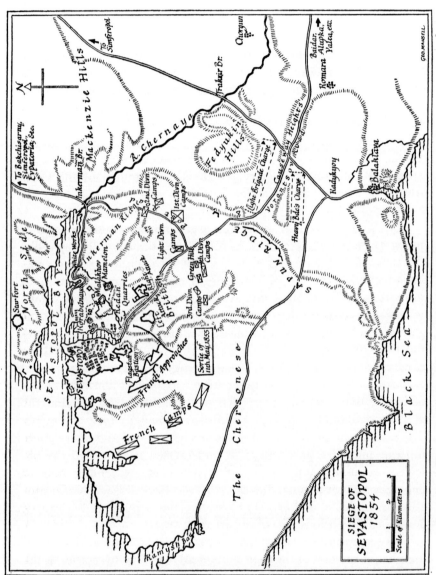

12. Sevastopol: the Situation during October and November, 1854

comparison. From the Sapun Ridge westward the Chersonese falls at first gradually and then sharply to the sea. It is scored by dry water-courses or ravines, which become deep and precipitous the nearer they approach the coast. They are like the fingers of a hand turned palm downwards and slightly clenched; and on the finger-nails, as it were, of the second and third fingers sit the town of Sevastopol and its suburb, the Korábelnaya, overlooked from above.

An army possessed of the Chersonese dominates the town. Indeed, the first British soldiers to arrive looked straight down onto it. "It looks a nice clean town," said Colonel Smyth when he viewed it first on 28th September from the Green Hill, his gaze uninterrupted by the works the Russians were even then busy raising. The ground does not, however, fall evenly. There are, so to speak, knuckles on the fingers, comparatively small eminences, and on those nearest the town the Russian Engineers, under Colonel Todleben, contrived with great skill to construct the bastions and redoubts that kept the Allies at arm's length for nearly a year.

If the Allies, once committed to a formal siege, had been able to confine themselves to the Chersonese, they could have constructed their lines of contravallation along the Sapun Ridge and defied all the attempts of the field army to dislodge them. Kamysh, the French base, lay within: Balaklava, however, did not. It lay in the plain below, in a situation which not only involved the British Army in the laborious task of dragging every pound of stores up the escarpment but also entailed an awkward enlargement of the lines. It was a weakness of which the Russians were not slow to take advantage.

The principal events of the siege may be summarised briefly. It consisted of six bombardments, three of which were accompanied by assaults. All failed, but the last was so nearly successful that the town was evacuated the night after. The First Bombardment lasted from 17th to 23rd October. Meanwhile the Russian field army approached from Chorgun and the Komara Hills, and on 25th October it attempted to storm the British lines at Balaklava (the battle of Balaklava). It failed, though it succeeded in cutting the Vorontsov[11] Road, the principal metalled road used by the British Army between the siege-works and the base. It made a further attempt on 5th November, when three combined corps tried simultaneously to force the British position on the Inkerman side of the Chersonese, storm the Sapun Ridge and raise the siege (the battle of Inkerman). This failed also, but at such a cost to the British Army that the French took over a portion of its front on the

[11]For these Russian names the English, rather than the French, forms of transliteration are used here. "Woronzow" looks awkward to the eye these days.

right flank as well as their own on the left. The Russian field army retreated for a time to Chorgun, but at the end of January came forward again, reoccupied Chorgun, crossed the Chernaya and placed their outposts and vedettes on the Fedyukin Hills, where they remained until April and even later. This period, from November 1854 to April 1855, was the critical period of the siege, in which the besiegers were on the defensive. The Second Bombardment, 9th to 14th April, was unproductive of any results. But the Third, 6th to 11th June, ended with the capture of the White Works, the Mamelon and the Quarries. At much the same time the Russian field army was pushed back beyond the line of the Chernaya into the Mackenzie Hills, and the French established themselves in the Baidar Valley (on 25th May Colonel Smyth speaks of meaning to ride out to the Chernaya "to sit under a tree and hear a bird sing".) The initiative was now firmly in the hands of the Allies. The Fourth Bombardment, 17th and 18th June, ended in failure to storm the Redan and the Malakhov redoubts. On the other hand the last attempt made by the Russian field army to raise the siege failed on the Chernaya on 16th August (the battle of the Chernaya). The Fifth Bombardment, 17th to 21st August, was sterile. But the Sixth, 5th to 8th September, brought the capture of the Malakhov (even though the British failed at the Redan); and the Russians abandoned the town in melancholy silence in the night of the 8th.

The 4th Division, which had remained on the Belbek until 25th September to preserve the communication with the Fleet and to protect the rear, joined the Army on the Chersonese on the 28th. With the arrival of the 57th on the 22nd it was rebrigaded in such a manner as to remove the 68th to the 2nd Brigade, in which it served for the remainder of the war:

> *1st Brigade* (Brigadier-General Goldie, formerly of the 57th): 20th, 21st, 57th;
> *2nd Brigade* (Brigadier-General Torrens): 46th (2 companies, the other six not arriving until 8th November), 63rd, 68th (less 2 companies at Headquarters), 1/Rifle Brigade.

(Torrens took a great liking to the 68th and, according to Colonel Smyth, "could say nothing bad of it".) About 4th October tents were issued for the first time since landing, and on the same day the Division encamped out of range of the fortress guns in rear of Green Hill, or Cathcart's Hill, on the extreme left front of the Army, forming, with the 3rd Division, the Left Attack. Ground was broken about a mile in front of the camp after dusk on 10th October, Colonel Smyth acting as the first field officer in the trenches; and from that moment the weary monotonous routine of "trenches and dinner" continued for eleven months.

When the bombardment opened on 17th October a party of the Regiment under Captains Croft and Shuttleworth assisted in the batteries under the heavy fire with which the Russian artillery replied. Sergeant Henry Sladden was commended for his conduct that morning, for having, while placing a 68-pounder gun in position, "courageously stood to the gun after one man had been mortally wounded and the remainder compelled to take shelter under the works, and not quitting it until the gun was lowered," as well as for "voluntarily carrying loose charges of ammunition from a magazine to the battery under heavy fire". The Regiment lost three men killed on that day and the day previous, and Assistant-Surgeon O'Leary was mortally wounded.

The 68th had only two companies engaged in the battle of Balaklava on 25th October when the 1st and 4th Divisions were brought down into the plain to assist in the repulse of Liprandi's attack on the rear of the Army at Balaklava and Kadykyoy. Colonel Smyth refers to the action in his letters as no more than a "cavalry skirmish," but he adds the interesting information that the position gained by the Russians in their advance on the so called Causeway Heights was "too strong to attack," an observation that will in some degree mitigate criticism of Cathcart's failure to exert pressure on the redoubts captured by the Russians and so divert attention from the injudicious charge made by Cardigan's Light Cavalry Brigade. The Regiment's casualties in that day's work was one man killed and one wounded.

The battle of Inkerman was a very different matter. It arose out of a powerful Russian offensive launched at the extreme right of the British position where the 2nd Division was posted. This was, relatively, the weakest sector (next to Balaklava) of the Allied position, and an attempt upon it was not wholly unexpected. The moment chosen, however, and the power behind the attack were a complete surprise. A corps under General Soimonov of 19,000 men was directed from the Korábelnaya at the 2nd Division front on the Inkerman Ridge, while a corps under General Pavlov of 31,000 men from the north of the Chernaya was moved across the river to assault the ridge in the flank. Together it was intended the two corps should roll up the Allied line from right to left and drive it into the arms of a corps of 22,000 men in the plain below the Sapun Ridge under General Gorchakov (Liprandi's successor), who, having first contained Bosquet's "Corps d'Observation" (a division), was to gain a foothold on the Chersonese. Soimonov's corps started the battle by creeping up on the 2nd Division picquets under the cover of a heavy mist in the early morning of 5th November.

The 2nd Division, in the absence of General de Lacey Evans, was temporarily commanded by the senior brigadier, General Penne-father, a hot-tempered Irishman with an extensive and expressive military vocabulary, who, in defiance of his superior's intentions in such an emergency, namely, to withdraw slowly to a "Wellingtonian" position on the "Home Ridge" in front of the 2nd Division camp, preferred to hold a forward line of skirmishers and "feed the fight", as he expressed it, there. Such was the confusion in the mist, the clumsiness of the Russian formations, and such was the dogged obstinacy displayed by the British infantry that this unorthodox procedure proved astonishingly successful. The reinforcements that were hurried from the left were thrown piecemeal into the fight as they came up. By the time the 4th Division arrived from its camp on the far left, what Kinglake describes as the "second period" of the battle was at its height. Soimonov's attack had been repelled with great loss and its commander killed; Gorchakov's movement in the plain had been recognised for what it was at that stage, no more than a demonstration; but a fresh attack by Pavlov's corps was developing and threatening the hard-pressed troops fighting in small groups in the right front of the Home Ridge. It would have been difficult and probably unwise to disengage them and bring them back to the Home Ridge at that moment; and Cathcart quite happily acquiesced in devoting the accession of strength (2200 men) he brought to patching the "leaks".

The 4th Division had been under arms early, before Cathcart's orders could reach it, because, according to Smyth, a bugler of a new regiment, frightened by the firing far away to the right, had already sounded the alarm. It had first been Cathcart's intention to turn out only Goldie's Brigade, Torrens's Brigade containing too large a pro-portion of men recently relieved from trench duty the night before. But after riding on ahead and hearing the firing increasing in volume he sent back word for Torrens and all men left in camp to follow immediately and make for the windmill in rear of the 2nd Division camp. In the 68th two companies under Major Wynne had just returned from the trenches (where he had heard the noise of guns being moved during the night and reported it) and a further two companies had already gone down to relieve them. Four companies, therefore, or about 200 men, were all that the Regiment could muster. The weather had turned cold about the 1st of the month; the previous day had been damp and raining; and the men, like the rest of the Army that day, were wearing their grey greatcoats. But after they had been marching for some time they were halted to enable them to throw off their coats that they might get at their ammunition-pouches more easily in action, a measure made necessary by the custom observed in the Regiment of wearing the greatcoats over the accoutrements. The 68th therefore arrived on the scene wearing their red coatees, and for some time was the only regiment of the Army to fight in red.[12]

By the time it arrived Cathcart had already placed Goldie's Brigade (with the exception of a wing of the 20th) and the 1 /Rifles in prolongation of the tenuous line formed in front of the 2nd Division camp and to the left of the post road. The 63rd, on the initiative of Colonel Windham, Cathcart's A.Q.M.G., was diverted to the protection of some guns in that sector of the front. The only force therefore remaining at Cathcart's immediate disposal for a counterstroke was Torrens's Brigade, and that had been reduced to four companies of the 20th, two companies of the 46th and the four companies of the 68th. A fresh assault was developing on the Sandbag Battery on the edge of the escarpment, and a murderous struggle was going on between Pavlov's men and the Guards: the Battery, which was uncompleted and contained no ordnance, changed hands again and again. How was Cathcart best to employ his small reserve? At that moment he noticed a strong Russian column—it was three battalions of the Selinghinsk Regiment—beginning to ascend the slope to take the Guards in the right flank, and, against the positive orders of Raglan's Q.M.G. not to leave the plateau, he launched Torrens's 400 men down the hill upon this attractive target.

The wing of the 20th were on the left of the assaulting line higher up the hill than the 46th companies and the 68th, who were well down the slope on the right. In their red coatees the 68th was plainly recognisable from the Russian batteries massed on the "East Jut" and had attracted their fire before Cathcart, riding to the front, gave the order to charge. At this they worked their way down through the thick scrub with great firmness and resolution, and fell on the Selinghinsk column in a headlong rush, under which it at first crumpled and then fled down the hillside. Colonel Smyth had his horse shot under him. Torrens fell wounded, but was able to receive

[12]Such was the explanation given by Lieut.-Gen. H. H. Morant to Kinglake in 1870, although it must be noted that Morant was not in action that day, having been wounded on 21st October and being confined to his tent. The regimental tradition that the 68th was the only regiment to fight in red at Inkerman clearly needs some qualification, as Capt. Clifford's recently published watercolours show all British troops in red at a later stage of the battle (*Henry Clifford, V.C.: Letters and Sketches from the Crimea*, ed. General Sir Bernard Paget (London, Michael Joseph, 1956).

Cathcart's congratulations as he lay on the ground. His brisk and powerful movement against an enemy about six times his number had carried his men well down into the valley, some even as far as the aqueduct and the meadows of the Chernaya.

Some had got beyond recall when Cathcart, who was short-sighted, discovered that the plain above and behind him was occupied not, as he had thought, by our own people but by a solid mass of Russians—of the Yakutsk Regiment—who had advanced unperceived up the hollow of the Quarry Ravine and now disclosed their identity by firing a volley into the confused ranks below. Making frantic efforts, he got those nearest him to face in the opposite direction and charge up the hill. Major Wynne, a very popular officer, "as good a man to hounds as ever crossed a horse," succeeded in rallying some, but was killed in attempting to "boil up a charge" as it was called; and at about the same time Brevet-Lieut.-Colonel Harry Smyth, the commanding officer's namesake, was mortally wounded. Sir George Cathcart, whose last words were "Well done, 68th!" and several of his staff were shot down under the merciless fire that poured in upon them from above at very short range. Most of the casualties suffered by the 68th were inflicted at this critical moment. The men started to go back, though walking, not running, and it was a matter of as much difficulty to stop them now as it had been to restrain their ardour before. But by the efforts of the officers, under Windham's leadership, most of them were assembled and brought to the rear. A French line battalion covered their movement, which was also in some degree screened by the high scrub and a projecting ledge of rock which hid all but those on horseback. They were withdrawn to the 2nd Division camp, and there issued with ammunition to replenish their empty pouches. Two men, Private John Byrne, a fine fighter who in peace spent most of his time in the cells, and Sergeant Daniel Dwyer, returned into the ravine under a heavy fire to assist some wounded comrades to the rear, an action for which both were later recommended for the Victoria Cross and Byrne's claim approved.

When the ammunition had been distributed Windham, on whom the mantle of command had fallen, led them back into the fight. With two companies of the 20th, two of the 46th, some Riflemen and a party of thirty or so Guardsmen and others who had become detached from their regiments, the 68th companies under Smyth were brought forward to the left of the Guards and on the left of the post road. In this new position, the one they should have occupied at the outset but for Cathcart's rash action, they came under the orders of Pennefather. He led the 68th still farther to the front, to

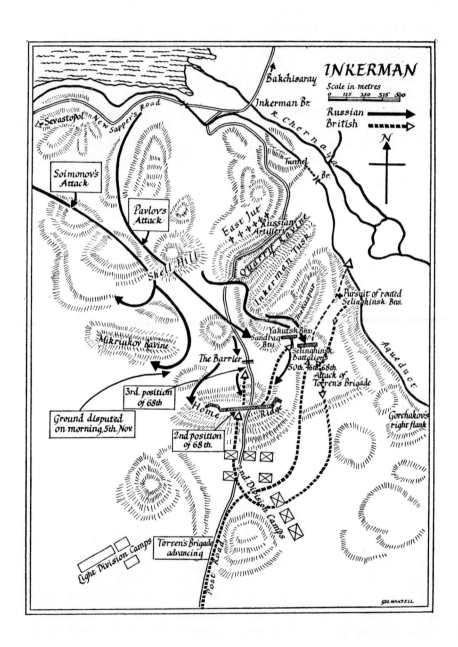

13. Inkerman, 5th November 1854

the head of the Quarry Ravine, with orders to observe the enemy's movements on Shell Hill and harass his artillerymen as best they could with fire from their smooth-bore muskets. As Kinglake says, "the presence of the 68th in an organised state near 'the Barrier' so soon after the false victory of the second period is obviously highly creditable to the Regiment".

The battle was passing through another critical phase as the Russians launched yet another attack on the Inkerman Ridge. After the losses in killed, wounded and missing during the charge there can hardly have been more than a hundred of the 68th to assist the scattered detachments that held the head of the Quarry Ravine against the fresh onslaught. If help from the French, at first declined as unnecessary, had not arrived at this juncture, the Russian attack bade fair to overwhelm by sheer weight of numbers the devoted men fighting there. As it was, however, though Bosquet's men suffered a rude check, reinforcements from the French Army were constantly coming up; and the devastating effect upon the massed Russian batteries on Shell Hill made by the fire of two 18-pounder siege-guns combined to bring about a decisive transformation in the Allies' fortunes. The enemy began to draw back. The men at the Barrier succeeded in maintaining their dogged fight; and the Russian batteries at last withdrew from Shell Hill down into Sevastopol, and their infantry slowly followed. The firing, which had been incessant since an hour before sunrise, died down and ceased altogether about half-past three in the afternoon.

The men of the 4th Division, marched back by Windham, reached camp about 3 o'clock. In the 68th three officers (Brevet-Lieut.-Colonel Harry Smyth, Major Wynne and Lieutenant Barker) and 17 n.c.o.s and men were killed or died of wounds; one officer (Lieutenant Cator) and 33 n.c.o.s and men were wounded; nine men were missing, of whom but one returned from captivity; a total of 69 from a body of men that did not exceed 16 officers and 227 n.c.o.s and men at the outset.

"There is no doubt we did our duty," wrote Colonel Smyth afterwards, justly apprehensive, as it proved, that with the loss of Cathcart, Torrens and Goldie the Regiment would receive scant recognition of its services that day. "Sir George Cathcart," he says, "was too courageous. He had no idea of common caution or prudence." Windham, who knew him better, says that he was a man more fitted to be first than second, but that he was easily "riled" and gave his orders in an over-explanatory fashion, and further confused everyone by naming regiments by their wrong numbers and forgetting which regiments were in which brigade. Nevertheless he had more recent experience—in South Africa—of high command in the field than anyone in the British Army, and had he survived the object of his rash charge would have received more careful consideration. As it is, it must be acknowledged to have been not only contrary to orders but unproductive of any favourable effect on the battle as a whole. Its one redeeming feature, however, was the admirable courage with which it was carried out, which makes it comparable in its way with the charge of the Light Brigade at Balaklava.[13]

After Inkerman the winter set in and the situation of the British Army at once wore a serious aspect. Whatever the tourist agencies may say, the whole of the Crimea (except the favoured part around Yalta and Alupka that is sheltered by the Yaila Mountains) is open steppe swept by the same icy winds that blow over the whole of Muscovy, though not for so long. The winter of 1854 began about 1st November with rain by day and frosts by night, and continued until about 15th February 1855, when Colonel Smyth noted that they "had jumped into spring". On 2nd April he was writing that the weather was perfect. From about then the sun shone clear from a limpid, almost indigo, sky on the yellow churned up earth of the trenches. Before, however, the snow started to fall in December the rain had turned the camp into a swamp. The men were always wet, and the trenches—not the deep slits which the Army of 1914-1918 knew in Flanders, but broad shallow ditches barely shoulder-high— were full of water. Lieutenant Battiscombe wrote to his father, who was Vicar of Barkway, that "it is as bad as if you were told to go in the big field opposite the house and lie down in the ditch all day and all night, only instead of being quiet you are being fired at by Russians and in constant dread of an attack". In the night of 14th November Sevastopol was visited by a tremendous thunderstorm and gale which tore down most of the tents and scattered stores and possessions beyond recovery, as well as destroying or damaging much of the shipping in harbour at Balaklava. An informal truce was observed by both sides for twenty-four hours. Those in the trenches lost their way and walked four miles back to camp. "Such a scene of confusion" says Colonel Smyth. "Caps flying away, and in the middle of the storm the big drum belonging to some other regiment came rolling through our lines. It was impossible to stop it," he said, adding, however, more philosophically than most, that no one was the worse except for a little lumbago, and "two dry days made us dry but dirtier than ever". Beards became the fashion as a protection

[13]For the Battle of Inkerman see: Smyth's letters in ms.; *The Crimean Letters and Diaries of Lieut.-Gen. Sir Charles Ash Windham*, ed. Sir W. H. Russell (London, 1897), pp. 59-62, 65-70; Digest; W.O.12/7667.

for the throat; and a service that had been traditionally clean-shaven for over 150 years, even when foreign services were sporting moustaches, came back from the Crimea covered in luxuriant hair to distinguish the veterans from those who had stayed at home. At first there was no other protection. The clothing that had been suitable in Malta was in rags, and the undressed sheep-skin coats and hoods supplied from home arrived when the worst of the winter was over, to turn the men, as it was said, into "Robinson Crusoes".

The discomforts of this period have been sufficiently laboured. At first there was ample fuel to be had from the roots of vines and the scrub-oak that covered the plateau in abundance and made "capital fuel—it smoulders and gives heat but will not blaze". That, however, did not last long, and it was supplemented from other sources. As late as January it was apparently possible for bold individuals in the advanced picquets to make a dash into the suburbs of Sevastopol and bring back sofas and tables for firewood. By that time tents had given way to huts, but the ground was "as bare as the road in Eaton Square". For a time the Commissariat was unable to supply full rations. Everything above what the Commissariat supplied, which was only meat, bread and coffee in the bean, was unobtainable. "Bread and cheese, and gin and water" was Colonel Smyth's luncheon on 20th November. Later, better things came up from Balaklava, and bottles were emptied in such profusion by our Crimean Army that huts were constructed from them and they were lying about the camp sites as recently as thirty or forty years ago—and perhaps still do. But for the first months there was no transport, nor any fodder for the transport, even for so short a distance as separated the camps from Balaklava. Everything, at any rate in the 68th, depended on the officers' private horses, which numbered eighteen, whether for luxuries like gin or necessities like the hut for the regimental hospital. For this humiliating state of affairs men in Smyth's position were inclined to blame Raglan for not getting about to see more with his own eyes. "His great panacea for all ills is an extra ration of rum," he wrote; and again, on Raglan's death: "He never came into collision with the men. They only knew him as a good old man who sometimes ordered them an extra glass of grog." By the end of March the situation was much improved. Some officers kept chickens. The rail-road from Balaklava—there were no steam locomotives until November 1855—was working; and there was a canteen selling beer and porter and other things at properly regulated prices.

It is hardly to be wondered at if in these circumstances the sickness was general. The amount of work to do—the trenches, the fatigue-parties, the working-parties—remained constant; and as the men to do it dwindled so those that remained were worked the harder. The sufferings of the Army as revealed by that newcomer to the battlefield, the war-correspondent, caused a quite extraordinary revulsion of feeling at home, which, really, is more remarkable than the losses themselves. Fundamentally it sprang from the new social conscience of the age. So remote had the Army been from society that, though the officers knew what their men were capable of, it was a revelation to the country at large. "It is a consolation," wrote Colonel Smyth on 20th November, "to read in the papers that the English Army here are not the pack of rascals they are sometimes considered in England." For all the wind, the rain, the snow, the lack of food, "the British soldier's pluck," he wrote, with the image of the men of the 68th before him, "does not desert him. He grumbles to be sure. But is not this meritorious? He does his work until he goes to hospital never to return." And: "the trouble is our men are such perfect machines. They fight as everyone knows: but if food is not put into their mouths, if fresh lodging is not found for them, they would lie down and die. It is only by being at them continually that one can get them to build a mud wall to protect their tents or anything else. To be sure they are hard-worked, but they seem unable to look beyond the event of the moment." In point of morale and fighting power it was probably the best army we had put into the field at the outset of a war. Nor was it squandered like so many of its predecessors. The mortality through disease in the 68th was bad enough: but the Regiment had experienced worse, even if the war-correspondent did not know it.

The figures (in studying which it is well to remember that the 68th was less severely struck than some, and that until 4th April 1855 it had a kind of reserve in the two companies at Lord Raglan's Headquarters) are as follows. It landed in the Crimea with about 750 rank and file "present fit". By 1st October this had dropped to 644; by 1st December to 632; 1st January 1855, 491; 1st February, 371. There were 207 men fit for the trenches on 4th January, 170 on the 12th, 150 on the 31st. On the 1st March the "present fit" figure rose to 439; 412 in April, 409 in May, 411 in June, 455 in July, 449 in August, 409 in September, 528 in October, 526 in November, 599 in April 1856, 602 in May, 674 in June, and 745 in July 1856.

The officers present dropped from 25 in October 1854 to 20 in February 1855, 16 in April and May, and 17 in July, August and September. In November there were 27; in June 1856, 30. So many of the original officers had gone by 31st December 1854 that Smyth wrote that a new race was springing up in the Regiment and "I find they look on me as an old man". Only two served with the Regiment throughout from beginning to end: Captain Somerville and Lieutenant Cassidy. Smyth, Macbeath (the son of the old quartermaster), Blount, Lewis, Finch, Shuttleworth, Vaughan (Adjutant from December 1854 to August 1855), Battiscombe, Tucker and Quartermaster Tunks saw most of the war but had short periods of leave. Hamilton (Adjutant on landing) served in the Crimea throughout, but from October 1855 held a staff situation. Five were killed. Most who came away did so to recover from wounds or sickness, and four of them (Lieutenant H. Smyth, son of the Colonel Smyth mortally wounded at Inkerman, Captain Storer, Paymaster Hadley and Assistant-Surgeon Johnston) died while on sick-leave. None sold out in the great "funk" period of the winter, when many seriously asked themselves if the military life was for them. On the contrary, when in January 1855 the service-companies were found, through promotions, to have a captain supernumerary to the establishment, Smyth gave the choice of going to every captain in turn by seniority: "*all* refused to go, so I was obliged to order the junior," Captain FitzRoy.

The sick-rate dropped from 74 in September 1854 to 61 in October (mostly cholera), but it rose to 110 in November, 150 in December, 327 in January 1855, and then dropped again: 251 in February, 211 in March, 182 in April, 157 in May, 187 in June, 131 in July, 147 in August, 121 in September, and remained around that figure until April 1856, when it stood at 86, and May, when it was 54. During the period 7th August to 30th September 1854 there were 31 deaths through sickness (mostly cholera); from 1st October to 31st December 57; from 1st January 1855 to 31st March 119; from 1st April to 30th June 22; and from then onwards about 4 a quarter. The total casualties in the ranks, killed, died of wounds, died of disease and missing not repatriated, may be summarised as follows:

Killed or died of wounds		45
Missing	26	
Less those repatriated	7	19[14]
Died in the Crimea and at Scutari		243
		307[15]

[14]The figures have been adjusted to allow for the return of Private McGeever, repatriated, who was originally reported killed on 11th May, 1855.

[15]There is a discrepancy between the pay-rolls (W.O.12/7667-7669), which have been used here, and the monthly returns (W.O.17/661, 17/670, 17/769), which appear to have formed the basis for the casualties commemorated on the Regimental Monument in Durham Cathedral. The monthly returns do not always take account of deaths occurring at the General Hospital at Scutari.

These are formidable figures, and they conceal much unrecorded courage and suffering. Is it, though, that we say too much of this, or that we say too little of the West Indies, of Walcheren and the Peninsula, where such losses were too commonplace to excite remark?

In providing reinforcements the depot system initiated in the 1820s worked fairly well, and at least sufficiently well for the Regiment to escape the drafting business of earlier wars. The four depot-companies at Fermoy supplied a spasmodic though fairly satisfactory flow of officers and young soldiers, which mitigated if it did not entirely meet the steady drain caused by death and sickness. The quality of the new men was indifferent. A draft of two young officers (Ensigns Vicars and Deshon) and 70 men that arrived in mid-November 1854 Colonel Smyth found "what might be called 'nice boys'—they have rifles but cannot yet load them"; and another of one officer (Ensign Saunderson) and 26 men, received later that month, were "quite boys". Apart from two-score men who returned from Scutari in March, few reinforcements were received between November and mid-May. These and later drafts were described as "a sad falling off in appearance from what used to be the sort of men we received".

Though the Regiment maintained recruiting-parties at Leeds, Ipswich, Warwick, Bolton, Ballyshannon, Portadown, Birr, Downpatrick, Lisburn and, from January 1855, at Durham, the normal methods of recruiting were not sufficient to make good the losses of old soldiers. Volunteering from the militia was again resorted to; since the militia had been embodied in 1852 on a voluntary basis and not by the ballot, it had lost some of its character, and the men were not on the whole of the old quality. The 68th received a total of 357 recruits from this source, principally from the Tyrone, 2nd West Yorkshire, York and South Mayo Regiments, but above all from the Armagh Militia, which supplied no less than 207 between 23rd and 27th June 1855. Not many, however, reached the service-companies. Some Warwickshire militiamen joined in the Crimea in February: they had been trained in the use of the Minié rifle but were sent out with the old musket. The volunteers from the 2nd West Yorks (whose colonel was Smyth's brother) were described as "decent". Most militia volunteers got only as far as Malta, where the four additional Reserve Companies authorised in the establishment of June 1854 set up shop as a kind of base-depot under the command of Captains Trent and Spratt on 11th March 1855. From that date all reinforcements from home, officers and recruits alike, underwent two or three months' training before being dispatched to the service-companies. A total of about 570 men, recruits and militia volunteers, joined the service-companies between December 1854 and March 1856.

There was never any shortage of applicants for commissions, though experienced officers were always at a premium. Several ensigncies were granted to militia officers: Clarkson, Nicholetts and Thornton, (in time to arrive in the Crimea in September 1855), and Duesbury, Hardy, Harrison, Turnor and Briggs, (too late to see any active service). The special ensigncy granted in January 1855 by the Queen to a non-commissioned officer in every cavalry and infantry regiment in the Crimea, "as a mark of her recognition of the meritorious services of the n.c.o.s of the Army," was given to the Sergeant-Major, Joseph Thompson. He had come out from the Depot to succeed Sergeant-Major Leggatt on the latter's receiving an ensigncy in the 1st Regiment on 3rd November 1854. However, he had barely received his gift and had been succeeded by Sergeant-Major Gibbons before he died. The other junior officers who joined the service-companies from May 1855 onwards (Grace, Seymour, Blood, Villiers-Stuart and Covey) had received their commissions in the usual manner.

Like all regiments, therefore, the 68th faced the remaining nine months of the siege in a progressively more and more diluted condition. It was not, however, so badly off as some, and its behaviour in the two serious engagements in which it was involved, both of them the powerful and determined sorties the garrison was in the habit of making, showed that it had lost none of its fighting quality.

The first occurred in the night of 12th January 1855. There was a slight thaw that night, and the Russians were celebrating their New Year. They had lighted great watchfires on the North Side and illuminated the hills above the Chernaya with rows of lights, which shone brilliantly through the darkness of the winter night. The windows of the public buildings in the town were ablaze with light, tantalising our advanced picquets with their gaiety. The parties in the advanced works had been put on the alert. A steady sergeant and about a dozen volunteers had been placed in the rifle-pits in front of the trenches to give warning of any movement. At a quarter-past one in the morning of the 13th the Russians inside their lines gave a loud cheer, and immediately an intense fire of musketry broke out on all sides. There were three officers and 175 men of the 21st and 68th in the advanced trenches on Green Hill at the time, who were suddenly assailed by two volleys from their front and another from their right. Under loud cries of "Rake!" they stood to their arms and replied as best they could. The sergeant's party in the rifle-pits had been surprised and taken in the din and confusion, and before they knew what had happened the men in the trenches were being attacked by three or four hundred of the enemy. They retired to a trench in their rear, and rallying, fired to such effect that the Russians withdrew to their lines without having made any impression. They took with them, however, a sergeant and fourteen men of the Regiment, of whom ten died in captivity, some, presumably, from their wounds. An officer (Lieutenant Battiscombe) and six men were wounded.[16]

The second sortie in which the Regiment was involved took place in the night of 11th May, when a force of about 2000 of the enemy made a determined assault on the forward trenches of the Left Attack. The trench was occupied by detachments from the 46th, 1/Rifle Brigade and the 68th. The 68th detachment consisted of about 250 men under Brevet-Lieut.-Colonel Macbeath, who had returned to the Regiment from guard-duty at Headquarters the previous month, and Captain Hamilton, formerly adjutant. The 68th were in the centre, the 1/Rifle Brigade on the right.[17] The night was so dark that nothing was visible, and there was a storm of wind and rain. All this made the officers uneasy, and the sentries were constantly visited. At about midnight the sentries in front of the left fired suddenly and fell back to the trench, and the whole stood to their arms. The Russians advanced in strong columns trying to force their way into the part of the trench held by the 68th, who, though at first in doubt whether they were friend or foe until Sergeant Gereghty gallantly crossed the parapet to make sure, gave them repeated volleys and resisted them in the most determined manner with the bayonet for an hour. Private Byrne, whose conduct at Inkerman has already been noted, maintained a hand-to-hand fight on the parapet with one Russian, finally stabbing him and taking his arms. About thirty of the enemy succeeded in actually entering the trench and gaining possession of No. 8 Battery, spiking one of the guns. Captain Hamilton, however, collecting a party of volunteers, including Sergeant Sladden, Corporal Glinane and Privates Cormick, Fitzpatrick, Sales, Smith and Sandys, boldly charged them and drove them out with the bayonet, killing both of

[16]Letter of Capt. H. L. Battiscombe, 19th Jan. 1855, in the *Regimental Journal*, Vol. 8 (1956), pp. 357-358.

[17]Col. C. F. Campbell, 46th (*Letters from Camp . . . during the Siege of Sevastopol* (London, 1894, p. 207), says the 68th were on the left; but Col. Smyth, who was in a position to have more accurate information, says they were in the centre. According to Vane (p. 88), there was some doubt whether Macbeath was in command that night. Col. Smyth's ms. letter of 14th May is quite categorical on the fact that he was, and Macbeath is moreover cited as a witness in Hamilton's recommendation for the Victoria Cross (W.O.98/2).

the Russian officers and several of the men. Outnumbered, they could not pursue, but waited for the reserves to come up from the rear; these, instead of taking the short cut across the open, were brought up by the zig-zag saps, by which time the Russians had gone off carrying their dead and wounded with them.

This gallant action earned Captain Hamilton the Victoria Cross and cost the Regiment one officer (Captain Edwards) and nine men killed or mortally wounded, eighteen n.c.o.s and men wounded, and one man missing. Though one of the most decisive repulses inflicted on the garrison in the whole course of the siege, it received poor recognition at the time, partly because the war-correspondents were away "covering" the Allied expedition that captured Kerch on the Sea of Azov, partly because the officer commanding the Left Attack that night was not present. Colonel M'Pherson was a game old gentleman with a bristling white beard, an old "Peninsular" who had commanded his regiment and had been employed on Sir Charles Napier's staff in Sind ten years before. But he could not face the wind and rain on that dark night, and as Lord Raglan could not mention him in his dispatch he mentioned no one. M'Pherson was superannuated a month later, and gave up command of the 1st Brigade of the 4th Division to Sir John Campbell. (Indeed, the rough work in the trenches of Sevastopol was proving too much for the older men. The commander of the 2nd Brigade since Inkerman, General Garrett, formerly of the 46th, another "Peninsular" and aged 60, was commonly known as "General Chaos": fortunately he had his son with him as brigade-major, who "puts things right" as Colonel Smyth wrote.)

There was not much fighting for the 68th after 11th May apart from the daily drudge in the trenches, which exacted a steady but not serious toll from the strength. Lieutenant Marshall and one man was killed in the attack on the Quarries in the night of the 7th June; but the Regiment was in reserve in the great unsuccessful assault on the Redan that was launched on the 18th, and was not engaged. "Everyone," wrote Colonel Smyth of this unlucky business,

> "was certain of succeeding. We left the camp at a quarter to two this morning [the 18th] and at daylight the attack began. We began our attack before the French [attack on the Malakhov], and mistakes were made, and the whole thing failed . . . I am grateful that the 68th, being in reserve, did not suffer—a selfish feeling—but taking it all in all it has given me a feeling of disgust at the whole business . . . We mismanaged somehow. Lord Raglan's plans were good but the Russians' better! General Bentinck [commanding the 4th Division] explained the whole plan of attack to us in the clearest manner, but as Sir J. Campbell's Brigade was to lead the attack he left the minor

details to us, and he made no arrangements, and rushed out with about thirty men to certain death. We went down to the Vorontsov Road at about 1.30, and remained there in reserve (all the shots going over our heads). We had no man touched. My place was close to the temporary hospital, and a very unpleasant one. We were ordered back to the camp, and I got as much rest and washing as I could, and was just going to eat dinner in the evening when I was ordered down to the trenches . . ."

Duty in the trenches became harder as the weeks wore on. The death of Raglan removed a commander who was so superior to all that no one questioned. His successors found it harder to impose their authority. There was an atmosphere of acrimony abroad, and everyone was very tired. But the end was in sight. The last casualties the Regiment suffered were on 20th August, and on 8th September the French delivered their final assault on the Malakhov, which, crowned with success, led to the evacuation of the town that night. Colonel Smyth, who had been the first field-officer on duty in the Left Attack on 10th October 1854 was the last on 24th September 1855, when the duty was discontinued.

Little more remains to be said. The Allies had at last achieved their object in the destruction of the base of the Black Sea Fleet, and although the Army remained, and even flourished, in the camps for another winter while the negotiations were proceeding, it had no further work to do. The 68th came again under the command of Lord William Paulet when he succeeded Garrett in command of the 2nd Brigade in October. Coming out on the staff of the Cavalry Division, he had been sent to Scutari much against his will in December 1854 to induce some order into the place. There, of course, he encountered the formidable Miss Nightingale, who, after some partial engagements in which she failed to gain her point, declared him a "broken reed"—which is probably the best compliment a soldier like him could have been paid. Miss Nightingale, incidentally, "went soft" on a soldier of the 68th, Private 3308 Robert Robinson, a young lad who had come out to Malta with the draft from the Depot on 20th July 1854 and was invalided to Scutari from the Crimea so early as 18th September, even before the Alma. He described himself as "Miss Nightingale's man," although he was hardly tall enough to carry an umbrella over her head. He eventually received his discharge on the payment of £20 on 15th September 1856.[18] Useful in his way, no doubt, he was not a man whom the 68th had as much reason to remember as Private John Byrne, V.C., a very different character, exemplary in war as he was to show again

[18] W.O.12/7667.

in New Zealand ten years after Inkerman, but, poor fellow, no peacetime soldier: as a colour-sergeant he was appointed to the staff of the 2nd North Durham Militia, from which he was discharged for insubordination and highly improper conduct in 1872, a few weeks before his death.

The dispersal of the Army had already begun before it was announced in General Orders of 2nd May 1856 that the 3rd, 46th and 68th were destined for Corfu, the most favoured of the Mediterranean stations, and the Regiment embarked in the *Rippon* at 7 in the morning of the 16th. They landed on the 24th. "I really think," said Colonel Smyth, who had thought there was a chance of their returning to England, "we ought to be very thankful to have dropped on our legs here. . . . It was a curious contrast, the bronzed faces and beards of the Crimean regiments with the pale smooth faces of the Mediterraneans whom we relieved." Detachments were sent to Zante, Ithaca and Cerigo, which, however, in July of next year, were brought together again and embarked for Portsmouth, where the Regiment landed in September 1857.

Eleven years had passed since they were there before as Paulet's regiment, just returned from Canada. There were still 100 men of that regiment serving, but this time the Regiment returned as veterans of a bloody war, the honours of *Alma, Inkerman* and *Sevastopol*, (granted on 16th October 1855) on their colours, and most of the men wearing the Crimean medal ribbon.[19]

---

[19]The first distribution of medals and clasps took place on 18th Sept. 1855. 116 received the clasps for Alma and Inkerman; 84 that for the Alma; 13 that for Inkerman and Sevastopol; 299 that for Sevastopol; and 354 for all three. On the face of it the Inkerman award, which amounts to 483, appears too liberal, not more than 230 men at the most having actually fought in the action.

CHAPTER VI

THE NEW ZEALAND WAR AND AFTER,
1857-1873

HAVING reformed everything else, the reforming hand of the Victorian age was laid upon the army. The Crimean War was supposed to have exposed defects in a system which had been elaborated but not radically changed for a century and a half, and a transformation was foreshadowed. For a decade, however, the army enjoyed a brief Indian summer before the chill set in, and in those years both the old 68th and its long-service soldiers made their last appearance.

The type of man serving with the Regiment at that time has been described by an officer who, as a newly commissioned subaltern, joined at Fermoy the Depot Battalion of which the 68th's two depot-companies formed a part. "Nearly all the older officers," he says, "had seen service in the Crimean War, which was then only a recent event. The majority of them were splendid fellows: that long siege had been a wonderful school for the forming of manly characters. They had a type and manner of their own. Their hair was not cut short, as in the present day, but was worn long over the ears: and they had large fuzzy whiskers with moustaches that went straight into them. They smoked much and some of them drank a good deal, but they carried their liquor well." The men were of the same solid stamp. A party sent to Limerick in May 1859 to the assistance of the civil power was composed entirely of men from the 13th and 68th. It was on the occasion of an election—in the days before the secret ballot. "There were a few broken heads, but on the whole the mob and the soldiers got on remarkably well. The ladies of the town came up with the most delightful freedom of expression to the line of soldiers which had closed across the streets after a batch of terrified voters had been got through, . . . any officer or soldier of exceptional size or feature being especially selected for the tongue-target. The old soldiers looked stolidly out upon the viragoes, though one could see at times in their eyes that some shaft of ridicule had struck home."[1]

In 1857, when the suppression of the mutiny of the Bengal Army was still far from complete, a regiment could not expect long at home; and in December of that year, when the 68th had been no more than three months at Portsmouth, it was embarked again, this time for Madras, under the command once more of Colonel Smyth. Two companies, C and I, Captain Spratt's and Cassidy's, were detached to Fermoy as depot-companies. The remaining ten, 39 officers and 805 n.c.o.s and men strong (the establishment, raised the previous month, was 1291) were embarked in two wings, the left in the *Argo*, the right in the *Australasian*, which reached Madras on 9th and 5th March respectively.

The Regiment was almost at once carried on to Burma, which, in East India Company days, was so to speak an outlier of the Madras Presidency. British Burma comprised at that time only the part known as Lower Burma. The frontier as fixed since the Second Burmese War of 1852-3 lay athwart the Irrawaddy about Thayetmyo, where the so called "Frontier Brigade" was posted; and throughout the 68th's tour of duty, from 1858 to 1863, it was customary to keep two, if not three, companies of the Regiment at Thayetmyo and one at Myede (now Allanmyo) opposite. The other six or seven remained at Rangoon, where they were quartered in the Cantonment, at a discreet distance from the polyglot population of Burmans, Brahmins, Jews, Parsees, Chinese, Bengalis, Moguls, and Madras sepoys with their hats

> "like the top of a pump
> Or the posts over which little blackguard boys jump."

The first step in the routine was carried out 23rd October, when three companies relieved three companies of the 29th Regiment, which was suddenly summoned to Bengal.

Of these monotonous five years there is little to say. The only event of historical importance was the transfer of power from the Company to the Crown, which took place on 1st November 1858. The Company's flag was hauled down that day, but the significance of the occasion, which was to have such an effect on the Regiment's history, passed unremarked at the time. Colonel Smyth handed over the command to Lieut.-Colonel Greer in December 1858. Lieut.-Colonel Lloyd commanded temporarily in 1861, and Lieut.-Colonel

[1]Lieut.-Gen. Sir W. F. Butler, *Autobiography* (London, 1911), pp. 15, 17 (*cit.* hereafter as "Butler").

Morant from February 1862 to March 1864. Lieut.-Colonel Morant, who had a dry and occasionally trenchant sense of humour, was responsible for a regimental order of interest to sociologists, in which, observing that he was "surprised to discover that not twenty men per company wash themselves daily, or at least certainly not the whole body," he prescribed a daily bathing parade. In other respects the 68th was wet enough, and a regimental wit produced a skit on "The Old Folks at Home" (a new song from America) of which the second verse went:

> "Talk of the climate of Calcutta,
> At least there it's dry.
> Here we are perched up in bungalows
> On stilts five feet high.
> And if ever it clears sufficiently
> For us to be reviewed,
> All that the General can say of us
> Is that we are all mildewed.
>> Oh, a dull and dreary quarter
>> Is this same Rangoon.
>> One single wish pervades its inmates
>> That they may leave it soon."

The quotation is from the earliest example of a regimental journal, *The D.L.I. Gazette, or the Wanderers' Magazine*. (It antedates by six years that of the 12th, for which a claim as the earliest magazine of a line regiment has been entered.) When the Regiment was under orders for Madras in 1857 some enterprising soul bought a printing-press "to assist in relieving the monotony of the long voyage before them". The printing-press went in the *Argo*, which, by the time the *Australasian* caught her up in the Cape Verde Islands, had produced a number of the *Argo* newspaper. So stimulated was the *Australasian* that under the combined editorship of Captains Trent, FitzRoy and Vaughan it produced in manuscript *The Sea, or Floating Gentleman's Magazine*, two numbers of which were run off on arrival at Cape Town, a further two at Madras, and a fifth at Rangoon. The *Argo* had meanwhile printed six. On the reunion of the two wings the same three officers assumed the editorship of *The D.L.I. Gazette*, a distillation of the talent of the whole Regiment; and although FitzRoy and Vaughan had both left the battalion by May 1859, the *Gazette* continued at least fitfully until March 1861.[2] The *Gazette* is an important document for the regimental historian. For the first time in its

[2] The *Bugle* was a product of the 2nd Battalion in India in 1894 and persisted until November 1900. The present *Journal* derives from the *Review*, which first appeared in 1922 and lasted until 1934.

history—even counting the narratives of "Jonas" and John Green, which are, alas, but limited in their view—the more articulate part of the Regiment speaks as a whole. There is revealed a body of men taking good-humouredly and philosophically the ups and downs of the military existence, organising theatricals, regattas, cricket-matches (the 68th carried its stumps with it to the Crimea and Burma and New Zealand), steeplechases, the D.L.I. Hunt, balls and horticultural shows (with prizes for Private Hartley and his carrots, peas and beetroots), indulging in a little homesickness, but at the same time implicitly showing itself a body of men with a lively regimental spirit which is clearly not of only recent growth. It is commonly said that in Purchase days the practice of officers ex-changing and getting promoted out of their regiments militated against *esprit-de-corps*. It is evident from the *Gazette* that there were always enough officers left, and those not only the paymaster, the adjutant and the surgeon, to transmit a strong sense of modest regimental pride. If there is foundation for the objection in other regiments, there is certainly none in the 68th of those years.

In August 1863 the 68th was fourth on the list for relief and would have returned home with the 74th, 1/13th, 69th and 43rd. But at that moment the Governor of New Zealand, Sir George Grey, asked for 3000 reinforcements to deal with a fresh outbreak of hostilities with the Maoris, and the 50th from Ceylon, the 68th and 43rd were sent in response to his appeal.[3]

§

In the 1860s the British settlement of New Zealand was barely twenty years old. The earliest settlements had been made on the Bay of Islands in the promontory north of Auckland. These had spread to Auckland (in 1863 a town of wooden houses with a population of about 14,000) and the country south as far as the Waikato River, which, with its tributary the Mangatawhiri, formed a kind of fron-tier with the Maori country in the interior. There were besides in the North Island the settlement of Taranaki, founded in 1841; Welling-ton, founded by the New Zealand Company in 1840; Wanganui, and elsewhere on the coast; all of which in the intervening years had extended their territory by successive purchases from the native tribes. The method of purchase was theoretically regulated by the Treaty of Waitangi, 6th February 1840, which guaranteed to the Maori tribes, in return for an acknowledgment of the Queen's government, a full, exclusive and undisturbed possession of their

[3]W.O.33/16, pp. 127-128, 167, 170-171.

lands until they should be disposed to sell any parts of them to the Crown. In fact, however, the title of the vendor was often disputed, and the Maoris, a proud, intelligent and warlike people, had as often gone to war in support of their claim. This had happened in the Bay of Islands in the 'forties, and again over the purchase of the so called Waitara Block of land in Taranaki. The latter dispute had been patched up by an uneasy truce in 1861. The Maori chiefs meanwhile, realising that their land was slowly but irrevocably passing to the European, made some attempt to unite in resisting the tendency, and elected a king in the person of the old warrior Te Wherowhero, who ruled from a "capital" at Ngaruawahia, in the heart of the tribal lands of the Waikatos, the most influential and warlike of all. With the pursuit of a "forward policy" on the part of the New Zealand government, and the spread of the "king movement" among the Maoris, relations between settlers and natives deteriorated sadly in the two years following the Waitara truce.

It must be said at once that the Maori enjoyed fighting. He had discovered, moreover, what other savage people have discovered, that the British soldier gave him a scrap after his own heart. His leaders were field engineers of a high order. They had learned by long practice to construct in a surprisingly short time the peculiar form of fieldwork, the *pa*, which gave the Maori wars their distinguishing mark. The *pa* was a chain of rifle-pits connected by a network of trenches and underground passages, protected by a timber palisade, dug deep enough to cover the whole body and as skilfully sited as any of Todleben's works before Sevastopol. Its construction had been ingeniously adapted to musketry on the arrival of the European, exposure to whose arms had brought the Maori down into the plains from the commanding heights he had previously favoured; and the palisade, originally used as barbed wire was from 1914 to 1918, so far from being strengthened to resist small arms and artillery fire, was (very sensibly) lightened to minimise what was recognised as the principal danger of artillery fire, namely splinters. With an enemy so skilful, so stoically brave and so industrious, the war took on, in a service recently released from the trenches of the Crimea, tactical features reminiscent of Cæsar's wars in Gaul. Every march and every movement made in territory even remotely hostile was crowned by the construction of a redoubt.

In implementation of the "forward policy" General Cameron, the General Officer Commanding, who had commanded the 42nd at the Alma, started at the end of December 1861 the building of a high road from Auckland southward to the limit of the European districts at Pokeno, near which place a large redoubt, the Queen's Redoubt, was laid out on 28th May 1862. Work on the redoubt and the pro-longation of the road was continued until March 1863, when an emergency arose in Taranaki calling for reinforcements. The settlers there were readmitted to the Tataráimaka Block, abandoned by them in 1861, and the Waitara Block was in return relinquished. This last gesture of conciliation, however, was insufficient. A party of the 57th under Lieutenant Tragett was ambushed by tribesmen from the Taranaki and the Ngatiruani, and slaughtered. Very soon after, in June, the Mataitawa tribe came out, shortly followed by the Waikato, the champions of the Maori race. A serious war was now at hand. Settlers were murdered almost in the outskirts of Auckland. Reinforcements from India were summoned; and Cameron, leaving New Plymouth on the defensive and transferring his headquarters to the Queen's Redoubt, assembled a force of about 1400 British in-fantry on the Great South Road with a view to penetrating deep into the heart of the "king country".

Active operations started with the crossing of the Mangatawhiri River and the occupation of Koheroa on 17th July. Cameron pushed on for Whangamarino, but his progress was slow owing to the precarious communication by road. The military posts on the Road near Drury were constantly under the threat of attack; and although the tribes on the south bank of the Waikato obligingly allowed the course of the river to be neutral from the Heads to Kohekohe, Cameron's supply route was not reasonably secure until his capture of Meremere on 1st November. On 21st November he won an important advantage at Rangiriri, and on 8th December he reached Ngaruawahia, the "king's" capital, which had been abandoned. The achievement was celebrated by felling the "king's" flagstaff. Tuhikaramea was reached on 1st January 1864, when Cameron was joined by a force he had detached through friendly country from Raglan to the Waipa River. He now looked to Rangiaohia, the chief place of the powerful Ngatimaniapoto tribe. Advancing in two columns from Whatawhata and Tuhikaramea with about 2400 men and turning the *pas* he encountered, he reached Rangiaohia on 21st February, surprised it and held it against a counter-attack on the 22nd. But once again the Maoris dispersed, eastwards towards the Maungatautari Range. Following, Cameron attacked a *pa* at Orakau, where the Maori chief delivered the famous reply, "The word of the Maori is, we will fight for ever and ever and ever." He was told, "Send away the women," to which he replied, "The women will fight too." Eventually the Maoris came out without surrendering although starved for two days, and all but thirty-three were killed. After this qualified success Cameron on 7th April led a reconnais-

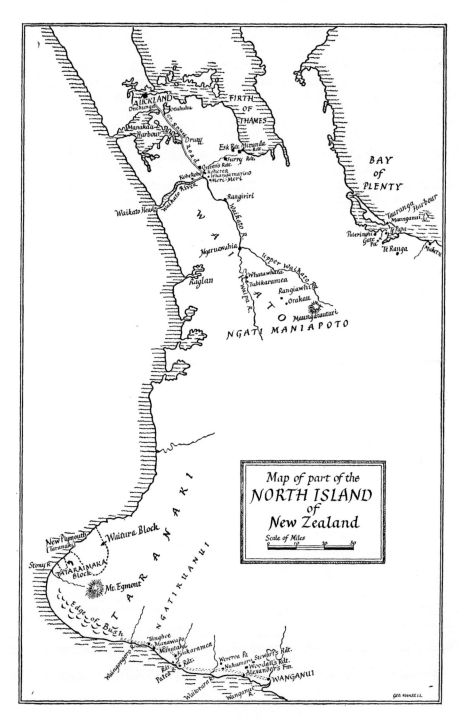

14. General Map of North Island, New Zealand

sance in force to the Maungatatauri Range, but found the *pas* there deserted. He had penetrated over seventy miles into enemy country; although he had been consistently successful he had failed to achieve anything decisive owing to his enemy's elusiveness; and his force was strung out in the redoubts along his line of communication. At this juncture his attention was diverted by the spread of the rebellion into the north-east of the Island.[4]

When at Meremere he had ordered a diversionary force of some 900 men under Colonel Carey from Otahuhu to the Firth of Thames; which, landing on the west side of the bay, had by 9th December 1863 established a chain of posts (Miranda, Esk and Surrey Redoubts) across the country to the Queen's Redoubt. This acquisition of territory had hardly been consolidated before news was received that the east coast Maoris had joined in the "king movement". Cameron was then planning his advance on Rangiaohia, and he sent Carey with another diversionary force to the Bay of Plenty partly to protect the Mission Station at Te Papa, partly to give countenance to those tribes that remained friendly, and partly to discourage the east coast tribes from moving across to the assistance of the tribes in his own front. Most of the reinforcements from India having arrived by this time, Carey's force consisted of about 700 of the newcomers, including a detachment of the 43rd and 14 officers and 407 n.c.o.s and men of the 68th. They were embarked in H.M.S. *Miranda* and the *Corio* steamer, and landed in Tauranga harbour on 22nd January 1864, encamping peacefully in the clover fields surrounding the Mission Station and constructing, in the manner that had become customary, two redoubts. One, that thrown up by the detachment of the 43rd (Monmouth) Regiment, was formed from an old *pa* on the bluff above the waterfront close by the Mission Station, and was called the Monmouth Redoubt; the other, thrown up by the detachment of the 68th, about half a mile away at the opposite angle of the ground taken up for the encampment, was called the Durham Redoubt. (The site of Monmouth Redoubt is still

[4]For the Maori War generally see: the reports of the Deputy-Q.M.G., Colonel Gamble, in W.O.107/7; W.O.33/16; A. J. Harrop, *England and the Maori Wars* (London, New Zealand News, 1937); Elsdon Best, *The Pa Maori* (Bulletin No. 6 of the Dominion Museum, Wellington, 1927). For the part taken in it by the 68th I have had the advantage of the ms. diaries of Major Sheffield Grace, kindly lent to me by his daughter, Lady Thompson, and of the ms. diary of Lieut.-Col. C. U. Shuttleworth, at the Depot, which also holds some of the beautiful drawings by Lieut.-Gen. H. G. Robley, then serving as a subaltern in the Regiment. See also Maj.-Gen. Sir J. E. Alexander, *Bush Fighting* (London, 1873). Presumably, too, the anonymous Victorian romance in two volumes, *Henry Ancrum*, reflects regimental sentiment, inasmuch as it was written by Brig.-Gen. J. H. Kirby, who was then a major in the 68th (Alexander, p. 210).

plainly visible in the flourishing modern town of Tauranga: Durham
Redoubt has been obliterated by development, but its existence is
preserved in the name of Durham Street.) In the months that
followed the bush and scrub were cleared, and the two redoubts
were made the strong-points of a defensive system of trenches and
rifle-pits covering the approaches to Te Papa.

For three months all was quiet. Colonel Carey, described by a 68th
officer as "the most fussy, uncivil commanding officer I ever came
across," "most vacillating and undecided," left for Auckland on 11th
March, and Lieut.-Colonel Greer, "looking very well and very
affable," arrived from leave on the 16th to take over command of
the 68th from Morant as well as to assume control of the Tauranga
District. Greer was an Irishman of 40, who, connected by marriage
to the two Smyths in the 68th who died in the Crimean War, had
served 23 years with the Regiment but had reached the Crimea too
late to take part in the siege of Sevastopol. He was greeted with
much satisfaction by his men, who cheered him when he spoke to
them, and animated his officers with a new spirit.

The 68th had been embarked with their womenfolk at Rangoon
during October and November in three ships: the *Australian*, which
reached Auckland on 8th January with 9 officers and 298 n.c.o.s and
men; the *Light Brigade*, which arrived on the 18th with 12 officers
and 268 n.c.o.s and men; and the *Armenian*, which arrived on 23rd
January with 7 officers and 348 n.c.o.s and men—a total of 28 officers
and 914 n.c.o.s and men. Most of the detachment in the *Armenian*,
which, though the first ship to leave Rangoon, arrived after Carey's
force had left for Tauranga, was sent up to Meremere on Cameron's
line of communication; but some were quartered in the Albert
Barracks in Auckland.

All, however, officers and men alike, before being sent up country
on service were issued with blue "jumpers" in place of red coats and
wore the forage-cap in place of the shako. In other words the 68th
had fought their last action in red. Nor was an encampment in New
Zealand quite what it was even in the Crimea. All marched with a
greatcoat and blanket folded bandolierwise over the shoulder and a
day's cooked rations in the haversack. Officers slept about four to a
bell-tent in which heaps of fern did for a bed, and "it was considered
a capital plan to take your tent-pegs out of the little canvas bag that
held them and, stuffing it with fern, to use it as a pillow". The men
slept on fern likewise, and "at night the occupants of almost every
tent would be engaged in listening to some story-teller . . . who
would begin his marvellous narrative with 'There was once a king
in the north of Ireland,' or 'There was a giant,' or some equally

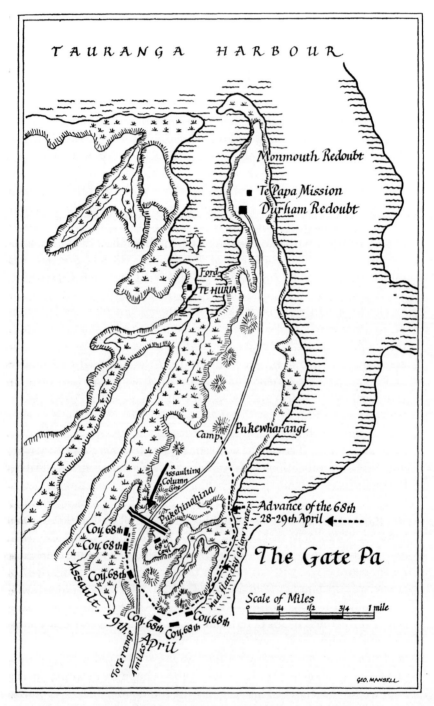

TAURANGA   HARBOUR

Monmouth Redoubt

Te Papa Mission
Durham Redoubt

Ford
TE HURIA

Pukewharangi

Camp

Assaulting
Column
line

Pukehinahina

Advance of the 68th
28-29th April

Coy. 68th

Coy. 68th

The Gate Pa

Coy. 68th

Coy. 68th

Coy. 68th

Coy. 68th   Coy. 68th

Assault, 29th April

To Terange
4 miles

mud flats dry at low water

Scale of Miles
0   1|4   1|2   3|4   1 mile

GEO. MANSELL

15. The Action at the Gate *Pa*, 29th April, 1864

distinguished person, and proceed to relate events the astounding nature of which would surprise even that prolific novelist Miss Braddon."

To explain the movements that followed it should be said that the Te Papa Mission (which was founded in 1838 by the same Archdeacon Brown who in 1864 still conducted it, entertained the troops and took the Sunday morning services), stood at the tip of a narrow tongue of land about three miles long formed by the muddy saltwater estuaries of the Kopurereroa stream on the west and the Waimapu on the east. The boundary between the Mission and the Maori lands ran across the base of the peninsula at its narrowest part, and was marked for all its length (say 500 yards) by a ditch. Where it was crossed by the ridgeway track leading south from Te Papa to the ranges a strong timber gate had been placed. The spot was well known to Europeans as the Gate and to Maoris as Pukehinahina. The ground, which rises and falls gently and slopes down to the water on either side of the ridge that carries the track, had in 1864 been for the most part cleared as far as the boundary. Beyond it was thickly covered with scrub and fern.

Towards the middle of April the "kingite" Maoris of Tauranga returned to their lands from the interior, where they had been assisting the Waikatos against Cameron's force, and started to reoccupy some of their old *pas*. One party sent a challenge to the commander at Te Papa inviting him to fight it out. At the same time they drew up, under the inspiration of one of their chiefs, Rawiri Puhirake, a code of fighting instructions in accord with the Christian principles learnt at the Mission, in which they were forbidden to mutilate the dead and encouraged to spare and even succour the wounded. Disappointed and hurt at receiving no reply, they moved closer and constructed two *pas* at the Gate itself under the noses of Greer's men, who, from 16th April onwards came out to watch them as they worked. ("Great excitement," says Major Shuttleworth in his diary.) Enlarging and strengthening the ditch and using the timber rails from the fence and the nearest houses in the township, which they entered by night, the Maori engineers placed a *pa* on either side of the ridge, a large one on the east and a smaller on the west, the whole work fronted by the usual palisade. By any standards it was a very elaborate field work.

General Cameron on hearing of this activity turned from his unfruitful campaign on the Waikato and hurried to Tauranga. At the same time he ordered up 900 infantry reinforcements to augment Greer's force. These included the remainder of the 68th, which was hurriedly withdrawn to Auckland, concentrated and embarked in

H.M.S. *Falcon* under Major Kirby (a very capable officer who had recently come in from the 86th). They anchored in Tauranga harbour late in the evening of 21st April.

With not much less than 1600 men at his disposal Cameron undertook an immediate attack on the Gate Pa, and on 27th April he moved forward to a small rise about 1200 yards from the *pa* known as Pukewharangi, where he pitched camp behind a screen of picquets. This time he was determined to bring his enemy to battle and allow none to elude him. From enquiry and reconnaissance it was found that a force could be moved to the *pa*'s rear at low water after dark by the mud flats on the *pa*'s right flank. He entrusted this tricky operation to Colonel Greer with the whole of the 68th, while he made a demonstration in front.

At dusk, about half-past six in the evening of the 28th, the 68th paraded 27 officers and 705 men strong, and marched off left in front down to the swamp of the Waimapu. They were guided by Mr. Purvis, a settler whose house had been one of the inlying picquets, and a Maori sergeant of police named Tu, who were accompanied by Major Shuttleworth and six men. Captain Trent's company formed the advanced guard. Crossing a mud flat nearly three-quarters of a mile long and knee-deep, they reached without mishap the spur running down from the high ground in rear of the *pa*. By 10, two hours before moonrise, the Regiment was all across and lying down along the crest of the ridge. At about 3 in the morning of 29th April Greer moved on, halting on a flat of *titri* scrub about 1000 yards from the *pa*, whence he could hear not only the voices of the Maoris in their pits but the challenges of the sentries in the headquarters camp. Major Shuttleworth was sent with three companies to the left rear of the *pa*, and picquets were posted at intervals along the whole length of the work and at 700 yards from it. The night was very dark and it started to rain. At daybreak Kirby was detached with three companies to the right, which was reinforced later in the morning by a party of thirty seamen from H.M.S. *Curaçao*. The remainder were re-distributed as shown in the drawing. Greer's movement, performed in the utmost silence and with great steadiness, had apparently succeeded. The enemy seemed unaware that they were surrounded: they were heard singing and making speeches. It looked as if their attention had been satisfactorily distracted by Cameron's demonstration in front.

At 7 in the morning Cameron opened with his artillery: one 110-pounder, two 40-pounder, and two 6-pounder Armstrong breech-loaders, together with two 8-inch mortars and six coehorns—a pretty devastating concentration of the best ordnance of the day. A mist came down at about 8 to interrupt the bombardment; but it was resumed at 9 and continued without intermission until 4 in the afternoon, the only alteration made being the dragging of one 6-pounder Armstrong across the swamp on the left, which successfully enfiladed the *pa* from that direction and drove the Maoris to their right. The guns registered on the Maori flagstaff in rear of the *pa*, with the result that there were a good many "overs", which caused three casualties in the 68th. Greer moved his men back somewhat, and again shifted the companies in response to a report from Shuttleworth that some of the enemy were escaping: indeed, according to Captain Grace, "Greer kept on changing the position of the companies".

By half-past three the *pa* seemed sufficiently battered to undergo assault. Some scrutinising it through their glasses even thought it was deserted. The storming-party was formed of 300 men: 150 seamen from H.M.S. *Harrier* under Commander Hay, and 150 men of the 43rd under Lieut.-Colonel Booth. The storm was covered by the fire of the so called Moveable Column (detachments of about 50 men each from the 14th, 12th and 65th, veterans of New Zealand warfare); and a force of seamen, marines and 43rd was formed into a reserve. At about 4, towards dusk—the May of the Antipodes is our November—the assault went in against the centre of the large *pa*. But, "when the position seemed to be on the very point of being carried, our men from some inexplicable cause fell back before the Maoris, who fought to the death; and they retired from the work under a heavy fire from the parapet, leaving behind several officers".

The cause of the panic that swept through these 300 men, faced by an enemy who did not exceed 250 in numbers and had been subjected to a heavy fire of artillery for eight hours, has exercised historians ever since. Some say the men, having entered the works, threw down their arms to plunder, and were taken by surprise when the Maoris emerged from their underground passages and poured in a sharp fusillade upon them. This seems unlikely, as a Maori *pa* was notoriously lacking in plunder. More likely is the explanation that, having entered and having lost an undue proportion of officers, they were surprised by a movement of the Maoris who had attempted to escape to the rear and found their path blocked by the 68th, and that this looked in the bad light like the arrival of a horde of reinforcements. If that is so Cameron's deliberate plan of encirclement proved in the event to be too much of a good thing. Be that as it may, the storming-party lost 10 officers and 23 men killed, and even the committal of the reserve could not retrieve the situation.

All this, however, was hidden from the 68th, who through the rain saw the rocket go up as the signal for the assault and could hear the cheers of the men as they advanced, but knew nothing more for some time. Captain Grace's experiences, written down in his diary a day or two after, are no doubt fairly representative. Greer had taken him from his company to a deserted *whare*, or native village, in rear of the *pa* to help in hoisting signals. He was returning from carrying a message to Shuttleworth when he heard the cheer at 4 o'clock,

"which cheer", he says, "was re-echoed by the various companies of the 68th, and I got into the midst of a heavy fire, bullets falling all round me. I found Greer had left the *whare* and had moved my company and a part of Spratt's so I could not find them. But getting into some fern I got fired at so often that I rejoined Casement's company [with Major Shuttleworth on the left], whom I advised to make his men lie down, as the fire was very hot—which he did. Presently about 20 Maoris were seen coming up and they were driven in by the fire of the company (B). Soon afterwards I heard Shuttleworth saying 'All the 68th this way,' and I joined him, and he assembled all the detached parties for the assault. We then heard that the storming-party of the 43rd and sailors had been repulsed, and [Ensign William] Clarke, 43rd, shot through the shoulder, joined us. Colonel McNeill, a.d.c., gave an order not to assault but to hold the spur we were on for the night. A sailor joined us who had gone through the *pa*. We had to remain where we were. Greer soon afterwards joined us. We lay down on our side of the spur, and another party (68th) on the other. In the night we heard a volley and a cheer, and that was [Lieutenant] Pownall's party [68th] charging us; and as I got to my knees I was knocked over by some men who ran over me, and then we shouted for them not to fire.

"The great mistake throughout the day was that the Maoris were not allowed to escape, but we should have let the storming-party had got well in [*sic*] before we attempted to show ourselves. All night it rained in heavy showers. No grog, no food, and many alarms. I lay wedged between [Surgeon] Best and [Captain] Light."

"*30th April*. At day-light we were moving off to our different posts when we heard that the Maoris had evacuated the *pa* during the night. I went up there, passing many dead on the way. Some wounded were in the *pa*. Those who were too bad to be moved amongst them a Scripture reader of Archdeacon Brown's of Te Papa [*sic*]. I found six of my company and skirmished with them in a swamp. James Davidson saw a Maori go into a *titri* bush and we drove him out into a party under [Lieutenant] Covey [68th, acting as Greer's field adjutant]. Soon afterwards we marched back into camp [at Pukewharangi] and had some breakfast at 2½ p.m. Two hundred of the 68th went back to Te Papa, my company amongst them."

In other words the 68th succeeded in driving back with some loss any groups of Maoris that attempted to make their way through the cordon in daylight, but in the wet, dark night were insufficient to prevent them escaping as they silently evacuated the work and, without returning any fire, crept through Greer's picquet-line. The total Maori loss was about 25 men killed, a tribute to the skill of their engineers and the astonishing *sang-froid* with which they endured the bombardment. The 68th lost 3 men killed or mortally wounded and 18 men wounded. All were mature soldiers of an average age of about 27, none of them with less than six years' service.[5]

The action of the Gate Pa has been written up as something of a tragedy,[6] highlighted only by the amazing staunchness of the Maoris and their praiseworthy humanity to the wounded. The repulse was certainly hurting to the self-esteem of a good regiment. Viewed, however, as an incident in the war, it was, in the event, a successful action even if, in common with all Cameron's previous encounters with the Maoris, it lacked finality and failed to achieve all the General intended.

On the evacuation of the *pa*, he proceeded in his methodical way to consolidate his position and thrust a wedge between the coast tribes and the Waikato country. A redoubt was raised on the site of the Gate Pa, another at Te Huria (or Judæa); and a third was started on 12th May on the site of an old *pa* at Poteriwhi, which was only abandoned on receipt of news of a fresh outbreak in the west of the Island at Wanganui. This development claimed the presence of the General himself and the better part of the troops at Tauranga, and left Greer once more in command. The 68th remained at Te Papa, but kept detachments of approximately company strength at the Gate Pa, Judæa and Maketu.

Indeed, Greer was on the point of sending a further part of his force in the General's wake in compliance with a request of his, when on 13th June he received threatening reports of the coast natives and their able and active chief Rawiri, who had escaped from the Gate Pa. Greer had been instructed to make sure by constant patrolling that no *pas* were raised in his vicinity, and to attack immediately if they made the attempt before they had time to establish themselves. On 21st June one of his patrols, about 600 strong, scouring the open ranges four miles beyond the Gate Pa, suddenly encountered a large body of 600 Maoris who had just begun to entrench themselves with a single line of rifle-pits at Te Ranga, across the track leading from Tauranga towards the forests to the south. The work was similar to

[5]Grace's diary, however, says that one of these, Private McGough, accidentally shot himself in the guard-tent on the 28th. The others were Sergeant James Harmer and Private McDonald. (W.O.33/16, pp. 233-238.)

[6]The contemporary report of the battle in the *Times* was very inaccurate, and the passage containing a description of the assault and repulse of the 68th was very properly contradicted by Col. Greer.

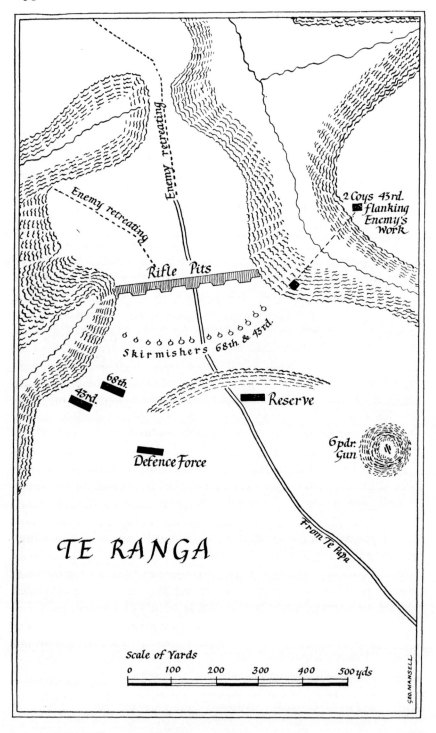

16. Te Ranga, 21st June, 1864

the Gate Pa, its flanks supported by precipitous gullies which, says the military topographer, "are more properly ravines". But, lacking the entrenchments of the other, it was not so strong, nor was it finished.

Greer energetically seized the opportunity vouchsafed him. Sending back to camp at Te Papa for 200 reinforcements and one 6-pounder Armstrong gun, he drove in with his skirmishers a party of Maoris who advanced to meet him. Then he extended the 43rd and part of the 68th to the front and flanks and kept up a sharp fire for two hours until the reinforcements came up. They must have seemed very long hours to Greer. He had observed another large body of Maoris emerging from the woods, who, by the time the troops from Te Papa approached, had got within 500 yards of the rifle-pits. But at a quarter to one, as soon as the reinforcements had arrived within supporting distance, he sounded the Advance, and the 43rd under Major Synge, two companies of the 68th under Captain Trent, and a party of the 1st Waikato Militia[7] under Captain Moore moved off to the attack in light infantry order as if on parade, Trent's and Casement's companies making for the left of the pits. The rest of the force remained in support under Major Shuttleworth.

In spite of the heavy fire directed against it the attack was carried out with irresistible dash and determination, and was received with equal determination and courage by the Maoris, who stood up in their pits without flinching. For a few minutes there was a desperate hand-to-hand fight—that occurrence so rare in war. The 43rd had a reputation to retrieve, the 68th a name to sustain, and the struggle was savage. Captain Trent fell severely wounded in the right arm as he led the two companies forward. Lieutenant Villiers-Stuart, one of the first into the pits, in a personal encounter with a Maori armed with an Enfield rifle and bayonet, was bayoneted by him but managed to cut him down with his sword. Corporal Byrne, the Inkerman V.C., the first of his company into the pits, had spitted his man but was about to be tomahawked by him when Sergeant John Murray, who had already accounted singlehanded for a pitful of eight or ten Maoris, ran to his assistance and cut the man down.

The fight was very even until Shuttleworth, 400 yards away, releasing the supporting companies and the two 43rd companies on the right flank at exactly the critical moment, rushed at the pits driving everything before him. The Maoris could not resist any longer and, disdaining to run, walked off down the gullies with the soldiers in pursuit, leaving 68 dead in the pits and another 40 in their retreat.

[7]Whose quartermaster was Thomas Tunks, quartermaster of the 68th in the Crimea.

Among them were Rawiri Puhirake, the chief whose signal courage had sustained them at the Gate Pa, and Henare Taratoa, a young Mission student, on whose body was found the humanitarian code of fighting instructions revealed to the soldiers now for the first time.

Considering the bitterness of the fighting, Greer's losses—10 men killed, 6 officers and 33 n.c.o.s and men wounded—were surprisingly light. The 68th lost 5 men killed, 4 officers (Captains Trent and Casement, Lieutenant Villiers-Stuart and Ensign Palmer) and 20 n.c.o.s and men wounded. Again, all of them were mature soldiers, one a man of 17 years' service—evidence of the type of man the Regiment was composed of at this time. "From the fact," Greer reported, "that the attack was made in light infantry order, and from the Maoris having waited for the charge and made a desperate hand-to-hand resistance, more opportunity was offered of showing individual gallantry than might occur in much more extensive operations;" and he found it difficult to make distinctions. He did, however, single out for their conduct the following officers and men of the Regiment: Major Shuttleworth, Captains Trent, Casement and Seymour (who took Trent's place), Lieutenant Villiers-Stuart, Surgeon-Major Best, Adjutant Covey, field-adjutant, and Ensign Palmer, Greer's orderly officer; Sergeant-Major Tudor, Sergeant Murray (who was recommended for the Victoria Cross and obtained it), Corporal Byrne, and Privates Thomas Smyth and Daniel Caffrey.[8]

"All much pleased," wrote Shuttleworth in his diary on the return to Te Papa, which was reached at 6 that evening. "All say the best thing done this campaign." It was; but quite how decisive the action of Te Ranga had been appeared only slowly. There were rumours, too well founded as it proved, of an enemy attack on Te Papa planned for the day of Te Ranga; and a party which went out on 22nd June to bury the dead had to skirmish with a few hostile natives. But on 25th July 133 Maoris, including many chiefs, came into Tauranga to make their submission to Greer, and from that moment the posts around not only Tauranga but Auckland and Drury also were unmolested.

The back of the rebellion in the north was broken, and it had fallen to Greer to break it. In the course of things it was hardly to be expected that the contemporary reports from Cameron's headquarters should give Greer all the credit that (it now appears in retrospect) he deserved. His name, however, is appreciatively remembered in New Zealand, where the new suburb that has grown up in the vicinity of the Gate Pa is called Greerton. The Regiment

[8]Greer's reports in W.O.33/16, pp. 260-263.

has every reason for remembering him. He had done little before except to command the Depot and, thanks to his decisiveness on 21st June, he had no opportunities of doing much after. In the Regiment he appears to have been considered something of a "fuss". "Greer scolding away in the Orderly Room," says Grace in his diary on 26th April. Even Shuttleworth, who clearly respected his commanding officer, speaks once (15th August) of: "marching past. I drilled and Greer looking on and making remarks, which does not work well." For a time (March and April 1865), he was oppressed by anxiety caused by the premature confinement of his wife, whom he had in camp with him—a period in which the band was not allowed to play and the Colonel seemed "quite as much afraid of the Maoris as he was this time last year". But when he was "in great force", as he usually was, his power of command was tremendous, and the whole battalion shook when his pronouncements were delivered. "Greer had a meeting of all officers," says Shuttleworth on 14th September 1864, "and spoke to them on the subject of gambling, and spoke well stopping it." And again, on 26th April 1865, "Greer had Trent up to Orderly Room and pitched into him for putting officers under arrest for trivial things, and spoke well on the subject." There was no question of who commanded the 68th. Nothing, however, in his career recurred to provoke those soldierly qualities so conspicuous that day at Te Ranga. He retired from the command in 1869. For a time he commanded Brigade Depot No. 63 at Downpatrick. He rose to the rank of lieut.-general, and he died on 26th March 1886.

Tranquillity settled once more upon Tauranga. The 68th took out their cricket-stumps again while the war went on in the west. After the departure for Taranaki of the last of the 43rd on 5th September 1864 the Regiment was the only regular infantry in the Bay of Plenty. In January 1865 the war entered a degenerate phase with the spread of the so called Hauhau movement among the Maoris, a bestial, cannibalistic fanaticism similar to that recently experienced in Kenya. Not only was the Tauranga garrison confined to camp, but four companies of the 68th (Seymour's, Casement's, Villiers-Stuart's and Grace's) were embarked for Auckland as reinforcements for Taranaki, the only theatre in which active operations were still proceeding. The remainder continued in camp at Tauranga until the whole Regiment embarked for home in March 1866.

The war just described was essentially a defensive war, carried on with the object of destroying the tribes that threatened the European settlements whether in Taranaki, Auckland or Tauranga: the war about to be undertaken was an offensive war, in implementation of a deliberate policy of confiscating the land north and south of New

Plymouth and a strip about sixty miles long near Wanganui. After Te Ranga the Ngatimaniapotos, the most powerful tribe after the Waikatos, moved south against New Plymouth, and Colonel Warre, in command there, had accordingly been reinforced. No serious hostilities ensued, however, until the end of 1864 when the New Zealand government undertook large-scale transfers of troops to Taranaki and Wanganui with the following objects: (a) the military occupation of the Patea valley from the sea to the forest, and of the country between the Patea and Wanganui, for the construction of the Waitótara road; (b) the occupation of the country from Tataráimaka southward as far as the Stony River; and (c)—the ultimate object—the construction of a road from Taranaki to Wanganui to favour the establishment of military settlements at points along it. The 57th, long in the Taranaki district, was reinforced by the 50th and a detachment of the 18th from Auckland, and later by the 70th and 43rd. Colonel Waddy, 50th, was appointed brigadier commanding at Wanganui and instructed to reconnoitre as far as the Waitótara, while Warre advanced from Taranaki to establish himself on the River. The Hauhau fanaticism was flourishing among the natives there; Te Ua, its leader, was strongly entrenched in the Weraroa Pa near Wanganui; and there was certain to be opposition.

This employment of H.M. troops to act as a kind of "Greathead Shield" to colonisation, which had been enjoined upon Cameron by the Governor, Sir George Grey, was novel and, in Cameron's view, improper. There were by this time considerable numbers of settlers formed into military bodies, and the jealousy between the professional and the colonial forces was, for familiar reasons, fairly keen, the one seeing formal, clumsy incompetence in the other, which in its turn felt itself exploited to serve the interests of a lot of land-grabbing colonists. Though these sentiments do not appear to have been very evident at regimental level, Cameron and Grey for their part represented their respective parties with an unseemly and fatal bitterness. They were, indeed, on the point of falling out. The result of all this was that the operations in Wanganui took on a curiously incoherent character which makes them unusually difficult to follow.

Operations started in January 1865 when Waddy moved out from Wanganui and raised a redoubt at Alexander's Farm. Another two were thrown up at Peake's and Mussen's Farms (Woodall's and Stewart's) to protect the outsettlers. A fourth thrown up at Nukumaru was held against a formidable attack from the Maoris in the Weraroa Pa, a check which was not followed up, as it would have been in old days, by an assault on the *pa* itself. On 5th February the line was continued to the Waitótara, and on 27th February to the Patea, where a redoubt was constructed on either bank. When the 68th's detachment arrived from Auckland the "military party" was beginning to feel there were not enough troops with which to prolong the line all the way to Taranaki.

The detachment disembarked at Wanganui on 20th February under Lieut.-Colonel Morant 11 officers and 229 n.c.o.s and men strong. On 25th February it marched out behind the band of the 18th to Alexander's Farm, and on the next day it encamped beyond the Waitótara, which took one hour to cross. On the 27th it reached the General's advanced camp beyond the Patea.

In an attempt to draw the enemy from the Weraroa Pa, which Cameron was reluctant to storm directly, a column under Colonel Weare was ordered up from the Waitótara to the Patea on 9th March, which, joining with the headquarter force, was to advance on the 10th towards Kakaramea. But at 5 that morning, after the tents had been struck, it started to rain hard, and the rain was followed by a gale "very nearly if not quite equalling in violence the memorable Crimean hurricane of 14th November 1854, but lasting longer," causing the postponement of the movement until the 13th. "No food could be cooked," says Grace, "and the tents leaked." Having dried out on the 11th, Weare's force started again for Kakaremea on the 13th. It consisted of nearly 1400 men, including two guns and 50 volunteer cavalry, the infantry made up of detachments of the 50th, 57th and 68th, the last-mentioned supplying 10 officers and 220 n.c.o.s and men organised in three companies under the command of Lieut.-Colonel Morant. Their route lay over flat fern-land, bounded on either side by a ridge running parallel with the line of march within musket-shot of the column. Suddenly the cavalry skirmishers covering the advanced guard came on about 200 Maoris on the ridge on the right, who at once opened fire. Infantry skirmishers with supports and reserves were brought forward and, changing front rapidly to the right, went at the ridge. The Maoris, who had extended until they occupied a line about 600 yards in length, rather naturally yielded in the face of such numbers in the open, and slowly retreated down into a swamp in their rear. Heavily fired on by Weare's men from the crest of the ridge, they lost a fair proportion of their number. Weare's men, on the other hand, continued their march until encamping at Kakaramea.

That is the official description of the fight at Kakaramea: Captain Grace's reads somewhat differently.

"When we marched off and got to the hill beyond the outlying picquets the Maoris began to fire and the 57th skirmished. Then

Seymour's and my companies were sent out to support them but became reinforcements. All confusion. Weare seems to have lost his
head. I thought perchance his brains might have gone into the green
pagri he wore. We went down a steep declivity into a swamp, across it
and up the next hill, the Maoris keeping up a fire. They kept walking
off but would not run, we after them, and so on till we got to the
village of Kakaramea. Many wounded Maoris were bayoneted by the
English soldiers. The village was found to be deserted though the fires
were still burning. Many pigs and fowls were caught and killed.
Lance-Sergeant Castles attached to my company was wounded in
the chest. . . . In the afternoon fatigue-parties were sent out and
searched the swamp, and prisoners were taken and several wounded
ones. One woman was found killed. She had been helping her husband to fight by loading one of his two double-barrelled guns while
he fired the other. . . . We got to the village by 9 a.m. and the baggage
soon came up. We encamped for the night. My company fired 283
rounds. . . ."

The next day Weare's force was relieved and marched on towards Manawapo, encamping at Manutahi. Tangahoe, six miles
from Manawapo, was reached by the 68th detachment on 29th
March. It shared in a reconnaissance in force of the village of Kata-
tauri on 6th April. That, however, was the limit of the advance. After
raising two redoubts on the Waingongoro, Cameron suspended the
operations towards Taranaki. The 68th detachment was withdrawn
to Wanganui, which it reached at 1 o'clock on 26th May.[9]

Desultory operations involving the detachment in reconnaissance
and fatigue-parties continued in the neighbourhood of Wanganui for
several dreary months yet. But orders had already been dispatched
for the recall of five regiments including the 68th and the war was
drawing to a slow conclusion. The detachment embarked at Wanganui for New Plymouth on 17th December 1865, and sailed thence
for Auckland on 13th February 1866. There it was joined by the
companies from Tauranga. A few men took their discharge and
settled in Tauranga, where they died respected members of the community fifty and sixty years after. And there were some heavy hearts
in March 1866, when the whole Regiment embarked. It was
conveyed in three ships, which landed it at Portsmouth in June and
July 1866.

They were pretty formidable men, these New Zealand veterans,
who had lived roughly for several years in detachments remote from
any refining influences. A subaltern who joined another regiment
recently returned from New Zealand found there was nothing these
hairy old soldiers "did not know of fording rivers and storming pali-
sades—also, a bottle of wine was apt to turn into a dead marine in a

[9] W.O.107/7; Major Grace's ms. diary.

brace of shakes whenever it dared to cross their path".[10] The Regiment's services in the Colony, which cost it altogether nine n.c.o.s and men killed or mortally wounded, four officers and 36 n.c.o.s and men wounded, and 25 men died from disease, were rewarded in May 1870 by the grant of the battle-honour *New Zealand*. By that time it was stationed in Ireland, having in the meanwhile moved to Aldershot in May 1867, thence to Manchester in January 1868 and to Queenstown in September 1869. For the purpose of having the new honour attached to the colours at the new Clothing Factory at Pimlico, the colours were sent through the post, which then proceeded to lose them in transit between Dublin and Holyhead.

In Ireland the companies were widely dispersed in a country that was troubled by the Fenian disturbances, and their respective movements are too numerous to particularise. Headquarters were first at Cork, in July 1870 at Kilkenny, from September 1870 to October 1871 at Templemore, and from October 1871 to 9th February 1872 at Cork. On that day the whole of the service-companies, about 30 officers and 900 men strong, embarked at Queenstown in the troopship *Euphrates* for Bombay under the temporary command of Major Trent. Passing through the new Suez Canal, it landed on 13th March and was immediately sent up country to Poona.

There for the time being the 68th must be left—on its first Indian tour of duty, which lasted for fifteen years—until it returned in the *Euphrates* on 13th April 1887 as the First Battalion of the Durham Light Infantry.

§

The New Zealand War was the last fought by the old long-service soldier in domestic surroundings that would have been familiar both to "Jonas" and John Green, in regiments they would have recognised, accompanied (if they had them) by their wives, and following a routine that had not materially changed in a hundred years. But the transformation was at hand. Long service, Purchase, regiments recruited haphazard according to circumstances, were on their way out: short service, a reserve, promotion of officers by merit, seniority and examination, and "territorial" recruiting were introduced in their place. In part they were changes brought about by the social upheavals of the Industrial Revolution. But that they should have occurred when and how they did was as much due to developments taking place on the Continent. An army, in fact, is not purely an expression of the social institutions of a nation: it is run in competition

[10]Gen. Sir Ian Hamilton, *When I was a Boy* (London, Faber, 1939), p. 292.

with other armies and observes alien rules. In 1866 and 1870 the Prussian Army, largely composed of men who by old standards would have been regarded as little better than recruits, defeated with ease the best professional armies of the day. One of the reasons for its success was the astonishing speed and efficiency with which it mobilised. The Prussian infantry regiments were recruited by conscription—a measure hardly entertained in this country even at the height of the Napoleonic Wars—on a system derived from the "cantonal" system of the early eighteenth century. Each had a recruiting district permanently allotted to it, and a depot to which reservists reported on mobilisation. In this country there was not only no reserve to speak of, but no fixed recruiting area and no fixed depot.

The absence of a reserve had caused anxiety ever since the Crimean War, and some steps had been taken to remedy the deficiency. But while service remained at 21 years it was idle to think of a reserve. If we were to mobilise our manhood on a scale comparable with Prussia, some quick thinking and some radical reforms were indicated. Both were forthcoming in the Secretary of State of the time, Cardwell, whose name has been given to the reorganisation of the army that ensued.

The reform which made its deepest mark on the old British regiments of the line was the creation of the so-called "territorial regiment", a regular regiment, that is, which recruits habitually from a defined district containing not only the first-line troops but all the reserve forces of the locality as well. The latter consisted of the old militia battalions and also of the new rifle volunteer corps formed in the early 1860s, whose history will be told later. It was reckoned that for a militia battalion of 1000 a population of 100,000 males was necessary; and as it was intended that each district should furnish two militia battalions, the country was parcelled into 66 districts each with a male population of about 200,000. It happened also that at that time the number of line battalions at home and abroad was about equal (72 abroad, 69 at home). By bringing home two battalions the number was equalised more exactly, enabling a pair of battalions to be "linked" as it was said: one at home on a low establishment in which the recruits were trained before being dispatched to replace the wastage in the high establishment battalion abroad.

The details were worked out by the "Military Forces Localization Committee" presided over by Major-General P. L. MacDougall, one of the foremost "intellectual" soldiers of the day, which produced its findings in a series of reports of which the last appeared in February 1873. England was divided into 50 "Brigade Districts", Scotland into

8, and Ireland 8 also. In linking the line battalions the Committee was charged with reconciling many conflicting claims: the nominal and the real connection of regiments with particular counties; their susceptibilities; their dress and facings (there was no intention at this stage of altering their precedence, their numbers, their traditions, their dress or their facings); and the exigencies of the foreign duty roster, so that regiments at home should not be sent abroad without a due period at home.

In the event the County of Durham was in March 1873 designated as Sub-District No. 3, with its Brigade Depot at Sunderland under Lieut.-Colonel Morant. The two Durham militia battalions (the 1st Fusiliers at Barnard Castle and the 2nd North Durham at Durham) together with the four administrative battalions and one unattached corps of Rifle Volunteers (1897 men) formed the reserve forces of the District. Understandably enough the 68th was one of the pair of line battalions assigned to it. The other was selected on grounds of administrative expediency. Of the sixteen battalions allotted to the eight districts in Ireland only seven were considered as being properly "national battalions." There were a further twelve which had established a real Irish connection through recruiting, most of them regiments recently transferred from the Honourable East India Company's service. There were consequently three surplus to requirements; and they (the 105th Madras Light Infantry, the 106th Bombay Light Infantry and the 107th Bengal Infantry), having "no predilection of long standing for any particular locality," were brought to English depots. The 105th was linked with the 51st at Doncaster; the 107th was linked with the 35th at Chichester; and the 106th was linked with the 68th at Sunderland.[11]

---

[11]*Parl. Papers* (C.2792), Reports of the Military Forces Localization Committee.

CHAPTER VII

THE SECOND BOMBAY EUROPEAN LIGHT
INFANTRY AND THE 106TH, 1839-1874

THE new partner was about as different in history and traditions
as any regiment could be that wore the red coat and drew its
officers and men from the British Isles. It was one of the European
regiments in the service of John Company.

In 1839 when its history starts, the Honourable East India Company had long since ceased to be a purely trading concern. Indeed,
in 1833 it had ceased altogether to trade. It carried, however, the
immense prestige that a wealthy corporation doing business in a
distant part of the earth for many generations cannot fail to accumu-
late. Its servants collected the revenue from several millions of people;
it administered justice, carried on wars with princes possessing
fabulous resources of men and money; it enlarged its own influence
in an ever widening circle. Its fleet of merchant vessels were the
aristocrats of the seas. It recruited, paid and employed an army,
part native, part European, as large again as the one fumblingly
administered by the Horse Guards and the other score of quasi-
military offices in London. It even entertained at its own expense a
sizeable proportion of the Royal forces. It appointed its civil servants
and trained them at its own school at Haileybury; it educated its
military servants at its own military seminary at Addiscombe. Never,
surely, in history has a corporation of directors and stockholders
wielded dominion over such a vast aggregation of wealth and population, nor exercised it with such breadth of view and largeness of
design. Everything about the Honourable Company was grand.
Kampanee Bahadur it was to its Indian servants and subjects, six
months' sailing away, who gave it one of the most respectful titles in
their vocabulary; and who shall deny its right to it, great impersonal
power that it was, which had broken the power of the mightiest
potentates that people knew?

So vast a concern could not continue without the resources, and therefore the control, of the Government. Since 1784 the Company had been placed in subordination to the legislature by means of the Board of Control, a body of six commissioners consisting of the Chancellor of the Exchequer, one of the Secretaries of State—there were but two at that time—and four other privy councillors. For some time the Board had ceased to assemble, and the active channel through which the Court of Directors' policies became permeated with the policies of Government was the President of the Board, a minister with a seat in the Cabinet. But the patronage of the twenty-four men who constituted the Court of Directors remained un-impaired until 1858. It was the Court that nominated all, appointed all, and recalled all. At the same time three of their number formed the Secret Committee, which was empowered to transmit certain orders from the Board to India without consulting the other twenty-one and retained the power to make war.

If the organisation was cumbrous in London it was hardly less so in India. The power of the Company had spread inland from the three great concessions it had won from the Indian princes: Bombay. Madras and Bengal. "The story of the English in India," says Philip Woodruff in an illuminating passage, "begins at Surat: circling counter-clockwise the focus of interest, a little ring of golden light, drifts to Bombay, swings round the coast to Madras, darts with Clive from Madras to Calcutta, and there dwells, spreading in a more and more widely diffused pool over newly acquired lands as new problems arise behind new frontiers."[1] Each became, and remained until the end, a presidency, with its own governor appointed by the Directors, its own army, its own peculiar institutions, and consequently its own character. Because of its immense preponderance of wealth and territories, it was the Bengal Presidency which became supreme, and the Governor-General of Bengal who ruled supreme over the Company dominions not only in Bengal and Hindustan but over the Governors of Madras and Bombay and their councils besides.

Of the three presidencies Bombay was the smallest and least pretentious, its army the smallest and roughest. Until the power of the great Mahratta Confederacy was finally broken in 1819, the proximity of its warlike neighbour had kept it pinned against the coast, and twenty years only had intervened in which this oldest settlement had been able to take advantage of the immense accession of territory beyond the Ghats that followed the peace. Maria Graham, who visited Bombay in 1812, found society there provincial; but she also

[1]Philip Woodruff, *The Men who ruled India: The Founders* (Cape, 1953), p. 238.

noticed after travelling wider that the distance kept up between the Europeans and natives was as nothing compared with that observed in Bengal and Madras. The Mahratta country, observes Woodruff, "was still a frontier province where things were done camp fashion".

The Bombay army, kept small by the Presidency's meagre revenue, in 1839 consisted of: one regiment of Queen's cavalry and four battalions of Queen's infantry; three regiments of native cavalry, twenty-six battalions of native infantry and one of European; four troops of European horse artillery, three battalions of European foot-artillery, and one of native; and an establishment of sappers and miners. In comparison, the Bengal army at the same time possessed no less than seventy native infantry battalions and everything else in proportion. While the Bengal army recruited from a fine-looking race of high-caste sepoys, the Bombay army habitually recruited from the hardier but less prepossessing races within its frontier, particularly Mahrattas, and caste was allowed less play in promotion. Likewise in appearance the "Ducks", as the Bombay army was called, suffered in comparison with the "Kai-hais". "The Bombay [European] Fusiliers are such queer fellows," remarks a Bengal officer on his first sight of their dirty, sunburnt faces when they relieved the Bengal troops at his cantonment in the first days of the Mutiny, "to us quite foreigners. They look more slovenly than our swell officers, wear crumpled jackets, no collars, black neckerchiefs, ride absurd *tats* (ponies), with swords and pistols, on the whole, and wonder at mules, at the number of buggies, etc." It was told of one old Bengal artilleryman, full of presidential prejudices, that on hearing a brother-officer commending the Bombay army, exclaimed, "The Bombay army! Don't talk to me of the Bombay army! They call a *chillumchee* a *gindy*, the beasts!" (Both words are perfectly ordinary ones for a basin.) Events were to show that behind an imposing façade the Bengal army concealed serious defects. The Bombay army was too much engrossed in policing its new-won territory to indulge in fancy-frills; and the efficiency and readiness of the Bombay division that came up into the Punjab in the Second Sikh War to take its share at the siege of Multan came as a revelation to those who had not seen the army of the Presidency on service.

Whether or not there was much difference between the men who officered each of the three armies it is hard to say. All the Company's servants, civil and military alike, were selected after nomination by the Board or one or other of the Directors, who each had a number of nominations in the year. To that extent all may be said to have been of a feather, in an age, moreover, when there was greater variety as well as cohesion within the vertical and horizontal divisions of society. The prospects too were broadly the same. In all the armies promotion went by seniority. It was a "seniority service", in which there were no supersessions save by brevets for meritorious, or by dismissal for disgraceful, conduct. Purchase as it was known in the Royal service did not exist. There was admittedly a stock-purse, managed by the officers themselves, to which they subscribed periodically according to their rank, and from which they drew a bonus upon retiring, thus in some degree accelerating the process of retirement and promotion to fill the vacancies. But there was no call upon fathers, uncles and grandfathers for large capital sums to buy commissions such as there was in the British army. These considerations made the Company's service appeal to a section of society with more modest means, to families with incomes rather than property.

The sons of the great titled and landed families seldom applied. The candidates came from the sons of the clergy, that abundant source of talent, of solicitors, of half-pay army and navy officers, merchants, small landowners, and, of course, of officers of the Company itself. Colonel Hodson has found that of all the schools contributing candidates for the Bengal army up to 1834 the Royal High School, Edinburgh, and Charterhouse produced the most. That is perhaps a fair indication, but it has to be translated into the terms of those days. While Eton is still admitting many local tradesmen's sons, many landed gentry are sending their boys to the local grammar-schools. All the public schools of the Victorian foundation have yet to make their mark, and it is commoner to find a boy of modest but good middle-class parentage attending, say, the school of the Rev. Dr Burney at Gosport, or the Rev. Mr Crooke at Bromley than Cheltenham, Shrewsbury or Rugby. If there was a difference between the officers of the presidential armies it is probably fair to say that the better-to-do went for Bengal and the most modest for Bombay.

But if there is one thing that is certain it is that the officers of the Bombay infantry were a very different set from those of the 68th and more especially from the 68th of Lord William Paulet's creation. That had, as we have seen, a markedly "landed" connection. There was little that was "landed" about the 2nd Europeans. Stalker was a shipbroker's son; Guerin a country parson's; Capon, Macan, Ramsay, Barr, Hervey, Whitehill, Sandwith, Jessop and Jervis were sons of Company's officers. Scott's father was a stockbroker; Eické's an underwriter; Macready's was the actor; Stiles's a captain in the Revenue Service; Parr's a coal-merchant, residing in Kentish Town (a more salubrious neighbourhood then than now); and so on and so on. There were plenty of men such as these in the 68th, but there were none like Henry Smyth, Wynne or Paulet himself in the 2nd Europeans. Those who entered the Company's service intended to live, marry, settle down and bring up families in the cantonments, return perhaps for a few years' furlough to recruit their flagging energies, but none the less live out their lives and livers in India. There were no promotions from the ranks—none at all. As one man died so the next in seniority stepped into his place. All this is quite strange to the Royal service. The backbone of the 68th, as of all the Queen's regiments, was the devoted number of officers who stuck by their profession and did their foreign tours as the rota came round. In that respect the professional soldiers of both services leave little to choose between them. But it was open to the Queen's officers to jump in and out very much as their preferences and circumstances allowed. The attitude of a body of men comprising such as these is very different—not necessarily superior or inferior—from one in which all have voluntarily exiled themselves with a view of making a fortune or at least of earning a fair competence for life.

§

Since the earliest days each presidential army had been part composed of Europeans. The European infantry regiment of the Bombay army, for instance, was first raised by Charles II for the defence of the dowry brought him by his Portuguese bride, and was transferred to the Company's service in 1668. The Madras and Bengal European regiments trace their history to an even remoter period, and there was not a warlike operation in the whole Indian continent in which one or the other had not taken a share. Indeed it was recognised that it was a waste of good soldiers to employ Europeans upon ordinary military duties in peace, and that they were properly "reserved for the sterner and more serious field operations on a considerable scale". (If only the West Indian governments, inhibited by the baneful influence of slavery, had recognised this too!) It was also recognised that "the native army required for its full efficiency a considerable admixture of European soldiery". The proportion usually observed was that recommended by Lord Wellesley when Governor-General, namely, one-fourth of an army engaged actively. By agreement the Royal troops maintained in India at the Company's expense were limited to 20,000 men. The Company likewise, by an Act of 1788, was limited in the number of European troops it entertained to a figure of 12,200. The sepoy army therefore, to be effective, could not be augmented beyond a certain point.

That point had been reached in 1838. The enormous expansion of British influence in India that took place during the Napoleonic War reached a pause with the close of the Burmese War in 1825 and the fall of Bhurtpore in 1826. There followed, as there did at home after Waterloo, a period of retrenchment, in which all establishments were ruthlessly pared and the immense armies run down. This halcyon period, which lasted long enough for the Company's finances to be restored, came to an end with the growth of the power of Russia at the expense of Persia. The Government in London, using smaller scale maps than was prudent, magnified it into a threat upon British possessions in India, which at that time did not extend beyond the Indus. It was this apprehension that was at the root of Lord Auckland's great expedition to place a British nominee upon the throne of Afghanistan. It was an undertaking defensible on grounds neither of expediency nor morality and it absorbed, moreover, a very large part of the army not only in Bengal but also Bombay at a moment when relations with Nepal, Burma and the Sikh States of the Punjab were such as seemed likely to provoke hostilities with all three simultaneously.

The "Army of the Indus", as the Afghanistan Field Force was called, was well on its way to Kabul when, on 9th March 1839, the President of the Board of Control, Sir J. C. Hobhouse, who was intimately involved with Palmerston in the government's Russo-phobe policy, suggested to the Court that both the Queen's and the Company's infantry establishments should be raised by ten men per company, equivalent to a reinforcement of almost three regiments. The Directors, clearly disliking the Government policy, acquiesced, adding, however, that they preferred the raising of whole regiments. This evidently was out of the question; but the President acted with such dispatch that on 11th April the Directors were instructing the Governor-General at Fort William. Hardly had the letters gone off before a more urgent demand for troops reached the Secret Committee from Lord Auckland, dated from his camp at Rohtak on 7th February. He retailed at length his uneasy relations with the Courts of Ava and Khatmandu, which kept immobilised a further large part of the Bengal army and all the Madras. Moreover, the expedition to Afghanistan had deprived Bombay of the greater part of its European troops, and a sizeable force was necessary in the Punjab both to ensure his communication with the Army of the Indus and to act in case Ranjit Singh's imminent death deprived him of the alliance of the Sikhs. He anticipated a breach with Persia. His European force was totally inadequate. "Whether," he said, "our operations are to be carried on in Ava, in Nepal, or in the countries of the Indus, the race of men by whom we shall be opposed are more hardy and robust, if they are not braver, than our sepoys. To ensure speedy and complete success against any one of those tribes we must rely mainly on the extent of European force which we array against them. But unfortunately the scenes of operation the possibility of which is alluded to are so far distant from one another that the European force destined for any one of these contemplated operations cannot be removed from one quarter to another . . . but each portion of the force must continue through an entire season of military operations in India with that branch of the whole army to which it was originally allotted." European cavalry and artillery he did not need inasmuch as the Company's were superior to any likely to be encountered in Asia; but infantry he needed urgently; and he put the number at four complete regiments.

The President's reaction was to propose the immediate raising of two infantry regiments under the Act of 1788. The Court made a more handsome counter-proposal of three new regiments, one at each Presidency, each on an establishment of 920 rank and file, which it reconciled with the 1788 Act thus:

Artillery establishment, officers included	.		6442
Proposed infantry establishment:			
Six regiments (3 old, 3 new) 920 .	.	5520	
Officers	.	237	
			5757
			12,199
By Act of 28 Geo. III ch. 8, sec. 2	.		12,200

To this Hobhouse acceded, and, such was the speed at which the departments could work if they chose that, though Auckland's dispatch was received only in the first week of April, by 10th May the Directors' instructions had been sent to Calcutta. Orders for the three new regiments were promulgated at Fort William on 29th July, and the new European Regiment at the Bombay Presidency received its first mention in Bombay General Orders of 30th August 1839.[2]

[2]The manuscript sources referred to in this chapter are the records of the East India Company, now in the India Office Library, where they are classed under various heads, e.g., Muster Rolls, Cadet Papers (cit. hereafter as "C.P."), Military Consultations (Bengal, Madras, Bombay, &c.), (cit. hereafter as "Mil. Cons. [Bombay])", Special Collections (cit. as "Spec. Coll."), &c. The whole circumstances surrounding the raising of the three European regiments in 1839 are set out in the correspondence in Spec. Coll. Vol. 37, No. 305.

It was not the first time the Bombay army had possessed a second battalion of European infantry. On the three previous occasions, however, (1768-1778, 1788-1796, 1824-1829), the second battalion had been rather a part of the first that had become unwieldy than a second regiment, which it was most certainly in 1839. Not that the old "Bombay Toughs" did not make an important contribution to the new regiment this time. They were stationed in the island of Kharaq, in the Persian Gulf, and at Aden, which they had stormed on 19th January, and only some details and recruits were left at Poona, where the new regiment was forming. But not only were the recruits made over but also an important stiffening of seasoned soldiers brought back from Aden and Kharaq. Twenty-eight sergeants (including 15 corporals made up to that rank), two drummers, and twenty-six privates made up as corporals were transferred in January 1840, several months before the great mass of recruits reached Poona from the Company's depot at Chatham.[3]

The officers of the new regiment were selected purely on the strength of their seniority in the service. The wholesale reductions of the Bentinck régime had led to great dissatisfaction among the officers, and the Company, always more indulgent towards the claims of its servants than the Crown, regarded the augmentation as something in the nature of a reparation. In their plan for officering the new regiments the object, it was said, was "to transfer no officer without bringing him nearer to a majority through the operation of line promotion than he would be if not transferred, while it will not place anyone in a position to supersede a senior officer in his own or in any other corps". The complexities of the plan are nowadays of hardly more than antiquarian interest. It need only be said that it resulted in the transfer of thirty-three officers, all but two of them from the sepoy regiments and most of them men of considerable experience.[4] Their experience, however, was not necessarily regimental, and it was commonly said, moreover, that service with sepoys unfitted an officer for command of Europeans. Their selection had certainly not been made with a view to their performing the exacting task of forming a new regiment out of several hundred raw recruits, a task which, to judge from later events for which there is evidence, was very formidable and can be reckoned as satisfactorily completed only when the Regiment received its first colours at Belgaum on 22nd January 1846.

The European regiments were always noted for their lavish establishment of officers, which caused them to be regarded as double

³Mil. Cons. (Bombay), Range 361/Vol. 25, No. 8651.
⁴Mil. Cons. (Bombay), 361/22, No. 6598.

regiments and as often as not employed in wings. But one of the weaknesses of the old Indian army, one which became only too apparent in 1857, was the extent to which officers—and those usually the ablest and most energetic—were allowed to take up staff, political, police, customs and other quasi-military duties. The new regiment was no more exempt than any other. No less than twenty-one of the thirty-three officers of the 2nd Europeans were absent for one reason or another at the time of its first muster. Of the four officers shown in Vane's *History* to have served continuously in the Regiment through-out its service under the Company one alone (Saunders) did regimental duty: Gordon was an Inam Commissioner; Barr was a pay-master; and Hervey, after a short period as quartermaster and inter-preter, was a Superintendent for the suppression of Thuggee. All the senior officers appointed under "the plan" on 8th October 1839 be-came ineffective soon after, either because they already held staff appointments, such as Stratford Powell, who was Adjutant-General at headquarters in Bombay, or because they preferred service with the native regiments and got themselves quickly re-transferred. This preliminary sorting-out process, though it occupied months when there was very little to command at the depot at Poona, nevertheless left vacant the vital situation of a commanding officer.

This was supplied by Sir John Keane, the commander-in-chief of the Bombay army, who, writing from Kabul, where he commanded the "Army of the Indus", recommended the appointment of Lieut.-Colonel Stalker, of the 19th Native Infantry. Aged 41, Stalker had recently distinguished himself in the command of his regiment during the storming of Ghazni. He was a brave and decided regimental officer "eminently qualified", as Keane said, "for the task of forming and commanding the new regiment," although all his service had been with native regiments. "His activity, professional ability and great zeal for the service are well known. His temper is excellent and he is calculated to gain the esteem and respect of the officers and men. All these qualities are not to be met with in every officer of his rank." Keane was right. A regiment's first commanding officer cannot but leave his mark upon it for the remainder of its existence, and it is not too far-fetched to see in the consistently good record of this battalion something bequeathed to it by Foster Stalker.[5]

In the meanwhile the organisation of the Regiment was carried out by the Adjutant, Lieutenant J. B. M. Gillanders, the son of a country gentleman of Ross-shire and lately adjutant of the 26th N.I., an officer to whom the battalion is beholden hardly less than Stalker. Several shiploads of recruits from Chatham arrived during the sum-

[5]Mil. Cons. (Bombay), 361/25, No. 8714.

mer of 1840. One ship, the *Lord William Bentinck*, foundered off Colaba with the loss of several men and families, but 77 survivors from the wreck reached the Regiment. By October of that year the strength was 590 (28 sergeants—all from the 1st Europeans—45 corporals, 6 drummers and 511 privates). Nearly half were from Ireland, a proportion that increased slightly over the years as the living conditions in that country deteriorated. None came from County Durham. Their officers on the other hand, unlike those of the 68th, were all English with the exception of Captain Macan, who came from Armagh, Gillanders, and Ensign Walker, who came from Dublin. A further batch of recruits arriving in the season of 1841 brought up the strength in October of that year to 916 n.c.o.s and privates, not far short of establishment.[6]

The history of the formation of the Regiment as a regiment of light infantry is interesting not only for its own sake but for the light it sheds upon that episode in the record of the 68th. It shows among other things that the selection of a battalion for light infantry training was not, in the view of the authorities, made in recognition of its past services—on the contrary, that its very newness constituted a reason for its conversion. But it shows also that there had grown up in those thirty years an idea among the younger generation of officers that conversion to light infantry was an honour granted to regiments with a distinguished record. Already, it seems, history and tradition were at variance, and it was unfortunately tradition that had become popular currency.

The decision to make the 2nd European Regiment light infantry was taken by the Governor of Bombay upon 13th December 1839, when as yet the Regiment was only a paper creation. Though made in Keane's absence it followed a recommendation of Keane's which embraced a much larger plan to introduce light infantry into the armies of Bengal and Bombay; that of Madras alone having any. Keane's opinion (which, coming from one who until the year previous had been Colonel of the 68th, deserves special attention), was that a tenth part of the army should be light infantry. He proposed that, in addition to the 2nd Europeans, two native battalions should be converted as well, and that the tenth company of the light battalions should be riflemen. "I am strongly in favour of light infantry, having served in it," he said. "A small number of light troops perform with ease and efficiency services that would have harassed and embarrassed a much larger body of the line. And it is clear that this must be the case, for while the aim of line drill is to keep the soldier steady in the ranks and to make him move with precision as part of a

[6]Muster Rolls (Bombay), Vol. 47.

large body, the light infantryman is taught to be constantly on the watch when skirmishing to take advantage of cover and position, without reference to points and dressing, and to think and act for himself."

The Governor's decision, which appeared as an order on 16th December, immediately encountered the opposition of the Supreme Government at Calcutta. It observed that the officers of the new regiment had been posted according to their claims in point of rank without reference to their fitness for a light infantry corps; that the men, "enlisted in England for European regiments in India, are entertained without any advertence to their adaptation to a corps of light infantry;" and that no local (that is to say, presidential) government, not even the government of India, was empowered to make the necessary changes in organisation, equipment and clothing without the sanction of the Court; and it directed the Governor to rescind his order. Rivett-Carnac accordingly did so, but he had no intention of giving in, and proceeded to assemble the materials for a reference to the Court. To the objection that the officers were posted only according to their "cadet standing" he replied that it was done every day at Madras, where they "led the way" in light infantry, having already one European and four sepoy regiments converted. To the objection that the men were unadapted for light infantry he replied that he and Keane considered the 2nd Europeans as a regiment "entirely of young recruits who can, in the course of their drill and instruction, be taught with comparative facility to adopt all that is requisite and essential to efficiency in the new formation". The step had been recommended by Keane before his departure for Kabul on the grounds that the "frontier situation" of the Presidency made it highly advisable, as well as the conversion of two sepoy regiments into light infantry, the introduction of riflemen, and the conversion of a cavalry regiment into lancers. No change of organisation or clothing were involved. The only change was in the adoption of the "double-sighted light infantry musket", of which there was a considerable stock in Bombay arsenal. Keane was asked to repeat his recommendation, which he did, adding drily that there was no fear of any laxity being admitted, as most inspecting officers put regiments through close movement drill—indeed, he said, the best light regiments in H.M. service were "second to none in precision as well as in the rapidity of movement". Carnac, moreover, on Keane's retirement, which took place in the midst of the controversy, obtained the opinion of his successor, Sir Thomas McMahon, who had proved himself in the field as a brigadier of Portuguese infantry in the Peninsula. McMahon's opinion reinforced Keane's. He would prefer a whole regiment of riflemen to Keane's three companies, but as to lancers and three light infantry regiments, including the 2nd Europeans, he was in complete agreement with Keane.

Before this formidable array of opinion neither the Supreme Government nor the Court (had it indeed originally thought otherwise) could resist. On 10th November 1840 the 2nd Europeans were ordered to be trained and known as the "2nd Regiment Bombay European Light Infantry". To complete the story it may be added that, the following year, the 4th N.I. were selected as a rifle regiment, the 5th and 23rd N.I. as light infantry, and the 1st Light Cavalry as lancers. The order, however, was received with much disappointment and dissatisfaction in the 1st European Regiment, who from Aden dispatched an elaborate memorial of their long and meritorious services in support of a claim for a similar distinction. The Adjutant-General justly observed that in the Queen's service seniority had nothing to do with selection as light infantry, and that the order of 10th November was not intended to derogate from the character of the elder corps. The Bombay Government compromised. They made the 1st Europeans fusiliers, and as the "Bombay Fusiliers" the "Toughs" were henceforth known.[7]

It is a small piece of entirely excusable regimental jealousy that would not be worth mentioning if it did not make clear the fact that the military authorities of that time, brought up in the days when the light infantry controversy was at its height in England, were blissfully unaware that they "distinguished" a regiment when they made it light infantry. They took the most malleable material at their disposal. It had been the magnificent service rendered by corps otherwise quite undistinguished that in the 30-odd years interval made it a point of honour on the part of all the rest to be like them.

The same order of 16th December 1839 which formed the Regiment as light infantry also prescribed their uniform and appointments. They were to be armed with the double-sighted light infantry musket. Their accoutrements were to be buff. The clothing was to be red with facings of pale buff, the lace white with a black worm; the caps were to bear a green silk ball as a tuft. The officers were to dress as officers of the line infantry with the distinction of bugle skirt-ornaments. Field-officers were to wear epaulettes, the remainder gold wings.

Why the facings were made pale buff it is hard to see. Facings, one feels, are not properly the department of the Governor, whose

[7]Mil. Cons. (Bombay), 361/25, No. 8633; 361/28, Nos. 721-726; 361/30, Nos. 2236-2238; 361/31, Nos. 3158-3159; 361/49, Nos. 3056-57; 361/48, Nos. 2450-51.

hand is certainly behind the matter of light infantry. In Britain the choice would have been the Colonels'. Colonels of the Company's regiments, however, were but shadows of their counterparts at home, who even in 1839 retained certain powers, particularly in the matter of clothing. They received an income from "off-reckonings", but, the Company providing the clothing, the off-reckonings were not the commodity familiar in this country. It is hard to see in the choice the hand of the first Colonel, General George Brooks, who held the appointment for only two months, and it is harder still to see in it that of General Ephraim Stannus, a magnificent old veteran wearing bushy whiskers and steel spectacles, who was too far away governing the Seminary at Addiscombe with his fiery temper and rich fund of invective to be concerned in that. It is far more likely to have been the work of Colonel Stratford Powell, the Adjutant-General, who was also senior major of the new regiment. But why? The facings of the 2nd European Regiment disbanded in 1829 were white: the 1st Europeans' facings were yellow. It seems, however, that the old 2nd Europeans were commonly known as the "Bombay Buffs", and it may well be that the choice was an attempt to perpetuate the old name. The question, however, is almost academic since on 21st July 1842 Stalker applied for the colour to be changed to white because of the difficulty of always obtaining the same shade, which "from cleaning continually changes, so that officers and men are seen with almost every shade of buff". So slow were the ordinary methods of supply that the first clothing of the new regiment had not been made up in England even at so late a date, and Stalker's application was immediately granted as involving no additional expense on that ground. Curiously enough, white remained the colour of the battalion's facings until 1902. When it became the 106th the facings were untouched; and when it became the 2nd Battalion of the Durham Light Infantry in 1881 the facings of all non-royal English infantry regiments were at the same time changed to white, so that it was not until the Durhams obtained permission to revert to their dark green facings that the descendants of the 2nd Europeans surrendered their familiar colour.

If the Regiment's "first clothing" had not been made up, let alone taken into wear, by July 1842, one may legitimately wonder how it was clothed all this while. Presumably the Poona *durzis* had produced something, otherwise the question of the facings would not have arisen. But the supply departments of the Company's army were notoriously slow. In 1843 and 1844 they sent out white balls for the 2nd Europeans' shakos. The Commanding Officer complained the second time. He was told he must dye them green. He replied that had been tried before but that the sun had turned them brown, and green worsted balls had been made up at the men's expense at a cost of eight annas a man. The official response to that was a reprimand for making up green tufts without previous sanction. Similarly the recruits' drill was retarded by a delay in the issue of the proper buff accoutrements. The 2nd Europeans were peculiar in adopting the broad belts used by Queen's infantry, and the Clothing Board at Bombay had received an unprecedented demand for them from detachments of the Queen's troops joining their regiments in Afghanistan, China and Madras, which drained the arsenals. Normally, of course, these articles were a charge upon the Colonels of H.M.'s regiments; but in the emergency the Company's storekeepers had taken it upon themselves to equip trained troops rather than recruits on the barrack-square, still learning marching in slow time to the pace-stick, the watch, the plummet and the drum.[8]

Meanwhile the forward policy of Lord Auckland was continued under his successor Lord Ellenborough, who, though warned against any expansion of territory beyond the Indus before his departure from England, nevertheless as one of his first acts annexed Sind. The conquest of the country was carried out by Sir Charles Napier entirely with troops from the Bombay Presidency, and the outbreak of war brought the 2nd Europeans from their peaceful cantonments towards the theatre of operations. In April 1842 the left wing, under Stalker himself, had left Poona to relieve the 1st Europeans at Bombay and had in turn been relieved by the right wing under Captain Wynter the following November. With the approach of hostilities the whole Regiment was warned for service. The left wing (under Major Spencer) was brought again to Bombay, while the right wing, when relieved, embarked for Kutch and reached Bhuj on 16th March 1843. Bhuj was not necessarily an unhealthy station, but after a heavy and protracted monsoon it became one, and by October the sick amounted to 276 out of 437, most with malaria. "Here we all are amidst fever and locusts," wrote Surgeon Cahill. "Sergeant-major, quartermaster-sergeant and all of our essential non-commissioned officers are laid up, only one bugler left to blow the calls, and the whole of the band sick. Up to September," he said, "this wing of the Regiment was in splendid health. I never saw men in such fine condition, ready for and fit for any work. But now I fear the effects of this outbreak will long be felt. The men will be in and out of hospital with periodical returns of fever and suffer from visceral disease and all the chronic ailments that follow head fever,

---

[8]Bombay G.O., 16th Dec 1839; Mil. Cons. (Bombay), 362/5, Nos. 5194-5196, 5996-6000; 361/48, Nos. 2862-65; Bombay G.O., 10th Mar 1854.

which are so difficult to eradicate. Pity to see a fine young regiment like this smashed by fever and its sequels." "Our regiment," wrote another surgeon, "will be completely ruined, and such fine young fellows as they looked the other day, now all with shaven heads."[9]

The epidemic was too serious to be disregarded, and under the advice of the medical authorities both the wing at Bhuj and the left wing, which had moved up to Karachi in May, were brought back to the Presidency in exchange for H.M.'s 86th, which vacated its quarters at Belgaum for them in January and March 1844. They left Napier's Army with the publicly expressed regrets of its eccentric and forthright chief, who never suffered fools gladly or gave praise where it was not due, and on this occasion acknowledged the Regiment's good conduct while under his command. The epidemic had deprived them not only of an opportunity for brilliant service, but also of their first commanding officer, Stalker, who, when at Bhuj, left them late in October to return to a native regiment. His successor was Major Henry Spencer, a good officer, now aged 44, the son of a London solicitor. But his health was broken, and so sickly was the state of the Regiment at this time that when he went on leave in June, 1844, he was succeeded by a captain, Wynter. Later in the year, about October, Lieut.-Colonel Robertson was brought in from the 20th N.I. to take command. Indeed, though the health of the men gradually improved at Belgaum, the Regiment was still in a weak state when in September 1844 it received its next call for service, in the so-called Kolhapur Field Force.

Kolhapur State lay outside the proper limits of the Presidency, in the wild and hilly regions of the South Mahratta Country where every hill was crowned by a fort and whose inhabitants looked on fighting as their profession. Situated at a point where Madras and Bombay territory almost touched, it was naturally the concern of both, and Madras troops had been moved in to Belgaum to take the place of the Bombay regiments sent up to Sind in January 1843. The Indian Government had an interest in maintaining friendly relations with the Raja, and since 1829 the Indian Government had had the power of appointing a minister. From the death of the Raja in 1838 it had actively intervened in the State's politics to preserve its influence. It was a situation that had occurred and continued to occur on every frontier throughout the period of British rule in India: as a

[9]Mil. Cons. (Bombay), 362/9, Nos. 7659-7662; 362/26, Nos. 8838, 8842; 362/28, No. 9989.

neighbouring prince's power deteriorated, so the Company's power advanced to fill the vacuum. As elsewhere, so in Kolhapur. In 1844 the Government's nominee was faced with armed opposition from the garrisons of the forts. These garrisons, or *Ghadkaris*, had been hereditary since the days of Sivaji, the great founder of the Mahratta Confederacy in the seventeenth century, and were maintained upon the revenue of certain villages, very much as certain manors used to be held on knight's service in this country. They complained that the British administration had encroached upon their ancient privileges, and that instead of their chief communicating direct with the Durbar he was placed under the orders of the Mamlatdar, a kind of revenue official who in former days had been subordinate to the chief. Alarm was created when the villages from which they drew their revenue were merged into larger districts; whereas previously each fort had a Mamlatdar to itself it now shared a Mamlatdar with other forts; and although the new Mamlatdar had not interfered with the dues themselves, their houses and fruit-trees had been counted and the privilege of sealing with their own seal orders carried from the forts had been discontinued. In other words, a régime of benevolent but unimaginative "rationalisation" was being dispensed, and the *Ghadkaris* were apprehensive of the future, as many another better informed citizen has been since when governments get rationalisation on the brain.

There were thirteen large forts in the State of Kolhapur, and the garrisons of all but two rose in revolt. The first to rise were the *Ghadkaris* of Budurgarh, who on 22nd July, shut their gates against the Mamlatdar. They were immediately joined in insubordination by the *Ghadkaris* of Samangarh. To repress them a field force under Colonel Wallace of the Madras service was sent north-west from Belgaum. He, unfortunately, was on 24th September checked in an attempt to take Samangarh, whose strength was seriously underestimated; while he was awaiting a battering-train and reinforcements the insurgents took courage; and the revolt, fomented by some unscrupulous courtiers, spread into a kind of Mahratta conspiracy.

Wallace's force, which left Belgaum on 16th September, included a "field detachment" from the 2nd Europeans under Captain Gillanders, consisting of two captains (Gillanders and Jones), seven subalterns (Shakespear, Brassey, A. P. Campbell, Tyacke, Savile, Aitchison and Thompson), a surgeon, ten sergeants, four buglers, twelve corporals and 189 privates. Not only was the Regiment so weak at this juncture that after the departure of the field detachment only 286 private men were left fit for duty in barracks—and 40 of them musicians—but the field detachment itself was in such a feeble state as to excite comment from General Delamotte, commanding the Southern Division of the Army, when he inspected it the evening before it marched off. "It did not escape my observation," he said, "the delicate and sickly appearance of many of the 200 men from the 2nd Europeans.[10]

After his repulse at Samangarh, Wallace sat down before the place to besiege it in all form. During the next fortnight the Regiment lost a private soldier and Lieutenant Shakespear killed, the first on 29th the latter on 30th September. By 12th October the breaches were considered practicable, and Wallace ordered an assault in twin columns for 4.30 a.m. the following morning. The first column, under Captain Jones, 2nd Europeans, consisted of 80 men from the Regiment, the grenadier and light companies of the 20th Madras N.I., with a company of sepoy riflemen as covering party. The second, under Captain Gillanders, consisted of 70 men from the Regiment under Lieutenant Savile, 150 from the 23rd Bombay N.I., who also found a covering party of 50 riflemen. Jones's column went in first and in a few minutes had mounted the breach, Lieutenant Campbell having the honour of reaching it first with Lieut.-Colonel Outram, who somehow managed to show up anywhere where there was trouble. Gillanders' column went in after. It was all over in half an hour. The assault was completely successful, the garrison losing 500 or 600 killed and a like number captured. Three only of the 2nd Europeans were wounded.

By this time, however, the whole country was in an uproar. A party of rebels surprised Chikodi in British territory and plundered the treasury. The *Ghadkaris* of Manoharh, overlooking the Savantvari country, whose inhabitants pride themselves on their pure Mahratta blood, rose up and started a kind of Robin Hood rebellion in that state as well. The *Ghadkaris* of Panhala and Pawangarh, two strong fortresses twelve miles north-west of Kolhapur, placed themselves in a state of defence. The garrison of Kolhapur itself overthrew the government and reinstated those deposed by the Indian Government. The revolt ceased to be merely a revolt of the *Ghadkaris*. The alarm it created in British territory was widespread, and there was something approaching panic in Ratnagiri, Vengurla and even Belgaum. The Field Force was substantially reinforced and placed under the command of the general commanding the Southern Division of the Army, General Delamotte. He was a cavalryman, just entering his sixties, too old for a rough-and-tumble of this kind, as his operations too plainly showed.

A light detachment under Outram was moved forward to Kol-

[10]Mil. Cons (Bombay), 362/42, No. 8392.

hapur, which surrendered, and Delamotte then moved against Budurgarh. He seized the fort on 10th November but only after one of the principal rebels was smuggled out at one gate while he entered at another, and on terms which the Directors considered unnecessarily lenient. Being near Manoharh, he was advancing to take that place when news reached him that Colonel Ovans, whom the Government had sent to assume temporary management at Kolhapur, had been kidnapped on his way and taken by the rebels into Panhala, where he was kept prisoner. Delamotte therefore marched north while the rebellion broke out behind him in the Savantvari, and he invested Panhala on 26th November.

Early that month Gillanders had had command of a composite battalion consisting of his own two companies, three companies of the 21st Bombay N.I., two companies of the 23rd Madras N.I., and the rifle company of the 16th Madras N.I. By the time the Field Force reached Panhala it was formed in three brigades, each of detachments from several regiments, European and sepoy, the 2nd Europeans contributing a detachment under Ensign Hassard of 20 men to Wallace's (1st) Brigade, the remainder acting with Brough's (2nd) Brigade.

After tremendous exertions the batteries were constructed high up on the steep hill on which the fort stands, at a distance of about 600 yards. On 30th November they opened, and continued the next morning at a range of 350 yards. In the afternoon of that day (1st December) the breaches were reported practicable for assault, and a storming-party under Lieut.-Colonel Brough, H.M.'s 2nd (Queen's), was formed, consisting of 200 of his own regiment, 100 from the 2nd Bombay Europeans under Gillanders, and 200 Madras sepoys. At about 4 p.m. the party advanced up the hillside, while the *Ghadkaris* rolled down rocks upon them as they struggled up the slope. It was a stiff climb, but as at Samangarh the resistance crumbled as soon as the breach was entered. As a matter of fact the reserve, which included Hassard's 20 men, though starting later than Gillanders' party, arrived at the breach first. But the whole business was over in an hour, and this time the number of prisoners taken was very considerable, amounting to not less than 2000. The casualties again were astonishingly small: 3 privates killed, 7 officers and 60 men wounded, of which the Regiment lost 2 privates killed, and Lieutenant Aitchison (who was acting assistant-engineer) and 10 privates wounded. Colonel Ovans, who had narrowly escaped with his life in the bombardment, was released.

Pawangarh nearby was stormed that evening not at Delamotte's orders but on the initiative of a brigadier and a Captain Bayley of the 20th Madras N.I. who found an easy way in. This officer's party, approaching the fort from the south while a detachment of H.M.'s 22nd, fresh from their laurels in Sind, approached from the north, consisted of 50 men from the 2nd Europeans under Lieutenant Thompson, and 100 Madras sepoys, and the two met unexpectedly at the foot of the walls. Bayley, who was in front, pressed a stone into the hands of Private Daniels, a large man of the 2nd Europeans standing by, and ordered him to split the wicket, which he did after several heavy blows. Daniels then squeezed through with some difficulty, catching his greatcoat, which was strapped to his shoulders, against the wicket. Inside, Bayley, following, discovered the lock of the gate in a sealed leather bag, which he tore open. The lock proved too strong for him to break; but Bugler Toole, 2nd Europeans, thrust back the bar of the gate, and the 50 men, 22nd and European Light Infantry mingled together, surged forward into the fortress. The 22nd claimed the capture of Pawangarh as theirs, but in the acrimonious correspondence that followed there can be no doubt that Daniels and Toole were the first men in.

On 5th December Wallace was ordered to march on the fort of Rangna, sixty miles or so to the south-west. At Patgaum on the 8th he united with a force under Captain Prior, who informed him the enemy held a strongly stockaded position 500 yards from the fort. "I immediately," he says, "determined to dislodge them," and on the 9th, forming his storming-party into three columns, he proceeded to do so. The right and left columns were composed of Madras and Bombay sepoys; the centre, which was to deliver the frontal attack, was composed entirely of 100 men of the 2nd Europeans commanded by Gillanders, with Brassey, Savile and Hassard under him. The attack, which went in early in the morning from right, left and centre covered by skirmishing parties of 20 from each column, the centre one led by Lieutenant A. P. Campbell, 2nd Europeans, was outstandingly successful. Not only was the stockade carried and the gate broken open, but the *petta*, or village, beyond was entered and the fort of Rangna evacuated the following night, at a cost to Wallace's force of two men wounded, neither of them in the Regiment.

By this time Delamotte's force was split up and operating over a wide area to reduce the remaining *Ghadkari* fortresses and round up those rebels who had escaped into the wild countryside and the State of Savantvari. Late in December one of his columns, containing the bulk of the 2nd Europeans, who, like all the European troops, were used as the shock-troops of the Field Force, besieged and reduced Manoharh and Mansantosh, in the course of which two men were killed. And on the 31st of that month he moved to attack a strongly built rebel stockade in a defile at Sassedrug nearby. This was a stubborn and bloody affair. The attack, covered by the rifle company of the 16th Madras N.I., was carried out entirely by the detachment of the 2nd Europeans, and it was repulsed with casualties almost as heavy as all those hitherto sustained by the Regiment. Lieutenant A. P. Campbell, a most promising young officer from Perth, and four men were killed, and Lieutenant Tyacke and four men wounded. The misfortune, however, was redeemed by one of those acts of bravery that have passed into Indian army history. When the storming party withdrew, Campbell's body was left in the open exposed to the musketry from the stockades. Three men of the Regiment, Corporal Thacker and Privates Walsh and Desmond, together with two sepoys from the 16th Madras N.I. (now the 3/1st Punjab Regiment), Cotapah and Veropah, crept out and managed to bring it back under a heavy fire. The three Europeans were honourably mentioned, while Cotapah and Veropah were admitted to the Indian Order of Merit, Cotapah receiving also a gold medal from the City of Perth for his bravery.

From the beginning of 1845 onwards the operations become even more scattered and difficult to describe as the fleeing rebels are harried and pursued—even into Goa—and the rebellion in the Savantvari is suppressed. Before they eventually fade out altogether the only indications of the Regiment's presence are stray references to such officers as Lieutenant Brassey, who commanded a detachment of pioneers engaged in clearing the road to Vengurla; Lieutenant Thompson, who was wounded in an affair at Sarapur; Ensign Fauré, a young South African from Graaf-Reinet, who was killed while on escort duty on the Vengurla road between Sassuli and Banda on the same day as the repulse at Sassedrug; and Captain Thornton, normally detached from the Regiment as Superintendent of the Salt-Chowkies at Ratnagiri, who "defeated a body of insurgents who had assembled at a temple four miles from Malwan with a very small detachment under his command".

Indeed, it was a difficult and muddled business, hardly worthy to be called a campaign. It brought no credit to the unfortunate Delamotte, whom the Directors found guilty of serious errors of judgment. It ended in an atmosphere of recrimination when Delamotte brought Wallace, who gave every appearance of being the most enterprising of his subordinates, before a court-martial for disobedience of orders. Nearly ten thousand troops in all had been occupied nearly eight months, and the bitterness aroused then was, as we shall see, to influence events in the perilous days of 1857. But so far as the Regiment was concerned they came out of it with an enhanced reputation. They were blooded, and they could begin to look the Toughs in the eye.[11]

§

There followed eleven years of peaceful garrison duty, interspersed only with moves from one station to another. The first took place in the monsoon of 1846 when they relieved H.M.'s 94th at Aden, which, like St. Helena and Mauritius, was an outpost of the Company's empire. There was some inconvenience in bringing them to Bombay for embarkation, and as there were only fair-weather tracks from Belgaum to the nearest sea-port, Vengurla, the march involved the construction of temporary bridges, hiring boats, and making rafts, before they were all safely on board on 9th November. Although they were under-strength at this period, (777 in 1846, 701 in 1847) their accommodation at Aden was severely cramped. But Major Macan, who was in command during their five years abroad, was an experienced and humane officer who had lived all his life in India and, when commanding the left wing at Bombay in 1842, had somehow contrived to get quarters enlarged "for the poor soldier who has not only no room for any game of exercise but not even a ball court to play at". The right wing under Captain Jones returned to Poona in January 1848, where it received all the European recruits destined for the Presidency. This accession brought the total strength up to a figure of 1039 n.c.o.s and men, but in September 100 men were given to the 1st Europeans as volunteers to make up their strength in preparation for service in the Punjab. The left did not rejoin until December 1849, by which time the right had come down to Belgaum. The excursion to Aden had deprived them of a second opportunity of active operations in the Punjab, where the elder regiment rendered such distinguished services at Multan in the Second Sikh War.

At Belgaum they remained until October 1853. Macan was succeeded in the command, immediately on their return from Aden, by Major A. P. Le Messurier, who, though one of the original officers transferred in 1839, had been on the staff latterly as A.A.G., Ahmedabad, and was not, it appears, an inspiring regimental officer. "While," says the Inspection Report, "I give the commanding officer of the 2nd European Light Infantry every credit for attention and zeal, yet I do not think he evinces that temper which calls forth re-

[11]The operations in Kolhapur and the Savantvari are detailed in the reports published in Bombay G.O. See also Colburn's *United Service Magazine*, 1845 (Part III), pp. 296-301.

spect and cheerful obedience of both officers and men. He is of an irritable disposition, and his corrections and reproofs I do not think are made with that temper which is calculated to ensure a proper impression without hurting the feelings of the individual." He went soon after the report was made and was replaced in February 1852 by a very different man. Major (he became Lieut.-Colonel in 1854) James Skardon Ramsay was the son of a captain of cavalry in the Bengal army, who, when commanding two regiments at the battle of Bitaurah in the Second Rohilla War, had been utterly routed, and afterwards, rather than face the court-martial, had absconded. He, his wife (the daughter of a brother officer of the name of Skardon), and the children thereafter lived a roving life in Scotland, in England and on the continent until the unhappy man died at Brussels about 1816. James was born in Somerset, he had been educated at the Military School at Brussels, and he entered the Bombay Service in 1819. He had every reason for making good, and, indeed, he had risen as fast as he could. "His general character," says the Inspection Report, "is steady and good, and he is a very efficient officer." He was now 53, on the threshold of a most happy period of command, and it is sad to have to relate how all this promise was shattered.[12]

In October 1853 the Regiment was moved to Hyderabad in Sind as part of the season's change of stations. Instead of moving by sea it marched the whole way to Karachi, where, in November, it lost several officers and 77 n.c.o.s and men transferred to the 3rd European Regiment, then raising. It reached Hyderabad in December, and remained there for two years until forming part of the 1st Division of the Persian Expeditionary Force.

§

Persia had been subjected to the southward pressure of Russian expansion since the beginning of the century. After the loss of hey Caucasian provinces she had turned east towards Afghanistan to recoup, and it had been the threat of a Russian-dominated Persia upon the independent state of Herat, regarded as the gateway to Afghanistan, that had started the whole series of events that led to the First Afghan War (and, incidentally, to the raising of the 2nd Europeans). The immediate threat had been removed by the stubborn defence of Herat; but the threat was renewed in 1855, when the ruler of Herat was removed by his subjects and replaced by a Persian nominee; and a Persian army at last succeeded in entering and taking

[12]Officers' Services (Bombay), *sb*. Le Messurier and Ramsay: C.P., xxxiii, 369.

possession of the city. The reaction of the Indian Government was, first, to arrange a treaty of alliance with Dost Mohammed of Afghanistan, to whom the ruler of Herat had appealed for help—the effect of this, however, was anticipated by the fall of Herat; and, secondly, and reluctantly, to make war on Persia. "Few wars," says Sir Percy Sykes, "have resembled that which followed. The usual question is how to injure an enemy most effectively, but on this occasion the efforts of our statesmen were directed to securing the evacuation of Herat without inflicting a heavy blow on Persia.[13] To have marched on Herat either through a friendly Afghanistan or from Bandar Abbas was equally expensive and difficult, and it was decided to operate from the Persian Gulf and Mohammera in the Shatt-al-Arab.

It was entirely a Bombay affair: the troops came from the Bombay army, the ships from the Bombay marine. So expeditiously was it all arranged that though final instructions did not reach Bombay until 9th November the expedition sailed four days later. It consisted of 8 war steamers, 7 hired steamers and 35 sailing ships under Admiral Sir Henry Leeke, which were loaded at Bombay, Vengurla, Probandar and Karachi. The troops, (2270 Europeans, 3400 sepoys, and 2750 followers) were organised into a division of two infantry brigades, four batteries of artillery and about three squadrons of cavalry, all under the command of the Regiment's former C.O., Major-General Foster Stalker, who, now in his 58th year, was perhaps, next to Outram, the most distinguished officer in the Bombay army.

The infantry was brigaded as follows:

> *1st Brigade* (Brigadier J. Stopford):—
> H.M.'s 64th
> H.C.'s 20th Bombay N.I.
> *2nd Brigade* (Brigadier R. W. Honner):—
> H.C.'s 2nd European Regiment Bombay Light Infantry
> H.C.'s 4th Bombay N.I. (Rifles)
> H.C.'s 2nd Baluch Battalion

The 2nd Europeans had come down the Indus by boat to Karachi in October, and there the evening previous to embarkation for Persia had taken on 183 volunteers from the 1st Europeans (who were stationed at Karachi), an accession which made them up to a strength of 929 all ranks. Several officers who were on leave or detached on other duties were recalled, and Ramsay, who had been temporarily

[13]Brigadier-General Sir Percy M. Sykes, *A History of Persia* (Macmillan, 1915), Vol. II, pp. 452-453.

in command of Hyderabad, returned to resume command of the Regiment in this their first service in the field as a unit.[14]

The first objective of the expedition was to gain possession of Bushire, a mean and ugly little town, but the only port in the Gulf and the best point at which to establish a base of operations. The commanders acted with commendable promptitude. After a cruise of several days in sight of the monotonous sand coloured cliffs of the Persian coast, the fleet cast anchor off Hallila Bay, 10 miles south of Bushire, on 7th December; and the troops disembarked without encountering any opposition except from 300 or so Persians hidden in a date-grove about 200 yards to the left of the beach, who were dispersed by fire from the gunboats. The Army bivouacked on the sand on that and the following nights, while the artillery and stores were landed.

Reconnoitring parties had found that the Bushire road was blocked six miles ahead by a force of Dashti and Tangistun tribesmen estimated at 1500 to 2000, who held a position at the former Dutch settlement of Reshire (Reshahr). Since the success of the expedition depended on its defeating every Persian force it encountered, Stalker very properly determined on an immediate assault. On 9th December his Army advanced, covered by the 3rd Cavalry, the horse artillery, two companies of the 2nd Europeans and two companies of the 4th Rifles. The enemy, posted in the village of Reshire among the ruins of deserted houses, behind garden walls, and hidden in ravines, put up a sharp resistance for a while until, driven back from wall to wall, they broke and fled, only some 800 of the staunchest retiring into their last defence, which was the old Dutch fort. This was a redoubt almost square in shape, its rear resting on the beach. The ditch was of considerable depth, but at several places the rampart had crumbled, so filling the ditch that an entry could be gained without a resort to scaling ladders. Stalker formed his troops in such a manner as to encircle the fort, the cavalry moving round to the north flank to cut off retreat to Bushire, the 4th Rifles, covering the south face, their left on the sea, to prevent escape in that direction. The assault was made in two columns: one, of the 2nd Europeans, stormed the north-east angle, the other, of the 64th and the 20th N.I., stormed the east, or landward, face. Assisted by fire from the fleet at a range of 1700 yards, the column attacked at about noon. They were received by a heavy matchlock fire, which cut down Brigadier Stopford as he mounted the parapet, but the 2nd Europeans entered by an easier breach and lost only two men killed and six wounded in the whole day's fighting. The redoubt was carried at the point of the

[14]Bombay G.O., 18th Oct 1856, 3rd Dec 1856.

bayonet in a few minutes. It was, said the Admiral, "one of the most brilliant and gallant charges I ever witnessed". The enemy was ruthlessly pursued, and his loss was estimated at 400.

Sailing on to the roadstead of Bushire, the Admiral at daylight next day (10th December), seeing the garrison drawn up near some wells, their centre supported by a high fortified tower and a redoubt, ordered his warships to open on them. After an hour the Persians retreated in good order into the town. He refused the Persian Governor's demand for an armistice, and proceeded to bombard the shore defences, which replied at first with some spirit but to very little effect. Having silenced them, he directed his fire against the south-west angle of the town wall to breach it. But before the troops were within 500 yards of the place the flagstaff was seen to fall in token of surrender. It was something of an anti-climax to the Army, but it was an entirely satisfactory conclusion. About 1500 men laid down their arms (British muskets, made over to them by the British mission of 1838), and 15 guns were captured.

The Army was encamped in an entrenched camp constructed about a mile and a half from the walls in a more healthy situation where water was easily obtainable. There they remained for some six weeks while the Persians accumulated troops to force them from Bushire. One of the Persian depots, at Chakota, twenty miles away, was raided and destroyed by Stalker on 24th December. But a larger and more dangerous one, at Barazjun, intended to be used by a force estimated at 8500 under the Shuja-ul-Mulk coming from his point of concentration at Shiraz, was reserved for a later operation.

Towards the end of January there arrived from India reinforcements amounting to a fresh division of infantry and a welcome addition of cavalry. With them came orders for the relief of Lieut.-Colonel Ramsay from the command of the Regiment. The Ordnance Department accused him of negligence in failing to apply for ball ammunition on embarkation at Karachi and for disembarking 25,800 rounds short. A more serious charge was his failure to make proper arrangements for the families left behind at Hyderabad. Their plight had become the subject not only of criticism in the *Sindian Newspaper*—these local newspapers were written and read almost exclusively by military men—but also of a court of enquiry. Censure fell principally on the surgeons, but Sir Henry Somerset, Commander-in-Chief at Bombay, considered Ramsay's command "beyond his abilities" and relieved him. He was replaced by Lieut.-Colonel Shortrede, who presumably came out with the reinforcements. Shortrede, now aged 55, the son of a Roxburghshire Sheriff-substitute, admitted into the Company's service at the recommendation of no less a person than Sir Walter Scott and having spent almost the whole of his career with the Trigonometrical Survey, was plainly unfitted for command, particularly at this juncture. Somerset had said so, and had appointed Lieut.-Colonel Stiles from the 7th N.I. to take Ramsay's place and "restore the interior economy of the Regiment". But Stiles was not to arrive until 6th March, and in the interval Shortrede, ably assisted by Major E. A. Guerin, the next senior, did as best he could.[15]

Meanwhile, shortly before the arrival of the 2nd Division, Stalker had been superseded in the command of the Army by Outram—who, though his junior, was a close friend from the time the two had sailed for India in the same ship thirty-seven years previously—but retained command of his original division, now renamed the 1st. Outram brought with him a new spirit of resolution. Determined to start operations upon the Shatt-al-Arab, he had first to dispose of the threat of the Shuja-ul-Mulk's Army at Barazjun; and, in the evening of the 3rd February, leaving a force of 1800 men under Colonel Shepheard to guard the camp, he set out with his Army of 419 cavalry, 2212 European infantry (H.M.'s 64th and 78th Highlanders and the 2nd Europeans), 2022 sepoys and 18 guns.

The detachment of the 2nd Europeans (under Shortrede) numbered 693. It was rather weaker than the two Queen's regiments from the sickness which had overtaken them at Bushire, but all the officers who had fought with them at Reshire and Bushire less two (Captain Thompson and Lieutenant Robertson) were present: Major Guerin, Captains Saunders and Tyacke, Lieutenants Whittaker, Hassard (adjutant), Laughton, Scott, Griffiths, Twyford, Fergusson, R. R. Gillespie, Gayer, W. A. Gillespie, Gardyne, Phillips, Warden and Woodcock, and three newcomers from India: Lieutenants Billamore and Utterson and Ensign Jervis. They had, besides, five officers serving on the staff: Major Barr, paymaster; Captain C. R. W. Hervey, a.d.c. to Outram; Captain Aitchison, Brigade-Major to the 2nd Infantry Brigade of the 1st Division; Lieutenant Frankland, recently appointed Brigade Major to the Cavalry; and Lieutenant Hutcheon, probationary sub-assistant commissary-general.

The march was a most trying one; the nights were cold, and the troops, without tents, were exposed to deluging storms of rain. But they did the 46 miles in 41 hours and reached the Persian entrenchments in the afternoon of the 5th. The enemy had fled. Or, as Outram said, they had withdrawn themselves and their guns to "the strong passes, where I did not deem it prudent to follow them; and, being satisfied with the moral effect of our occupying their position

[15]Mil. Letters and Enclosures (Bombay), Vol. 39 (1860), No. 17.

for two days, I decided upon our moving the troops back to Bushire".
The magazines of stores and ammunition were destroyed—a work in
which Hassard, the adjutant, was employed: and the return march
started at dusk on the 7th.

It so happened that Shuja had intended attacking that very night.
His horsemen came up with Outram's Army in the dark, making
every effort, such as sounding the English bugle-calls, to create
a panic as the men were formed in a circle to protect the baggage. At
daybreak of the 8th February the enemy were seen on our left rear,
six or seven thousand strong, drawn up in order of battle on a small
eminence near the village of Khushab (or Khooshaub, as our ancestors pronounced it). Outram accordingly deployed the Army for
the attack, the infantry in two lines covered by the light companies,
the guns in front, and the cavalry some distance on the right. The
2nd Europeans, with the 2nd Brigade of the 1st Division, found themselves in the front line, with the 26th Bombay N.I. (of the 2nd
Division) on their right and the 4th Bombay Rifles (of their own
brigade) on their left. So soon as they had deployed the lines moved
forward in support of the guns. "In beautifully steady order," an eye-
witness described it, they breasted the slope on which the Persian
artillery was trained. In this movement the Regiment lost three men
killed and an officer (Woodcock) and eight men wounded, casualties
heavier than any other infantry regiment. The brunt of the action,
however, was borne part by the cavalry, who, though only two regiments strong, made two overwhelmingly impetuous charges, one of
which went right through a battalion drawn up in square, and part
by the artillery. The fire of these guns was something the Persians
were utterly unprepared for, and they fell back in disorder too
quickly for the infantry to have much say in their defeat. By 10
o'clock the battle was won. Only the scarcity of cavalry prevented
the Persian's complete destruction. The total cost to Outram's Army
was 16 killed (among them, however, Lieutenant Frankland of the
Regiment, on the cavalry staff) and 56 wounded. No offensive action
was ever after attempted by the Persian army, and to that extent the
battle of Khushab was decisive.

It was a weary army that trudged back into camp two days later,
many having lost their shoes sucked off in the mud, and all of them
damp and cold. But Outram had the knack of getting the most out of
his men, and before long he was off on his expedition to the Shatt-al-
Arab. This time he did not take the 2nd Europeans with him, an
omission of an important part of his European force which is perhaps
to be ascribed to the shortcomings of Shortrede as a commanding
officer. They were left to guard the camp at Bushire under General

Stalker. Stalker's health had broken down before the expedition to Barazjun, and on 27th March while Outram was away, he put an end to his life, a sad finish to a gallant career.[16]

After the fall of Bushire the Persian government had started negotiations for peace. Since the evacuation of Herat was agreed to, it remained only to part the contestants. The 2nd Europeans, who in their first and last campaign as a regiment had at one time or another brought 1005 men to Persia (including 38 officers and the volunteers from the Fusiliers), remained at Bushire until 15th May, when they embarked for Karachi.[17] It was the last expedition undertaken by the Company's army, and there is perhaps to be detected a note of nostalgia in the liberality with which the battle honours (*Persia, Reshire, Kooshab*) were distributed in October 1858,[18] at a time when these operations seemed to form part of a more wholesome past.

§

The mutinous spirit of the Bengal native regiments, that was eventually to spread through the entire Bengal army until that imposing and mighty structure fell crashing in pieces, had begun to show itself in late March 1857, and continued all through April. By the time the first troops returned from Persia the situation was very grave indeed. The Bombay officers said "that will not happen in our army", but so many devoted Bengal officers had said the same of their own regiments that it was impossible to see where the mutiny would stop. It was therefore an act of the greatest faith and courage on the part of Lord Elphinstone, the Governor of Bombay, to dispatch the two Queen's regiments to Calcutta immediately they returned from Persia. The 1st Bombay Fusiliers were sent up into the Punjab as a European reinforcement to the hard-pressed stations there—we have already seen them marching into the Lines of Lahore with their crumpled jackets and black neckerchiefs, gaping in wonder at the sumptuous appointments of a Bengal cantonment. Bombay was left with only two Queen's regiments and two of the Company's European regiments if the Bombay native army should prove unreliable too. This force was used in detachments, some in garrison, some in

[16]The operations in Persia are detailed in the reports published in Bombay G.O., Dec 1856, Jan and Feb 1857. See also Lieut.-General Sir James Outram, *Persian Campaign* (1860); Capt. G. H. Hunt (73rd), *Outram and Havelock's Persian Campaign* (1858); and a (not very reliable) account by General (then Lieut.) Ballard in *Blackwood* for 1861.

[17]Digest; Persia Medal Roll, Vol. 5, 20.

[18]*Bushire* was added in October 1861.

the numerous "field forces" that were hastily organised to lend assistance in Bengal or in the few localities in the Presidency affected by mutiny.

It may be said at once for clarity's sake that the Bombay army remained remarkably loyal. "Out of thirty-two infantry battalions only six gave ground for anxiety"; only two, the 21st and 27th N.I.— and in each a portion only—mutinied; and the 27th alone disgraced themselves by killing any of their officers.[19] It should also be said that only one wing of the 2nd Europeans was actively engaged in operations, and no more than a detachment from that involved in any fighting.

On 29th July the left wing was embarked for Bombay under Captain Jones, with Lieutenant Gayer acting as adjutant. A detachment from this of about three companies under Captain Jones was sent on by sea to Goa, whence, with the assistance of the Portuguese authorities, who were usually most accommodating, they marched up to Belgaum. They arrived "in tatters, shoeless and nearly kitless from the severity of the monsoon, but eager for work". The remainder of the left wing, under Major Guerin, who had apparently come on from Karachi, was brought in ships of the Bombay Navy to Ratnagiri. A small detachment was left there under Captain Saunders and Lieutenant Watson; but the greater number, consisting of 2 colour-sergeants, 3 sergeants, 9 corporals, 2 buglers and 90 privates —106 men—under Major Guerin, Captain Hervey (who, as a superintendent for the suppression of Thuggee in these parts was especially familiar with the country), and Lieutenants Gayer and Warden with Assistant-Surgeon Brigstock, was marched up over the Ghats to Kolhapur. This last movement, it should be noticed, was carried out at the height of the monsoon, "an achievement unheard of, I believe," says Colonel Le Grand Jacob, "in Indian history, as it was previously considered a thing impossible to land on that coast, . . . Bombay and Goa being during that season the only ports available".

The reason for these forced marches to the scene of their operations thirteen years before was the unsettled state of the South Mahratta Country, where, as it chanced, were stationed the three newest native regiments, the 27th at Kolhapur, the 28th at Dharwar, and the 29th at Belgaum. It transpired later that conspirators in the 27th N.I., who were in communication with the rebel sepoys in Bengal and also with disaffected persons in the town of Kolhapur—a legacy of the rebellion of 1844—intended to mutiny on 10th August; but, hearing that the adjutant, a Jew, whom they distrusted, was

[19]Sir Patrick Cadell, *History of the Bombay Army* (Longmans, Green, 1938), p. 202.

sending his family away on 31st July, and that European troops were being sent up from Bombay, they determined to rise that night before their plans were properly matured. At all events they rose that night, killed three of their officers, plundered the officers' bungalows and issued forth from the Cantonment to join with their fellow conspirators in the town. In this they were foiled as the gates were shut against them. Some dispersed towards Ratnagiri; some into the Savantvari jungle; others took up a position in a small outwork where the Rajas' horses and menagerie were kept, and were destroyed there by loyal men from their own regiment and a detachment from the Kolhapur Local Infantry on the day they had originally planned to rise.

Four days later, at midnight of the 14th August, Colonel Le Grand Jacob, appointed by Lord Elphinstone and Sir Henry Somerset to command in the Kolhapur and Ratnagiri area, arrived, followed three days after by two horse artillery guns and Guerin's detachment of the 2nd Europeans. The guns had come by "the upper road", but Guerin's detachment, which had come up over the Ghats through the thick black soil of the country, driving before them the mutineers of the 27th who had made for Ratnagiri, were a sight to behold. "Such a spectacle," says Le Grand Jacob, "it was painful to see. The men had marched in deep mud and torrents of rain across swollen streams, and such of their kit as they had managed to bring was ruined."

After balancing the question whether he was strong enough to disarm the remainder of the 27th, Le Grand Jacob, who now had 100 European infantry and about 450 loyal sowars and sepoys, determined to act immediately. On the 18th "I drew up," he says, "the Europeans with the Kolhapur Local Corps in one line, loaded the guns with grape and canister, and at a right-angle to these the South Mahratta Horse. In the space thus commanded the mutinous regiment was formed in quarter-distance column. Calling commanders to the front, I told them that I should address the regiment in words that I trusted would come home to their hearts, and that I had every hope no resistance would be attempted . . .; but that, should I be disappointed, I should give the sound by bugle, when they were to direct one round from each gun and one volley from each corps, taking what care they might to avoid shooting the European officers of the 27th and my staff as we retired upon them. The cavalry were then to sweep along the whole front of the line. . . . It was an anxious moment, for hundreds of these men of the 27th knew they were standing with halters round their necks. . . . I then addressed them. . . . Before I had finished speaking I observed tears on the faces of some of the front ranks close to me. . . . The order was given to pile arms—obedience to which was the crucial part of the proceedings: that once done all was safe. After a slight but ominous pause they obeyed, and the column being filed off to the flank all danger was over." In the court-martial that followed twenty-one were convicted, and the afternoon after the disarming the troops were assembled to carry out the sentences, four of the Rajas' guns having been borrowed for the purpose. Eight were blown from them, two were hanged and eleven shot by musketry. Unfortunately, the Enfield cartridges issued to the 2nd Europeans were fitted with the iron cups condemned after trials at home, and all the ammunition being in any case much impaired in the forced march from Ratnagiri, some of the victims were left untouched after the first volley.

The detachment remained at Kolhapur for the next four months in an atmosphere of growing tension. Early in December the storm broke with a rising of the rebels within Kolhapur. By this time Guerin's detachment had been reinforced by the arrival of 67 n.c.o.s and men from Ratnagiri and Belgaum under Captain Thompson and Lieutenants Scott, Jervis and Grant, and were quartered with the South Mahratta Horse and the Kolhapur Local Infantry in the Civil Lines and the Cantonment outside the walls.

Kolhapur, a fortified city containing 60,000 inhabitants, was surrounded by walls, built in the form of a pentagon rather over $1\frac{1}{2}$ miles across at its greatest extent and rather under at its least, and pierced by six formidable gateways. They were in places double, and the whole was surrounded by a wet ditch. The suppression of a rising inside such a place, whether countenanced by the Rajas or not, presented a prodigious task.

Le Grand Jacob decided to risk the safety of the Cantonment. Only a few hours after hearing of the rising, in the night of 5th December, leaving only a guard of a trusty n.c.o. (not named) and twenty men of the 2nd Europeans, with instructions to defend it to the last extremity, he assembled all his force for an attack. Mrs. Guerin, who had recently joined her husband, came to take shelter at the post just as Jacob left, and exclaimed to him, "I can trust our men. We will never surrender!" At the main gate Jacob posted a party of 50 of the 2nd Europeans under Lieutenants Scott and Jervis with orders to make up a powder-bag and "get in by skilful management if possible" and at any rate to distract attention, and then went on to the rear of the town with the remainder, the guns and the Kolhapur Infantry under their able officer, Captain John Schneider. The morning of 6th December was just dawning as he reached another gate, which he attempted, unsuccessfully at first, to blow in with a gun. A second attempt succeeded, in the course of which Captain Thompson, acting as a zealous staff-officer to Jacob, was thrown into the ditch from the narrow causeway, and the storming-party rushed in. Fortunately the rebels' attention was elsewhere or hardly a man would have survived. As it was, only a dozen or so disputed the entry, and they ran off firing a few random shots. In a short time Jacob's men reached the palace. Scattered parties brought in prisoners; a drum-head court-martial, of which Guerin was president, found thirty-six guilty, who were immediately executed; and the men piled arms in the palace courtyard and had breakfast under the eyes of the rajas' officials, who even then had half a mind to cut them down as they ate. But the rebellion was over. Jacob's resolute action had suppressed it with the loss of only two lives.[20]

Meanwhile, at Belgaum, though there had been no fighting, things had not been quiet. An explosion was averted only as a result of the precautions taken by Major-General Lester, commanding the Southern Division of the Army, who at first had only a battery of artillery and the depot details of H.M.'s 23rd with which to awe the wavering loyalty of the 29th N.I. The arrival of Captain Jones's detachment of the Regiment from Goa in August had been a welcome reinforcement, which enabled him to take action against the conspirators, who were in communication with others at Kolhapur and Poona. Later in the year the right wing and headquarters of the Regiment, after disarming the 21st N.I. at Karachi on 13th September, was brought by sea to Vengurla and arrived at Belgaum on 8th December. The detachment at Kolhapur was then reinforced, and at the same time detachments were sent out to Kaladgi (under Captains Aitchison and Jessop) and Dharwar (under Captain Westropp and Lieutenants Billamore, Utterson and Woodcock). A detachment remained at Ratnagiri until the second quarter of 1858.[21]

The 1st Bombay Fusiliers were engaged upon the fringe of great affairs in Hindustan; the 3rd Europeans were winning distinctions in Central India at Kalpi and Jhansi; but the 2nd Europeans were kept in the Presidency, and once and once only crossed the border. This occurred in February 1858, when Captain Aitchison's detachment at Kaladgi formed part of Colonel Malcolm's Field Force, which was

[20]For operations at Kolhapur generally see Maj.-General Sir George Le Grand Jacob, *Western India before ond during the Mutinies* (1871), pp. 178 *et seq.* The services of the Regiment may be disentangled from: Muster Rolls, 70; Bombay Medal Rolls (Mutiny), Vol. 27; and the Digest. For a description of Kolhapur see Mil. Letters and Enclosures (Bombay), Vol. 49 (1862), No. 52.

[21]Muster Rolls of 1st Jan and 1st Apr 1858; Officers' Services (Bombay); Bombay G.O., 19th Feb and 5th Mar 1858; Bombay Medal Rolls (Mutiny) Vol. 27.

sent to crush the rebellion at Shorapur, a principality of the independent state of Hyderabad. Though the Nizam had shown himself
consistently unsympathetic to the conspirators, his territory, for long
the resort of military adventurers seeking opportunities outside the
soberly administered dominions of the Company, had filled with
mutineers and others from Bengal. The Raja of Shorapur, taking
advantage of these ready mercenaries, raised a sizeable army, which
had been the occasion for Lester's stationing a force at Kaladgi, near
the frontier, late in the previous November. Anticipating the Raja's
revolt, the British Resident at Hyderabad dispatched a force from
Hyderabad and another from the Madras Presidency under Major
Hughes, and called upon Malcolm's assistance from Kaladgi.
Malcolm's Field Force consisted of the detachment of the 2nd Europeans under Captains Aitchison and Jessop (1 colour-sergeant, 6
sergeants, 5 corporals, 2 buglers and 73 privates), some South
Mahratta Horse, two guns and the 15th Bombay N.I. In spite of a
forced march, however, Malcolm found on his arriving in the evening
of 8th February that the Raja, defeated by Hughes, had fled from
Shorapur, leaving the town almost deserted. The 2nd Europeans had
been in support and got no farther than Darur on the Kistna.
Though cheated of the glory, this little force had played an essential
part in preserving the tranquillity of the Deccan, for, as Malleson
says, the rising of Hyderabad under the Nizam would have been a
blow struck at the heart: the whole of western and southern India
would have followed.[22]

Does not the constable on the beat contribute as much to the
protection of society as the posse of police who has to have a glorious
fight before it makes the arrest? It is in that light that the unstirring
history of the Regiment in the Mutiny must be viewed. Its duties were
not finished with the return of Malcolm's Force, for Malcolm's Force
continued operations in the South Mahratta country until late in the
year. There is evidence that at least Captain Scott and Lieutenant
Laughton had a share in them; and Lieutenant R. R. Gillespie, a
worthy grandson of the famous Sir Rollo, is mentioned by Le Grand
Jacob as having taken an active part in the capture of Miruj in June
1858 together with "two companies of Europeans". But if their
services in Bombay, contrasted with the sieges of Delhi and Lucknow
or even Sir Hugh Rose's slogging, indefatigable pursuit of Tantia
Topi, may seem pedestrian, they were none the less necessary and

[22]Officers' Services (Bombay), 5. 31 (sb. Aitchison); Bombay Medal Rolls
(Mutiny), Vol. 27: memorandum, Superintendent, Bombay Army Records, to
D.A.G., Southern Army, Poona, 30th June 1909; Malleson, History of the Indian
Mutiny, Vol. 3 (1880), pp. 125-130.

productive of good; and they are a salutary reminder of the rigours
of service in a presidency almost untouched, it is commonly supposed,
by the infection of mutiny.

§

Quite apart from the anxieties of active operations, service in all
the Company's European regiments at this juncture was beset by the
fundamental uncertainty of their survival, which made the next five
years a period of doubt and unsettlement. The Mutiny brought with
it almost inevitably the transference of all power from the Company
to the Crown. The transfer was effected by the India Act, which
reached the Indian army in the form of a proclamation on 1st
November 1858. The Company's European force had by this time
been substantially augmented. Some new artillery battalions, three
new regiments of cavalry and three new battalions of infantry had
been raised for the Bengal army, and it was in these that dissatisfaction was most loudly expressed, the 5th Bengal European
Infantry at Berhampore even appointing their own officers. This
was mutiny almost as blatant as that recently suppressed; and although no others went so far, the dissatisfaction was general among
the soldiers, who, on the grounds that the terms of their enlistment
had been altered, claimed the right of a free discharge or re-
enlistment with a bounty. The Indian Government was thus faced
with an unpleasant dilemma: either to insist on the terms of the
proclamation, which made the Company's troops subject to the
same terms of service as the Queen's, and risk a mutiny among men
whose good example was sorely needed; or to deprive itself of a
sensible proportion of its European army before the population had
settled down.

Previously it had been intended to continue the Company's
Europeans as a local force until the retirement of the existing generation of officers and men, before assimilating them as an integral part
of the Queen's forces. The "White Mutiny", as it was called, made
everyone think again. The Government consulted the law officers,
both in India and at home, on the rights and wrongs of the men's
grievances. They pronounced that, inasmuch as the men on enlistment had sworn to serve the Queen and the Company, the men's
claim had no substance. This only shows how wrong a right may be.
The man on enlistment *could* have chosen to serve in the Queen's
army, but he *did* not: he preferred the Company's. That being so, it
was hard to persuade him he had equally contracted to serve in
the Queen's. Lord Clyde, Commander-in-Chief in India, very

9

sensibly declined to press the legality of the lawyer's argument, and in an Order of July 1859 he allowed every man not wishing to transfer to the Queen's service to take his discharge. Ten thousand proceeded to do so. But it was no good now pretending that there could be any besides Queen's troops in India. Clyde had been one of those who thought the maintenance of a European local force feasible, and he had been compelled to change his mind. It is clear, he said, that it is dangerous to trust to local corps, and that "we can alone put faith in a discipline which is constantly renovated by a return to England, and the presence of officers with their regiments who look on them as their home".[23]

In this manner "amalgamation", as the process of assimilation was called, was ushered in. The pros and cons were heatedly debated at the time, and anyone who cares may see the best of both in Sir William Mansfield's Memorandum of 20th October 1857, Sir Robert Biddulph's of 31st August 1860 (both for), and Sir James Outram's of 2nd January 1860 (against).[24] Outram's most telling argument against amalgamation was the loss to India of the officer who came out to make it his home for the next twenty or thirty years, and acquired a knowledge of its people, its languages, its religions and its civil and military history; the officer who came out on a tour of duty would despise the native, as all the Europeans did who had not served in native regiments. Mansfield and Biddulph, on the other hand, were both agreed that if British regiments returned from ten years' foreign service with discipline relaxed in every respect (three years in the West Indies were considered enough to break it), what must be the effect on the Company's European regiments which never returned? "These regiments during the excitement of war are second to none, but their discipline . . . is exactly what I should have expected," says Mansfield. "The various points of discipline," says Biddulph, "in which the E.I.C. regiments are so inferior are well known to military men, such as neglecting to salute officers, showing a want of respect in their demeanour, making loud remarks in the hearing of their officers, answering coarsely and in a disrespectful manner, and many other things of that sort." It was also said officers accustomed to command native troops were unfitted to command Europeans. Running through the Royal army's attitude to the Company's there is undoubtedly a strong prejudice against anything even faintly smelling of "trade"—Mansfield speaks

[23]Cit. in Willoughby Verner, *Military Life of H.R.H. George Duke of Cambridge* (1905), Vol. 1, p. 227.
[24]*Ibid.*, pp. 208-209; J.S.A.H.R., Vol. 18, pp. 13-15; Goldsmid, *James Outram* (1880), Vol. 1, pp. 421-430.

of its "mercantile instincts"; but it is impossible to ignore this evidence from contemporaries upon such a subject. It must consequently be reluctantly admitted that after the White Mutiny, which showed up a lamentable want of confidence between the officers and their men, there was no alternative to amalgamation.

Once the men taking their discharge had been smuggled out of India, with every precaution taken against their contaminating the Queen's regiments, it was decided to amalgamate the following: three cavalry regiments, which were formed into H.M.'s 19th, 20th and 21st Hussars; the artillery and engineers; and nine infantry battalions, namely: the three "*vieux*" of Bengal, Madras and Bombay, formed respectively into H.M.'s 101st, 102nd and 103rd; the three "*petits-vieux*" of 1839, formed into H.M.'s 104th, 105th and 106th; and the three regiments of the 1853 creation, which were formed into H.M.'s 107th, 108th and 109th. What remained of the 4th, 5th and 6th Bengal Europeans were taken into the 104th and 107th. All being predominantly Irish, they were allotted recruiting districts in Ireland. In the "territorial" reorganisation of 1881 all but three became Irish regiments, which were disbanded in 1922.

"In Bombay," reported Lord Clyde, "we have as yet heard of misbehaviour only in a small body of artillery." And there is every reason to believe that the Bombay Europeans withstood the temptations with exemplary steadiness. But the discharge figures are eloquent testimony of the widespread extent of the men's dissatisfaction here as elsewhere. The 1st Fusiliers lost 400-500 men; the 2nd Europeans lost 382, all men who had arrived since 1855; the 3rd Europeans suffered losses that would have crippled them had they not had their ranks filled from the volunteers of the German Legion. When the orders for the disposal of the discharged men reached them in August 1859, the 2nd Europeans were distributed between Kolhapur and Belgaum, a wing at each with a small detachment at Sangli. Five officers were detailed to accompany them to the port of embarkation (originally Bombay, but changed to Goa on account of the scarcity of shipping). And when that operation was concluded, "Her Majesty's 2nd Regiment of Bombay European Light Infantry", as it became on 3rd November 1859, was reduced to a strength of 601 n.c.o.s and men. Numbers continued to decline as men were time-expired or invalided, until on the last day of its existence at Nimach on 30th July 1862 they stood at 490.[25]

At the same time the officers started to transfer. Lieut.-Colonel Stiles relinquished the command in March 1858, and Guerin, his successor, an old and experienced officer who had taken them

[25]Muster Roll, 1st Oct 1859; Bombay G.O., 18th Aug 1859; Digest.

through many trials, finally retired on a £200 pension in December 1861. Captains Billamore and Robinson transferred, and Lieutenant A. M. Shewell went on the Invalid Establishment for lameness in 1860. Colonel Barr, Captains Aitchison, Gordon, Herbert, Scott, Hervey and Westropp, Lieutenants W. A. Gillespie, Woodcock, Griffiths, Mackenzie, Phillips and Watson—most of whom had served both in Persia and the Mutiny—transferred in the course of 1861. Moreover, in that year all officers were circularised by the Adjutant-General offering them a choice of one of three courses: to volunteer for general service in the Royal army; to remain in the local service; or to join the Staff Corps, the body from which the Indian army of the future was to be officered. Most of those qualified preferred the Staff Corps, and a further large accumulation of experience was thus taken from the Regiment.

Indeed, in the 2nd Europeans only one captain, nine lieutenants and one ensign volunteered for general service. Although six of these (Captain Tyacke, a Cornishman, the last survivor of those who had served with the Kolhapur Field Force of 1844, Lieutenants R. R. Gillespie, Gardyne, Robertson, Warden and Jervis[26]) were all either Persia or Mutiny veterans, it cannot be said that by themselves they formed a very satisfactory foundation on which to build a new regiment. The others, Lieutenants Ducat, Burnett, Caldecot and Gaitskell and Ensign Elliott, had seen no active service. In the older regiments the officers showed a slightly greater inclination to follow the fortunes of their old colours. But there was not one regiment that did not undergo a radical reorganisation on its transfer to the Crown. It is, in fact, no more than a convenient shorthand, and not strict historical truth, to say that the Company's European regiments became Her Majesty's 101st to 109th. They formed the foundation, but there was more to it than the change of a shako-plate.

The establishment of the new Royal regiment was quite different. Instead of two lieut.-colonels it had one. It had two majors, twelve captains (instead of ten), fifteen lieutenants (instead of sixteen), ten ensigns (instead of eight), a paymaster, an adjutant and a quartermaster in addition, 109 n.c.o.s, 24 buglers, and 810 privates. The ranks were not filled up for some years to come, but the vacancies in the commissioned grades were filled—at least on paper—immediately. The Commander-in-Chief in India had persuaded the Duke of Cambridge at the Horse Guards, who had a strong prejudice against the Company's service, to grant promotions to those volunteering for

[26]Jervis was the unfortunate a.d.c. of Sir William Mansfield whom Mansfield brought before a court-martial and dismissed, in the course of proceedings which can only be described as a misuse of his powers.

general service on a surprisingly liberal scale. Tyacke received a majority, R. R. Gillespie, Gardyne, Robertson, Warden, Jervis and Ducat received companies, Elliott a lieutenancy, and Gaitskell the adjutancy. The paymastership went to Hepworth, an officer in the Adjutant-General's Department at Bombay. The quartermastership was given the 2nd Europeans' respectable old sergeant-major Francis Mackey.[27]

But these promotions still left many vacancies, the most important of which was the command. This was given out of the Regiment to Lieut.-Colonel R. W. Disney Leith, of the 1st Bombay Europeans. The son of Sir Alexander Leith, who commanded the 5th Division in the Peninsula, he was a man of imposing physique, standing 6ft. 5ins. and broad in proportion, who had led his company the first into the breach at Multan, wielding a long cavalry sabre that only he could use, and there had lost his left hand by a sword-cut. A finer soldier the Regiment could not have been given. But he and the twenty-three other officers who were transferred from the native regiments (among them Captain Jopp, who had served with the mutinous 27th) as well as the Bombay general list, did not join immediately. Indeed, in September 1862, there were only three captains, three subalterns and three staff present, and the Regiment was temporarily commanded by Captain Henry Shewell, who had not opted for general service. For a short time from 11th October the command was exercised by Lieut.-Colonel the Hon. Eyre Massey, 95th, who, by a curious coincidence, had started his military career in the 68th as an ensign under Paulet. Most of the officers joined during the course of October. But Tyacke and R. R. Gillespie did not return to duty until January 1863, and Lieut.-Colonel Leith did not assume command until February 1863.

By this time the Regiment had left the familiar South Mahratta country. Since January 1861 it had been stationed at Nimach in Rajputana, a district which the Bombay army had garrisoned since 1850 but had temporarily relinquished to the "Kai-hais" at the time of the Persian expedition. Nimach was an unhealthy station, and the sick-rate rose sharply. As the Inspector-General reported at the end of 1862, the monsoon was of unusual length, "and the supply of animal and vegetable food not properly kept up. . . . The supply of malt liquor failed in August, and that combined with the excessive moisture and the use of bad-fed and overdriven animals for rations have rendered the majority of the men particularly liable to disease." From a battalion whose average strength over the period was 465, admittances to hospital totalled 2086 (as against the 1st Europeans' at

[27]G.O., Simla, 31st July 1862.

Poona 733 and 1045, and the half-German 3rd Europeans' at Karachi 772 and 769—quite exceptionally good, as the figure included a high incidence of venereal). By March 1863 the total strength, n.c.o.s and men, had sunk to 388. Yet it was at this unpleasant place that, at a parade on 30th July 1862, eleven officers, 47 sergeants, 29 corporals, 17 buglers and 397 privates grounded arms as the 2nd Bombay European Light Infantry and took them up as Her Majesty's 106th. Three officers, one sergeant and 18 privates chose to remain in the local service in the cadre of the old regiment.[28]

The days of the Company, an indulgent master, quick to criticise yet quick to make amends, are over: the days of the Crown, a harder master and more remote yet not unkindly, begin.

§

Twice before the British Line had owned a 106th. The earlier was a regiment raised in 1761 by Colonel Isaac Barré, an Irish politician who, from a wound he had received at Quebec, a bullet that had lodged loosely in his cheek and gave a savage glare to a countenance already dark and swarthy, and from his possessing a rich flow of parliamentary invective, struck terror and dismay in all opponents. His regiment appropriately enough had black facings and were known as the Black Musketeers. They appear for a brief moment in Gibbon's *Journal* in the autumn of 1761 recruiting at Devizes, where the South Hampshire Militia behaved to them with becoming civility, lending them drums, fifes, sergeants and privates for their recruiting, and messing with them. It was civility ill requited, for early next year they fell out, what with the strong beer and their jealousy at the South Hampshire's greater success in recruiting, and the two parted in March 1762 on the worst of terms. The Black Musketeers were disbanded in 1763. The second 106th was raised in September 1794 by a half-pay captain, William Earle Bulwer, of Heydon Hall, Norfolk, who had served three years as a subaltern in the 68th, and is better known as the father of Lord Lytton, the novelist and statesman. Being raised at his own cost largely of volunteers from the Norwich Royal Regiment of Volunteers, it was a Norfolk battalion. It had but a short existence. Like most of the other regiments raised that year it was drafted the next. There is even less connection between the three 106ths than there is between the three 2nd Bombay Europeans.

What sort of an accession was this third and latest comer to the British Line? It was a regiment well below establishment, sickly in

[28]Mil. Letters and Enclosures (Bombay) Vol. 53 (1863), No. 56; Digest.

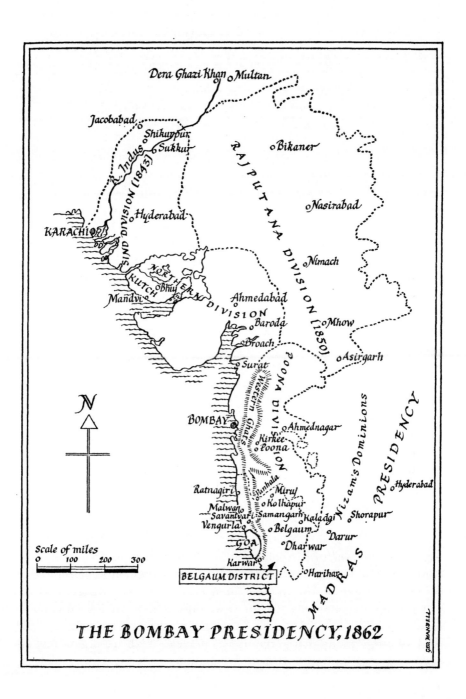

17. The Bombay Presidency in 1862

health and under-officered. Half the n.c.o.s and men were Irish; seven were "Indo-Britons". Physically it made as good an appearance as any British line regiment, and its ranks were filled with mature soldiers, only one under 20 and only seven over 40, and two-thirds of them with more than five years' service. Eighty-six men bore the Mutiny Medal for their services at Kolhapur or Shorapur, and a further 150 had served in the Mutiny in such manner as it was given the Regiment to do so. They were, moreover, volunteers, purged of their malcontents.[29]

They remained at Nimach until January 1864, when they marched to Nasirabad. In March 1867 they marched to Mian Mir, thence to Ambala in March 1868. There they stayed until November 1870, when they were moved by rail to Jhansi. The strength, in spite of cholera epidemics, gradually improved with accessions of drafts from the depot, though the old hands of the Company's service were fast disappearing. Lieut.-Colonel Leith handed over to Lieut.-Colonel Tyacke in May 1866, and he in June 1872 to Lieut.-Colonel Bolton (formerly of the 2nd Bombay N.I.), who, however, died in August 1873. Purchase made a fleeting appearance among the officers for the first and last time, so that when it was finally abolished in 1871 there were three officers who had bought their steps. On paper therefore the Regiment was slowly assimilating itself to the others in H.M.'s service, if in outward appearance it looked curiously old-fashioned.

In December 1873 it left India for the first time in its existence. On the 12th of that month it embarked at Bombay under the command of Lieut.-Colonel R. R. Gillespie with a strength of 20 officers, 672 n.c.o.s and men, 52 women and 102 children in the Indian troopship *Euphrates* (the same ship, by some strange historical quirk, that had taken the 68th on its first Indian tour of duty the previous year). It landed at Portsmouth on 12th January 1874 and was quartered at Parkhurst Barracks in the Isle of Wight. New colours were presented on 14th August by the Crown Princess Frederick of Germany (the Queen's eldest daughter). The old colours, presented in 1860, were laid up in St. Thomas's, Newport—where they still remain—at a service which was concluded by the Regiment marching up in single file to the altar where they lay, each man saluting them while the band played "Can I forget how dear thou art to me?" It was a ceremony without any hidden significance, but somehow it seems to mark the conclusion of an epoch.[30]

[29]Monthly Casualty Returns, 106th, 5/7 (1863).
[30]*United Service Gazette*, 22nd Aug 1874.

CHAPTER VIII

THE FIRST SERVICES OF THE DURHAM LIGHT INFANTRY, 1873-1899

WITH the Cardwell reforms of 1873 the three types of soldier furnished by the County of Durham, professional, militia and volunteer, were for the first time assembled, if tentatively and under duress, into a single military body. In the *Army List* of 1873 there they may be seen:

> the Brigade Depot (No. 3) at Sunderland,
> the 68th, with its depot at Sunderland.
> the 106th, with its depot at Sunderland,
> the 1st Durham Militia (Fusiliers), with its depot at Barnard Castle,
> the 2nd North Durham Militia, with its depot at Durham,
> the 1st Administrative Battalion of Durham Rifle Volunteers, with headquarters at Chester-le-Street,
> the 2nd Administrative Battalion of Durham Rifle Volunteers, with headquarters at Bishop Auckland,
> the 3rd Administrative Battalion of Durham Rifle Volunteers, with headquarters at Gateshead,
> the 4th Administrative Battalion of Durham Rifle Volunteers, with headquarters at Stockton,
> and the 3rd Durham Rifle Volunteer Corps, with headquarters at Sunderland.

They were more fortunate than some, having at least the nominal connection with an entire county. But as yet they were like ten people introduced at a party and not very willing to talk. For a time, indeed, there was a doubt on the host's part if the right thing had been done. The Stanley Committee of 1876 wished to go further and favoured a "territorial" designation for the whole. But the Airey Committee, which reported in March 1880, pointing out that since 1872 the proportion of line battalions at home to those abroad had fallen from 70 : 71 to 59 : 82, considered the linked battalion system was in danger of breaking down, and recommended that the battalions should be unlinked. At the same time the Duke of Cambridge was wishing he had never put his name to the Cardwell proposals.

Then in 1881 another committee sat on Stanley's proposals of 1876, and brought out a report favouring not only "territorial" designations and a tightening of the bond between linked regiments but also a greater uniformity of dress and facings throughout the army. The recommendations were adopted *in toto* in General Order No. 41 of 1st May 1881 issued under the Royal Sign Manual.

From that date the County of Durham became a Brigade District (No. 58[1]) furnishing:

> two line battalions, the 1st Battalion of the Durham Light Infantry (formerly the 68th) and the 2nd Battalion (formerly the 106th);
> the two militia battalions, the 3rd Battalion (formerly the 1st Durham Fusiliers) and the 4th Battalion (formerly the 2nd North Durham Militia):
> and the five volunteer battalions.

All the old numbers and all the old distinctions of dress disappeared in the frenzy for uniformity. Since it was a non-royal English regiment, the 68th's facings were changed to white (those of the 106th already were); and since the combined regiment was considered to have no special distinctions, it was given a badge of a rose and its lace was rose-patterned. The battle-honours of the 106th were added to those of the 68th. The depot, though remaining temporarily at Sunderland, was removed a year or two later to Newcastle because, it was said, no suitable site could be found in or near the county town "which could be relied upon as not being undermined". The headquarters of the old North Durham Militia were moved from Durham to Newcastle at the same time.[2]

As part of the same process of standardisation the Regimental March was pronounced, either in 1882 or 1883, to be "The Light Barque," a melody written expressly for the famous contralto, Madame Eliza Lucy Vestris (1797-1856) by G. T. Craven, an otherwise obscure composer, between the years 1820 and 1830. Before the Duke of Cambridge addressed himself to improving the general standard of military music, commanding officers did very much as they chose; and the 68th from Crimean days had played the

[1]By G.O.70/1881 it was renumbered 68, and was known from 1884 onwards as the 5th/68th District.
[2]*Parl. Papers* (C.2793 and C.2791), Reports of the Stanley (1877) and Airey (1880) Committees; W.O.32/121/263; G.O.70/1881.

stirring march of the 95th, "I'm Ninety-Five". This was the march the 68th submitted for their own when the order came out calling on them to do so, but it was rejected, by the Duke it is said, in favour of "The Light Barque," which the Regiment had apparently favoured before the Crimea and was still used by the 83rd (1st Royal Irish Rifles). The sentiments of the 106th, who before 1878 played "Paddy Carey" and "Ap Shenkin" after, seem hardly to have been consulted.

These were changes more radical than those of 1873, and were correspondingly resented. Some were quietly ignored. The badge of the rose (changed to the united red and white rose in 1888) was never worn on any article of clothing. The bugle, cherished by each battalion (the light infantry bugle-horn in the 68th, the French bugle-horn in the 106th), continued to be the badge worn on the buttons, the collar, the waistbelt-plate, the forage-cap and the "universal" helmet-plate. The strings of the new bugle were led into a crown in the style favoured by the 68th since about 1830. The rose was borne only on the colours and disappeared from the *Army List* in 1934 with the introduction of the centre-badge.[3] The 68th's green facings were restored in December 1902. Other unsatisfactory aspects of the reforms could not be lightly disregarded; and one important defect, the location outside the County of the depot—the principal ingredient of cohesion—was not remedied until 1939.

I. The union of the two line battalions performed by Cardwell was at first so partial as to be hardly noticeable. In 1873 they were both abroad. The 68th was at Poona: the 106th had not set foot in this country since it was raised. Each continued to lead an independent existence.

The organisation that was eventually to exert a decisive unifying influence, the depot, consisted as yet of twelve officers and a few n.c.o.s and recruits, who were listed separately under three heads; "Depot 68th", "Depot 106th", and "3rd Brigade Depot".[4] Before moving to Sunderland neither battalion's depot had shared anything in common. The 68th's since 1872 had been successively at Cork, at Templemore and, from October 1872, at Sheffield. The East India Company's military depot had been moved in 1843, much against its will, from Chatham, whence it was crowded out by H.M.'s troops, to Warley in Essex, where, it was objected, the recruits felt the want of the example set by the Queen's regiments; and when the 2nd Europeans were brought onto the British establishment their depot had been moved successively from Birr (1863) to Limerick

[3] By A.O.100/1934 (April).
[4] W.O. 12/10220 (Pay Lists, 3rd Brigade Depot, 1873-1874).

(1864), to Mullingar (1865), to Chatham (1866), to Shorncliffe (1869), to Kinsale (1870), and the Curragh (1872), until finally being fixed at Sunderland in December 1872. In these circumstances it was hardly surprising that the enforced union should have been greeted with such a marked absence of cordiality. Though all the recruits brought in to Sunderland came from the County, the depot acted as agent not only for the 68th and 106th but for Engineers and Artillery, and the 4th and 6th Dragoon Guards besides. Nevertheless, within a year the depot had developed a greater cohesion, which grew as the years went by until eventually it spread into the battalions it served.

In the battalions the introduction of short service, that is to say a service of six years with colours and six in the reserve, accelerated the turnover of men and to that extent assisted the process of assimilation. The effects were first felt in the ranks. For some years after 1873 the home battalion, the 106th, supplied no drafts to the 68th; but in 1879 two drafts amounting to 467 men were transferred from the 106th to the other. The 106th was by that time, to judge from the lists of discharges and deserters, a predominantly English regiment; the only Irish were old soldiers who remained from Company days; and the whole was quite one-third composed of pit-men, enginemen and puddlers and labourers from County Durham. Drafts on such a scale over a number of years eventually made the two battalions indistinguishable in point of composition.[5] At first the officers posted from one to the other in the "linked" days can be numbered on the fingers of one hand. After 1881, however, the practice became more common, and in the year 1885 alone there were three such transfers (Captain Menzies and Lieut.-Colonel Lee from the 1st Battalion, and Lieutenant Maunsell from the 2nd).

The process of assimilation was, however, slow, and many pre-judices had to be overcome before the county connection could be established sufficiently to mould all battalions of the Durham Light Infantry into one regiment. Short service was not an unmitigated blessing, and in lowering the standard of man in the ranks it at first exacerbated inter-battalion jealousies. "What subtle change has come upon the race?" asked an officer who had known the old long-service man with "his splendid physique and his well chiselled feature." "Not only are the figures gone but the faces also are vanished—those straight clean-cut foreheads, the straight or aquiline noses, the keen, steady eyes, the resolute lower jaws and shapely turned chins." A battalion composed as the 68th could not be ex-

[5] See W.O.16/2095.

pected to take to the new kind. The 68th recorded its draft of 467 from the 106th merely as coming "from England", and another of 138 in March 1881 likewise, rather as if it were an occurrence best forgotten. "We never had anything to do with the other battalion," said the commanding officer of the 1st in 1891, "before we were linked to it, and although the men do not complain I think there is a strong dislike to going to it." Significantly, it was not until 1897 that the Officers' Dinner Club, founded by the 68th in 1864, admitted officers of the 2nd Battalion, and then only "officers past and present since 1st July 1881". The bad feeling between the two was then said to be "wearing out," and in time ("but not just yet") it was reckoned would disappear altogether. It would, however, have gone on much longer but for the 2nd Battalion's achievements in India in the 1890s, of which more will be said later.[6]

In the early years, moreover, the reforms of 1873 and the 1881 did nothing to predispose the County of Durham in favour of its "territorial"[7] regiment. Those were years in which the antipathy to the army was as strong as it ever was: when soldiers were commonly turned out of music-halls and public-houses on account of their uniform and informed "we don't allow soldiers to go anywhere except in the gallery," or "we don't serve soldiers except in such-and-such a room"; when a sergeant-major of the Rifle Brigade was treated as a fellow travelling companion by others in a railway compartment when mistaken for a rifle volunteer, but cold-shouldered when he was found to be a regular soldier. The records of the depot at Sunderland show why. They reveal men who deserted within a few days of enlisting, of men rejected for poor physique—hardly a recruit but spends a week out of two in the cells for drunkenness, and hardly twenty out of a hundred recruits can have reached the battalions. In County Durham the prejudice against the soldier was strong enough to discourage the recruit from the agricultural districts, where the wages were comparable with the soldier's pay (a shilling a day less stoppages, which were never under 3½d). In the industrial districts—at any rate in the 1890s, which were prosperous years—the recruiters could not compete with the 8s. or 10s. a day that was a common wage at Hawthorne, Leslies', the Elswick Works and at other yards on Tyneside. Even a labourer at Elswick got 4s. a day; a skilled man could earn £1; and

[6]Butler, pp. 41-42; evidence of Lieut.-Col. Upcher before the Wantage Committee, 1892 (Parl. Papers (C.6582) pp. 147-153).

[7]Perhaps it is as well to repeat that between the years 1873 and 1908 a "territorial regiment" meant a regular regiment and not what we have come to understand by the expression.

a man in a riveter's gang could earn as much as £1 10s. "The British workman is very independent in the north," said the commanding officer of the Regimental District, "and the employers tell me that in many instances they will not work more than three or four days in the week. They go away when they like and the employers take them back."[8]

In such circumstances it was idle to expect the County, though possessing a population of 900,000, to supply recruits for the engineers, artillery, cavalry and Coldstream Guards as well as to support exclusively the Durham Light Infantry. The greater part of the home battalion at that period (the 1st) was drawn from the mills of Bradford, where the battalion was stationed, and from Tyneside at large. Usually they were 17 or 16½ on joining—though giving out that they were 18—of inferior physique and needing at least two years' "building up". Occasionally a man of a stronger and more intelligent type came forward from among the Durham colliers, and the men enlisting from the militia were mostly Durham men. But neither came in sufficient numbers to make it a Durham regiment.

Similarly in the early days the reserve mechanism was worked too awkwardly either to make the Regiment efficient or to give it a Durham quality. Almost all the 660-odd reservists recalled to the 106th in April 1878 went in a month or two to other regiments (the 21st, 30th and 96th). The reservists recalled from August 1882 to February 1883 during the Egyptian War not only went outside the Regiment but caused serious disorganisation in the battalions they entered. "They had lost a great deal of their discipline and they looked down on the non-commissioned officers who were not in the services when they went away." They were "grand men" on active service but proved a bad influence on a young battalion.[9]

There was another aspect of the reforms which adversely affected the bond between the County and the line battalions. Hardly had the 68th and 106th been united to form the "territorial" regiment of the County before the depot was moved out of the County from Sunderland to Newcastle. The move took place on 9th January 1884 on completion of the barracks in Newcastle, where a double depot was established for the 1st and 2nd Battalions of the Northumberland Fusiliers as well as the 1st, 2nd and 4th Battalions of the Durham Light Infantry. The decision was ill advised. The report of 1876 which adverted to the absence of building land that was not undermined has proved to be unfounded: no search for alternative sites

[8]Evidence of Lieut.-Col. C. E. Hope before the Wantage Committee, 1892 (*Parl. Papers* (C.6582), pp. 233-240).
[9]*Ibid., loc. cit.*

in the County was energetically undertaken. Already in 1891 the Inspector-General of Recruiting was recommending the removal of the depot from Newcastle to Durham to stimulate recruiting. Similar representations were made in the same year by the Mayor of Durham and the General Officer Commanding the North-Eastern District (Major-General Wilkinson), the latter adding that pressure was put upon the best of the recruits to enter the Northumberland regiment in preference to the Durham. But the decision to move, once taken, proved too expensive to reverse: all the representations were turned down on grounds of expense.

Further efforts on the part of the County in 1898 were equally unavailing. On 29th July a deputation, consisting of the Hon. Arthur Elliott, Member for the City, Mr. J. L. Wharton, a native of the County and Member for the West Riding, and Colonel C. Rowlandson, the Mayor of Durham, met the Secretary of State and his advisers in London. They presented not only copies of resolutions passed by the Town Council and by a crowded public meeting held in the Durham Town Hall on 4th May 1898, all urging the removal of the depot to Durham, but a number of supporting letters from Lord Barnard and others such as Canon H. D. Tristram, Canon A. S. Farrar, Professor of Divinity at the University, and the Rev. H. A. Mitton, Master of Sherburn Hospital. The most interesting in view of the contemporary popular estimation of the soldier was the letter of the Rev. Thomas Dodd, Vicar of St. Cuthbert's, Durham, who thirty years before had been curate in the garrison town of Tynemouth, where, he says, "even then, before the great efforts of the famous workers among soldiers such as Miss Robinson had attained their marvellous success, the presence of soldiers amongst us was considered an influence of good". The advocacy of Mr Elliott, the City's Member, falls less convincingly on modern ears: "I cannot help," he said, "being struck with the love of athletics and vigorous exercises the young men of the County display, and to my mind they are just the sort of young men who ought to have a chance of seeing a regular battalion amongst them." A suitable site for the depot, sixteen acres near Neville's Cross, where Neville's Cross College now stands, was put forward as obtainable at £200 the acre. The University of Durham, strongly opposing the introduction of the depot into Durham, dissociated itself from the Deputation, however; and the combined endeavours of Mr Wharton, Mr Elliott and Colonel Rowlandson failed to move the Secretary of State. Lord Lansdowne politely thanked them for their encomiums upon the army, but declined to ask Parliament for £20,000 or £30,000 for what he could not describe as indispensable. "We are," he said, "at the moment thinking towards double depots, as we think the depots scattered over the face of the country in Mr Cardwell's time scarcely wanted."

In this manner the baleful effects of the 1881 decision were prolonged until 1939. At the end of the century it could be said that the Regiment had not, nor so much as a single company of it, been seen in the County. Though both battalions contained many Durham men, it was as Colonel Upcher said in 1891: "We have nothing to do with the County of Durham except through the militia. The Durham Light Infantry is not a territorial regiment."[10]

II. Since 1853 the county militia had consisted of two battalions of infantry, each with an establishment of a thousand men: the 1st Durham Fusiliers, with its depot at Barnard Castle, and the 2nd North Durham, with its depot at Durham. Although the ballot had been dispensed with, the militia had lost none of its Durham quality. Its ranks were filled almost exclusively from men of the County, it was officered principally by gentlemen of the County, and its barracks and stores continued, even after the reforms, to be the property of the County. The transference of its administration from the Lord Lieutenant to the War Office in 1872, the transformation of the two battalions into the 3rd and 4th Battalions of the Durham Light Infantry, and the removal of the 4th Battalion's depot to Newcastle, affected but did not deprive it in any material sense of its connection with County Durham.

Before 1873 its links with the 68th and 106th hardly existed: after and until 1881, they were occasionally unsatisfactory and always tenuous. Bugle-major Gibbons, for instance, formerly sergeant-major of the 68th, had acted as bugle-major of the North Durham from 1855 to 1861, but had been discharged for misconduct; and Colour-sergeant John Byrne's ill-fated attachment has already been noticed. More happy were the appointments of Sergeant John Murray, V.C., 68th, to the North Durham in 1872, and of Henry Sladden, who had been the 68th's quartermaster in New Zealand, quartermaster of the North Durham from 1878 to 1881. Of the officers who had seen previous service in the line—two in the 1st Durham, five in the North Durham—two alone had served with the 68th or 106th: Captain H. C. Molyneux and Captain Charles Hood, who had been with the 68th in New Zealand and had acted as adjutant from 1870 to 1873. Neither of the militia battalions' adjutants came from the 68th or 106th.

After the reforms of 1881, which marked the militia battalions as creatures rather of the War Office than of the County, the bonds with the "territorial" battalions were more sedulously cultivated.

[10]W.O.32/122/7698 (822 and 832): Upcher's evidence *cit. sup.*

Indeed, it appears that what the militia lost in County connection they gained in attachment to the regular regiment. In 1882 the adjutants of both battalions, Ruddach (3rd) and Parker-Jervis (4th), were former officers of the 106th; and William Shea, quartermaster of the 3rd, was an old sergeant-major and quartermaster of the 68th and Patrick Connell, quartermaster of the 4th, was an old sergeant-major and quartermaster of the 106th. From that time the regular battalions continued almost consistently to supply those important appointments, and the list of officers from the 1st and 2nd Battalions who served with the militia may be extended almost indefinitely: John William Byrne, formerly sergeant-major and quartermaster of the 68th, who served with both the 3rd and 4th Battalions; Joseph Magee Byrne, who had enlisted in the 68th as a boy of 14 in 1865, rose to sergeant-major and quartermaster in 1885, served with the 3rd Battalion on active service in South Africa in 1900, and died in retirement as honorary major in 1926; Captains Johnson-Smyth and F. H. Whitby (or Westloe), both former officers of the 106th, adjutants of the 3rd and 4th Battalions; and many others besides.

While on the one hand there can be little doubt that these bonds with the "territorial" regiment both assisted in creating a regimental spirit and materially increased the efficiency of the militia (the militiaman regarded with enhanced respect an officer who had served in the line), on the other hand control by a government department—which, when pushed, looks largely to "expediency"—often operated to interfere with cherished local prejudices. The removal of the North Durham's depot from the county town to Newcastle in 1884, if expedient, was heedless of county sentiment. An even greater cause of dismay was the renumbering of the militia battalions in 1908. For reasons that shall be mentioned the militia in that year was cast in a draft-finding role and converted into "Reserve" battalions, maintaining depots at the depots of the regular battalions. The Reserve Battalions were all numbered 3rd, and if any regiment possessed more than one they were designated "Extra-Reserve Battalions" and numbered from 4th upwards. Because, therefore, the 4th Battalion Durham Light Infantry had its depot at Newcastle it was numbered 3rd; and the old 3rd at Barnard Castle, the lineal descendant of the old Durham Militia, with a history that might be traced back to Neville's Cross and beyond, became, in the best adjutant-generalese, the "4th (Extra Reserve) Battalion". But what else was to be expected when up and coming staff officers were calling fine old corps "units"?

The melancholy fact must be recorded that the militia, partly as a result of its very zeal to act in the line, was ceasing to be an efficient force on its own account. Many officers regarded it merely as a convenient means of entry into the professional army without any training at Sandhurst—out of twenty subalterns joining the South Durham Militia between 1898 and 1901 seventeen obtained commissions in the line; and although it received in return a refreshing flow of experienced officers from the regular battalions, its equivocal position depressed its ancient character. In 1891 it was said the Durham Militia recruit differed little from the recruit for the line. Most of the men came from the towns, those for the old 3rd Battalion from Hartlepool and Sunderland, those for the old 4th from Gateshead and Sunderland. The wages paid in the collieries and shipyards were too high to attract recruits, and many that did enter did so with a view to a month's holiday. (The usual period was 56 days' preliminary drill and 27 days' camp.) Although enlisting entailed the sacrifice of a good sum of money, commanding officers were usually accommodating, Lord Percy, for instance, bringing his Northumberland men back from Strensall Camp at 3 o'clock in the morning to obviate their losing more money than necessary.

Nevertheless, at the turn of the century the militia was still a live institution. The great landowners of the County continued to take an active interest in it. Lord Barnard, the descendant of the earls of Darlington and dukes of Cleveland, who had commanded the old Durham Militia for four generations, continued the tradition by acting as honorary Colonel of the 4th Battalion. The list of officers, with its Sowerbys, Surteeses and Greenwells, retained much of its former county character. The strength of each battalion (957 for the old 3rd, 990 for the old 4th, out of an establishment of 1060) gave evidence of the continued support of the so called "professional militiaman".

In the South African War both battalions were embodied: the old 3rd from 5th December 1899 to 12th June 1901, the old 4th from 23rd January to 4th December 1900 and from 6th January to 3rd October 1902. Both served abroad. The 3rd, which had volunteered to a man on 18th December, 1899, took over the 1st Battalion's quarters in Tournay Barracks Aldershot, and was one of the first three militia battalions to arrive in the theatre of war. It disembarked from the *Umbria* at East London, 29 officers and 703 n.c.o.s and men strong, on 3rd February 1900. It was employed on the lines of communication of Gatacre's and Brabant's forces in Cape Colony and the Free State, and with Brabant's Colonial Division as well as garrisoning Rhenoster and Dewetsdorp; losing, mainly from disease, its commanding officer, Colonel R. B. Wilson (who was awarded the C.M.G.), Lieutenant F. H. A. Sowerby, 2/Lieutenant J. C. Wilson and 26 n.c.o.s and men. Five officers and six n.c.o.s were honourably mentioned in Lord Roberts's dispatches before being brought home in May 1901 with 19 officers and 542 men. The 4th Battalion in its first embodiment was quartered in Aldershot and Rushmoor Camp, forming part of Major-General Oliphant's (3rd) Division in the 1st Army Corps for home defence. During its second embodiment it embarked for South Africa with a strength of 31 officers and 821 n.c.o.s and men. After landing at Cape Town on 18th February 1902, it was moved by rail to Orange River Station in Cape Colony. Besides furnishing detachments, it was employed on the line of block-houses from the Orange River to the Modder River and formed a company of mounted infantry which operated on convoy duty between Kimberley, Boshof and Christiana. Before returning home in September 1902 it had lost five men killed or died of wounds and eleven died of disease and other causes. Major H. J. Sowerby of the 3rd Battalion received the D.S.O., and Sergeants T. Beeby (attached to the 3rd from the 4th) and T. Sweeny (3rd) received the D.C.M.

The militia lasted for a further six years and then disappeared in the Haldane reforms of 1907-1908. The changes in social habits in the preceding generation had made it a curious hybrid. "The militia have been plundered at one end by the line and encroached on at the other by the volunteers," Lord Lansdowne had said; and Lord Haldane, who could find no place for it in his great scheme of army reorganisation, summed up the attitude of his predecessors towards it in confessing that "by sure and slow degrees the militia have been made the hewers of wood and drawers of water to the regular forces". It became a "Special Reserve" with the dual function in war of coast defence and supplying reinforcements to the regular battalions. All ranks undertook to serve anywhere.

From that moment the militia ceased to occupy its traditional position. In Durham procuring officers became a matter of difficulty. As Lieut.-Colonel W. H. Briggs (himself a militia officer and the son of one) shrewdly said, everyone knew what the militia was but no one knew what "Special Reserve" meant: explanation was necessary and, as he said, "explaining is apologising". No officers, he went on, came in from the line, and in the thirteen years before 1914, out of twelve officers that joined, only six obtained regular commissions. The War Office's insistence on a six months' probationary period with the home line battalion discouraged many young men from offering themselves: they had their careers to consider, and if they wanted to "do part-time soldiering" they went to the Volunteers (or Territorials, as they had now become), or else, having been in an O.T.C. and trained for commissions on the outbreak of a war, they now preferred to take their holiday "enjoying themselves with sports," "either shooting and fishing or going abroad". In Durham, he continued, "wealth is rapidly acquired. Most parents in Durham are making money, and the monied classes move away from the County to more congenial districts as soon as possible"; and the militia was losing its identity with the County. Colonel Briggs's picture was, perhaps, somewhat highly coloured, but it describes a development that is only too apparent in retrospect. Haldane, having failed to persuade the militia to play by his rules, meant to destroy it, and destroy it he did.

If the Durham Militia was not intended to go on active service in 1914, most of the men composing it nevertheless served with the Durham Light Infantry, most of them with the regular battalions—from which indeed it had become hardly distinguishable, so many were the time-expired regulars who had gravitated towards it. It may have ceased to be a County concern but it was certainly a regimental one. Without it the regular battalion in France, supplied by it with drafts containing many faces familiar from former days, would have hardly survived the first months of the war. It was not the militia our forefathers knew, however, and its place in the military constitution of the nation was taken by the Volunteers.[11]

III. The volunteer movement may be said to have started in 1852, when certain public-spirited gentlemen of Exeter, at the instigation of Mr John Bucknill, a Rugbeian and the son of Dr Arnold's physician—the connection with the Headmaster of Rugby is significant—assembled to form a corps of volunteers under the impression, which had been fostered for some years in the press, that the regular and militia forces were inadequate for the defence of the country. There was an echo of the sentiment in London. But the response was negligible until 1859, when the press took alarm from the hostile tenor of some letters of sympathy addressed by a few French officers to their Emperor on his escape from Orsini's attempt on his life, which had been hatched in England by Italian refugees. The officers were suffering from one of those attacks of bellicose anglophobia which periodically overtake people; but it was magnified here into a threat of invasion. The response this time was overwhelming. The enthusiasm was tremendous. Tennyson's "Form, form! Riflemen, form!" was printed in the *Times* on 9th May 1859. On the 12th the Secretary of State, yielding to pressure, empowered Lords Lieutenant of counties to enrol volunteer corps under the old Act of 44

[11]For the Militia see: W.O.16/1382 and evidence in the Wantage Committee Report (*cit. sup*). Lord Barnard kindly allowed me to inspect some papers in his possession. For the 3rd and 4th Battalions in South Africa see W.O.73/59; 108/1.

Geo. III cap. 54, which was still on the statute book, and from that moment not a day passed without some public meeting being called or some new corps being brought into existence. In 1858 the number of volunteers had been 15,122. In 1859 it had fallen to 14,981. But in 1860 it had jumped to 133,242, and on 23rd June of that year 20,000 volunteers, armed, equipped and travelling at their own expense, paraded before the Queen in Hyde Park.

The more one reflects on the volunteer movement the more curious it appears. The two years of its greatest growth, 1852 and 1859, were years of the profoundest peace—at least so far as this country was concerned—and called, one would have thought, for no expression of martial ardour. Again, if one can sympathise with the "scares" that gave it impetus, one could understand an ephemeral enthusiasm such as that which launched the Volunteers of the Revolutionary and Napoleonic Wars, but not an enduring movement which, lasting long after the effervescence of the more youthful had fizzled out, has survived now for a century, with roots deeply embedded in our institutions. The model, if it can be said to have taken a foreign model, was the American militia of the War of Independence, those formidable and self-reliant riflemen our ancestors early in the century had striven to emulate, and all the familiar arguments for raising "rifle volunteers" were gone over again, this time with success, since the rifle had become a reliable weapon and the Enfield was as good as any to be had. So Rifle Volunteers they became, even if their drill was the close-order evolutions of extreme complexity in vogue at the time. Lastly, though possessing the goodwill of the population, the movement was not "popular" in the sense that the *Garde Nationale* of Revolutionary France was, or the volunteer levies raised contemporarily in Germany and Italy. Nor was it, initially, an "aristocratic" movement: although the great families later gave their resources and their influence, at the outset they were committed to the militia. The original impulse came from men of comfortable circumstances—of whom there were many more than in the days of the first Napoleon—out of a desire to form "clubs" of "members" similar to themselves, under the orders of a "committee" of officers of their own electing.

As clubs they regarded themselves and as clubs they were regarded by the government. At first the government did no more than sanction their existence. Though it later assisted in many directions and made a small capitation grant in respect of every man that made himself efficient, in the beginning every corps found its own uniform, its arms, its places of drill, its ranges, everything, at its own expense. Members were (at least they were in Durham) of three classes: (a) effectives, who subscribed 10s. a year and either found their own uniform or were assisted from the general fund; (b) honorary members, who subscribed £1 a year, found their own clothing and drilled as often as possible; and (c) non-effective, who merely subscribed. Candidates for membership had to be approved by the corps committee. Candidates for commissions were proposed by the elected commanding officer to the Lord Lieutenant, and the officer on appointment contributed to the funds at the rate of five guineas for a captaincy, four for a lieutenancy and three for an ensigncy (and a fee to the Clerk of General Meetings of the Lieutenancy). Everything revolved round this question of solvency. The capitation and other grants were never enough; bazaars and the other money-raising expedients were resorted to even after the Volunteers had become "Territorials".

Perhaps the government was right to withhold public funds: some plants flourish best when the water is spared. One result, at any rate, was an intense individuality in each corps, which showed itself in every aspect of its appearance, in particular its dress, in which the Lord Lieutenant had some say but not, in the circumstances, the government. There was another result. Some corps were entirely composed of men of one profession, like the Inns of Court, the Civil Service Rifles, or the Advocates Company and the Writers to the Signet Company of the Edinburgh Volunteers. Some, however, recognised that admission should be extended to embrace artisans and labourers, like the colonel who proclaimed that the Volunteers were for all classes and that he would himself equip twelve working men. Yet the terms of service virtually confined the force to the fairly well-to-do, and its ranks were drawn from a much higher class then the force of 1803. Readers of Chesney's "Battle of Dorking" (1871) will remember that all the regular officers, brigadiers and staff-officers alike, are made to address the Volunteers as "gentlemen".

The movement was a little late in reaching County Durham. Sixty-three out of ninety-four lieutenancies in Britain had organised corps before the County raised its first. One of the earliest, if not the earliest, meeting held in the County to propose a volunteer rifle corps was that which took place on 24th October 1859 in the Police Court at Gateshead. It was presided over by Councillor Benjamin Bigger, of Deckham Hall, but the moving spirit was Dr William Robinson, who was appointed a secretary and later acted as the corps' surgeon. By 7th November 53 members had been enrolled, and the following week Mr George H. L. Hawks, of the firm of Hawks, Crawshay & Sons, ironfounders, a captain in the South Durham Militia, whose ancestors had formed the Gateshead Volunteer Infantry of 1803, was elected to command the corps. At Stockton the first public meeting was held in mid-November, presided over by the mayor, Mr Alcock, where 100 declared themselves ready to enrol and £140 was promised from subscribers. By the following Thursday 200 volunteers had come forward and £350 promised. The Barnard Castle Corps was proposed at a meeting held there on 21st November. Sergeant-major Morris, South Durham Militia, was appointed drill-master, and the first drill took place on 5th December. At a later meeting in December the chairman, Mr W. J. S. Morritt, J.P. and deputy-lieutenant, of Rokeby Park, subscribed £20 and Mrs Morritt £5. At the same meeting, however, the name was changed to "the Teesdale Volunteer Rifles" to preserve an historical continuity with the Teesdale Legion raised by Morritt's uncle in 1803; and the corps, forming its headquarters at Startforth, across the bridge from Barnard Castle, was administered by the Lord Lieutenant of the North Riding of Yorkshire and did not return to the County for some years. The South Shields corps was proposed on 28th November at a meeting at the Central Hall, South Shields, presided over by the mayor, Mr John Williamson, where 60 young men came forward and £300 was promised, including £100 from the Jarrow Chemical Company. The Durham corps was proposed at a meeting held in the Town Hall on 6th December, at which the mayor, Mr H. J. Spearman, of Burn Hall, took the chair and large subscriptions were offered. Hartlepool in June 1860 went so far as to raise a corps of ladies, who were drilled "once a week in the Prissick Schoolroom by Mr Stephenson, the government drill-sergeant of the artillery corps".

The first Durham corps to be officially recognised was that of *Stockton*, which was granted its commissions on 27th February 1860. It chose as its captain-commandant Mr R. Thompson, formerly lieutenant in the 48th Madras Native Infantry.

The second (though numbered 3rd—the 2nd, wherever it was, came evidently to naught) was the *Sunderland* Corps, formed on 6th March 1860 under Mr T. E. Chapman as captain-commandant, who was soon after succeeded by Mr Edward T. Gourley, lieutenant in the North Durham Militia.

The third, though numbered 8th, was the *Gateshead* Corps, formed on 14th March 1860, under the command of George Hawks, already mentioned, from whom it derived its nickname of "Ha'ak's Men". It had procured from Mr Ellison a field in High West Street as a drill-ground, Mr Squires as drillmaster, and was fast raising three companies.

The fourth, though numbered 6th, was the *South Shields* Corps, formed on 20th March, under the command of the Mayor, Mr John Williamson.

The fifth, though numbered 7th, was the *Durham* Corps, formed on 24th March, under the command of Mr John Fogg-Elliot, J.P., deputy-lieutenant, of Elvet Hill, whose Elliot forebears came from Middleton-in-Teesdale.

The sixth, though numbered 9th, was the *Blaydon* or *Blaydon Burn* Corps, formed on 3rd May under the command of Mr. Joseph Cowen, of the firm of Joseph Cowen & Co., firebrick and clay retort manufacturers, which owned collieries at Blaydon. Sometimes known as the *Tyne and Derwent Rifles*, it drew its men from Blaydon and Winlaton and drilled on Blaydon railway platform, every evening after the westbound train had passed, until 1864, when the Winlaton "up-hillers" and the Blaydon "down-hillers" fell out, and each secured separate drill-grounds.

The seventh, though numbered 10th, was the *Beamish* Corps, formed on 12th May under the command of Mr J. Joicey, whose family had recently purchased the South Tanfield Colliery from the Swinburnes and owned a considerable part of the township of Kyo.

The eighth, though numbered 4th—there was no 5th—was the *Bishop Auckland* Corps, formed on 24th May under the command of Mr William Trotter, of Byers Green Hall, near Spennymoor, a captain of the South Durham Militia and a son of the John Trotter who raised the Darlington Legion and the 1st Durham Local Militia. Captain Trotter, after rising to command the 2nd Administrative Battalion, Durham Rifle Volunteers, was killed in the hunting field in February 1866.

The ninth, though numbered 11th, was the *Chester-le-Street* Corps, which, though proposed on 22nd December 1859, was not formed until 5th June 1860, under the command of Mr P. S. Reid, whose father, as an agent for the London Chartered Gas Company, had introduced it to the coal of Pelton Colliery.

The tenth, though numbered 12th, was the *Middleton-in-Teesdale* Corps, formed on 14th July (largely of employees of the London Lead Company, which developed Middleton) under the command of Mr H. G. Bainbridge. It was dissolved in 1899.

The eleventh, numbered 13th, was the *Birtley* Corps, formed on 17th August under the command of Mr E. M. Perkins, of the firm of Perkins & Co., ironfounders, of Birtley.

The twelfth, numbered 15th, was the *Darlington* Corps, formed on 6th October under the command of Mr G. J. Scurfield, Lord of the Manor of Grindon, whose forebears, Greys and Scurfields, had long owned property in Norton, Coatham Mundeville and Grindon.

The thirteenth, numbered 14th, was the *Felling* Corps, formed on 31st October under the command of Mr W. W. Pattinson, of the firm of Hugh Lee Pattinson & Co., the Felling Chemical Works, a name that is well known to metallurgists from the "pattinsonisation" of lead.

The fourteenth, numbered 17th, was the *Wolsingham* Corps, formed on 24th November under the command of Mr Thomas H. Bates, whose family had long owned land in those parts. It was dissolved in September 1866.

The fifteenth, numbered 18th, was the *Shotley Bridge* Corps, formed on 1st December under the command of Mr. Jonathan Backhouse Richardson, whose family had long owned property at Shendon Hill, Sunderland, and Medomsley and Shotley Bridge. It was dissolved in 1865.

The sixteenth, numbered also 16th, was the *Castle Eden* Corps, formed on 14th December under the command of Mr Calverley Bewicke, J.P. and deputy-lieutenant, of Close House, Northumberland, and Urpeth Lodge, Co. Durham.

The seventeenth, numbered 19th, was the *Hartlepool* Corps, formed on 26th January 1861 under the command of Mr G. W. Jaffrey. It was dissolved on 9th November 1872. (The ladies' corps was never recognised.)

The eighteenth, numbered 20th, was the *Stanhope* Corps, formed on 19th February 1861 under the command of Mr J. T. Roddam.

Finally, there was the 21st Corps, the second in order of raising, the *Startforth* or *Barnard Castle* Corps. It had been formed as the 7th or Startforth Corps of the North Riding of Yorkshire on 29th February 1860, under the command of Morritt as captain-commandant, with Mr Morley Headlam, of Whorlton Grange, as lieutenant. In March 1860 it had consisted of 29 members who found their own uniform and six who found everything but their caps and belts, which were supplied by the Corps. On Morritt's retirement he was succeeded in the command by Morley Headlam, 26th December 1863, under whose leadership it was readmitted to the Lieutenancy of Durham as the 21st (Barnard Castle) Corps on 29th December 1863, and placed in the 2nd Administrative Battalion. At the first meeting of the National Rifle Association at Wimbledon in 1860 Edward Ross, a private of the Corps, the son of a great deerstalker and a friend of Morley Headlam's, won the Queen's Prize of £150 and a gold medal, an achievement which was the occasion of enthusiastic rejoicing on his return to Barnard Castle.

These corps varied greatly in size. Some, like the Sunderland Corps, which was large enough to lead an independent existence as a weak battalion of five companies, consisted of several companies. Others barely contained the necessary 60 effectives to qualify as corps of company strength. Encouragement was given by the War Office to form these smaller corps into loose-knit battalions, complete with lieut.-colonel, adjutant and other staff. Whereas previously captains-commandant had been accustomed to receive applications from former adjutants of militia or half-pay officers of the line, the formation of the so called "Administrative Battalion" was accompanied by a half-promise on the part of the government to fill the adjutancies itself.

The first Administrative Battalion in Durham was formed on 5th October 1860 out of a combination of the Durham, Beamish, Chester-le-Street and Birtley Corps, to which Captain Perkins, of the Birtley Corps, was appointed lieut.-colonel and Captain William Benjamin Wilkin, formerly lieutenant in the 2nd Lanark Militia, adjutant. The 2nd Administrative Battalion was formed on 14th December 1860 out of the Bishop Auckland, Middleton, Darlington and Wolsingham Corps, under the command of William Trotter, of the Bishop Auckland Corps, as lieut.-colonel and Captain George Horne, formerly of the 12th Lancers, as adjutant. The 3rd Administrative Battalion was formed on 1st June 1861 from the South Shields, Gateshead and Blaydon Corps, under George Hawks, of the Gateshead Corps, as lieut.-colonel and F. B. Henderson, formerly lieutenant of the 1st West York Militia, as adjutant. The 4th Administrative Battalion was formed in February 1862 from the Stockton, Darlington, Castle Eden and Hartlepool Corps under G. J. Scurfield, of the Darlington Corps, as lieut.-colonel. In 1873, when the Volunteers were combined (on paper) to represent the reserve forces of Sub-District No. 3, the Rifle Volunteers of the County were arrayed as follows:

 1st Administrative Battalion (Durham, Beamish, Chester-le-Street, Birtley and Felling Corps), with headquarters at Chester-le-Street, under the colonelcy of the Earl of Durham and the command of Lieut.-Colonel Joicey (Beamish), and with W. B. Wilkin as adjutant;
 2nd Administrative Battalion (Bishop Auckland, Middleton, Stanhope and Barnard Castle Corps), with headquarters at Bishop Auckland, under the colonelcy of Colonel Robert Duncombe Shafto and the command of Lieut.-Colonel John Jobson (Bishop Auckland), and with George Horne as adjutant;
 3rd Administrative Battalion (South Shields, Gateshead and Blaydon Corps), with headquarters at Gateshead, under the command of Major J. A. Cowen (Blaydon), and with James M. Webster, late 18th Regiment, as adjutant;
 4th Administrative Battalion (Stockton, Darlington and Castle

Eden Corps), with headquarters at Stockton, under the colonelcy of the Duke of Cleveland, with Robert Thompson, formerly 48th Madras N.I., as adjutant; and

3rd Durham Rifle Volunteer Corps (Sunderland Corps) with headquarters in Sunderland, under the command of Colonel Gourley and with Henry Roberts, late 98th Regiment, as adjutant.

These Volunteers of the early days had as much intention of joining the Durham Light Infantry as they had of jumping over the moon. Such assistance as they derived from the regular army came from the army at large as they could procure it and not from any particular district or regiment. For a time, indeed, in the 'seventies, it seemed that, help or no help, the whole movement would dissolve into nothing, and the 4th Administrative Battalion, it is said, was saved from dissolution only by the energies of its adjutant, Major Thompson. Annual camps for the whole battalion—a marked step towards efficiency—did not become customary till the late '80s, and throughout their history it was as much as anything the families that composed these corps that preserved them for the regular forces to assist. In the 2nd Battalion there were the Vanes, the Trotters (William Trotter, lieut.-colonel from 1861 to 1866, his son Henry John Trotter, lieut.-colonel from 1887 until meeting a death like his father's in the hunting field in 1888), and the Watsons, of an old firm of Barnard Castle solicitors who had been active in bringing the railway to the town (William Watson, commanding from 1885 to 1887, his nephew Harry Crawford Watson, who commanded from 1911 to 1915, and his son W. I. Watson, who, having commanded the Battalion in the Second World War and re-formed it in 1947, is now its present honorary colonel). In the 4th Battalion there was a long tradition of Rowlandsons and Pattinsons, and the late Air-Marshal Sir Lawrence Pattinson was serving with its lineal descendant (the 5th Durham Light Infantry) when it went to France in 1915. No less praiseworthy was the service devoted to their battalions by individuals like Andrew Henderson, who enlisted in the 5th Durham Rifle Volunteers in 1884 and served in every rank until resigning in 1946 as Colonel A. Henderson, C.M.G., T.D., D.L.

The reforms of 1881 brought the battalions into a real connection with the Durham Light Infantry which increased over the years. They had undergone a reorganisation in 1880 by which

the 1st Administrative Battalion became the 4th Durham Rifle Volunteers

the 2nd Administrative Battalion became the 2nd Durham Rifle Volunteers

the 3rd Administrative Battalion became the 5th Durham Rifle Volunteers

the 4th Administrative Battalion became the 1st Durham Rifle
Volunteers

the 3rd Corps became the 3rd Durham Rifle Volunteers.

In December 1887 they underwent a second, by which

the 1st Durham Rifle Volunteers became the 1st Volunteer
Battalion, D.L.I.,

the 2nd Durham Rifle Volunteers became the 2nd Volunteer
Battalion, D.L.I.,

the 3rd Durham Rifle Volunteers became the 3rd Volunteer
Battalion, D.L.I.

the 4th Durham Rifle Volunteers became the 4th Volunteer
Battalion, D.L.I., and

the 5th Durham Rifle Volunteers became the 5th Volunteer
Battalion, D.L.I.

This was a palpable step towards affiliation with the "territorial"
regiment. While the artillery and engineer volunteers, who also
formed part of the 68th Regimental District, had always looked to
the Royal Artillery and Royal Engineers for professional assistance,
the infantry volunteers not only progressively lost their "club"
character but also became increasingly a preserve of the Durham
Light Infantry. In 1882 only the 5th had a D.L.I. adjutant (Major
R. A. Crawford and Captain A. de B. Paget, 68th): the others had
one from the 51st, one from the 3/60th, one from the 101st and one
from the Lanark Militia. In 1884, with the appointment to the 3rd
of Major S. B. Triphook (who appears in Sir Ian Hamilton's memoirs
as the embodiment of all the adjutantly virtues), the number rose to
two; and although there was never a time when all the volunteer
battalions had a D.L.I. adjutant, they like the militia, were tightening, albeit slowly, their bonds with the Regiment.

These were substantially strengthened by the Volunteers' conduct
in the South African War. While the Volunteers of the Napoleonic
Wars had been raised for service within the parish, certainly not
beyond the County, the rifle volunteers had enrolled to serve anywhere within the kingdom in the event of invasion, but even they
had not envisaged serving abroad. When, however, in January 1900
an appeal was issued to Volunteer battalions to provide a company
of 116 all ranks per regiment as a reinforcement to their regular
battalion in South Africa, many more in Durham responded than
were needed. The first "Volunteer Service Company," which was
formed at the depot at Newcastle from the five Durham battalions,
embarked at Southampton on 23rd February 1900 under Captain
J. Turnbull, 4th Volunteer Battalion, and reached the 1st Battalion
early in April, soon after the relief of Ladysmith, while it was en-

camped at Elandslaagte. It shared in the 1st's fortunes until 9th October 1900, when it was sent to Van Reenen as part of the Drakensberg Defence Force. It remained there until April 1901, and embarked at Durban on 8th May. A 2nd Volunteer Service Company, also drawn from all five Volunteer battalions, sailed from the Albert Dock on 15th March 1901 and joined the 1st Battalion on 23rd April under the command of Captain J. Cook, 4th Volunteer Battalion, at Eden's Kop, near Heidelberg. Becoming, like its predecessor, an integral part of the regular battalion, it was relieved at Bankop, on the Swaziland border, by a 3rd Volunteer Service Company, under Captain E. S. Strangwayes, 3rd Volunteer Battalion, in April 1902, and embarked at Cape Town on 12th May, the 3rd following soon after on 9th July. A 4th Volunteer Service Company, formed from Northumberland volunteer battalions as well as Durham, embarked at Southampton on 14th March 1901 and on arrival was attached to the 2nd Buffs, on blockhouse duty between Balmoral and Brugspruit, near Pretoria, on the Lourenço Marques railway. It was later attached to the 2nd Northumberland Fusiliers, in whose movements it shared until it embarked at Cape Town in May 1902. These services, to which the Durham Volunteer Battalions contributed ten officers and not less than 400 men, were no less arduous than those of the 68th in St Vincent in 1773, and earned each battalion the honour "South Africa", which all but the 2nd[12] bore on their colours from 1909 onwards.

On 31st March 1908 the Volunteer Force was dissolved, and Haldane's Territorial Force, administered by newly formed County Associations, was inaugurated on the following day. Haldane's object, which he successfully attained, was to remodel the Volunteers along the lines of the regular army, in brigades and divisions with staffs of regular officers, complete with all their ancillary services. From a collection of volunteer corps of differing strengths, establishments and loyalties, loosely regulated by the Volunteer Act of 1863 (which had replaced the old one of 1804), he created a tightly organised force of fourteen homogeneous infantry divisions ready, after training, to assume the defence of the country on the dispatch of the regular formations.

Under the new scheme No. 5 District, which comprised the populous counties of Northumberland, Durham and Yorkshire, supplied two divisions, the Northumbrian and the West Riding, to the former of which all the Durham Territorial battalions were assigned. From

[12]The 2nd Vol. (the present 6th) Battalion, like other rifle regiments dispensing with colours, carries its honours on the cross-belt badge, which bears the oaktree and acorn device of Bishop Auckland.

being battalions of twelve, eleven and seven companies, they were reformed into battalions of eight companies with a total establishment of 29 officers and 980 n.c.o.s and men. They were more closely identified with the Regiment than ever before, as their new designations indicated:

> the 1st Volunteer Battalion (roughly corresponding to the old 4th Administrative Battalion) became the 5th Battalion Durham Light Infantry with headquarters at Stockton (Stockton 3 companies, Darlington 3, Castle Eden 2);
> the 2nd Volunteer Battalion (roughly corresponding to the old 2nd Administrative Battalion) became the 6th Battalion Durham Light Infantry, with headquarters at Bishop Auckland (Bishop Auckland 2 companies, Spennymoor 1, Crook 1, Stanhope 1, Barnard Castle 1, Consett 2);
> the 3rd Volunteer Battalion (roughly corresponding to the old 3rd Rifle Volunteer Corps) became the 7th Battalion Durham Light Infantry, with headquarters at Sunderland (Sunderland 6 companies, South Shields 2);
> the 4th Volunteer Battalion (roughly corresponding to the old 1st Administrative Battalion) became the 8th Battalion Durham Light Infantry, with headquarters at Durham (Durham 2 companies, Chester-le-Street 1, Birtley 1, Beamish 1, Stanley 1, Washington 1, Hamsteels 1);
> the 5th Volunteer Battalion (roughly corresponding to the old 3rd Administrative Battalion) became the 9th Battalion Durham Light Infantry, with headquarters at Gateshead (Gateshead 4 companies, Blaydon 2, Felling 1, Chopwell 1).

They were brigaded in the Northumbrian Division in the following manner:

> *Northumberland Brigade:* 4th, 5th, 6th and 7th Northumberland Fusiliers,
> *York & Durham Brigade:* 4th East Yorks, 4th and 5th Yorkshire Regiment [Green Howards] and 5th Durham Light Infantry,
> *Durham Brigade:* 6th, 7th, 8th and 9th Durham Light Infantry.

It is an order of battle worth remembering. It was to prove itself one of the hardest and hardiest divisions of the whole army, and it had an immense reputation. Though in May 1915 the Division was numbered as the 50th, and the Brigades received respectively the numbers 149th, 150th and 151st, the whole remained substantially in that order throughout its magnificent fighting history until the Division was finally destroyed on the Aisne in May 1918.

These men, dressed in the now familiar khaki service-dress and flat caps, were a far cry from the hirsute Durham Rifle Volunteers of 1860 with their "brown and grey mixture" uniforms embellished with Austrian knots, their brown leather belts and gaiters, and their rigid shakos 3¼ in. high in front, 4½in. high at the back. In Durham, apparently in response to representations to the Lord Lieutenant that the atmosphere was too smoky for a smart showing in grey, rifle green was adopted by all corps in 1863. The 3rd (Sunderland) Corps went over to scarlet with blue facings before 1875, and the 3rd and 4th Administrative Battalions followed in 1876 and 1877. The last to change was the 4th Volunteer Battalion (the old 1st Administrative Battalion), which kept the green uniform until 1910 on becoming the 8th battalion of the Regiment in the Haldane reforms. The only battalion never to change was the present 6th Battalion, whose commanding officer at the time, Colonel the Hon. W. L. Vane, a former 68th officer and, incidentally, the Regiment's historian, strongly opposed any alteration, with the result that it retains to this day, for formal occasions, the rifleman's uniform and, on service, the rifleman's black shoes, buttons, and black metal capbadge. It retained until May 1915—what was perhaps historical justice in a regiment with the 68th's association with Rottenburg, Hompesch's Maltese Cross on its cap badge. It still follows rifle regiments in carrying no colours.

The change from Volunteer to Territorial Force was not universally popular. There was at first uncertainty over the new terms of engagement, and in the reorganisation of companies some old associations were broken, such as the detachment from the 8th of the company (C) formed by Durham University and the detachment from the 5th of the three Middlesborough companies, which were joined to the Yorkshire Regiment, Nevertheless a large majority of each battalion re-engaged. By April 1914 the 5th, 6th, and 7th were only a hundred below establishment and only a few officers short, while the 9th was less than fifty below and the 8th forty over. The next year was to show what sort of men these were.[13]

§

In 1885 both the regular battalions were abroad. The 1st was still in India. The 2nd was in Egypt, where it shared in the action of

[13]For the Durham Volunteers see: *Gazettes* of the period; the *Times*, 26th Oct, 7th, 14th, 16th, 21st and 26th Nov, 1st, 8th and 23rd Dec 1859; Barrie Rose, "The Volunteers of 1859" in J.S.A.H.R., Vol. 37 (1959), p. 103; *Regimental Review* (1924), pp. 45-47; the *Volunteer Service Magazine*, Vol. 4 (1895), pp. 55ff. Col. W. I. Watson kindly allowed me to inspect his collection of papers bearing on the 21st Durham R.V. and its descendants. For the Volunteer Service Companies' returns, 1900-1902, see W.O.108/1.

Ginnis, now remembered only for its being the last action in which British infantry fought in red.

The 2nd Battalion had been moved from Lancashire to Ireland in March 1880, and from there, after changing quarters several times, it had embarked in August 1881 for Gibraltar and Malta. It had remained divided, with a wing in each station, until March 1883, when the whole was concentrated in Gibraltar. It had embarked for Egypt 22 officers and 863 n.c.o.s and men strong on 15th February 1885, and, having landed at Alexandria, was quartered in the Citadel in Cairo by 23rd February. After a short period from September to November spent under canvas near the Khedive's old harem at Abbassiya, it entrained on 8th November at the Bulak railway station for service in Upper Egypt.

Egypt was a new station for the army. The events of 1882 which gave rise to the bombardment of Alexandria and the battle of Tel-el-Kebir need no recounting here; but the developments in the Sudan, which had been a dependency—one might say an empire—of Egypt since 1819, are an integral part of the story. Since assuming responsibility for the internal affairs of Egypt the British Government had been understandably but culpably slow to recognise or assume responsibility for the Sudan, an enormous tract of country then, extending from the desert wastes on either side of the Nile around Wadi Halfa to the dense equatorial jungle of Uganda—a huge territory about the size of Europe. For three or four years it had been in the throes of a religious revolution led by a Moslem prophet calling himself the Mahdi, an ascetic with a compelling personality who, accumulating a vast army from the fighting population, gradually wiped out every Egyptian garrison in the northern part of the country until he threatened the security of Egypt itself. The last important garrison to fall was Khartum, the seat of the Khedive's governor-general, General Gordon, with whose murder the Mahdi's conquest of the Sudan as we know it may be said to have been complete. From that moment the Mahdi's eyes were turned upon Egypt. To a desert-born Arab Egypt represented all the wealth, the delights and power of the world, and it loomed as a distant but by no means unattainable prize on his horizon. After the fall of Khartum there was rather less emphasis upon asceticism among the leaders of the rebellion; the patched *jibba* of the dervish was exchanged, in the privacy of the harem, for the white silken robes of the debauchee; and the Mahdi's girth was visibly swelling from his excesses during the few months of triumph allowed him. He died five months after Gordon; but the invasion of Egypt was no less energetically pressed forward by his successor, the Khalifa.

Upon the failure of the belated British expedition to relieve Khartum, Dongola, the last garrison between Egypt and Khartum, was evacuated; and a mixed force of British and Egyptian troops, called the Frontier Field Force, with headquarters at Aswan, was placed under the command of Major-General Grenfell, while an advanced brigade, under Brigadier-General W. F. Butler, maintained outposts some forty miles beyond the railhead at Akasha. When Wolseley had gone and the Nile Expedition had been dispersed, the command in Egypt was resumed by Lieut.-General Sir Frederick Stephenson, whom the 68th had known in the Crimea as the commander-in-chief's courteous and competent military secretary. The Khalifa's dervishes meanwhile came on down the Nile past Dongola as far as Kaibar, where, in October, they were said to number 15,000.

Butler's instructions were to protect the ninety mile stretch of railway which ran from Wadi Halfa to Akasha. For some months his force consisted of a weak battalion of British infantry (the Camerons), a weak battalion of Sudanese and a weak battalion of Egyptian infantry. The country, an inhospitable tract of desert forming a natural boundary between Egypt and the Sudan, is aptly named the Batn-al-Hagar or "Belly of Stones," a confused mass of rugged, boulder-strewn hills some sixty miles deep. "A more terrible desert it would be difficult to find; blackened rocks and yellow sand meet the eye in every direction, and the heat and glare in the afternoon even in the winter months are very fierce." In its midst at Kôsha, where the track to Kaibar takes off and where the Nile turns from an easterly course to a northerly, affording a good command in either direction, Butler hurriedly constructed a mud-brick fort which he intended to hold whether the dervishes sat down to besiege it or by-passed it to raid the railway behind. He also fortified and garrisoned the posts on the Nile and the stations on the railway. Railhead at Akasha was held by an infantry battalion and a company of mounted infantry which included the "Durham division" of the 1st Battalion Mounted Infantry. The "division" was a detachment of some thirty picked men from the 2nd Battalion under Lieutenant H. de B. de Lisle, which from July onwards had undergone training with the 19th Hussars at Abbassiya and had been sent up the Nile with the rest of the mounted infantry in September.

The fort at Kôsha was finished only in the nick of time. On 28th November about 8000 dervishes were reported at Amara, six miles upstream, and at the same time Butler learned of the enemy plan. The dervish emir, he discovered, intended holding him at Kôsha with the main force while a flying column swung round through the desert to cut the railway in his rear.

Operations began on 3rd December with an attack delivered by a thousand dervishes on the post at Ambuqôl, where they tore up the railway for some miles. The following day they attacked and cannonaded the small garrison of eighty men from a nearby hillock. Butler, hastily collecting a force of about 600 combined infantry, cavalry, camelry and artillery, moved on Ambuqôl, but on reaching Tanqur was informed that the enemy had cleared off. He was about to return, and indeed the camp had been struck and the train was standing in the station with steam up ready to start, when Lieutenant de Lisle rode in with the news that the enemy was far from having cleared off. He had ridden out with a patrol from Akasha towards Ambuqôl on his own responsibility, he had penetrated the enemy line and got in touch with the garrison commander, Captain Ferrier, R.E., who told him the water supply was cut off and the ammunition reduced to thirty rounds per man. He had then ridden back with two men of the company, just managed to push his way through a gap in the dervish position and, though pursued by a horde of mounted spearmen, succeeded in reaching Butler at Tanqur before the train moved away. As a result of his plucky action Ambuqôl was relieved at 6 the next morning (the 5th).

But meanwhile the number of the enemy in the village of Ginnis, in front of Kôsha, who increasing daily. Kôsha was to all intents and purposes besieged, and the narrow strip of cultivation between the two villages became for the next two weeks the scene of perpetual sorties, attacks and skirmishes.

Matters were clearly moving towards a crisis. In response to Butler's representations reinforcements of British troops were arriving from the north. The 1st Royal Berkshire[14] and the 1st Royal West Kent came up first. The last were the 2nd Durhams, under Colonel Coker, who had reached Aswan on 20th November, having travelled part of the way by rail and part in barges towed by steamers. The battalion was considerably under strength. Many had been left sick in Cairo. Five men had died on the way up, and at Aswan there cannot have been more than 17[15] officers and 690 n.c.o.s and men in

[14]Understandably, the battalions were still unofficially called by their old numbers (*cf.* contemporary account in F. Loraine Petre, *The Royal Berkshire Regiment* (Reading, 1925), Vol. 1, pp. 345-347). They seem also to have retained some of the distinctions on their uniform, as some men of the 1st Battalion found in the sand near Alexandria in 1927 a 106th badge, which can only date from this period.

[15]Col. Rogers Coker (commanding), Lieut.-Col. Lee, Major Peyton (E Company), Major James (D Company), Major Fulton (F Company), Capt. Johnson-Smyth (A Company), Capt. Murphy (C Company), Lieut. Mead (H Company),

the ranks (though a draft of 98 from the depot, which arrived on 5th December, and another of 21 from the depot at Ramla, which joined the 15th, brought the numbers engaged at Ginnis on the 30th up to 18 officers and a round 800 men). On 5th December four companies were sent on to Wadi Halfa by steamer, and thence by rail to Sarras; the remainder were distributed along the line of railway between Ambuqôl and Akasha; and the whole was not concentrated at the railhead until the 24th. From there the Battalion moved up to Mograka, near Kôsha, on the 29th. At about the same time Sir Frederick Stephenson himself and Major-General Grenfell, commanding the Frontier Field Force, arrived from Cairo and Aswan, and everything was made ready to relieve the pressure on the place.

Stephenson left the arrangements to the able and energetic Butler, who had devised a plan for placing the newly arrived British Brigade, entrusted to his command, on one of the desert hills that flanked and overlooked Ginnis. Butler calculated that if he started an hour and a half before daybreak he could win the ridge by dawn; and if, as he said, "that point was reached before the Arabs got to it from Ginnis we held them in the palms of our hands: if not, they had every chance of holding *us*".

During the evening of 29th December he went out into the desert south-east of Kôsha and laid two stones to mark the flanks of an infantry battalion drawn up in quarter column, and then laid two other pairs on either side, some thirty or forty yards behind the first, to mark the position of the other two battalions of his Brigade. Before dawn on the 30th, he dressed six companies of the Berkshire in the centre pair and fell in six companies of the West Kent and six companies of the Durhams in quarter column on the Berkshires' right and left respectively. Within the three sides of the square so formed he placed the camel-guns, ambulances and other impedimenta, and he closed the square by a composite "Reserve" battalion of six companies commanded by Lieut.-Colonel Lee, 2nd Durhams, made up from two companies from each of the three battalions. He was ready at a quarter to five. There was no moon, and a slight mist lay over the desert, but the ridge he was using as a pointer was plainly outlined on the horizon to the west.

About six hundred yards in rear stood the 2nd Brigade (the 1st

Lieuts. Cooper, Wilson, Baker, Tweddell, Mathew, Moss (B Company), and Lockhart-Mure (G Company), Lieut. and Adjutant Bush, and Quartermaster Sheehan. Lieut. Buck, who had been Asst.-Provost-Marshal in Cairo, arrived in time for the action. Lieut. de Lisle had been attached to the 1st Battalion Mounted Infantry since 8th July. Lieut. Searle was on staff employ. (W.O.16/1930).

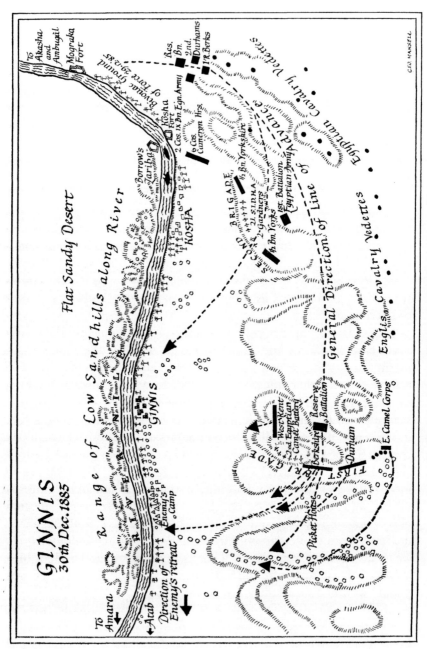

18. The Action at Ginnis, 30th December, 1885

Yorkshire Regiment and the 1st Egyptian Battalion) under Colonel Huyshe, and the English and Egyptian Camel Corps, which were to follow Butler. The 20th Hussars and the mounted infantry were out on the desert flank. On coming level with Ginnis, both infantry brigades were to wheel right, Butler's aimed upstream of the village to cut off the enemy if they attempted to bolt up the river-bank, Huyshe's aimed below the village; while the 9th Sudanese Battalion and the Cameron Highlanders, who had formed the garrison of Kôsha, were to issue from the fort and press the dervishes frontally through the palm-groves and the clusters of mud houses that lined the Nile in the strip of cultivation.

At 5 Butler, without waiting for the 2nd Brigade, started his march. It lay across broken ground intersected by steep khors or ravines. The enemy's fires could be plainly seen along the river bank. But beyond the barking of dogs there was not a sound to indicate that the movement was discovered. At about 6, as dawn began to break behind it, the column was level with and about three-quarters of a mile from Ginnis, and the ridge that was Butler's objective lay about 600 yards to his front. He made the flank battalions, the West Kent and the Durhams, deploy outwards from the centre, and then resumed the march in the old direction. They came to the foot of the ridge, the black and grey rocks were now fully visible, but no enemy showed anywhere and the silence was unbroken except for the sound of the men's boots on the boulders.

As, however, the first men reached the top the scene changed in an instant. The race had been won, but only by a few hundred yards. Immediately the leading scouts of the emir's army opened fire from concealed positions, only about two hundred yards from the leading companies, along a front of about a thousand yards, and the khors quickly filled with Arabs running up from the palm-groves. The three battalions inclined to the right, lined the ridge and lay down, though not before a few men had been hit. In a minute or two the Berkshire in the centre delivered their first volley. The Durhams on the left took up the fire, the West Kent followed, and Wodehouse's camel-battery unlimbered and joined in soon after. It was a magnificent spectacle, according to those there: for greater effect all the battalions save the Durhams had been ordered by Sir Frederick to exchange their khaki tunics for red serge "frocks" from the stores at Halfa, and the thin red line of the two battalions in line on the right, away to the left Coker's khaki battalion, and even farther beyond the 20th Hussars guarding the left flank, gave an imposing impression of might. The mounted officers remained mounted; and for the last time our enemies looked upon us as they had for nearly two centuries.

For a quarter of an hour "the fire was hammer and tongs on both sides". But the immense power that could be exerted by the musketry of British infantry when deployed in line soon took effect and, searching the slopes and khors in which the dervishes had gathered, mercilessly mowed them down. They started to edge to the left of the line, but Butler checked the movement by shifting the Reserve Battalion beyond the Durhams and sending the Camel Corps farther out still. Some continued to come on in an ecstasy of martyrdom. But, as Butler says, "the battle was soon over; we had had it all to ourselves".

He ordered the Brigade to advance and, while the Arabs fled up the river bank, he moved down the slope towards their camps behind Ginnis. The 2nd Brigade was doing the same, reaching the village about twenty minutes later at half-past 9 a.m. It was as the adjutant of the Berkshires wrote, "a most thorough success in every way". It was estimated that some 6000 dervishes were engaged, of whom 500 were killed and 300 wounded, including the emirs in command. The victory was bought at a total cost of seven men killed and thirty wounded among the British troops. The Durhams lost four men wounded, one of whom, Private Samuel Mason, died at Kôsha two days later.

The pursuit was not pressed. The cavalry was for some reason not ordered on to Amara until nightfall and it did not reach Abri, only ten miles from Ginnis, until the evening of the 31st. That night a mounted force under Major Smith-Dorrien, whose officers included Lieutenant de Lisle, was sent forward to overtake the enemy and capture the large sailing nuggers that carried the Arabs' supplies. Though his instructions forbade his pursuing beyond Suwarda, he did not catch up the nuggers until he was nearing Sayid Effendi in the afternoon of 1st January, where they lay windbound. De Lisle succeeded in capturing the nugger assigned to him, which he managed to bring back in spite of its being carried by the current to the left bank under the eyes of the retreating dervish army. On the bank beside it was an Arab boy of two whose father had been killed in the battle. Brought back and baptized with the names of James Francis Durham, he was kept and schooled at the expense of the sergeants of the Battalion on their own request. He in due course enlisted in it, married an English girl, and served until dying at Fermoy on 8th August 1910 as a corporal of buglers.

The Battalion advanced no farther than Kozak and then returned to Kôsha on 5th January 1886, where it remained until April. After six months at Aswan it returned to Cairo in late November before embarking for India at Suez on 6th January 1887. It arrived at Ghorpuri Barracks, Poona, much under establishment, on 20th January.

Ginnis is hardly remembered now, and although it was as creditable an action as Bushire or Reshire and involved as large a force, it is commemorated by no battle honour. Later events in the Sudan overshadowed it. A more formidable attempt to invade Egypt was thwarted at Toski in 1889, and the reconquest of the Sudan, which was undertaken and accomplished over the years 1896 to 1898, has overlain all memory of the period when Egypt was first threatened. Historically Ginnis lies in a trough between those two crests of excitement, the Gordon Relief Expedition and Omdurman. It did not remove the threat to Egypt. Yet, if the Frontier Field Force of 1885 had failed—if Butler had lost the race to the razorback ridge, if the reinforcements from Lower Egypt had not come up in time, and many more ifs besides—what a different story then! As it was, all those taking part received the Egyptian Medal and the Khedive's Star. Of the 2nd Battalion Colonel Coker and Lieutenant de Lisle (who was recommended for the Victoria Cross for his conduct at Ambuqôl) were made Companions of the new Distinguished Service Order in the first *Gazette* of the Order, and two men[16] received the D.C.M. The campaign had cost the Battalion one officer (Captain R. B. Barker, commanding the Nile Reserve Depot at Wadi Halfa) and 55 n.c.o.s and men died from sickness.[17]

§

The 2nd Battalion now entered upon one of the most brilliant periods of its history, and by one of those odd historical acts of justice the scene was the Poona Cantonment and the Bombay Presidency, which had reared the Battalion in its infancy fifty years before.

It is hard, in default of those detailed inspection reports which afforded so valuable an insight in earlier years, to form an idea of the Battalion as it was on its first return to India in 1887. The impression one gets, however, is that it was a good, ordinary, workaday battalion, reliable and yet on the other hand rather rough. An officer has described his first encounter with the justice dispensed in its Orderly Room. It was at Gibraltar in 1883, when the Battalion was

[16]Sergeant Stuart and Private Warberton. Stuart's name, however, does not appear in the pay lists.

[17]For Ginnis see: Butler, *cap.* xviii; Gen. Sir Frederick C. A. Stephenson, *At Home and on the Battlefield* (London, 1915), pp. 340-344; Gen. Sir Horace Smith-Dorrien, *Memories of Forty-eight Years' Service* (London, 1925), pp. 57-67; Gen. Sir F. R. Wingate, *Mahdiism and the Sudan* (London, 1891), pp. 265-285; Gen. Sir Beauvoir de Lisle, *Reminiscences of Sport and War* (London, Eyre & Spottiswoode, 1939), pp. 20*ff.* (*cit.* hereafter as "De Lisle"); W.O.16/1930.

commanded by Lieut.-Colonel Girardot, one of the last of the old Company's officers. The prisoner was a soldier's Irish wife brought in on a charge of being drunk and disorderly outside the canteen. The Colonel looked up from his paper and said,

"Hullo, you old b—, you here again?"

"Yes, your 'anner, yes, your 'anner."

"What is the evidence, Sergeant-major?"

"Found drunk and disorderly outside the canteen, Sir."

"Anything to say?" asked the Colonel. "No? Then seven days cells."

"All right, your 'anner, all right. I'll tak' it from you, for after all you *are* a man," and off she was marched to the cells for an altogether irregular punishment. The same officer's first inquest he attended was upon a man of the Battalion who had been found dead in a drinking shop in Gibraltar two days after receiving a legacy of £28. The landlord in evidence declared the man had handed over a roll of money saying, "Supply me with drink and let me know when the money's gone." When he could not drink any more he lay on the floor asking, "Pour it over me. I likes the smell," and after two days of that he was dead. Yet the Battalion had done good service in Egypt, and the story of Jimmy Durham shows that behind a rough exterior it concealed a warm heart. It was not a battalion of hard bargains: on the contrary, in both the commissioned and non-commissioned ranks it was one in which sons quite happily followed fathers (the McBains, the Whitbys and the Ainsworths). It lacked the tone imparted to the contemporary 68th by Paulet; rather it was passing through the phase the 68th passed through a hundred years earlier.[18]

This was the Battalion whose polo team in 1894 startled Indian society by winning the Infantry Cup after meeting the Gordon Highlanders in the finals in Lucknow. It was generally supposed that polo was a rich regiment's occupation, and if there was one thing about the 2nd Battalion it was that they were not rich. The result at Lucknow had been preceded by some modest successes, the Quetta Open Tournament in 1891 and the Barnard Challenge Cup in 1893 at Jubbulpore; but the victory over the Gordons not only confirmed the Durham team's faith in the principles on which they had trained but proclaimed that a dazzling new meteorite had been launched.

During the seasons that followed, the Durham team was not once defeated in the fourteen open tournaments they entered. They won the Barnard Trophy outright in 1895 and replaced it with the Durham Light Infantry Cup, which they won. They won the 7th

[18]De Lisle, pp. 16, 17, 34.

Hussars Cup at Mhow, and the Infantry Cup again in three successive years, 1895, 1896, and 1897; and in 1896 at Ambala they won in a match with the 5th Dragoon Guards the All-India Inter-Regimental Cup, competed for by all regiments in India and regarded as something of a perquisite of the cavalry. That year they also won the Bombay and the Jodhpur Open Cups, and in 1897 they repeated their success by defeating the 16th Lancers in the Inter-Regimental at Meerut.

At Poona that year they met a British cavalry regiment which, almost fresh from England, came up from Bangalore breathing vengeance and accompanying their threats with loudly voiced and not very choice insults. Two of the Durham team were on leave, and the captain had recourse to two newcomers, one of whom, Lieutenant B. C. Fairfax, had joined not long before and had played no first-class polo. Despite this handicap they were soon four goals up, at which the captain, according to his practice of making no more goals than necessary, passed up the word to "wait in front". But the cavalry team's insulting language in front of the stand, which grew with their discomfiture, could not be overlooked, and at a throw-in the captain called out to his forwards, "If that is the attitude you may make some more goals." The crowd laughed, and before the chukka was half over two more goals had been added to make the score 6-0, where it stood when play closed. Fairfax, when asked afterwards what he thought of first-class polo, replied, "Oh, is that first-class polo? I have never been called a b— so often in my life."

That was the Poona Open Cup of 1897, and the next year they not only defeated the same opponents in the Inter-Regimental at Meerut but won the Championship of India at Lucknow. The Championship was opened that season for the first time to admit not only all the army teams but the teams from the Indian states like Jodhpur and Patiala, whose rulers could afford to lavish huge sums on ponies and commanded the services of some of the best native players in the continent.

The victory in the Championship was the culmination of five seasons of unbroken success on the part of an infantry battalion of but modest means. The lustre of their achievement has even now barely faded. It brought the Regiment a fame with which not all the battle honours of the 2nd Europeans nor all the devoted services of the 68th over a hundred and fifty years had endowed it, and secured to it a character and a reputation productive of nothing but good. The cynical may smile if he pleases that the prowess of a handful of men on ponies striking a ball from one end of a flat pitch to the other should, in popular estimation, outshine the achievements, say of Johnston's little redcoated battalion slogging up the goat-tracks of the Pyrenees; but he will smile in despite of reality.

These astonishing successes were principally due to that same Captain de Lisle who had distinguished himself at Ambuqôl, and they owed their origin to the moment when in June 1893 he was offered the adjutancy of the Battalion on condition that he gave up racing. He was at the point of making himself a useful gentleman rider, but he renounced all his aspirations on reflecting that he could equally train his ponies for polo. A Guernseyman, the fourth son of a respectable old soldier who had served throughout the Crimean War in the Royal Dragoons (in the ranks, it appears), he was without any means but his pay, but from the moment he set his heart on an army commission he had determined on success in whatever lay at his command. At this period he was twenty-eight years of age, with the red hair and bushy moustache that gave him his nickname "Foxy", short in stature, 5ft. 7ins., very powerfully built, with a wrist and forearm of prodigious dimensions that enabled him to handle polo-sticks of a weight most rival players found unmanageable. His interest in horses had brought him in touch with some of the most famous trainers and riders of his day in India, of whom there were many. They had taught him everything there was to know of riding—and of falling—in fifty years he never broke a bone; and his constant attendance in the stables had familiarised him with the ways of the syces, who, it is said, can speak to their charges and be understood. An Australian pony of his, "Mary Morrison", which could "play polo" riderless and on her own at his bidding, is supposed to be the origin of Kipling's story "The Maltese Cat" in "The Day's Work" (1898). His judgment of horses and ponies was uncanny, his command of them perfect. His command of his team, severe and uncompromising, was less perfect: some, it is said, chafed at his restraints; but there was no gainsaying he was right. The rules by which he led them to victory were ruthlessly applied: but so long as he captained them they were invincible, and their successful career was only interrupted when he left India for the Staff College and the Battalion was moved to Burma. The rules that governed his own career were hardly less successful, bringing him fame as a mounted infantry commander in South Africa, a rich heiress for a bride, a cavalry brigade in the Expeditionary Force of 1914 and the command of the famous 29th Division in France, that staunch division that never lost its character in spite of all its losses. He lived rather longer than most would wish to if granted the dispensation, and he died on 16th July 1955, widowed and blind in his great house in

Mayfair, but retaining to the end an uncanny faculty of hearing and recognising. A thruster such as he cannot but be an uneasy bedfellow, and there is no denying he was not universally popular. But the Regiment has every reason to congratulate itself on nurturing such a soldier in its midst. Here was a man who, if anyone did, filled the unforgiving minute with sixty seconds' worth of distance run.

The succession of victories obtained by the Durham Light Infantry team—"particularly nice fellows," an opponent called them—on whose unity all contemporary books on polo speak with admiration, was achieved partly by de Lisle's application of principles that were novel in their time, partly by his shrewd management of the Battalion's meagre financial resources, and partly by the outstanding ability of the eighteen or so members of the team trained by him.

In 1891, when the Battalion gained its first, very moderate, success at Quetta, polo was a "new" game, its forms and observances still fluid. (It was, indeed, an old game originating in Persia, whence it had migrated to China, India and Japan; it was taken up by the Assam planters in 1859, whence it spread *via* the army to England as "hockey on horseback" in 1870, Hurlingham producing the first rules in 1873, and thence to Australia in 1876 and the United States in 1883.) The number of players in a side was generally recognised by then as four, but team-work was rudimentary. The man on the ball, who had only one idea, to make a goal for himself, was always followed by another to back him up in case he missed, while the No. 1 was expected to ride off the opposing back without taking much other part in the game. Some captains even thought it was unnecessary for No. 1 to carry a stick. "This," says de Lisle, "was the bad old gallop-and-hit game", and differed essentially from his own ideas. He had closely watched the excellent football eleven then fielded by the Battalion, which had obtained a run of successes by means of accurate passing, by working at a fast pace and by accurate shooting at goal. The application of these principles to polo, worked out with great care in practice before matches, was responsible for the team's first significant victory, that over the Gordons, whose best player, Lieutenant F. W. Kerr, pinned his faith to a dribbling game. At this he was most skilful, but it was slow, and de Lisle's men, who had trained on the principle that pace would always defeat the slow game, were rewarded by the outcome of their team-work and their skill at combining. In de Lisle's game there was no aimless hitting or striking the ball into the corner of the ground at the opponents' end; he stressed the vital importance of the penultimate stroke so as to ensure a reasonably easy shot at goal; he practised his team to anticipate what any member in control of the ball would do; and his call to a player to ride a man and leave the ball to the player backing him up was a firm order to be obeyed as an order on the parade-ground. Above all practice, constant practice, every afternoon. The men and ponies were kept in hard condition. Early hours and careful living were enforced. All other expenditure was discouraged. Pigsticking and steeplechasing were regarded with disfavour lest they should disable men and ponies wanted in the polo team. During play de Lisle insisted on absolute silence. "It is noticeable," he observed, "that in a tight match the side that begins to shout is almost sure to lose. A silent team has a great advantage." The contrast between the yelling, blaspheming cavalry team from Bangalore and the silent Durham Light Infantry team in the match at Poona in 1897 must have been most impressive.

As novel in its day as his principles of play was his management of the Battalion's modest resources. He was assisted by Captain W. C. Ross (later Brig.-General Sir Walter Ross of Cromarty), of the 1st Battalion, returned to India for a spell in the 2nd, who drew up the rules. In the Indian cantonments the barracks for the men were generally situated at some distance from the officers' bungalows and mess, and most officers kept one if not two ponies to carry them from the one to the other. In the early days of the Battalion's tour un-trained Arab ponies could be bought in Bombay for £20 or £30, and they, when trained, were suitable for second-class tournaments and saleable at about double the purchase price. If, it was found, each officer kept one pony bought by the regimental club, trained it and played polo on it, the club could dispose of the ponies at a profit of about £200, including their keep, at the end of every year. Constant and careful buying and selling, at which de Lisle was adept, had by 1893 yielded a sufficient sum wherewith to mount the Battalion team on good ponies in sufficient numbers for first-class matches. With the team's successes a Durham Light Infantry-trained pony was a commodity whose value served to enhance the resources of the club even more as the years went by. The gain was later offset by the team's competing in first-class tournaments, which entailed retaining ten or twelve of the best ponies for a second year, and increased entry-fees and rail-fares—losses and expenses that together amounted to about £400 annually. Nevertheless over 400 ponies passed through the hands of the club in those eight years. De Lisle himself, it is said, preferred Australian ponies to all others for polo in India, and his bay mare "Mary Morrison" played in nineteen tournaments. The most famous was his white Arab stallion "Snow", which had won thirty-one races, mostly steeplechases, before being put to polo, and then played in the winning team in three polo tournaments in the seasons of 1894 and 1895. He ended an honourable career at stud in Australia.

In accordance with that curious dispensation of providence that always gives a good leader the right men, de Lisle was fortunate in the officers composing his teams. At first, he says, there was only one other player in the Battalion, and he concentrated his attention on the newly joined officers. The most outstanding was Lieutenant H. B. des V. Wilkinson, a Durham man, oddly enough, from the Oswald House branch of that Durham family. Very strong and a good horseman, he yet lacked a naturally good eye, played but an indifferent game of billiards, racquets and cricket, but by constant practice developed into a remarkable player of polo. He was, according to de Lisle, "the best shot with a polo-stick when going at the fastest pace I ever met. He required twice the amount of practice other players put in but when wound up he had not his equal at No. 2. The faster the pace the more he showed to advantage and the straighter he hit." He could pick up a ball passed at right angles and make a goal, when galloping at it, with a single stroke. In the Poona match of 1897 he took the ball the length of the ground on the near side, ridden off all the way, and scored from eighty yards with a shot on his near side. Both he and de Lisle, who played No. 3, could score from the centre line, and when they hit out their balls usually reached the centre flag. Lieutenant W. J. Ainsworth, the son of a 106th officer, who entered the Battalion in 1893, played No. 1 in most of the tournaments, though in the last season he and Lieutenant L. F. Ashburner, who had played as a comparative newcomer in the Poona match, had to toss for it, and Ashburner won. Captain C. C. Luard, a good cricketer, not so strong a horseman as either Wilkinson or Ashburner but "a beautiful striker," usually played Back. This is to mention, however, but five of the best known players. The fact that in the seventeen successful tournaments between 1891 and 1898 no less than eighteen different officers played shows that the team owed its pre-eminence to more than the mere possessing a few good performers. It was the product of a combined effort on the part of the whole Battalion.[19]

Two or three generations earlier it is hardly conceivable that even such a run of successes as that of the Durham Light Infantry team would have made much impression upon a regiment's history. The 68th's cricket never did. But by the end of the last century organised games had acquired so enlarged an importance in popular estima-

[19]For the Regiment's polo see: De Lisle, pp. 35, 58ff., 186-187; Vane, App. IX (pp. 275-280); De Lisle, *Tournament Polo*, (1938). Most text-books on polo published between 1898 and 1930 will mention the D.L.I. team.

tion that de Lisle's achievements could not fail to produce the profoundest effect upon the Regiment and endow it with an aura of
glory. First, they raised the reputation of the 2nd Battalion in the
eyes of the 1st. De Lisle himself, having served a short while with the
1st when at Colchester in 1886 and 1887, had personally experienced
the resentment the elder battalion felt at the amalgamation with the
younger. Neither, perhaps, could be described as rich; but the 1st's
officers were still largely sons or younger sons of families owning
broad acres, while the 2nd's came largely from families with more
modest perspectives; and, whereas the 1st was accustomed to do
things in a suave manner born of long practice, the 2nd was still
inclined to do things in the old Bombay camp-fashion. But after 1898
the reputation of the whole Regiment derived from the prowess of
the 2nd Battalion in the polo-field, and the 1st could only bask in its
reflected glory. The old inequality disappeared. The 1st collectively
had little opportunity of acquiring a name for polo until after it went
out to India in 1902, but during that tour of duty it received much
assistance from de Lisle, who was then commanding the Royals, and
it too developed a taste for the game which it never lost. Soon,
wherever a battalion of the Durham Light Infantry appeared polo-
sticks would not be far away: on the veld at Eden's Kop in 1900,
when the 10th Battalion was near the 2nd in Flanders in 1915, when
the 2nd was in South Russia in 1919, on the North-West Frontier—
it was as a later commanding officer has said, "always we played
polo wherever possible, in peace and war and in strange places".
Polo was the catalyst which broke down the barriers between the 68th
and the 106th.

At the same time the whole Regiment enjoyed an enhanced reputation in
the army at large, partly through the polo, partly as a result of the
achievements of the team's members in the South African War. All
were mentioned in dispatches; two (Ross and de Lisle) were awarded
the C.B., three (Ashburner, Ainsworth and Way) were awarded the
D.S.O., and two (de Lisle and Luard) received brevet promotion.
For bad reasons as well as good the Regiment became a pre-
eminently desirable one to enter. As a result the quality of the
officers who joined was assured even more securely than in Paulet's
day. The consequences flowing from that circumstance need no
emphasis, and it would be invidious to enlarge upon them.

At the time, the prestige of the 2nd Battalion was immense. In February 1890 it had moved in ordinary obscurity by the sea-route from
Poona to Quetta, and in February 1892 from Quetta to Mhow. But
in January 1896 its reputation was such that it succeeded in getting itself restored to Poona, a plum which could not be expected twice in a

tour. The commanding officer of the battalion in Bombay indignantly asked why the Regiment was so favoured, but the General Officer Commanding at Bombay, Sir Charles Nairne, would not budge, saying, "There is only one reason: it is that I want the D.L.I. there." The Battalion's tour of duty in India was not all polo and football. In March 1897 700 men volunteered for plague duty in Poona, of whom six officers and 135 men under Major Paget were selected for the disagreeable task. And in October of that year, on the outbreak of hostilities on the North-West Frontier, Major Paget and Lieutenants A. K. Robb and W. Gibson, seven n.c.o.s and three men were selected for service in the Tirah Expedition, and attached to the 2nd Yorkshire Light Infantry. (Lieutenant Robb was recommended for the D.S.O., but the recommendation was not entertained.) At the turn of the year 1898 the Battalion was moved to Mandalay. It remained there two years, during which it supplied an escort for the Eastern Burma Boundary Commission, in the wild country inhabited by the head-hunting tribe of Was, and found a mounted infantry company for service in South Africa with the so called Burmah Mounted Infantry. Late in 1900 the Battalion was brought back to the mainland and stationed at Wellington near Ootacamund, a healthy station where they quickly recovered from the sickly climate of Burma. They remained two years—part of the time guarding Boer prisoners of war—until returning home by way of Calicut and Bombay in December 1902.

The Battalion that landed at Southampton on 16th December 1902 was a very different concern from the one that had embarked at the Albert Dock for the Mediterranean twenty years before.

CHAPTER IX

THE BOER WAR, 1899-1902

THE 68th, or 1st Battalion, saw no active service in the thirty-five years between the New Zealand War in 1865 and the Boer War in 1899. A whole generation of officers and men entered, served and disappeared without any opportunities of distinction in the field.

The Battalion's tour in India (1872-1877) was peaceful routine. It remained in Poona until November 1874, when it was moved to Mhow. At the turn of 1875 it moved to Nasirabad and Nimach. In 1878 it moved to Mian Mir, the great cantonment outside Lahore, where it remained until December 1880. In April 1879 Lieut.-Colonel Trent, compulsorily retired, was succeeded by the last of the Crimean veterans, Lieut.-Colonel Tucker, who held the command until July 1884. From Mian Mir it moved by way of Muzaffernagar to Meerut, where it stayed for three years until entraining in October 1883 for Allahabad. It did not move again before it embarked for home—once more in the *Euphrates*—in February 1887 under the command of Lieut.-Colonel Crawford. In spite of recurrent cholera epidemics, the Battalion's effective strength remained fairly constant at around 900 n.c.o.s and rank and file; but on its departure it transferred an aggregate of 429 men to the 2nd Battalion, which had newly arrived in India from Egypt; and what with discharges and other reasons this fine battalion on its first appearance in Colchester on 14th April 1887 had been reduced to about 200 effectives.

During its two years in Colchester Lieut.-Colonel Upcher, who had served twenty-five years in the 24th Regiment and was one of the few officers of his battalion to escape the disaster at Isandhlwana, was brought in to command. In May 1889 the Battalion was moved north to Bradford and Lichfield, and it remained divided until uniting in September 1891 at Aldershot, where it had the distinction of being the last corps of the garrison to exchange the old Martini-Henry rifle for the Lee-Metford. It did not move again until late in September 1893, when it embarked for Ireland under Lieut.-Colonel Gordon. Headquarters and the main body of the Battalion were stationed at Buttevant, remaining there until October 1895, when the whole were moved into Dublin.

On the outbreak of the war in South Africa in October 1899 it was high on the roster for India. In 1898 it had moved to Tournay Barracks, Aldershot, and when warned to prepare for service it consisted of eight companies, 24 officers and 689 n.c.o.s and men strong on an establishment of 832. On mobilisation, however, the establishment was raised to 1110 all ranks, and the recall of 525 Section B reservists brought the strength up to over 1200. Though it had formed part of the 2nd Infantry Brigade at Aldershot, it was sent abroad to join the 4th (Light) Brigade (Major-General Lyttelton) of the 2nd Division (Lieut.-General Clery). Leaving behind a detachment of 379 men, which, with similar detachments from the Queen's and South Lancashire Regiments, was formed into the "3rd Provisional Battalion," it embarked at Southampton on 24th October in the Cunarder *Cephalonia*—amidst scenes of popular enthusiasm to which the soldier of 1899 was altogether unaccustomed—with a strength of 27 officers and 921 n.c.o.s and men (over half of them reservists).[1] Also on board the *Cephalonia* were Captain de Lisle and two companies of the 2nd Battalion of Mounted Infantry of which he commanded the so-called Dublin Company, and the Brigadier and his staff.

"The troops on board," Lyttelton has recorded, "were mostly Durham Light Infantry, a fine regiment under Colonel Woodland, one of the old anti-reform school, with no war service and not far from my own age. . . . He told me candidly that he was old-fashioned and no tactician, but whatever I told him I wanted his regiment to do he would see that it was done, and I found him as good as his word."[2] Together with this confirmation from its brigadier, there are other indications that the Battalion was in remarkably good shape at this time. Pronouncedly more *Durham* than it had been ten years

[1] Lieut.-Col. Woodland (commanding), Bvt.-Lieut.-Col. H. S. FitzGerald, Majors T. R. Johnson-Smyth and G. C. Mansel; Capts. B. W. L. McMahon (adjutant), R. F. Bell, W. C. Lascelles, H. R. Cumming, O. B. Harter and A. C. Tucker; Lieuts. E. A. C. Blake, G. L. Cochrane, W. Northey, R. Tyndall, L. C. Soltau-Symons, J. S. Unthank and C. B. Thresher; 2/Lieuts. C. D. Shafto, J. W. Jeffreys, C. L. Matthews, A. W. B. Wallace, R. R. Lambton, K. J. W. Leather, R. E. Rasbotham, P. W. Nickalls and E. W. Appleby; and Quartermaster J. H. Liebrecht. (W.O.73/59).

[2] Gen. the Hon. Sir Neville Lyttelton, *Eighty Years* (London, 1927), p. 202 (*cit.* hereafter as "Lyttelton").

before, it had for some years enjoyed the reputation of being the best bayonet-fighting battalion in the army. In the Military Tournament at Aldershot in 1898 it had won two of the bayonet combat competitions, and in 1899 a team of nine under Corporal Melia won the All-Army Bayonet-fighting Championship.[3]

Its condition was in no small part due to its commanding officer. Colonel Woodland was by birth an Irishman and in 1899 was just fifty years of age, rather old for commanding officers at that time, in appearance somewhat old-fashioned with his side-whiskers, but possessing a dominating presence that subalterns were apt to find alarming. Formerly (1872-1875) adjutant of the 68th, a bachelor who, apart from a spell at the depot, had lived all his life in the regimental mess, he belonged to a generation of officer which, already fast disappearing under the Wolseley régime, the South African War was to make extinct; but he was a true soldier, and he was to prove himself an able and gallant commanding officer in the field. (Lyttelton it need hardly be said belonged to the new school; Clery, the divisional commander—"Old Bluewhiskers" the men called him from the colour he dyed them—was the very reverse.)

The war with the Boer Republics of the Orange Free State and the Transvaal is commonly regarded now as a faintly ludicrous and somewhat discreditable episode in our military history. It is neither the one nor the other. It is only ludicrous if we remember no more than the mistakes that were made and forget the profitable lessons learned, and only discreditable if we underestimate, as our grandfathers did, the enemy who opposed us.

The Boer, whatever the contemporary press may have said, was a formidable opponent. Stubborn and intelligent (if not very wise) by heredity, reared for generations in a healthy climate where all his physical faculties were tested from boyhood, he was, in his own country, man for man superior to any mercenary soldier in the European continent. That deserves to be recognised. Outnumbered and surrounded, both geographically and domestically, by the "Kaffir" races from whom he had recently won the land he lived on, he was as combative, as proud and as sensitive as the white planter in the Southern States of America; and though lacking the other's graces, he had the same sense of belonging to an aristocracy. Wide stretches of open veld and an atmosphere as clear as crystal had

[3]Their names, kindly supplied to me by Mr Maurice Donovan, one of their number, are interesting: Corporal Melia (born in Middlesbrough of Irish stock), gymnastic instructor: Privates Alcock (Irish) tailor; Collins (Tyneside), bandsman; Donovan (Irish), orderly-room clerk; Fellingham (born in the army of Irish stock), bandsman; Humphries (London), cook; Martin (Tyneside), bugler; O'Brien (Irish), machine-gunner; and Taylor (Hartlepool), blacksmith.

developed his physique and his eyesight; no cutting blasts checked his circulation; no damp stiffened his joints with rheumatism.[4] As a marksman he was unrivalled anywhere. "From boyhood every man was expected to conform to a strict standard of one shot one kill, meat being a necessity and cartridges dear. Nor had the hunter necessarily an easy or a stationary target. . . . He must learn to pick up his target, swing onto it and bring it down in a matter of seconds. . . . The result in the days when game was plentiful," says one who knows more about South African warfare than anyone living, "was that the Bushveld men were lightning quick in cover and the High Veld men could bring down a buck or an enemy at five hundred yards with a degree of certainty that can have had few equals and no superiors anywhere."[5]

It was not as if the marksman was merely a peaceful farmer or game-hunter. Constant native warfare had sharpened his military aptitudes and practised his military tactics. Trained to horses, despising footslogging, the burgher was a born mounted infantryman. With a sack of biltong and coffee he was, moreover, more mobile than his opponent, chained to his toiling convoy of ox-wagons. When European armies were still teaching close-order movements and the bayonet attack, the Boer had practised dispersion to a degree that foreshadowed "the empty battlefield" of the days of smokeless powder. What was more disconcerting to his enemy, he had developed the idea of covering the attack with a "hose-pipe" of rifle fire to keep the heads of the defence down. His best shots from among the older men were carefully posted to fire over the advance, and "their slow, controlled, deadly accurate fire made it difficult if not impossible for the defenders to show themselves . . ."[6] The practice was extended with the introduction of the rifle and breechloader, and was continued when the burgher, on joining his commando in 1899, exchanged his own weapon for the Mauser from the government armoury. It was the most modern principle of "fire and movement" translated into terms of pure musketry. To European soldiers, preoccupied with re-fighting great battles like Gravelotte, it came as a revelation. The Boer had no use for the European's belief in the brusque effectiveness of the bayonet. Instinctively conservative of life, as a craftsman, a family man and a member of a sparse and beleaguered white society might well be, he avoided the sharp losses of the bayonet fight by discreet withdrawal if attacked, and in the

[4] Lieut.-Col. E. S. May, *A Retrospect on the South African War* (1901), p. 8.
[5] Major G. Tylden, "The Development of the Commando System in South Africa, 1715-1922" in *Africana Notes and News* (Johannesburg, 1959), Vol. 13, p. 305.
[6] *Ibid., loc. cit.*

offensive learned—eventually—to replace the bayonet by firing from the hip. As one of de Wet's junior officers once said, "What sort of a fool do you think me when you offer me a bayonet? I can have two of your men down before they can get even a few yards towards me with their bayonets!"[7]

The Boer, however, underestimated the power of the British army as seriously as it underestimated him. He had encountered it but partially in the war of 1881, when his marksmanship and tactics had embarrassed small British forces in several actions before finally routing Colley's force from an apparently impregnable position. His commandos had decisively defeated Jameson's Raiders. After Majuba the British Government chose not, and after Krugersdorp was in no position, to take any further action; and the Boer was left with the fruits of his prowess and a hearty contempt for the British nation as a whole. His experience of the restless and unstable element in the British population of the goldfields of the Rand confirmed his opinion of his enemy; and the whole tradition of his upbringing was in favour of isolation and opposed to informing himself better.

He did not know that the army had undergone very substantial improvement in the twenty years' interval. The standard of marksmanship had improved, and the improvised battalions of mounted infantry which it became the practice to incorporate in every field force were almost equal in training, if not in numbers or experience, to the Boer commandos. Open order formations were practised by the infantry battalions, though not, perhaps, as generally as was desirable. The short-service soldier and reservist of 1899 was probably physically superior to their counterparts of 1881. He was certainly better trained. The staff and ancillary services were better organised—though in these respects as in others there was much room for improvement: for instance, in the manœuvres at Wareham in 1898 the transport of the 1st Battalion Durham Light Infantry had been provided by Messrs. William Whiteley and the canteen arrangements had been placed in the able, but not very military, hands of Messrs. Lipton.[8]

The Boer was right, on the other hand, in regarding himself as superior to the infantryman in the veld. The regimental officer and soldier had not been taught in the new training to act on their own. "The colonel's coals must be conducted from the quartermaster's store by a mounted non-commissioned officer to ensure that the driver, a man perhaps of five-and-twenty years of age, does not go to the wrong quarters, or delay on the road, or let his horses run away,

[7] *Ibid.*, pp. 306-307.
[8] Digest.

or commit some other enormity. His younger brother driving a grocer's cart to twenty houses in various parts of the town perhaps meets him, and smiles derisively at the untrustworthy soldier. For in the army, when you want a man to do a thing you must invariably send another man to see him do it."[9] Even in the best mounted infantry battalions, seasoned by months of a kind of soldiering that tried the qualities of every single man, it was uncommon for his leaders to let him know what he was about. Though the war was one in which the self-reliance of individuals was tested to an unprecedented degree, it was a quality not encouraged. The Boer took advantage of his superiority in this respect when he could. He had a sincere regard for his opponent's courage. But he vastly underrated the ordinary British soldier's capacity for coming up smiling in the face of death, wounds, discomfort and disappointment suffered over and over again. Nor had he a conception of the might and the determination that were to be exerted to oppose him.

Psychological and military considerations favoured an immediate Boer offensive—south-eastward into Natal, with Durban and the sea as a distant objective; south-westward to the Bechuanaland railway at Mafeking and Kimberley, with the object of entering Cape Colony and raising the Cape Dutch in the cause of the Republics; and southward into the Colony, across the Orange at Bethulie and Norval's Pont, with the same object. The first, in view of the vulnerability of Natal and the strength of the Boer force undertaking it, was the most dangerous. On that front the situation rapidly deteriorated after Joubert's commandos crossed the Natal frontier at Botha's Pass and Laing's Nek on 12th October.

Sir George White, the senior officer in South Africa, already heavily outnumbered and anticipating a movement from the Free State commandos over the other Drakensberg passes (De Beer's, Van Reenen's and Tintwa's), preferred concentrating at Ladysmith to holding the nothern part of the province containing the coalfields. But he did not withdraw the advanced brigade at Dundee until—despite two partially successful actions (Talana and Elandslaagte)—the offensive from the Free State developed sufficiently to compel him to assemble the whole Natal garrison, about 13,000 men, around Ladysmith. There, on 30th October, as a result of the action which is variously known as Farquhar's Farm, Lombard's Kop, Modderspruit, Nicholson's Nek, or Ladysmith, it was effectively bottled up.

At home it had been recognised that, if the Boers assumed the offensive, the troops in South Africa, working on exterior lines, would have difficulty in maintaining positions widely separated by

[9]May, cit. sup., p. 45.

impenetrable country; but it had been considered that the dispatch of an army corps, *the* Army Corps (of three infantry divisions and one cavalry, organised with all its supporting services, under the command of Sir Redvers Buller) would be more than enough to redress the balance. The Army Corps was to have marched straight to Pretoria either through Natal or across the Free State by the railway running through Springfontein, Bloemfontein and Johannesburg. But on arriving at Cape Town on 31st October Buller found the situation had developed so unfavourably that he determined on breaking up the Army Corps, sending Hildyard's Brigade of Methuen's Division and Barton's of Gatacre's to Natal. Finally, hearing that the Boers had come down beyond Ladysmith as far as Estcourt, he divided the Corps still further by sending Hart's Brigade of Gatacre's Division and the whole of Clery's Division to the Natal front, and betook himself there to command.

It was for this reason that the *Cephalonia*, which had reached Cape Town on 18th November after coaling at St. Vincent with the assistance of the colliers in the ranks of the 1st Battalion, was sent on to Durban, where it arrived on the 23rd. The Battalion was immediately conveyed by rail to Nottingham Road, and thence on the 25th to the encampment at Mooi River, where the other battalions of Lyttelton's 4th Brigade were assembled into what became commonly known as the Light Brigade:

> 2nd Scottish Rifles (Cameronians)
> 3rd King's Royal Rifle Corps
> 1st Durham Light Infantry, and the
> 1st Rifle Brigade

"Physically," says Lyttelton, "they were a very fine lot." But like all but one of the brigades of the Army Corps (Hildyard's) the 4th had never served together as a formation; the staffs and the units were unfamiliar with each other; and the initial awkwardness was not improved by Buller's habit of altering the composition of the brigades to suit the requirements of the operations of the next few months.

During November—which in South Africa is the beginning of summer, the season of heavy rains that turn the tumbled hills of Natal into a luxuriant green and fill the rivers—the advanced Boer force had withdrawn from Estcourt to a position behind the Tugela at Colenso, covering the siege of Ladysmith. Buller, who arrived at Pietermaritzburg on 25th November, determined on an immediate advance against them. Three courses were open to him. He could assault the Colenso position frontally; he could move on Weenen, cross the Tugela by the wagon drifts thirty miles below Colenso, and make for Elandslaagte; or he could turn the left of the position by the upper Tugela drifts (Potgieter's, Trickhardt's, etc.) to approach Ladysmith from the south-west. Preferring the last-mentioned, he set his force in motion from their rain-sodden encampments on 12th December in the direction of Springfield. However, that evening he suddenly changed his mind. He resolved on a frontal assault of Colenso, which took place early in the morning of 15th December, and failed.

The Battalion was barely involved in the battle of Colenso. The Brigade had moved from Mooi River to Frere on 6th December, thence to Chieveley on the 13th, and in the action it was placed in a reserve position by Shooter's Hill, which it occupied throughout the early hours of the morning until about half-past seven, when the failure of the two principal infantry attacks on the Boer trenches became apparent. At about 8 half the Brigade was moved to the right to cover the withdrawal of Hildyard's Brigade, while the other half, consisting of the 1st Rifle Brigade and all but one company of the 1st Durham Light Infantry, was directed to the left to favour the withdrawal of Hart's (Irish) Brigade. Hart's men were already under orders to retire after their gallant assault into the great bend of the Tugela known as The Loop, where, enfiladed from both flanks, they had been unable to cross; but the orders took some three hours to reach those farthest forward; and by that time, at about half-past ten, Lyttelton's two battalions were posted on the Doornkop Spruit. The Riflemen and four companies of the Durham Light Infantry crossed the Spruit and opened out to six or eight paces interval. Four companies of the Riflemen and two of the Durhams advanced farther and formed a firing line about five hundred yards from the Tugela as Hart's men passed through them to the rear, pausing in the Spruit to slake their thirst and then moving on "as cool and indifferent as ever" to form up out of range. Thanks to the fire of the artillery and Lyttelton's two battalions, the enemy made no attempt at direct pursuit, and indeed so smoothly was the withdrawal carried out that many in the ranks were unaware they were doing anything but countermarching to another crossing of the river. It was not a beaten Army that Buller withdrew to its camps that afternoon. Some, like the Durhams, who had two men wounded, had hardly been engaged. All were in the best of spirits and eager for another attempt.[10]

After Colenso Buller returned to his original intention of an advance by the upper drifts of the Tugela, which he undertook as soon

[10]The best detailed military accounts of the war are still the *Official History* (*cit.* hereafter as 'Off. Hist.") and the *Times History*, which are used here throughout.

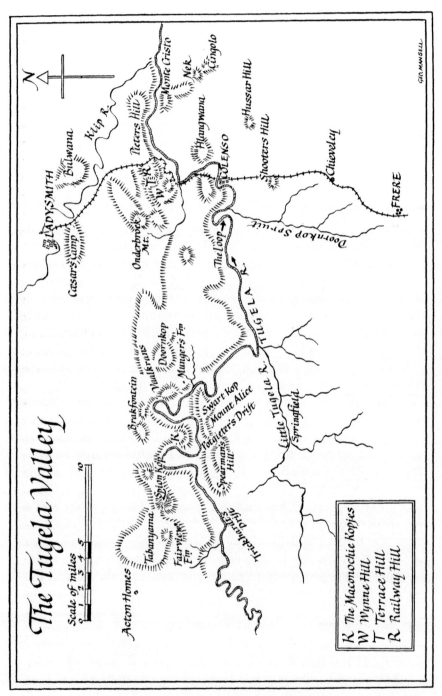

19. The Tugela Valley, December, 1899—February, 1900

as the new 5th Division (Warren) had joined him and received its transport. The operation, for the purpose of which Lyttelton's Brigade was withdrawn from Clery's and placed under Warren's command, started on 10th January 1900 with a march in heavy rain from Frere to Springfield (11th) and thence to Spearman's Hill (12th), overlooking the winding course of the river below and, beyond, the hills on which the right of the enemy position rested. At Colenso they had stared up at the bare green escarpment that dominates the south bank of the Tugela much as the White Horse Hills dominate the Vale below (and might be mistaken for them but for the aloes plants and thorn-bushes that destroy the illusion). From Spearman's and one or two isolated kopjes on the right bank they could view the prospect more as equals. But there was still the river, very full at that season, and the formidable array of hills—Tabanyama, Spion Kop, Brakfontein, Vaalkrans and Doornkop—to overcome before they could see Ladysmith clear in their front.

Buller's intention of forcing a crossing at Potgieter's Drift was forestalled by the Boers, who rushed reinforcements at four hours' notice from the Colenso position. But he attempted to turn their right by crossing still higher, at Trickhardt's. The operation was entrusted to Warren, who, assisted by a feint at Potgieter's made by Lyttelton, three of whose battalions were the first troops to stand on the north bank, successfully executed it on 17th January. At the same time the mounted brigade ranged around the Boer right at Acton Homes. However, Warren's movements developed painfully slowly. On the 19th, in order to favour his advance on Ladysmith by the Fairview road, he decided to clear Spion Kop, from which the enemy embarrassed his right flank. Once again assisted by Lyttelton, who brought up the Durhams into the "bridgehead" of the Maconochie Kopjes[11] on the 20th and launched a demonstration against Brakfontein with the 3/60th, he attained his object in the night of the 23rd/24th. But in the morning the Boers, making a supreme effort, hurried reinforcements to the Kop, and there developed a gruesome struggle for the summit which continued throughout the remainder of the day and into the hours of darkness. At 4 in the morning Lyttelton had endeavoured to draw the Boers from the Kop by another feint against Brakfontein carried out by the Durham Light Infantry, who, he records, "advanced as if to attack covered by heavy artillery fire, but with strict orders not to commit themselves. This was well carried out, and answered its purpose by keeping a considerable number of Boers off Warren." Further diversionary

[11]Previously called The Kopjes, they were renamed after the tins of provisions supplied by the well-known army contractor.

attacks made by Lyttelton during the 24th, though successful locally, proved insufficient, however, to affect the issue on Spion Kop; and in the early hours of the 25th the hill was evacuated against orders. The Boers drew off at the same time, but were the first to discover the ghastly battlefield was untenanted.

After the failure at Spion Kop Buller withdrew his whole force across the river with the exception of the "bridgehead" on the Maconochie Kopjes, which continued to be held by the Rifle Brigade and the Durham Light Infantry until relieved by the 11th Brigade on 3rd February. Surveying the Boers' heights from the summit of the Swart Kop, Buller next determined to assault the Vaalkrans ridge, on the left of the semi-circle of hills that constituted the enemy position, and push the main body through the valley to the east of it, while Doornkop, the ridge on the other side of the valley, was to be cleared also. The 2nd, 4th and 5th Brigades were detailed for the attack, but the whole was to be preceded by a smart bombardment and a sham attack on the main Boer position on Brakfontein by the 11th Brigade, after which the artillery was to be secretly withdrawn to the right and its fire concentrated on Vaalkrans.

At 7 in the morning of 5th February the three assault brigades started from their bivouacs at the foot of Mount Alice and Swart Kop and, marching east through Harding's Farm, halted in dead ground opposite a newly constructed pontoon bridge known as Pontoon No. 2 to await the completion of the feint. The 11th Brigade had meanwhile moved out from the Maconochie Kopjes to practise their deception, and, at about half-past one moved back again according to plan. There was a delay, however, in withdrawing the artillery across Pontoon No. 2 and in switching it to its new positions. During the lull Buller, according to Lyttelton, began to shilly-shally, and he was only persuaded to continue the attack on Vaalkrans on Lyttelton's undertaking to "have his men on the top by 4".

It was about 2 therefore before the Durham Light Infantry and the Rifle Brigade of the 4th Brigade started on their march for Pontoon No. 3, which had been constructed under heavy fire in the morning. They quickly crossed in rushes of companies, re-formed on the far side under the cover of a bank some twenty feet high, and then pushed on in single file for about half a mile, hugging the river bank until reaching a deep donga which entered the Tugela a little above Munger's Drift. Until this moment their progress had been sheltered from the fire of snipers scattered in the mealie-fields and in the slopes above them, and also from a Boer gun which, dropping shell into the valley, churned up the waters of the river without causing any casualties. But above the donga where the companies wheeled left and deployed into the open, there was no cover; and, though they were supported by the naval guns on Swart Kop and the field guns below, they had to make their way up Vaalkrans against a steady and accurate rifle and pom-pom fire directed at them not only from in front but from Green Hill and the Kaffir kraal in their right and right rear.

With the Rifle Brigade slightly behind on their right, the eight companies of the Durham Light Infantry, extended to four or five paces and advancing on a two-company front with M and L Companies under Major Johnson-Smyth leading, immediately sustained heavy losses, among them Major Johnson-Smyth himself. "It was rather a stiff job," Lyttelton said afterwards, "and the Durham Light Infantry at first were a bit staggered at the heavy fire which greeted them, and I ran forward to join them; but before I reached them they pulled themselves together, and covered by accurate shelling and closely supported by the Rifle Brigade, they breasted the hill splendidly, and exactly at 4 p.m. I saw Lascelles, a young D.L.I. officer, waving his hat on the top, and the hill was ours."[12] The first man to reach the summit, according to regimental tradition, was Colour-sergeant J. P. L. Shea of K Company, born in the Regiment, the son of Quartermaster W. Shea, a fine old soldier who had received the Empress of India's Medal in 1877 as the best soldier of the 68th.[13] Breaking through Munger's Farm the Battalion had stormed up the double peaked hill at the point of the bayonet, routing those of Viljoen's men that survived and taking some prisoners.

In their wake there followed Lyttelton's other two battalions as well as the Devons of Hildyard's Brigade, which was to have gone on to take Green Hill on the other side of the valley. But for some reason Buller had lost heart and suspended the complementary movement, ordering Lyttelton to consolidate his gains and hold his position. Thus for the remainder of the 5th, all through the night and for most of the 6th, Lyttelton's men lay behind the *schanzes* they hastily improvised. On the left lay the Durhams with the 3rd King's Royal Rifle Corps in close support, to their right the Rifle Brigade supported by the 2nd Cameronians, while two companies of the Devons prolonged the right. There was little sleep that night. Throughout the hours of darkness heavy bursts of rifle and pom-pom fire were directed on them by the enemy on Brakfontein, Kranskloof

[12]Lyttelton, pp. 218-222.
[13]Colour-sergeant Shea transferred to the 2nd Battalion, in which he rose to be sergeant-major and, later, quartermaster. As Capt. J. P. L. Shea, M.C. and Bar, D.C.M., he died 1st Dec 1917 from wounds received at Gouzeaucourt, 30th Nov.

and, more particularly, the hill a short distance in front, Hill 360, whence, behind a veil of smoke rising from the saddle connecting it to Vaalkrans (which had been set alight), they poured in a fire of the most disconcerting accuracy, which increased as reinforcements arrived from Spion Kop.

In the morning Lyttelton signalled that even with artillery support he could not seize Hill 360, an essential step if the advance was to continue. Buller hesitated. He referred by telegraph to Lord Roberts, who had recently arrived at the Cape to assume command in South Africa. While Buller waited the Boers delivered, at about 3.30 in the afternoon, a counter-attack on the Durham Light Infantry from behind the screen of burning grass. They beat it off with some ease with the assistance of the King's Royal Rifles, some of them hardly noticing that it had taken place.[14] But the Vaalkrans approach to Ladysmith had lost its enchantment for Buller, whose doubts were not to be dispelled. Ordering Lyttelton's Brigade to be relieved, he summoned a council of war, which obligingly advised an abandonment of the operation.

Towards evening Hildyard's men relieved Lyttelton's from their fatiguing service of twenty-six hours on the ridge, and the Durham Light Infantry, handing over their *schanzes* to the 2nd Queen's, withdrew across the river to their bivouac under the Swart Kop. Their attack on Vaalkrans was as fine a thing as their charges at Orthez and Inkerman, but their losses, as losses were reckoned before 1914, had been fairly heavy. Two officers (Major T. R. Johnson-Smyth and Lieutenant Charles Duncombe Shafto) and 18 n.c.o.s and men were killed or mortally wounded; six officers (Bvt.-Lieut.-Colonel H. S. FitzGerald, Captain W. C. Lascelles (crippled), Lieutenant E. A. C. Blake and 2/Lieutenants R. R. Lambton, C. L. Matthews (commanding a half-company of M) and E. W. Appleby) and 70 n.c.o.s and men were wounded. The last number included the Battalion's sergeant-major, Mr Joseph Freel, later awarded the D.C.M., who had risen from private to sergeant in one year (1885) and was to rise to the rank of lieut.-colonel-quartermaster, one of that extraordinary line (not yet extinct) of dyed-in-the-wool Durham Light Infantrymen who have made the Regiment their home and have preserved it as a home for others.

Buller announced his intention of abandoning the attempt on Vaalkrans at 4 in the afternoon of 7th February. At dawn the next day the whole Army was in motion towards the rear, and, after a hot

---

[14] The *Times History's* account (Vol. 2, p. 324) of the Durhams' "wavering" is an exaggeration not supported elsewhere.

march it was back under canvas at Chieveley on the 11th. No time was to be lost if Ladysmith was to be relieved, and Buller's next operation started three days later. It was directed against the lower Tugela, and involved forcing the enemy from the heights he occupied on the south bank, Hlangwana, Cingolo and Monte Cristo, possession of which would outflank and command the Boer position at Colenso.

The Monte Cristo movement was entrusted to the 2nd Division, under the temporary command of Lyttelton, whose Brigade came under the orders of Colonel Norcott. The operation started auspiciously enough with the surprise of Mission Hill and Hussar Hill by Warren's 5th Division on 14th February. But Buller was slow to profit from this success, and Lyttelton was not allowed to develop his attack on Monte Cristo until the 17th, by which time the enemy had recovered and reinforced his left. Nevertheless, by a judicious combination of fire and movement Lyttelton drove the Boers off Cingolo back to Monte Cristo on the 17th, and the next day worked forward across Cingolo Nek and carried Monte Cristo with Norcott's Brigade, while Barton's on its left took Green Hill. Norcott's had an easier task than the others, attacking in the valley and being supported by a well directed fire from the artillery. In the attack the Battalion stood between the 3rd King's Royal Rifles on its left and the Rifle Brigade on its right, and, owing largely to Lyttelton's competent handling, its casualties were low, amounting to only eight men wounded. After the action Norcott pushed north-westwards towards the river through a thick belt of trees and scrub which favoured skirmishing. The Rifle Brigade and the Durham Light Infantry remained on the river bank until the 23rd. "The battle of Monte Cristo," says Lyttelton, "was the first unmistakable victory we had won, and we thought the relief of Ladysmith was ensured. So it was, but there was a bad disaster and some hard fighting before the goal was attained."[15]

Meanwhile, with the capture of Hlangwana on the 19th, the south bank cleared and the Boer trenches at Colenso flanked, two courses lay open to Buller. He could either cross near Colenso and fight his way through the hills beyond, or he could make a flank march by Cingolo Nek to the confluence of the Klip River with the Tugela and then advance by the Klip on Bulwana, the great height that dominated Ladysmith. Preferring the former, he crossed on 21st February and seized the Colenso Kopjes. From there he pushed forward to occupy Horseshoe Hill, Wynne Hill and Hedge Hill the next day, but further progress was checked largely as a result of the effect-

[15]Lyttelton, p. 226.

iveness of the hastily improvised entrenchments of the Boers, whose genius for this kind of business was never shown to greater advantage.

On 23rd February Buller's objective was Terrace Hill, for the assault of which he detailed the Irish Brigade of Hart, who was always ready for any offensive movement. Early that day Hart led his brigade from its bivouac near Colenso round the bend of the river by the north bank until it stood opposite the Imperial Light Infantry and Norcott's two south bank battalions, the Rifle Brigade and the Durham Light Infantry, who crossed to support it at about 7 a.m. The attack went in at about midday. Leading were the Inniskillings, followed by half of the Imperial Light Infantry and the Connaught Rangers in close support, while a second line consisting of the Dublin Fusiliers and a third consisting of the Rifle Brigade and the Durham Light Infantry followed as close as possible. The charge across the open of these gallant Irishmen was one of the bloodiest episodes in the war, but courageous as it was it failed in front of the well concealed entrenchments thrown up by the Boers across the summit, and many of Hart's men fell back to a position about half-way up the slope, where they manned a line of *schanzes*. Norcott's two battalions for some reason did not come up until after 9 in the evening, by which time it was too dark to employ them; but the next morning Hart, seeing his forward parties retiring from the false crest on which they had spent the night, ordered up the Durham Light Infantry, with the Rifle Brigade in support, to occupy the *schanzes*. The Battalion, greeted with cheers by Hart's men, relieved the unfortunate Irishmen at about 10 a.m., having accomplished their task with but small loss owing to a covering fire provided by the 5th Brigade's maxims on their left.

Surrounded by the dead, dying and wounded left on the ground after the attack, the Battalion occupied this unpleasant position until the evening of the next day (the 25th). Much of the remainder of the 24th was spent in removing, under heavy fire, Hart's wounded, and at 9 that evening the Battalion was attacked by a party of the enemy who crept down the donga to the west of the hill. It drove them off, as indeed it drove off two further enemy attacks on the 25th. In this critical and exposed situation, when the rest of Buller's Army presented an admirable target for a determined counter-stroke on the part of the enemy, Colonel Woodland showed himself at his best. Much to the embarrassment of his officers he insisted on standing erect, and when one of his subalterns delicately warned him that the Boers had a machine-gun trained on them, he replied, "My dear boy, I can't help it if they have." Before the Battalion was relieved it had lost two men killed, one officer (Lieutenant L. Soltau-Symons) and 34 n.c.o.s and men wounded, and four missing.

For two days there was a lull while Buller concentrated on his right to enlarge his front and massed his artillery on the south bank preparatory to a bombardment of Terrace Hill, Railway Hill and Pieter's Hill, which were to be assaulted respectively by Norcott's two battalions (reinforced by the East Surreys), Kitchener's and Barton's Brigades. The preparations occupied the 25th and 26th February. At about 10 in the morning of the 27th Barton, who had farthest to go, started his attack on Pieter's Hill; Kitchener developed his attack about three hours later; and Norcott, who had the shortest distance to cover, moved up at about 5 in the afternoon. Barton's attack was only partially successful; but Kitchener's had captured Railway Hill before Norcott had started, and Norcott's Brigade, led by the Rifle Brigade and the East Surreys and supported by the Durhams in reserve, carried Terrace Hill in fine style against a stubborn resistance before darkness came down.

During the night the Boers evacuated Pieter's Hill. In six hours, at the cost of 500 casualties, the Natal Army had at last won the decisive victory which opened the way to Ladysmith. The Durhams' share in this triumphant operation had cost them only nine men wounded.

Buller's pursuit was leisurely and hardly worthy of the name. Though his mounted force made contact with the Ladysmith garrison late the next day (28th February), he himself did not enter until 3rd March; and he allowed his opponent to take up a line on the Biggarsberg from Sunday's River to Helpmekaar, which he did not force until early in May. When the Boers retreated to the Transvaal frontier, to the Laing's Nek position which had led to Colley's downfall twenty years earlier, Buller attempted nothing until early June though repeatedly urged to activity by Roberts. When he did he wisely out-flanked it by crossing the Drakensberg at Botha's Pass, and drove them from it in the action of Alleman's Nek (11th June). Volksrust, the first town in the Transvaal, was entered on 12th June. Standerton was occupied on the 22nd, Greylingstad on 2nd July. The last action fought by the Natal Army took place at Bergendaal on 27th August, after it had been ordered north to the Delagoa Railway; and on 1st September Roberts proclaimed the annexation of the Transvaal.

The share of the 2nd Division in general and of the Durham Light Infantry in particular in these deliberate but none the less satisfactory operations was almost negligible. The Battalion lay on Sunday's River, near Elandslaagte, from 9th March to 10th April, where it was joined (as already mentioned) by the 1st Volunteer Service Company, an accession which brought its strength up to a total of 29 officers and 1400 n.c.o.s and men. While drilling in camp on 10th April it was unexpectedly shelled by the enemy, losing four men wounded, and it underwent a similar experience on 13th May at Vermaak's Kraal after it had moved up to face the Laing's Nek position. But it took no part in the fighting at Alleman's Nek, and it reached Vlakfontein, near Greylingstad, peacefully on 4th July. Indeed, it never again went into action as a battalion during the remainder of the war, although forming, for about a month from 7th August, part of a column under Clery operating in the Greylingstad and Standerton area.

After the entry into the Transvaal the 2nd and 5th Divisions were allotted the boring but necessary task of guarding the line of communication through Natal, the shortest and most reliable supply route for the Army in the Transvaal. The 2nd Division was made responsible for the section of railway from Heidelberg to Kromdraai. From the end of September until the end of December the Battalion (less one company detached to Kaffirspruit and Vlaklaagte) lay at Standerton. In the last days of 1900 it was moved farther up the line to Eden's Kop near Fortuna, and closer to brigade headquarters at Heidelberg. Detachments were supplied at Vlakfontein, Suikerbosch Spruit, Rustfontein and Kilfontein, but otherwise for close on a year it remained stationary, if not undisturbed, at Eden's Kop until the end of October 1901.[16]

By then Colonel Woodland, on being invalided on 31st August 1900, had handed over the command to Lieut.-Colonel H. S. FitzGerald, whose staff experience contrasted strangely with his predecessor's purely regimental career. The son of a Bengal army officer, he had entered the 68th during its uneventful tour in India; but he had contrived to see service in the Second Afghan War (attached to the 15th Sikhs), he had served in the Marri Expedition of 1881, he had been on the staff of the Frontier Field Force in the Sudan in 1885 and 1886, and he had taken part in the operations on the Niger in 1897 and 1898 before accompanying the Battalion to South Africa and receiving a wound at Vaalkrans. During the period of his command the total, though not the effective, strength of the Battalion was enormous. In June 1900 it stood at 34 officers and 1636 n.c.o.s and men. This figure takes no account of the very considerable number of enterprising spirits, both officers and men, who got themselves attached to mounted infantry battalions, nor of the very considerable numbers in hospital with enteric, or typhoid fever, which was to

[16]Off. Hist., Vol. 3, App. 8 (pp. 556-558).

carry off one officer (Lieutenant Thresher, the adjutant) and 57 n.c.o.s and men—more than those killed by the enemy (44). But, although the strength fell slowly during 1901, the Battalion was the most powerful the Regiment had ever put into the field, the numbers never dropping below 1200 until the end of the war. The 2nd Volunteer Service Company (3 officers, 113 n.c.o.s and men) arrived from Cape Town to replace the 1st, which left the Battalion on 9th October, in April 1901, and remained until relieved by the 3rd (2 officers, 92 n.c.o.s and men) in April 1902. At the same time the Battalion received drafts amounting to no fewer than 8 officers and 1132 men—evidence of the process that is euphemistically described as "wastage". At the end the proportion of old soldiers cannot have been high, and even that was reduced in March 1902, when in common with thirty-seven other regiments in South Africa the Battalion exchanged 150 men for a like number from the 2nd Battalion in India.[17]

Guarding the Natal Railway lacked both the excitement of action and the repose of peaceful military routine. The line was constantly under the threat of sudden attack—three attacks on trains were made by the Boers in February 1901 alone: one on the 6th near Vlakfontein Nek, another on the 20th near Steyn's Kraal, and another on the 24th between Suikerbosch and Steyn's Kraal. And on 22nd June 1901, while patrolling near Eden's Kop with nine men, Lieutenant R. E. Rasbotham was mortally wounded and two of his men wounded in a gallant affray as a result of which Private St. Clair was promoted to the rank of corporal by the Commander-in-Chief. Throughout these months the Battalion's existence was one which lent itself to the "regrettable incidents", the "Duffer's Drifts" so common in the war, which—if one excepts the loss of a blockhouse on 2nd April 1902—it was mercifully spared. The boredom, discomfort and uncertainties of the kind of life led by those left with the Battalion are portrayed more vividly than in any description by a letter, dated Standerton, 20th December 1900, from Lieutenant R. S. Hamilton-Grace, the son of the Captain Sheffield Grace whose New Zealand diaries were quoted earlier:

> ". . . I have had a most sickening day of it. I had to get up at 3.45 and parade at 4.10 in the pouring rain. I then took a party of fifty men up to the station to escort some guns. We got thirty of us into a truck uncovered and uncleaned. We then started amid pouring rain. We went steadily on till 11.30 a.m. absolutely drenched. The engine broke down twice. When I arrived at Greylingstad I was told they could not relieve my escort and I must go on. However I managed to

[17]W.O.73/59; 108/1.

11

get out of it and got an empty truck back. We got back here at 1 p.m. after having spent nearly nine hours in a truck, rain pouring down all the time. I may mention that I had nothing to eat or drink, being only warned for escort duty at 11 p.m. the night before. However, I suppose I ought not to complain, for the train in which I ought to have gone (but which started twenty minutes too early) was derailed, and the truck in which I should have been turned over, killing two men and wounding two. I suppose it was a close thing.

"We are having exciting times here. The Boers are more active than they have been for the last six months. We have definite news that Standerton is to be attacked. I have not had an undisturbed night for the last four nights, and shall be out again tonight. Picquet and outposts and standing to arms, sleeping ready accoutred—it is no joke, and I am beastly tired. In the day one is on eternal court-martials or boards. Lang and I do orderly officer every other day, no one else being available at headquarters. It has now rained steadily for twenty-four hours and everything is a bit damp. Small parties go out and meet Boers daily. This sort of game will apparently last for ever. We are all utterly 'fed up' and long to get away to India. However, there does not seem much prospect of that, for the present at all events. I wish Kitchener would do something.

"Thresher is taking over adjutant from McMahon today. He comes up from Durban tonight. He has been with the M.I. right through the war . . ."[18]

§

The annexation of the Transvaal marked the defeat of the Boer armies in the field and, it was hoped, the end of the war. The hope was disappointed. At about the time that the Battalion started its vigil at Eden's Kop a renewed spirit of hostility ran through both Boer Republics, and the struggle entered a second, more bittter, phase of guerrilla warfare. The commandos were out again under younger and more enterprising leaders tested in war, who ranged over a country, as large as Spain in extent, amidst a population prepared to support them and resist to the uttermost. In suppressing them the British Army underwent a chameleon-like transformation. The divisions and brigades of the first year disappeared to give place to the "column", which, not far removed from the commando, became progressively lighter, more mobile, more self-reliant as the months went by.

From the point of view of the regimental soldier the war became increasingly a mounted infantryman's war; weeks in camp or bivouac were exchanged for weeks and months *on trek*, nights spent beneath the clear blue skies of the golden high veld under a greatcoat or the blanket carried folded under the saddle; and the limit of the sub-

[18]From a ms. letter kindly lent to me by the writer's sister, Lady Thompson.

altern's horizon was the *spitzkop* or *tafelkop* he was to take in the after-noon or the next day. In this kind of warfare there was no formal deploying in extended order; mounted men were always deployed. There were no "safe" areas. No faculty could ever afford to be at rest. One moment the column was quietly trotting: the next the fight was on. Then it was a matter of hurriedly dismounting, handing over your mount to an unhappy horse-holder, who stood in the best cover he could find hardly knowing what was going on in the firing line, and then a scramble up a rocky hill, while the bullets splashed viciously on the rocks at the side and in front, or, perhaps, a Boer gun played its shells with almost humorous accuracy, back and forth, until it struck something or somebody. This was mounted infantry warfare: restless, rough, grimly competitive, healthy, exciting: the kind of thing which old campaigners prefer recalling as "true soldiering" to all the Colensos and Magersfonteins of the early days.[19]

The Regiment's contribution to the mounted infantry force, both in officers and men, was important. Our interest is directed to three mounted infantry commanders and four battalions of mounted infantry, namely:

(a) the Burmah Mounted Infantry, to which the 2nd Battalion supplied one of the three companies composing it. The battalion was commanded by Major Cruickshank, of the Essex; and the Durham Company, of five sergeants and 98 men, was under the command of members of the famous polo team, Captain C. C. Luard and Lieu-tenants W. J. Ainsworth, L. F. Ashburner and A. S. Way, and Lieutenant P. C. Grover attached from the Shropshire Light In-fantry. Mounted on hardy little Pegu ponies, none above 12.2 hands high, which gave them a comical stunted appearance, the Burmah M.I. embarked at Rangoon in the *Palamcotta* on 24th January 1900 and landed at Cape Town on 13th February, in time to share in Lord Roberts's great advance on Bloemfontein. They enjoyed an immense reputation. Even a seasoned mounted infantryman from another battalion described them as "a fine body of men, all two-badge men," "tremendous gamblers, particularly on a pay-night," and their first serious engagement, at Sanna's Post, proved that they could fight as well as play polo.

(b) the Composite Regiment of Mounted Infantry, better known from the name of its commander, Major Hubert de la P. Gough, 16th Lancers, but numbered officially in about July 1901 as the 24th Battalion of Mounted Infantry. The company to which the 1st

[19] *A Soldier's Diary, 1899-1901* by Murray Cosby Jackson (London, 1913), who served in the ranks of the Hampshire Company of the 7th M.I., gives an excellent description of M.I. fighting.

Battalion contributed a section of one officer (Lieutenant E. B. Thresher) and thirty n.c.o.s and men was originally formed at Frere, soon after Colenso, of a section from each of the four battalions of Lyttelton's Brigade, and was known as the Fourth Brigade Company M.I. before being incorporated into a battalion under Gough's command after the relief of Ladysmith. On Thresher's return to the Battalion as adjutant in December 1900 his place was taken by Lieutenant R. R. Lambton[20] until his death at Bloedrivierpoort in September 1901, when command was given to Lieutenant E. W. Appleby. Lieutenant K. J. W. Leather, who acted as transport officer of the battalion, joined in July 1901.

(c) the 26th Battalion Mounted Infantry, originally formed at Standerton in November 1900 as the Second Division Mounted Infantry—Buller's Army always favoured cumbrous titles—which was numbered 26th in July 1901. No. 2 Company of the battalion, commanded by Captain Ionides, East Surrey, consisted of a half-company from the 2nd East Surrey and a half-company, of two officers (Lieutenants L. Soltau-Symons and C. L. Matthews) and 56 n.c.o.s and men, from the 1st Battalion. At the end of November 1901 the Durham half-company was joined by Appleby's section from the 24th, and in March 1902 it was further reinforced by a draft of thirty men from home under 2/Lieutenant W. R. Lovering, thus forming a detachment of company strength under Captain L. Soltau-Symons (promoted meanwhile in the Royal Warwickshire) until its disbandment at Mooi River on 6th September 1902.

Both the section in the 24th and the half-company in the 26th were kept up to strength from volunteers from the Battalion who had passed the riding and sharpshooting tests at the M.I. Depot near Pretoria. Many of the men, having been accustomed to pit-ponies before enlistment, had little to learn in the management and care of their mounts.

(d) the 23rd Battalion Mounted Infantry, formed at Aldershot in March 1900, to which home details of the Regiment contributed a half-company; this, together with a half-company of the 1st King's Own, was commanded by Captain H. M. Trenchard, Royal Scots Fusiliers (better known as the Marshal of the Royal Air Force). The Durham half-company served in South Africa from mid-June 1901 under 2/Lieutenant H. J. Coddington and three militia officers

[20]This young officer, the sixth son of Lieut.-Col. Francis William Lambton, Scots Guards, of Brownslade, Pembrokeshire, and Lady Victoria Alexandrina, daughter of the 2nd Earl of Cawdor, was the first descendant of John Lambton to serve in the Regiment.

who shortly afterwards obtained commissions in the Regiment: C. O. Rowlandson, J. G. Gillespie and C. R. Shirreff.

Of the three commanders from the Regiment first and foremost was de Lisle, one of the most distinguished mounted infantrymen of the day. He came out to South Africa in command of a company in the two fine mounted infantry battalions which, formed at Aldershot in October 1899 and composed of sections of picked shots from thirty-two regular battalions, represented the sum of our mounted infantry force at the outset of the war. On the retirement of Lieut.-Colonel Tudway, of the Essex, at the end of the year, de Lisle succeeded to the command of his battalion (the 2nd), which he held for about a month until selected to organise one of the new mounted infantry battalions called for by Lord Roberts on his arrival late in January 1900. From the command of this, the 6th (which consisted of companies from 2nd Bedford, 1st Welch, 2nd Wiltshire and 1st Gordons), he soon rose to command one of those columns that were to become the principal instrument in the suppression of the commandos, and from that moment his movements belong to the larger history of the war. The staff-officer of his column was the Captain H. B. des V. Wilkinson whose exploits on the polo field have already been noticed.

Hardly less distinguished were the services of Major W. C. Ross, formerly adjutant of the 1st Battalion from 1885 to 1887, who had accompanied Brigadier-General Hector Macdonald from India as his staff-officer on his appointment to command the Highland Brigade. Ross had hardly landed before he was selected to organise another of Lord Roberts's new mounted infantry battalions, the 8th, consisting of companies from the 2nd Cheshire, 1st East Lancashire, 2nd South Wales Borderers and 1st North Staffordshire. At Bloemfontein Ross's command was extended to comprise a "corps", which later formed part of Colonel Le Gallais' famous column, and it was in this formation that the 8th shared in the action of Bothaville, 6th November 1900, in which the commando of the crafty de Wet was defeated with the capture of all its guns and wagons and 150 prisoners. The heavy losses sustained in this ferocious and very creditable engagement included not only Le Gallais, who was killed, but Ross, whose lower jaw was carried away by a sniper's bullet. The wound was thought to be mortal, but he survived to receive the C.B. and to command a brigade in the First World War.

The third mounted infantry commander was Major E. St G. Pratt, who was selected to command the 13th Battalion Mounted Infantry. It was one of the four new battalions formed near Pretoria in November 1900 in the second great quest after mounted infantry, carried out when, many experienced colonial and yeomanry corps having been allowed to leave the theatre, the renewal of the war exposed the need of a new levy. The 13th contained no companies from the Regiment, but Major Pratt, who commanded the battalion from its formation throughout its operations under Alderson, Bullock and Spens and until it was disbanded at Heidelberg in August 1902, appointed three Durham Light Infantry officers to subordinate situations in it: Lieutenants W. Northey (adjutant), J. W. Jeffreys (quartermaster), and J. S. Unthank.

So diverse and widespread were the services of these corps that it is hardly possible to enter into them without describing in detail a complex and difficult period of the war. To understand them at all, however, it should be said that, after the initial setbacks, the struggle passed through five, not very clearly defined, phases, in all of which one or another of the Durham mounted corps had a share.

The first phase began in January 1900 with a resumption of the offensive—in Natal with the operations already sketched, in the central theatre with Lord Roberts's great advance from the Modder River through Paardeberg (27th February), Bloemfontein (13th March), Johannesburg (31st May) to Pretoria (5th June). It ended with the proclamation announcing the annexation of the Transvaal and with Roberts's return home.

There followed a six-month period (August 1900 to January 1901), in which the assumption that the war was over except for stamping out the embers was gradually replaced by a recognition of the true state of affairs, namely that the Boer resistance had revived, presenting the immense problem of suppressing the rebellion of an agricultural community. The phase was marked by the employment of numerous columns operating in disturbed districts while garrisons, immobilising a large proportion of the Army, were left stationary to protect the long supply routes through both Natal and the Free State. In January 1901 there were thirty-eight such columns of varying sizes, most of them, however, composed of strong detachments of artillery and infantry (as well as cavalry and mounted infantry) and lengthy convoys of ox-wagons, formidable on paper but cumbrous in reality.

In January 1901 a third phase opened with the organisation of "drives", such as French's great drive in the untouched eastern Transvaal, an enormous conception employing simultaneously seven powerful columns (Alderson's, Dartnell's, Knox's, Allenby's, Pulteney's, Campbell's and Smith-Dorrien's). The drive, the first attempt to deprive the commandos of their resources, embraced such diverse objects as the destruction of farms, the capture not only of wagons but of the burghers' women folk and their consignment to so called concentration camps, besides the military one of destroying the commandos. Against an active and enterprising enemy, with troops of varying aptitudes for operations in the veld, the pursuit of so many objects made excessive demands upon both the force available and its supply organisation.

In the fourth phase (May 1901 to January 1902) the drive was reduced in scope and improved in application. At the same time the blockhouses, hitherto used for the passive defence of the railways, were multiplied by mass-production upon a new pattern and extended along roads as well as railways to form barriers through which hunted commandos could penetrate only with difficulty. The columns, increased to nearly seventy in number, and supported and reinforced by means of these fortified corridors, maintained a constant pressure within the compartments; and, following the example of enterprising column commanders like Benson, who used a highly organised intelligence system, they developed a facility for surprising laagered commandos at night or at dawn when they were most vulnerable. Benson himself was killed in the hard fought action of Bakenlaagte (30th October 1901), and the blockhouse line could be penetrated, particularly at night, by a determined enemy, and often was. Yet the improved drive, devoted to the limited object of flushing commandos, and the conversion of a purely passive defence line into a means of aggression together exerted a pressure upon the guerrillas that gradually proved irresistible.

The last phase (January to May 1902) was distinguishable from that preceding it only in the further elaboration of the blockhouse line, which ceased to follow even roads and railways, and in the further elaboration of the drive, which now consisted of columns as lightly equipped as commandos, strung out, like beaters, in long lines stretching from one blockhouse line to the next and "sweeping" inexorably across the veld. Such sweeps were masterpieces of organisation, tours de force of staff-work, but made great demands on the endurance of the men, mostly M.I., and their mounts. The results, measured in terms of enemy losses and captures, were only once spectacular. But in time the new methods wore down the Boer resistance and finally broke it altogether.

To complicate this picture of an apparently orderly evolution there was the enemy, the stubborn and resourceful "Joe," as the soldiers called him. The jargon of the "drive", with its "beaters" and "stops", was derived from the grouse-moor; but here the game was far from docile, and could, and often did, retaliate sharply on the "guns". Every drive was marked by small actions and most lapses into carelessness brought their own retribution. Nor did the Boer wait patiently to be "driven". There was hardly an offensive undertaken by the Army but was anticipated, dislocated or interrupted by some Boer offensive. The most implacable and crafty of their leaders were de Wet, who operated, at enormous ranges, from his home country in the eastern Free State; Delarey and Kemp in the western Transvaal; Smuts in the western Cape; and Louis Botha in the eastern Transvaal. French's drive in the eastern Transvaal, for instance, was interrupted by de Wet's invasion of Cape Colony and the "Great de Wet Hunt" that followed (December 1900 to March 1901); and in September 1901 the "fourth phase" was rudely disturbed by Louis Botha's invasion of Natal, which, after Alleman's Nek, had quietly relapsed into its pre-war tranquillity. (The Natal invasion, it should be said, was stopped at Itala and Fort Prospect, at the latter of which the garrison was part composed of a detachment of the Durham Artillery Militia, once a corps belonging to the Regimental District, men who by birth were brothers of those serving in the Durham infantry battalions; and it was from their ranks, in the midst of that stubborn engagement, that one man's voice was raised as one feels his ancestors' were at Arklow crying, "Surrender be damned! I'm a pitman at home and have been in deeper holes than this before.") Moreover, throughout the guerrilla period of the war the Boers, who even at the end had some 24,000 men able to take the field, improved their own methods. Blockhouses were commonly attacked by men armed with shotguns with which to spray the loopholes; and as an alternative to the bayonet-attack they developed the charge while firing from the hip and even from the saddle, as they did with devastating effect at Bakenlaagte.

It is consequently vain to seek any geographical pattern or any grand strategical conception in operations after August 1900. Wherever there were British troops—and there were troops throughout the length and breadth of both republics—fighting was liable to occur, whether it was as a result of ambushes of columns on the march, attacks on blockhouses, surprising commandos in their laagers, or the ordinary M.I. daily routine of rushing kopjes. The whole of the Free State and the Transvaal was one vast thunder-cloud in which lightning might flicker at any moment.

The first serious fight involving a Durham mounted corps occurred on 31st March 1900 at Sanna's Post (or Sannaspos) near Bloemfontein, which the Burmah M.I. had entered with Martyr's Mounted Infantry Brigade of Roberts's Army two weeks earlier. At the end of the month the Burmah M.I. was serving with Alderson's Mounted

Infantry Brigade,[21] which, together with a detachment consisting of the Composite Regiment of Household Cavalry, the 10th Hussars, Q and U Batteries, R.H.A., composed a force about 1700 strong under Brigadier-General Broadwood on a "showing the flag" expedition to the east of the Bloemfontein perimeter, on the far side of the Modder River at Thaba N'chu. On 30th March Broadwood, hearing of a Boer concentration at Ladybrand, had started retiring to the near bank of the Modder (which was in spate) by the drift on which stood the buildings of the Bloemfontein Waterworks. The crossing was successfully accomplished by 3.30 in the morning of the 31st. At daybreak Broadwood's bivouac was unexpectedly shelled by Boers on the eastern bank, and he resolved on a further retirement to the Bloemfontein perimeter at Boesman's Kop, half-way between the Waterworks and Bloemfontein, which was occupied by a detachment of mounted infantry.

This was exactly what the Boers hoped he would do. Unknown to him a Boer force of about 400 under Christiaan de Wet, a name that as yet signified little to the British Army, had crept up the bed of the Koornspruit, a small tributary of the Modder—imperceptible until a man was almost on it—and lay in wait to ambuscade his convoy as their comrades on the Modder persuaded it westwards. Without firing de Wet's men silently captured the first troops to approach the spruit, almost a whole battery of horse artillery (U). Then they poured a well directed hail of bullets into Q Battery and Roberts's Horse, who, warned by fugitives from U Battery, had turned about and galloped back to the cover of a group of buildings to return the fire. In the eleven hundred yards that separated the spruit from the corrugated-iron roofed sheds of the as yet half-finished station of Sanna's Post there is no cover; and on this small battlefield, more like a black-powder battlefield of the '80s,[22] there developed one of the most savage fights of the whole war.

When the firing broke out the Burmah M.I. were facing the Modder, as part of the renguard covering the retirement; but Colonel Alderson at once sent the Durham Company and a party from the other two companies to Q Battery's assistance. They galloped their little ponies to the station buildings through a mob of loose horses, dismounted and extended to right and left of the guns, which, meanwhile, were keeping up a steady but largely ineffective fire at the difficult target. For about four hours these men were

---

[21]The Brigade consisted of: the 1st M.I. (Amphlett), one company 2nd M.I. (Brooke), the 3rd M.I. (Pilcher), Rimington's Guides, the 1st New Zealand Mounted Rifles and Roberts's Horse.

[22]So Major Tylden has pointed out to me.

heavily engaged in the exposed position, the gun-detachments falling one by one until at last only the battery commander, Major Phipps-Hornby, his captain, who was bringing up ammunition from the wagons, one sergeant, one corporal and eight gunners remained unwounded to fight the guns. De Wet's situation was also precarious. But Broadwood's attempts to turn his position had, for reasons best not entered into, miscarried, and the only course left to him 'seemed to be to order a retirement (without the guns if necessary) on Boesman's Kop by a wide detour to the south.

Phipps-Hornby, however, had no intention of abandoning his guns without a struggle. The horses that remained could not be brought up from the wagon-lines in rear of the station unless they were all to be killed. But the survivors of his detachments succeeded in man-handling the guns about forty of the seventy-odd yards between them and the station. They were then quite exhausted, and Phipps-Hornby called on the escort for volunteers. His call was immediately answered by Lieutenant Stirling and Private Bright of the Essex Company, Private Parry of the Duke of Wellington's Company, Lieutenants Ainsworth, Ashburner, Grover and Way, Lance-corporal Steele and Privates Pickford and Horton of the Durham Company, and Lieutenant Maxwell (18th Bengal Lancers) of Roberts's Horse. They sprang forward, and with the assistance of one or two gunners dragged back to cover four out of the five guns, one wagon and one limber, though their determined efforts to bring back the remaining gun and three limbers were, alas, unavailing. Lieutenant Grover (attached) fell mortally wounded, Major Cruickshank was blinded by a bullet behind his eyes, and Privates Pickford and Horton were both severely wounded. But their united exertions and devotion were rewarded when Phipps-Hornby, having hooked in what was left of his fine battery, retired it at a walk to the rear. The mounted infantrymen, it is said, "though it was to court death to show a hand, in a spontaneous outburst of admiration rose to their feet and cheered the gallant survivors".

The retirement was the signal for the Boers to surge forward from their cover to reap the harvest of their success. The whole brunt of the fighting now fell to the mounted infantry, whom Alderson gradually withdrew leap-frog fashion, each detachment covering the retreat of the other, until they reached the upper Koornspruit, about a mile and a half from the drift. Here the burghers halted, contenting themselves with a long range fire, while Alderson's men continued their retirement with exemplary steadiness. Some held their ground too long and suffered capture, but the small losses of the Durham

Company (three men wounded and eight missing[23] in the whole morning's work) are testimony of the skill with which they fought.

If it had not been redeemed and dignified by such acts of gallantry Sanna's Post would have gone down as one of those "regrettable incidents" that disfigured the Army's record in South Africa. Everything but the gallantry was regrettable. The retirement carried with it the loss of the Waterworks, which were not recovered for another month, during which time Bloemfontein, deprived of a proper water supply, became that hot-bed of typhoid fever for which it afterwards became renowned.

In the advance on Johannesburg and Pretoria the Burmah M.I. was attached to the 7th Battalion Mounted Infantry in Major-General Ian Hamilton's Division, and was engaged in twenty-eight actions, including Thaba N'chu, Houtnek, Vet River, Zand River, Lindley, Doornkop, Diamond Hill, Bethlehem and in the operations in the Brandwater Basin. Early in 1901 it was involved in the Third, or Great, de Wet Hunt in the Free State, from Leeuw Kop to Tabaksberg (29th January, where Lieutenant A. S. Way was killed in a smart little action), through Bloemfontein to Bethulie, Philippolis and Doornkloof to Prieska and Hopetown.

During its services the Durham Company lost two officers (Grover and Way) and six men killed and ten men invalided through wounds and disease. Their Burmese ponies had long since gone: in December 1900 only one was left. By July 1901 the strength had dropped to two officers and 85 n.c.o.s and men, by May 1902 to one officer and 76. They were returned to England with drafts from the 1st Battalion, and did not rejoin the 2nd until its arrival in Aldershot from India in December 1902.

The operations of the M.I. detachments from the 1st Battalion were largely confined to the Natal border and the eastern Transvaal, where their principal enemy was Louis Botha and the commandos under his influence.

The M.I. section which eventually came under Gough's command (in *Gough's*, or *the 24th M.I.*) was at first involved in Lord Dundonald's flanking movements during the Spion Kop fighting and the successive attempts to relieve Ladysmith. In the advance into the Transvaal it was engaged at Alleman's Nek (under Gough), and on 4th August it played a prominent part in a small fight known as Delange's Laager. Early in 1901, with Dartnell's, Spens's and Bullock's columns, it was operating in the eastern Transvaal, where it established a reputation for itself; and it was in the Free State when

[23]These eventually rejoined the Company at Pretoria.

in September 1901 it was suddenly ordered to entrain and return to
Natal to help in the repulse of Louis Botha's invasion.

On arrival at Newcastle it was sent by Lyttelton to Vryheid, with
the object of covering the return of a large convoy of wagons from
Vryheid—one of the attendant operations of provisioning the cumbrous columns at that stage of the war. The first morning out, 17th
September, Gough, having crossed the Buffalo, was approaching
Scheepers, a great bare hill seven miles from Vryheid, when his
advanced guard noticed a party of about two hundred Boers ride up
it and off-saddle. No one had seen so many Boers at once for over a
year, and Gough, who knew the country like the back of his hand,
considered it too good a chance to miss. Being, however, only very
little stronger and too experienced to tackle them in daylight, he
watched them until sunset, when they remounted, rode back towards
the defile of the Blood River near Dejager's Drift, and then off-
saddled again and lounged about the *poort* (Bloedrivierpoort),
evidently settling down for the night. Making a wide detour to
arrive on the spur overlooking them, Gough prepared his attack.

Gough was unaware that they were but the advanced guard of
Botha's invasion force, over a thousand strong, which was at that
moment moving down the river valley unobserved by Gough's
scouts. As Gough's men approached the spur Botha's force, still
mounted, was hidden from them but caught a glimpse of them
charging across the open ground in time for Botha to rush a firing
line up on to the ridge in Gough's front, which met the charge at
point-blank range. A very hot fight ensued. At the same time Botha
unleashed from behind the hill about five hundred horsemen on
Gough's right, who galloped down and swamped the mounted
infantry in the flank and rear, and another Boer force climbed the
lower slopes of the Drakensberg on Gough's left and threatened that
flank as well. In a few minutes a dashing charge was changed into a
crushing defeat. In the confusion the battalion's transport officer,
Lieutenant Leather, and several men of the Regiment succeeded,
with praiseworthy resource, in bringing out the convoy it had been
their duty to guard. But 250 mounted infantry had been killed,
wounded and captured. In the Durham Section Lieutenant Lambton
"a most gallant boy," as Gough calls him, was mortally wounded
and three men killed, and three n.c.o.s and men wounded. Gough
managed to escape in the bad light, and the rest of the prisoners—
the Boers had long since ceased to keep their captives, usually
sending them back without their trousers—found their way out.
Nevertheless the action, called variously Dejager's Drift and Blood
River Port, put an end to a fine battalion with a long record of

success, and the Durham Section was transferred to the 26th M.I.[24]

The first trek undertaken by the *26th Mounted Infantry*, No. 2 Company of which contained a half-company from the 1st Battalion Durham Light Infantry, began on 26th January 1901 when it joined Colonel Colville's Mobile Column at Greylingstad. At first employed in escorting provisioning convoys for French's drive in the High Veld of the eastern Transvaal, it exchanged its first shots at Uitkyk, on the Standerton-Ermelo road, with Brits's Blaauwkop commando. Before it returned to Standerton it had taken part in one of the hardest treks of its existence. Later, in May, it made an unsuccessful attempt to surround Brits on the Blaauwkop, but on the return Ionides's Company managed to capture Adriaan Delange, who had caused Buller much trouble the year before. On 26th May the battalion joined Colville's Column at Delange's Drift on the Klip River, which, after running into Malan's commando, trekked westwards along the left bank of the Vaal. Near Villiers the Company attacked and carried a kopje protected by a barbed wire fence, from which the last Boer fled pursued by the battalion commander, Major Wiggin, 13th Hussars, and Lieutenant Matthews, 1st Battalion, and then moved on to search the farm of Buys, an implacable opponent who hung on and harassed the rear of the column. After crossing the Vaal and while moving along the Waterval they were attacked in camp under the cover of fog but successfully resisted; and they reached Greylingstad on 11th July having made, in company with Brigadier-General Kitchener's Column, an assault (which failed) on Pretorius's headquarter camp at Waterval Hoek. Another trek ended at Standerton a few weeks later after a skirmish at Kromdraai, on 25th July, in which Corporal Nicholson of the Durham half-company, having lost his horse in retiring and though taken up by Lieutenant Matthews, fell off and was killed. A trek with Colville's Column in August aimed at Pretorius's commando on the Waterval was productive of only the capture of a large number of wagons.

The next trek, which started on 26th August, took the battalion over the Klip River into the Gemsbokhoekberg, through the Drakensberg into the Free State by Muller's Pass, and thence across the Klip again by Delange's Drift. On 6th September it crossed the Vaal at Robert's Drift. Ionides's Company acted as rearguard in the operation, "and a section of the Durhams, sent in to drive some cattle, had two men wounded by Boers concealed in a mealie-field. An ambu-

[24]Gen. Sir H. de la P. Gough, *Soldiering On* (London, Arthur Barker, 1954), pp. 83 *ff.* I am much indebted to Lieut.-Col. A. Howe of the Regiment, who served as a sergeant in Gough's and the 26th M.I., for the help he gave me towards understanding the treks he took part in.

lance had to be sent for, and being a long way ahead it took a long time coming. In the meanwhile other casualties occurred." Lieutenant Matthews was dangerously wounded, Sergeant Sykes was killed, and two Durham men and two men of the East Surrey were wounded. After a few days rest at Standerton the column was on the move again towards Ermelo, where, however, it received news of the invasion of Natal, which brought it south to Volksrust, where it arrived on 25th September.

The elaboration of the blockhouse system in the spring of 1901 involved the battalion in the duty of covering the construction of the line to Piet Retief and the Swaziland border, and it remained on the border, taking part in the two actions of Mahamba's Drift and Kwakeni, until December. At the end of January 1902 it shared in Plumer's drive of the Boers into the blockhouse angle at Castrol's Nek, which was accomplished successfully with the surrender of many Boers on the Assegai River on 24th January. Later Colville's Column acted as a stop to one of the great Free State drives by holding a range from Sandspruit and Alleman's Nek to the Drakensberg, after which it descended into Natal, through Newcastle to Dejager's Drift (where Gough's M.I. had come to grief). In March it moved to Paulpietersburg and Piet Retief. After encountering Chris Botha's commando on the Assegai in an only partially successful action, it trekked to Wakkerstroom, where on 11th April Colville handed over the command to Colonel Mills of the Dublin Fusiliers. In an expedition to harass the Vryheid district, for some time left undisturbed, the column marched by Utrecht and Bloedrivierpoort but were anticipated by the Zulus, who rose and killed over sixty of the Vryheid commandos at Holkrans near the Pivaan. The 26th M.I. were at Vryheid when peace was proclaimed.[25]

The treks of the 26th M.I. have been detailed at some length partly because, latterly at any rate, the battalion contained a larger proportion of 1st Battalion men than any other, and partly because they illustrate more aptly than anything else could both the constant and varied services these mounted infantry companies were called on to perform and the changing nature of the measures taken to suppress the guerrilla war. The services of the other two battalions in which we are interested were hardly typical in either of these respects. The *13th M.I.*, which acted first with Alderson's Column in the Magaliesberg in December 1900, in French's drive and, later, with Bullock's and then Spens's Columns in covering the Standerton-Ermelo blockhouse line and in five of the great sweeps across the

[25]Col. Hugh W. Pearse, *History of the East Surrey Regiment* (London, 1916), Vol. 1, pp. 446ff.

High Veld and the eastern Free State, was equally hard worked but was not properly a Durham corps. [26] Similarly, the *23rd M.I.*, which contained a half-company from the Regiment, was employed principally on the intelligence service of the officer commanding the Vereeniging District; and though it lost two men killed and one officer (2/Lieutenant Coddington) and three men wounded and was on duty at the Vereeniging Conference, its operations were not typically those of mounted infantry.

Every aspect of the guerrilla war was represented in the services of the Regiment as a whole. The M.I. companies represented its active aspect: the infantry battalions its passive—the 3rd Battalion guarding the communications and escorting convoys in Cape Colony and the western Free State, the 4th in its blockhouses between the Orange and the Modder, the 1st in its blockhouses on the Natal Railway.

While, however, the services of the militia battalions were almost wholly passive, those of the regular battalion began to change with the increasing elaboration of the blockhouse line and its gradual transformation into an offensive system. At the beginning of October 1901 the 1st Battalion re-entered operations for the first time for over a year. On the 3rd of that month a party of four officers and 196 n.c.o.s and men under Major G. C. Mansel joined Rawlinson's Column at Greylingstad, and at the end of the month the remainder of the Battalion, nineteen officers and 625 n.c.o.s and men, left Standerton to join Campbell's Column to take part in Kitchener's great summer offensive against Louis Botha and the High Veld commandos, a vast undertaking employing twelve columns. Three companies (A, K and G) under Major Saunders, joined Allenby's Column, M Company under Major the Hon. W. L. Vane joined Colonel Wing's Column, while L and the other Volunteer Service Company were later divided between Wing's and Simpson's Columns.

The operations consisted principally of night raids in the new improved style. The detachments under Wing and Rawlinson shared in the dawn attack on Piet Viljoen's laager at Trichardsfontein near Bethal on 10th December, the most brilliant of all the raids, which took 130 prisoners, a large bag for that period. The operations of the following weeks were not so successful, and of all the Boer leaders Ben Viljoen alone was caught. But the gradual eastward advance, which carried the Battalion forward through Bankop to the blockhouse line between Roodeval and Athole, had seriously thinned the commandos before the line was established on the Swazi border in March 1902. They left the High Veld for ever and sought refuge in the Vry-

[26] *Two Years on Trek*, ed. Capt. H. F. Bidder (London, 1907).

heid district. In their final resistance the Regiment was represented only by the company with the 26th M.I. The Battalion remained in the blockhouse line, and headquarters were at Camp Buchanan, fourteen miles east of Athole, when the Peace was signed on 31st May.

On this note of anti-climax the war, which had long ceased to occupy people's minds at home, petered out. It has been called the last of the gentleman's wars. It may be so. Certainly there were still some restraints, some niceties, observed to mitigate and inhibit the effects of what was essentially a civil war, observed, moreover, not entirely with a view to expediency. Sickness, for the last time, exacted a heavier toll of life than military weapons—if that is a qualification. The new weapons, however, were far from gentlemanly; and indeed, at this greater distance, the South African War seems in retrospect to be the first of those wars in which almost every deed of gallantry, almost every act of devotion to duty, was requited by death or dis-ablement dispensed with an almost cynical sense of inevitability. It called for new qualities in our regiments as well as new tactics, qualities of stolid endurance and imperturbability in the face of losses and occasionally humiliation. Fortunately those hard-headed little men who were the regulars of those days showed that they could take a prodigious amount of punishment. Buller's reverses on the Tugela left them entirely unmoved. With the rest of the army the Durham Light Infantry went through the purifying fire and came out hardened and prepared. These were qualities of which they had much need in the years to come but were never in want.

The dispersal of an Army of a quarter of a million men naturally occupied some months. The Battalion was not brought down to the railway at Standerton until 30th June. Demobilisation began the next day. The time-expired men and reservists were sent down in detachments of one hundred to Eden Dale, near Pietermaritzburg, the first reaching Southampton on 24th August, the last on 9th October. The Volunteer Service Company embarked at Cape Town on 9th July and landed at Southampton on the 31st. The Battalion itself, much reduced, remained at Standerton until 26th October, when it entrained for Durban and embarked on the P. & O. ship *Assaye*, fourteen officers and 422 men strong, on the 29th. It arrived at Bombay, three years after it had expected, on 11th November 1902.[27]

The services of the 1st Battalion and of the Durham Company of the Burmah Mounted Infantry earned the Regiment the battle honours *South Africa 1899-1902* and *Relief of Ladysmith*, which were granted in December 1904. Colonel Woodland, Lieut.-Colonel

[27]W.O.108/1.

FitzGerald, Major W. C. Ross and Captain de Lisle were awarded the C.B. In addition to Captains Ashburner and Ainsworth and Lieutenant Way, Major Mansel, Major Pratt, Captains L. E. C. Elwes (who had served with the Balloon Section, R.E. from 5th February to 27th June 1900), W. C. Lascelles and Northey received the D.S.O.; de Lisle, Pratt, Luard, McMahon, Cumming and Blake received brevet promotion, and Quartermaster J. H. Liebrecht was granted the honorary rank of captain. The following warrant-officers, n.c.o.s and men were awarded the D.C.M.: Sergeant-major J. Freel, Colour-sergeants A. Noble, J. P. L. Shea and R. Ward, Sergeants W. H. Littlejohn and M. J. O'Brien, Corporals H. Hawkins and A. Neal, Lance-corporal C. Steele, Privates G. Bennett, J. Cottle, E. Horton, J. S. Parker, S. Pickford, J. W. Robson, and J. Bell; and Privates L. St. Clair and Quinn were specially promoted to the rank of corporal for gallantry.

Before consigning the 1st Battalion, which left England at the height of Victorian prosperity and was not to see it again until the post-war era of strikes and ration-cards, there remains one curious historical incident to recount. It relieved the 2nd Battalion on the Malabar Coast, one company relieving a 2nd Battalion company at Connanore on 15th November; and at Calicut on 16th November 1902 there took place that unusual occurrence, the meeting of a 1st and 2nd Battalion. It was the first time the two had confronted one another after a union of thirty years.

The 2nd Battalion remained at Aldershot until October 1905, when it moved to Cork. Thence, in January 1909, it moved to Fermoy, much under establishment, only 430 all ranks. In January 1911 it was moved to Colchester, where it was quartered in Hyderabad Barracks for the next two years except for a short period in August of that year when, nineteen officers and 588 n.c.o.s and men strong, it was ordered north to Bradford on strike duty. Having won the Army Hockey Cup and reached the final of the Army Football Cup in 1911, in 1913 it actually won the Football Cup for the first time in the Regiment's history. When war broke out in August 1914 it occupied Whittington Barracks near Lichfield, where it had been since September 1913, with a strength (before mobilisation) of 545 all ranks on an establishment of 802, under the command of Lieut.-Colonel B. W. L. McMahon.

Meanwhile the 1st Battalion moved from Wellington to Lucknow (January 1905), from Lucknow to Nasirabad (January 1909), and from Nasirabad to Nowshera (December 1911). It appeared in all its glory at the Delhi Durbar of 1911, an occasion on which King George V presented it (11th December) with new colours to replace those presented at Colchester in 1888 by the Duke of Cambridge. At the outbreak of war it was still at Nowshera under the command of Lieut.-Colonel C. C. Luard with a strength of 1053 all ranks, rather over the establishment of 1031, a battalion as hard and as experienced as any in the service and probably more so than most.

CHAPTER X

THE GREAT WAR, 1914-1918

THE Great War was the first in which both Regiment and County were united not only by bonds of sentiment, which as has been shown, were growing strong before 1899, but by official inducement, which culminated in the Haldane reforms of 1908. From an aspiration the identification of the two had become first a cherished fiction and then a reality, until at last the County was fully and officially associated with a first-class line regiment, and the Regiment, in which the last grumbles against "linking" had sunk to a barely audible murmur, with a stubborn and muscular people of more than a million from which to fill its ranks. Who shall say which benefited the more? In a relationship so singularly happy and so mutually beneficial it is mistaken to question too closely. Neither, certainly, has lost: both perhaps have gained. Even those with only the faintest of recollections of a Durham battalion in that war remember always that it was "tough", and dug so well that it appeared to sink into the earth before the astonished gaze of its southern comrades; and the County has continued to feel an intense pride in its regiment and deep affection for it. Both also are united in their past achievements and sufferings.

The Raising of the Durham Battalions

I. The telegram ordering mobilisation was received by Major Morant, commanding the depot, at 8 in the evening of 4th August. The procedure had been perfected over a number of years and in the event worked smoothly and efficiently. Yet the wording, "*mobilize stop acknowledge*" came as a complete surprise—one depot-commander wired back "I have stopped mobilizing"—and even at Newcastle it was a puzzle. "I went over to the Mess," says Morant, "and asked

Coddington [adjutant of the 3rd Battalion] if he was sending out
Special Reserve notices. He said No, he was awaiting another telegram ... I said I was certain this was the signal for General Mobiliza-
tion and that action as regards the Special Reserve should be taken.
They then went and looked at their orders and did as I suggested."
By the morning of the 5th every reservist's kit was complete and in
order in his pigeon-hole in the Mobilisation Store. Rations and the
cooking of them had been arranged, and at about 6 a.m. the first
reservists, summoned by posters distributed by the police, made their
appearance. Their medical examination, clothing and equipment
proceeded throughout that day, and at 7 that evening the first
batch of about 300 (under Major A. K. Robb, lately adjutant of the
Durham University O.T.C.) left for the 2nd Battalion, which had
meanwhile wired from Lichfield its requirements of 685 to bring it up
to its war establishment. The remaining 384 left on the 6th. Altogether about 1020 reservists came up, absentees numbering less than
1 *per cent*. The whole operation went without a hitch; "the men gave
no trouble and arrangements worked well".

On 7th August Colonel Cardiff arrived to take command of the
3rd Battalion, whose mobilisation was due on the fourth day, and
Lieut.-Colonel F. G. Kenyon-Slaney, a 68th officer who had retired
in 1899, arrived to take command of the depot from Morant. The
mobilisation of the 3rd Battalion on the Saturday was less orderly.
The battalion comprised not only the 400-odd reservists surplus to
the 2nd's requirements but the "special reservists" or militia, who
did not come up as well or as punctually and were considerably more
drunken. Their war station was the coastal defences at South Shields
and Jarrow, where they arrived some 200 or 300 short, and continued to do so in small and neither very military nor sober parties
over the next few days. The 4th Battalion at the same time came over
to Seaham from Barnard Castle.

II. At the end of July the five Durham Territorial battalions,
forming nearly half of the Northumbrian Division of Haldane's
creation (*cf. sup. p.* 266), had gone into camp for their annual fifteen
days' training, the York and Durham Brigade (which included the
5th Battalion) at Deganwy, the Durham Light Infantry Brigade (the
6th, 7th, 8th and 9th Battalions) at Conway. On 3rd August, when
they had been under canvas for hardly a week, they were recalled to
their peace stations: the 5th to Stockton, the 6th to Bishop Auckland,
the 7th to Sunderland, the 8th to Durham and the 9th to Gateshead.
Early on the 5th they bade farewell to their homes and dispersed to
the sectors of the Tyne and Wear defences allotted to each under the
mobilisation scheme, which some of their officers had reconnoitred

earlier in the year when the prospect of actually digging them had seemed remote and fantastical. The 5th, for instance, went to the Hartlepools and the South Gare, the 6th to Bolden Colliery, the 8th to Roker and Whitburn Gasworks Village, before all went under canvas in Ravensworth Park. Early in October they withdrew to winter quarters in billets in the Newcastle and Gateshead area to undergo training. During the next few months they re-formed on the new four-company organisation adopted by the regular battalions in 1913, and practised sham fights and undertook route-marches that remained etched on their memories for many years. This continued until April 1915. Between the 16th and 19th of that month, the fourth complete Territorial division to be declared fit for service, they embarked for France, and within a week were engaged in one of the bloodiest actions of the whole war. It was not until after this (on 14th May 1915) that the Division received the number which it was to make famous, 50, and the Brigades their hardly less well known numbers, 149th, 150th and 151st.

The Haldane scheme had originally contemplated that any great expansion of the army would be carried out by the county Territorial Associations, who consequently, so soon as war broke out, proceeded to recruit. The response was so overwhelming that by November not only had the Force made good the deficiencies on its establishments but was even 90,000, or nearly 25 *per cent.* overstrength. However, the Secretary of State, Lord Kitchener, viewing the struggle in larger terms (very properly as it proved), conceived the formation within three years of no less than seventy new divisions simultaneously with the maintenance and reinforcement of the six regular and fourteen Territorial. So gigantic an expansion lay far beyond the capacities of the Associations—and Kitchener meant that it should. In his view the Territorial engagement—under which Territorial battalions at the front were losing men (only a few admittedly) claiming their discharge right up to the moment conscription was introduced—and the quasi-domestic organisation of the county Associations cramped the exertions necessary in a contest with a military power like Germany. His intention, which he realised in his first days at the War Office, was to raise the so called New Army from the streets, as it were, six divisions at a time, and the first volunteers were called for by proclamation on 7th August. In the early months of the war therefore the Associations and the War Office were in direct competition both for men and for stores, the Associations being inevitably at a disadvantage. Nevertheless, by the end of 1914 the strength of the Territorial Force had doubled and, indeed, no special efforts in recruiting were needed until the autumn of 1915. On 15th September 1914 the Force was called on to volunteer for foreign service. Battalions containing over 60 *per cent.* of such volunteers were designated "general service", ordered to recruit to 25 *per cent.* over establishment and ceased to be administered by their county Associations.

The five Durham battalions quickly found the necessary percentage and proceeded, like most others, each to form reserve battalions containing those unable for medical or other reasons to volunteer, who were soon joined by many former members who had resigned before the war. The new battalions were known as "second-line" battalions, distinguished from the "first-line" by the figure 2 / before it. The 2 /5th was formed at Stockton and Darlington in September; the 2 /6th at Ravensworth Park, near Gateshead, on the 26th of that month; the 2 /7th at Sunderland on the 16th; the 2 /8th at Durham during October; and the 2 /9th at Ravensworth Park on 11th September. Second-line brigades were formed early in 1915; the 2 /1st York and Durham at Malton on 5th January, the 2 /1st Durham Light Infantry Brigade at Durham on 18th January. The divisional headquarters of the 2 /Northumbrian Division opened in Newcastle that month. The two Durham brigades soon after assembled respectively at Cramlington in Northumberland and in The Leam Camp, near Heworth. It was not until August 1915 that the Division received a number, the 63rd, the Brigades being numbered 189th and 190th. At first responsible for the coast defences in the Seaham, Sunderland and Newcastle area, the 63rd never went into action as a division, and, after moving south and inland to Retford, Gainsborough and Doncaster, it was dissolved in July 1916. The Brigades, however, persisted until the end of the year. Four of the Durham battalions later served abroad, having in the meanwhile supplied such large numbers of excellent recruits to the first-line as to lose most of their Durham quality. They had also spawned, on the 26th May 1915, the 3rd North Coast Defence Battalion, which, composed of their more experienced officers and n.c.o.s, became the 23rd Provisional Battalion Durham Light Infantry, T.F.

On the embarkation of the Northumbrian Division in April 1915 the second-line battalions underwent a transformation similar to that of the first-line, and shed those officers and men who, from wounds and other reasons, were fit only for home service into reserve battalions. These became the 3 /5th, 3 /6th, 3 /7th, 3 /8th and 3 /9th, and trained drafts for the first-line. By this time the rush to join up had materially subsided. Some battalions raised their men by Beat of Drum, as their eighteenth century ancestors had, while Lieut.-Colonel G. G. Plant, 5th, who, himself unfit for service, had already raised the 2/5th, enterprisingly advertised in the leading newspaper for prospective officers, an ingenious expedient which met with a surprisingly good response. After a year in their respective depots the battalions were in May 1916 removed to Horton in Northumberland, where, in August, they were amalgamated into one battalion, named the 5th Reserve Battalion, T.F., under the command of Lieut.-Colonel H. C. Watson, who had retired from the command of the 1/6th Battalion in April 1915. The 5th Reserve Battalion later moved to Catterick and, later still, to Sutton, near Hull.

Two further battalions were raised by the Durham Territorials from men of low medical category, the 26th and 27th, which were formed at Durham and Gateshead out of the 23rd Provisional Battalion on 1st January 1917. Conscription had been introduced for a year; the Territorial quality had been diluted beyond recognition: and neither of them was a battalion in which the Regiment may take much pride. At this distance of time, for instance, the chief claim on our attention possessed by the 27th is the fact of its having been joined in 1918 by a young organist named Malcolm Sargent, suffering from some temporary disability, who had recently taken a musical degree at Durham University.

III. Kitchener's conception of the New Army has already been described. The first call for volunteers, made by proclamation on 7th August 1914, was for 100,000 men, who were formed into six divisions (each of twelve "service" battalions organised in three brigades) numbered from 8[1] to 13. The response from the "First Hundred Thousand" (K1) had hardly died down before a second and a third call (K2 and K3), made on 11th and 13th September, had raised twelve further divisions, which were numbered from 15 to 26.

In Durham the first call produced the 10th (Service) Battalion Durham Light Infantry, allocated to the 43rd Brigade of the 14th[1] Division, which was to be trained at Aldershot and, consisting of the service battalions of rifle and other light infantry regiments, was for that reason designated "Light". The second call produced the 11th (Service) Battalion Durham Light Infantry, allocated to the 61st Brigade of the 20th (Light) Division, which was also to be trained at Aldershot. The third call produced four Durham service battalions: the 12th and 13th, allocated to the 68th Brigade of the 23rd Division, which was to be trained at Frensham, near Farnham, after being temporarily quartered at Pirbright Camp; and the 14th and 15th, allocated to the 64th Brigade of the 21st Division, which was to be

[1]Before the K1 divisions were organised the 8th Division had been formed out of regular battalions brought back from overseas garrisons, and the 8th New Army Division was consequently renumbered 14th.

trained at Halton Park, between Tring and Wendover, but at first temporarily accommodated in billets in the vicinity of Tring.

It is mistaken to be too particular over the dates at which these six battalions were raised. In the enthusiasm of the men composing them K1, K2 and K3 differed not at all; the stream of volunteers continued in overwhelming numbers almost uninterruptedly throughout the first three months of the war; and the principal distinction between the first and the later levies lay in the amount of assistance each received from the Regiment and the speed with which they were equipped. The 10th Battalion, for instance, the earliest, soon reached a strength of 2000, from which the commanding officer picked 1100 of the best men and handed over the remainder to the new formed 11th, and it afterwards underwent a similar thinning process to provide both officers and men for the 12th, 13th, 14th, 15th, and even the 16th and 17th Battalions. It was a question of first come first served: the earlier the levy the quicker it was equipped and the closer were its ties with the Regiment, which became progressively more slender as the levy proceeded.

The 10th Battalion was fortunate in its commanding officer, Lieut.-Colonel H. H. S. Morant, lately commanding the depot, who was appointed on 19th August. The son of the Colonel H. H. Morant whose services in the Crimea and New Zealand have already been noticed, himself a regular officer who had served ten years (1898 to 1908) with the Egyptian Army, a great sportsman, large in build if a little ponderous—though painstaking and accurate—in thought, he combined a high sense of duty with a mature military experience, and was admirably suited to form a New Army battalion, to which his human qualities attracted many excellent officers and men. His battalion was comparatively well off in officers and n.c.o.s from the Regiment: Captain A. L. Cartwright, Captain the Hon. R. T. St. John; Captain J. S. Unthank, who had served in South Africa with the mounted infantry; Captain W. T. Wyllie, a son of W. L. Wyllie the painter, in August 1914 a supernumerary officer serving in the Colonies, who was appointed adjutant; Captain G. W. F. Phillipps, temporarily attached to the 3rd Battalion; Captain J. G. Harter, on leave from the 1st Battalion; and J. P. Cherry, the quartermaster, was a former quartermaster-sergeant of the 1st Battalion. There were besides a certain number of serving regular n.c.o.s., among them R.S.M. A. Noble, who had won the D.C.M. in South Africa, a man of outstanding character who was later killed in the Salient "beloved," as Colonel Morant has recorded, "by every man in the battalion". The New Army officers included among their number: three rowing blues, J. B. Rosher, J. H. Jerwood and G. E. Fairbairn;

J. A. Parke, a son of Morant's adjutant in the 1st Battalion; and W. Stobart, who came of an old Durham family with many connections in the Regiment. The Battalion, which soon received the nickname of the "Shiny Tenth," in October was among the first to wear a distinguishing badge on its clothing, consisting of the regimental bugle cut in silhouette out of scarlet felt. When cloth became scarce in 1916 these badges were made out of old hunting coats sent to Morant by hunting men in Northumberland and Durham.

The later levies were not so well endowed either in the matter of trained officers and n.c.o.s or equipment. Some of the drafts from the depot contained "old soldiers;" but they were "mostly useless," celebrating their return to the army by "colossal drunks," and though eager to get to the front they were not suitable as New Army n.c.o.s. There were no uniforms left to clothe K2 and K3. Colonel Davison, commanding the 11th Battalion, was to be seen teaching his men to right and left turn dressed in a bowler-hat and a suit of "dittoes". Emergency blue clothing did not reach the 23rd Division until October, khaki not until the spring of 1915.

Regular officers, let alone officers of the Regiment, were even more sparsely distributed. In the 11th Colonel G. M. Davison, who had retired from the command of the 2nd Battalion in 1906, had only three, only one of whom was from the Regiment. Two Durham Light Infantry officers had applied for the adjutancy but on hearing who was to command had withdrawn, leaving the appointment to Lieutenant G. Hayes, a 1st Battalion officer on leave, who reluctantly assumed it. The others were newly commissioned. The 12th Battalion received as its first commanding officer Lieut.-Colonel L. E. C. Elwes of the Regiment, an officer with a distinguished Boer War record who had retired in 1905 as a captain after twenty years' service; and though his officers included Lieutenants C. R. Shirreff, already mentioned, and T. F. C. Carr-Ellison of the Regiment, almost all the others were newly commissioned. (One of the company sergeant-majors was Sergeant Chivers, formerly of the 1st Battalion.) The 13th Battalion's first commanding officer, Lieut.-Colonel G. A. Ashby, was a retired officer of the Cornwall Light Infantry, though among his officers were Major N. T. Biddulph, who, though he had retired from the 2nd Battalion in 1909 was to take the battalion out to France in 1915, and the quartermaster, S. Snow, a veteran of Ginnis, formerly a colour-sergeant of the 2nd. The 14th Battalion's first commanding officer, Colonel R. Eccles, and his successors who took it to France, came from outside the Regiment; and although the officers included Major R. F. Bell, who had retired from the Regiment in 1913, and Captain G. M. Saunders, who had retired in

1903, all the remainder were new commissions. The 15th Battalion, raised by Lieut.-Colonel R. A. Smith, half-pay Shropshire Light Infantry, and taken into its first action at Loos (where he was killed) by Lieut.-Colonel E. T. Logan, a Cheshire Militia officer, was only once commanded by a Durham Light Infantryman and contained no serving officers from the Regiment.

All the battalions, however, had this in common: the men with only a few exceptions came from County Durham. They were Durham to the core. In point of quality the recruits differed not at all. All the men and most of the officers and n.c.o.s were volunteers who had never come near the army in their lives, joining from a settled society to welcome the opportunity of generations with an enthusiasm and a joy it is impossible for this crabbed and disillusioned age either to describe or imagine. Most of the men were pitmen, a class of man that did not often enlist, which was nevertheless to prove itself in that war the staunchest and hardest of the community. Everyone who served with them has said what magnificent fighting men they made, dogged and determined, not just once but returning over and over again, after casualties unknown in any war before, with an ardour and resilience barely diminished, to do the same once more. "I had a very sad parting from my old platoon," wrote an officer of the 20th Battalion when transferred to a company composed mostly of shipyard workers. "My pit lads would have followed me anywhere, and I am sad at leaving, as they were too." Those who have since met survivors from their ranks, unemotional and determined, have been glad to have them as companions in other dark days.

At first they lacked all conception of army discipline. Drunkenness and absence off leave they were unable to take seriously at all. Colonel Morant relates that one day at Aldershot when he was passing the guard the sentry took no notice. The adjutant went up to him and expostulated, saying, "Don't you know the Commanding Officer?" "Noa," was the reply. "What! you don't know the C.O.?" "D'yer mean," said the man, nodding to a tent, "he what sits in yon white hoose and ta-akes our pa-ay?" Most of the officers and n.c.o.s, themselves scarcely more experienced, naturally found it difficult to accustom them to habits so foreign to anything they were used to, and the difficulty was not eased for the officers, who came from every part of the country besides County Durham and took a month or more to understand their speech. Indeed, more time elapsed than was spent in training before the New Army divisions became military formations. The whole atmosphere was too friendly—in retrospect perhaps excessively so—for military notions of discipline to take root.

Those Durham battalions that later joined regular divisions found there a very different state of affairs, where orders were carried out not merely to oblige. Curiously enough, the difference persisted long into the time when all divisions, regular, Territorial and New Army, varied very little in point of composition. Even as late as 1st December 1918 Rawlinson noted it, when the King visited the Fourth Army. The 50th and 46th Divisions, he records, "gave him a tremendous reception": the 1st, 2nd and 4th "received him far more stolidly". In none was there "more than a sprinkling of professional soldiers. Yet the 1st Division parades as it used to do at Aldershot, and the 46th, when the time to unbend comes, just remember that they are citizens."

In October 1914 "K4" was raised from the Special Reserve, and the 3rd and 4th Battalions of the Regiment, by then very much over-strength with a heterogeneous collection of "old soldiers", reservists, wounded convalescents from the 2nd Battalion and recruits, were permitted to form service battalions provided the strength of the parent battalion did not fall below 1500 all ranks. In this manner the 16th Battalion (to which the 3rd supplied its first draft of 485 men on 26th October) and the 17th were raised, being directed for training to Cannock Chase as part of the 89th Brigade, of the Fourth New Army 30th Division. K4, however, became a very poor brother of the other three. By spring 1915 it had become apparent that its battalions were needed to provide trained reinforcements for the others when they should take the field, so it was broken up, the 89th Brigade becoming on 10th April the 1st Reserve Infantry Brigade of the Training Reserve, whose subsequent history is continued later.

On 10th December 1914 the Fifth New Army (37th to 42nd Divisions) was authorised. It contained for the most part battalions raised earlier, by cities like Manchester, provinces like Ulster and great landowners like Lord Derby, in a style more reminiscent of the feudal centuries than even of the eighteenth. Remarkable among those remarkable battalions—and in some respects unique—was the 1st County of Durham Battalion, numbered 18th. It originated in a proposal made by Major F. T. Tristram, J.P., a former regular officer and a captain in the 1st Volunteer Battalion, to Colonel Rowland Burdon, Unionist Member for the Sedgefield Division, whose ancestors had raised volunteer corps a century before. As an outcome a committee was formed early in September, under the chairmanship of the Earl of Durham, the Lord Lieutenant, of a number of gentlemen of the County (among them Colonel Burdon himself, Sir Walter Gray, Bart., and Mr H. Pike Pease, Unionist Member for Darlington, later Lord Daryngton), who agreed to raise and equip at their own expense a battalion from the County. An appeal made at the same time for subscriptions met with an immediate and extraordinary response. £10,000 was quickly collected from a list of subscribers which included Greenwells, Salvins, Wilkinsons, Fenwicks, Ropners and other names familiar from Napoleonic days, as well as former officers of the Regiment such as Colonel C. W. Darwin, adjutant of the 68th from 1875 to 1880, who had retired in 1894. Lord Durham placed Cocken Hall at the disposal of the committee, so saving an expenditure of over £6,000. From the outset a high standard of physique was required in the recruits, none under 5ft. 9ins. being admitted. Those who came forward were, moreover, of a superior class of man, most of them clerks, tradespeople, students, teachers and so on. The contingents from Durham, South Shields, Sunderland, Hartlepool and Darlington assembled at Cocken Hall on 24th September.

The first commanding officer, Mr C. W. Tilly, was soon succeeded by Major F. T. Tristram; he soon stepped aside as second-in-command when the services of Lord Southampton, a former officer of the 10th Hussars, were secured; and at the end of October the command was effectively assumed by Lieut.-Colonel Hugh Bowes, a keen Volunteer officer who, after having commanded the 5th Battalion from 1905 to 1908, had, while Secretary of the Durham Territorial Force Association, energetically realised the intentions of Lord Durham's committee. One of his most zealous supporters was W. D. Lowe, Senior Censor and Bursar of Durham University and major in the O.T.C., who later commanded the battalion in France. Several of the officers and n.c.o.s had served in the regular battalions: the first quartermaster, R. Robson, a colour-sergeant of the 2nd Battalion, had been sergeant-major of the 5th, and his successor, J. H. Chaplin, had joined the 1st as a side-drummer and risen to colour-sergeant. It was soon clothed and equipped, despite the cool reception Lord Kitchener gave it—who, however, afterwards warmly commended and thanked those who had prompted it, and even offered to reimburse the committee, an offer that was politely declined. Other battalions, in Durham as well as elsewhere, were raised on money from private sources which was refunded later; but the 18th Durham Light Infantry has the distinction of being the only one raised and equipped free of any expense to the nation.

It also has the distinction of being the first New Army battalion to come under enemy fire. Two companies sent on 16th November under Major Tristram to man coast defences were at Hartlepool when, on 16th December, the German battle-cruisers *Derfflinger*, *Von der Tann* and *Blücher* loomed out of the mist to bombard the unfortunate town. It was an occasion which gave the new battalion an opportunity to display a praiseworthy cool bearing in a purely passive role while losing five men killed and eleven wounded.

Local training came to an end in May 1915 when the 18th was marched to Newcastle and passed before Lord Kitchener in review. Provisionally allocated in December 1914 to the 122nd Brigade of the 41st Division, it joined, at Ripon on 22nd May, the 93rd Brigade of the 31st Division of the *new* K4 (which had formerly been the 38th Division of K5).

By the end of December 1914 the first enthusiastic rush to join up was spent; those coming forward were more sober men who, after reflecting maturely, had surrendered good situations and left families; and, to stimulate and control recruiting, recruiting-committees were set up, that of County Durham being under the chairmanship of Lord Durham, the secretaryship shared between members of each of the three political parties, Liberal, Unionist and Labour. The first battalion raised by the Committee (after much correspondence) was one composed of men of short stature, below 5ft 3 ins. and above 5ft., who, debarred under the original conditions, were nevertheless men of excellent physique, many of them pitmen. Sanction was given on 15th January 1915 for the raising of the 2nd County of Durham Battalion, numbered 19th, from the so called "bantams," under the command of Lieut.-Colonel W. Thomlinson, a former major of the 4th Durham Volunteer Artillery and a member of the Durham T.F. Association. The first recruits assembled at the Co-operative Society's Buildings in West Hartlepool on 3rd March. Originally allocated to the 125th Brigade of the 42nd (K5) Division, which on the break-up of K4 became in April the 105th Brigade of the 35th (*new* K4) Division, entirely composed of "bantam" battalions, it moved to Masham Camp in Yorkshire on 22nd June, and later, to Perham Down on Salisbury Plain.

The 20th Battalion arose out of an invitation extended in June 1915 by the War Office to the mayor and recruiting-committee of Sunderland to form an infantry battalion from the district. Although Wearside had only recently contributed a complete brigade of field artillery, the invitation was accepted. After Major K. J. W. Leather, 4th Battalion, whose valuable Boer War services have already been mentioned, had been secured as commanding officer, recruiting was opened in July and the men began to assemble at St. John's Wesleyan Schools in Ashbrooke, Sunderland, on 23rd August. Commonly known as the "20th Battalion Durham Light Infantry (Wearsiders)," the new battalion entrained for Wensley in Yorkshire about 150 strong on 28th August; and though it was allocated to the 123rd

Brigade of the new 41st Division, formed at Aldershot in September, it did not move south until the War Office took it over from the recruiting-committee early in January 1916.

Some idea of the pride localities took in their battalions in those days may be gathered from the attentions paid to the 20th by the civic dignitaries of Sunderland. When it paraded to entrain for Wensley it was seen off by the Mayor and Mayoress and all the members of the recruiting-committee, who gave the men their best wishes, served them with a dinner at the Co-operative Café and provided them with cigarettes. Later, in April 1916, when 400 of the Battalion came to Sunderland on furlough before embarking, the Mayor, Alderman S. Richardson, after giving each man a package containing sandwiches and cigarettes, addressed them in front of forty or more members of the corporation and the recruiting-committee saying, "We shall not forget you, and we shall have pleasant memories of you, and hope you will have pleasant memory of those you leave behind." Not a masterpiece of civic oratory perhaps, but it is a reminder of the intense, almost proprietary, interest the County took in the men it sent on service in that war.

The next service battalion raised by the County arose out of an approach made on 6th August 1915 by the War Office to the County Recruiting-Committee for a battalion of pioneers, with one of which each New Army division had already been (and each regular and Territorial division was gradually being) equipped in view of the peculiar conditions of trench warfare. Recruiting for the 3rd County Battalion, or 22nd Battalion Durham Light Infantry, was opened on 1st October, and the first recruits went into billets in West Hartlepool on the 11th. Although the levy was handicapped by the "Derby Scheme" of "group attestation" (the first shadow of conscription, which induced many to await the calling up of their groups), progress was sufficiently satisfactory for the new battalion to be taken over by the War Office on 9th March 1916. On the 21st Lieut.-Colonel Thomlinson, who had raised the bantam battalion and had raised this also, was succeeded by Colonel C. B. Morgan, a retired officer of much experience from the West India Regiment, and it moved to Scotton Camp, Catterick, on the same day. It embarked for France on 16th June, being only then allocated temporarily to a division, the 19th, until, on 2nd July, the second day of the great offensive on the Somme, it was finally posted to the 8th Division (regular).

The later New Army battalions, like the first-line Territorials, commonly formed reserve companies as a basis for reserve battalions from which drafts could be supplied to the parent battalion. This was the origin of both the 21st and the 23rd Battalions. The 21st was formed when the 19th Battalion left Cocken Hall on 29th July 1915, from the reserve companies of both the 18th and 19th. Never serving abroad as a unit, it moved successively from Wensleydale, to Richmond and to Hornsea. The 23rd was formed at Scotton from the reserve companies of the 19th early in November 1915. After supplying drafts to the 20th in January 1916, it moved to Atwick, near Hornsea, for coast defence duties in April. A 24th Battalion was similarly to have derived from the 22nd, but the reserve companies of that battalion on embarkation were instead transferred to the 16th Battalion at Rugeley, and the formation never in fact took place.

It has already been hinted that by this time the surge of volunteers had subsided, and still hardly half of Kitchener's seventy divisions had been raised. The National Registration Act of July 1915 subtly transformed volunteering from a courageous act of supererogation into a duty. A last chance to volunteer was offered in the "Derby Scheme" of October 1915, which produced a further 250,000. On 27th January 1916 the Military Service Act came into force, under which every man, married or single, born between 1875 and 1897 was compulsorily enrolled.

The effects of conscription on recruiting were not spectacular, and it must be said at once that in the Regiment only one more service battalion was raised between that date and November 1918. Volunteering had already claimed the cream of the country's manhood. But it inevitably increased the pressure on the regimental reserve units, Territorial as well as New Army, so as to make them unworkable. One expedient adopted was the formation of the Corps of the Training Reserve, a scheme by which 112 of the battalions in the reserve infantry brigades became "Training Reserve Battalions," receiving recruits not required for the regimental reserve. The staffs of the battalions continued to belong to their regiments but were attached. In this manner the 16th and 17th Battalions of the Regiment lost their county identity in September 1916 and became respectively the 1st and 2nd Training Reserve Battalions, of which the 1st was disbanded at the end of November 1917.

The scheme was then further developed to provide progressive training for recruits under 19. Forty-two of the 112 battalions were selected for this purpose, fourteen becoming "Young Soldier Battalions," twenty-eight becoming "Graduated Battalions". A pair of the latter was linked to one of the former, so that, when a recruit had finished his training in the Young Soldier battalion, he passed on to one or another of the Graduated battalions. These were organised in four companies according to age, say, D Company for those of

18 to 18¼, C for those of 18¼ to 18½, B for those of 18½ to 18¾, A for those of 18¾ to 19. Thus every three months a company of 19-year-olds in each battalion was ready for drafting to France. In October 1917 it was found that Graduated battalions of the Training Reserve were suitable for home-service divisions, and, dropping their former designations, they assumed high numbers (201st upwards) as infantry battalions. A little later Young Soldier and Graduated battalions were identified with line infantry regiments, the Young Soldier battalions becoming the 53rd, the linked Graduated battalions the 51st and 52nd, battalions of the regiment to which they were affiliated. In this manner the 11th (Reserve) Battalion of the North Staffordshire Regiment and the 31st (Reserve) Battalion of the Northumberland Fusiliers became, successively, the 4th and 86th Training Reserve Battalions, the 258th and 273rd Battalions, and, finally, the 51st and 52nd (Graduated) Battalions Durham Light Infantry; while the 2nd Training Reserve Battalion, the descendant of the old 17th Durham Light Infantry, became the 53rd (Young Soldiers) Battalion Durham Light Infantry.

None, naturally, fought abroad as battalions. But the 51st, at Durham, virtually did so in the critical days of spring 1918 when the whole battalion, although composed of lads under the age for foreign service, emptied itself in four days.[2] A telegram from the War Office regretting but explaining their hurried departure was read out to each company as it paraded for the station, and "on each occasion," the adjutant writes, "the lads spontaneously took off their hats and cheered their heads off". He adds: "a week after the first company had left the Colonel and I were inspecting the empty messhalls when one of the company appeared in hospital kit with his arm in a sling. He had been wounded immediately on arrival at the front, and by a strange coincidence was evacuated to a hospital in Durham, which he had left exactly a week previously."

The 51st, after serving in the 215th Brigade of the 72nd (home service) Division, was transferred on 15th January 1918 to the 206th Brigade of the 69th (home service) Division, which was quartered in Middlesbrough, Barnard Castle, Durham and Stockton, afterwards moving to Gainsborough and Catterick. The 52nd, after serving in the 220th Brigade of the 73rd (home service) Division, was transferred to the 69th Division at the same time. Both were moved from Catterick in March 1919 for garrison duty in Germany. The 52nd arrived in Cologne on 6th March, the 51st on the 8th, and they performed the guard duties in rotation thereafter. The 53rd arrived in Cologne on 4th April, but, being immediately reduced

[2] 160 of them, certainly, went to the 1/8th Battalion on 5th April.

to cadre, gave about 200 officers and men to each of the other two.

Three other battalions were raised in the Regiment after conscription. The 25th (Works) Battalion was a labour depot raised for Northern Command in May 1916. It carried no arms nor underwent any military training. The 28th was formed in April 1918 as a home service battalion under the command of Lieut.-Colonel R. H. W. Cardiff, a Durham Militia officer with South African service who until then had commanded the 3rd Battalion at South Shields.

The 29th Battalion, the last battalion to be formed, was raised on 19th June 1918 at Brookwood in Surrey from the training cadre of the 2/7th Duke of Wellington's Regiment (formerly 62nd Division), to constitute part of the 41st Brigade of the 14th Division, which had returned battered from the spring battles in France for reorganisation. It was hardly a "territorial" battalion in the old sense. It was commanded by Lieut.-Colonel F. S. Thackeray, 2nd Highland Light Infantry, who, to his original cadre of nine officers and fifty men, was able to add a draft of 1100 men of low medical category from a variety of north country regiments (including 100 from the 27th Durham Light Infantry and 167 from the 28th). Over a third were found unfit, but the Battalion embarked on 2nd July and was able to share in the last fighting in Flanders with the reconstituted 14th Division from the end of September onwards.

In the aggregate the Regiment, which at the outbreak of war consisted of two regular, two special reserve and five Territorial battalions, may be said to have raised a further: thirteen Territorial,[3] eleven service,[4] one Works,[5] and nine New Army reserve, home service, young soldiers and graduated battalions[6]—a total of forty-three battalions.[7] Of these twenty-two served abroad in one theatre or another:

On the Western Front (see Table overleaf) .		18
(of which there served in Italy (12th, 13th, 20th)	3	
and in Egypt (18th)	1)	
In Macedonia (2/5th, 2/9th) . . .		2
At Archangel (2/7th)		1
In India (1st)		1
		— 22

[3] 2/5th, 2/6th, 2/7th, 2/8th, 2/9th, 3/5th, 3/6th, 3/7th, 3/8th, 3/9th; 23rd, 26th, 27th.
[4] 10th, 11th, 12th, 13th, 14th, 15th, 18th, 19th, 20th, 22nd, 29th.
[5] 25th.
[6] 16th, 17th, 21st, 23rd, 24th, 28th, 51st, 52nd, 53rd.
[7] This figure may be reconciled with the official number of 37 (with which the Regiment is credited in the Army List) by regarding all the third-line Territorial battalions as one, by overlooking the duplication of the 23rd, and by deducting the abortive 24th.

Brigading of Battalions serving on the Western Front

Battalion	Dates	Brigade	Div.
2nd Durham L.I.	4th Aug. 1914–11th Nov. 1918	18th	6th
1/5th Durham L.I.	4th Aug. 1914–12th Feb. 1918	150th	50th
	12th Feb. 1918–15th July 1918	151st	50th
	16th Aug. 1918– 9th Nov. 1918	117th	39th
1/6th Durham L.I.	4th Aug. 1914–15th July 1918	151st	50th
	16th Aug. 1918– 6th Nov. 1918	117th	39th
1/7th Durham L.I.	4th Aug. 1914–16th May 1915	151st	50th
	16th May 1915–20th Jun. 1918	Pioneers	50th
	20th Jun. 1918–11th Nov. 1918	Pioneers	8th
1/8th Durham L.I.	4th Aug. 1914–15th July. 1918	151st	50th
	16th Aug. 1918– 6th Nov. 1918	117th	39th
1/9th Durham L.I.	4th Aug. 1914–12th Feb. 1918	151st	50th
	12th Feb. 1918–11th Nov. 1918	Pioneers	62nd
2/6th Durham L.I.	6th May 1918–11th Nov. 1918	177th	59th
10th Durham L.I.	11th Sept. 1914–12th Feb. 1918	43rd	14th
11th Durham L.I.	11th Sept. 1914– 6th Jan. 1915	61st	20th
	6th Jan. 1915–11th Nov. 1918	Pioneers	20th
12th Durham L.I.	13th Sept. 1914–11th Nov. 1918	68th	23rd
13th Durham L.I.	13th Sept. 1914–14th Sept. 1918	68th	23rd
	19th Sept. 1918–11th Nov. 1918	74th	25th
14th Durham L.I.	13th Sept. 1914–26th Nov. 1915	64th	21st
	26th Nov. 1915– 1st Feb. 1918	18th	6th
15th Durham L.I.	13th Sept. 1914–11th Nov. 1918	64th	21st
18th Durham L.I.	27th Apr. 1915–11th Nov. 1918	93rd	31st
19th Durham L.I.	Jun. 1915– 8th Feb. 1918	106th	35th
	8th Feb. 1918–11th Nov. 1918	104th	35th
20th Durham L.I.	Sept. 1915–17th Mar. 1918	123rd	41st
	17th Mar. 1918–11th Nov. 1918	124th	41st
22nd Durham L.I.	20th Jun. 1916– 2nd July. 1916	Pioneers	19th
	2nd July 1916– 3rd July. 1918	Pioneers	8th
29th Durham L.I.	19th Jun. 1918–11th Nov. 1918	41st	14th

Parenthetically there should also be mentioned as part of the County's contribution the battalions of the Durham Volunteer Corps, which, however, never formed part of the Regiment. The Volunteer Corps was revived on 17th June 1916 on the same terms (the 1863 Act) under which the Territorials had formerly existed. By 9th August four Durham Battalions had been recognised: the 1st (Gateshead), 2nd (Sunderland), 3rd (Bishop Auckland) and the 4th (Darlington). Stockton followed in October, Hartlepool in December. The 7th and 8th (Sunderland and Houghton-le-Spring), recognised in March 1917, came from Doxford's shipyard. The 9th (Birtley), 10th (West Hartlepool) and the 11th (Sunderland) brought the total strength of the Corps in Durham to 256 officers and 10,408 n.c.o.s and men in August 1918.

§

Unavoidably perhaps, but regrettably, the Regiment was unable to play as large a part in its expansion as it could have done. In the first six months of the war the army absorbed over four times as many men as the German Army, with its infinitely greater resources, was accustomed to handling in a year. The whole atmosphere of those early days was one of hurried improvisation. The Special Reserve was sufficiently preoccupied in finding replacements for the regular battalion in the Expeditionary Force, which by Christmas 1914 had suffered casualties equivalent almost to a whole battalion. With all military experience at a premium, the services of many former officers and n.c.o.s became inevitably devoted elsewhere and outside the Regiment.

For instance, Colonel A. de B. V. Paget, one of H.M. Gentlemen at Arms, raised the 2nd Sportsman's, or 24th, Battalion Royal Fusiliers. Lieut.-Colonel H. A. Cartwright, who had retired in 1892 yet had served with the 7th Imperial Yeomanry in South Africa and in 1914 was Master of the Wilton Foxhounds, came forward to command the 3/4th Dorset. His brother-in-law, Lieut.-Colonel L. Parke, a former adjutant who had retired in 1901 and gave a son to the 10th Battalion, was commanding the 4th Hampshire (T.F.). Captain B. C. Fairfax, who had retired early in 1914, returned and rose to command the 17th King's. Captain A. C. Tucker, the son of the Colonel H. A. Tucker who commanded the 68th from 1879 to 1881, who had himself retired in 1907, commanded the 1st Garrison Battalion, Yorkshire Regiment. Colonel F. G. A. Wiehe (descended from a Brunswick family), a very fine officer who, though his active service belonged to the halcyon days of the 68th before 1899, had yet contrived to serve in the Second Afghan War and wore the Kandahar Medal—he not only gave a son to the Regiment (2/Lieutenant G. I. Wiehe, who joined the 2nd Battalion in March 1915) but himself served with the Canadian forces in France. Colonel the Hon. W. L. Vane, the Regiment's historian, who had retired from the 1st Battalion in 1903 to command the 6th until 1911, raised the 2/6th Battalion and later crossed to France as an area commandant. Some of those officers, moreover, who began the war in the Regiment had subsequently to give their services outside it. Major J. S. Unthank, Morant's second-in-command in the 10th, commanded from May 1916 to April 1919 the 4th Seaforths, where "his courage and coolness," his "reticent and self-effacing" conduct earned him a deserved popularity. Captain J. W. Jeffreys, in 1914 adjutant of the 6th, later rose to command both the 1/6th and the 2/8th Battalions as well as the 53rd Queen's. And the services of the officers of the 1st Battalion, marooned as it were on the North-West Frontier, shall be mentioned in due course, for all but one went on active service at one time or another.

Similarly the services of the n.c.o.s granted commissions were largely given to other regiments. There can be no better testimony of the high quality of the Regiment's senior n.c.o.s in 1914 than the long list of those who were commissioned and received awards for their conduct in the field. Perhaps the most spectacular was the career of Colour-sergeant James Jones. He had entered the 2nd Battalion as a boy in the band and went out in 1914 as C.S.M. of a company, was commissioned on 1st October 1914 and, by the time he was killed on 14th October 1918, he was acting-lieut.-colonel, D.S.O. and M.C., commanding the 17th Lancashire Fusiliers. Hardly less meritorious was the career of Sergeant-major Ernest Crouch, who had enlisted in the 1st Battalion on 10th November 1891, transferred to the 2nd when at Mhow in 1893, had served in South Africa and, having been appointed in 1913 R.S.M. of the 9th Battalion, accompanied it to France in 1915, and finally commanded it in succession to Lieut.-Colonel R. B. Bradford, V.C., receiving the D.S.O. and D.C.M. Colour-sergeant H. Shearwood, formerly of the 1st Battalion, and quartermaster of the 6th Battalion, who went out to France with the 7th Yorkshire Light Infantry and "was to prove that in spite of his sixty years of age no night in France was so bad as to prevent him coming forward into the trenches . . . nor any task too difficult for him to tackle," became brigade-major eventually to a second-line Territorial division; C.S.M. E. Higginbotham, who had entered the 68th as a boy, rose to command a prisoner-of-war camp—and the list may be extended at greater length than space allows.

"Dug-outs" was the impolite name given to (and assumed by) those who returned after long retirement. That some of them seemed curiously antiquated only shows how novel were the problems faced by those who raised our forces in that war. It emphasises how long in fact may be what, to a historian, seems but a short span of time, and also by how small a generation of soldiers the brunt of that war was borne. The services of these men, however, form an essential part of the combined effort exerted by both the County and the Regiment.

The Aisne and Aisne Heights, September 1914

In August 1914 there were six divisions at home available for the formation of the Expeditionary Force, of which four—the 1st, 2nd, 3rd and 5th—were embarked with the utmost dispatch. The other two—the 4th, which was wholly stationed in Ireland, and the 6th, which had two brigades in Ireland and one, the 18th (containing the 2nd Durham Light Infantry), dispersed in England[8]—were detained

[8]The 1st West Yorkshire Regiment and the 2nd Durham Light Infantry were stationed at Lichfield, the 1st East Yorkshire Regiment at York, and the 2nd Sherwood Foresters at Sheffield. On 4th August all four had barely returned from brigade training at Llanidloes.

for some weeks, partly against the contingency of a German force landing and interfering with the shipment of troops, partly in view of the exposed situation of Ireland, which had only recently approached the verge of civil war. The 4th Division reached the field in time to take part in the battle of Le Cateau and, with the 19th Brigade, became the nucleus of the III Corps formed on 31st August. The 6th Division, however, did not embark for France until the second week of September, and did not join the III Corps until after the operations on the Aisne.

When the order to mobilise was received by the 2nd Battalion in Whittington Barracks at 6.30 in the evening of 4th August, a detachment of 263 men under Major Mander already occupied its "precautionary period" stations in South Shields. The reservists arrived from the depot in two parties at 4 in the mornings of the 6th and 7th August, and at 10 on the 7th the Battalion (including Major Mander's detachment, which had returned at 7 a.m. on the 6th) paraded ready to move to Edinburgh, the 18th Brigade's prearranged war station. All four companies arrived in Dunfermline in the afternoon of the 8th. They remained there until the 13th, when, the other two brigades having completed their mobilisation in Ireland, the whole 6th Division began concentrating around Cambridge. After three weeks strenuous training, of which the 600 reservists were much in need, the Battalion entrained at Newmarket for Southampton in the night of Monday 7th September, and embarked for Saint-Nazaire, two companies (Major Mander's and Captain Northey's) in the *City of Benares*, the others (Major Blake's and Major Robb's) in the *Bellerophon*. The two wings disembarked 27[9] officers and about one thousand n.c.o.s and men strong on 10th and 11th September. Entraining independently in the well-known "Hommes 40, Chevaux 8" cattle-trucks—some inside, some on the roofs—and passing through Châteaubriant, Chartres and the outskirts of Paris, where they got a clear view of the imposing new fortifications then erecting, they detrained at Coulommiers and marched to billets in Saint-

[9]Lieut.-Colonel B. W. L. McMahon, commanding; Majors J. A. Crosthwaite, second-in-command, D'A. W. Mander (B Company), E. A. C. Blake (C Company), and A. K. Robb (D Company); Captains W. Northey, D.S.O. (A Company), H. V. Hare and J. H. Wood; Lieutenants H. J. Taylor, W. H. Godsal (adjutant), C. R. Congreve, W. B. Twist, W. A. Grey-Wilson, and L. G. Norton; 2/Lieutenants W. E. Parke (machine-gun officer), V. A. C. Yate, R. B. Bradford, N. C. P. Conant, C. M. Stanuell, C. W. Beart and R. Marshall; and Quartermaster J. P. L. Shea. Attached: (from the 3rd Battalion), Lieutenant C. Smith and 2/Lieutenant J. R. Gales; (from the Reserve), 2/Lieutenants C. Mearns and C. H. Baker; and from the R.A.M.C., Captain G. P. A. Bracken. Captain F. G. Maughan was staff-captain, 18th Brigade; 2/Lieutenant C. H. Green was doing duty with the 6th Divisional Cyclists.

Germain-sous-Doue, where on 15th September the Battalion was assembled for the march north to the Army on the Aisne.

By then the military situation had to some extent stabilised. The German armies, checked in their triumphant advance, had retired from the Marne and had been thrust back to a position beyond the Aisne. The Expeditionary Force, which lay between the 5th French Army on its right and the 6th French Army on its left, occupied a line roughly following the ancient ridgeway called the Chemin des Dames, with the Aisne in its rear. All formations which had shared in the exertions of the previous four weeks being exhausted and much reduced in strength, the fresh 6th Division was distributed between the I and II Corps. The 18th Brigade (Brigadier-General W. N. Congreve, V.C.) was attached to the I Corps (Haig), which held the right of the British line.

The Battalion, marching in heavy showers of rain by way of Château-Thierry, Tigny (16th), Chacrise (17th) and Dhuizel (18th), through a countryside that bore the marks of the passage of great armies, reached Bourg-et-Comin on the Aisne in the early hours of 19th September. That same evening at dusk it was moved on up the ridge to relieve a battalion of the weary 2nd Brigade in its hastily improvised trenches actually on the Chemin des Dames north of Troyon. On its right lay the 1st West Yorkshire, the extreme right-hand battalion of the British Army, beyond whom lay a battalion of Moroccans, the extreme left of the French 5th Army. In front lay the German 7th Army, which, rushed from the eastern part of the front to fill the gap found by Haig's men on the 13th, was still fresh compared with Kluck's tired troops lower down the Aisne. Major Robb's Company occupied the Battalion's left trenches; next him was Major Blake's; then Captain Northey's; and on the right, next the West Yorkshire, was Major Mander's. Picquets were posted in front of each company, who, being a little jumpy on their first active service, fired on their own men during the night causing several casualties.

Since the moment, a week before, when the Germans had been forced from the ridge, they had made several attempts to win it back by heavy counter-attacks, and on 20th September their 7th Army made a further effort on a corps front opposite the junction of the French and British Armies. It was a cold morning and at times there were heavy showers of hail. The first attack soon after dawn drove in the Moroccans, but was repelled by them and the West Yorkshire; and a second was also effectively checked. But a third, delivered at about 1 in the afternoon, drove back the Moroccans sufficiently to cause the West Yorkshire to be enfiladed; and the Germans, working down the line and taking advantage, it is said, of the white flag ruse, swept three of its companies into captivity. The Durhams' flank being exposed by this disaster, the right-hand company suffered heavy casualties from artillery and machine-gun fire. The 2nd Foresters, ordered up from the reserve position to restore the situation, succeeded in recovering the West Yorkshire's trenches, but not before Major Robb on the left had, through some mistake, advanced his company against the enemy in two sharp counter-attacks. A young sergeant in his company, who was later commissioned and became adjutant of the 18th Battalion, Sergeant F. G. Stone, has described his experiences:

> "We then got the order from Lieutenant Mearns to advance. Did so under a storm of bullets and shrapnel to within, I should think, thirty yards of them. I could see their heads and round caps sticking out of their trenches. Felt rotten advancing, but all right once I started firing. Had to retire. No sooner back in the trenches and absolutely breathless than we had to advance again. Same thing occurred, and retired again. Our casualties were pretty heavy . . ."

They were. The situation was restored by half-past four, but the Battalion had lost in its first day's engagement almost as heavily as the 1st Battalion in the whole of the Boer War. Major Mander and Major Robb, Captain Hare, Lieutenants Stanuell and Marshall and 36 n.c.o.s and men were killed; and six officers (Lieutenants Godsal, Twist, Grey-Wilson, Gales, Mearns and Baker) and 92 n.c.o.s and men were wounded. In Robb's Company only 2/Lieutenant Bradford remained. It was an introduction to a new kind of warfare.

The Battalion remained in the same trenches for the next five days, which passed without any further attacks materialising, though the enemy fire was fairly continuous and troublesome. It was relieved at about 10 p.m. on 25th September and marched back to Pargnan, several miles behind the line but still within range of the German guns. Next day it was moved forward to a reserve position in a wood north of Vendresse-Beaulne in support of the 3rd Brigade, which was successfully withstanding a powerful attack. It was not called upon, but some casualties were sustained before it was withdrawn across the Aisne to billets in Vauxtin at about 10.30 p.m. on 1st October.

The Race for the Flank: Armentières

To the stalemate which had been reached on the Aisne there succeeded that great series of movements often called "the race for the Channel ports," the outcome of which set the scene of operations for the next four years. The Germans prefer to call it *das Ringen um die Flanke*, the struggle for the flank, which, indeed, it was also. By the time the 2nd Battalion was relieved at Vendresse the race was already well under way, and the north flank of both armies had been prolonged from Noyon as far as Lens. It was then decided to move the Expeditionary Force from the Aisne front to the left of the Allied line that it might enjoy the advantages of the short communication with England, an awkward and difficult operation which was begun in the night of 1st/2nd October. The II Corps between Missy and Vailly was secretly relieved by the corps on either side extending to their right and left.

This movement brought the 2nd Battalion from Vauxtin at 7 p.m. on 2nd October, and carried it through Braine to relieve the 2nd Duke of Wellington's (II Corps) in a position south of the confluence of the Aisne with the Vesle about Ciry. The line here was still fairly fluid, and German and British patrols exchanged shots daily and nightly in the debated land on either bank of the river. The main position lay on the railway line, but picquets were placed well in advance on the Vesle bridges. The Battalion's turn to move north came at 2 a.m. on 7th October, when it started a long march south-westwards to Saint-Rémy, near Villers-Cotterêts, and thence to Largny-sur-Automne. Continuing on the 8th to Saint-Sauveur, it entrained at 9.20 p.m. on the 9th at Le Meux, south of Compiègne, for Arques, which was reached next day.

The race was still proceeding when the 18th Brigade, now for the first time with the 6th Division in the III Corps (Pulteney), detrained and entered the country which was to be the British Army's battlefield for the next eighteen months, a flat, low-lying country, intersected with dykes and sluggish rivers bordered with willows and thorn hedges, so waterlogged that trenches were barely practicable and breastworks had necessarily to take their place. The three British Corps started to take their share in the struggle on 11th October, when the III Corps was directed east to join in an outflanking movement towards Lille.

The Battalion that day marched to Wardrecques. Carried on French lorries to Hazebrouck on the 12th, and marching on the 13th to Vieux-Berquin, it went into action at 2 that afternoon when it came up on the left of de Mitry's cavalry corps in front of the enemy, who was entrenched behind the Météren Becque. The attack, which was delivered on Ferme Labis and Les Trois Fermes, was successful, though it was attended with some loss. Two officers (Lieutenants Parke and 2/Lieutenant H. Storey—a sergeant who had received his commission only ten days before) and eleven n.c.o.s and men were killed; one officer (2/Lieutenant C. E. Smith) and sixty n.c.o.s and men were wounded.

The enemy gave back towards Lille under the steady pressure of the British infantry, the northernmost of which bent his line back along the line of the Lys towards Menin. On 14th October the Durhams advanced to Le Doulieu. They then turned cautiously south-east to cross the Lys by a broken bridge at Sailly, which the Germans had abandoned in flames, and in the evening of the 15th took up an outpost position south of the town, where they remained until the evening of the 17th. The advance was continued in the direction of Lille. The advanced guards walked on the grass verges to deaden the noise, occasionally passing groups of French cavalry, one of whom—a detachment of cuirassiers, their cuirasses and helmets now a little rusty—called out to a company of the Battalion, "Hullo, Tommee, I was at Oxford."

On the 18th the Battalion, which had reached Bois-Grenier against some opposition the previous night, was ordered to make a demonstration to test the enemy's strength at La Vallée, at the edge of the slightly elevated ground on which stood the perimeter fortresses of Lille. The demonstration, which soon developed into an attack by the 18th Brigade to gain the ridge from Ennetières-en-Weppes to Capinghem, was begun under a heavy fire of shrapnel at about 3.45 in the afternoon, and was directed south-eastward towards Fort d'Englos. The battalion on the Durhams' left failed to reach Capinghem; but in spite of an intense musketry fire the Battalion succeeded in getting as far as Ennetières and even beyond before dusk. Sergeant Stone, who was wounded in the attack, has described the confused scene:

> "Advanced in extended order to about a hundred yards to our front when suddenly a hail of bullets began coming from right, left and front. Dropped flat, and shrapnel began to burst over us. Rushed forward over turnip-field—no cover whatever. Drop again. Bullets so thick now that all we could do was bury our faces in the mud and lie flat. Risked a look over turnip-tops and was hit in the shoulder by a piece of spent shrapnel. Sore but not wounded. Advanced again and reinforced men in front of us. Remained here for about two hours, but were unable to get forward the bullets were so thick. Just before dusk was struck by rifle-bullet in the calf. Sergeant Harrington on my left struck in the foot, so when dark enough, we both hobbled back [to Ennetières] . . ."

In this successful (perhaps too successful) enterprise, which thrust a small salient into the line, four men were killed and two officers (Captain Northey, D.S.O.—who died later—and Lieutenant

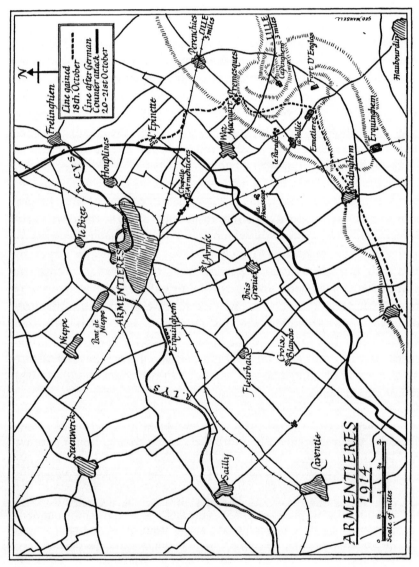

20. Armentières: the Ennetières Salient, 18th/20th October, 1914

Conant) and 74 n.c.o.s and men were wounded; 29 were missing. After nightfall the Battalion, relieved by the 2nd Foresters, went back to a reserve position at Fétus, a mile north-west of Ennetières.

The pressure exerted by the III Corps, whose line projected in a salient from Prémesques to Ennetières, appeared to the Germans to threaten Lille (theirs since the 11th), and inevitably provoked a counterstroke, which fell chiefly on the 18th Brigade's small salient on 20th October. Being in reserve the Battalion was distributed by companies to reinforce the other battalions as they came under attack. Major Blake's Company went to the Foresters at Ennetières and La Vallée; Captain Birt's (D) went first to the East Yorkshire at Paradis and then to the West Yorkshire on their right; Captain Wood's (B) went to the East Yorkshire; and Captain Taylor's (A) was soon after ordered to follow.

It is now known that in the storming of Ennetières the Germans employed no less than three-quarters of an army corps (the XIII), and there can be little wonder that the 2nd Foresters, who formed the garrison, were overwhelmed. The attacks came upon them soon after 1 p.m. from the east, the south-east and south-west, but it was not until dark that a German attack from the west, delivered by an estimated three battalions, burst into the village, took the platoons on the east in the rear and captured most of them. The survivors retired in good order on La Vallée, but were surprised and surrounded by another enemy force from the north; and though some managed to hold out in the house in La Vallée until the early hours of the 21st, almost the whole battalion was destroyed. Major Blake, whose company of the Durhams shared their fate, is said to have taken two platoons into a sugar-factory and to have brought a valuable overhead fire upon the attackers from the upper storey until a heavy shell fell into the building, smashing the machinery and killing and crushing the men inside, including the Major himself. The other two platoons under Lieutenant Norton were involved in the bitter fighting after dark on the south of the village, and all were either killed or captured. Only 23 n.c.o.s and men from the company returned. At the same time the companies supporting the battalion on the Foresters' left were heavily engaged until compelled by the fall of Ennetières to secure their exposed flank and relinquish their hold on the Prémesques ridge. Three platoons of A Company made two unsuccessful attempts to force their way back into La Vallée but had to be withdrawn to Fétus to prevent any further advance by the enemy, who, to everyone's surprise, made no effort to exploit his success. The Battalion's loss in this fight fell mainly on C Company. Two officers (Major Blake and Lieutenant Norton, who was left

mortally wounded in enemy hands) were killed, and two (2 /Lieu-
tenants Beart and Gilbertson) wounded. Of the n.c.o.s and men four
were certainly killed and 46 wounded, but of the 177 missing most
were undoubtedly either killed or severely wounded.

After a short rest in Bois-Grenier the Battalion moved on 21st
October into the trenches at Rue du Bois. Here on the 27th and 28th
October they underwent two exceptionally heavy bombardments
followed by an infantry assault, the second of which forced back the
men from the two advanced trenches but was repelled with very
heavy losses with the assistance of the two supporting battalions. A
hundred German dead were counted in front of the East Yorkshire's
trenches and 56 in front of the Durhams'.

For the 6th Division, the 18th Brigade and the 2nd Battalion this
marks the end of what is officially known as the battle of Armentières,
which is really the fighting provoked by the III Corps on this sector
in the general attempt to roll back the northern German flank. The
Battle of Armentières merges insensibly into that of Ypres (in which
the Corps had no share), which was already in full swing when the
2nd Battalion successfully withstood the assault on Rue du Bois. At
Ypres the race to the sea, the struggle for the flank reached its climax.
The Allies, always, as it was said, "twenty-four hours and an army
corps behind the enemy," had failed to outflank and envelop him,
but they did succeed in denying him the principal Channel ports and
in securing them for themselves. Stubborn fights like that at Ennetières repeated by the score placed the line while still molten where
it remained set and solid, almost without change, for years to come.

The Battalion remained in front of Armentières, at L'Armée,
Chapelle d'Armentières, Frélinghin, until 24th May next year, when
it was brought up into the Salient and took over the trenches near
Potijze on the 31st. By then there were few familiar faces from
September. Lieut.-Colonel McMahon returned home in January
1915 to take command of the School of Musketry at Hythe, handing
over to Major Crosthwaite. All the original officers but four had
either been killed, or wounded once by the end of 1914. In June 1915
the Battalion was well up to strength, 32 officers and 1050 n.c.o.s and
men, but of these only 180 had come out with it.

Ypres 1915: Gravenstafel, St. Juliaan, Frezenberg, and the Bellewaarde Ridge

The failure of the British attack at Neuve-Chapelle in March and
of the French offensive in Champagne had convinced Falkenhayn
that the Allies were incapable of breaking the German line, and left
the German command with an unwonted freedom of decision. In the

west it chose to resume the attack on the Salient, where success would bring all it had hoped for in October, the Channel ports and the Flemish coast, "the goal of the old German army in its days of glory in the first weeks of war". We who are familiar with the outcome of "Second Ypres" will consequently be surprised to learn that it was a German victory. In Durham it is remembered as the scene in which its Territorial battalions received their rude baptism of fire without any quiet initiation in a "nursery" sector.

Ypres in 1915 was not a town of importance in itself, but, the line having solidified where it had, it was the northernmost point at which the line ceased to be protected by the barrier of inundations that stretched northward to the sea. The town lies on the canalised Yser, which is a fair obstacle, but on its far bank. The country is flat, but on the German side it slopes gradually up to the ridge running north-eastward to Passchendale from the "Flemish Switzerland". Opposite Ypres the ridge is not high, 150 feet at the most above the plain; but it was high enough and close enough to overlook and command not only the town but the roads that diverge in all directions from it into the Allied rear. Hence the salient, The Salient, for which the Army had fought to the death in October and November. From the ridge some low spurs run westward, in the dips between which trickle several insignificant streams draining eventually into the Yser. The spurs within the Salient were, from north to south: the Poelkapelle Ridge, on which stand Poelkapelle and Langemarck; the Stroombeek Ridge; the Gravenstafel Ridge; the Zonnebeke Ridge; the Frezenberg Ridge; and the Bellewaarde Ridge. Their gentle slopes cannot be compared with the ridges that featured so largely in that other soldier's battle, Inkerman, but in such a landscape any fold that offered shelter from ground observation assumed an importance out of all proportion to its size. The country in the spring of 1915 was green, flat, open and wet, and studded with numerous farm buildings, usually solidly built, often surrounded with water, almost every one of which formed a strong-point fought for over and over again.

"Second Ypres" consists essentially of: the initial breach in the north sector of the Salient on 22nd April, in the "soft" part between Poelkapelle and the Canal, held by two French divisions who, demoralised by poison-gas, gave back until the enemy unexpectedly halted scarcely a mile short of Ypres; the improvisation of a retrenchment in that sector, and a further German assault on its jagged flank, which was temporarily held on the Gravenstafel Ridge in some murderous fighting lasting a week (23rd to 30th April)—to which the names of *St Juliaan* (on the west) and *Gravenstafel* (on the east) have been given; a withdrawal to an inner line running by

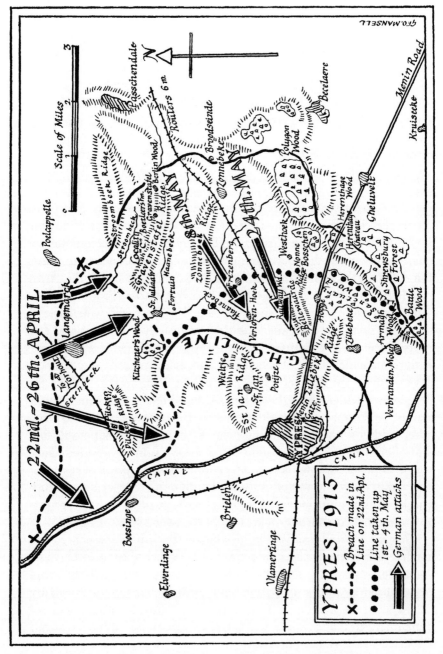

21. Second Ypres, April—May, 1915

Frezenberg and Hooge; and two unsuccessful assaults upon it, named *Frezenberg Ridge* (8th to 13th May) and *Bellewaarde Ridge* (24th to 25th May). Since the Northumbrian Division was split at the outset to succour different parts of the line, the five Durham battalions at one time or another shared in all four battles. The Regiment owes its honour *St Julien* principally to the engagement of the 1/5th there on 26th April; *Gravenstafel* principally to the fine performance of the 1/8th at Boetleer's Farm on that ridge at the same time; and *Frezenberg Ridge* to the share of the 1/5th in its defence on 13th May.

On 22nd April, when the Division was warned to move at a moment's notice, it had only that day completed its concentration in billets around Steenwoorde and Cassel. The 1/5th Battalion (150th[10] Brigade), which was the first Durham battalion to move, had disembarked at Boulogne on the 18th, 31 officers and 1000 n.c.o.s and men strong, under the command of Lieut.-Colonel G. O. Spence, a keen and very capable Volunteer officer, in peace a director in a large firm of shipbuilders. Conveyed during the night of 23rd/24th April in London motor-buses, which still bore the familiar advertisements for Mellin's Food and so on, through Poperinge to Vlamertinge, it marched on to a hutted camp at Brielen, near the Canal, which was reached before dawn on the 24th. The camp was under enemy artillery fire, but no casualties were suffered until the afternoon when, the Brigade having been split, the Battalion was ordered forward with the 4th Yorkshire and the 4th East Yorkshire to some reserve trenches near Potijze. Later that afternoon it was moved through St Jan to Wieltje in support of the 3rd Canadian Brigade, which was heavily engaged on the Gravenstafel Ridge near St Juliaan.

This was the "hard shoulder," as it were, of the breach, where the fighting had fluctuated all that day and the day before. To restore the line a counter-attack was planned, to be undertaken at dawn on the 25th by the 10th (regular) Brigade under Brig.-General Hull, who also had at his disposal several battalions from other brigades and the whole of the 150th. Communications, however, were so disorganised that the 1/5th did not receive its orders until 2 a.m., and none outside the 10th Brigade had any clear idea of what was intended. During the night the Battalion marched at a disconcertingly quick pace behind the 1/5th Yorkshire to Fortuin, whence it was to have co-operated on the right of the 10th Brigade. By dawn it was in position in time to witness the failure of that magnificent assault. But through some mistake in the orders it received, after advancing un-

[10]Properly "York and Durham Brigade" until 14th May. It was commanded by Brig.-General J. E. Bush, commissioned in the 106th in 1880, who had served at Ginnis as adjutant.

opposed it found itself *en l'air* and fell back to Verloren-Hoek, though later in the day both it and the 1/5th Yorkshire moved forward to fill a gap in the line on the right of the new line won near Fortuin. As the Battalion advanced it came under a heavy machine-gun and artillery fire which caused a number of casualties. In the evening the two battalions were relieved, having between them lost four officers and 284 n.c.o.s and men.

Meanwhile the 151st Brigade, which had been placed under the command of the 28th Division, assembled at Rietveld, near Cassel, soon after 2 p.m. on the 23rd. It consisted of the 1/6th, under the command of Lieut.-Colonel H. C. Watson, whose uncle had commanded it twenty years before; the 1/7th, under Lieut.-Colonel E. Vaux, of the great brewing family; the 1/8th, under Lieut.-Colonel J. Turnbull, a cheerful, powerfully built man who had taken the 1st Volunteer Service Company to South Africa in 1900 and, though his (like Lieut.-Colonel Watson's) term of command had expired in 1912, had succeeded Lieut.-Colonel W. C. Blackett the previous October owing to the latter's ill-health; and the 1/9th, under Lieut.-Colonel A. Henderson, who, it will be remembered, had joined as a simple volunteer in 1884. At about 5 p.m. the battalions had moved forward by bus from Steenwoorde through Poperinge to Vlamertinge, which was reached shortly before midnight. The sound of the battle raging had been clearly audible at Cassel, and from Poperinge onwards the Very lights rising from the trenches traced the whole outline of the Salient. It was not, however, until the afternoon of the next day, the 24th, that the Brigade was sent by Plumer to General Snow, senior officer in the Salient, who placed it on its arrival after dark at Potijze, near the rear position dug the previous autumn known as the "G.H.Q. Line". "The arrival of these very fine Territorial troops," says the Official Historian, "ready to go anywhere and do anything, did much to hearten the troops with whom they came in contact, and their subsequent help and sacrifices were gratefully acknowledged by their Regular comrades."

At Potijze the Brigade was split. The 1/6th was sent to relieve part of the 2nd Shropshire Light Infantry covering Potijze to enable it to be lent to the hard pressed 28th Division in the line. The 1/7th and 1/9th bivouacked near Potijze. The 1/8th, on the other hand, was sent up to assist the 85th Brigade at Verloren-Hoek. The 8th's first experience of coming under fire had been an unpleasant ordeal, but it had not damped their spirits. "Through the darkness came the voice of some irrepressible Bede College member of A Company as a shell passed over: 'Aye, it reminds yer o' Durham Regatta. Now, lads, up goes another! All together! Bang! Mind the stick!' Then someone called 'Who's won the Grand?' and there were rival cries of 'City!' and 'Bede!' "

The 85th Brigade ordered the 8th on through Frezenberg and the outskirts of Zonnebeke to reinforce the 8th Canadian Battalion, holding Boetleer's Farm on the Gravenstafel Ridge, which it reached at about 3 a.m. on the 25th. The situation, even if it had not been dark, was extremely confused, and it was not until daylight that the companies completed their dispositions in full view of the enemy, who were from 80 to 250 yards distant across some fields of young corn and mustard. D Company (Captain T. A. Bradford)[11] and A (Captain F. G. Harvey), leaving the others and headquarters in the Farm, occupied an advanced position on the far side of the Stroombeek.

The early morning, which witnessed the famous attack of the 10th Brigade farther to the left, was comparatively quiet. But at about 9 heavy shelling began which gradually increased in volume until 2 in the afternoon, when enemy infantry started to gather in the dead ground to the north-west. The first attacks were repelled. But at 3.30 three trains were observed drawing up on the Ypres-Torhout railway from which troops, including marines in blue, detrained and advanced towards the ridge in large numbers on the front and left flank of the position. The Canadians received orders implying that a switch-line, or retrenchment, had been prepared in rear which was occupied by the other battalions of the Brigade, and accordingly withdrew from the magnificent defence they had maintained during the previous two days. Lieut.-Colonel Turnbull, however, having received no such orders from the 85th Brigade, remained in action and was eventually reinforced by the 1st Monmouthshire and 8th Middlesex, and later, indeed, by the Canadians, who returned. The forward positions, after putting up a very stout resistance, were abandoned in the evening, being attacked on three sides and the companies there having lost very heavily; but throughout the night the Battalion under Colonel Turnbull's leadership held on to Boetleer's Farm despite every inducement, moral and otherwise, to retire. His left flank was open for a thousand yards and his right was

[11]The only survivor of four brothers, sons of George Bradford of Milbanke, Darlington, whose services are remarkable. The eldest, Lieut.-Commander G. N. Bradford, R.N., received the V.C. at Zeebrugge, where he was killed at the age of 31; Lieutenant J. B. Bradford, M.C., 18th Battalion, died of wounds in France, 14th May 1917, at the age of 27; Brigadier-General R. B. Bradford, who had fought with the 2nd Battalion on the Aisne and later commanded the 1/9th, receiving the M.C. and the V.C., was killed on 30th November 1917 at the age of 25, the youngest brigadier in the army. Captain T. A. Bradford received the D.S.O.

scarcely more secure. However, he held on in this salient till 4 a.m. on the 26th, when the Germans—some of them said to be dressed in khaki—came on again and forced him to give ground. The Battalion fell back to the Hanebeek, fighting, however, so effectively under the adjutant, Captain G. A. Stevens, who exhorted them to "aim at the middle button, boys," as to keep off all pursuit; and later, on instructions from the 85th Brigade, they were brought back to the Zonnebeke Ridge. Still under fire the Battalion remained there throughout the 26th until the early hours of the 27th, when it was relieved by the 1/5th Battalion from the left. Withdrawn first to a position hear Frezenberg, it rejoined the Brigade at Verloren-Hoek.

"The greatest possible credit," recorded General Bulfin, who commanded this sector of the confused soldier's battle, "is due to the 8th Durham Light Infantry and the small detachment who, in spite of having their flanks turned and being enfiladed, remained in the northern line beating off all attacks and inflicting heavy loss on the enemy, and thereby saved the flank of the 85th Brigade." No less valuable to them were the opinions of the Canadians who had fought with them and set the standard. The respect of the one for the other was reciprocal. "They call us the mad Durhams," one man wrote home in a letter. Their determined resistance was bought at a heavy price. The relief, says their historian, contrasted strangely with the ordered reliefs down communication trenches of later days. This time "the Battalion stepped out of mere ditches and formed up roughly on a track behind, officers and n.c.o.s calling out for "any more 8th Durhams that were left". When the roll was called in the relative security of Frezenberg only six officers and about 142 n.c.o.s and men answered. These were formed into a fighting company under Colonel Turnbull. Other survivors turned up after. But 19 officers and 574 n.c.o.s and men had been killed, wounded or found missing[12] in their gallant fight.

The 1/6th was meanwhile engaged alongside the 2nd Shropshire Light Infantry in the north-eastern sector of the flattened salient, half-way between Frezenberg and Zonnebeke, to which they had been ordered to advance at about 11.15 in the morning of the 26th. Here, with their right resting on the Ypres/Roulers railway, they succeeded in holding on all day in spite of heavy casualties. At the same time the 1/7th, farther left, ordered northward at about 2 p.m. towards Gravenstafel, advanced undismayed through heavy shell-fire to a point north of Zonnebeke, where they stayed until brought

[12]9 officers and 81 n.c.o.s and men killed and 153 n.c.o.s and men wounded; 2 officers and 340 n.c.o.s and men missing, many of them wounded more or less seriously.

back to Verloren-Hoek in the evening. The 1/9th remained in reserve at Verloren-Hoek throughout the day.

Throughout the 27th, 28th and 29th these three battalions of the 151st Brigade were kept in the line. On the 30th they moved to Frezenberg, in front of the G.H.Q. Line. The 5th Battalion, meanwhile, relieved in the night of the 28/29th from their trenches south of the Hanebeek—"sorry trenches they were, freshly made, very bad and narrow, with scarcely any traverses, nothing at all behind and only funk-holes for shelter"—were brought back to the camp at Brielen, and a day or two later marched to billets near Steenwoorde.

To the week's confused and bitter fighting there succeeded a lull, during which a shortening of the battered salient was contemplated. The new line chosen, though two miles behind the original and hardly two miles in front of Ypres itself, ran in front of the G.H.Q. Line and included the Frezenberg Ridge, the first on which a stand could be made. Postponed several times, the withdrawal was successfully carried out between 1st and 4th May. The rest of the 50th Division having been brought back to Poperinge on 2nd and 3rd May, it was a movement that did not affect the Durham battalions until the resumption of the German offensive on the 8th. On that day they made a heavy onslaught on the Frezenberg Ridge by which they drove a breach in the line between Frezenberg and Verloren-Hoek.

The breach was plugged, and the 151st Brigade was not brought up into the Salient until late on the 11th, when all but the 1/8th, which, now reduced to a company, remained in reserve at Brielen, was placed in the G.H.Q. Line astride the Menin Road. The 150th did not come up again as a brigade, though the 1/5th Battalion was moved during the night of the 12th into the sector of the front line held by the 81st Brigade near Hooge and Sanctuary Wood. Letter A Company went to the 2nd Camerons; B to the 1st Argylls; C and D to the 1st and 9th Royal Scots. The next morning at dawn the Germans brought down a very severe bombardment under which their infantry attacked the line between Verloren-Hoek and the railway, which gave but did not break. The Battalion was held in readiness to move to the threatened sector, but apart from suffering from the shelling it was not involved. The 151st Brigade was equally unaffected save that the 8th Battalion was brought up to Potijze. "So far as the 50th Division was concerned the Battle of Frezenberg Ridge was a period of moving and marching about, much shell-fire, and great discomfort, but not actual fighting with the enemy."

There followed a lull from 14th to 23rd May, during which the Division was again split. When the Germans attacked the Bellewaarde Ridge on the 24th the 1/5th Battalion was allotted to the 2nd Cavalry Brigade in the line near Hooge; the 1/6th remained in the G.H.Q. Line; the 1/7th was divided between the G.H.Q. Line and the 3rd Royal Fusiliers in the line near Bellewaarde Farm; the 1/8th (two companies) closed the gap between the 3rd Royal Fusiliers and the 2nd East Surrey on their left; and the 1/9th had two companies with the 2nd East Surrey.

The attack was made at dawn on the 24th accompanied by a tremendous bombardment and gas, which, in the absence of any wind, moved slowly and lay low. The fiercest attack fell in the 85th Brigade's sector. The 8th Middlesex were overwhelmed, but to their right three companies of the 2nd East Surrey and the companies of the 9th and 8th Battalions not only stuck to their position all day but counter-attacked, "it being specially recorded by the 28th Division that there were few stragglers to the rear and none from one of its battalions". Colonel Henderson, 9th, and nine of his officers and 204 n.c.o.s and men became casualties; the 8th lost four officers and 103 n.c.o.s and men; but the survivors of the four companies held on with such exemplary tenacity that the enemy was forced to exploit farther to the south. Here he overwhelmed the 3rd Royal Fusiliers and the 1/7th Battalion's companies, the majority of whom (about seven officers killed, two wounded, and over 200 men lost) were either gassed, wounded or killed, and thrust the remainder out of their trenches to a second line. Farther south at Hooge the cavalry line held; the companies of the 1/5th Battalion attached to the 9th Lancers successfully assisted in forming a flank which thwarted the attack; and its company (C) that was posted in Sanctuary Wood managed to hold their trench against a subsidiary attack made in that direction.

With the Battle of Bellewaarde Ridge "Second Ypres" came to an end. Both sides were exhausted. If the Germans had failed in their Durchbruch to the Channel ports, the British had lost the ridge which made the Salient tenable. Thereafter it was held "by luck and courage but by no other effective means". The brunt of the powerful enemy attacks had been borne by the regular divisions, but the 50th in its first action had shown that even without comparable training and initiation a first-rate Territorial division had immense reserves of resilience. It lost altogether nearly a third of its strength. Of the Durham battalions most heavily engaged between 22nd April and 25th May the 1/5th lost two officers and 89 n.c.o.s and men killed or died of wounds, ten officers and 205 n.c.o.s and men wounded; while the 1/8th, in spite of having received a draft of officers on 8th May, on 7th June was reduced to a strength of 27 officers and 312 n.c.o.s and men. It was accordingly organised on 8th June into a single battalion with the 1/6th, known as the 6/8th Composite Battalion, under the command of Lieut.-Colonel Turnbull, to which the 8th contributed one and the 6th three companies. The two battalions did not resume their separate identity until 11th August. The 1/7th had been made the divisional pioneer battalion on 16th May.

The 50th Division went into the line for the first time as a formation when it relieved the 3rd in Sanctuary Wood during the night of 6th June. Sanctuary Wood then bore some resemblance to a wood, and was not the collection of battered stumps of trees which it became later when an exasperated 8th Battalion man, labouring up the communication trenches bearing a heavy load of sandbags, dumped his burden in the mud and exclaimed with disgust, "Sanctuary Wood! No — Sanctuary and no — Wood!" From then on the Durham battalions entered upon the routine of "normal" trench warfare which lasted until the Division was brought down into the Somme fighting twelve months later.

Trench warfare in 1915 was still an improvised business with us, and it was some time before the British Army, hampered by a lack of ammunition for the artillery, fought the Germans on equal terms. They already had their stick-grenades, their rifles with telescopic sights and their *Minenwerfer*. We had the Battye bomb, the hairbrush bomb and the jampot bomb (called "Tickler's Artillery" from the jam-maker's name), which were hardly more dangerous to the enemy than to us. Nevertheless, despite the inequality the 50th Division was not prepared to let him have it all his own way. Its active and aggressive patrolling was greeted with dismay by the enemy, whose men shouted across No Man's Land or put out boards saying, "Go away, you — Northumbrians! Why don't you let us sleep?" or "What do you — Northumbrians want here?" The night was for work, the day for rest. There were quiet spells and others. "Quiet" days were those in which a battalion experienced little more than the morning and evening "hate" and numbered its casualties in ones and twos and threes. What losses could be sustained in such warfare is shown by the 1/9th Battalion, which on 19th April 1916, the anniversary of its arrival in Flanders, had lost: 8 officers and 129 n.c.o.s and men killed or died of wounds, 16 officers and 566 n.c.o.s and men wounded, and 26 officers and 575 men sick—a total of 50 officers and 1264 n.c.o.s and men, or rather more than a whole battalion in a year.

The Division remained in the Salient until the middle of July 1915, when it moved south to the Armentières sector, which it held until

the second week of December. Returning north, the Durham
battalions were involved in some stiff fighting early in 1916 on Hill
60, never "quiet", and in the trenches on the Bluff, where the line
crossed the Ypres-Comines Canal. In April they were moved to the
Vierstraat sector, remaining there until the first week in August. In
May the 151st Brigade bade farewell to its very popular brigadier,
J. S. M. Shea (promoted to the command of the 30th Division), who
had always referred to his men as his "tigers". There was a story that
a man going up a communication trench in the dark who was
challenged by a sentry replied, "One of Jimmy Shea's — tigers!"

Hooge, 1915

One of the finest feats of arms performed by the 2nd Battalion in
the war was the attack upon Hooge, in which it shared on 9th August
1915.

The Château of Hooge, like the other châteaux in the Salient,
was not so much a feudal mansion as a country house for those
wealthy Belgian merchants who before the war came to Ypres and
its surroundings for a life, ironically enough, of leisured comfort.
From May 1915 it lay on the front line—so much so that the Château
lay in German hands and the stables in ours. On 30th July this sector
was held by the 41st Brigade of the 14th Division, one of the first
New Army divisions to come out. About 3.15 that morning there
descended upon it with dramatic suddenness one of the most terrify-
ing onslaughts of the whole war. The site of the stables was blown up,
and, amidst a hissing sound clearly heard by one of the battalions in
the first line, a bright crimson glare turned the whole scene red.
"Jets of flame as if from a line of powerful fire-hoses spraying fire
instead of water shot across the front trenches . . . and a thick black
cloud formed. It was the first attack on the British with liquid fire . . .
The surprise was complete and would probably have led to an entry
even at the strongest part of the line." As it was, the 41st Brigade was
for the time being practically wiped out and demoralised, and the line
thrust rudely back across the Menin Road to the verge of Zouave and
Sanctuary Woods.

The disaster brought into its first serious action the senior of the
Durham service battalions, the 10th, under Lieut.-Colonel Morant,
in the 43rd Brigade of the 14th Division. It was not its first experience
of the trenches, for since landing at Boulogne on 21st May it had
done two tours of duty in and near the Salient in which it had already
suffered 70 casualties. Ordered to move at half-an-hour's notice from
its bivouac at Vlamertinge at 3 a.m. on 30th July, it was unable to
reach its appointed place on the southern edge of Zouave Wood until

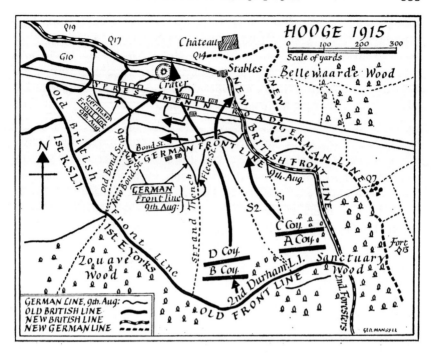

22. Hooge, 9th August, 1915

11 p.m., only 3½ hours before it was to have shared in a dawn counter-attack. This it was mercifully spared. In very confused conditions in the dark Colonel Morant succeeded in relieving one of the stricken 41st Brigade battalions, the 7th Rifle Brigade, in an awkward position in Zouave Wood, where the trenches were filled with the corpses from the previous day. Despite a terrific bombardment it also re-established the line on the front edge of the wood. In the two nights and a day spent in this unpleasant situation it lost a further 8 officers and 170 n.c.o.s and men killed and wounded. Though it was some time before the Division as a whole regained its composure— even after the replacement of two brigadiers who had not shown to advantage—the 10th Battalion itself, if not directly implicated, came out well in the episode, and one of its patrols, led by Lieutenant C. E. Pumphrey up Strand Trench so close to the enemy that he could see the German sentry through the loop-hole in the barricade, obtained information essential to the success of the 6th Division's attack on 9th August.

To restore the line the 6th Division was withdrawn from its trenches near Wieltje and Potijze to relieve the luckless 14th on 6th August. During the next two days every deception was used to mislead the enemy; the co-operation of the artillery was meticulously planned; and for the first time for months ammunition was provided on a lavish scale. The infantry assault was entrusted to the 2nd Durham Light Infantry advancing from the head of the re-entrant, whence it had 500 yards to cover, and to the 1st Shropshire Light Infantry of the 16th Brigade, who were to converge from the left "shoulder" when the Durhams came level.

The 2nd Battalion was in excellent condition and well up to strength. Since 11th June it had been commanded by Lieut.-Colonel M. D. Goring-Jones, a 2nd Battalion officer lately serving with the 1st in India, a small wiry man with a black moustache and an eye-glass, usually seen smoking a cheroot, whose bungalow in India had been filled with the skins and heads from his trophies on *shikar*. During the autumn the Battalion had somehow acquired the nickname of the White Gurkhas. It has also formed an extraordinary friendship with the Queen's Westminsters, Territorials who had joined the brigade as a fifth battalion early in November—a friendship difficult to account for except on grounds of reciprocal respect, for the Territorials were mostly City businessmen and well educated clerks of a different stamp entirely from the Durham men. In the march from Potijze it had suffered some casualties, and the prospect of tackling the German trenches (heavily wired) in its front while exposed to an enfilade fire from the German trenches in the wood to its right was not pleasant; but every man knew that the Division had been brought over especially for the task and that the Battalion had been selected for the hardest part, which was to be performed under the eyes of the newcomers from England.

By 2.15 a.m. on 9th August the Battalion was deployed, with two companies up, on the edge of the Wood, which consisted of fully grown oak, beech and ash with a thick undergrowth of briar and hazel, except at the verge, where it had been shelled away. The two assaulting companies under Captain R. V. Turner, C (2/Lieutenant W. Davison) on the right and D (Captain Turner) on the left, each had two platoons up in single rank at fifty yards interval. The two supporting companies in rear under Captain A. H. M. Bowers, A (2/Lieutenant R. Gregg) on the right and B (Captain Bowers) on the left, were deployed similarly. Three machine-guns were sent under Lieutenant G. I. Wiehe with the first line, three (two borrowed) with the second.

At 3.25 half an hour after the opening of the artillery bombardment, the Battalion advanced in short rushes to the attack, guided in its general direction by the line of Trench S2. In what seemed only a few minutes it reached its objective. A bitter bayonet fight ensued, while the enemy replied with his machine-guns at Q7, in Fleet

Street and in the Menin Road, as well as from his mortars in Belle-waarde Wood and in the right rear at Fort 13. The issue, however, was never in doubt. The Shropshires' attack from the left converged at exactly the right moment, though contact was not established with them till about 6.10, and the Durhams began to consolidate their capture. In a short while about 150 prisoners had been sent back. Five hundred enemy dead were afterwards counted, most of them bayoneted. At the same time the bombing parties under Lieutenant Storey had fought their way down G8, G7 and Bond Street according to plan.

> "I was commanding the two attacking companies," Captain Turner wrote long afterwards of the assault. "Things were so indistinct with the dust of missiles bumping about, the half-light and the mass of trenches about, that it was difficult to know when we had reached our objective. I remember prodding with my walking-stick to locate the roadway and so get a basis for taking up our line, digging and reversing trenches, etc., and preventing eager souls pressing on into our own barrage. I got hit in the knee about this time, and in the face, but fortunately had my stick and could get along to the Crater and see C.S.M. Kent, who was doing blood-curdling work . . ."

By noon, though the battalions were somewhat mixed, the front line had been made into a continuous fire-trench held by three improvised companies under Lieutenants Layng (left), Sopwith (centre) and Davison (right). At about 2.30 reports from both the centre and left companies that the enemy was massing on both flanks for a counter-attack brought the commanding officer to the front line, but the artillery broke up the concentration before the counter-attack could develop. Nevertheless the enemy *Minenwerfer* and artillery fire, which had never ceased since 9.30 in the morning, continued to cause uncertainty—as well as casualties—until 8.30 in the evening, when the order was sent up for the Battalion to withdraw on being relieved.

So dense was the smoke and so difficult and precarious the communications that only Lieutenant Davison and about 120 men responded; and when the Battalion marched back to billets in Ypres that night, played out of the trenches by its band, its strength was a mere four officers and 166 men. However, next morning (10th) at about 9.30 Lieutenants Briggs, Sopwith, Wiehe and Sheriff, and about forty men made their appearance from near the Crater, where the message had failed to reach them; and in the evening a party of about 24 men under 8702 Lance-corporal J. G. Smith came away from an isolated trench near the stables. No message had reached him either, but he had remained quite happily in command of his party, whose existence would have gone unnoticed had not the officer commanding the relieving battalion received a note from him asking for more bombs and reinforcements! He was later awarded the D.C.M.

The Battalion's casualties in this very creditable and successful attack were heavy. All the officers of the supporting companies had been either killed or wounded by 6 a.m. on the 9th. Altogether it lost: six officers (Captains A. H. M. Bowers, and R. H. Legard, 2/Lieutenants R. Gregg, R. W. May,[13] J. A. Cartwright[13] and J. C. Holcroft[13]) and 92 n.c.o.s and men killed; six officers (Captain R. V. Turner, Lieutenant G. Sopwith, 2/Lieutenants G. M. Garland, K. Storey, R. K. Robson and M. Coverdale) and 262 n.c.o.s and men wounded; and 100 men missing, of whom many were later found to have been killed. "The old commanding officer," one man wrote home, "who is nearly seventy years of age [Goring-Jones can hardly have been fifty] and a trump, was crying. I can tell you we got anything we wanted. I know I got a gill of rum and went to sleep." They received the cheers of their comrades as they marched into camp at Poperinge and the thanks and congratulations of the brigadier, the divisional commander (Major-General W. N. Congreve, V.C.), the corps commander, the Army commander (Plumer) and Sir John French himself, who considered it "one of the best conducted of the smaller operations of the campaign".

The Battalion remained in the Salient until 30th July 1916.

Loos

The offensive in the Lens coalfields which goes by the name of the battle of Loos was the first in the series of great Allied offensives which continued almost unbroken until the great German offensive of March 1918. It was undertaken against Sir John French's better judgment to synchronise with the attack of d'Urbal's 10th French Army in Artois, which in turn was prompted by the critical situation on the Russian and Italian fronts. Its interest for us lies in the employment of the 21st New Army Division, containing the 14th and 15th Battalions Durham Light Infantry, which was brought up with the 24th New Army Division on the second day to exploit such success as had already been attained.

The 21st was a division of K3, which, as has been said, had suffered in training from being a "youngest brother" who receives his pre-

[13]Three young officers recently commissioned from Sandhurst. Cartwright, whose brother was killed with the 20th Battalion, 21st September 1917, was a nephew of Colonel H. A. Cartwright. Captain Legard came from the 4th Battalion, Captain Bowers from the 3rd.

decessors' cut-down clothes. At first billeted around Tring, the Division did not move into hutments until May 1915, nor did it undergo brigade training nor complete its musketry courses until its arrival in Aldershot Command in July. Nevertheless it was brought out to France early in September. The 14th Durham Light Infantry was commanded by Lieut.-Colonel A. S. Hamilton, a retired Indian army officer of 50, the 15th by Lieut.-Colonel E. T. Logan, D.S.O., Cheshire Regiment, who had shown himself a thrusting and enterprising mounted infantry commander in South Africa. They had left Witley Camp on 11th September, and had received no experience in even a "nursery" sector of the front when, after assembling in the Saint-Omer area at Nielle-lès-Ardres and Nordausques, they were ordered forward into the battle on 25th September. Our ancestors used to reckon it took two years at least to make a soldier; although perhaps the enthusiasm and intelligence of the average volunteer of 1914 might have allowed a reduction of the period by a few months, yet staffs and higher formations cannot be improvised in much less; but here was an entirely new formation rushed into a most difficult and trying situation after no more than a year's existence. The Commander of the Forces was not blind to the risk. He had balanced the dangers and took the step advisedly, and reluctantly.

The assault on 25th September was carried out after a four day bombardment by six divisions across a country of coal-tips and miners' houses very like parts of County Durham. It was to have breached the German line. In places it nearly did; the German counter-attacks were repelled; and a timely application of a powerful reserve might have done the trick. But it was not until 1.20 p.m. that French released the 21st and 24th Divisions, which at that moment were several hours away (the 14th Battalion was at Nœux-les-Mines, the 15th at Houchin nearby), fatigued after long marches. They could not be ready in place until 11 a.m. on the 26th, and consequently the opportunity was already 24 hours old before it could be exploited.

Wet, tired and hungry, the 64th Brigade moved off in the rain after dark at 7.15. Along the congested road through Mazingarbe they passed Vermelles about an hour later, and at 9 they halted to prepare for the advance to the line, for the issue of bombs, tools, stores and so on, which took three hours. At midnight it moved on on a front of two companies in a line of companies in column, the 14th and 15th leading. At about 1 a.m. the old British front line was passed. The obstacles here were numerous, and in the dark every delay seemed interminable. At about 2 the old German front line was reached, and at about 3 the Brigade halted. It was to have followed the 63rd Brigade but it had lost contact. The 14th finally

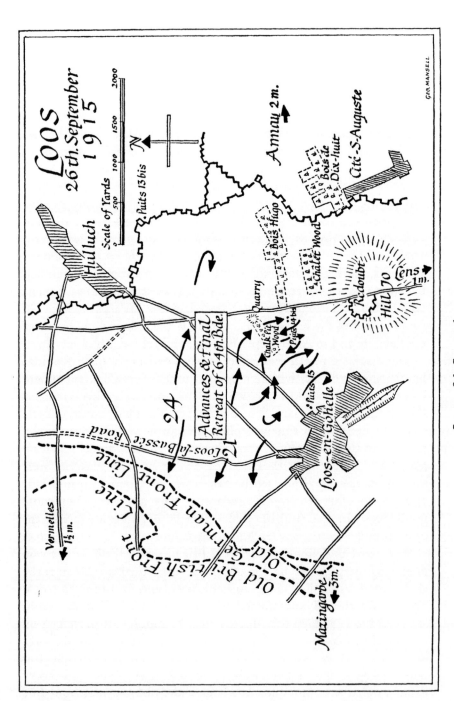

23. Loos, 26th September, 1915

occupied a deserted German battery position, while the 15th settled down about a quarter of a mile in rear, one company on the Loos / La Bassée road in the nothern outskirts of Loos. Soon after dawn on the 26th the 63rd Brigade was discovered well in advance on the Lens /Hulluch road north of Bois Hugo, and touch was gained with a K.O.Y.L.I. battalion of the 24th Division on the left. The first casualties from the German batteries occurred at this time.

The orders which reached the battalions at 7 a.m. gave Annay as the Division's final objective. First, however, a redoubt on the northern slope of Hill 70 had to be taken before the 63rd Brigade could undertake its attack on Puits No. 14-bis at 11 a.m. Alas, not only did the assault on Hill 70 fail but the Germans forestalled the 21st Division's advance by delivering a counter-attack on the 63rd Brigade, which lay in the Durhams' front. Before long the 63rd sent back for a battalion to reinforce its right in Chalkpit Wood. The 14th Battalion was selected and was soon advancing steadily; but at 10.30, when it was approaching the wood under a considerable shell and machine-gun fire, the left of the 63rd began to retire and, what was worse, apparently mistaking the Durham men in their great-coats for Germans, fired on them; and then, discovering their mistake, continued their backward movement, involving the 14th Battalion in it. It soon rallied and moved on again through the retiring men. It was met, however, by a heavy machine-gun fire, particularly enfilade fire from Bois Hugo, from which it lost in a few minutes Lieut.-Colonel Hamilton, the adjutant and the four company commanders. Forced back, it retired in good order behind the 64th Brigade.

At 11 a.m. the 24th Division on the left started its attack according to the original orders and carried the 63rd and 64th Brigades along with it. In this movement the Durham battalions—the 14th in front, the 15th in support—formed a link between the right of the 63rd and the troops advancing from Loos, but unfortunately, in keeping touch with the latter they got pulled round towards Hill 70 and suffered heavily from machine-guns hidden in Chalkpit Wood. Lieut.-Colonel Logan fell mortally wounded at the head of the 15th; the movement lost momentum; the men on the right retired; and by 12.30 the whole line was in retreat. The battalions rallied on the Loos /La Bassée road and at about 2 they came on again in a spontaneous advance in which the survivors joined with the 9th K.O.Y.L.I. of the 64th Brigade. But, once again, unsupported by the artillery, which had not been warned of the attempt, and smitten in flank by shrapnel and machine-gun fire, they had no chance of success. With the exhausted survivors of the two divisions—who had not been able to refill their water-bottles—they fell back, like sheep without a shepherd as one officer said, to the old German front line, where they were relieved at night.

More could not be expected from the 21st and 24th Divisions. An attack, made next day (the 27th) by the third division in reserve (the Guards), restored most of the ground won in that sector on the 25th; but there was no longer any question of a breach of the German line, let alone a break-through.

The casualties in the New Army divisions had amounted to about a third of their infantry strength. The 14th Battalion lost in killed and wounded 17 officers and 277 n.c.o.s and men; the 15th 12 officers and 450 n.c.o.s. and men. Hard things were said of these raw troops, not all of them deserved. As the brigadier of the 64th wrote in his report, " the spirited way in which the 14th D.L.I. returned to the attack three times, and the 15th D.L.I. twice, is in my opinion deserving of the highest commendation. That the attack failed was no fault of the men's or their training." Some stiffening, however, was felt to be necessary in the divisional organisation, and with that view the 1st East Yorkshire of the 18th Brigade (6th Division) was exchanged with the 14th Battalion in the 64th Brigade. From 28th November therefore the 14th shared the fortunes of its regular brothers-in-arms. Lieut.-Colonel G. F. Menzies, South Lancashire Regiment, a courtly, old-fashioned retired officer who had served in the Tirah Campaign and in China, took Colonel Hamilton's place in command. The 15th Battalion remained with the 64th Brigade for the rest of the war to be battered about more than any other Durham battalion. Its command was given to Lieut.-Colonel A. E. Fitzgerald, East Surrey Regiment, who had been in the South African Police at the time of the Jameson Raid.

§

By the end of 1915 the Regiment had six service battalions on the Western Front. The 10th were in the Salient, where they remained until 20th June 1916.

The 11th, which having, owing to the number of pitmen in its ranks, become the divisional pioneer battalion, had disembarked at Havre with the 20th Division on 20th July, occupied a section of the trenches near Laventie until it entered the Salient on 20th May 1916.

The 12th and 13th, 68th Brigade, 23rd Division, had disembarked at Boulogne on 26th August, and were in the trenches near Bois-Grenier and Armentières on the Lys. While there the 13th had the honour of winning the Regiment's first V.C. of the war, when at La Houssoye in the night of 4th November 1915 Private T. Kenny gallantly rescued his officer, who had been severely wounded during a patrol in No Man's Land.

The 14th, warmly welcomed to the 18th Brigade on 28th November at Herzeele by the 2nd Battalion, with whom a temporary exchange of officers and men was arranged, remained in the Salient until August 1916.

The 15th, after a temporary attachment to their brothers in the 50th Division near Armentières in October, stayed on the Lys until accompanying the 21st Division into the new British line on the Somme, which it entered opposite Fricourt on 2nd May.

Before the Somme offensive started on 1st July 1916 four more Durham service battalions had followed:

The 18th came to France in March 1916. They had left Fovant Camp on Salisbury Plain for Liverpool on 5th December 1915 and embarked with the rest of the 31st Division for Alexandria, where they landed on the 22nd. After two months spent in the Qântara sector of the Canal defences without any opportunity for active operations, they reimbarked on 5th March 1916 and were landed at Marseilles on the 11th. In a climate very different from the one they had left they entered the line first on taking over the trenches northwest of Beaumont-Hamel on 30th March.

The 19th (Bantams), who left Perham Down on 31st January and landed at Havre, first entered the line for instruction near Neuve-Chapelle on 29th February, and later moved to a quiet sector near Richebourg-Saint-Vaast and Festubert.

The 20th, which left Aldershot on 4th May and crossed by Havre, entered the line as the first battalion of the 41st Division to do so near Le Bizet on the Belgian border just north of Armentières on 29th May.

The 22nd (Pioneers), which left Catterick Bridge on 16th June and landed at Havre early on the 17th, were at Millencourt, two miles west of Albert.

The Somme was the first real test of the Durham service battalions. "The 10th had endured the horrors of Hooge but had never been called upon to attack; to the 14th and 15th Loos was the tragic memory of a single day; the other battalions entered the great offensive with the experience of nothing but trench warfare behind them."[14]

The Somme, 1916: Albert

The Battle of the Somme, which had been matured since February, the second in the series of Allied offensives from September 1915 to March 1918, was the first great undertaking of the British Army. In

[14]Captain Wilfrid Miles: *The Durham Forces in the Field, 1914-1918*, p. 45.

size and complexity it overshadowed everything previously attempted by a British army. The country here, open, rolling, unfenced downland not unlike Salisbury Plain, was very different from the earlier battlefields in the Watteringues, and the chalk subsoil favoured trenches and works of a more elaborate construction which contrasted advantageously with the muddy holes and breastworks of the northern sectors. In any case the whole business of trench warfare was by this time much more highly organised. Lieutenant Arnold Pumphrey,[15] a young solicitor in peace, commissioned in the 20th Battalion after serving in the ranks of the London Rifle Brigade at Second Ypres, described as follows the new state of affairs after his first experience of the Somme with the 20th: "How different from the trenches of old! Instead of mud everything is clean and dry and tidy and well protected. Instead of sleeping in mud I recline in an immense dug-out, and instead of the pitiful swapping of half-hours of sleep between weary duties I can, as second-in-command [of a company], have a fairly decent amount of rest and hot meals properly cooked and properly served for me; instead of dirt indescribable and a week's beard, one washes and shaves just as at home; and altogether the past is an evil memory only." "It appears," he writes after the first issue of steel helmets early in May, "that trench warfare is a succession of tryings-on of different headgear. In boring but not dangerous circumstances war, as I knew it before, *was* war. Now I doubt if it is really."

In so vast and lengthy a concern it is difficult to grasp properly the achievements of single battalions scattered over an enormous battlefield which has now lost most of its tactical significance with the disappearance of the trenches. The Somme offensive marks for us the beginning of that phase of the war in which the British Army for the first time had at its disposal both men and the fruits of the nation's industries in quantities that were little inferior and often superior to its opponents'. The Germans have disgustedly named this and subsequent offensives *Materialschlachten*, as being things suprahuman and therefore unfair; and certainly we are dealing with a moment in the history of warfare when the behaviour of humans in the struggle is subjected to scrutiny more as if it were a bar of metal in the hands of an analyst. On both sides divisions are anxiously watched until they are declared "exhausted" or "*abgekämpft*" and sent to quiet sectors where, employed in digging trenches, they may forget their losses and recruit their strength. On the Somme "three turns in the fighting line" was the general custom. We are immediately con-

---

[15]The youngest son of Thomas Edwin Pumphrey, J.P., of Mayfield, Sunderland, he had several brothers and cousins serving in the Regiment.

cerned with ten divisions (the 8th, 21st, 31st, 23rd, 35th, 14th, 20th, 6th, 41st and 50th), and with three turns of each in accomplishing the task of pushing the line to the top of the chalk ridge that runs from Ginchy to Thiepval.

The great assault started, after a week's heavy and continuous bombardment, at dawn on 1st July under a cloudlessly blue sky. Nineteen divisions, walking forward in "waves" at a hundred yard intervals, were to have advanced two miles to the line Montauban / Pozières /Serre. Two Durham battalions were involved in this first day's fighting.

The 15th Battalion (21st Division), under Lieut.-Colonel Fitz-gerald, which lay towards the right of the British line opposite Fricourt, climbed out of their trenches at about 7.30 a.m. with A and B Companies in front, and fought their way forward over the German front line system until, early in the afternoon, they came up against opposition in Shelter Wood. Here they succeeded in beating off a

24. The Somme Battles, July—November, 1916

sharp counter-attack (with the loss, however, of the commanding officer), and remained until relieved early the next morning. They had captured 200 prisoners and they had lost in killed and wounded 440 all ranks including seven officers killed. Progress on this flank was fairly good.

The other Durham battalion, the 18th (31st Division), under Lieut.-Colonel Bowes, lay in a sector where no progress was made at all. It was near the left of the British line, opposite the ruins of Serre, which dominated the British trenches, and occupied Maitland Trench, about 700 yards behind the front line. Here the German artillery and machine-gunners, put on the alert by the springing of the great Beaumont-Hamel mine at 7.20, opened to such effect among the infantry climbing out for the assault that try as they might they could not advance. Some of D Company got as far as Pendant Copse, but were wiped out. At 9.30 a.m. the three companies of the Battalion that had not taken part were ordered from the reserve trenches to repel any counter-attack that might develop after the disaster. None fortunately did, though the German counter-bombardment continued to obliterate their trenches throughout the six days and nights the Battalion occupied them. By 3rd July the strength of this fine battalion, containing some of the best of the manhood of the County, had been reduced to fourteen officers and 357 men. When assembled behind the line at Louvencourt at 5 a.m. on 5th July it had lost twelve officers and 58 *per cent.* of its n.c.o.s and men killed and wounded.

So much for the first day. The 12th Battalion (23rd Division) entered the battle on 6th July in Horseshoe and Triangle Trenches near La Boisselle on the right, and on the 7th supported an attack made by the 11th Northumberland Fusiliers on the flank of the 19th Division on Bailiff and Peake Woods, securing and consolidating ground which was found of great value when the 69th Brigade attacked Contalmaison on 10th July. Seven officers and 235 men had been killed or wounded. The 13th Battalion in the same brigade was involved in the same fight until relieved on the 11th.

Bazentin, 14th-16th July

The opening of the offensive, measured in terms of gains of ground and losses (which were tragically high), had been disappointing, none of the objectives having been reached. Some progress, however, had been made between the River Somme and Mametz, and here it was determined by continuing the battle on a smaller scale to break into the German second position. In an attack made at dawn on 14th July by four divisions on the Bazentin Ridge the object was attained and the German line was indeed for a moment breached.

It was the 110th Brigade which represented the 21st Division in this signal achievement, and the 15th Battalion (in the 64th Brigade) was not called upon until the evening of 15th July, when it relieved in the trenches in Bazentin-le-Petit Wood.

The 12th and 13th Battalions (in the 68th Brigade, which was placed at the disposal of the 34th Division, thrusting towards Pozières) was also not called upon until the 15th, when it relieved the 112th Brigade. At 8 p.m. on the 17th the 12th Battalion delivered an assault on the German trenches south of Pozières. Although one company succeeded in getting within bombing range the wire was found to be twenty yards thick and uncut by the artillery, and the enemy machine-gunners were on the alert, mowing down one company before it had gone seventy yards. The attack consequently failed with the loss of ten officers and 130 n.c.o.s and men.

The 19th "Bantam" Battalion, temporarily attached to the 9th Division, was also not called upon until after the original assault. It helped to consolidate the position reached at Longueval on 20th July, and on the 30th, although it played no more than a supporting role in the 106th Brigade's attack from Maltz Horn Farm to Guillemont, it lost twelve officers and 250 n.c.o.s and men.

Pozières, 23rd-31st July

After the success on the 14th a further series of operations was launched to drive the enemy from the main ridge. They developed into a number of individual fights with limited objectives which continued until the end of August, by which time almost the whole of the crest was in our hands.

Pozières itself was captured by the Australians on 23rd July. On the 26th the 23rd Division relieved the 1st to the south-east of the village. In an attack in the morning of the 28th a company of the 13th Battalion under Lieutenant G. S. Kaye-Butterworth succeeded in advancing the line by 200 yards on the right of Munster Alley before it was relieved that evening; a second attack made on its return to the line in the evening of 4th August carried it sixty yards farther; but a third effort, which became a bomb-fight in Munster Alley, could do no more. Thirteen officers and 126 n.c.o.s and men were lost. The 12th Battalion, though sharing in no assaults, lost at the same time one officer and 68 n.c.o.s and men.

Delville Wood

Delville Wood, which lies on the ridge, was the scene of a bitter

struggle involving five divisions in succession and lasting from the end
of July until the end of August. The 10th Battalion, in the 14th
Division, which was brought down into the Somme from the Arras
sector on 8th August, entered this scene of desolation on 13th August
and again, after a brief rest, on the 25th. Edge Trench, on the
northern verge of the wood, which the Battalion was to have occupied on relieving the 9th Rifle Brigade, was found to be still partly in
German hands. An attack to dislodge the enemy hastily organised by
Colonel Morant for 7.30 p.m. on 26th August—which had, however
to be postponed no less than three times for want of Stokes mortars
until 5 p.m. on the 27th—succeeded not only in seizing Edge Trench
but in pushing forward along the old German communication
trenches known as New Trench and Ale Alley. Though the post-
ponements aroused the displeasure of the Brigadier, Brig.-General
P. R. Wood, the Battalion's attack finally completed the month-long
fighting in Delville Wood, which at last was in our hands. The
Battalion's casualties before it was relieved in the night of the 28th
were six officers and 203 men.

Guillemont, 3rd-5th September

Guillemont, one of the fortified localities covering the third of the
enemy's defensive line running from Morval by Lesbœufs and Flers
to Martinpuich, had been the subject of four attacks between 23rd
July and 18th August, all of which had failed. One of the last of these
localities to fall, it was finally attacked on 3rd September by the 20th
Division, which had been brought south from the Salient at the end
of July. The 11th Durham Light Infantry, under Major G. Hayes
(formerly of the 1st Battalion), was the divisional pioneer battalion,
but it had already taken its turn of trench duty, and in the action that
ensued was to show that it could not only carry out its normal tasks,
such as the digging of the assembly trenches north of Guillemont for
the forthcoming attack, but fight as well.

The assault was carried out at noon on the 3rd from the north,
west and south of the village, and was planned to carry the line level
with the western verge of Wedge Wood, the objective of the 5th
Division on the 20th's right. Two companies of the 11th were in
divisional reserve in Bernafay Wood, but one company (A) was
attached to the 59th Brigade in the right attack, and another (D)
was attached to the second assaulting brigade, the 47th, on the left.
Guillemont was quickly overrun; and although the final objective
was not reached, largely owing to the failure of the flanking divisions
to take Leuze Wood on the right and Ginchy on the left, a line was
established on the road from Ginchy to Wedge Wood. It was a

surprisingly successful operation, which cost the Battalion apart from much hard work the loss of four officers and 87 men wounded.

Flers/Courcelette, 15th September

The assault of 1st July was the first; Pozières on the 14th was the second; and a third great effort had been maturing since the middle of August while the Army struggled for the top of the ridge in the succession of limited but expensive operations which have been described. The third, which takes its name from the two small villages of Flers and Courcelette, was to be delivered on a ten-mile front by "fresh forces and all available resources (including 'tanks') with the object of securing the enemy's last line of prepared defences between Morval and Le Sars with a view to opening the way for the cavalry". A strong force of all arms would then establish a flank position on the line Morval/Le Transloy/Bapaume and assist in rolling up the enemy defences to the north-west, which would simultaneously be attacked from the front. The plan involved penetrating not only the German Third Position, which, under construction when the offensive opened on 1st July, ran from Combles in front of Morval, Flers, Eaucourt l'Abbaye and Le Sars, but also a back line covering Lesbœufs and Gueudecourt, and another farther back still as yet only in process of digging. For this formidable undertaking twelve infantry divisions were assembled, not to mention a concentration of heavy and field artillery as yet unheard of in the British Army, nor the tanks, which, 42 of them, were to be used for the first time in war. Of the twelve divisions employed we are interested in seven.

On the right of the attack was the 6th Division, containing the 2nd and 14th Battalions, which had come south from the Salient at the end of July and had spent August on the Ancre opposite Beaumont-Hamel. Having entered the XIV Corps front on 8th September, it lay opposite a spur held by the enemy between Ginchy and Leuze Wood (ours since the 9th), on top of which he had constructed a four-sided system of trenches, 300 yards by 150, known to us as the Quadrilateral. This strong-point had already been the subject of several unsuccessful attacks before it was decided to include it in the general offensive of 15th September as a subsidiary operation. To facilitate the movement of the three tanks allotted to the 6th Division a gap of about 200 yards was left in the creeping barrage. This gap unfortunately coincided with the strongest point of the Quadrilateral; two tanks were "non-starters" and the third was driven back damaged; and the 16th Brigade's attack failed. The repulse of the Division appearing to prejudice the chances of a break-through, rumours of which on other fronts had reached the divisional commander, an attack by the 18th Brigade was planned for that night, to be carried out by the 2nd Durham Light Infantry and the 11th Essex. Alas, the 11th Essex, attacking from the south-east, lost direction in the dark, while the 2nd Battalion, from the north, having had insufficient time for reconnaissance, bombed down a trench successfully only to discover that it did not lead to the Quadrilateral. However, a third attempt was made by the 1st West Yorkshire and the 14th Durham Light Infantry at 5.30 a.m. on 18th September. Under both a stationary and a creeping barrage they at last overcame this redoubtable work, which, held by the 21st Bavarians, had cost the Division over 3500 casualties, and carried the line forward to within striking distance of Morval and Lesbœufs. The 2nd Battalion, under Major A. E. Irvine (a regular officer who, joining the battalion from the adjutancy of the 4th Battalion after Hooge, had succeeded Lieut.-Colonel H. R. Cumming on 14th September) had lost four[16] officers and 30 n.c.o.s and men killed, and six[16] officers and 99 n.c.o.s and men wounded, and 34 missing; the 14th four officers and 31 n.c.o.s and men killed, and five officers and 161 n.c.o.s and men wounded.

The 20th Division did not enter the battle until relieving the Guards Division after their initial success near Ginchy on the night of the 16th, and consequently the 11th Battalion was involved only in the unexciting but dangerous work of preparing new trenches for the next advance.

The 14th Division, however, on the left of the Guards, after expelling the enemy from a pocket east of Delville Wood, had achieved most encouraging progress east of Flers until held up on Bulls Road where it met the road from Gueudecourt. The 43rd Brigade was in reserve on the 15th, but it was brought up at midnight, and at dawn on the 16th the men of the 10th Battalion could look down the slope to Gueudecourt over the Gird and Gird Support Trenches which were to acquire such a malignant reputation. Aeroplane reconnaissance had reported that the trenches, which lay half-way between the Army's third and fourth objectives, did not appear to be held by the enemy. An advance beyond Gueudecourt was accordingly ordered for 9.25 that morning to be undertaken by the 6th Somerset Light Infantry and the 10th Battalion. So soon, however, as the Durhams moved forward they were assailed by that bane of trench-warfare, enfilade machine-gun fire. They went on, but when only a

---

[16]Killed: Captains E. Hughes and B. C. Baty (23rd Battalion) and 2/Lieutenants R. J. Meikle and L. Birtles. Wounded: Captain J. M. Garland and 2/ Lieutenants L. A. Hartshorn (4th Battalion), A. R. Watson, J. Dudley (17th Battalion), J. Crawford and H. F. W. Chamberlin.

quarter of a mile had been gained the "survivors had to seek cover in shell-holes and stay there". A second attack at 6.55 p.m. organised by Colonel Morant (who was himself wounded) from a hundred men at Battalion headquarters under the only officers remaining, the adjutant and the bombing-officer, did not get beyond the survivors of the morning, and all fell back after dark to Bulls Road. The Battalion was relieved next morning, having lost five officers killed and eleven wounded, and 381 killed, wounded and missing in the ranks.

It was in the second attack that Sergeant J. Donnelly, a native of Benwell and one of the original volunteers of August 1914, was sent out to the right to establish the position of the Somersets. Mistaking a German outpost for them in the dark he called out, "Are you the Somersets?" and immediately received a bullet in the arm, but eventually delivered his message and carried back the reply, an action for which he was rewarded with the D.C.M. He was detained convalescent with the 16th Battalion at Rugeley, but he left them without leave and made his way back to the Battalion without any ticket or orders of any sort, declaring he "could not serve with a bloody conscript battalion." It was a twelvemonth before the court of enquiry proceedings reached Colonel Morant regarding a deserter of the name of Donnelly said to be deficient of a great deal of kit. By that time he was a company-sergeant-major, with the M.M. and a bar to the D.C.M., to which he later, when commissioned, added the M.C.

The 41st Division attacked on the left of the 14th towards Flers. The 20th Battalion, probably the best in the Division, had come down from the Ploegsteert sector and entered the line near Longueval on 11th September. It was not involved in that dramatic entry into Flers, "without precedent in war," when the one surviving tank lurched up the main street of the village followed by parties of cheering infantry; but after *lassitudo certaminis* had succeeded the original impulse of the attack, the 20th, under Major J. W. Hills, M.P. for Durham, was brought up in the evening to the old front line and the next evening advanced through a heavy German barrage to the far side of Flers, where for the next two days they consolidated their position. "The Boche," Captain A. Pumphrey wrote home on the 20th, "will, I think, take some time to forget our activities of the past few days."

The 64th Brigade (21st Division) was placed under the command of the 41st Division in the evening of the 15th. The 15th Durham Light Infantry, now under the command of Lieut.-Colonel R. W. Pedley, Royal West Kent, started for the line from Pommiers Redoubt at 2 a.m. on the 16th to make a fresh attack at dawn on the

Gird Trenches, but, having lost direction in the dark, was not in position until 5.30 a.m. Late in starting and in ignorance of the whereabouts both of their own troops and of the enemy, they suffered heavily before they had even passed through the forward troops of the 41st Division. Yet they pressed on until within seventy yards of the Gird Trench, where they could do no more. Any incautious movement attracted fire; their flares were too damp to ignite; and the British barrage descended indifferently on them and the enemy. When the Battalion was withdrawn after dusk it was barely 200 strong. It had lost six officers killed and thirteen wounded or missing, and 419 killed, wounded and missing in the ranks. These, the heaviest losses in the brigade, were evidence of the determination with which the Battalion had gone forward.

Farther to the left, playing a limited but important part in the offensive, lay the III Corps (47th, 50th and 15th Divisions), whose objectives on 15th September were the trenches on the reverse slope of the ridge linking the Flers defences with Martinpuich. The 50th, whose first experience on the Somme this was, advanced in the centre. On its right was the 47th (containing temporarily the 13th Battalion), confronted by the formidable obstacle of High Wood, which held it up now as it had held up every attempt for some weeks. The delay allowed an enfilade fire to interfere with the 50th's attack, which was delivered notwithstanding by the 149th and 150th Brigades (the 1/5th Battalion in a supporting role). Nevertheless, despite heavy losses, they reached their third objective by 10 a.m., after the 150th had been reinforced by the 8th Battalion, and by 1 p.m., High Wood having at last fallen to the 47th, the front was consolidated on the Starfish Line. In the evening at 9.40 the remaining battalions of the 151st Brigade advanced to take Prue Trench, east of Crescent Alley. The 1/5th Border Regiment[17] failed to arrive in time, but the 1/6th and 1/9th Durham Light Infantry (Lieut.-Colonels J. W. Jeffreys and R. B. Bradford) "went forward gamely in the face of accurate machine-gun fire which caused them heavy casualties". Small parties of both entered Prue Trench but were all killed or wounded, and those in the Starfish Line, unable to hold it against a counter-attack, had to fall back.

The next day the 151st Brigade with the 1/5th renewed the attack on Prue Trench but failed again. A third attempt made at dawn on the 17th was only partially successful, and further desperate attacks on the 18th failed to carry it. It was not until the 21st that the enemy evacuated this deadly stretch of line, the scene of so many

[17]Which had taken the place of the 1/7th in the Brigade on its becoming pioneers.

bombing-attacks and the grave of so many fine men. By then the Durham battalions had been relieved. When the 1/5th was brought out of the line on the 19th four officers and 88 men only answered to their names. The 1/9th had lost 44 *per cent.* of its strength. The whole 151st Brigade had lost 43 officers and 903 n.c.o.s and men.

Morval, Lesbœufs, Gueudecourt

Rain had fallen steadily since the night of 17th September, turning the battlefield into a morass which connoisseurs of mud were later to regard as even worse than that encountered in the Salient in the autumn of 1917. The offensive was nevertheless prosecuted to gain the objectives not attained in the previous week's fighting: Morval and Lesbœufs on the right, and Gueudecourt in the centre, an advance of about 1200 to 1500 yards. Zero hour was fixed at 12.35 p.m. on 25th September.

On the right of the advance the 5th, 6th and Guards Divisions rapidly overcame the enemy in Morval and Lesbœufs. The 2nd Battalion in the 18th Brigade, facing their old opponents in the Salient, the 52nd Reserve Division, took their first objective, and two companies of the 14th Battalion and the 1st West Yorkshire carried on to the second. It was, says the 6th Divisional history, "one of the most successful battles of the Somme, thanks to good weather and observation, a carefully arranged creeping barrage and a sound preliminary bombardment."[18]

On the left of these divisions the 21st Division was to have captured Gueudecourt, taking the Gird Trenches and then advancing to the far side of the village. The 15th Battalion was in reserve to the 64th Brigade, in the first day's advance, which succeeded only in winning a footing in Gird Trench. But the next morning, 26th September, following an attack by the bombing parties of the 7th Leicester, whose path was cleared for them by a single tank, the Battalion went forward from Gird Trench at 9, reached and passed Gird Support, and, during the afternoon pressed on to the east of Gueudecourt until relieved after dark.

Scattered but occasionally savage fighting continued on the days after these important successes. The enemy had been badly shaken, and though he had contrived to withdraw his artillery intact he was forced back on a line of hastily improvised trenches. On 27th September Thiepval, on the left of the front, which had resisted since 1st July, was secured, a capture which favoured an enlargement of the frontage of yet a further offensive.

[18]Losses were so light that the 2nd Battalion Diary does not even condescend to state them.

The Battles of the Le Transloy Ridge

A wet autumn had set in, and the continuation of the offensive was carried on towards Bapaume in ever deteriorating conditions. It opened on 1st October with an attempt to straighten the left of the front by the capture of Eaucourt l'Abbaye and that part of the German Third Line known as the Flers Line as far as Le Sars.

The 50th Division lay at the left centre of this front and attacked towards Le Sars with the 151st Brigade, consisting of the 1/6th Durham Light Infantry, the 1/5th Northumberland Fusiliers and a composite battalion made up from the 1/5th Border Regiment and the 1/8th Durham Light Infantry. As seen from above by an air observer the attack looked magnificent. "The first troops," he reported, "to extend from the forming-up trenches appeared to be the 50th Division, who were seen to spread out from the sap-heads and forming-up trenches and close up under the barrage apparently some fifty yards away from it. They appeared to capture their objective very rapidly and with practically no losses while crossing the open." It was not quite so easy as it appeared. Owing to the failure of the division on its right the 1/6th Battalion, the right-hand battalion, became exposed to enfilade machine-gun fire which, before zero hour, deprived it of its commanding officer, Major G. E. Wilkinson; and when it went over at 3.15 p.m. it immediately lost so heavily as to make its situation critical. Seeing this, Lieut.-Colonel R. B. Bradford, commanding the 1/9th, which was in support, asked and got permission to take command of both the 6th and the 9th, which together he managed so ably under a very heavy fire that, with a renewed effort, both battalions had secured Flers Trench by 9.30 in the evening, and beat off a counter-attack. During the night they consolidated their capture by barricading Flers Support. For this inspired act of leadership, by which he secured the Brigade's right flank, Lieut.-Colonel Bradford, only 24 and still but a substantive lieutenant, earned a well deserved award of the Victoria Cross. The 151st Brigade was relieved by the 68th during the night of 2nd October, the 12th Battalion relieving the 1/5th Northumberland Fusiliers and the 13th relieving the 1/8th Durhams.

These two battalions, now reduced to 50 *per cent.* of their strength, continued their predecessors' achievements with the capture of Le Sars on 7th October. Assisted by a tank, which reached the front line a minute after the infantry had advanced at 1.45 p.m., the 12th Battalion in stubborn fighting cleared the Tangle (a nest of machine-guns). But they were held up at a sunken road until the arrival of the

13th Battalion, which largely owing to the energetic leadership of a young New Army officer, Captain D. H. Clarke, M.C., fell upon the enemy and overcame all resistance. The defence collapsed and the Durham patrols advanced beyond the village, even outrunning the barrage. "It was," according to the *Official History*, "the striking success of the day." It was certainly the great day of the 12th and 13th Battalions.

Not all the objectives, however, were carried on the 7th, and after the reliefs had been carried out the offensive was resumed, somewhat optimistically, on the 12th. On the front to the east of Gueudecourt where the 6th Division had relieved the 20th, an attack made over heavy ground for the line of trenches north-west from Le Transloy encountered stiff resistance from fresh troops. One attack was repulsed with heavy loss. On the extreme left flank of the Division the 14th Battalion, now under the powerful command of Major J. B. Rosher, M.C., (formerly one of Colonel Morant's more promising New Army officers) who had succeeded to the rather over-courteous régime of Colonel Menzies, managed to enter Rainbow Trench and bombed up the Beaulencourt road to Shine Trench, but could go no farther. A resumption of the attack on 15th October, made at dawn instead of the afternoon, failed to occupy Mild and Cloudy Trenches, and an attack of the 2nd Battalion's from Needle Trench at the same time was equally unsuccessful.[19] The 6th Division was finally taken out of the battle on 20th October, giving place to the 8th, of which the 22nd Battalion, as divisional pioneers, succeeded to the disagreeable legacy.

Ancre Heights

By this time "conditions in and behind the battle front were so bad as to make mere existence a severe trial of body and spirit. . . . The infantry, sometimes wet to the skin and almost exhausted before zero hour, were often condemned to struggle painfully forward through the mud under heavy fire against objectives vaguely defined and difficult of recognition." Yet the manner in which they kept up their spirits was deserving of all praise, and indeed goes beyond belief. Captain A. Pumphrey of the 20th Battalion, returned "from where I was when I was where I don't much like being," was able at this time to say his men were "splendidly fit and wonderfully steady and cool" and that "a cheerful spirit of triumph seems to

[19]The Battalion's casualties between the 14th and 16th were: three officers (2/Lieutenants H. F. W. Chamberlin, C. Green and H. Barclay) and 19 n.c.o.s and men killed; five officers (2/Lieutenants T. Veitch, A Dunn, J. Crawford, C. W. Heppleton and L. Haggie) and 95 n.c.o.s and men wounded, and 28 missing.

carry everyone along"; and no doubt the other battalions were animated by a similar spirit. A professional French soldier who saw our armies on the Somme describes them as lacking *savoir-faire*, but he gives them every credit for possessing "a certain spiritual strength in which they said, 'Oh well, failed today: it'll be all right to-morrow'."

The offensive was continued both astride the Ancre and on the right. On 30th October a limited attack was projected with the object of eliminating the German sailents north-east of Eaucourt l'Abbaye and north of Gueudecourt. The former salient enclosed the Butte de Warlencourt, a barrow or tumulus about forty feet high, which in that rolling downland afforded an important point of vantage to whoever held it. The attack was put into execution on 5th November after a wet night succeeded by a gale, which was still blowing strong when the 151st Brigade, which had spent the night in trenches filled with cold mud up to the thighs, with great difficulty clambered out to its last battle on the Somme. The objectives of the 1/6th and 1/8th Battalions were the Gird and Gird Support Trenches,[20] while the 1/9th was to capture the Butte and the quarry just west of it. Several men of the 6th were drowned before the assault started. The going was heavy and progress slow. The advance of the 8th was hampered by the partial failure of the Australians on their right. The 6th, at least on their left, managed to establish themselves in Gird Trench. The 9th, under Lieut.-Colonel Bradford, advanced on the left in fine style and carried all its objectives by 10.30 a.m. But at about 3.30 in the afternoon the enemy, who had already made several unsuccessful counter-attacks, came on again. Watchers from the other Durham trenches saw the solitary figure of a 9th Battalion man pause for a moment on the summit of the Butte and then pass down the other side out of sight into a desperate mêlée that continued all afternoon and far into the night. The Gird and Butte changed hands more than once. But shortly after midnight the enemy's attacks at last prevailed. The weary survivors of the Brigade were forced out of all the captured trenches and made their way back to their own.

In the Regiment's last fight on the Somme it was pitted against the German 1st Guard Reserve Division, a worthy foe, and though it was a disappointing close to the offensive in which so much had been accomplished, there was no dishonour in having failed against

---

[20]It should be explained that the Gird Trenches were very lengthy, extending along the whole length of the front from Gueudecourt almost to the Ancre, and that only the portion near Gueudecourt on the right was taken in the attack of 25th Setember.

such opponents. The Brigade as a whole lost 38 officers and 929 n.c.o.s and men, of whom:

the 1/6th lost eleven officers killed, wounded and missing, 34 n.c.o.s and men killed, 114 wounded and 111 missing;

the 1/8th lost nine officers killed, wounded and missing, 37 n.c.o.s and men killed, 100 wounded and 83 missing;

and the 1/9th lost seventeen officers killed, wounded and missing, 30 n.c.o.s and men killed, 250 wounded and 140 missing.

§

By that time most of the Durham battalions had long since left the Somme.

The 10th had been finally relieved on 18th September to take over a sector near Arras;

the 12th and 13th, which had left the Somme for the Armentières sector on 11th August, returned for the Le Sars operations on 10th September, but finally departed for the Salient on 15th October;

the 2nd and 14th left the Somme on 23rd October for the La Bassée sector;

the 15th had left early in October for the same destination;

the 18th had left on 7th July for Neuve-Chapelle, though they returned for a spell in front of Hébuterne early in January 1917;

the 19th left the Somme late in August and went into trenches near Arras in September; and

the 20th Wearsiders moved away on 13th October for Flanders, and took over trenches near Sint Eloois (Saint-Eloi) on the 24th.

Only the 11th and 22nd remained. The 11th (Pioneers) were kept at work until 1st November, though the 20th Division was withdrawn to rest early in October, and remained near the battlefield;

and the 22nd (Pioneers), entrusted with strenuous work on communications across the desolation, was involved in the 8th Division's attack at Bouchavesnes on 4th March, 1917.

The German Retreat to the Hindenburg Line

Already on 5th September Ludendorff had given instructions for the preparation of a system of rearward defences running from Armentières in the north to Réthel in the south. They were a tacit recognition of the hammering the Germans had taken on the Somme. Construction was begun at the end of September and continued until March 1917 in almost peaceful circumstances with the employment of 65,000 workmen, civil as well as military.[21] The Germans distinguished four systems: the *Wotanstellung*, from Armentières, past Lille, by Hénin-Liétard and Quéant to Sailly-Saillisel; the *Siegfriedstellung*, from Arras, by Quéant, Havrincourt, Saint-Quentin, La Fère, Condé-sur-Aisne and Vauxaillon to Cerny-en-Laonnais; the *Hundingstellung*, from Péronne, by Ham, La Fère, Crécy-sur-Serre, Chivres and Château-Porcien to Réthel; and the *Aisnestellung*, between Berry-au-Bac and Château-Porcien. By the British Army, who did not appreciate its significance until February, the whole gigantic undertaking, 143 km. long, was known as the Hindenburg Line, except for the *Wotanstellung*, which we knew as the Quéant Switch. For some time the German Command, having concluded for a number of reasons that throughout 1917 their western armies should remain on the defensive, hesitated between standing on their present line and withdrawing to the new Hindenburg Position as the commander opposite the British Armies repeatedly urged. Their minds were made up for them by the Fifth Army's operation on the Ancre in January and February, which caused a German withdrawal of three miles on a 15-mile frontage. On 4th February 1917 the Emperor signed the order for the prepared retreat to the Hindenburg Line. The country surrendered was systematically "scorched"— trees felled, wells polluted, houses booby-trapped—and an area of some 65 miles by 20 skilfully and malignantly devastated. On 14th March, two days before they should have, the withdrawals started.

Fortunately the Arras offensive, which had been planned to take place in April to synchronise with the French offensive on the Chemin des Dames, was scarcely affected, Arras lying just beyond the northern limit of the retirements. But, comprising as it did the capture of Vimy Ridge and an advance from Arras towards Cambrai, it involved the penetration not only of the existing front line defences but also of the new Hindenburg Line, the so called Wancourt/Feuchy Switch and the Drocourt/Quéant Switch besides.

Arras, and the First Battle of the Scarpe,
9th-12th April 1917

Of the fourteen divisions engaged in the first assault on that Easter

---

[21]The size and elaborate nature of the works came as a revelation to the Army when they were first encountered. The remarks of Colonel Morant, whose battalion penetrated part of them on 9th April, reveal the awe, almost, with which our soldiers examined their skilful construction. "The mystery is, Who does the work? Our brigadier [Wood] insists the infantry do the work—to make out that we do little. I do not believe that the infantry do it. If so they must be far more skilled and harder workers than ours. Our defences are childish compared to theirs." It was the brigadier who was wrong.

Monday two, the 14th and 21st, contained Durham battalions, and a third, the 50th, was in reserve.

The 21st lay on the right of the assault, near Hénin-sur-Cojeul, where least progress was made. In spite of the four days' bombardment, which was conducted with great skill and power, the wire on this front had not been properly cut. The 15th Battalion (64th Brigade) under Major J. Falvey Beyts advanced at 3.54 p.m. on 9th April from wet assembly trenches, two companies up, two in support, quickly occupying the first enemy line a thousand yards in their front with few casualties. The supporting companies, however, after passing through were unable to get through the wire of the second line, and suffered moreover from machine-gun fire from the flanks where the other battalions of the Brigade had been held up. They tried to bomb their way up, but unsuccessfully. They repeated the attempt in vain the next morning and had to content themselves with the first line, which they barricaded so effectively as to beat off all counter-attacks. Their losses in the two days amounted to eight officers and 241 n.c.o.s and men killed and wounded.

Farther to the left, by Beaurains, the 10th Battalion (43rd Brigade) shared in the more spectacular advance made that day. The task was particularly formidable inasmuch as the 14th Division lay opposite the point where the old German support system was joined by the Hindenburg System. The Battalion attacked at 7.34 in the morning. "I must say," Colonel Morant wrote afterwards, "it is a change. We gave them a terrific bombardment before the original attack and they were fairly cowed and sick of it."

> "Just as it was getting light the first thing was a solemn procession of half-a-dozen tanks right down the slope towards the enemy in full view of them. But they did nothing to them and they sat in our line till zero . . . They crossed our trench in their stride. When the time came for the infantry to advance the tanks did so too but behind the infantry—anyhow I think they did quite well for a time and then came to a standstill . . . We took the first trench [Nice Trench] quite easily, though we had some of our best men killed over it, including poor Stewart, the late adjutant . . . As soon as I saw the trench was taken—which I recognised by the prisoners bundling out of it—I got out of my trench and went forward. I was supposed to stop at the first trench taken, but seeing the Battalion wandering on I went after it. They had to go on about a thousand yards further, over all sorts of blown-in trenches which one knew by heart from the map . . . but so mangled as to be difficult to recognise. Boches kept appearing out of dug-outs, and after being searched they only wanted to know the direction back—which they really knew of course—and they would dash off at once approaching any of us with their hands up and calling out 'Kamerad' terrified. Lots of course were put on to

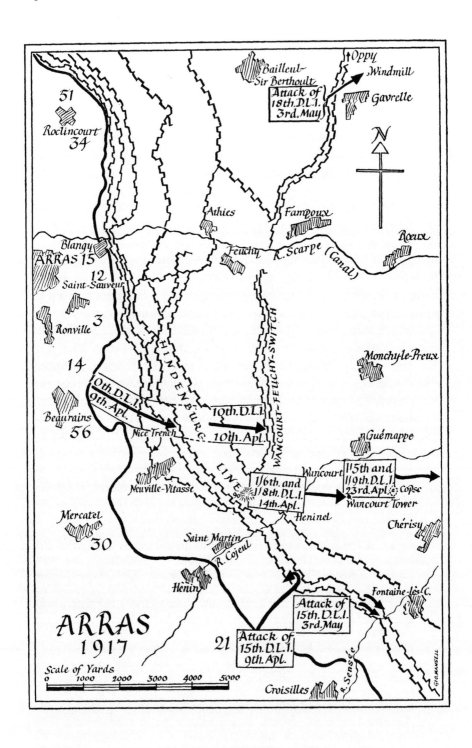

51
Roclincourt
34

Bailleul–
Sir Berthoult

↑Oppy
Windmill

Attack of
18th. D.L.I.
3rd. May

Gavrelle

N

Athies

Fampoux

Roeux

Blangy
ARRAS 15
12
Saint-Sauveur

Feuchy

R. Scarpe (Canal)

Ronville 3

14

Monchy-le-Preux

HINDENBURG

WANCOURT-FEUCHY-SWITCH

10th. D.L.I.
9th. Apl.

Beaurains
56

10th. D.L.I.
10th. Apl.

Guémappe

Nice Trench

LINE

Wancourt

1/5th and
1/9th. D.L.I.
23rd. Apl.   Copse

Neuville-Vitasse

1/6th. and
1/8th. D.L.I.
14th. Apl.

Wancourt Tower

Chérisy

Mercatel
30

Heninel

Saint Martin
R. Cojeul

Hénin

Fontaine-lès-C.

ARRAS
1917

21

Attack of
15th. D.L.I.
3rd. May

Attack of
15th. D.L.I.
9th. Apl.

R. Sensée

Scale of Yards
0   1000   2000   3000   4000   5000

Croisilles

25. Arras, April—May, 1917

stretcher-bearing. One party came past me, one smoking a cigar—I knocked it out of his hand and asked him what the h— he meant by it—he looked quite alarmed! When we had got to our furthest point we were ordered to go to [the Hindenburg Line] . . . I discovered quite a lot of Boches holding the same trench we were in about 800 yards off, so I got two machine-guns and two Lewis guns and got them onto them. It was very exciting, as we looked right down along the trench and could seen them dodging our bullets. They eventually vacated the trench . . . In the afternoon it came on to snow, and the men spent a wretched night in the open, as also did the officers.

"Next day [at 11.50 a.m.] we had to do another attack, another 300 yards or more [to the Wancourt/Feuchy Line]. That went off very well. Then, when it was over the cavalry appeared! I leapt out of the trench with excitement at a chance of seeing what would happen. Well, they sent out a patrol or two to nearly as far as we had got!—after asking us all about the situation (we were always taught to ask the cavalry all about it before we did anything, but now the cavalry ask the infantry!) Shortly after, two riderless horses came back, and there was a good deal of 'come-hup-ping' and hauling at the horses to get them over the trenches . . . They went forward to behind the crest of the hill we had taken. Then, when we were just starting home thinking the battle was over, suddenly the Boche started to shell our trench where there were still some [cavalry] crossing. This was the unpleasantest shelling I have had. It went on for half an hour, long after the cavalry had gone, all at this one place. We lay tight at the bottom of the trench cursing the cavalry like anything . . ."

Some of the exhilaration felt by the Army is communicated in Colonel Morant's words, normally so matter-of-fact. The Hindenburg Line had been breached and the Wancourt/Feuchy Switch taken. Although by the time the 43rd Brigade was relieved in the night of the 10th a counter-attack on the Battalion's right had driven it back two hundred yards, the net advance of 4000 yards was the most spectacular one made by the Army with the possible exception of Cambrai later in the year. Casualties, measured by Somme standards, had been light: the 10th Battalion had lost seven officers and some 350 n.c.o.s and men killed and wounded. Less than justice was done—probably owing to the Brigadier's prejudice—to what was undoubtedly the Battalion's greatest achievement in the war and a magnificent success by any standard.

Wancourt Ridge, 13-15th April

The weather continued bad; the enemy reinforced his fighting line; and progress made during the next days was slow, methodical and costly. The 50th Division relieved the 14th on the 13th while it was in the act of surrounding Wancourt and crossing the dry bed of the Cojeul. At 4 a.m. on 14th April at very short notice the 151st Brigade was ordered to advance to protect the left flank of the 56th Division in an attack on Chérisy. The capture of Guémappe had been considered a necessary preliminary, but the 29th Division, newly arrived on the 50th's left, was not ready to undertake it, and the 151st's attack started under many misapprehensions. It was executed by the 1/6th and 1/8th Battalions and the 1/5th Border Regiment, but it became confused with the 56th Division's troops at Wancourt Tower, and although a party of the 6th Battalion with great gallantry reached a point some sixty yards east of the tower none were ever seen again. The day ended with only the capture of a portion of Wancourt Ridge at a cost of sixteen officers and 213 n.c.o.s. and men killed, wounded and missing.

The Second Battle of the Scarpe,
23rd-24th April

There was a pause in the operations until 23rd April while a combined offensive was organised with a view to reducing special centres of resistance. On the 23rd the 50th Division, between the 30th and 15th, was given the task of attacking three of the German lines east of Wancourt and north-west of Vis-en-Artois. The first objective was carried, but before the advance to the second was begun the enemy delivered a counter-attack which drove it back to the starting line although it had been reinforced by the battalions in support, of which the 1/5th was one. For a final effort in the evening two more battalions were added, one of them the 1/9th, the only two battalions that consisted of more than "small parties of weary men". This time the steadiness and determination of the advance were too much for the enemy. With surprisingly small losses they succeeded in reaching the Blue Line, a 1600 yards' advance on a 500 yards frontage. It was a very satisfactory conclusion to the Territorial battalions' tour of duty in this sector.

The Third Battle of the Scarpe,
3rd-4th May

Nivelle's great offensive on the Chemin des Dames having obviously failed, the intention of the British Command was to obtain a good defensive line on the Arras front before transferring the offensive to Flanders. This involved the 21st Division in an attack across the Sensée to seize Fontaine-lès-Croisilles and take 500 yards of the Hindenburg Line. The attack was made at 3.45 a.m. and was over in 24 hours. The 15th Battalion (64th Brigade, 21st Division), which since the previous November had carried the replica of the banner of St Cuthbert that is now in the Museum, was ordered to bomb down the Hindenburg defences west of Fontaine, but on going forward encountered a heavy barrage which caused many casualties. The company on the left was held up by unbroken wire; even with the assistance of a tank, which ran shooting down the trench, little headway was made; and an attack by the supporting companies failed with over a hundred casualties. It was in these disappointing circumstances, however, that on 6th May a stretcher-bearer of the Battalion, Private Michael Heaviside, a miner of 37 from Craghead who had served in the South African War, won the Regiment's third V.C. of the war for succouring and bringing back after dark a wounded man who had lain in the open for four days and three nights.

Farther north at Gavrelle the 31st Division attacked simultaneously towards Oppy Wood. The 18th Battalion, in its first large-scale offensive since its unfortunate experience at Serre on 1st July 1916, was called up to reinforce the 93rd Brigade's advance, which had encountered serious opposition. In a counter-attack the Germans succeeded in seizing Gavrelle windmill, from which they could enfilade the whole advance, but they were driven out by C Company of the Battalion under Captain H. E. Hitchin, D.S.O., in the last of three bitterly contested attempts. The attack as a whole, however, failed as lamentably as that to the south without any material gains.

Indeed, the Battle of Arras was closing, and fighting was continued only to conceal from the enemy that the weight of the offensive was being transferred elsewhere.

Hill 70, 15th-21st April

Before passing on to the two other great offensives of the summer of 1917, Messines and Third Ypres, there remain to be mentioned the spring attacks carried out in the Lens coalfields by the 6th Division. Here the enemy had carried out minor withdrawals as they had farther south, the British infantry pressing so hard as to accelerate somewhat his departure. His resistance started to stiffen on 15th April when his hold upon Hill 70 was threatened. An attack by the 14th Battalion (Major J. B. Rosher, M.C.), on the 21st disposed of a strong machine-gun nest on the Double Crassier railway which had held up the right, and the next day a combined attack by the 14th and the 11th Essex secured the whole of the objective. Unfortunately the division on the right had been unable to get forward and the Battalion was eventually machine-gunned out of its capture and compelled to relinquish Nash Alley after suffering the loss of ten officers and 231 n.c.o.s and men killed and wounded. The five months' tour of duty of the 2nd and 14th Battalions in this sector, which lasted until 25th July, was a continuous succession of raids and counter-raids, and although the fighting had no influence on the larger issues fought out elsewhere, the Regiment's honour of "Hill 70" was hard won.

Messines, 7th-14th June

The failure of the French armies, shipping losses and the collapse of the Russian front left the British Command with no real alternative but the resumption of the offensive, which took place, first, at Messines (7th to 14th June) and then at Ypres (31st July to 10th November). Messines, with its tremendous artillery bombardment and its unprecedented explosion of land-mines containing a million pounds of high explosive, was a triumph of careful organisation, in which the infantry had little more to do than go forward and take possession. The bombardment began on 21st May; it became intense on the 31st; and at 3.10 a.m. on 7th June, the mines were sprung in an explosion that was clearly felt in London. Immediately after, nine divisions advanced and by the end of the day had captured all their objectives.

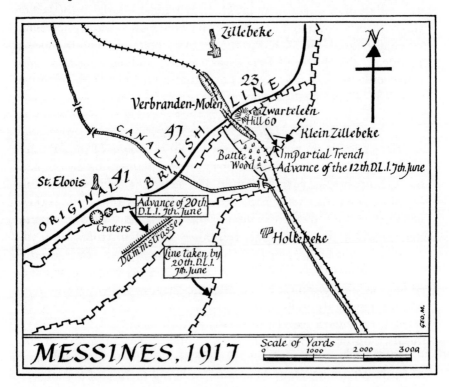

26. Messines, June, 1917

The 20th Battalion (123rd Brigade, 41st Division), which, under the command of Lieut.-Colonel P. W. North, Royal Berkshire, lay near the St Eloois mine, pressed forward before the shock had passed away. Within a hour the Dammstrasse, a level drive honeycombed with dug-outs, was captured, and the line was consolidated. Losses during the 7th and 8th were only eight killed and 13 wounded.

The 23rd Division, containing the 12th and 13th Battalions, under Major R. Tyndall (1st Battalion) and Major J. A. L. Downey, was on the extreme left of the British attack. Its objective was only 300 yards distant and was captured in twenty minutes. The 12th, at first in reserve, captured Impartial Trench, beyond the second objective, with the loss of only 15 killed and wounded. A party which got as far as Klein Zillebeke had to be withdrawn, however, and a heavy shell-fire in the evening caused so many casualties that the Battalion was relieved in the night by the 13th. Heavy retaliation from the enemy artillery followed, but the line held fast.

Thus at last, after two years, the enemy was removed from the dominating southern face of the Salient, with a swiftness and completeness unmatched by any previous major operation.

Third Ypres: Pilckem Ridge

The main British operation, known as the "Northern Operation," to which Messines was but an essential curtain-raiser, comprised the capture of the Ypres Ridge, then a landing on the Channel coast, and finally a general advance against Ghent, the right flank moving along the Lys and the left guarded by the neutral Dutch territory at the mouth of the Scheldt. The Ypres offensive was entrusted to the dynamic Gough in preference to the methodical Plumer, fresh from his master stroke of Messines, and six precious weeks of summer were taken up in altering arrangements to suit the methods of the new commander. The enemy was given time and warning not only to organise his defence in depth and to dispose nearby his special counter-attack divisions (*Eingreif-Divisionen*), whose absence had so contributed to our early successes at Arras, but also to bring up reinforcements as he pleased from the southern fronts, where clearly nothing was to be expected from the French armies. It was the last day of July before the infantry assault began.

The first day started with an assault by nine divisions against an objective 6000 yards distant. The 20th Battalion (Lieut.-Colonel North), in the 41st Division, had occupied since 25th July a position on the right of the road from Zwarteleen to Klein Zillebeke, a little forward of the ground won by the 12th Battalion on 7th June. The task of the Division on the 31st was to advance astride the Ypres /

Comines Canal and protect the right flank of the main attack by capturing Hollebeke. At 3.50 a.m. the buglers of the Battalion sounded the charge and the Wearsiders went forward, C and D Companies leading. The first German position was taken against a strong resistance, which increased as the Battalion entered the zone fortified by concrete pill-boxes held by determined snipers and machine-gunners of the 6th Bavarian Division, who "were not the rabbits the special correspondents seem chiefly to hear of". When the Battalion started to dig in the enemy poured out of his pill-boxes. They were repelled, but owing to a shortage of bombs the "mopping up" so essential was only partially successful. It began to rain, and at about 4 in the afternoon a determined counter-attack was launched. The Wearsiders inflicted heavy losses with their musketry, and though the enemy made some progress on the right, where the neighbouring battalions had not been so successful, the artillery-fire opened in response to the Battalion's messages dispersed him and enabled it to restore the line. Another counter-attack made at dusk the next day was smashed completely in the same way before the Battalion was relieved and taken back to Elzenwal on the Ypres/Kemmel road. Colonel North, badly wounded, was succeeded by Major R. C. Smith, a regular officer from the 1st Battalion. Eight officers and 431 in the ranks had fallen.

Menin Road, 22nd-25th August

Heavy rains delayed a resumption of the advance, which had been disappointing, and it was not until 16th August that a second attack was launched. The 10th Battalion, the next to enter the battle, had come up to Zillebeke Bund on the 20th. At 2 a.m. on the 22nd it was ordered forward through Sanctuary Wood to occupy a support position for the attack on Inverness Copse, which it reached though suffering 60 casualties on the way. The attack itself was carried out by two other battalions of the 43rd Brigade, who, however, unable to reach their objective, had before evening called up all the 10th's companies. No progress was made on the 23rd. Early on the 24th the Battalion headquarters at Clapham Junction (on the Menin Road) were turned out to repel a counter-attack delivered by parties of flame-throwers and light machine-gunners. It was broken up by artillery though not before the forward companies, fighting hard, had been forced to withdraw. In spite of the very stout resistance maintained by Captain Jerwood, one of the Battalion's best officers, by nightfall the only part of Inverness Copse remaining in British hands was that behind Jasper Avenue and Jasper Lane. Losses were very heavy. Before the Battalion was relieved early on the 25th and brought back to Ouderdom it had lost fourteen of its twenty officers and 355 out of its 688 n.c.o.s and men. (C.S.M. Donnelly, it should be added, received a bar to his D.C.M. for his conduct in this action.)

Menin Road Ridge, 20th-24th September

The loss of Inverness Copse and the failure to make progress on the Gheluvelt plateau caused severe disappointment to Haig. The principal role in the offensive was restored to Plumer, who asked for three weeks in which to make his preparations. It was not therefore until 20th September that Plumer's methodical advance could be executed. It was planned in three steps, each consisting of three bounds of 1500 yards carried out at six days' interval. The assaults were to be made on narrow fronts, no division attacking on a frontage of more than a thousand yards. The attack of 20th September was led by the 41st, 23rd and two Australian divisions.

The 20th Battalion entered the line near Bodmin Copse, but did not take part in the first assault, which carried the first and the second objectives, to the so called Blue Line, but not the third. At midday, however, the Battalion was ordered up to the Blue Line, and managed by fighting patrols sent out after dusk to establish contact with the brigade on the right and the battalion on the left. At 7 next morning, the 21st, it was ordered to take part in an attack on the centre of the Green Line. It advanced accordingly at 9.8 a.m. against stiff and unbroken resistance, which caused many casualties, among them Captain Arnold Pumphrey, D.S.O., who was killed rushing a machine-gun nest near the Tower Hamlets. It dug in about 200 yards ahead, broke a counter-attack in the afternoon and managed to maintain its position despite a heavy box-barrage put down later. When they were brought out the next night (22nd) the Wearsiders' casualties, seventeen officers and 303 n.c.o.s and men, were the heaviest in the Brigade.

Advancing on the same day immediately north of the 20th Battalion was the 68th Brigade of the 23rd Division. The 12th Battalion (Major Tyndall) was in reserve; but the 13th,[22] under Captain D. H. Clarke, M.C., a New Army officer who had given proof of his military qualities on many previous occasions, had the task of passing through the two battalions making the first assault after they had reached the Blue Line and then of attacking the Green Line, on the

[22]Both battalions had been in the Klein Zillebeke sector on 7th July, when 2/Lieutenant Frederick Youens of the 13th won the Regiment's fourth, and the Battalion's second, V.C. of the war during a German early morning raid. He was receiving medical attention in a dug-out after a patrol, and he rushed out without shirt or jacket to rally his men. One bomb thrown at him he hurled back, but a second exploded in his hands, mortally wounding him. The raid failed.

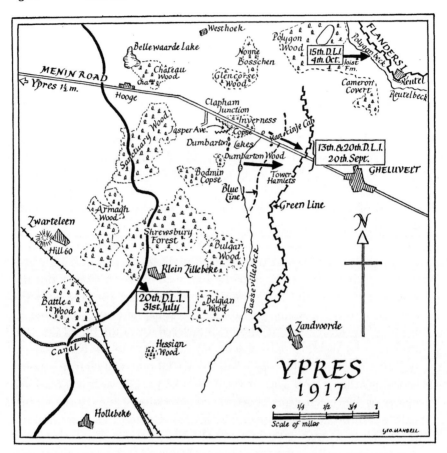

27. Third Ypres, July—October, 1917

forward slope of the Gheluvelt plateau astride the Menin Road. It
was a very difficult undertaking. It was 8.30 before the Battalion
reached the Blue Line and punctually and in perfect order advanced
to the Green. They encountered some machine-gun fire from cellars
in the ruined houses on the Menin Road, but these nests were
quickly eliminated in savage fighting. By 11 a.m. the Battalion was
consolidating on the Green Line although unable at first to establish
contact with the 41st Division on their right. The first of the inevitable counter-attacks, delivered at 3 in the afternoon, was beaten off;
a stronger one early next morning from one of the *Eingreif-Divisionen*
met the same fate; and two more attempts were repelled with the
assistance of a platoon posted well out north of the road to take the
assailants in enfilade. A timely barrage dispersed a fifth late on the
same day. The Battalion was relieved on the 22nd after suffering the
loss of five officers and 289 n.c.o.s and men. A word of commenda-

tion from the artillery supporting them, who told them "all were full of the 13th D.L.I." and that they hoped they went off "thinking half so much of the 33rd Divisional Artillery as they do of you," is a valuable testimonial of their conduct.

The 12th, though in reserve, became involved in heavy fighting in support of the 11th Northumberland Fusiliers, and before they were relieved on the 24th had lost nine officers and 140 n.c.o.s and men.

Broodseinde, 4th October

The second of Plumer's "steps" is represented by the Battle of Polygon Wood, 26th September, in which the Durham battalions had no important share, although the 23rd Division was brought up to take the place of the 33rd Division, which had been forced back by a counter-attack on the 27th.

In the third "step," the Battle of Broodseinde—4th October, "one of the black days of the German army"—which put Plumer's Army on the crest of the Ypres Ridge, the 21st Division was the centre division of the X Corps' attack on the southern flank by Polygon Wood. The 15th Battalion was one of the 64th Brigade battalions selected for the assault.

The attack went on in heavy rain at 6 a.m. on 4th October against Reutel. The Battalion had already suffered so severely the previous day from German heavies searching the whole area as far as Hooge that it had been reorganised as two companies. These encountered fierce fighting, with further casualties, before they reached Joist Farm, only 300 yards in front of their trenches; but they managed to carry the farm and cross the Polygonbeek and dug themselves in south of the farm where, during the remainder of that day and the whole of the 5th, they successfully maintained their ground against at least three counter-attacks. Colonel Falvey Beyts[23] was killed and his adjutant wounded, and so attenuated was the Battalion by the time it was taken out in the night of the 5th that the command was held by a subaltern, Lieutenant John Sedgewick. Twenty officers and 410 n.c.o.s and men had fallen. Nevertheless they had made an important contribution to the action which gave the Army possession of a dominant position overlooking the Reutel valley, which completed the security of the southern flank of the battle-front.

[23]The third commanding officer of the 15th Battalion to be killed in action. The Battalion was unlucky in its commanding officers. Apart from Lieut.-Colonel Logan, mortally wounded at Loos, Lieut.-Colonel Fitzgerald, killed on the Somme, and Lieut.-Colonel Falvey Beyts, killed on this occasion, it later lost Lieut.-Colonel Festing, killed on 21st March 1918, and Lieut.-Colonel Holroyd-Smyth, mortally wounded on 18th September 1918.

Second Passchendale, 26th October

Already conditions in the Salient had become what later generations know only too well from photographs, and still the ultimate
objectives of the "Northern Operation" were far distant. Only the
crest of the Ypres Ridge had been won. Should the offensive be
prosecuted to Passchendale? It was a question that is debated to this
day. For better or for worse the offensive was continued.

This time the only Durham battalions involved in the assault were
those in the 50th Division, brought up, as it had been on the Somme,
when ceaseless gun-fire had churned the battlefield into a morass and
winter was setting in. Little progress had been made in the first
battle of Passchendale (12th October), but it was hoped that a second
attack would gain possession of the Passchendale/Westroozebeke
Ridge. The 50th Division, lying on the northern face of the Salient,
took no part in the assault of 26th October which eventually won the
Ridge itself, but was ordered to share in the Fifth Army's attack
towards Houthulst Forest. The attack, carried out by the 149th
Brigade, was unsuccessful and made no progress at all. However,
the Durham battalions of the Division remained in this sector until
9th November, some of them, the 6th particularly, sustaining heavy
casualties.

That was the last assault delivered in Third Ypres. Yet there were
other Durham battalions which by their presence on that turbulent
battlefield helped to earn the Regiment the hard won honour of
Ypres 1917, where holding the line while new advances were
prepared was scarcely less of an ordeal than the advance itself. The
19th (35th Division), for instance, which had long ceased to be
Bantam, lost, in the two days from 2nd to 4th November when at
Koekuit and Weidendreft, no fewer than sixteen officers (including
the commanding officer and the adjutant) and 125 in the ranks
without being actually engaged. The 10th also held a sector at
Passchendale in December which Colonel Morant, who never
laboured his discomforts, described as "perhaps the *most* poisonous
sector we had *ever* been in". Some pioneer battalions like the 22nd in
the 8th Division (whose presence at the Division's assault on 16th
August is responsible for the battle-honour *Langemarck*) and the
11th Battalion in the 20th did work much appreciated at the time
and suffered without sharing in glory.

Three battalions, the 12th, 13th and 20th, were withdrawn from
the Salient before the offensive closed, when five divisions were transferred to the Italian front on 26th October to help repair the disaster
at Caporetto. The 20th returned in time to share in the March

retreat; the 13th came back in September 1918; but the 12th remained in Italy for the remainder of the war.

Cambrai, 20th November/4th December

The battle which lifted for a dramatic instant the heavy shade of trench warfare and afforded a glimpse, all too brief, of green unshelled country, had been pondered by the British Command as an alternative to the "Northern Operation" since the failure of Nivelle's spring offensive. The German front line opposite Cambrai was the Hindenburg Position itself, which at this point formed a slight salient where it turned from a north-west course (from the canalised Scheldt at Banteux) to a northward course (towards Mœuvres). Though the Hindenburg Position was some 4000 yards deep, consisting of trenches strongly wired and purposely constructed so wide as to be impassable by tanks, and though it was backed by another line on the far bank of the Scheldt, the British Command nevertheless determined: to breach it by a *coup-de-main* in the neck between the Canal du Nord and the Scheldt valley; to pass cavalry through the breach to isolate Cambrai and seize the crossings of the Sensée beyond, while infantry and tanks cleared Bourlon Ridge, which overlooked Cambrai; and, finally, to exploit the success by driving north-east to Valenciennes, so cutting off all the enemy troops between Havrincourt and the Sensée. For the first time tanks employed in mass occupied an integral tactical part in an operation. A further element of surprise was introduced in the omission of a long preliminary bombardment, the artillery finding their targets by "silent" registration from the map.

Five infantry divisions made the initial assault, of which two (the 20th and the 6th) contained Durham battalions. The 11th Battalion did not take an important share until the later stages. But the 2nd and 14th of the 6th Division, which attacked on a two brigade front between Villers-Plouich and Beaucamp, were engaged from the beginning.

The task allotted to the 18th Brigade, containing both the 2nd Battalion, now under the command of Major H. R. McCullagh, a 1st Battalion officer who had joined the 2nd in January, and the 14th, still under Lieut.-Colonel Rosher, was to pass through the 71st Brigade (on the Division's left) on its attaining the second objective a thousand yards beyond Ribécourt, and secure the third objective a mile beyond on the Prémy Chapel Ridge. It was then to throw out a defence flank towards Flesquières to favour the further advance of the 51st Highland Division on its left and to secure the flank of the 29th Division on its right. The 29th Division would then converge to

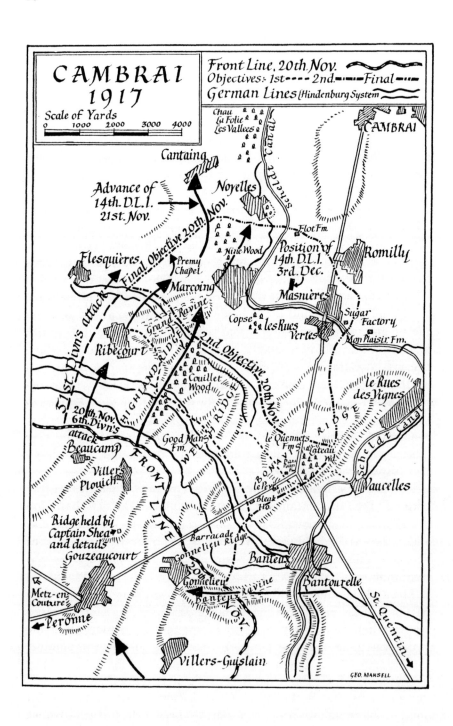

28. Cambrai, 20th November—4th December, 1917

seize the crossings over the canalised Scheldt at Marcoing and occupy the high ground at Rumilly on the far bank.

The attack went in at 6.10 in the morning of 20th November. The Division's operations were attended with complete success. The 2nd Battalion, which had moved forward from south of Beaucamp in artillery formation at 6.20 and had encountered the Hindenburg Position soon after 10, passed through the 71st Brigade at 11.15 towards its final objective according to plan. After advancing for about a mile it came under machine-gun fire from the left, but the shooting was very poor and came from some distance off. Soon, not far short of its objective, it reached the trenches of the Hindenburg Support Line, where a German battery of five field guns opened upon it at point-blank range, pinning the left company (C) to the trench. Captain E. Fawcett, a 3rd Battalion officer commanding the Company, after sending a party to reconnoitre the battery, organised two parties, one under himself, one under Captain G. S. Fillingham, a young officer commissioned from Sandhurst in August 1915, which, working round the flanks of the battery, gallantly charged it and at the second attempt took it at the point of the bayonet while the guns were still firing. The Battalion then resumed the advance to the Prémy Ridge, where it consolidated, at the same time capturing an abandoned howitzer battery. At the cost of 23 casualties it had taken eleven guns and thirteen prisoners as well as reaching its objective— an altogether novel experience.

The 14th had meanwhile reached the Prémy Ridge with the loss of only seven men wounded. The next day, 21st November, because the 51st Division had failed to take Cantaing the Battalion was ordered to send two companies to fill a gap in that direction. Suddenly, soon after midday thirteen tanks came roaring over the Prémy Ridge and made for Cantaing from the south-east. They were joined almost spontaneously by a squadron of the Bays and one of the 14th's companies, to whom Colonel Rosher, seizing his opportunity, on his own initiative added two further companies under his personal command. The enemy hotly resisted but, pressed unmercifully, gave way, and the 14th entered Cantaing in triumph soon after, taking four hundred prisoners. Ably handled, the Battalion had lost but few casualties in this decisive and prompt action, for which Colonel Rosher received a well merited D.S.O.

The astonishing success won by the Third Army in those first days, which carried it across the Scheldt and made the church bells ring in London, was followed by bitter disappointment. The Germans managed to mass reinforcements against both flanks of the new salient, and on 30th November launched a powerful counterstroke which not only regained much of the ground lost but also penetrated the original British position to the south.

Both Durham battalions of the 6th Division occupied part of the line that held firm. But in the south, Gouzeaucourt, which the Germans reached at about 9 a.m. on the 30th, contained the headquarters and one company (C) of the 11th Battalion (20th Division pioneers), under the command of Lieut.-Colonel G. Hayes, as well as the 18th Brigade's transport under the battalions' respective quartermasters. Colonel Hayes, whose first warning of the attack was the sight of a mass of horses galloping from Villers-Guislain towards Fins, immediately led his party out to Hill 135, about 700 yards south-west of the village, from which he could see the Germans advancing in perfect order entirely unopposed. Joined by a field-company of Sappers, he withdrew to an old British trench astride the main road west of Gouzeaucourt, where the transport details of the 18th Brigade under the senior quartermaster, Captain J. P. L. Shea of the 2nd Battalion, enabled him to extend his left flank beyond the Gouzeaucourt-Metz road.[24] That stout old soldier, the first man up Vaalkrans, the last surviving officer of the battalion of September 1914, after packing the vehicles and sending them to the rear in an orderly fashion, had organised a party of every available man, shoemakers, tailors, and the like; and together this odd assemblage succeeded by their very indifferent musketry in checking every attempt made by the enemy to come farther until it was relieved by the Guards at noon. Unfortunately in the scrimmage Captain Shea fell mortally wounded and died on 1st December. "A braver man," the regimental historian has said, "never existed, nor loved his regiment more. He never missed an opportunity of doing anything for the Battalion, nor for a single man of the Battalion if he could help him." He was succeeded by R.S.M. J. Watson, R.S.M. of the Battalion since September 1914.

Odd though it may seem the apex of the salient, the "bridgehead" made by the 29th Division on the far bank of the Scheldt at Masnières, was one of the last points to give way before the enemy counterattack. Here the 14th Battalion and 1st Shropshire Light Infantry had been brought up from in front of Villers-Plouich to relieve part of the 29th during the night of 2nd December. The 14th lay with its right on the canalised river and its left touching the Shropshire battalion. Soon after 10 in the morning of the 3rd

[24]A marked map among the regimental records places the "ridge held by Captain Shea and details" about half a mile north-east of Gouzeaucourt. The *Official History*, however, combines Hayes' stand with "Joey Shea's battle" south and south-west of Gouzeaucourt.

a heavy barrage came down, and an infantry attack developed against the right flank of the Battalion and the troops on the left bank

Like most units the 14th had thrown up a number of n.c.o.s and officers who always came to the fore when there was fighting, and in this precarious situation there was ample opportunity for such natural leaders. One, Lieutenant A. Rothfield, Austrian by nationality and Jewish by race, had already won the M.C. and earned a bar to his decoration on this occasion for walking in the open along the parapet during the bombardment to reorganize his company and for remaining with his men until he collapsed from his wounds. Another was Captain A. M. Lascelles, M.C., brother of 2 /Lieuteant Reginald Lascelles of the Regiment, who had been drowned in India in 1904. A natural fighter, he had left Uppingham after some escapade and had served as a trooper with the Cape Mounted Rifles throughout the Boer War and in German South-West and, leaving the Union only to return home and join up, had found his way from the 3rd Battalion to the 14th in time for the Somme. He was one of those happy souls who enjoyed their war. If there was a raid to be done or a prisoner to be taken for identification Lascelles was the man, asking only for a couple of glasses of beer to be ready for him on his return. On this occasion, in command of A Company in a feeble trench on the right of the position, although wounded he delivered a sharp counter-attack with twelve hastily collected men, drove the enemy from the trench, was captured, escaped, and received two further wounds. Meanwhile Colonel Rosher, in spite of having beaten off a fresh attack at midday, had been forced to give ground on his left and bring his men back to a reserve trench, fighting, however, every step of the retreat so successfully that in a momentary lull he was able to withdraw unmolested across the canal by the railway-bridge. Even then the Battalion had not shot its bolt. Returning to the attack at 4 p.m. by means of a barge bridge, it recovered the reserve trench and maintained itself until 10.15 in the evening, when it received orders to withdraw again. Before dawn it had reached a position in the old Hindenburg Support line north-east of Ribécourt. Out of a fighting strength of 450 the Battalion had lost fourteen officers and 262 n.c.o.s and men. Colonel Rosher received a bar to his new D.S.O., Captain Lascelles the Victoria Cross.

During the next few days the Army withdrew to the "Flesquières Line". Almost as much ground had been lost at Gouzeaucourt as had been gained on 20th November. It was a bitterly disappointing conclusion to a most promising conception. But the Regiment bears no honour more richly deserved by their three battalions concerned than "Cambrai 1917", which has no stain upon it.[25]

The Reorganisation of the Army,
February 1918

The period of more than two years in which the British Army was able to enjoy (if that is the word) the opportunity for an unbroken succession of offensives was now at an end. The Russian front had collapsed, releasing for employment on the Western Front all the German formations hitherto tied there. In January 1917 the enemy had 124 divisions in the West; in December the figure had risen to 162; and in March 1918 it was 194 and still rising as others were transferred from east to west. At the same time, in January 1918 the British Army took over from the French a new line forty-two miles in length stretching from about Gouzeaucourt to the River Oise, which was entrusted to the Fifth Army under General Gough. To correspond with the enlarged commitment no accession of reinforcements was forthcoming. On the contrary, by March the infantry of the Expeditionary Force threatened to fall below establishment to the extent of some 40 *per cent.*, a deficiency the government of the day was not prepared to make good. The number of infantry battalions in each division was accordingly reduced from twelve to nine to form brigades of three, instead of four, battalions. The surplus were drafted to bring up to strength the others that were retained.

It was an unhappy start to the new year. The reductions were carried out on orders from the Secretary of State without reference to the battalions' efficiency. Two fine Durham battalions went, the 10th and the 14th. The 14th was 43 officers and 839 n.c.o.s and men strong when it was disbanded on 1st February. Colonel Rosher went to command the Machine-Gun Battalion of the 6th Division. Most, however, went to other Durham battalions—seven officers and 143 men, for instance, to the 18th, ten officers and 200 men to the 19th, and seven officers and 150 men to the 22nd. The 10th, which Colonel Morant had left in December on promotion to brigadier after three years of painstaking command, was disbanded on 3rd February near

---

[25]Cambrai, alas, was the grave of Brig.-General R. B. Bradford, V.C., M.C., who had commanded the 186th Brigade of the 62nd Division in the battle with conspicuous success. He was killed when his headquarters near Lock 7 on the Canal du Nord were shelled on 30th November. He had left the 2nd Battalion on 2nd May 1915 to become adjutant of the 1/9th, then its commanding officer and, finally, the commander of the 186th Brigade, to which he was appointed on 10th November 1917 at the age of 25. An appreciation by his divisional commander of his quite exceptional qualities is printed in the 62nd's *History* by Everard Wyrall (London, 1924), Vol. I, p. 120n.

Vendeuil. No drafts had been received since the fighting in Inverness Copse, but though it was under-strength its commanding officer reckoned it "at the top of its form". Its divisional commander, Sir Victor Couper, a good judge and presumably less partial, who had had "The Shinies" under his command since its formation at Woking and had seen it at Ypres in 1915, in the Somme at Delville Wood, at Arras, Wancourt, Inverness Copse and Passchendale, wrote to say "for the purposes of regimental history" that "in the trenches there were no harder workers; they were never surprised by the Germans; and, as far as I know, no man of this battalion was ever made prisoner. When they were disbanded I lost one of the finest battalions in my division." Major Ward, Cornwall Light Infantry, who had commanded it for six weeks, confessed he left it with the profoundest regret. There was, he wrote, to Morant, "such a wonderful spirit in the battalion and the men were splendid. I love the little ditty they used to sing on the march, 'We are the lads from Durham we are.'[26] It seemed to pull them together so well when they sang it, specially at the end of a long march. One can easily understand the pride you took in them." Officers and men went in different directions. Captain Jerwood, one of the best of Morant's officers, went to command the 6th Somerset Light Infantry, with whom he was killed. The rest were distributed between the 2nd, 5th, 6th, 7th, 8th and 15th Battalions.

Apart from the disbandments other old associations were broken up by the reorganisation. In the 50th Division the 1/5th Battalion was transferred on 12th February from the 150th to the 151st Brigade, and the 1/9th, a first-class fighting battalion, converted into pioneers, was taken out of the division altogether and attached to the 62nd as divisional pioneers. Similarly the 19th (formerly Bantams) was transferred from the 106th to the 104th Brigade, but in the same division, the 35th; and the 20th was transferred from the 123rd Brigade to the 124th, 41st Division, on 17th March.

On the eve of the battle the Durham battalions were distributed as follows:

the 2nd was north of Boursies, on the Cambrai/Bapaume road, the only Durham battalion actually in the line when the storm broke;

---

[26]"We are the lads from Durham, we are,
    We have just arrived in town.
    We make a show wherever we go,
    We're in the front line, we're in the know,
    We know all the pretty girls from Ypres (Shields, etc.)
        Up to Durham, to Durham,
    So wake up and shake up the dear old town—
    We are the lads from Durham, we are, left, right, left . . ."

the 1/5th, 1/6th, 1/7th and 1/8th were with the 50th Division in Fifth Army reserve well behind the line at Marcelcave;

the 1/9th was with the 62nd Division, First Army, near Arleux, north of Arras;

the 11th (20th Division, Fifth Army) was at work on the Ham/ Noyon railway;

the 12th and 13th were still in Italy;

the 15th (64th Brigade, 21st Division) lay behind the Fifth Army line at Liéramont, near Epéhy;

the 18th was in billets at Bajus and Frévillers in First Army reserve behind Lens;

the 19th were resting behind the Salient at Elverdinge;

the 20th was in camp at Warluzel, north of Doullens, having only just returned from the Italian front and reached Doullens on 7th March; and

the 22nd had just carried out some important works under Lieut.-Colonel Morgan in the Salient and was resting at Poperinge before rejoining the 8th Division in the south.

The Somme, 1918: Saint-Quentin, Bapaume, Rosières and Arras, 21st March–1st April

By the middle of March the Germans, profiting from the collapse of the Russian front, had massed a total of seventy-one divisions against the line between Croisilles, south of Arras, and the Oise, which was held by twenty-six British divisions of the Third and Fifth Armies. On the weakest part of that new southern sector, where the position was held not by a continuous line but according to the "blob" system of defended localities, the twelve divisions of the Fifth Army were pitted against forty-three German. The stronger, Third Army, sector in the north, held by fourteen divisions, was attacked by nineteen. The enemy also possessed a superiority of 5:2 in heavy artillery, which was handled by the redoubtable Colonel Bruchmüller, a master of the gunner's art.

This *Kaiserschlacht*, designed to end the war in one gigantic convulsion, was conducted in two phases. The first offensive was directed towards Péronne and Amiens; and although the German armies attacked astride the Somme, the *Schwerpunkt* was aimed north of the river, on which the armies were to form a defensive flank and then wheel half-right to the north-west. Then, Haig's reserves having been drawn south, a second offensive was directed towards Hazebrouck in the north. The first gave rise to a series of actions over a front of over forty miles which are known under the generic title of the Second Battle of the Somme. The second, fought along a front of twelve

miles from Armentières to the La Bassée Canal, bears the generic
name of the Battle of the Lys.

The only Durham battalion actually in the line when the storm
broke on the foggy morning of 21st March was the 2nd, which, after
a short rest at Berles-au-Bois, held a naturally strong part of the
Third Army line in the Morchies sector, north of the Cambrai /
Bapaume road. Since 5th February it had been commanded by
Major D. L. Brereton, a gentle 1st Battalion officer who by ancestry
and upbringing had clerical and educational connections that afterwards took him into the Church. B and D Companies were in the
front line, each with a platoon in support; A and C were in reserve.
Almost immediately after the Battalion had stood to at 5 that morning the enemy, not unexpectedly, opened a heavy gas bombardment,
principally on the reserve line. Increasing in intensity at 7 and
cunningly directed upon points where the telephone cables crossed,
it cut all communication—except by pigeon and runner—between
companies and battalions to right and left as well as with brigade
headquarters behind. Such a concentration of hostile artillery had
not been experienced before. It continued until 9, keeping the men's
gas-masks on and causing heavy casualties. It then developed into
a creeping barrage under which the infantry advanced. Practically
no frontal attack was made against the front line, but the enemy broke
through on either flank and advanced up the valleys between the
reserve and the supports. B and D Companies were surprised and
surrounded, and soon after 11 o'clock, having suffered crippling
casualties, had no alternative but to surrender. The reserve meanwhile had succeeded in holding the enemy up as he advanced across
the open. Eventually, by bombing up Leech Avenue, a communication trench, he forced his way right up to battalion headquarters at
the junction of Leech Avenue and Winter Reserve Trench. But a
counter-attack under 2 /Lieutenant H. McBain, the bombing officer,
whose father and grandfather had both given honourable service to
the Battalion in former days, pushed him back along Leech Avenue
and established a block about 150 yards up. By this gallant effort
four enemy machine-guns and several boxes of ammunition were
captured which were used to good effect by the reserve companies.
A German killed at the very entrance of the headquarter dug-out
was found to belong to the 3rd Regiment of the Prussian Guard, and
a map taken from an officer showed the objective to be Achiet-le-
Grand, fifteen miles to the rear.

The terrific bombardment had by now subsided; but parties of the
enemy could be seen marching in fours accompanied by field-
batteries which dropped into action amongst them. Clearly the flank

at Lagnicourt had been broken through. At 3 p.m. orders were received to prepare to withdraw. At 4 the post at the block had to fall back fighting, and the 1st West Yorkshire on the right reported at the same time that they were almost surrounded. Both flanks had evidently gone. On the other hand the wire remained intact and all the enemy's efforts across the open were successfully checked. At 4.30 what remained of the West Yorkshire side-stepped into the battalion sector. Though the 11th Essex had come up to cover the withdrawal, any movement in daylight was considered impossible, and, when at 6.50, with dusk still an hour away, the supply of bombs ran out, there seemed no alternative but to stay and fight it out. Then, mercifully, at about 7.15 the mist of the morning fell again, presenting an opportunity which Major Brereton seized to order every man back on his own. Although the machine-guns opened on them as they emerged and although the infantry followed them at about 300 yards distance, most managed to reach the Corps Line in front of Morchies over a mile in rear. All next day heavy fighting continued. At dusk on the 22nd the 41st Division came up to relieve the weary survivors of this magnificent resistance, who were taken out and, on 25th March, sent north behind the Salient.

The forward companies had orders to hold on to the last and none were seen again. In the rear companies not a man left the trenches until Major Brereton gave the order. There was Private Sawyer, a pre-war soldier, who stood on the firestep outside the headquarters dug-out, coolly adjusting his sights as he steadily aimed and fired throughout almost the whole 14-hours' engagement, in a kind of final farewell salute from the old army. Out of thirty officers and 639 n.c.o.s and men in the trenches on 21st March only Major Brereton, Lieutenant Spencer and 58 men were present in the evening of the 22nd. The fate of the others cannot be established with certainty. Twelve officers[27] and 52 n.c.o.s and men were certainly killed; six officers and 286 n.c.o.s and men were wounded; the rest were missing, including many who were killed or wounded or who died in captivity. No finer example of dogged devotion to duty was ever given by British infantry, and it is pleasing to record that the battle

[27]Killed: Captains E. H. Gilpin (adjutant) and M. P. Griffith-Jones, Lieutenant D. Osborne, 2/Lieutenants G. Cates, J. E. Eccles, R. A. Appleton, K. E. Alexander, W. T. H. Davis, W. Henderson, A. Black, R. M. Hogg and H. E. Jebb.
Wounded: Captain G. S. Fillingham, Lieutenants W. Rice and N. A. Pearson, 2/Lieutenants N. O. Mackinnon, H. McBain and B. Reynolds.
Missing: Captains G. Sopwith (second-in-command), H. A. Pickering, and E. Fawcett, Lieutenant M. M. Hutchinson (wounded), 2/Lieutenants H. H. Carmichael, J. J. Lunn and E. W. Tuffs.

was not so vast that this feat of arms failed to leave its mark on the outcome.

The 41st Division had been brought down in a hurry from their tranquil quarters around Doullens and by 2 in the morning of 22nd March the 20th Battalion, under Major A. V. A. Gayer (Middlesex), was in the so called Green Line north-east of Beugnâtre to take over the fight from the weary 6th Division. Theirs started at 8 a.m. on the 23rd, when a fierce bombardment was followed by a mass attack of infantry. The position was well sited and enabled the Wearsiders to pour in a well directed rifle and Lewis-gun fire upon the enemy, who advanced with great determination no fewer than six times until his dead were piled high in front of the wire. In the evening the line was still intact, and casualties in the Battalion amounted to only three officers and 83 n.c.o.s and men. The next day, however, the line on the right gave and the Division had to retire to conform. Before the 24th was out the Battalion had withdrawn to Favreuil, north of Bapaume, and the next day the retreat continued, first to Sapignies, then to Achiet-le-Grand and finally to Gomiecourt. Early on the 26th it was in the old German front line of 1st July 1916. Constant shelling took a steady toll of the weary men of the Battalion, which, by the time the German offensive petered out on this front on 29th March, had lost eleven officers and 320 n.c.o.s and men.

Rather to the north (or left) of the sector fought for by the 6th and 41st Divisions, the 31st had been brought up from reserve to Ervillers on the Green Line to relieve the 34th in the night of 22nd March. The 18th Battalion, under Lieut.-Colonel H. F. G. Carter, K.O.Y.L.I., experienced its first critical attack early on the 24th after retiring to a position astride the Arras-Bapaume road in front of Hamelincourt. At least three determined attacks were repelled by artillery and musketry; but during the night the enemy having penetrated to Gomiecourt, the Battalion was ordered back next day to Courcelles, and thence, on the 26th, to a reserve position behind Moyenneville. Colonel Carter was wounded there, and for a day (27th) the command was exercised by Captain F. G. Stone, the adjutant, whose experiences as a sergeant in the 2nd Battalion in 1914 have already been quoted. When the attack on this front had spent itself on the 28th, the Battalion occupied a good position on the road from Ayette to Boiry-Sainte-Rictrude. B Company under Lieutenant A. A. McConnell had shared in the gallant defence of Moyenneville by the 15th West Yorkshire, who held on all through the 26th and the following night; and though the remainder were not seriously engaged in the few days before they were finally relieved on 30th March, the Battalion's losses totalled 320 all ranks in killed,

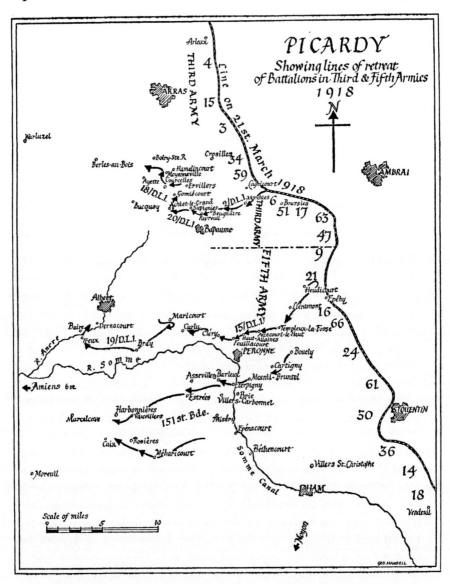

29. The Retreat on the Third and Fifth Army Fronts, March-April, 1918

wounded and missing. Many had been caused on the 26th in an attempt to recover Moyenneville, which had been abandoned mistakenly during the night on the orders of a brigade-major suffering from the effects of a shell that had burst near him.

These withdrawals on the Third Army front had been serious enough. Those farther south on the Fifth Army front bore an even more alarming aspect, giving rise to even greater exhaustion and weariness of body and soul.

The first Durham battalion in the Fifth Army to encounter the enemy was the 15th Battalion (21st Division) under the command of Lieut.-Colonel H. W. Festing, D.S.O. (1st Battalion) which was brought from the reserve at Liéramont early on the 21st and ordered to deliver a counter-attack to regain the Yellow Line south of the Heudicourt-Vaucelette Farm road before 7.15 p.m., a task which it successfully accomplished, with the loss, however, of Colonel Festing. The Division as a whole succeeded in remaining firm all that day, and it was not until the evening of the 22nd that the Battalion had to withdraw to the Green Line near Templeux-la-Fosse. The next morning the situation to the south caused a further fighting retreat, first to Aizecourt-le-Haut, then to Haut-Allaines, then to the cross-roads at Feuillacourt, where a stand was made by the depleted 64th Brigade, and finally, during the night, to Cléry. Early on the 24th Cléry had to be abandoned, and when darkness fell and the 35th Division began relieving, the 15th Battalion was back on the north bank of the Somme at Curlu. By that time the Brigade was organised into a composite battalion to which the Battalion, having lost sixteen officers and 486 men killed, wounded and missing, could contribute no more than a company.

The 35th Division contained the 19th Battalion, under Lieut.-Colonel W. B. Greenwell (formerly adjutant of the 1st Battalion in India), which, arriving from the Ypres front, had taken over a line at Maricourt by the evening of the 24th. Ordered to counter-attack in the afternoon of the 25th to restore the line at Favières Wood, it successfully accomplished the task, though with many losses; but at 1 a.m. on the 26th a further retirement was ordered which brought the Battalion to Bray. After a brief but ineffective resistance it was again compelled to retire, this time to Treux, where on 28th March it triumphantly resisted every attempt to surprise it. It was finally relieved on the railway between Buire and Dernancourt on 30th March, having suffered a total of 160 casualties.

South of the Somme the 50th Division, which had been hurried up from G. H. Q. reserve and detrained late on the 22nd at Brie, south of Péronne, in the evening was holding the Green Line five miles east of the river, the 151st Brigade on the left in front of Boucly on the Cologne. That night, however, the corps on its right was forced to give way and cross the Somme, and the battalions' positions had hardly been occupied before they were abandoned, first for a line running south from Cantigny, and then another on the near bank of the Somme. The 151st crossed at Eterpigny during the afternoon, the battalions leap-frogging through one another and the rearguards holding off the enemy as best they could—one, the 6th, was ambushed in Mesnil-Bruntel—until by dark they occupied a position on the left bank running through Barleux. At dawn on the 24th the enemy contrived to pass small parties across the Somme. Although they were quickly shot down, a German battalion succeeded in crossing south of Péronne during that night, and a counter-attack by the 5th at about 9 a.m. on the 25th failed to dislodge it. Farther south at Béthencourt the enemy forced the Somme in numbers, and the 50th Division, now reinforced by the 8th, withdrew to a line running north and south through Estrées-Deniécourt and Assevillers, the 1/8th on the right, the 1/6th on the left. Once again developments on the right intervened. There, the 8th Division, containing the 22nd Battalion, failed in an attempt to recover the west bank at Epénancourt (in which one company of that battalion was involved). The 50th Division's line consequently fell back to a position in front of Miséry, while hot fighting—involving both the 1/5th and the 1/7th (pioneers) at Villers-Carbonnel—continued throughout the 25th nearer the Somme. The retirement was carried out during the night of the 25th across part of the old Somme battlefields, and a difficult and wearisome march it was.

There followed what is known as the Battle of Rosières, which lasted over the 26th and 27th March and involved all the Durham battalions of the Division, by this time much confused. The 1/6th and 1/8th formed part of the 150th Brigade under the command of the 8th Division and lay in front of Rosières; two companies of the 1/5th lay nearby under the 149th Brigade; the 1/7th were in reserve. Desperate fighting began on the 27th with the enemy making gigantic efforts to break through to Amiens. Vauvillers fell in spite of a gallant, and at first successful,[28] defence by the 1/5th under Major A. L. Raimes, who was wounded; and a counter-attack delivered by the 1/8th under Lieut.-Colonel H. Martin, who was also wounded, failed to recover Méharicourt. The defence made by these weary and attenuated remnants was magnificent; but though it checked the German advance it did not stop it; and once again the line fell back. Stubborn rearguard fighting continued as far as the line of

[28]"We accordingly pushed on, platoon by platoon and section by section, in quite the old field-day style, the men firing freely at the Germans, who could now be seen advancing towards us five or six hundred yards away. We came under machine-gun fire, and the bullets were kicking up the dust all along the line. We had many casualties, and as one looked back over the level ground behind, one could see the motionless forms of many men who had fought their last fight, while here and there were wounded men trying to make their way to the rear. After a while it became very exciting, as we could see the enemy halt and turn back through the trees near Vauvillers. Our men gave a sort of grunt, and advanced ten times as quickly as before . . ." Major A. L. Raimes, *The 5th Battalion Durham Light Infantry* (1931), pp. 137-138.

Caix/Harbonnières and until 1st April, when the Division was finally relieved. By that time the battalions had become so reduced that it was barely possible to organise (on 29th March) single composite battalions from each brigade.

"Who that took part in the retreat of the Fifth Army in March," writes the historian of the 8th Battalion, "when they see the almond blossom in an English spring, will fail to recall the trees in bloom on the road leading back from Saint-Quentin, the beauty of which seemed only to accentuate the miseries of the retreat?"

Throughout those critical days the pioneer battalions, understandably, fought as ordinary infantry, and all gave a good account of themselves. The 1/9th, with the 62nd Division on the Third Army front, distinguished itself in the defence of Bucquoy (26th to 31st March), an action in which Private T. Young, of High Spen, a stretcher-bearer, gained the Regiment's sixth V.C. of the war for rescuing wounded in the open under fire on no fewer than nine occasions. A small part of the 22nd Battalion's share in the 8th Division's fight on the Fifth Army's front has already been mentioned. A better indication of the heavy fighting sustained by the Battalion before it was relieved at Moreuil on 1st April is given by its casualties, which totalled 23 officers and 469 n.c.o.s and men, including its able and popular commanding officer, Lieut.-Colonel C. B. Morgan, D.S.O., who had taken it out to France in 1916 and was mortally wounded near Harbonnières on 27th March. The 11th Battalion (20th Division), also on the Fifth Army front, was involved in equally heavy and continuous fighting from Villers-Saint-Christophe, near Ham, on 22nd March to Moreuil on the 30th, in which it lost 19 officers and 455 n.c.o.s and men.

The Battle of the Lys: Estaires, Hazebrouck, Kemmel and the Scherpenberg, 9th-29th April

Measured in gains of territory in square miles, the success the Germans had won was enormous, nullifying all the painful Allied gains of the previous two years as well as much besides. All this was not enough, however. Although the line bulged ominously it had not been breached, and every gain had been won at a disproportionate cost. The second part of the offensive, originally conceived in even mightier terms, had to be reduced from a front of about thirty miles to one of twelve, from Armentières to the La Bassée Canal. Even so it was a very formidable blow and came near to succeeding.

At the outset it met with singular luck. Launched on 9th April with fresh troops, it struck at Estaires a tired Portuguese division which was due for relief, and drove it off the field. The right "shoulder" of the breach, held by the 55th Division, well rested and well trained, stayed firm and exacted an immense toll from the attackers; the left "shoulder", however, held by the 40th, weak and shaken after its experiences in March, was rolled back.

The 50th Division, which was to have relieved the Portuguese Division during the night of 9th April and was for that reason billeted nearby in the untouched town of Estaires, had only recently been withdrawn from the fighting in Picardy and was composed to a large extent of drafts of lads from the Graduated Battalions like that mentioned earlier in this chapter. The 1/8th Battalion, for example, under Lieut.-Colonel P. Kirkup, one of the few survivors from 1915, had been brought up by these means from the strength of a weak company to that of a weak battalion of 26 officers and 622 n.c.o.s and men. The performance of the Division in the fighting that followed reflects every credit therefore not only on its untried troops but also on the weary survivors of the previous month's retreat who formed its cadre.

Its introduction to the battle took place in the worst of circumstances. Launched (with the 51st Division) into the blue, no one knew exactly where, to hold the progress of a victorious enemy through the midst of the retreating Portuguese, it had a task of sufficient difficulty; and at the outset one of the two leading battalions of the leading brigade, the 1/6th Durham Light Infantry of the 151st, lost all but five of its officers when an unlucky shell struck the convent in which they were billeted. It went into action with its commanding officer (Major T. B. Heslop) and its adjutant, but with all its platoons and one of its companies commanded by non-commissioned officers. Contact with the enemy was made at noon a few miles beyond the Lys and the Lawe, and the Durham battalions proceeded to defend a "line" of fortified posts as follows: the 6th in front held some fortified farms and posts on the far side of the Lys two miles south-east of Estaires, including Le Drumetz; the 8th held the Lawe bridges near Lestrem; and the 5th on their left, under Lieut.-Colonel Spence, held the Lys and Lawe bridges at La Gorgue and Estaires. Not, however, for long: the enemy, driving in two columns, one against the crossing at Estaires, the other past Bout-Delville towards the Lawe crossings at Lestrem, forced the 8th out of Le Marais Farm and the 6th out of Le Drumetz; so that the 6th, turned on both flanks and reduced to four officers and 60 men, had no alternative but to fall back on the river. The 5th meanwhile managed to hold on to the Pont-Levis, at the eastern end of Estaires, and to defy several attempts to seize it; but at 7 p.m., when it became clear the enemy had brought up artillery to destroy the bridgeheads systematically, the whole brigade was ordered behind the rivers with the exception of the 8th's at Pont-Riqueul. Even that, however, had to go during the night.

The next day, 10th April, the enemy renewed his attempts to force a passage at Estaires. By 11 a.m. he had succeeded despite desperate counter-attacks on the part of its defenders. The Durham battalions on the Lawe swung back their left behind Estaires to keep touch, but the 8th continued to defend successfully the passage at Lestrem until late that night, when less two companies, it was withdrawn into brigade reserve at Beaupré.

Dawn on the 11th found the much attenuated 151st Brigade north of the Lys and west of La Gorgue. The Germans, outnumbering them four to one, continued to press on during the day and, taking advantage of a gap between the 5th and the 6th Battalions, forced them

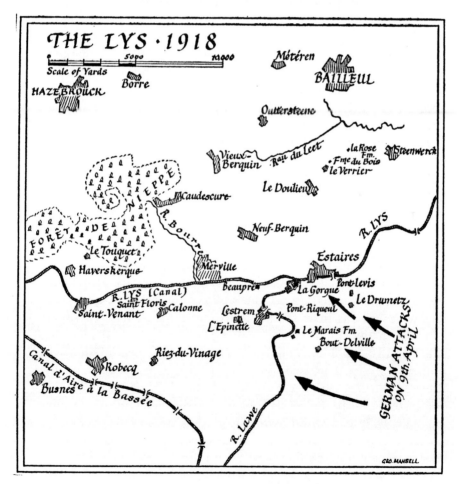

30. The Lys Battles, April, 1918

back through Merville. The 5th on the left resisted splendidly and succeeded in delaying the enemy until a line was prepared by Sappers short of Neuf-Berquin. But this also went under a heavy attack at 4 in the afternoon. "I think," said one of the 5th's officers, "the only thing that saved us that night was the amount of liquor the Boche found in Estaires and Neuf-Berquin, as I have never heard such a noise in my life as they made singing." There is indeed some reason to suppose that their excesses delayed them, for although they renewed their attacks early on the 12th in great strength, sufficient time had been given for the tired defenders to form a continuous line. Under pressure the scanty remnants of the Durham Brigade retired (the 5th Battalion being brought south by Pont-Tournant to rejoin the rest behind Merville), but fighting so stubbornly that by 3 p.m., when the 5th Division, thirteen fresh battalions from Italy, started to relieve them, they had only gone back 1500 yards.

The relief of the tired 50th—the whole division by then hardly more than a battalion in strength—was completed in the early hours of 13th April. There was much truth in the Corps Commander's words that the fine stand of the 50th during those four days had gained the time necessary to enable the reserves to be brought up and had saved the situation. The cost of course was the annihilation, almost, of the battalions.

Meanwhile, immediately to the north, the 31st Division had been brought out of G.H.Q. reserve behind the Arras front and rushed to meet the threat against Hazebrouck. The 18th Battalion (under Lieut.-Colonel Lowe) entered the battle in the evening of 11th April very near where the 2nd Battalion saw their first fighting in the Watteringues in October 1914, a fact which did not go unnoticed by the adjutant, Captain F. G. Stone. Ordered from Outtersteene to recapture Le Verrier, Ferme du Bois and Ferme La Rose, they advanced on the left of the 13th York and Lancaster at 7 in the evening and, eliminating all the troublesome machine-gun posts, they were well dug in on their objective by dawn. At daylight on the 12th the enemy could be seen massing for the attack. Artillery fire failed to disperse him, and by 8 a.m. all battalions of the 93rd Brigade were hard pressed. Soon the 18th was forced back on the Ruisseau du Leet with 270 casualties. Isolated detachments fighting desperately in scattered posts kept up a resistance some hours after the main body had withdrawn, but the line as a whole was forced back, first to the railway at Outtersteene, then on the Bailleul/ Outtersteene road, and finally to the southern outskirts of Météren. The night was quiet; the 13th passed without any attack by infantry —though there was an hour's heavy bombardment; and on the 14th the Battalion was taken out of the line back to Borre, where the survivors were joined with the 15th West Yorkshire into a composite battalion about 450 strong under Colonel Lowe's command. It was not finally relieved until 28th April.

These were critical days. The 11th April was the day on which Haig, usually markedly uneloquent, issued his famous "backs to the wall" message. Bailleul fell on the 15th. Although the German progress was slow and costly and although the advance had failed to gain its objectives, it was approaching the high ground of Kemmel and the Scherpenberg, that strange "Flemish Switzerland" which had been the Second Army's "keep" from the beginning. Messines Ridge was lost on the 16th. The ground so dearly bought in the Salient was given up. Kemmel itself, defended by French troops brought from the south, fell on the 25th. On the 29th the Scherpenberg fell too. Elsewhere, however, that day their attack was smashed. The Germans tried no more, and the Channel ports were saved.

The Regiment had no battalions directly involved in this second phase of the Battle of the Lys, and it owes its honours *Kemmel* and *Scherpenberg* principally to the fighting endured by the 2nd and 15th Battalions a little to the north, the 2nd near Polygon Wood, the 15th between Vierstraat and Wijtschate. The fighting was heavy and caused many casualties in both battalions, but it cannot be compared with that experienced by the Durham battalions farther south.

The Aisne, 27th May-6th June

The third powerful German offensive to fall on British troops was that on the Aisne late in May. This was a front held by the French armies, but, in implementation of Foch's policy of *roulement*, the exchange of tired British (or French) divisions for fresh French (or British) ones, it was part-occupied by four British divisions, the 8th, 21st, 25th and 50th. Three (the 8th, 21st and 50th, which composed the IX Corps of the French Sixth Army under the choleric General Duchêne) contained Durham battalions, and all had suffered crippling losses during March and April. The British Command, suspecting the possibility of a German blow in this quarter, entertained misgivings on the suitability of the front, but it had received reassurances from Foch's chief of staff that it was both suitable and quiet. Quiet, forsooth! Unknown to the French Intelligence forty-one German divisions had been assembled against sixteen Franco-British, and 1036 heavy batteries against 266, these under the direction of that same Colonel Bruchmüller who had startled our armies on that foggy March morning and was preparing now an even more devastating gunner's brew. The upshot was very far from quiet. The 50th

Division was smashed to smithereens and the others fared little better.

The 151st Brigade, railed from Lapugnoy, near Béthune, on 26th April and reaching Arcis-le-Ponsart on the 28th, had taken over the line from the 73rd Regiment of the French 51st Division on 6th May. The position lay in front of the Chemin des Dames rather to the east of the sector occupied by the 2nd Battalion in its first battle. In front ran the marshy Ailette "with its astonishing nightly chorus of frogs"; behind were the Bois de Beau Marais, the Aisne and the Aisne Canal. From 22nd May onwards the 151st Brigade, in the centre of the Division's front with Craonne on its left, kept two battalions in the line and the third in reserve at Chaudardes, while the transport and quartermasters' details lay across the Aisne at Muscourt. "For three weeks, in trenches shadowed by green trees and the Bois de Beau Marais gay with flowers and singing birds, the war bore a different aspect. Here surely was that hitherto phantom sector all had some day hoped to find."

The idyll was broken in the evening of the 26th, when the 5th Battalion, in reserve at Chaudardes, was ordered forward to Centre d'Evreux, the reserve fighting position, and the 8th, in the line by Chevreux, was reinforced by a company of the 7th. At about 9 the French 75s on the right near Rheims opened up. The Germans a mile away around Corbeny could be seen massing in enormous numbers. At 1 a.m. on the 27th a German flare went up, evidently the signal for Bruchmüller's infernal symphony to begin. The most experienced connoisseurs in bombardments had known nothing like it. For three hours a rain of gas and high explosive shells of all calibres showered upon every conceivable target. Front trenches and wire entanglements were swept away in the fury of the tornado, dug-outs broken in, buried cables cut, batteries destroyed. Soon after 4 a.m the German infantry started their climb up to the ridgeway. Three divisions attacked the front held by the 50th. The 151st Brigade, taken on both flanks, was soon overwhelmed, though the few sur-vivors of the bombardment fought, as a German account is reported to have said, "till their weapons were torn from them". The supports gave what resistance they could on the intermediate line at the edge of the Bois de Beau Marais, but, outflanked and surrounded, they too were overwhelmed. By 5 only isolated machine-gun and Lewis gun posts survived from the 8th and 6th Battalions and the company of the 7th. Two companies of the 5th coming up from Centre d'Evreux ran into three German battalions pushing on beyond the Battle Zone and were driven back in confused fighting in the wood in the half-light; another joined them and was equally repulsed; the fourth was captured in its dug-outs while awaiting orders it never received. Brigade headquarters were overrun and the brigadier killed.

Those officers that remained gathered what men they could and fell back to the Aisne bridges. A group under Captain W. N. J. Moscrop (5th) apparently took up a position covering the bridge at the south end of Maizy, for their graves were found there after the war. A party from the 6th and 8th was assembled by Lieut.-Colonel Birchall, 7th, at Cuiry-lès-Chaudardes at the southern edge of the forest, and managed to keep the enemy in check till about 11 a.m. Another under Lieut.-Colonel Kirkup, who, though sick, had left the ambulance against orders, put up a stiff resistance at Concevreux until nearly 5 p.m. Other scattered parties held the line of the canal under Lieut.-Colonel F. Walton, 6th, and on the hill behind small groups of survivors held a quarry under Lieut.-Colonel B. B. Robinson, 5th, and Major G. D. Gould, 8th.

About midday the remnants of the Division were organised into a composite unit under Lieut.-Colonels Walton and Kirkup called "149/151 Brigade Force". For some hours it held the heights on the south bank of the Aisne, but later in the afternoon it was flanked and forced back, first to Vantelay and then to Jonchery on the Vesle,

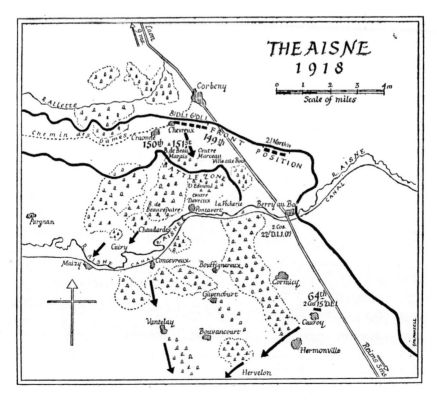

31. The Aisne, 27th May, 1918

where during the night some officers of the Durham battalions joined from leave and courses. There the force managed to resist until the familiar outflanking game started at about 4.30 p.m. on the 28th, by which time the Germans were in its rear at Vendeuil. It succeeded, however, in extricating itself and retiring on Savigny-sur-Ardres. The movement was continued under the pressure of further attacks on 29th and 30th May, by some through Poilly and Sarcy to Chaumuzy and by others to Vert-la-Gravelle, south of the Marne, where all that remained from the 151st Brigade in the line on the 27th, a body of men amounting to 103 all ranks, were collected.

Meanwhile, on the right of the IX Corps the 21st Division had undergone a similar experience. On the morning of the 27th the 15th Battalion, under Lieut.-Colonel C. E. R. Holroyd-Smyth, 3rd Dragoon Guards, weak and recently made up from drafts from lads' battalions, was at Cauroy-lès-Hermonville in reserve to the 64th Brigade. At 10 a.m. it had been ordered to send up a company to reinforce, but by that time the Germans were across the main Rheims/Laon road and almost in the village. A bitter struggle took place in the redoubts and trenches with which the village was honeycombed, and although the Battalion was driven to the south edge the Germans tried in vain to debouch from it. During the night it retired into the heights behind to a position between Hervelon and Luternay Farm, where Colonel Holroyd-Smyth was wounded at the outset of a fresh enemy attack early on the 28th. Forced back but fighting hard, it retired to a prepared position between Prouilly and Trigny, whence the next day, the Germans having reached Jonchery in the rear, it was ordered—before becoming engaged—to retire to the Vesle at Muizon. By this time it consisted of a mere six officers and 40 men in a composite unit under the command of Lieut.-Colonel W. N. S. Alexander, East Yorkshire. The withdrawal was continued during the 29th and 30th through Rosnay, Méry-Prémecy and Marfaux into the Forest of Epernay at Chaltrait. It had lost 456 in killed, wounded and missing, including eight officers killed or missing and seven wounded.

The 22nd Battalion (8th Division pioneers), which on the 27th lay at Bouffignereux, half-way between the 50th and the 21st, lost a company in the line (with the 1st Worcester and 2nd Northampton) at the first attack, fighting to the end. The rest were driven back and back across the Vesle to Moslins, where it was absorbed into the 8th Division Composite Battalion after losing nineteen officers and 494 n.c.o.s and men.

After this calamitous affair it remains only to add the epilogue. The 50th Division was broken, and though it was re-formed the new contained none of the old battalions. The 1/5th, 1/6th and 1/8th Battalions were reduced to cadre on 15th June, all those surplus to cadre strength (ten officers, fifty n.c.o.s and men) being distributed among other battalions. They were moved to Rouxmesnil in the Dieppe area in July, and from August until 9th November, when demobilisation started, they formed the 117th Brigade of the 39th Division at Rouen. The 22nd was brought back on 23rd June to Friancourt, near Le Tréport on the coast, and although at the time it had a strength of 23 officers and 474 n.c.o.s and men, it was absorbed by the 1/7th Battalion, which on 3rd July became the 8th Division's pioneer battalion.

Of all the fine Durham infantry battalions involved in the Aisne fighting the 15th alone survived. Brought once more up to strength, it returned to the trenches on the Somme near Hamel on 17th July and continued to serve to the end.

The Marne: Tardenois, 20th-30th July

Two more German offensives were launched in that critical summer of 1918, and a third was confidently meditated by the German Command. The first fell on the French armies between Montdidier and Noyon in June, and punched a flat salient in the line. This, the Battle of the Matz, was followed on 15th July by what would nowadays be called a pincer attack east and west of Rheims, a gigantic affair planned on the scale of that of 21st March. The eastern attack, after gaining but little ground, was decisively checked by the French Fourth Army under Gouraud. The western, on the other hand, created an immense salient, at the tip of which 50,000 German infantry crossed the Marne and carried the advance almost as near Paris as it had been in the dark days of 1914. The situation was critical. However, to the west of the new salient in the Forest of Villers-Cotterêts Foch prepared a large force of eighteen French and two strong American divisions under the command of Mangin for a counter-stroke; and, much against his will Haig, who was expecting —rightly as it proved—a further blow in the sensitive Hazebrouck sector, depleted his scanty reserves by sending four British divisions to reinforce the stricken front. On 18th July Mangin's Army attacked the west flank of the German salient. Before nightfall it had pierced the front south of Soissons and advanced an average of five kilometres on a front of forty-five. It was the first successful counterstroke the Allies had made for six months, and though not decisive it was sufficiently dangerous to cause the German Command to suspend their third offensive (in Flanders), to which those on the southern fronts had been intended as no more than feints.

The 62nd Division, one of the British divisions which had been sent south, detrained south of Châlons on 17th July. It was directed upon the eastern flank of the salient, where it came under the orders of the French Fifth Army under General Berthelot, and arrived in time to share in the attacks launched to pinch off the salient from the east. Their attack started on 20th July. Trench warfare, the only kind known to these troops, was done with for the time being. The country was thickly wooded—so thick that the divisional commander acknowledged he had "seen nothing thicker since I fought thirty-five years ago in the Burmese jungle" but, so far as such could be called open, it was open warfare. Small progress was made that day in stubborn fighting through the woods around Marfaux, and the next day, owing to the heavy losses, the 1/9th Durham Light Infantry, under Lieut.-Colonel E. G. Crouch, were fittingly employed in their former capacity of ordinary infantry in the 187th Brigade's attack through the Bois de Rouvroy and the Bois d'Avermont against Bouilly Ridge. Through an error of the guides the Battalion started 600 yards behind the proper start-line, and on debouching from the wood and rushing down the hill was immediately met by the fire from

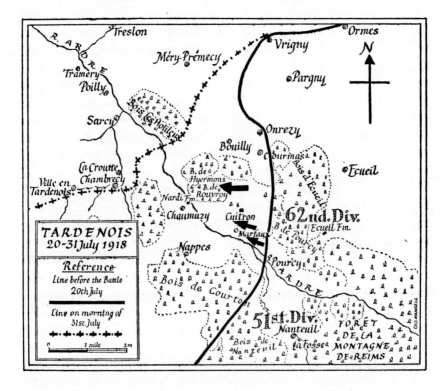

32. The Marne: Tardenois, July, 1918

"hundreds of machine-guns". No troops could have withstood the murderous fire poured upon them, and the Battalion, which had made a gallant advance of 600 yards, could do no more than consolidate their gains. They were taken out that night and moved back to the Bois d'Ecueil, having lost 28 n.c.o.s and men killed, and seven officers and 131 n.c.o.s and men wounded, and 11 missing.

After a day's rest it was attached to the 186th Brigade for an attack on the Marfaux/Cuitron line which took place at 6 a.m. on the 23rd, the 1/9th acting on the right against Cuitron. One company (A) suffered sixty casualties while assembling in the wood, and suffered a further thirty before it advanced into the open. But the Battalion's attack was completely successful. The village of Cuitron was captured along with 85 prisoners and nine machine-guns, at a cost of 15 n.c.o.s and men killed, one officer and 93 n.c.o.s and men wounded, and 8 missing. "They fought magnificently as Durham men always do," the divisional commander wrote afterwards.

Stubborn and costly fighting—not, however, directly involving the 1/9th—continued on this front for the next few days; Berthelot's Army could make little impression; and the enemy retired slowly and very much in his own time. It was not until 5th August, when the Germans were reported well entrenched behind the Vesle, that the great Soissons salient could be said to have been obliterated. By that time the 62nd Division, speeded on its way by a touching tribute from the French Army Commander, had left the Marne for the Somme, having added *"en lettres d'or dans les annales de vos régiments"* *"les noms prestigieux"* of Marfaux, Chaumuzy and Montagne de Bligny, and having shared in that other Battle of the Marne, no less momentous than the first.

The Third Battle of the Somme: Albert, Bapaume and Arras, 21st August-3rd September

The Allies' prospects, so dismal for six months, now underwent a dramatic change. In the decisive battle which was fought out near Amiens on 8th August, "the greatest defeat which the German army had suffered since the beginning of the war," the Regiment took no part. But in the resumed offensive which carried the British Army across the old Somme battlefields almost to the line held on 20th March, the Regiment was represented by three battalions. Two were pioneer battalions: the 1/9th (62nd Division) in the Third Army, and the 1/7th (8th Division) in the First Army to the north. Pride of place, however, must go to the battered old 15th Battalion (21st Division, Third Army), which had suffered everything since its ill-starred baptism of fire at Loos to its near-annihilation on the

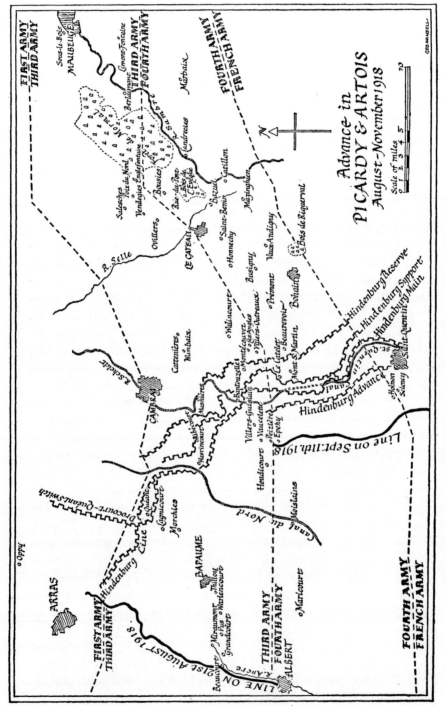

22. The Advance on the Third and Fourth Army Fronts, August—November, 1918

Aisne, but was now to go forward from the farthest limit of the retreat to the very forefront of the final advance.

The conditions in these last actions closely resembled those of open warfare, for which the lads of nineteen who largely composed the infantry were totally untrained. Yet the artillery, handled with skill, made up for any training the infantry lacked; and the infantry, rested and reinforced since their exertions in March and April, soon got the hang of the business and learned their craft as the offensive progressed.

On 21st August the 21st Division lay second division from the right of the Third Army on the west bank of the Ancre. The 15th Battalion (64th Brigade), under Lieut.-Colonel Holroyd-Smyth, entered the battle in the evening of the next day when they relieved some Yorkshire Territorials in a ravine north of Beaucourt. On the 23rd the Brigade was given the task of taking that part of the Thiepval Ridge south of Miraumont. Crossing the Ancre by foot-bridges at 11 that night, they encountered the enemy in obstinate fighting west of Grandcourt, but by dawn on the 24th, after pushing ahead very fast, they reached their objective. To have made "a night advance to attack a line known to be held and seize an objective over 3000 yards beyond it was an exceptional task," says the Official Historian of the war, who shall not be gainsaid, and its successful accomplishment reflects the greatest credit upon the brigade-commander and his battalions. In the initial stage of the advance the Battalion formed the reserve, but on closing up (an hour late owing to the difficulty of identifying the position) on the intermediate line, it resumed the advance at 3.15 a.m. on the right of the Brigade. Soon after daybreak the brigadier, whose able arrangements were largely responsible for the success, was wounded, and Lieut.-Colonel Holroyd-Smyth succeeded him. The situation was precarious. Indeed, having outmarched the supporting brigade they were almost surrounded. No other troops made their appearance; several counter-attacks were launched against them; and they were called on to surrender by the Germans. It was midday before the brigade on the right began to make itself felt; and about the same time, on the left, the 42nd Division captured Miraumont. The enemy's fire at last slackened, allowing some improvements to be made more freely to the position, and soon after the enemy cleared off and left the Brigade in comparative peace. The divisional commander described the exploit as "one of the finest deeds performed by any brigade during the war." Colonel Holroyd-Smyth won a well earned D.S.O. Casualties up to 27th August, by which time the Battalion had advanced with the rest of the Army by Pys, Le Sars, past the Butte de Warlencourt of evil memory almost to Ligny-Thilloy, totalled 14 officers and 268 men.

On 26th August the First Army joined in the battle north of Arras with the object of capturing the Drocourt/Quéant Line. The 8th Division, containing the 1/7th Battalion under Lieut.-Colonel B. C. James, Devonshire Regiment, advanced north of the Scarpe to form a defensive flank to favour the advance of the Canadian Corps to the south. There was some bitter fighting in Oppy Wood, but the Battalion itself did not become seriously involved in it. However, the First Army's assault on the Drocourt / Quéant Line on 2nd September was a complete success. The Canadians penetrated the Line everywhere except on the extreme left. The Third Army's complementary movements on that day involved the 62nd Division, which was given as objective the capture of Morchies/Lagnicourt Line where the 2nd Battalion had made its fine stand on 21st March. The attack was not completely successful. But the 187th Brigade succeeded in taking Vaux Wood. A counter-attack drove it out ten minutes later, but C Company of the 9th Battalion, in support, recaptured it at 2.30 p.m. with only few casualties and held it fast.

The Hindenburg Line: Havrincourt and Epéhy, 12th-26th September

Recognising defeat on the 2nd, the German Command ordered a retreat to the Hindenburg Position, which, begun during the night of the 2nd/3rd, represented the abandonment of the whole salient gained in March. The British First and Third Armies followed. They were compelled, however, to fight much of the way, and before they came up against the Hindenburg defences on 10th September several costly actions took place. One, affecting the 15th Battalion, occurred on 9th September north of Heudicourt, near the scene of their successful counter-attack at the beginning of the March retreat. Their objective was Chapel Hill, which they managed to attain despite an obstinate resistance. A counter-attack, however, drove them back a little, and by the time the Battalion was relieved it had lost seven officers and 270 men.

From 12th to 18th September the Armies were engaged in seizing the outlying defences of the Hindenburg Position. In the action of Havrincourt (12th September), fought to gain the spur which dominated that front, the Regiment was represented by the 1/9th Battalion. The Division had captured Havrincourt in the Battle of Cambrai, and its commander's operation orders started with the words "the 62nd Division will recapture Havrincourt". The 1/9th, in support of the 186th Brigade, which after stiff fighting succeeded only in establishing itself on the eastern edge of the village, attempted to carry the line forward a half-mile beyond the Hindenburg front system. After evacuating the position the enemy returned in force, but the right-hand company reached and held its objective besides gaining touch with the 37th Division on the right. At the end of the day Havrincourt was firmly held. Stiff fighting, however, continued during the next few days before the position was secure.

On the 18th the Third and Fourth Armies co-operated to win the enemy outpost position which, bristling with fortified localities, lay between Le Verguier and Epéhy, an operation which involved the 15th Battalion (21st Division, Third Army) and the 2nd Battalion (6th Division, Fourth Army).

The Third Army attack on the left was carried out by three divisions with the ultimate objects of securing the ridge overlooking the valley of the Scheldt and the Saint-Quentin Canal. All the 21st Division's objectives were successfully taken. The 62nd Brigade, which had a company of the 15th with it, took Vaucelette Farm without much difficulty; and the 64th Brigade, with the rest of the Battalions, passed through to attack Villers-Guislain. Some embarrassment was caused on the right by the failure of the 58th Division to get beyond Peizière, and Lieut.-Colonel Holroyd-Smyth, a most promising young officer (its fifth commanding officer to fall), was mortally wounded early in the assault. But on the whole the attack was satisfactory, gaining ground and taking many prisoners.

To the south in the Fourth Army sector, the 6th Division, on the extreme right of the British Army opposite Holnon, had an unenviable task. The 2nd Battalion (under Major R. V. Turner since 12th July), which had barely recovered from the March fighting, had been railed south from the Kemmel sector on 1st September and had been in divisional reserve at Monchy-Lagache since the 13th. In order to secure a line well away from the wood on which to form up on the 18th, the 18th Brigade was entrusted with the task of clearing the wood, establishing posts at its edge and of pushing forward. The first part of the preliminary operation, carried out on the 16th, was successful; but an attempt made on the 17th to capture Holnon by one company (B, under Captain Potts) was repulsed by heavy machine-gun fire, with the result that the attack on the 18th started under disadvantageous circumstances.

The terrain of the attack was "a bare, glacis-like slope devoid of cover except for two or three shell-trap copses," which stretched for 3000 yards to the high ground overlooking Saint-Quentin. Although the Fifth Army was known to have had trenches here in March, none could be seen, and there was no sign of life. It was afterwards found that the Germans had camouflaged their trenches with thistles, which in places covered the ground to a height of eighteen inches. The 2nd Battalion's objective on the 18th was Selency and the trenches behind it, and it attacked under the orders of the 71st Brigade. It advanced at 6.20 a.m. under a creeping barrage with two companies up (D and A), and two (C and B) in support. The assault companies passed through Holnon but, meeting with heavy machine-gun fire from Selency Ridge and Round Hill, which the French 34th Division on the right had failed to capture, they very soon lost all save one of their officers and many n.c.o.s. At the same time enemy machine-gunners lying doggo in the cellars of the ruined houses in Holnon, who should have been mopped up by the support companies, emerged and turned their weapons on those in advance, throwing them into further disorder. They started to dribble back in small parties. The net gain of the attack was a mere 200 yards. In the afternoon C Company under Captain Garland managed to establish some posts in the village, and the next night, in bright moonlight, he pushed forward some more to the far side, which he somehow, despite enemy observation from Round Hill, maintained until the Battalion was relieved in the night of the 20th. By then it had lost ten officers[29] and 295 n.c.o.s and men.

The results of the 6th Division's attack were disappointing, particularly in view of the successes obtained elsewhere on the Army's front with comparative ease. The Battalion, moreover, suffered a further disappointment on 24th September when the attack on Holnon was renewed. It was much under-strength, and the lack of officers had only partially been made good by means of attachments from other regiments. A platoon under Lieutenant Silburn, which got as far as the second objective on the Selency Ridge, was surrounded and taken and another under Lieutenant Cohen, which had secured a footing in Douai Trench, 200 yards in advance, also became isolated and had to withdraw after putting up a stout resistance and losing all its leaders. The total casualties were seven officers[30] and 230 n.c.o.s and men. More mortifying still, the obstacles holding the Division up, Douai Trench, the Quadrilateral, Round Hill, and Manchester Hill, were overcome without the Battalion's assistance in very stubborn fighting in the next two days. Meanwhile the Battalion itself was

[29]Killed: 2/Lieutenants J. Folliott and G. P. Franklin-Evans. Wounded: Captain S. R. Streatfeild and R. Haylett, Lieutenants F. H. Richards, E. H. Krause and S. Brewin, M.C. (Northumberland Fusiliers), and 2/Lieutenants G. W. Bale, B. R. J. Simpson and D. W. Reid (Northumberland Fusiliers).

[30]Killed: Lieutenants M. Cohen, M.M., J. R. Lambdin and G. B. Taylor (11th Leicester). Wounded: Captain G. C. Handcock, M.C., Lieutenant H. Hall (York and Lancaster) and 2/Lieutenant W. Archer. Missing: Lieutenant L. Silburn.

withdrawn to reorganise and digest the large reinforcement drafts it had received, and did not share in serious fighting until the middle of the following month.

The Hindenburg Line: Canal du Nord, Saint-Quentin Canal, Beaurevoir and Cambrai, 27th September-9th October

At the end of September the Allied armies were suitably poised for a grand resumption of the offensive along the whole line. Immediately before the British armies lay the formidable obstacle of the Hindenburg Position, three strong lines which, though partially breached in the north opposite the First Army, were still intact in the south. Behind these, moreover, lay the Canal du Nord, the Saint-Quentin Canal and other canal and river lines. The Germans still had 197 divisions on the Western Front, 113 of them in the front line, and among the rest many *Eingreifdivisionen*. Ludendorff relates several incidents as evidence of the fragile morale of his troops. But these were hidden from those who fought them, and though it was plain the enemy was not resisting as he had on the Somme, the experience, say, of the 2nd Battalion at Holnon had shown he was not giving in lightly and was defending every inch of ground he gave.

The Third and First Armies attacked on 27th September, the Fourth two days later. The right of the First Army and the left of the Third had at the outset to cross the Canal du Nord, and the Third Army had besides to tackle the unbreached part of the Hindenburg Position. The Fourth, apart from the Saint-Quentin Canal, had before it the intact Hindenburg Position with its advanced, main and reserve (Beaurevoir) lines. By the evening of 28th September, however, the First and Third Armies, though not advancing as rapidly as had been hoped, had made a breach six miles deep in the German defences. The Fourth Army, by the evening of its first day, the 29th, had thrust three miles into the advanced and had taken half the main line of the Hindenburg Position. Soon the Saint-Quentin Canal was crossed and on 4th October the Fourth Army breached the Beaurevoir Line and entered Cambrai on the 9th.

In the Battle of the Canal du Nord the Regiment was represented by the 1/9th Battalion, which was not employed as infantry in the assault but was given the task of clearing the bed of the canal for use as a road. Between 29th September and 13th October it had road construction parties successively at Ribécourt, Marcoing, Masnières, Wambaix and Cattenières.

In the Battle of Saint-Quentin neither the 15th Battalion (21st Division) nor the 2nd (6th Division) was properly engaged, both being in reserve at the time of the assault. But the 15th moved up on

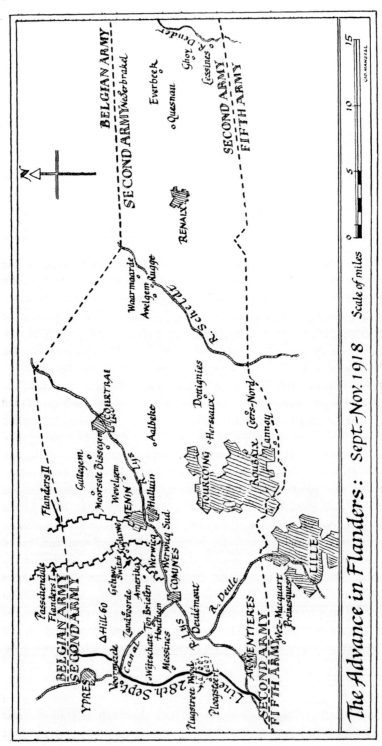

34. The Advance in Flanders, September–November, 1918

5th October and, crossing the canal south of Bantouzelle, came up before the Beaurevoir Line that evening. And at the same time but a little farther south the 13th Battalion, under Lieut.-Colonel D. H. Clarke, D.S.O., M.C., (which had been brought back from Italy on 18th September to be placed in the 74th Brigade of the reconstituted 25th Division) having moved up from Millancourt, through Albert, Ribemont, Maricourt and Moislains, had entered the line on 3rd October at Mont Saint-Martin, south of Le Catelet.

The first to take part in the forcing of the Beaurevoir Line was the 13th, which attacked from Prospect Hill, east of Le Catelet, with the 74th Brigade at 6 o'clock in the morning of 5th October. The objectives included the village of Beaurevoir itself. Although this was not taken, the progress made was encouraging in the face of a heavy machine-gun fire. Lieut.-Colonel Clarke was badly wounded early on, but his men pushed ahead, took the line of trenches behind the road from Guisancourt Farm to Beaurevoir and even reached the road from Beaurevoir north to Villers-Outréaux. Here, however, they found themselves enfiladed, and they had to retire to a line about 400 yards in advance of their start-line. Guisancourt Farm, taken by the 11th Foresters on their left in the same brigade (old comrades from the 23rd Division), had likewise to be abandoned. Casualties were heavy and included 15 officers killed and wounded. The attack was renewed at 4.10 the next morning (the 6th). This time the Foresters established themselves firmly in Guisancourt Farm, and the 13th Battalion similarly took the Villers-Outréaux road and dug in farther on facing south-east. It was relieved that night for a few days.

Rather to the north the 15th Battalion under Lieut.-Colonel H. H. Neeves (21st Division, Third Army) attacked the same morning and carried Montécouvez Farm, and a party under 2/Lieutenant E. Roughley gained a footing in the front trench of the main Beaurevoir system. At 1 a.m. on the 8th, when the Battalion resumed the attack, it penetrated the Beaurevoir defences, seizing the Château des Angles in a stubborn struggle. Walincourt, entered that evening, was occupied as billets by the Battalion on the 10th, their first glimpse of a village almost untouched by shell-fire, with furnished houses; lying, moreover, in a green unspoilt landscape. Breaching the Beaurevoir Line had cost it a total of 213 all ranks killed and wounded.

These most encouraging advances, which properly belong to the Battle of Cambrai, involved the 13th Battalion under Major L. M. Greenwood (who had served with it almost from its formation and now continued in the field despite influenza). It joined in on 9th

October with a successful attack on the enemy line near Honnechy, on the old Le Cateau battlefield, followed on the 10th by an attack on Saint-Benin, which carried it across the Selle. Indeed, in those exhilarating days battle succeeded battle with such astonishing rapidity that it is hard to draw a distinction between the end of one and the beginning of another.

The Advance in Flanders: Ypres and Courtrai, 28th September-19th October

On the Flanders front, where the 18th, 19th, 20th and the new 29th Battalions lay, progress had been hardly less satisfactory. The Lys salient won by the enemy in April was abandoned (not, however, without heavy fighting) during the period from 30th August to 9th September, while the southern armies were recovering Bapaume and breaching the Drocourt/Quéant Switch in front of Arras. The northern armies' final advance started on 28th September. In spite of bad weather and torrential rain they succeeded in thrusting eight miles into the German front, so enabling the whole of the Ypres Ridge to be recovered by 3rd October. The Germans fell back to their well prepared Flanders Position. The advance, delayed by transport difficulties, was resumed on 14th October. Although the principal part had been reserved for the French and Belgian divisions thrusting towards Brussels while the Second Army formed a flank guard on the Lys, in the event Plumer's men proved to be the spearhead, entering Roubaix and Courtrai on the 19th.

On 28th September the Durham battalions were distributed as follows:

in the north the 19th Battalion (35th Division) was in the line with "the tortured mass of earth still called Hill 60" in its front;

the 20th Wearsiders (41st Division) which, under Lieut.-Colonel A. V. A. Gayer, had lost many officers and men on 4th September in an obstinate struggle for the Wijtschate/Voormezeele road at Bois Carré, lay in reserve behind the 35th Division near the Ypres/Comines Canal;

the 29th, who had entered the line on 13th September near the Menin Road, were in the 14th Division's reserve south of the Ypres/Comines Canal; and

the 18th (31st Division) who had been the first troops to re-enter Bailleul on 30th August, lay to the north of Ploegsteert village with Plugstreet Wood in front of them as their objective.

In the attacks delivered on the 28th and successive days heartening progress was made in every sector. The 19th (under Lieut.-Colonel H. R. McCullagh, 1st Battalion), advancing under an intense bombardment at 5.25 a.m., fought their way to the top of the ridge without suffering many casualties, and on the 30th, Zandvoorde having been cleared by the 105th Brigade, resumed the advance through Ten Brielen. An attempt to pierce that part of the Flanders Position called the Geluwe Switch at Amerika Cabaret, half-way between Werwicq and the Menin Road, failed, however; and after vainly renewing it at dawn the next day the Battalion was relieved. Since the 28th it had lost two officers and 141 n.c.o.s and men. Brought up again on 11th October, they shared next day in an attack from the direction of Moorsele, which carried the high ground south of Gullegem, commanding some of the Lys crossings. In spite of determined resistance on the part of isolated machine-gun nests, in the elimination of which many acts of bravery were performed, the Battalion achieved its objective with the loss of 90 all ranks, and continued the advance towards Bissegem. By the time it came forward again on the 18th, the Lys crossings were secured, and at 5.30 a.m. that morning the Brigade, attacking in a heavy mist across pontoons laid during the night, reached the Aalbeke/Courtrai road. By noon W Company of the Battalion had patrols in Courtrai. They were the first British troops to enter the town.

The 20th Wearsiders, commanded since 4th September (when Lieut.-Colonel Gayer was gassed) by Major C. Pannall, entered the advance on 29th September when one of its companies cleared Houthem. It did not share in the first attack on the Geluwe Switch which held up the 19th, but it lost several men before it was relieved. It rejoined the attack, which had been renewed on 11th October, at 5.30 a.m. on the 13th, when, passing through the 122nd Brigade, it fought its way together with the 26th Royal Fusiliers through a mass of fortified farm-buildings which were supported by field-guns firing over open sights. Two 18-pounders attached to each battalion dealt with the gunners while the infantry closed in on the farms from the flanks. Progress became quicker as the morning mist lifted. A fresh attack organised by Major Pannall at 11 was successful, and by 4 in the afternoon all objectives had been taken. Patrols were pushed forward to the Lys which cleared the north bank as far as Wevelgem on the left. Before it was relieved in the evening of 15th October the Battalion had lost four officers and 71 n.c.o.s and men wounded.

The 29th Battalion remained in reserve when the 14th Division launched its attack near Comines on 28th September, and did not enter the line until 1st October. On 14th October, "now very tired and dirty but still keen," the Battalion, ordered to throw out patrols across the Lys if resistance slackened, accordingly approached the river in the afternoon. Lieut.-Colonel B. W. Ridley, an architect in peacetime who had succeeded Colonel Thackeray in July, finding the enemy's fire had almost ceased, managed under cover of a trench-mortar barrage to pass some patrols over by a bridge improvised of duckboards; but heavy hostile shelling immediately began again and drove the patrols back. At 5.30 next morning, when the fire had slackened once more, the whole Battalion made good the crossing; the enemy withdrew; and by about 11 the 29th were on the railway south of Comines with their left on the road to Wervicq-Sud. They were relieved that evening, and though they re-entered operations on 31st October at Dottignies, east of Tourcoing, they were not called upon to fight again.

In its attack on Plugstreet Wood on 28th September the 18th Battalion under Lieut.-Colonel W. D. Lowe, pushing forward over very wet ground in the rain, had successfully cleared the wood by the morning of the 29th, and on the 30th advanced towards the Lys across muddy open country in the direction of Deulémont. Progress was not so good as expected. But while it rested the Lys was crossed, and when it rejoined the line was far ahead across undevastated country. On 18th October the Battalion reached Tourcoing; on the 19th it was at Lannoy, on the 20th at Leers-Nord. Like the 29th it had done with fighting.

Before proceeding to the final battles which brought the war to a close there remains to be interpolated the short story of the 59th Division in the Fifth Army. Both the Army and the Divisions were new, having been radically reconstituted after the March retreat, the Division with B2 battalions from England. One of them was the 2/6th Durham Light Infantry which, from being a Garrison Battalion stationed at Frinton, disembarked at Calais on 6th May and was placed in the 177th Brigade at Hestrus on 10th May. First employed for some months on the construction of rear defences, at the same time undergoing a purifying process to eliminate the unequivocally unfit, the new division first entered the line on 25th July and took part in its first attack on 30th September. On 10th October the 176th and 177th Brigades delivered the attack which gained Wez-Macquart and the Prémesques Ridge. The 2/6th may consequently have some slight claim to have avenged their brothers of the 2nd Battalion who had fought vainly for the same ground almost exactly four years before. The Division went on, passed Lille on its right, and was one of the first Allied formations across the Scheldt. After these operations the Corps Commander issued an order that the 59th was never again to be described as a B Division so long as it remained in the XI Corps.

The Battles of the Selle, 17th-25th October,
and the Sambre, 4th November

The two final convulsions of the war, which take their names from the principal obstacles overcome, covered so enormous an area that for single battalions the names have little significance: and in what appeared as hardly more than a steady advance it seems best to narrate the fortunes of each battalion separately.

In the south, on the right of the Fourth Army's advance, the 2nd Battalion under Major R. V. Turner had already, on 12th October, shared in a minor operation carried out by the 18th Brigade at the unusual hour of 4.30 p.m. to push the line forward to the Bois de Riquerval level with Vaux-Andigny. Reconnaissance had been imperfect, and the enemy (according to the regimental diary) was assisted by spies dressed as civilians. Whatever the reason the attack failed, but the failure was redeemed by "a very pretty tactical move" devised by the IX Corps Commander, in the attack of 17th October (the Battle of the Selle). The 6th and 4th Divisions were moved to the north flank and attacked in a south-east and easterly direction instead of frontally, or north-east. The 6th had to attack fan-wise from Vaux-Andigny on a front of 1500 yards and then advance about 3000 yards to a front of 5000 yards.

The 2nd Battalion attacked on the 17th at 5.20 a.m. in a heavy mist which did not clear till about 8 and at first so embarrassed the advance that it became a matter for platoon- and section-commanders. At the same time and for the same reason, the enemy machine-gun fire was inaccurate, and the assault companies (B and A), though temporarily held up on uncut wire in front of Bellevue Trench, entered the breach and then passed on. When the mist cleared the machine-gun fire became more deadly. But the 1st Division passed through according to plan, and all objectives were successfully attained with the capture of 82 prisoners at the cost of six officers[31] and about 90 n.c.o.s and men killed or wounded.

After a brief rest in reserve at Bohain the Division was brought up in the night of the 20th to relieve the 27th American Division on the front from Bazuel to Mazinghien. East of the Selle the country they entered differed essentially from the open, rolling downland they had passed through, being instead a multiplicity of small enclosures bordered by quickset hedges trained on wire. The enemy moreover

[31]Killed: Lieutenant T. Shepherd (York and Lancaster), and 2 / Lieutenant L. Pollack. Wounded: Lieutenant W. G. Lapham, 2 /Lieutenants J. S. Lancaster, J. L. Evans and L. J. Harvey (all, with the exception of Lancaster, attached from the York and Lancaster).

enjoyed excellent command from his position in the Bois de l'Evêque and on the far side of the Sambre Canal; and from the volume of his artillery fire, which was heavier than any experienced since the fighting at Holnon, it was evident he intended to resist strongly on the so called Hermann Line.

In the Fourth Army's attack, a quarter-right wheel designed to establish a defensive flank facing east in order to protect the main operation being performed by the First and Third Armies, the 6th Division's part was to advance to the Sambre Canal. The 2nd Battalion's advance on 23rd October started at 1.20 a.m. So many casualties were caused by a heavy enemy bombardment with gas and high explosive on the assembly positions that B Company, in support, was used to reinforce the assault companies (D and C), and there was some disorganisation at first from the gas. But once the hostile barrage was passed the Battalion encountered little resistance until close to its objective (a little short of the Canal). Here a nest of machine-guns in Gimbremont Farm, north-west of Catillon, held it up until the arrival of the reserve company (A). Once, however, the machine-gunners had been eliminated the resistance crumbled, and the Battalion was able to secure all its objectives. During the period it occupied the position only one attempt at a counter-attack was made, and apart from patrols it remained unmolested until withdrawn into billets at Busigny on 29th October. It was still at Busigny at the Armistice. The attack of the 23rd, its last in the long series which had started at Troyon on 20th September 1914, had cost it eight officers[32] and 140 n.c.o.s and men. It had lost approximately the strength of a battalion since the beginning of the counter-offensive on 1st September.

Attacking immediately on the left of the 6th Division on 23rd October was the 25th Division. The 13th Battalion, which during its rest at Prémont was taken over by Lieut.-Colonel P. F. Hone— Major Greenwood having been invalided to die of pneumonia soon after—had been moved up through Honnechy to a point north-west of Le Cateau in the night of 22nd October. Owing to its position in the wheeling movement, the Division had a longer distance to cover than the 6th, and the 74th Brigade had orders not to advance until the situation in front became clear. It did not pass through the 75th Brigade until about 11.15, when short of Rue du Pont, on the northern edge of the Bois de l'Evêque, where, confronted by the belts of wire marking the Hermann Position, its farther advance was checked

[32]Killed: 2/Lieutenant J. H. Jeffrey. Wounded: Captain G. M. Garland, Lieutenant N. A. Pearson, 2/Lieutenants S. G. Snowball, W. N. Leng, A. Wilson, D. L. Shield and F. S. Richardson.

and then postponed till the next day. At 4 in the morning of the 24th the 74th's attack went in, the 13th Battalion on the left of the 9th Yorkshire. Losses were heavy as the wire was untouched by the artillery; but the position was rushed; and after some hand-to-hand fighting it was taken by about 7.30 a.m. The Battalion, moreover, resumed the advance at 2 in the afternoon to the high ground beyond Le Faux. Before it was moved back to a camp near Saint-Benin on 31st October it had lost six officers (including Colonel Hone) and 285 n.c.o.s and men killed or wounded.

When it came up again, to cross the Sambre on 4th November at a point about 400 yards south of Landrecies, the advance was a very different matter. Abandoned enemy heavy and field batteries lay beside the route, a squadron of 12th Lancers led the way, and cyclists and armoured cars swarmed along beside the infantry. The 13th's turn to attack did not come until 6th November at Marbaix (which made but a perfunctory resistance), and though it formed the advance guard on the 7th it was soon relieved and brought back into reserve at Bousies on the west side of the Forêt de Mormal, where it was quartered at the Armistice.

Not far to the north, but in the Third Army, the 15th Battalion (64th Brigade), brought up to Amerval, took part in the 21st Division's attack on 23rd October, when, passing through the 1st East Yorkshire in Ovillers, they fought their way into Vendegies-au-Bois. From there the 62nd Brigade carried the line beyond. In the next day's advance to the Englefontaine/Salesches road the Battalion was held up for some time on the wire of the Hermann Position. However, the enemy machine-gunners were silenced by a bayonet attack led by Captain John Sedgewick, who had distinguished himself the previous year at Polygon Wood. Poix-du-Nord was taken along with many prisoners. An enemy counter-attack early on the 25th was repelled with heavy loss. In the evening the Battalion was withdrawn to Vendegies-au-Bois, having lost seven officers (including Lieut.-Colonel Neeves, wounded) and 246 n.c.o.s and men.

Before it was moved up to take its share in the final advance which it so richly deserved, it received a substantial draft of officers and men; and when it crossed the Sambre on 7th November by a pontoon-bridge at Berlaimont its ranks contained Captain A. M. Lascelles, V.C., M.C., and it was commanded by Lieut.-Colonel A. C. Barnes, D.S.O., M.C. It was involved that morning in some fighting at the Ruisseau Grimour, but, after repelling a counter-attack, it pressed on to Limont-Fontaine and drove the enemy out of the village in a fierce bayonet attack. In this, their last fight, the 15th Durhams lost three officers and 124 n.c.o.s and men killed and

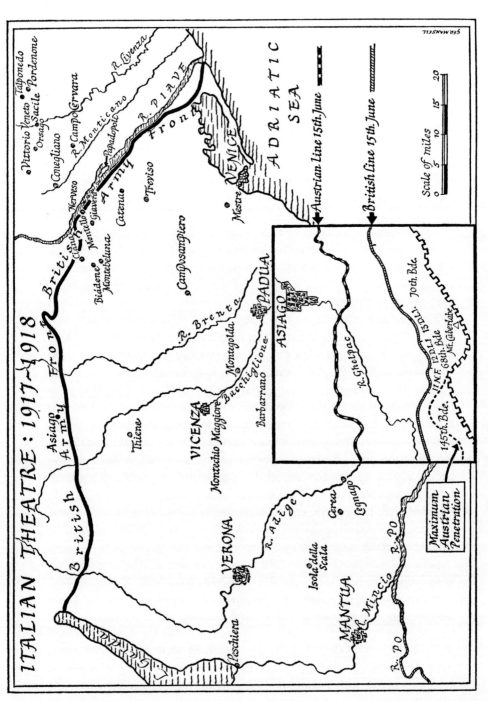

25. The Italian Theatre with (inset) Asiago. 15th June. 1918

wounded. Among the former, killed four days before the Armistice, was Captain A. M. Lascelles. It was at rest in billets at Berlaimont on 11th November.

§

At 11 o'clock on 11th November the Durham battalions all along the Western Front were situated, from north to south, as follows:

the 20th Wearsiders, who had come against determined resistance outside Avelgem on 25th October—among the wounded that day was 2/Lieutenant J. Donnelly, M.C., D.C.M., M.M.—were about 1¼ miles west of Nederbrakel;

the 19th, which had also been involved in an obstinate struggle for the left bank of the Scheldt at Rugge and Waarmaarde on 31st October, were in billets at Everbeek, on the Dender;

the 2/6th were near Lessines, on the Dender;

the 18th were at Quesnau, east of Renaix;

the 29th were resting at Herseaux, east of Tourcoing, after an uncomfortable spell in the line;

the 1/7th were at Harchies, between Condé and Mons;

the 11th were near Feignies, north-east of Maubeuge;

the 1/9th were at Sous-le-Bois, a suburb of Maubeuge;

the 15th were at Berlaimont;

the 13th were at Bousies; and

the 2nd were at Busigny.

Alone of the divisions containing Durham battalions the 6th and the 62nd were designated to form part of the Army of Occupation under General Plumer. The 62nd was the only Territorial division to be selected and the 1/9th the only non-regular Durham battalion to share in the triumphant march to the Rhine. Its route lay by: Colleret, to which it moved on 16th November, Biercée, Haies, Villers-Poterie, Mettet, Bioul, Yvoir, Ciney, Haid, and Haversin (29th November); then on 6th December by Fallon, Ocquier, Saint-Roch, Rahier, Grand-Halleux, Petit-Thier, it entered Germany at Meyerode and Medell on 16th December, proceeding by Büllingen, Udenbreth, Sistig, Eicks and Floisdorf, Berg, to Kommern, which was reached in a snowstorm on 25th December.

The 2nd Battalion started its march to the Rhine with band and colours on 14th November with a short march to Saint-Souplet, thence on the 15th to La Groise, and by Marbaix (16th), Beugnies, Grandrieu, Boussu, Florennes, Falaen, Sommière, Sovet, Miécret, Marchin, Ouffet, Aywaille and Stoumont, it entered Germany at Malmedy (then German), and on 16th December reached Elsenborn

Camp, where so many of the German Army had begun their march in August 1914. Continuing on the 19th to Imgenbroich, and marching by Schleiden, Kommern, Enzen and Dürscheven, it reached Lechenich, its destination, on the 23rd.

*Italy: The Piave, 15-16th June, and
Vittorio-Véneto, 26th-29th October*

To be ordered from the mud, corruption and horror of the Salient as it was in October 1917, to travel past the sunshine and the blue seas of the Riviera, and to arrive on a front where houses were intact and shell-holes were wired in as a precaution against people falling into them, where the enemy knocked off for lunch for two hours at 11.30—this was the happy fortune of the 12th, 13th and 20th Battalions of the Regiment in November 1917, when the 23rd and 41st Divisions (among others) were transferred from the Western Front to help restore the situation in Italy after the disaster at Caporetto. Little wonder an officer wrote saying the men's morale had risen 50 *per cent.*, and that he was "quite tired rushing from one side of the carriage to the other to see some new and wonderful sight". Unfortunately, this idyllic state of affairs did not last long for all. The 20th Battalion was returned in February after hardly more than two months in the Montello sector, to take part in the March retreat. The 13th, after sharing in the repulse of the Austrian offensive on the Asiago Plateau, returned to France in September 1918 when the reductions were applied to the divisions in Italy. Only the 12th stayed on to share in that fine feat of arms which carried the Army across the Piave and led to the crowning victory of Vittorio-Véneto.

The 12th and 13th, detraining at Ásola, west of Mantua, and marching across the plains of Lombardy, were directed upon the River Bacchiglione at Montegalda, where the line was to have been established if the Italian Army had failed to arrest the Austrian advance on Piave. The Piave line, however, held; and since the British divisions were allotted the Montello sector, the 12th and 13th marched forward to Biádene, taking their first duty in the trenches on 27th December between Ciano and Rivasecca. As one private soldier said, "it was a picnic to Passchendale".

The 20th Wearsiders detrained at Isola della Scala and Cerea, near Legnago, on 19th and 20th November. Marching by Barbarano, Camposampiero and Giávera, they relieved the 1st Italian Division in the trenches on the Piave at Nervesa. Conditions were quiet compared with the Western Front and remained so. Casualties in the ranks amounted to only four killed and five wounded during the whole of the Battalion's tour of duty in Italy. One of the few suffered, however, was its commanding officer, Lieut.-Colonel R. C. Smith (1st Battalion), mortally wounded on 1st December during a reconnaissance. He was succeeded by Major A. V. A. Gayer, D.S.O., 23rd Middlesex, who took the Battalion back to France when the 41st Division was transferred from the theatre to meet the impending storm in France at the end of February.

Partly with a view to an offensive movement planned to break through from the Asiago sector, partly in deference to the Italian Command's jealousy of that sector, where the enemy lay within ten miles of the plains, the British divisions were relieved at the Montello and brought up onto the plateau about the middle of March. The two remaining Durham battalions were accordingly moved to Thiene on 25th March. On the 26th, paying farewell to the genial spring weather in the plain, they were carried up in lorries through the snow-covered valley of Carriola, and, equipped with fur boots, "goggles stonebreaker's," alpenstocks and crampons, they entered the line facing Asiago for the first time on 27th March. No Man's Land, which by vigorous patrolling was gradually brought under Allied control, was about a mile deep. The front trenches were cut with characteristic Italian ingenuity in the rock on the forward slope of the south bank of the Ghelpac. The British divisions, favouring the practice developed in France of keeping few men in the front trenches and of relying on counter-attacks from reserve trenches to recover any ground lost in the initial assault, found the Italian system too rigid for their taste, and had to build fresh trenches to give the necessary defence in depth. For the first few months, however, the prospects of all were focused upon an impending Allied offensive on the Asiago front.

These prospects were rudely shattered on 15th June when the Austrians unexpectedly launched an ambitious offensive of their own. It was a pincer movement, one arm of which was intended to break through the Asiago front and penetrate to the plain at Vicenza, while the other, forcing the Italian line on the Piave (from which the battle takes it name), was to cross the river, seize Treviso and exploit to Padua and even as far as the Ádige. The latter for a time looked dangerous, and indeed blew an ominous gap five miles deep on a front of fifteen before it was repaired. The Vicenza movement, on the other hand, made hardly any impression at all.

On 15th June the 68th Brigade had three battalions in the line, the 11th Northumberland Fusiliers on the left, the 12th Battalion (Major J. H. E. Holford, a very good officer from the Sherwood Rangers Yeomanry), and the 13th Battalion (under Major D. H. Clarke, whose qualities have already been mentioned) on the right, all on the forward slopes of Monte Caberlaba. Of the Austrian attack so far as it affected the Durham battalions there is really very little to say. They just shot it to pieces. It was preceded by a heavy bombardment at 3 a.m. which included gas-shells. It quickened at 4, slackened, and then quickened again until the Austrian infantry came on at about 6.45, headed by storm-troopers with detachments of bombers, machine-gunners and *Flammenwerfer*. They mostly belonged to the 38th Honvéd Division, Hungarian reservists whose martial vigour enjoyed a high reputation in former days. Opposed by the rapid musketry and machine-gun fire of the Durhams—the artillery had been shot up in the opening bombardment—they advanced with great gallantry, but not a man of them penetrated the wire on the Durham front. Ten got in amongst the Fusiliers on the left but were immediately killed. The 70th Brigade on the 13th's right lost their forward trenches for a while, but a counter-attack at once restored them. Fighting continued until the later afternoon while the enemy strove to make headway, but by 5.45 the 13th had patrols out in No Man's Land picking up prisoners. During the whole day's work the 12th's casualties amounted to one officer and four men killed and two officers and 35 men wounded; the 13th only two men killed and an officer and 23 men wounded: hardly more than the losses of a "quiet" day on the Western Front.

Before the final Allied offensive in Italy took place, the 13th Battalion, one of the three in the 23rd Division rendered surplus by the "reductions," which were applied to the divisions in the Italian theatre on 6th September, had returned to France. It was relieved in the line on 11th September and entrained at Thiene on the 14th. A little later, the 12th, in view of the forthcoming offensive on the Piave in which the British divisions were cast in the role of storm-troops, was relieved on the Asiago front and moved, on 5th October, to Montecchio Maggiore, and thence by Vicenza, Mestre and Treviso to Catena, which it reached on 23rd October.

The plan was to break through across the Piave and, by penetrating to Vittorio-Véneto, separate the enemy's river front from that in the mountains. The offensive started in the night of 23rd October when a British brigade was poled across the swollen river by skilled Italian boatmen in scows to the island of Papadopoli, in midstream. There a sudden spate isolated it and delayed the main attack until the night of the 26th. The 12th Battalion, under their fire-eating commanding officer, crossed to Papadopoli with the rest of the 68th Brigade at 11.30 that night and were in their assembly positions by

2 a.m., though not before the covering bombardment—and the enemy's counter-bombardment—had opened.

The assault across the further arm of the Piave was no light task. The Durhams, attacking in the centre of the Brigade, which was at the extreme left of the two-division front, had to cross several streams (reported fordable) and then mount an earthen *bund*, or embankment, twelve feet high in some places and about six feet wide at the top, protected by uncut wire and defended by machine-gun posts. When the Battalion advanced at 3.30 a.m. half the leading company were struck wading through the streams, but Captain Gibbens, M.C., D.C.M., cut a passage through the wire at the head of a small party (who were all killed) and so enabled the following company to pass through. The first objective was in their hands by 7.30, the second by 9, when A and B Companies came through them to carry the Battalion to the third. This was the road between Casa Padovan and Casa Benedetti, which was won by 11. The enemy infantry, who were no good in a rough-and-tumble, showed but a feeble resistance; but his machine-gunners, assisted by the terrain, which was enclosed with hedges and buildings, fought skilfully and obstinately, and had to be rushed and surrounded individually. They were matched in obstinacy and skill by the 12th, whose display of both qualities is shown in the very moderate casualties they suffered (by Western Front standards), of two officers and 27 n.c.o.s and men killed and three officers and 111 n.c.o.s and men wounded. and 11 missing.

The advance, resumed in a north-easterly direction at 12.30 p.m. the next day, carried them against similar resistance forward to their next objective. On the 29th the Battalion forced the passage of the Monticano at Casa Balbi with the co-operation of the 11th Northumberland Fusiliers on their left; and by 3.30 a.m. on the 30th they had reached the objective of the road from Conegliano to Campo Cervaro. By this time it was not just a bridgehead that had been secured but a penetration of the enemy's whole defensive line. The pursuit moreover was pressed hard. The 12th Battalion, placed in reserve on the 30th, went into billets at Orsago that night. It is surprising to have to record that although all ranks had been wet through since crossing the Piave, had lain in the open in the frost and had fought for three successive days, not a man fell out during the trying march to Orsago. After moving to Sacile on 31st October, they were at Talponedo, a small village west of Pordenone, when the armistice with the Austrians came into effect at 3 p.m. on 3rd November.

Macedonia, 1916-1918

The Ruritanian politics in which we became embroiled when a Franco-British force was sent in October 1915 to the Greek port of Salonika, to assist the Serbian Army when crushed by a combined Austrian, German and Bulgarian offensive, need not detain us. Nor, really, need the operations, in which the two Durham battalions that served in the theatre, the 2/5th and the 2/9th, were involved only marginally.

Both were second-line Territorial battalions which, after supplying Category A1 drafts to the first-line battalions in France, became almost entirely B1 and "homeless" upon the break-up of the 63rd Division on 21st July 1916. The 2/5th, under the command of Lieut.-Colonel P. W. Williams-Till, had been under canvas at Babworth near Retford until moving to Catterick in July. Equipped with sun-helmets and tropical kit, it embarked at Southampton on 1st November. Disembarking at Salonika on the 17th, it was employed for some months on guard duties on the road from Salonika to Seres until 1st March 1917, when, although classed fit only for garrison duties, it was brigaded in the 228th Brigade and brought up into the line. Its brigadier, Brigadier-General W. C. Ross, was that same Durham Light Infantryman who was last mentioned receiving his terrible wound at Bothaville. The 2/9th Battalion, embarking at Southampton under the command of Lieut.-Colonel F. R. Simpson[33] on 4th November, remained near the base at Salonika for the remainder of the war. Its record consists of little more than the routine for fatigue-parties, guard detachments and other similar duties in unpleasant surroundings for months on end.

The record of the 2/5th was rather less monotonous. The sector in which the 228th Brigade relieved the 83rd (28th Division) lay to the west of Lake Butkovo, and the portion of the line held by the Battalion from 25th March lay on the forward slope of the Krusha Ridge (with headquarters on a hill called Belvedere), overlooking the valley of the Struma. Beyond rose the towering Belašica (Belashitza) Mountains, occupied by the Bulgarians. The positions of both opponents were almost impregnable; neither could do much; and apart

[33]Afterward Sir Frank Robert Simpson, Bt., Hon. Col., 9th Battalion, and High Sheriff of the County, 1935 (1864-1949). Four other members of this Durham family have given their services to the Regiment: his two sons, Captain Claude Frank Bell, 9th, killed 3rd December 1917, and Basil Robert James (the present baronet), who served as a lieutenant in the 2nd Battalion and was wounded on 18th September 1918; and two nephews, Robert Barry Yelverton (born 1898) who served in the 2nd Battalion from April to June 1918, and Frank Harold (born 1902). Both have commanded the 1st and 2nd Battalions.

from reliefs and patrols, with which the Bulgarians interfered little, almost the only variations in the routine were the seasonal retirement to the summer line, higher up the Krusha Ridge (June), and the seasonal reoccupation of the winter line (November). Deaths from wounds totalled two during the whole campaign. The principal foe was disease, which accounted for 21 deaths in the Battalion, mainly from malaria, from which in June 1917 as many as 76 in one company were in hospital.

The routine remained unbroken until September 1918. The main offensive, which was begun on 14th September, took place many miles to the left of the Butkovo front. But on the 24th the 2/5th was ordered forward from their summer line near Kamberli to the winter line. On 1st October, the day after the Bulgarian armistice, the advance of the 228th Brigade, now on the extreme British right and under Greek command, started with a move to Dojran, which was reached on the 5th. On the 14th it crossed the Belašica Mountains by the Kosturino Pass. The Battalion had got to Radomir when, on 31st October, the Turkish armistice having been signed, both it and the 2/5th Seaforths of the Brigade were ordered by General Franchet d'Espérey to occupy the Black Sea ports of Varna and Burgas. Railed by way of Sofia and Plevna, the Durham battalion arrived at Varna on 12th November.

On 8th February 1919 it embarked for Batum, the Russian port on the Black Sea which, ceded to Turkey in March 1918, was occupied by the Allies as bailees. There, from the 20th of that month for four months, it was given—amongst others—the embarrassing duty of protecting the person of the Turkish General Nuri Pasha. Demobilisation had reduced the Battalion to a mere 19 officers and 100 men when on 17th September it left Batum for Constantinople. It landed at Devonport on 30th October, and was disbanded a few days later after nearly three years foreign service.

The 2/9th at the same time, under the command (since 28th February 1918) of Lieut.-Colonel A. Henderson, moved a few miles out of Salonika to Kalamaria on 15th July, 1919. Its disbandment was completed on 5th January 1920.

Archangel, 1918-1919

The 2/7th, like the 2/9th, had formed part of the 190th Brigade of the 63rd Division when the division was broken up in the summer of 1916. The brigade was not broken up until 4th December, but the 2/7th had already left on 29th November to join the 214th Brigade at Andover. The brigade was taken out of the 71st Division to join the 67th in the Colchester and Ipswich area on 12th February 1918.

At the end of September the 2/7th left the brigade and on 7th October it embarked for North Russia as a garrison battalion, disembarking at Bakaritsa, opposite Archangel, on 24th October. Neither the depressing conditions of an Arctic winter nor the conflicting and discouraging tasks with which the Archangel force was entrusted need emphasising; and since the Battalion appears never to have had even the satisfaction of serving with the part of the force that was active in the interior, it is unnecessary to enlarge upon the melancholy fate reserved for this battalion except to observe that it was present in the theatre.

India: the North-West Frontier and
the Third Afghan War

The feelings of the 1st Battalion can be imagined when, one after another, the British infantry battalions in India were taken for service in one theatre or another until only eight[34] out of the fifty-two remained, and still the 68th had not gone. So acute was their disappointment that when volunteers for drafts were called for 880 out of 900 responded, and when a braggart from home taunted them on their detention in India he was found next morning outside the canteen with his brains battered in. A magnificent body of seasoned soldiers, most of them men of seven years' service or more, under a most able and inspiring commanding officer, the last survivor of de Lisle's famous polo team, in August 1914 the Battalion had been abroad nearly fifteen years. Earlier in the year it had taken part in a hard campaign against the Bunerwals near the Malandri Pass, and it was as hard as nails. It could reasonably look forward to active service or relief. Yet, according to the policy of the Indian government under which the seasoned European units of the three Frontier divisions should be retained at their stations at all costs, it was kept for a prolonged tour of duty on the Frontier, subjected at the same time to a steady drain of officers and its best n.c.o.s and men attached to units in active theatres.

When war broke out six officers were on leave. Captain J. H. Wood joined the 2nd Battalion in France, where he was wounded; Captain R. V. Turner also joined the 2nd Battalion, which he eventually rose to command; Lieutenant J. A. Churchill held a number of staff appointments in the Expeditionary Force from August 1914 till the end; Lieutenant G. Hayes was appointed adjutant of the 11th Battalion, which he afterwards commanded; Lieutenant J. G. Harter

---

[34]The 2nd King's, 2nd Somerset Light Infantry, 1st Yorkshire (Green Howards), 1st Duke of Wellington's, 1st Royal Sussex, 1st South Lancashire, 2nd North Staffordshire and the 1st Durham Light Infantry.

was appointed brigade-major of the 151st Brigade and died of wounds he received in the fighting at The Bluff on 2nd March 1916. Only Lieutenant J. O. C. Hasted returned to the Battalion in India. He left it early in October 1916 to command a company of the 2nd Leicester in Mesopotamia, where he gained a very good D.S.O., and returned on 20th August 1917 to become adjutant.

Of the officers with the Battalion in 1914 one followed another home until, early in 1917, only Major E. du P. H. Moore (commanding), Lieutenants J. F. Ferguson and E. H. L. Lysaght-Griffin and Major Freel, the quartermaster, remained from the original number. Major Goring-Jones, the second-in-command, returned in May 1915 to take command of the 2nd Battalion until promoted to the command of the 146th Brigade. Major H. R. Cumming, an able officer with an attractive personality who had been a company commander at Sandhurst, returned from India to command the 2nd Battalion until he too was promoted to a brigade, the 110th. (He was killed by Sinn Feiners in an ambush near Cloonbannin on 5th March 1921 when military governor of Kerry.) In August 1915 Captain R. C. Smith went home and took command of the 20th Wearsiders, with whom he was killed in Italy in December 1917. Major C. L. Matthews left in September 1915 to command—most successfully— the 1/4th Hampshire in Mesopotamia. In June 1916 Colonel Luard himself vacated the command for the command of a brigade, first in India, then in Mesopotamia and later in Palestine (the 8th Brigade, 3rd (Lahore) Division). In October 1916 Majors W. B. Greenwell (adjutant until 1st June 1916), R. Tyndall and E. V. Manger were ordered home: Greenwell to take command of the 19th Battalion, Tyndall the 12th, and Manger to serve with the 2nd Battalion, which he commanded from December 1916 to February 1917, when he left to command the 2/9th King's. In March 1917 they were followed by Captains H. C. Boxer, H. R. McCullagh, E. H. Gilpin and A. G. de Bunsen. Boxer later transferred to the Tank Corps; McCullagh joined the 2nd Battalion, commanded it from 15th August 1917 to 5th February 1918, and commanded the 19th from June to October 1918; Gilpin joined the 2nd Battalion as adjutant and was killed on 21st March 1918. Major D. L. Brereton came back early enough to be wounded during the march from Wieltje to Hooge on 6th August 1915 and commanded the 2nd Battalion in its magnificent fight at Morchies on 21st March 1918. Major H. W. Festing, Brigade-major of the 2nd Infantry Brigade at Nowshera from 1914 to 1916, having returned home to command the 15th Battalion, was killed on the same day. Major H. E. Lavie returned to command the 6th York and Lancaster and later became one of Ironside's stalwarts in the North Russia campaign of 1919. Lieutenant P. A. Smith left in October 1916 to command a company of the 2nd Dorset in Mesopotamia, and afterwards joined the Royal Flying Corps. Lieutenant A. J. Clifton played an important part in the formation of the Tank Corps in India and subsequently commanded an armoured car battalion.

By the end of the war all the officers of 1914 save only Major Moore, Major Freel and one other had served outside the Battalion. Captain Lysaght-Griffin left in October 1917 to be seconded to the Signal Service in Mesopotamia, first in command of a mobile signal section in the I Corps area, later in command of the 31st Signal Company working under G. H. Q. at Baghdad. Captain Ferguson, appointed adjutant *vice* Greenwell on 1st June 1916, left the Battalion in September 1917 to be attached to the 2nd Leicester in Hasted's place as a company commander. While on patrol near Jaffa in April 1918 he was wounded and taken prisoner by the Turks but miraculously survived his captivity.

Similarly many of the best of the senior non-commissioned officers were commissioned, some to serve outside the Battalion. While Sergeant-major Waiton, Quartermaster-sergeant Tilley, Colour-sergeant Sibbald and Sergeant Mahoney were early commissioned in the Battalion, at the same time Colour-sergeant A. Howe, who had served as a sergeant in Gough's Mounted Infantry in South Africa, was commissioned in the Royal West Kent and served in Mesopotamia attached to the Royal Fusiliers; and Colour-sergeant R. C. Loverock, commissioned in the Oxford and Buckingham Light Infantry, was wounded serving in Mesopotamia, where he was awarded the D.S.O. Private Norman Lobb, one of the best athletes in the Battalion, left it in 1914 for the Signal Service in East Africa. He got the D.C.M. at Tanga, but later, unfortunately, died of cholera at Kut just before it fell. Private Allison, who had been with him, died in captivity. Moreover, two substantial drafts of n.c.o.s and men were dispatched to Mesopotamia for service with regular battalions, one of them the Black Watch.

The fates of these men have been detailed at some length to show that the training and experience of this fine battalion were not thrown away and that, quite apart from its services on the Frontier—which were essential however unpopular—it contributed its weight to the great struggle. That standards had to be lowered in consequence was to be expected. But the frank inspection report made on 18th March 1917 by Brig.-General Beynon, a most able and experienced Frontier soldier, shows that there was nothing that could be described as deterioration. The Battalion, he said, "has been in the field since June 1915 and is thoroughly fit and serviceable. The men are in hard condition. There has been a steady drain on officers and n.c.o.s to supply drafts, and few of the old officers remain. The present officers consist mainly of youngsters from England or of promotions from the ranks, but so far the training of the men shows no deterioration." Sir F. Campbell, commanding the 1st (Peshawar) Division, of which it formed part, found the rank and file "a smart hard-bitten lot," and the Battalion as a whole "a first-class fighting unit". In June 1917 it was inspected by Lieut.-General Sir A. A. Barrett, commanding the Northern Army, who knew it well and wrote that "the old light infantry spirit is very much to the fore in the Battalion, which is in very good order and quite fit for active service". Major-General Sir Charles Dobell, its divisional commander at Rawalpindi, reported in July 1918 that he considered it "to be up to pre-war standard;" and even in August 1919, when almost 400 of the old n.c.o.s and men had returned home as "pivotal men" or on release-slips, he could write that "the pre-war spirit and standard prevail". Before the war it had been a current saying on the Frontier: "a tap of the drum, a pair of green hose-tops, and the D.L.I. has passed". It still would not have been out of place five years later.[35]

The operations in which the Battalion took part appear insignificant beside the gigantic offensives in Europe, where battalions lost half their strength in a single attack. The absence of a butcher's bill, however, was partly due to the skill with which experienced infantry could carry out their task, which, essentially, was the defence of India on a frontier that was always unsettled and at once became turbulent so soon as it got round to the tribes that the garrison was reduced.

The Mohmands, one of the large tribes of the belt of Independent Tribal Territory on the Indian side of the Afghan border, early gave evidence of restlessness, and from 1915 to 1917 gave plenty of occupation to the 1st (Peshawar) Division, to the Nowshera Brigade of which the Battalion belonged. The Battalion was mobilised at Nowshera under the orders of Lieut.-Colonel Luard on 17th April 1915. After some preliminary operations in which the companies were detached, headquarters were moved north to Malakand on 23rd August, and thence to Haibatgram, on the left bank of the Swat

[35]The origin of the phrase is obscure, though it is said to date from a review at Peshawar. Green hose-tops, incidentally, became a free issue in the Battalion on 23rd March 1918, "correspondence from A.H.Q. rendering this necessary to prevent the total abolition of hose-tops as being an unnecessary expense to the Division".

River, where the Brigade[36] was assembled under the command of
Brig.-General W. G. L. Beynon to meet an advance of the tribal
lashkars from the upper Swat valley. This was successfully checked in
a small engagement near Landakai, and the Brigade moved back to
Chakdarra. When temporarily under Luard's command on 26th
October it advanced north to disperse a *lashkar* of about a thousand
Swatis and several hundred Pathans, who had come down to
Kotegram, nine miles away. The Battalion, acting as advanced
guard on the 27th, covered the advance of the 46th Punjabis with
musketry and machine-gun fire—a combined operation which,
though failing to catch the enemy, so effectively dispersed him that
the camp at Chakdarra remained unmolested by his snipers until the
Brigade returned to Nowshera on 26th February 1916. At the same
time B Company, under Captain Manger at Mardan, where it
formed part of the Mardan Mobile Column,[37] was engaged on
19th October in a similar action on the Peshawar/Abazai road near
Matta. It did not rejoin the Battalion at Nowshera until 20th April
1916.

In October 1916 a strict blockade of the Mohmand country was
imposed. A chain of posts was erected at intervals of about 400 yards
between Abazai, where the Swat River leaves the hills, and Michni,
on the Kabul River. A double apron barbed-wire fence was run
between the posts and, in front, a curtain of live wire supplied with
current from the powerhouse at Abazai. During the winter of 1916/17
the blockade line was garrisoned in turn by a brigade of the Peshawar Division, each brigade taking a tour of two months' duty.
Improvements made in the line in May 1917, by the construction of
rough country towers in the place of the open works used at first,
enabled it to be garrisoned by only two battalions; and after July,
when the Mohmands had come to terms, the regular troops were
relieved by the newly raised Mohmand Militia, who were holding the
towers and the wire at the outbreak of the Third Afghan War in 1919.

Before, however, the line was properly completed the 1st Battalion
was mobilised on 22nd October 1916 and marched, 18 officers[38] and

[36]Wing 1st Durham Light Infantry, 46th Punjabis, 82nd Punjabis and 2/1st
Gurkha Rifles.

[37]One squadron 14th Lancers, one section 8th Mountain Battery, R.G.A., B
Company 1st Durham Light Infantry and 38th Dogras, under the command of
Lieut.-Colonel Longden, 38th Dogras.

[38]Major E. du P. H. Moore (commanding), Captain H. R. Richardson (second-
in-command), Captains H. C. Boxer (A Company), H. R. McCullagh (D Company), E. H. Gilpin (C Company), A. G. de Bunsen (B Company), J. F. Ferguson
(adjutant) and P. A. Smith, Lieutenants C. W. Sibbald, S. V. Mercer, A. W. T.
Harwood and G. Stevenson, and 2/Lieutenants B. T. Sketchley, G. T. Gold-
schmidt, F. Taylor, W. English, G. W. Daintree and H. V. Page (attached).

THE GREAT WAR, 1914-1918

THE GREAT WAR, 1914-1918 443

613 n.c.o.s and men strong, to Pabbi, on the Nowshera/Peshawar road. From then until 7th February 1917, acting with the 2nd Infantry Brigade,[39] it was in perpetual movement along the blockade line, and on 15th November 1916 took part in a serious little action at Subhan Khwar, near Shabkadar. The enemy had been reported occupying the Hafiz Kor *nulla*, and the brigade was ordered at 10 that morning to advance against him on a 2000 yard front. The Battalion attacked on the left of the brigade line with two companies up (A and D), one (C) in support and the fourth in brigade reserve. The position was taken with few casualties, and the enemy's fire remained desultory until about 4 in the afternoon, when the order was given to retire to the camp at Subhan Khwar. The enemy promptly followed boldly and occupied the vacated position within minutes of the brigade's withdrawal. A heavy covering fire from C Company prevented any serious interference, however, and by 5.30 the Battalion was back in camp having lost one man killed and one officer (Lieutenant G. Stevenson) and nine n.c.o.s and men wounded. C.S.M. J. R. Kilgour was later awarded the D.C.M. for his conduct on this occasion, and Sergeant E. Devereux, Corporal F. E. P. Gordon and Private A. Lawty the M.M. The action was the fourth and last in a series fought at Subhan Khwar since the beginning of the Mohmand rising in April 1915.

The months from February to November 1917 were the last of the Battalion's six year stay in Nowshera. On 24th November it was relieved by the 2nd North Staffordshire and moved back to Rawalpindi, where it formed part of the 2nd (Rawalpindi) Division; and it was quartered there, under the command of Lieut.-Colonel Moore, when the Third Afghan War broke out.

The war occurred at an awkward moment. Though the armistices in Europe had been signed, the larger part and the best of the Indian regiments were still absent. The European regiments were for the most part Territorials anxious for relief and demobilisation. The few survivors of the Old Contemptible battalions, the backbone of the garrison, were, as already indicated, under-strength and already suffering from the pangs of demobilisation. There was much political unrest, inflamed early in 1919 by the passing of the Rowlatt Acts, which, enabling judges to try political cases in certain circumstances without juries, appeared to conflict both with the aspirations of the Congress and declared government policy. Serious riots broke out in Delhi, Ahmedabad, Lahore and Amritsar. The civil disturbances

[39] 1/4th Queen's, 1st Durham Light Infantry, 46th Punjabis and 95th Russell's Infantry, under the command of Brig.-General W. G. L. Beynon.

alone were an acute embarrassment. At Rawalpindi, for example, the 1st Battalion from an effective strength of only 320 had to keep in a state of readiness parties of a hundred men for the locomotive shops, fifty for the emergency column and another hundred for aid to the civil power. A detachment of 25 was sent down to Lahore on 15th April 1919; and the Battalion hockey-team, fourteen men under Sergeant Davies, who happened to be in Lahore for a tournament at the time, exchanged their sticks for rifles and played an important part in suppressing a riot, killing and capturing some armed rioters.

It was in the midst of this delicate period of transition that the political structure, which had kept the border tribes and the whole Afghan frontier comparatively tranquil, collapsed with the murder of the Emir of Afghanistan, Habibulla, who despite temptation had honoured his covenants with the Indian government. He was succeeded by his son Amanulla, who was in the hands of a faction clamouring for war. Taking advantage of the government's embarrassment, even fomenting the political agitation and, as usual, rousing the border tribes, the new Emir moved Afghan troops and irregulars across the frontier at the beginning of May 1919. It says much for the high quality of the frontier garrison that, notwithstanding its weakness, the formidable Afghan hosts made little headway. They were beaten wherever they debouched. A counterthrust to Kabul was even contemplated (but given up), and the war, though its legacy of unrest among the frontier tribesmen persisted until 1939, was soon over.

The first Afghan incursion took place on the Khyber front. The brunt of it was gallantly borne by the Peshawar Division, which in a series of hard fought actions not only repelled the invasion but chased the Afghans back to Dakka before the Rawalpindi Division came up. Unfortunately the contagion had spread to the Afridi clans, who largely composed the Khyber militia performing the normal police work of the Pass. When the Khyber Rifles were disbanded their duties fell to the Rawalpindi Division, which, on arriving at the Khyber in the nick of time, was entrusted, first with the relief of the 1st Division at Peshawar and Nowshera, and later, when itself relieved by the 16th Division, with the protection of the communications along the pass.

The 1st Battalion, which, had it not been relieved in the Peshawar Division, would have been as much in the thick of it as their successors were, was consequently deprived of an opportunity of fighting. Having completed its mobilisation at Connaught Barracks, Rawalpindi, within nine hours of receiving the order at 3.40 in the morning

of 6th May, it was railed forward to Peshawar with the rest of the
4th Brigade[40] in the evening of the 9th. Armed with "Mark III
H.V. (converted)" rifles, which had been returned from one of the
fronts in very bad condition, it was a weak battalion with a strength
of 20 officers[41] and 432 n.c.o.s and men. It arrived at Peshawar at
10 a.m. on 10th May, and, after a few days of policing duties, went up
by lorry to Jamrud, which was reached at 8.30 a.m. on the 17th.
Ali Masjid was reached after a hot and dusty march at 3.45 p.m.
without any encounters with Afridis, though the second-line transport was sniped. The next day it went on with the 33rd Punjabis to
Landi Kotal, where it remained until 28th May. In the projected
advance to Jalalabad it got only as far as Landi Khana (29th to 30th
May) before the movement was cancelled owing to a fresh incursion
by the Afghans to the south, on the Kurram front. The Emir asked
for an armistice on 3rd June; but although hostilities officially ceased
on the Khyber, he continued to incite the tribes on either side of the
Durand Line, and the fighting went on. The Battalion was not
directly involved, and it was still at Landi Kotal when on 11th
August news reached it that the Emir had signed a peace treaty at
Rawalpindi on the 8th.

From that moment the dissolution of the Battalion proceeded
apace. It had known for some time it was to return to Europe in the
trooping season, and the advance party sailed from Bombay on 21st
September. In October three officers and 155 men departed on
demobilisation, and when the Battalion left Landi Kotal for Rawalpindi on 3rd November it comprised only seven officers and 159
n.c.o.s and men present. On 12th November Lieut.-Colonel Moore
left to take command of the 2nd Battalion (then at Batum); Major
Hasted followed him soon after; and for a few weeks the Battalion
was commanded by Captain Waiton, who in 1914 had been its
regimental sergeant-major. When it finally embarked at Bombay on
29th December under Captain Charles it consisted of no more than
four officers and 87 n.c.o.s and men. On 12th February 1920 it

---

[40]4th Brigade, 2nd (Rawalpindi) Division, under Brig.-General E. C. Peebles:
1st Durham Light Infantry, 1/33rd Punjabis, 40th Pathans, 2/54th Sikhs
(F.F.)

[41]Lieut.-Colonel E. du P. H. Moore (commanding), Major H. Richardson,
Captains J. O. C. Hasted, D.S.O. (adjutant), C. Waiton, P. Hartridge, C. W.
Sibbald, A. W. T. Harwood, S. V. Mercer, Lieutenants F. Gunn, W. M. Wardle,
F. D. Charles, H. Critchley, F. A. Marks, Curry, Ashton, Geraghty, Hartigan,
Brown and Clark; and the Quartermaster, W. H. Lowe, R.S.M. for many
years, who had succeeded Lieut.-Colonel Freel, D.C.M., on 11th March.
Lieutenants A. J. Goldie, G. W. Daintree and J. Mahoney joined a few
days later.

landed at Liverpool. This country had not seen it since it left for the Boer War in October 1899.

The return of the 1st Battalion is a suitable moment at which to mark the end of the War, a war in which the Regiment in four years earned four times as many battle-honours as it had gained in the whole of its previous history. The casualties it suffered were in proportion. According to the figures compiled officially immediately after, the 12,006 n.c.o.s and men who lost their lives while serving in the Regiment may be distributed among the Battalions as follows:

1st Battalion	42	b/f	8078
2nd Battalion	1306	15th Battalion	1508
3rd Battalion	64	16th Battalion	8
4th Battalion	27	17th Battalion	11
1/5th Battalion	831	18th Battalion	525
2/5th Battalion	23	19th Battalion	496
1/6th Battalion	830	20th Battalion	677
2/6th Battalion	52	21st Battalion	5
1/7th Battalion	600	22nd Battalion	526
2/7th Battalion	26	25th Battalion	37
1/8th Battalion	816	26th Battalion	25
2/8th Battalion	9	27th Battalion	8
1/9th Battalion	682	28th Battalion	2
2/9th Battalion	28	29th Battalion	51
10th Battalion	688	51st Battalion	3
11th Battalion	288	52nd Battalion	7
12th Battalion	534	53rd Battalion	7
13th Battalion	635	5th (Res) Battalion	19
14th Battalion	597	Depot	13
c/f	8078	Total	12,006

There had been some doubts at first as to the advisability of regiments raising service battalions, and had it been known how soon the old regular army would be destroyed in the field the doubts would have been hard to allay. That the new battalions should have not only maintained but even raised the Regiment's reputation speaks highly for those few officers and n.c.o.s who early set an example of service to those who had never come near the army in their lives. Once the example was set the Regiment's reputation depended entirely upon the Durham men who filled its ranks. The manner in which they met, and rose above, the trials of the bloodiest war in our whole history is still a live memory for those who saw them. From it has sprung the exceptional bond that has since existed between County and Regiment: the one secure in the knowledge that it has confided its sons to a first-class concern, the other that its reputation, hardly won and jealously preserved, is safe in the hands of Durham men.[42]

[42]In so partial and condensed an account as this of a huge struggle like the First War it seems pedantic to give any references, unless it is by way of making acknowledgment. The history of the Service Battalions is admirably and accurately covered by Capt. Wilfrid Miles, *The Durham Forces in the Field, 1914-1918* (London, 1920), originally intended as the second volume to a work of which the first was to continue Col. Vane's history of the regular and Territorial battalions. Col. Vane died, however, before his contribution was completed, and the gap was never made good, although it was partially filled by two good battalion histories (Major A. L. Raimes's of the 5th (1931) and Major E. H. Veitch's of the 8th) and Col. W. I. Watson's *Short History* of the 6th (1939). Those who find the present account insufficient are referred to these, as well as to Lieut.-Col. W. D. Lowe's *War History of the 18th (S) Battalion* (Oxford, 1920). The Territorial battalions' services are covered by Everard Wyrall's *History* of the 50th Division (1939). The regular battalions, on the other hand, have not so far had their services fully recorded, and if it might seem as though they receive undue emphasis or space, that is the reason. In contemporary ms. material I have had the privilege of seeing Brig.-Gen. H. H. S. Morant's detailed diaries, which Mrs Morant generously allowed me to see; and the letters written by Major Arnold Pumphrey (20th Battalion), which his sister, Mrs E. A. Pumphrey, very kindly lent to me.

CHAPTER XI

THE YEARS BETWEEN, AND THE SECOND
WORLD WAR, 1919-1945

THE nation emerged from the war with an influence enlarged,
both in moral and territorial terms, as it had never been in the
whole course of its history. Great empires had fallen, and the victors
entered as heirs or trustees to their dominions. It is now clear in
retrospect that the resources which this country was prepared to
devote, in its fond belief that all wars had ended, were inadequate,
irrespective of the new commitments. Having reduced its immense
armies, it had reverted to a professional army enlisted voluntarily
from a war-weary population substantially diminished by the loss of
Ireland. The Cardwell System, which had barely survived the strain
of the Boer War, was given another lease of life but only by means of
such makeshifts as making home stations of Germany and Gibraltar.
In the disappearance of the militia, moreover, which was placed in
"suspended animation," an essential feature of the Cardwell
System was abandoned. The consequent strain on the regular army
during the two decades that followed not only deprived it of the
orderly rotation of reliefs that were another feature of the system, but
denied it the leisure and the opportunity to absorb and practise the
new techniques developed in the war.

In some respects but not all, the history of the times was reflected
in that of the Regiment. It had its share of emergencies and hurried
departures, and it took part in the belated experiments made in the
'thirties towards a new organisation. One sorry consequence, however, it was spared. Durham being one of the countries hardest hit
by the economic depression as well as being one in which unemploy-
ment gave a welcome, however regrettable, stimulus to enlisting, the
Regiment could have recruited itself six times over. Recruiting had
even to be suspended for several months in the year. As it was,

recruits were so numerous that the old militia barracks at Barnard Castle were opened up as additional accommodation. The low establishments of the post-war infantry battalions were insufficient to absorb all into the Regiment—indeed there was hardly a regiment in the army that did not receive recruits from Durham; and the Regiment, possessing a high reputation as a sporting regiment—its football and polo successes continued throughout the 1920s and 1930s—was in a position to take its pick of the recruits. No other line regiment enjoyed such advantages.

§

The reconstitution of the two battalions on a regular basis took place in 1919 and 1920. The 2nd Battalion, which had moved from Lechenich to Pingsheim and thence to Brühl near Cologne early in 1919, was scarcely recognisable as a regular battalion, being composed largely of men due for demobilisation. On 14th April the cadre of 6 officers and 50 n.c.o.s and men was brought back to Catterick. At the same time the foreign service details under Major D. L. Brereton, together with drafts of men re-enlisting for overseas service, were moved from Bordon to Catterick to form a new 2nd Battalion under the temporary command of Lieut.-Colonel Morant. Embarking on 13th October with a strength of 23 officers and 777 n.c.o.s and men under the temporary command of Major R. V. Turner for an unknown destination (which turned out to be Batum), it started a tour of foreign duty which was destined to last until it returned to Woking on 16th November 1937.

The 1st Battalion was reconstituted for home service. The home service details, a collection of men whose numbers fluctuated daily but aggregating some 30 officers and 700 n.c.o.s and men, had been formed from the 3rd Battalion on 27th September 1919 (the last act performed by the militia in the history of the Regiment), and assembled at Tidworth under Lieut.-Colonel Morant. The backbone of what at first was not a very military body was formed by the cadre on its return from India, who joined on 20th February 1920 to make a new 1st Battalion. Before it had properly shaken down and while it still contained a strong short-service element, it was embarked at Dover under Colonel Morant on 2nd March for Cologne, where, quartered in barracks at Riehl, it was brigaded in the 2nd Rhine Brigade.

In the troubled post-war years it could not long remain quiet. On 28th May 1921 it was railed by way of Mainz, Leipzig and Breslau to Oppeln in Upper Silesia, where hostilities had broken out as a result of the realignment of the Polish-German frontier. Four British battalions had been sent from the Rhine the previous March to help preserve order during the plebiscite, which had disappointed the Poles in giving the Germans a two-thirds majority. The Poles, under a freebooter of the name of Korfanty, had retaliated by raising one of those "free corps" that abounded in central Europe at the time, which on 3rd May entered German territory and claimed large portions, including the vital industrial belt, for Poland. They were resisted by a similar "free corps", the *Selbstschutz*, led by General Karl Höfer, a German officer with a distinguished war record who had lost an arm at Kemmel in 1918. The ensuing struggle looked dangerous. While Korfanty's *freicorps* appeared to be receiving undue support from the French occupation forces, Höfer's stood every chance of being reinforced and countenanced by the German government in a manner that became only too familiar fifteen or so years later. Each party numbered, it was said, not less than 80,000, and though they wore no more than brassards to distinguish themselves, they were heavily armed and equipped with artillery. The German party confidently assumed that the British force would take the German side against the French. But in any case what, between such opponents, could a weak occupation force expect to accomplish even if it were united in sentiment?

That a situation so potentially explosive should have been peacefully resolved reflects every credit upon the good sense and bearing of those on the spot. In the first place the British contingent, a "division" of two brigades,[1] each of three weak battalions (two of which had to be brought from England), resolutely refused to be drawn into taking sides against the French. Secondly, although compelled to occupy a curious neutral zone in a No Man's Land between two well armed opponents, the Allied force succeeded nevertheless in preventing either party from gaining a mastery, and gradually imposed its will.

The 1st Battalion, four weak companies commanded by officers who had all commanded battalions in the War, with a total strength of 27 officers and 355 n.c.o.s and men, went into billets at Kempa and Krzanowitz (later renamed Erlengrund), north of Oppeln, on 1st June. Its position in the neutral zone, which it occupied on 4th June, lay on the southern slopes of the commanding Annaberg; and although both Kennedy and Morant failed to persuade Höfer to

[1]Upper Silesian Division (Major-General Sir W. Heneker): 1st Brigade (Col.-Commandant A. G. Wauchope): 1st Royal Irish, 3rd Middlesex, 2nd Connaught Rangers; 2nd Brigade (Col.-Commandant A. B. Kennedy): 2nd Black Watch, 1st Durham Light Infantry, 2nd Leinster Regiment.

cancel a retaliatory offensive which threw Korfanty's men back at Gleiwitz, both parties were eventually prevailed upon to evacuate the plebiscite area. The remainder of the Battalion's stay, while the dispute was referred to the League of Nations (which gave an award unexpectedly favourable to the Poles), was comparatively quiet. In September for some months part of the Battalion was quartered in Schloss Koschentin belonging to Prince Hohenlohe-Ingelfingen, a name well-known to soldiers of the previous generation, who, in recognition of his treatment, frequently took the officers shooting on his estate. It was a quasi-military operation in which the hares, red-deer, wild duck or partridge were pursued by a long line of beaters, impeccably dressed from the right or the left, who were periodically advanced or halted by the Prince's foresters clothed in green, who sounded his orders on bugles. In December B Company under Captain V. A. C. Yate was sent to Ödenburg (Sopron) in the province of Burgenland for two months, when the Hungarians refused to surrender the town to the Austrians, to whom it had been promised in the peace treaty. Another company for a time occupied Lublinitz, where Lieutenant E. A. Arderne, a young officer who had served with the 2nd Battalion in the closing stages of the War, distinguished himself by a cross-country run from there to Ratibor and back (120 miles) in forty-eight hours.

Except for a sudden move to Bobrek in June 1922, the Battalion's year-long duty in Upper Silesia was unmarked by further emergencies. On 3rd July, having received General Heneker's congratulations on its "reliability, smartness and good discipline," it returned to Cologne. A fortnight later, on 17th July, it was brought back to England and stationed in York.

There is little to be said of its stay either at York (19th July 1922 to 29th December 1924), Ballykinler (31st December 1924 to 16th January 1926) or Belfast (16th January 1926 to 4th November 1927). Lieut.-Colonel Morant was succeeded in the command by Lieut.-Colonel A. E. Irvine in January 1923, Lieut.-Colonel Irvine by Lieut.-Colonel Matthews in January 1927. It was a period of steady improvement both in strength and composition upon the immediate post-war years. One link with the past was broken in these years when the old "Iron Band," which had been the Battalion's pride since the days before the Boer War, was finally discontinued after a vain attempt to revive it on the Battalion's return from India. Only the Military and String Bands were retained.

In the 1927 trooping season it was to have moved to Devonport, but owing to the dislocation of the reliefs caused by the Shanghai emergency—which disturbed the 2nd Battalion at Sialkot—the

Battalion was sent to Alexandria. Leaving Belfast on 3rd November and embarking the next day at Southampton, where it was seen off by the Colonel (Major-General Sir Frederick Robb), Colonel Irvine, Lieut.-Colonel Jeffreys and Lieut.-Colonel Freel, the 1st Battalion took over Mustapha Barracks from the 1st Leicester on 16th November.

The G.O.C. British Troops in Egypt, Lieut.-General Sir E. P. Strickland, was well-known in his day as a martinet, and the Battalion entered upon its new duties with some apprehension. Soon, however, under the inspiring command of Lieut.-Colonel Matthews it contrived by winning many military and sporting competitions to charm him out of his reserve. His first inspection report said it had "settled down quickly on its arrival in Egypt and has developed in every way since it has been here". Two years later, on its departure, after it had twice won the Gordon Polo Cup (1929 and 1930),[2] the Command Football Cup, the Command Football Shield, the British Troops in Egypt Rugby Cup, the Congreve Cup for all-round shooting, and a number of competitions at the 1929 Command Rifle Meeting, he wrote to congratulate it on its successes and to own that "the presence of such a battalion in Alexandria has given me a feeling of the greatest confidence and reliance".

On completing its tour in Egypt on 9th April 1930 the Battalion returned to England to be stationed at Catterick. Its self-reliance developed by its conduct in Egypt, the Battalion continued to win golden opinions from those whose command it came under. But its four-year stay was unmarked by anything more outstanding than its selection, in 1932, as one of two units to carry out tests of the experimental service clothing, the "deerstalker" outfit. This was newspaper talk for a short while, and the report on the tests rendered by Major J. O. C. Hasted, among others, led to modifications which resulted in the familiar battledress of 1939. Before the Battalion went south to Blackdown on 20th November 1934 and just after the command had been assumed by Lieut.-Colonel J. A. Churchill from Lieut.-Colonel W. B. Greenwell on 16th November 1933, the Army Commander reported that it was "by far the best unit in Northern Command". An event hardly less important in the history of the county connection was the march the Battalion undertook through County Durham in July 1934. The first occasion in its existence on which the 68th had been displayed before the County, the march was routed through Gateshead, Birtley and Chester-le-Street,

²The teams were: (1929) Captain J. E. S. Percy, Lieutenants R. B. Y. Simpson and J. H. N. Poett and Lieut.-Colonel C. L. Matthews; (1930) Captains E. T. Heslop, J. E. S. Percy and R. B. Y. Simpson, and Lieutenant R. T. B. M. Dand.

Usworth, Sunderland, Whitburn, Seaham, Blackhall, Spennymoor, Kirk Merrington, Bishop Auckland, Darlington and thence back to Catterick.

At Blackdown, where it joined the 6th Brigade of the 2nd Division, the Battalion occupied the hub of the military universe. The Division, commanded by Major-General Archibald Wavell, was *the* experimental division, for which a galaxy of the best brains in the whole army had been selected to staff and command it. The 6th Brigade, under Brigadier H. M. (afterwards Field Marshal Lord) Wilson, was a mechanised formation in which the Battalion, equipped with the only Bren-gun carriers in the army, was cast in the part of a "support" or, as it was later called, a machine-gun battalion among three rifle battalions. Since 1928, when at Alexandria, it had been organised as three rifle companies and one machine-gun company (S). For the next two years it was to comprise a headquarter company, three machine-gun companies each of three platoons armed with four Vickers guns, and an anti-tank company (A) of four platoons each armed with four anti-tank guns. All transport was mechanised, and the anti-tank company was entirely carried on tractors and trailers. A foretaste of its unwonted mobility was obtained in May 1935 when, during an exercise lasting ten hours, it covered no less than 160 miles. Though the Battalion's conduct was well reported on, the change did not endure beyond the autumn of 1936, when the Division was stripped of much of its equipment to meet the emergency in Palestine. It reverted to the organisation of an ordinary rifle battalion on 1st October 1936. Within the Battalion its share in an historic experiment was evidently regarded with mixed feelings. When it went under canvas on Thursley Common in June 1937, it was remarked that "after two years of mechanisation during which few personnel marched anywhere, it was interesting to note the benefit of a fortnight's camp. The improvement between the march down and the march back was quite marked."

In July 1937, shortly after the Battalion had provided a party of eight officers and 228 n.c.o.s and men for the Coronation Parade in London (12th May), it received warning to embark for Shanghai in the forthcoming trooping season. Embarking in the *Dilwara* at Southampton on 16th October with a strength of ten officers and 364 n.c.o.s and men, it landed at the Bund in Shanghai on 26th November, having picked up en route at Port Sudan the "turnover personnel" from the 2nd Battalion, which brought its strength up to 19 officers and 717 n.c.o.s and men. Owing to the illness of Lieut.-Colonel Grey-Wilson, who had commanded since 15th October 1935, the Battalion was taken out by Major E. T. Heslop, who commanded until Colonel Grey-Wilson rejoined on 2nd April 1938.

Shanghai was not a good station and the international situation was tense. There was at first some sickness; and the temporary accommodation—A, B and C Companies in the Boys' Department of the Municipal Schools, D and Headquarter Companies in the Girls', the officers in private houses in Yu Yuen Road—was unsatisfactory. The Japanese had recently renewed hostilities against the Chinese and taken up a position in the eastern part of the International Settlement, in the remaining parts of which as well as in the French Concession an uneasy neutrality was preserved along a perimeter some twenty miles long. On 29th November 1937 the Battalion took over from the 2nd Loyals five section posts in the southern half of the Western Perimeter, with the 2nd Loyals on its right and the French Concession on its left. In addition an emergency platoon stood by permanently at fifteen minutes' notice in barracks. On the departure of the 2nd Royal Welch Fusiliers late in January 1938 the garrison was reduced to two infantry battalions, and the 1st Battalion's responsibility was extended to comprise the whole Western Perimeter from Jessfield Park to the French Concession. Nevertheless the Battalion received favourable reports of its efficiency, and it succeeded moreover in defeating the unbeaten football team of the Loyals as well as winning the Army Polo Cup. The last success was particularly gratifying as the Battalion was naturally expected to produce a team of de Lisles whereas, in fact, hardly anyone had played before.

The relief in October was upset by the Munich Crisis. The Battalion's departure for Tientsin and Pekin was successively postponed five times between the 7th and the 17th. Landing at Chinwangtao on 20th October 1938 with a strength of 22 officers and 701 n.c.o.s and men, by the 23rd it had railed a company (A) and a platoon to Pekin and the remainder to Tientsin, where it reorganised as a rifle battalion on the 1938 pattern. (Other "new patterns" were coming in. It was remarked that when the 1st Lancashire Fusiliers departed on relief they "had adopted the new fashion of wearing trousers with no puttees.") The international situation was as tense at Tientsin as it had been at Shanghai. The Japanese twice seized private soldiers of the Battalion for alleged offences within the Japanese-controlled area of the city, and then returned them without either apology or explanation. The most memorable event, however, occurred in August 1939, less than a month after Lieut.-Colonel E. H. L. Lysaght-Griffin had succeeded Colonel Grey-Wilson in the command, when the Pei-Ho overflowed its banks, flooding the barracks (among other places) to a depth of over six feet, converting the streets of the city into waterways and cutting off the electricity and other services. It was an emergency which brought out the best in the Battalion as well as the administrative ability of its commanding officer and of Lieut.-Colonel W. H. Lowe, its quartermaster since 1919. The men were evacuated by wading and swimming to one of Jardine, Matthesons' large godowns on the Bund. The Mess, in a two-storey building, did not move but it had to be approached on sampans, which were tied to the banisters. "Some officers therefore heard the news that war had broken out from a passing sampan whilst playing deck-tennis on the Mess roof."

§

The 2nd Battalion's stay in Batum was mercifully short. The town, with Kars and Ardahan, had been ceded under the Treaty of Brest-Litovsk to Turkey, which, according to the terms of the Armistice of 30th October 1918, evacuated the whole of Transcaucasia to British forces as trustees for the emergent republics of Georgia and Armenia. The disputes between Georgia, Armenia and Azerbaijan having been settled by British mediation, all Transcaucasia except Batum was handed over on 28th August 1919, Batum itself being relinquished to Georgia on 7th July 1920, when the country's independence was recognised by Soviet Russia. The 2nd Battalion (22 officers and 627 n.c.o.s and men under the command of Lieut.-Colonel E. du P. H. Moore) consequently embarked on 7th July for Constantinople, where the Allies had sent troops the previous March to preserve it from the nationalist army of Kemal. From July to October the Battalion was stationed at Pavlo on the Izmid peninsula, an Allied bastion against any advance of the Kemalists on Constantinople and the Straits, which had been internationalised under the Treaty of Sèvres (10th August 1920). On 10th November it embarked at Constantinople under Lieut.-Colonel H. E. Lavie for India. Its first station was Ahmednagar, where it remained until December 1923, when it moved to Cawnpore, and thence on 14th March 1926 to Sialkot.

It had been at Sialkot barely a year, and was preparing to repeat the previous year's football and polo successes when the "Shanghai Crisis" supervened. The crisis had arisen from a development in the struggle of the war-lords which took place in January 1927, when the Russian-inspired armies of the Kuomintang under a new young war-lord of the name of Chiang-Kai-Shek, turning east in their victorious progress against the armies of the northern confederacy, moved from Hankow towards Shanghai. Against an attack from without, the International Settlement, in which all nations possessing extra-territorial rights maintained their interests, (save the French, who had a Concession of their own), lacked any unified and organised defence. For various reasons, ignoble and otherwise, only the British government was prepared to act to protect the Settlement (which, incidentally, was the responsibility of Major-General C. C. Luard, G.O.C. Forces in South China). Its prompt action in dispatching the Shanghai Defence Force has been quoted—and rightly so—as a model of how a "fire-brigade force" should be employed.

The Shanghai Defence Force, approximately the strength of a division, was composed of three infantry brigades, two of which came from England and one, the 20th,[3] from India. The 20th was originally stationed at Jhansi, but it was reinforced by an additional European battalion, the 2nd Durham Light Infantry, which, hurriedly mobilised, was brought down to Calcutta and embarked in the *Takliwa* on 27th January 1927 under the command of Lieut.-Colonel J. W. Jeffreys. Together with the 2nd Gloucesters the Battalion was the first of the Force to land at Shanghai on 14th February. "No strangers," wrote the *Daily Mail* Shanghai correspondent, "have ever stirred this cynical cosmopolitan city so deeply and so diversely as did the lads from two English counties, 1500 of them in the familiar khaki, when they marched this morning with shining bayonets through the heart of the International Settlement, a living pledge for the protection of British life and property." From 25th February until 17th April the Battalion was on constant duty on the barbed wire cordon line, and on several occasions had to take action. The most serious occurred on 22nd March, when the army of the Northern Confederacy, fleeing before the Cantonese, tried to rush the sector held by the Durhams. Fire had to be opened several times and two men of C Company were wounded. That was the climax of the emergency, which remained dangerous until the triumphant Chiang succeeded in ridding himself of the extreme Communist element and ruled supreme at Nanking. Although from that time a British garrision was maintained at Shanghai, where it proved essential to the city's security when threatened by the Japanese ten years later, the purpose of the Shanghai Defence Force had been fulfilled. In the summer of 1927 it was gradually dispersed. The 2nd Battalion, which had shown itself a first-class fighting unit

[3] 2nd Gloucestershire, 2nd Durham Light Infantry, 4/1st Punjab Regiment, 3/14th Punjab Regiment, under the command of Col.-Commandant P. B. Sangster. The staff of the whole Force, which was commanded by Major-General J. Duncan, included the 1st Battalion's former adjutant, Captain J. F. Ferguson, as G.S.O.3 (Ops), and Major J. A. Churchill as D.A.A.G.

(however red it may have painted the place), was reimbarked for India on 22nd July, and on 12th August was back in Sialkot. In April the command had been given, much to its disappointment, outside the Regiment to Lieut.-Colonel R. T. Lee, Queen's.

In 1930, when the disturbances in India became acute for the first time in several years, the Battalion was stationed on the Waziristan frontier. Since the 1st Battalion's day Frontier defence had undergone an important change. The old Curzon system of setting a thief to catch a thief, under which the normal policing of the Tribal Area was entrusted to militia recruited from the tribes themselves while the "hoplites" of the field units were kept in reserve on short notice, had been abandoned after the Third Afghan War had demonstrated the risks it involved. Instead, the field units had been moved up into cantonments situated in Tribal Territory, from which they maintained columns, constantly patrolling and living very hard indeed. One of the largest and most active of the columns was that based on Razmak, a new cantonment which had been occupied as the permanent base of a brigade only since 1923. The 2nd Battalion, which has been described at this time by a young Indian Army officer doing his year's attachment as a "beautiful battalion," had come up to Razmak on 10th November 1929. It had marched the last 72 miles from Bannu, and having since been constantly employed with "Razcol," was in hard condition when the Madda Khel Wazirs, prompted largely by Congress money and propaganda, first gave indications of unrest.

The first incident occurred on 11th May, when a large gathering attacked Datta Khel, a post held by a company of Tochi scouts. They, however, put up a stout resistance until the 15th, when the Razmak Column, containing the 2nd Battalion under the command of Lieut.-Colonel R. V. Turner, arrived after a 66-mile march over difficult country without much water, and dispersed the *lashkar* that surrounded the place. Not long after, the work of subversive agents became apparent among the Mahsuds as well, normally implacable enemies of the Wazirs. Early in July their *lashkars* descended and invested the *Khassadar* post of Sororogha, south-east of Razmak. The Column, which had been north, at Gardai, returned to Razmak on 9th July and was again set in motion south to Tauda China. From there reconnaissances were made in the direction of Maidan and Ladha, where 300 hostiles had assembled to oppose it, and on the 12th and 14th the Battalion met and engaged the Mahsuds in two small actions. In the first it lost one man killed and ten wounded (out of the Column's loss of 4 killed and 17 wounded) in a successful attack on a hill from which the Column had been fired upon. Corporal Brooks, commanding a picquet, received the M.M. for his conduct on this occasion. In the second the Mahsud *lashkar* showed little inclination to come to close quarters, and the Column returned to Razmak without further interference. The Mahsud revolt started to subside from then on. The Column, which left Razmak on 22nd July, occupied Ladha without opposition on the next day. When the last of the hostile tribes submitted on 27th July the suppression of the Mahsud outbreak was complete.[4]

The remainder of the Battalion's tour in India was comparatively peaceful. In November 1930 it left Razmak for Barrackpore, where it stayed (latterly under the command of Lieut.-Colonel C. R. Congreve) until moving to Bombay in October 1934. In September 1936 it was taken by Lieut.-Colonel J. O. C. Hasted from India to Khartum. After only a few months there it embarked for home at Port Sudan, arriving at Woking on 16th November, a bare month after the departure of the 1st, whose place it took in the 6th Infantry Brigade (2nd Division). It was still at Woking, but under the command of Lieut.-Colonel V. A. C. Yate, when war broke out in September 1939.

The War: the Raising of the Durham Battalions

Two wars between the same opponents could hardly have started more differently. In 1939 there was none of the excitement of August 1914, none of the overwhelming rush to join up; and in place of Kitchener's solemn countenance and minatory forefinger the nation's eye fell on some large red bills appealing—as though they were unobtainable commodities—for "*your* courage, *your* cheerfulness," beyond which, apparently, nothing was needed. In fact, the establishment of the Territorial Army had been doubled the previous March from thirteen to twenty-six divisions; the Military Training Act, requiring registration and six months' training for men between the ages of 20 and 21 on 3rd June, had been passed the previous May; and on the first day of the war conscription was introduced with the National Service (Armed Forces) Act. As a result, although many, anticipating their call-up, volunteered at the outbreak, there was no dramatic rush to the colours nor any dramatic proliferation of infantry battalions that September: sufficient had been done already; and such proliferation as there was—in competition with the greatly increased demands of industry—did not take place until the critical summer of 1940.

[4] These operations entitled those taking part to wear the Indian General Service Medal 1908-1935. A bar—the ninth since 1908—bearing the inscription 'North-West Frontier 1930-31" was issued.

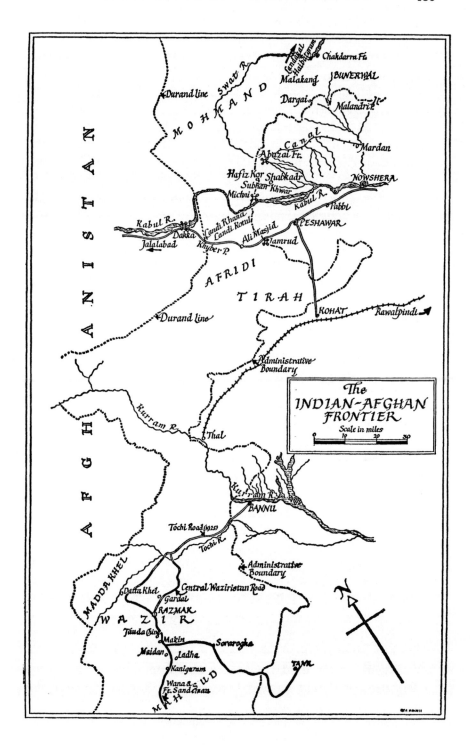

36. The Indian-Afghan Frontier

I. The Regiment started the Second War with eight battalions as compared with the nine of the First. Of the two regular battalions the 1st was at Tientsin, the 2nd (6th Brigade, 2nd Division) at Woking. The militia was in that state known as suspended animation, that is to say it no longer existed. The other six were Territorial.

II. The original five Durham Territorial battalions, re-formed in the years immediately following the First War, had succeeded in keeping up their numbers surprisingly well. With the expansion, however, of Air-Defence-Great-Britain the 7th Battalion had been invited to convert into a searchlight battalion, and in 1936 it had become the 47th (D.L.I.) A.A. Battalion, R.E. (T.A.). The 5th Battalion had adopted the same course in 1938, providing, however, not one but two battalions: the 1/5th under Lieut.-Colonel C. D. Marley becoming the 54th Searchlight Regiment; and the 2/5th, mainly drawn from the West Hartlepool and Horden companies, becoming under Lieut.-Colonel O. J. Feetham the 55th Searchlight Regiment. Deprived officially—but by no means spiritually—of two fine battalions, the Regiment was consequently left with but three to contribute to the 50th Division, the 6th, 8th and 9th. This fine formation, owing to other reforms taking place at the same time, was radically reorganised. All the Northumberland Territorial battalions having ceased to be infantry, the old 149th Brigade disappeared (to be replaced in 1940 by the 25th); while, with the conversion of the 5th, no Durham battalions remained in the 150th Brigade; the 151st alone contained all three of the old Durham battalions.

Upon the doubling of the Territorial establishment in March 1939 each of the three supplied a cadre of about three officers, two warrant-officers and about twenty n.c.o.s and men on whom to form second-line battalions from the large numbers coming forward at that time to offer their services. Whereas most other regiments long continued to designate theirs as 2/6th and so on, the Durham Association from the first numbered them 10th (the 2/6th), 11th (2/8th) and 12th (2/9th). The organisation of these proceeded unequally. The 12th, under Lieut. Colonel H. L. Swinburne, a 9th officer of more than twenty years' service, was organised down to sections by September 1939: the 10th and 11th, on the other hand, were not organised down to platoons until several months later. The three formed the 70th Brigade of the 23rd Division, a new formation.

The 12th, it should be said here, left the Regiment before the campaign started. Ever since the disbandment of the four battalions of Tyneside Scottish, which had been raised in the First War as the 20th-23rd Northumberland Fusiliers (New Army), a strong pressure had been exerted upon the Secretary of State by the Tyneside Scottish

Committee in Newcastle to re-raise at least one battalion. The duplication of the Territorial establishment offered an ideal opportunity. None of the Northumberland units being infantry, which the Tyneside Scottish traditionally were, the Committee asked and obtained permission for the 12th, a Gateshead battalion, to become the "12th Battalion (Tyneside Scottish) Durham Light Infantry". A further step towards separation was clearly desirable if it was to survive in peace. Bagpipes were unsuitable for the light infantry pace; bagpipes and bugles harmonise but ill; both the Liverpool and the London Scottish already had affiliations with Highland regiments; and for the Tyneside Scottish to become an integral part of the Black Watch, which had no clan association, was an obvious move, which was officially recognised on 31st January 1940. In the fighting in which the 1st Tyneside Scottish shared near Arras in May it was still 80 *per cent.* 9th Durham Light infantry. But although the old connection with the Regiment vanished more and more with each successive draft it received after Dunkirk, and although it adopted the Tyneside Scottish cap-badge and—somewhat coyly—the dress of a Black Watch Territorial battalion, it continued throughout the war to wear a green lanyard to signify its D.L.I. origin.

III. Most closely resembling the New Army of 1914 were the so called Dunkirk battalions, sixty of which were raised in June and July 1940 from an intake of conscripts increased from 70,000 per month to 345,000 in two months. Conscripts they may have been, but it is not derogatory of the conscripts of 1916-1918 to say that they were much more like the volunteers of 1914. Coming from all walks of life except the "reserved occupations," they were on the whole superior men of excellent physique, intelligent and reponsive to good leadership.

In the Regiment they made up three fine battalions, the 14th, 16th and 17th, which on 12th October 1940 were brigaded together near Edinburgh to form the 206th Independent Infantry Brigade, at first belonging to no one division. The 14th was raised at Brancepeth and for three years commanded by Lieut.-Colonel R. J. Appleby, who after serving with the 2nd Battalion in Flanders until being wounded in 1917 had continued with the Regiment ever since. The 16th was first organised at Morton Hall, under the Braid Hills near Edinburgh, by Lieut.-Colonel J. G. Morrogh-Bernard, East Yorkshire Regiment. Later commanded by Lieut.-Colonels E. C. Sebag-Montefiore of the Regiment and A. S. P. Murray, Grenadier Guards, it received a good start. The 17th was first organised at Shrewsbury and Harlescott by Lieut.-Colonel H. B. Morkill, who, himself a Green Howard, became devoted to it during the three years he commanded it. At first ill equipped, all rapidly acquired a good corporate spirit under the command of active and experienced regular officers.

The early history of the 17th is fairly characteristic of all three. When Lieut.-Colonel Morkill arrived at Copthorne Barracks on 26th June he found he was the sole representative of a battalion of whose war-establishment even he had not been informed. After a fortnight, however, he had an assortment of twelve officers and 145 n.c.o.s from no fewer than nine different regiments (some kilted—none D.L.I.), whom on 17th July he took north to Morton Hall. The 16th Battalion was in the next field, the 14th four miles away at Duddingston. Between 18th and 26th July 800 men arrived in their civil clothes—an excellent type of man, Lieut.-Colonel Morkill records, most about 27 years of age and most married. By the time the Battalion moved south to the Isle of Oxney on the Kent coast on 17th December, he had a battalion shaping well and in a fair state of training. In February 1941 it was moved to Shorncliffe with $2\frac{1}{2}$ miles of coastline to defend. It had its share of the ordinary frustrations. When, for instance, in a practice, all the fire-hoses were found to be defective, the barrackmaster at Shorncliffe, an old soldier of some forty years' service, issued a new one but "on condition," as he said, "you never use it for water but let it stand on the wall". Views, too, on the advantages and disadvantages of the various defences were apt to change with each new commander. One liked such and such pillboxes; another did not; and one day spent painting them with the letters A (approved), B (requiring strengthening), C (not wanted), or X (loop-holes not wanted) might be followed by another spent in painting C on those already marked A or B, or in painting out the Xs. But one of the most rewarding moments in a commanding officer's service came on 10th May 1941 when the Battalion was visited by the G.O.C. the XII Corps, General B. L. Montgomery, whose decided opinions on all matters had already made a refreshing impact on his command. After watching the Battalion for some time he rose to go, saying as he did so, "Well, that's very good. You could do anything with that lot."

Alas, one only of the Dunkirk battalions went on service. This was the 16th, which had earlier left the Brigade to join the 139th in the 46th Division. The 14th survived until the end of the war, but after the autumn of 1943 only as a training battalion, first at Durham, later moving into Northumberland, to Otley (1945), and later still to Blandford, where it was disbanded in 1946. The 17th, after pro-viding reinforcement drafts aggregating 100 officers and 1200 n.c.o.s and men over the years of its existence, was disbanded at Seaford on 14th December 1943.

The diminishing threat of invasion and the correspondingly reduced need for infantry affected another battalion raised at the same time. The 15th was not a Dunkirk battalion. It was organised on 9th October 1940 by Lieut.-Colonel E. T. Heslop of the Regiment from the 15th (formerly 3rd) Holding Battalion at West Hartlepool, containing men who had completed their primary training at the Depot. Belonging for a time to the 217th Brigade of the Durham and North Riding County Division, it was removed after the break up of the county divisions in November 1941 to the 225th Brigade of the 42nd Division, before being converted a fortnight later into a regiment of the Royal Armoured Corps and numbered 155th. Its weapons henceforward were the "funnies" of its new division, General Hobart's 79th Armoured, which, though belonging to 21st Army Group, did not serve abroad as a formation. In May 1944 the 155th, after drafting 400 officers and men as reinforcements, was reduced to cadre, but it survived until the end of the war still conscious of its D.L.I. origins and still wearing the D.L.I. flash.

There remains to be mentioned one other battalion of the Regiment formed for active service. The 18th, the second to bear that number in the war, was raised at the Infantry Depot at Geneifa in March 1943 largely from convalescents and details of the 6th, 8th and 9th Battalions in Egypt. Though most of the officers were not from the Regiment, several were, and its medical officer, Captain W. Rankin, had served with the 6th Battalion and had been presented with its cap-badge and lanyard. The Battalion became the principal infantry element in that essential instrument of amphibious warfare, the Beach Group, a group of specialist units formed to relieve the assaulting troops of every responsibility connected with the clearing, defending and maintaining the beach-head until the more permanent base installations arrived to take over. D Company under Major W. Leybourne of the Regiment belonged to No. 34 Beach Group in the Sicily and Anzio landings. Headquarters and two other companies belonged to No. 36 Group, which shared in the operations at Bone and Bizerta and played a prominent part in the Salerno landing. After coming to this country in 1944 the Battalion took part in the Normandy landings, and was later moved to Boulogne and Calais, where it operated transit camps. One company in February 1945 was sent to the Dunkirk perimeter to assist in holding a German sortie, which it accomplished successfully with the capture of many prisoners. The 18th was disbanded at Calais in August 1945.

IV. Four other battalions were raised in the Regiment for home

Brigaded Battalions, 1939-1945

Battalion	Dates	Brigade	Division
1st Battalion	31st Jan. 1940–21st July 1940 23rd July 1940– 1st Sept. 1940 2nd Sept. 1940–27th Feb. 1941 28th Feb. 1941–23rd May 1941 5th Jun. 1941–22nd Jan. 1942 27th Jan. 1942–12th May 1942 14th May 1942– 9th Sept. 1943 19th May 1944–31st Aug. 1945	23rd 22nd Matruh 22nd Guards 23rd 233rd 234th 10th Indian	6th (70th) 10th Indian
2nd Battalion	3rd Sept. 1939– 7th Sept. 1941 8th Sept. 1941–19th Oct. 1941 20th Oct. 1941–31st Aug. 1945	6th 127th 6th	2nd 42nd 2nd
6th Battalion	3rd Sept. 1939–14th Dec. 1944	151st	50th
8th Battalion	3rd Sept. 1939–14th Dec. 1944	151st	50th
9th Battalion	3rd Sept. 1939–30th Nov. 1944 2nd Dec. 1944–31st Aug. 1945	151st 131st	50th 7th Armoured
10th Battalion	3rd Sept. 1939–11th Sept. 1940 25th Oct. 1940–19th Dec. 1941 9th Jan. 1942–18th Oct. 1944	70th 70th 70th	23rd Iceland Force 49th
11th Battalion	3rd Sept. 1939–26th Jun. 1940 9th Jan. 1941–19th Dec. 1941 18th May 1942–18th Oct. 1944	70th 70th 70th	23rd Iceland Force 49th
12th Battalion (1st Tyne. Scot.)	3rd Sept. 1939–31st Jan. 1940 31st. Jan. 1940–26th Jun. 1940 9th Jan. 1941–19th Dec. 1941 18th May 1941–18th Oct. 1944	70th 70th 70th	23rd Iceland Force 49th
14th Battalion*	12th Oct. 1940–19th Sept. 1942 25th Sept. 1942–14th Nov. 1944 15th Nov. 1944–31st Aug. 1945	206th 209th 203rd	56th 77th 45th
15th Battalion* (155th R.A.C.)	20th Oct. 1940–17th Nov. 1941 19th Nov. 1941–30th Nov. 1941 1st Jan. 1942–13th July 1945	217th 225th 35th Army Tank	42nd 79th Armoured
16th Battalion	12th Oct. 1940–17th Dec. 1940 28th Dec. 1940–31st Aug. 1945	206th 139th	56th 46th
17th Battalion*	12th Oct. 1940–10th Sept. 1942 10th Sept. 1942–25th Sept. 1943	206th 164th	56th 55th

*Did not see foreign service.

defence and training. The earliest was the 13th, formed in December 1939 from the Durham Group (No. 41) of the National Defence Companies, which, composed mainly of veterans from the First War for the purpose of guarding vulnerable points, had been gradually expanded under the ægis of the County Territorial Association since 1935. Since August 1939 the Durham Group had been commanded by Lieut.-Colonel J. E. Stafford, who continued to command until the 13th formed a second battalion (the 2/13th) under Lieut.-Colonel W. F. Simpson in September 1940. The 2/13th became in

March 1941 the 18th Battalion and led an independent existence in Lincolnshire until moved north in November 1941 to be reabsorbed into the 13th, which at the same time was renumbered 30th, to correspond with the numbering of Home Defence battalions of other regiments. Under a new commanding officer, Lieut.-Colonel R. Boys-Stones, the 30th was for a time in 1942 reorganised as a field-force unit and a counter-attack battalion, but the competing demands for arms other than infantry caused it to be broken up on 20th November 1942.

The 70th (Young Soldiers) Battalion was raised in December 1940 under Lieut.-Colonel H. McBain of the Regiment to accommodate those young men who, after Dunkirk, anticipated their call-up by volunteering at 18 or 19. Suitable officers and n.c.o.s to train such first-class material were naturally spared grudgingly by field-force battalions; but the Regiment's 70th was singularly fortunate in its first commanding officer, who, starting with a cadre of forty all ranks from the Depot, contrived by his drive and enthusiasm to form a battalion which acquired an excellent reputation. First organised at School Aycliffe near Darlington, in a children's mental home as yet barely completed, it was occupied for the first two years of its existence guarding aerodromes near Catterick. When the age for conscription was lowered from 20 to 18 in 1942 it would have been disbanded had it not, as a result of its good name, been specially selected as the first demonstration battalion of the newly formed G.H.Q. Battle School at Barnard Castle. Commanded first by Lieut.-Colonel P. J. Jeffreys and later by Lieut.-Colonel G. S. Fillingham, both of the Regiment, it carried out these important duties with exemplary spirit until, moved from Barnard Castle to Tow Law in July 1943, it was disbanded in August 1943. The majority went on the 10th of that month as reinforcements to the 151st Brigade in Sicily. Some of the others went to the 10th, 11th, 14th and 17th Battalions. Others were received by the 16th Battalion in Italy, where Lieut.-Colonel Preston reported very well of them; and over one hundred went to the 6th Lincoln (in the same brigade with the 16th), whose commanding officer wrote: "if we got drafts like this one every time, the war would soon be over".

Finally the Depot. On the outbreak of war the Depot was made a lieut.-colonel's command and placed under Lieut.-Colonel J. O. C. Hasted, barely a year retired from the command of the 2nd Battalion. His first duty was the historical though heavy task of transferring it from Fenham Barracks at Newcastle to Brancepeth Castle in the County. The Castle, the ancient seat of the Nevilles, had early the previous century passed into the hands of the rich coal-owning family of Russell, who had transformed the crumbling medieval buildings into a neo-Norman mansion of prodigious dimensions. After being used as a hospital in the First War it had been offered to the War Office by Viscount Boyne. But, the offer having been declined, it had remained unoccupied until September 1939, when it fell to Lieut.-Colonel Hasted and the former Depot commander, Major G. I. Wiehe, to convert a structure by no means in the best state of repair, besides lacking water, light and heating, into the Regiment's first home in the County for sixty years. A man of many varied talents, whose brilliant Northern Command Tattoos presented but one aspect of a complex personality, Hasted was ideally suited to meet the challenge; and the Brancepeth that exists today was largely his creation. It was an unfortunate stroke for the Regiment when he took his own life while still in command in January 1942.

From the first an infantry training centre with the object of training recruits and supplying cadres for the new levies, the Depot became in August 1942 the combined Training Centre (4th I.T.C.) for both the Regiment and the Duke of Wellington's, who had been displaced at Halifax, in providing the first six-weeks' basic training of every recruit. So successful were the methods employed that it was selected by the War Office in August 1943, then under Lieut.-Colonel McBain's command, for the so called "Brancepeth Experiment," an improved recruit training in which a time-and-motion study was introduced. The upshot was a new syllabus which was adopted by the whole army. But, over and above its ordinary tasks of training and draft-finding, the Depot at Brancepeth, commanding probably the finest situation that any depot has ever enjoyed in England since regiments first had depots, owes its importance in the Regiment's history to its being the first home the Durham Light Infantry has occupied in the County since that fateful day in 1884 when it was removed to Newcastle.

§

If the exigencies of a highly organised war effort required the Regiment both to wear a sadly reduced *Durham* aspect and to depend far less on local and personal endeavour than it had in 1914, the manner in which the war developed allowed the Regiment, particularly the regular element, to take a substantially larger part in its own expansion. The 1st Battalion was commanded throughout by regular officers of the Regiment. The 2nd Battalion could not be, but it was the only battalion to be commanded by one of its own

emergency-commissioned officers. The Territorial battalions, particularly after the opening disasters, contributed rather fewer of their
own officers to command them: Lieut.-Colonels T. H. Miller, W. I.
Watson and G. L. Wood (6th); Lieut.-Colonel R. S. McLaren (8th);
Lieut.-Colonel W. F. Simpson (9th); Lieut.-Colonel C. D. Marley
(10th); Lieut.-Colonels J. Bramwell and C. D. Hamilton (11th);
and Lieut.-Colonels H. L. Swinburne and C. W. Oxley (12th).
Compared with the First War the regular contribution was sub-
stantially larger throughout. Among the Territorial battalions the
Regiment provided: Lieut.-Colonels P. J. Jeffreys (the son of the
officer who had commanded the 6th in the First War) and C. R.
Battiscombe (6th); Lieut.-Colonel C. W. Beart (8th); Lieut.-Colonel
J. E. S. Percy (9th); Lieut.-Colonel F. W. Sandars (10th); and
Lieut.-Colonels R. F. Ware, J. H. N. Poett and J. M. Hanmer (11th).
It also supplied them with a number of company commanders
including: Major R. G. Atkinson (6th), who distinguished himself
both at the Primosole Bridge and at Geel; Major C. M. D'Arcy
Irvine (9th); and Major R. B. Humphreys (11th). All the new
battalions received their first commanding officers from the Regiment save only the 16th and 17th, and all without exception were
regular officers. The reasons for the increased regular contribution
may be sought partly in deliberate policy, partly in the smaller
number of battalions raised, but above all in the merciful preserva-
tion of experienced officers of middle regimental rank who, in the
earlier struggle, had almost all been killed or disabled in the first few
months.

Some of the best talents possessed by the Regiment before the
war, being wholly or partly devoted to objects outside it, would not
otherwise receive mention in its history. Major J. F. Ferguson, the
1st Battalion's first adjutant in 1919, was lost to the Regiment when
in 1933 he accepted the flattering offer made to him by Lord
Trenchard to assist in his reforms of the Metropolitan Police Force,
becoming Commandant of the new Police College at Hendon and
Chief Constable of Sussex. Major T. S. Airey, who in 1939 had
recently passed the Staff College, rose to become Lord Alexander's
Director of Military Intelligence and Military Governor of Trieste.
Captains J. H. N. Poett and A. H. G. Ricketts were still at the Staff
College when war broke out. Captain Poett, formerly adjutant of the
2nd Battalion, after commanding the 11th Battalion, was given the
command of the 5th Parachute Brigade on its formation in June 1943,
and led it when it was dropped near Ranville in the 6th Airborne
Division's operation east of Caen on 6th June 1944. Captain Ricketts,
a kinsman both of the Major William Gough who commanded a

company of the 68th in the Peninsula and of the Morants, father and son, rose to become second-in-command of the 3rd West African Brigade at the time of Wingate's second long-range penetration into Northern Burma early in 1944. He came forward to take command and extricate it from an apparently hopeless situation at the "White City" (late April 1944), and he later commanded the 4th West African Brigade in Burma. Lieut.-Colonel E. H. L. Lysaght-Griffin, commanding the 1st Battalion, left to take up an appointment on the staff, in which he rose to become the chief administrative staff-officer of the XXX Corps. Other promising careers, however, including those of two former adjutants, Major H. E. F. Fox-Davies and Captain F. H. Simpson, were cut short early, the one by death, the other by an untimely captivity.

Lastly, throughout almost the entire length of the war, presiding over the Regiment's destinies and fortunes with a father's care and interest, there was its Colonel, Colonel C. L. Matthews, who as a young subaltern had led his half-company up the slopes of Vaalkrans, had trekked with the M.I. and fought with Dunsterforce before many of his officers were out of the nursery.

The Campaign in France, 1939-1940

All seven of the Durham battalions in existence at home in 1939 took part in the Dunkirk Campaign. The 2nd Battalion, mobilised and brought up to strength with reservists, crossed to France with the 6th Brigade[5] on 25th September under Lieut.-Colonel V. A. C. Yate, who as a subaltern had crossed with the Battalion in September 1914. It disembarked at Cherbourg on the 26th. After concentrating at Chantenay, south-west of Le Mans, it was moved up to the Belgian frontier. Headquarters were at Bercu, south-east of Lille, where the Battalion remained, engaged in improving the incomplete defences (the "Gort Line"), until the storm broke in May 1940. Before then, however, Lieut.-Colonel Yate was forced by ill-health in March to hand over the command to Lieut.-Colonel R. B. Y. Simpson, who had fought with the 2nd Battalion in the closing stages of the First War.

The 50th Division, its two brigades organised as a motorised formation under Major-General G. le Q. Martel, one of the small group of officers who had made tanks their study since their inception, was one of the first Territorial divisions to go to France. It left the Cotswold country where it completed its training and crossed to Cherbourg in the last week of January 1940. After a month spent in

[5] 1st Royal Welch Fusiliers (the old 23rd of Lambton's day), 1st Royal Berkshire, and 2nd Durham Light Infantry.

training near Amiens, it was moved north to work on the II Corps
reserve line near Loos-lès-Lille, a task in which the North Countrymen
were only too pleased to show what they could do in comparison
with "soft South Country" troops. The 151st Brigade, which was
responsible for the southern sector of the line from Seclin to Wavrin,
was very much a D.L.I. concern. Its commander, Brigadier J. A.
Churchill, had commanded the 1st Battalion, and his staff-captain,
Captain W. M. F. Vane, the son of the Regiment's historian, was a
6th Battalion officer. Of the battalions all but the 8th (Lieut.-Colonel
C. W. Beart), which Lieut.-Colonel E. A. Leybourne had left in
December, were commanded by their own officers: the 6th by Lieut.-
Colonel T. H. Miller, the 9th by Lieut.-Colonel W. F. Simpson.
The Division, said their commander, justifiably prejudiced, "was a
grand division and contained some of the best men in the British
army".

The other three battalions, the 10th, 11th and 1st Tyneside
Scottish (formerly 2/9th), crossed with the 23rd Division, which with
two others was brought out in April, half trained and only sketchily
equipped, largely to meet the pressing need of constructing airfields
and other rear installations. The Durham battalions (the 10th under
Lieut.-Colonel C. D. Marley, the 11th under Lieut.-Colonel J.
Bramwell, the 1st Tyneside Scottish under Lieut.-Colonel H. L.
Swinburne) composed the 70th Brigade, commanded by the officer
who when younger had so distinguished himself at the head of the
8th Battalion in the critical days of 1918, Brigadier P. Kirkup. From
the last days of April they occupied a tented camp in the orchards
around Nuncq, south of Saint-Pol. Of the 2000 men in the Brigade
1400 had not fired a Bren gun and 400 had not completed their war
course with the rifle.

The Withdrawal to Dunkirk: (i) The Dyle,
10th-16th May 1940

Since November 1939 it had been decided that in the event of an
invasion of Belgium the Franco-British armies, pivoting on Givet,
should carry out a wheeling movement to a north-south line to the
east of Brussels. Running from Antwerp to the Meuse, the line was
largely protected by water-courses: in the north, from the sea to
Louvain, by canalised rivers; from Louvain to Wavre by the Dyle;
and from Namur to Sedan, where it joined the Maginot Line, by the
Meuse. Between the upper Dyle and Namur the line ran across the
elevated watershed which, known in military parlance as the
Gembloux Gap, had been recognised as a sensitive spot. The sector
destined for occupation by the B.E.F. lay on the Dyle between

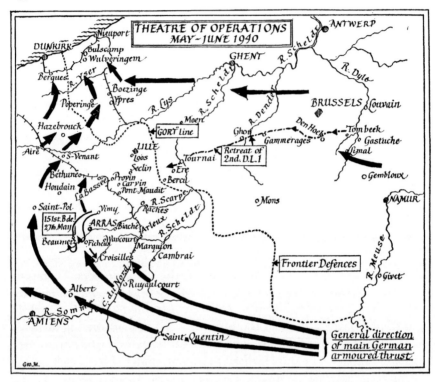

37. The Theatre of Operations, May—June, 1940

Louvain and Wavre, with the Belgian Army on its left and the French
1st Army on its right covering the Gembloux Gap.

The German invasion started at 5.35 a.m. on 10th May, and the
plan was put into operation at 1 p.m. Because the 6th Brigade, on the
right of the Army, had least distance to cover, the 2nd Battalion was
not required to move until the end of the second day. But after dark
on the 11th it moved off from Bercu in troop-carrying transport,
and in the afternoon of the 12th was debussing behind the Dyle in
the Bois de Bilande. By evening it occupied its position on the
wooded slope of the Dyle valley opposite Gastuche, with headquarters in the village of La Tombe. On its left lay the other battalions of the Brigade: the 1st Royal Welch Fusiliers on the left, the
1st Royal Berkshire in the centre. On the 14th the 2nd North African
Division, the left of the French 1st Army, came up to extend the line
on its right. Each British battalion held its sector on the "blob"
system with mutually supporting posts for all-round defence. D
Company (Captain W. B. Hutton), on the Battalion's left, was
posted below the river bridge, which lay in its field of fire: B (Captain
F. R. Tubbs) was in the centre; A (Major J. R. Cousens) on the

right; and C (Captain R. H. Blackett) in reserve near battalion headquarters.

A fortnight or ten days in which to consolidate had been expected, but the crisis approached a good deal quicker than that. The 12th May was quiet. Late on the 13th the 4th/7th Dragoon Guards started to retire through the Battalion. Late on the 14th all bridges were blown. Little, however, was attempted by the enemy against the forward defensive line, although C Company, acting as outpost company, established contact with his armoured cars and motor-cyclists at 4 that afternoon, and although his men occupied the wooded slopes of the opposite bank. The battle started in earnest suddenly at dawn on the 15th, when a platoon of B Company was rushed and overrun. This attack was successfully repelled by 2/Lieutenant R. J. Hyde-Thomson[6] at the head of the platoon on its right; but D Company meanwhile was subjected to a heavy attack which penetrated the forward posts as deep as the Château de Laurensart, despite a counter-attack by the reserve company. Two company commanders were wounded early on, and the situation was not restored until about 4 in the afternoon, when a company was brought up from the brigade reserve. A second, and again unsuccessful, attack was delivered on the Battalion's front after dark.

In both the conduct of 2/Lieutenant R. W. Annand, a young subaltern who had joined from the Supplementary Reserve, had set an inspiring example, and his personal courage had been largely responsible for the failure of the attacks on D Company in which he commanded a platoon. It was posted to defend the bridge by which the enemy bridging-parties, under a heavy mortar and machine-gun barrage, made several determined efforts to cross and infiltrate into the Battalion's position. In the morning, at the head of his men, he had repelled two attempts, and once, when ammunition had run out, he had dashed forward in the open regardless of the fire to disperse an enemy party with grenades, which he carried in a sandbag. Though wounded, he had remained in command, and when the second attack developed he had not only gone forward to stand on the parapet of the bridge and toss grenades onto the German troops below but later, after his platoon had withdrawn, he had returned to bring out, on a wheelbarrow, his batman, who he was told had been left behind wounded. For his gallantry Annand was awarded the Victoria Cross, the Regiment's first and among the first to be won in the army in the war.

[6]In captivity Lieutenant Hyde-Thomson "graduated" to the *Sonderlager* at Colditz, where he made several, unfortunately unsuccessful, attempts at escape. He died with the rank of major in Uganda in 1951.

The casualties in the Battalion in repelling the only serious attacks made against the 2nd Division front had been surprisingly low, and the men's self-confidence had been justifiably raised. But although the British Army's position had been maintained intact, elsewhere the fighting had turned out less favourably and there were indications that the Dyle position itself could not be held much longer. Apart from the disaster suffered by the French Armies on the Meuse front around Sedan, which at that stage seemed remote and in any case was obscurely reported, the French 1st Army covering the Gembloux Gap had been pierced near Limal and forced to withdraw. A sympathetic withdrawal of the British right flank to a weak position on the Lasne was ordered in consequence, much to the disappointment of the Battalion, who, the men said, "had Jerry beat to a frazzle". The 6th Brigade managed to disengage during the night, and in the morning held the line from Tombeek to Terlaenen.

(ii) The Withdrawal to the Scheldt, 17th-19th May

It was the beginning of a larger scale withdrawal to the line of the Scheldt as a result of the increasing threat to the I Corps' right flank. Though the enemy did not make contact on the Lasne until 2 in the afternoon of the 16th, the 6th Brigade began to thin out at 9.30 and at 11 p.m. started for the intermediate line of the Senne. The 2nd Battalion's route lay through Overijse, Hoeilaart and Terblock and, at about 1.30 a.m. on the 17th, very tired, it reached Den Hoek in the Forêt de Soignes, where it was to have been met by transport. No transport, however, made its appearance, and the Brigadier ordered the march to continue by Elingen, Leerbeek and Oetingen to Gammerages. Two companies, A (Major Cousens) and D (now under Lieutenant J. H. H. Bonham), delayed by a mortar barrage and retiring by compass, was unable until several days later to rejoin the Battalion, which staggered into Gammerages at about midnight. Worn out with marching over forty miles in 27 hours after being engaged for 36 hours, the men had had little more food than the splendid meal organised by Quartermaster Pearson at Den Hoek.

During the 18th the Battalion, with the rest of the exhausted brigade, was moved west of the Dender to a reserve position behind the 2nd Division line at Ghoy; and on the 19th, having crossed the Scheldt at Tournai, it occupied a sector of the Scheldt line on the left of the brigade front near Ere.

(iii) The Defence of Arras, 19th-20th May

By this time the whole military situation had developed dramatically for the worse. The Germans, smashing through the French front at Sedan with their armoured formations and driving rapidly due westward towards the Channel, were laying bare the soft rear of the whole Army. On 17th May, while the 2nd Battalion was in the Forêt de Soignes, a force of two partially trained divisions was hurriedly improvised to cover the southern flank on the line Saint-Amand / Raches /Arleux /Ruyaulcourt. One of the two divisions was the 23rd, of which the 70th Brigade was moved up from the line of communication through hordes of refugees and miscellaneous transport and placed behind the Canal du Nord, south of the Cambrai /Arras road, to form the extreme right flank.

There is no such thing as a hopeless situation, and if there was anyone qualified by past experience to meet the impending crisis it was Brigadier Kirkup. But the prospects were not bright. The enemy, whose exact position was as yet unknown, numbered five armoured divisions at the top of their form with two others in close support. In every respect but ordinary courage the British divisions opposing him compared unfavourably. The men's training was incomplete. They lacked most weapons but their rifles. There was no divisional artillery and the guns that supported the 23rd had no optical instruments. The formations were without such essential services as signals. The 23rd contained only two out of the normal three brigades. The position, moreover, which the Durham battalions occupied was weak, requiring much work for which there was little time to spare and no tools to do it with. The Canal du Nord, which in 1918 had been no good as a defence from its incompleteness, in 1940 was again no good from its imminent abandonment: it was almost dry. This however, was all that stood between seven German armoured divisions and the English Channel on 18th May.

The conclusion was almost foregone. At 6 a.m. on the 19th the enemy tanks approached and opened fire. The 70th Brigade retired behind the railway from Croisilles to Marquion; and the Division was preparing to withdraw to the La Bassée Canal when it was ordered to take up a position facing south-east and running from Saulty to Arras and thence along the Scarpe to Biache-Saint-Vaast. The 70th Brigade was to occupy the right of the line west of Arras, around Saulty, Lattre and Beaumetz. The La Bassée movement had already begun when the fresh orders, involving a night march of a further fifteen or twenty miles, were received. The Brigadier attempted to lighten it by ferrying the men in stages in the limited transport available. Before dawn of the 20th the 10th Battalion (at Mercatel), the 11th (at Wancourt) and the Tyneside Scottish (at Neuville-Vitasse) were on the move to the new positions. But a little after dawn the transport came under a heavy air attack, followed soon after by enemy tanks and infantry who descended on the scattered battalions. The Tyneside Scottish received very heavy casualties in the resistance they offered near Ficheux, during which their commanding officer, Lieut.-Colonel H. L. Swinburne was captured. Those of the 11th still at Wancourt, with only rifles with which to defend themselves, were either killed or captured—almost half the battalion. The 10th lost most of two companies that were caught with the Tyneside Scottish between Blairville and Ficheux. They did what they could, but in the nature of things it could not be much. At 5 a.m. the 10th had only two companies at Lattre-Saint-Quentin; and the 11th only the elements of three weak companies at Beaumetz-lès-Loges. When, later in the day, the 70th Brigade assembled at Houdain according to orders received by Brigadier Kirkup, who had gone to divisional headquarters to report the disaster, it consisted of a mere 14 officers and 219 n.c.o.s and men.

The claim that these Territorial battalions delayed the German advance five hours is considered "modest" by the Official Historian, who, however, accepts it, only adding the rider that at that critical juncture every single hour's delay was of incalculable service to the rest of the British Army. The Germans who encountered them acknowledge that on the 20th they were able to gain ground but slowly and with continuous fighting against an enemy who defended himself stubbornly. If, therefore, the battalions were sacrificed they were sacrificed neither needlessly nor in vain. In any case they were not finished. On 23rd May at Gondecourt the remnants of the 70th Brigade were formed into one battalion of six companies under the command of Lieut.-Colonel C. D. Marley, 10th Battalion, and fought the rest of the campaign under the title of "Marleyforce".

(iv) The Arras Counter-attack, 21st May

Already on the 19th the German penetration was very deep. It had reached Amiens, and Army headquarters was meditating a general retreat north-westwards to Dunkirk. On the 20th British troops were thrown back across the Somme at Abbeville; Albert was lost; Doullens surrounded. The eastern "shoulder," however, at Arras still held fairly firm. A counter-attack at this point clearly promised important results if the troops to execute it were available. The only troops to hand were the 50th Motorised Division, which at that moment was holding the La Bassée Canal line on the new southern front; and the movement it was ordered to undertake at 4 in the afternoon of the 20th against at least three German armoured divisions, though called a counter-attack, was necessarily of a more modest description, with the object rather of clearing or spoiling than of intercepting or crushing.

Till then the 50th Division had undergone a bewildering series of marches. On the 16th it had been moved up from Loos, near Lille, to be in reserve to the main front on the Dender. When, however, the withdrawal to the Scheldt was ordered, the Division was brought back early on the 18th to a line in which the Durham battalions were disposed: the 6th at Moen, the 8th at Helchin, and the 9th at Saint-Genois. On the 19th, as part of the plan for the withdrawal to Dunkirk, in which that flank of the Allied Army lying to the north of the German penetration was to form a hollow square with the 50th Division acting as a flank-guard on the La Bassée Canal, it was ordered south; and during that night the 151st Brigade moved to occupy the canal bridges between Cuinchy and Pont-Maudit. Early on the 20th the 6th was at La Bassée the 8th at Provin, the 9th at Meurchin. Finally, on the 20th, just as the Division was preparing to move to Lens, orders arrived for it to join General Franklyn's force at Arras, and by 6.30 a.m. on the 21st all the Durham battalions were assembled in and around Vimy.

The "limited operation to relieve the pressure on Arras" was planned to take the form of a sweep round the west and south of Arras, the second "phase" of which was designed to place the attackers on the line of the Sensée between Saint-Léger and Croisilles. It was to be carried out by the 151st Brigade supported by two battalions of tanks and artillery, the whole organised into two assault columns and a reserve. The left, or inner, column, under the officer commanding the 6th Battalion, Lieut.-Colonel T. H. Miller, was headed by the 4th Royal Tank Regiment and was to move from Thélus by Les Tilleuls, Ecurie, Anzin-Saint-Aubin, Wagnonlieu, Dainville, Achicourt, Beaurains and Hénin-sur-Cojeul. The right, or outer, column, under the officer commanding the 8th Battalion, Lieut.-Colonel C. W. Beart, was headed by the 7th Royal Tank Regiment and was to move from Petit-Vimy by La Targette, Marœuil, Duisans, Warlus, Berneville, Wailly, Ficheux and Boisleux-au-Mont. The reserve, consisting of the 9th Battalion under Lieut.-Colonel W. F. Simpson and two batteries, was to follow the right column.

The right column started at 1.15 p.m. on the 21st and its advanced guard soon entered Duisans, where the 8th Battalion followed by clearing the woods, an operation embarrassed by the appearance of some French tanks from the west, who caused confusion by firing on the column until the mistake was discovered. By 5.30 Warlus was made good: Berneville was occupied by 6, while B and C Companies under Major McLaren remained to secure Duisans. At 6.15, however, enemy resistance started to harden. A heavy machine-gun and mortar fire pinned down the infantry near Berneville, causing 50 *per cent.* casualties; Warlus and Duisans were dive-bombed; and at 6.45 the enemy followed up with attacks from west and south. These were held, and at midnight some French tanks from Warlus provided a valuable reinforcement. But more could not be done. The Duisans garrison was cut off from the 9th in Marœuil by German armoured patrols, and there was no alternative but to carry out a retreat, in the course of which Colonel Beart was wounded. By 6 a.m. on the 22nd the column, fighting as it went, was back at Vimy.

The left column, starting at 11.30 a.m. had cleared Anzin-Saint-Aubin by 12.30, and although the leading company of the 6th began to come under shell fire at about 2.30 while approaching Wagnonlieu, the column continued to press forward in artillery formation to Beaurains. The tanks got as far as the Arras/Bapaume road at Mercatel. The enemy responded, however, by dive-bombing Achicourt, Beaurains and Agny. At 8 he shelled the column. That was followed at about 10.15 by tank, mortar and machine-gun fire, which caused the column to withdraw on Achicourt. There two companies of the 6th were subjected to a heavy attack which caused many casualties. Some got back to Ecurie; others lost the way—one party under a field officer found itself at Boulogne next day, where, having taken a modest part in the defence of the port with No. 1 Company 1st Welsh Guards, embarked when the place fell on the 23rd and arrived in England. The main body and the 9th Battalion, which, apart from a carrier-platoon sent in to assist at Duisans, had spent a relatively quiet day at Marœuil, reached Vimy in the early hours of the 22nd and took up a defensive position on the famous ridge.

As a desperate attempt made at a critical juncture by tired Territorial troops who had been on their feet for almost three days and three nights, the Arras counter-attack inevitably invites comparison with that other occasion in April 1915, when the same battalions received their baptism of fire under very similar circumstances at Second Ypres. That they should have ended differently reflects no discredit upon the sons of the fathers. One of the Durhams' enemies at Arras was the same General Rommel the Division was to know better in two other theatres. So vigorous, he says, was the action of Brigadier Churchill's Brigade that the Germans were under the impression they were being attacked by no fewer than five British divisions. Those present with the Brigade may therefore reflect, plausibly if somewhat fancifully, that each man fought that day as fifteen. The immediate effect of the operation was to postpone any concerted action against Arras. Its wider implication was to transmit a nervous shiver throughout the entire Kleist Group area, which gave rise to a modification in the orders of the German XIX Corps, inhibiting both the attack on Boulogne two days later and the vital armoured thrust on Dunkirk.

(v) The Saint-Omer—La Bassée Line, 23rd-29th May

The Allied Armies in the north were by this time fighting in a box-shaped position whose sides contracted as each successive line was penetrated; and this is the proper moment at which to advert to the fortunes of the 2nd Battalion and its destruction at Saint-Venant on 27th May.

The Scheldt line held until 21st May, when the combined Army fell back, first, to the Lys—"Gort" Line and, later, to the Yser Canal —"Gort" Line. The contraction of the line freed two British divisions (the 2nd and the 48th), which were hurried towards the southern front during the night of the 23rd /24th. The line improvised on this front was that well defined and, indeed, historical stretch of canals running from the coast at Gravelines, through Saint-Omer, Aire, Béthune and La Bassée, to which Vauban and other French military engineers had devoted their skill in past generations. By the morning of the 23rd the German threat to the southern front was fully disclosed: he had forced bridgeheads at Saint-Omer and Aire, and his tanks were within three miles of Hazebrouck. The defence of the front was the responsibility of the III Corps, a formation whose composition fluctuated but under whose command the 2nd and 48th Divisions were placed at 5.10 a.m. on 24th May.

The 6th Brigade, in spite of congestion on the roads, arrived in the area of Vieille-Chapelle at 11.30 that morning, and at 6 in the evening started its advance towards the Aire Canal in transport. The 2nd Durhams arrived at Calonne-sur-la-Lys at 11 at night. At dawn on the 25th, while the Germans forced a crossing near Busnes, the march was continued on foot. A weary march it was, and it was not until 9.30 in the evening that the Battalion occupied its allotted position in the southern outskirts of Saint-Venant.

The situation was obscure. It was said the enemy tanks that had penetrated the Canal line had been cut off and were trying to fight their way back south. Far, however, from retreating the enemy was coming on in force. By 10 a.m. on the 26th he had found, and entered, a gap between the 2nd Battalion and the 4th Brigade on its left (or south-east), and had infiltrated to Merville, twisting back the 4th Brigade's line to Riez-du-Vinage. During the day two companies of the 1st Royal Welch Fusiliers were repulsed in an attempt to gain the Canal line from Saint-Venant, and one of their companies at

Robecq was surrounded and cut off. By the evening of the 26th the remainder of the Fusiliers had withdrawn to Saint-Floris, while the 2nd Durhams held Saint-Venant with three companies, the fourth (D) covering a gap between them and the 1st Royal Berkshire on their right (or north-west).

On the 27th the enemy launched two powerful attacks on the 2nd Division. The first, delivered at 4.30 a.m. while it was still half light, descended on the 4th and 6th Brigades and lasted until about 11. On the 6th Brigade front, from Fauquelin to Saint-Venant, all three battalions were heavily engaged. A Company, on D's left, was early involved with a strong German patrol, on which it inflicted many casualties at, however, considerable cost to itself. Later, as the light became stronger, tanks and armoured cars approached B and C Companies. The anti-tank guns were soon knocked out, and the tanks fought their way towards battalion headquarters by a barn on the road beside the canalised Lys. Two tanks shelled the position from the left flank, and though an anti-tank rifle detachment managed to destroy the crew of one before being itself overcome, others closed in remorselessly, straddling the slit-trenches in which the occupants, though unharmed, were yet powerless to offer resistance. D Company, meanwhile, on the far right, was heavily engaged in a fight which soon reduced its effectives to 45 all ranks. Most of them fell in a vain attempt to counter-attack.

At 11.45 the Brigadier ordered the Fusiliers and the Durhams to withdraw north of the Lys. Some managed to do so. But every attempt to cross drew a heavy fire. One enemy tank, which eventually went on as far as Haverskerque before it was put out of action, crossed the canal bridge and destroyed the post there from the rear. Most of the Battalion was pinned to its position by the overwhelming fire, and it had no choice but to fight it out with rifles against tanks. The last stand was made at the barn near headquarters. Lieut.-Colonel Simpson—whose conduct throughout had been so conspicuous as to earn the D.S.O. on his release from captivity—being an army pistol shot, disposed with his revolver of some of the infantry who swarmed in after the tanks. At last, however, "two tanks turned into the barn, German infantry poured in and the struggle was over".

By evening all that remained of the Battalion, the survivors of D Company, three carriers—the last in the Brigade—and some men from B Echelon, was assembled at Le Touquet and brought to Caudescure with the remnants of the Fusiliers. At midnight the 2nd Division was reported no longer operational. There is little more to say. What was left of the 6th Brigade was marched north by way of Strazeele, Fletre, Bailleul, Westouter and Poperinge to Sint-Jan-ter-

Biezen, which they reached at about 5 p.m. on the 28th. The whole division, when collected within the Dunkirk perimeter on the 29th, amounted to hardly 500 men, and, being non-operational, was among the first to be embarked when the embarkation was ordered to begin the night of the 29th/30th. The 6th Brigade details were taken on board from the Dunkirk and La Panne beaches that night.

(vi) The Ypres/Comines Canal, 26th-28th May

After the Arras operation the Durham Territorial battalions of the 50th Division were withdrawn to Vimy Ridge, where, early on the 23rd, Brigadier Churchill's Brigade occupied a sector from Givenchy-en-Gohelle to Farbus. The enemy meanwhile, massing in Souchez and thrusting towards Lens, threatened to cut off the Brigade's retreat. Orders for its withdrawal behind the La Bassée Canal did not reach it until early in the morning of the 24th; but it succeeded in extricating itself, by making a wide detour south; and from 8.30 that morning until later in the 25th it was in billets in the area Don/Herrin/Bois d'Epinoy/Carvin.

The Division, with the 5th, was earmarked for a repeat performance of the Arras operation across the "neck" of the German penetration to link up with a simultaneous French counter-offensive from the south. Events, however, moved too swiftly. In the evening of the 25th the Commander-in-Chief abandoned any notion of such an operation. Instead, the Division was ordered into G.H.Q. reserve in the area Armentières/Radinghem/Laventie against a possible collapse of the Belgian Army on the left of the main front between Menin and Ypres.

By the time the orders reached divisional headquarters early on the 26th all but the 6th Battalion of the 151st Brigade had become too involved in fighting which had developed on the La Bassée Canal to move with the rest of the Division. During the previous night the 9th Battalion, in response to a request from the French, had reinforced the French troops holding the canal with two companies posted in Bauvin, near Provin, which was heavily shelled at 6 a.m. on the 26th. The 8th Battalion in response to a similar request had sent a carrier platoon to reinforce the French position at Carvin; and later during that morning the main 8th Battalion's position had been so heavily dive-bombed that it was forced to withdraw to Camphin. At 11.45, however, the Battalion, supported by some French tanks, counter-attacked and retook Carvin. Some hours after this success the 9th Battalion, which had retired from the canal bank owing to the number of moored barges which reduced its value as an obstacle, underwent another dive-bombing attack. Nevertheless, at nightfall, so effective had the resistance of the two battalions proved that General Langlois asked them to remain in action at Carvin and Provin until the disordered 1st North African Division could be relieved, and their release could not be given until the early hours of the 27th.

Meanwhile the rest of the Division with the 6th Battalion had moved north to prolong the left flank of the main front. The 5th Division had been used to plug the gap between Comines and Ypres; the 50th extended the line along the Ypres/Comines Canal to Boezinge and came into position during the course of the 27th. By midnight the 8th and 9th Battalions had come up to complete the 151st Brigade. At the same hour the Belgian Army capitulated.

Throughout the 28th there was considerable enemy activity along the whole Yser Canal line; but though the pressure on the Durham Brigade front increased from about 4 that afternoon the line was maintained intact; and the only alteration made was the withdrawal of the 8th Battalion into a reserve position near Dikkebus Lake facing south. The principal danger, in fact, since the collapse of the southern front the previous day, came not from the east but from the south, and the enemy was driving north-eastwards upon Poperinge. At midnight the Division swung back according to orders to the line Poperinge/Woesten/Bikschote, a line which it held until the evening of the 29th, when it was finally ordered back into the Dunkirk peri-meter. This, the final withdrawal of the campaign, was carried out with some difficulty. The enemy had been in contact with the Dur-ham Brigade from about midday on the 29th onwards, and the severity of the fire had increased as the day wore on. The disengage-ment, which began at 8.15 p.m., was consequently a matter of some delicacy. It was not made the easier by the enemy, who with his usual tactical skill had found the junction of C Company of the 8th Batta-lion with the 3rd Division battalion on its left, and launched a heavy attack upon it, cutting the company off and, despite a stubborn resistance which lasted all night long, killing or capturing the whole except two men. The rest of the 8th, however, successfully extricated themselves. By 12.30 a.m. on 30th May the last of the Division was across the Yser River and the bridge was blown.

(vii) Dunkirk

The Brigade's position on the perimeter lay on the Canal de Bergues à Furnes opposite Wulveringem: the 6th Battalion (now under Lieut.-Colonel P. J. Jeffreys, the son of the officer who had commanded it in the First War) on the right, the 9th (now under Lieut.-Colonel J. E. S. Percy) on the left near Bulscamp, the 8th (under Lieut.-Colonel R. S. McLaren since Arras) in reserve on the Canal du Ringsloot. It was to have been embarked during the night of the 31st, but during that day the enemy increased the pressure on that front. Breaking through the 1st King's Own Scottish Borderers at about 9 a.m., he compelled the 9th Battalion on their right to form a flank. A counter-attack by both battalions (the 9th's organised by Major C. R. Battiscombe) restored the line; but a fresh enemy attack on the 9th at 2 p.m. not only forced it back over the Canal du Ringsloot but also caused the withdrawal of the 6th. A gap between the 9th's left and the Borderers was closed by the 3rd Grenadier Guards in the evening, and though the units were by then much mixed up they were subjected to nothing more serious than a harassing fire. Early on 1st June the three battalions, whose sole diet for some days had been tinned pilchards in tomato sauce, were at last withdrawn from the line. At 2.30 in the afternoon they started to move down to the beaches for embarkation. The 50th was the last division to go.

What remained of the 2nd Battalion had gone on the 29th; Colonel Marley's battalion had embarked during the night of the 30th/31st. Having assembled at Gondecourt on the 21st, and then embussed to move north to the Canal de l'Aa, it had returned to Gondecourt on the 23rd, been moved to Seclin on the 24th, and to the Haute Deule Canal on the 26th. That evening it was brought back behind the Lys to Le Petit Mortier near Steenwerck. On the 28th, being behind the Yser Canal position at Krombeke, it had provided reinforcements to the Durham battalions in the 50th Division, among them a detachment under Captain Shipley (11th), Marley's adjutant, which went to the 8th. At midday on the 29th it was at Killem-Linde; after dark it was withdrawn into the perimeter; and the next night it was embarked with the rest of the 23rd Division.

The North African Campaigns, 1940-1943

With the entry of Italy into the War in support of the Axis on 11th June 1940, a new theatre of hostilities opened up on the African shore of the Mediterranean, which, at first remote and almost independent, exerted an ever increasing influence on the decisive theatre in Europe as more and more of the resources and energies of the opponents were placed in the scale. From the outset the Regiment was represented by one battalion (the 1st). With the arrival of the 50th Division in January 1942 a further three battalions were added until, in January 1943, when the 16th Battalion joined the First Army in Algeria, the Regiment had five battalions in the North African theatre.

The swaying fortunes of the fighting may be summarised in the following seven phases:

(i) the original Italian thrust across the Libyan border in September 1940;

(ii) the defeat of the Italian Army at Sidi Barrani in December 1940, and its pursuit through Bardia, Tobruk, Derna and Benghazi as far as Agheila;

(iii) the German-Italian counter-offensive in April 1941, which left Tobruk isolated and besieged, and drove the British Army back to the border, where it made two unsuccessful attempts to reverse the situation (15th May and 15th June);

(iv) the British offensive of November 1941, which relieved Tobruk and pressed the Axis Army as far as Agheila again;

(v) the German-Italian counter-thrust of January 1942, which forced back the British Army to the Gazala Line, outside Tobruk;

(vi) the great German offensive of May and June 1942, in which Tobruk was captured and the British field army thrown right back to the Alamein Line;

(vii) the great British offensive of October 1942, which, starting with the Battle of Alamein and prosecuted in a succession of offensive movements, drove back the Germany Army first into Tripolitania and finally into Tunisia, where the combined British Armies from Egypt and Algeria forced it into surrender near Tunis in May 1943.

The 1st Battalion, which was involved in the first four phases, had landed at Suez from Hong Kong on 30th January 1940 under the command of Lieut.-Colonel E. H. L. Lysaght-Griffin. After six months spent on the Canal at Moascar and at Port Said—during which time it lost both its commanding officer, who took up an appointment on the staff, and its tried old quartermaster, Lieut.-Colonel W. H. Lowe—it was moved up into the Western Desert as far as Mersa Matruh in the third week of July.

At that time it was confidently expected that the Italian Army would at any moment advance across the border with Matruh as its first objective. Even when in September Graziani, having set his ponderous force in motion, settled down by Sidi Barrani, the halt was considered only temporary; and throughout the summer and autumn the garrison of Matruh was engaged in preparing the place against attack, subjected all the while to an average of at least one, if not two, air-raids a day. Finally, however, in December, when the Italians had done nothing, the British Commander-in-Chief attacked himself.

In the Battle of Sidi Barrani, one of the most spectacular feats of arms ever performed by the British army, the Battalion was represented only by a composite company of four officers and 70 n.c.o.s and men. Under Lieut.-Colonel E. A. Arderne, the fearless and enterprising officer who commanded the Battalion for the next two years, the company formed part of a force of about 1700 men assembled from the Matruh garrison under its commander, Brigadier A. R. Selby. Its task in the battle was to contain the Italians occupying the camps at Maktila during the attacks on the more southerly camps by the main British Army. The D.L.I. company belonged to a column (C) under Lieut.-Colonel Arderne's orders whose first duty—which it carried out during the night of 8th/9th December—was to establish a "brigade" of dummy tanks in a *wadi* west of Matruh as a bait for the enemy airforce. By 11 in the morning of the 9th, the day the great offensive opened, "Selbyforce" had reached a *wadi* a few miles short of Maktila, from which the Italians, ever prudent, retired. During that day and the 10th the main Army had swept down on the line of Italian camps from the south, had overrun and destroyed them, and had reached Sidi Barrani, in rear of Shireisat. Early on the 11th Selby, whose limited attacks had so far failed to produce any similar catastrophic effect on his immediate opponents, ordered an advance, which, much to the surprise and relief of Arderne's men, was shortly followed by the surrender of the 1st Libyan Division. The spectacle, like many things in that curiously comical campaign, was grotesque. A senior Italian officer stepped forward, saluted and gravely declared while standing in front of a vast pile of unexpended ammunition, "*Monsieur, nous avons tiré la dernière cartouche.*" A platoon under 2/Lieutenant R. A. G. Birchenough which flushed another Italian position was greeted by an officer, who rushed at them shouting, "Sir, you have killed a man." The company's casualties in the exhilarating episode were negligible.

Reorganised and placed under the command of Major R. Q. F. Johnston, the second-in-command, the company continued, in conjunction with the 7th Hussars, to take part in the next operation, which resulted in the fall of Bardia (3rd January 1941). Here, however, it suffered the misfortune to lose its commander, mortally wounded on patrol.

At the end of February the Battalion was withdrawn from Matruh to the Canal, where it underwent training with the 22nd Guards Brigade for a projected attack on the Dodecanese Islands. That venture, however, was interrupted by the turn of events in the Desert, where the enemy, reinforced by German formations and commanded by Rommel, contrived to thrust back the weak screen of British troops in his front of Agheila, and advance to the top of the Escarpment above Sollúm. The Battalion was hurried back first to Matruh (8th April) and then to Sollúm, while A Company, under Captain P. H.

M. May, was detached to hold Bardia with the assistance of a troop of light tanks. After Captain May had blown the wells and successfully extricated his "garrison" during the night of 11th/12th April, the Battalion retired to position at the top and bottom of Halfaya Pass. From there on 23rd April it was brought back to Kilo 90 on the Matruh/Barrani road.

Halfaya, 15th–16th May 1941

The operation undertaken to wrest the summit of the Escarpment around Halfaya from the grip of the enemy, which went by the code-name *Brevity*, was set in motion by Brigadier Gott on 15th May. The 22nd Guards Brigade, forming the centre of three columns, was to advance along the top of the Escarpment, clear the summit of

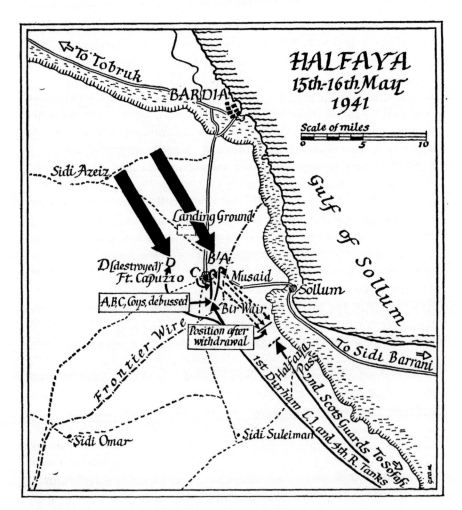

38. Halfaya, 15th—16th May, 1941

Halfaya Pass, secure Fort Capuzzo and exploit northwards in conjunction with twenty-four I-tanks. The 2nd Scots Guards, in front, with the support of the tanks broke into the enemy position at the top of the Pass. The 1st Battalion, which moved up from Sofafi in transport on a front of 800 yards, passed through the frontier Wire and, dismounting, deployed again, managed despite the non-appearance of the tanks to get one company into Capuzzo. Then, however, a heavy enemy fire pinned down the three assault companies: and in the afternoon a strong counter-attack delivered by the II/5th Panzer Regiment not only destroyed the reserve company (D, Major H. E. F. Fox-Davies), which had made a wide flanking movement on the left, but drove the others eastward to Musaid. No further progress could be made, and the operation was abandoned in the early hours of 16th May. The Battalion's losses (11 officers and 185 n.c.o.s and men) temporarily crippled Arderne's fine battalion. Nothing material had been gained except the top of Halfaya, and that was lost on the 27th.

Syria, 28th June-6th October 1941

Early in June the Battalion, which had been withdrawn on 16th May to Buq Buq—where its losses were partially made up by reinforcements from several regiments   was taken out of the Desert and moved to Syria with the newly re-formed 23rd Brigade.[7]

Syria had been entered on 8th June by a force, consisting largely of Free French, one Indian infantry brigade and two Australian brigades, in an attempt to overcome the Vichy administration before it succumbed totally to Axis influence. The 23rd Brigade was not assembled until the end of the month, when it concentrated at Tulkarm, in Palestine; and it did not enter active operations until the final phase, the 1st Battalion relieving an Australian battalion at Merjayun on 1st July. The village had already twice defied attempts to capture it, and the prospect of renewing them was daunting. Fortunately other operations were successful in isolating it, and on 11th July the Battalion was able to move forward against only slight opposition to Yuhmur and cross the Leontes. On the same day General Dentz, the Vichy commander, asked for an armistice.

Tobruk, 18th November-10th December

The Battalion was at Idlib near Aleppo when on 2nd October it was given a fortnight's notice to move. Railed from Aleppo on 6th October to Tahag on the Canal, and embarking in two crowded destroyers at Alexandria, the Battalion re-entered the very forefront

[7]4th Border Regiment, 1st Durham Light Infantry, and 11th Czech Battalion, under Brigadier A. Galloway.

of military events when it landed at Tobruk on the 12th. The movement was part of the larger scheme for the relief of the 9th Australian Division by the 6th (or, more properly, 70th) British. It carried the Battalion to a place which, having successfully resisted investment since 11th April, imparted to anyone who set foot in it during those eight months an aura of glory, however wrily it may have been worn.

The great offensive, the Battle of Sidi Rezeg, which was directed towards the object, amongst others, of relieving Tobruk, was not launched until 18th November. In the meanwhile the Battalion occupied a sector on the southern perimeter known as Figtree Sector, which had been previously held by the 2/48th Australian Battalion. The daily round was monotonous, but the commanding officer was not one to allow monotony to become oppressive. An athlete as we have seen, he would appear at headquarters with a Bren, look round for a likely volunteer and then set out to draw the enemy fire to check, as he expressed it, "the usual contradictory reports of night patrols". Once visiting a forward company, on being asked if there were any mines in that area, he replied, "Oh yes," and scraping away the sand with the toe of his boot to disclose a teller-mine beneath, added, "There's one," and walked on "as unconcerned as if it had been a stone". There was constant patrolling. On 9th November D Company of the Battalion (Major H. M. Vaux) and a platoon under Lieutenant J. E. Stafford delivered a heavy—but unsuccessful—raid on the exposed enemy post known as "Plonk" at Bir Azazi, a mile outside the perimeter and two miles east of the El Adem road.

Before the offensive began it had been arranged that, on receipt of the code-word "Pop", the garrison should advance from the south-east of the perimeter at first light on the following morning and, successively seizing certain well defined enemy positions up to and including the dominating feature of Ed Duda, so form a kind of appendix to which the relieving Eight Army could attach itself. The 23rd Brigade was cast in an unspectacular supporting role. In the event, "Pop" was not received until the late afternoon of 20th November, and even then it was somewhat premature, as patrols carried out by the Battalion towards "Plonk" sufficiently showed. The break-out was made punctually on the 21st, but Ed Duda, which lay on the escarpment dominating the By-Pass road and the Trig Capuzzo, was not secured until the 26th, when a precarious contact was established with a New Zealand brigade from Eighth Army. The corridor formed was thereafter subjected to a series of powerful enemy counter-attacks and several times almost severed. But it gallantly held until, after one final convulsion on 2nd December, Rommel's armour at last gave best, leaving the field to the infantry.

The 1st Battalion did not enter these operations before the final stage was reached. On 5th December, as part of an endeavour to force back the enemy's investing line westward, the Durhams were ordered to lead a sortie from Ed Duda against Point 157, 6000 yards distant, on the capture of which the 4th Border Regiment of the Brigade was to pass through and exploit to Point 162, north of El Adem.

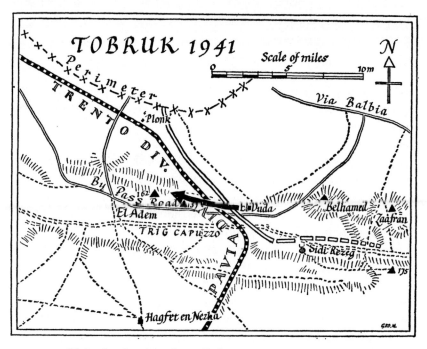

39. Tobruk: the Attack on Point 157, 7th December, 1941

Postponed until the 7th, the attack went in from Ed Duda after dark at 7.20 p.m., the men advancing on foot on a bearing of 275°. At about 10.30 the three forward companies encountered stiff opposition and, though C Company (Major A. L. S. Keith) managed to make further progress, his whereabouts was unknown and the others were held up by machine-guns firing on fixed lines. With the assistance, however, of some tanks summoned by Lieut.-Colonel Arderne, the enemy was cleared out of his positions by 2.30 a.m. the next morning (8th), and, the Battalion having consolidated, the Borders were able to pass through to carry the final objective with small loss. "A classic night operation" as it was described in the Desert Army Magazine, it earned Lieut.-Colonel Arderne an immediate award of the D.S.O. It cost the Battalion the loss of three officers (including Major Keith, killed rounding up prisoners) and eight n.c.o.s and men killed, and one officer and 26 n.c.o.s and men wounded.

Lack of transport prohibited any further share in operations by units of the 70th Division. After a period of salvaging on the derelict battlefield, the Battalion (except for a part of B Company, employed on the prisoner of war cage at Tobruk) was brought back to the Canal Zone at Qassassin on 19th December. On 24th January 1942 it was embarked for Malta and so removed from the North African theatre of operations.

Gazala: Gabr el Fakri and Zt el Mrassas, 14th and 15th June 1942

On the departure of the 1st Battalion from the Desert the Regiment was nobly represented in the field throughout the last three phases of the campaigns by the Territorial battalions in the 151st Brigade.

Having been the last division to leave Dunkirk and having taken all its German prisoners with it, the 50th not unnaturally returned with a very good and healthy conceit, as well it might. It believed itself to be the only formed and effective division in Britain. Everyone has borne witness to the impressive bearing of the men composing it. To join it was an honour. Orders to mobilise for service overseas were accepted as a due right.

On its arrival in the Middle East in June and July 1941 it was not, however, received enthusiastically. No formed divisions were. While the 150th Brigade was (temporarily) sent up into the Desert, the others were sent, first, to Cyprus (July to November), where the 150th rejoined, then to Iraq (November to January 1942), against a threatened German advance from Russia into Persia. It was not until the end of February 1942 that the Division was finally reunited to occupy a position in the Gazala Line, west of Tobruk, the strong and conspicuous line on which the Eighth Army awaited the renewed German offensive in May. The 151st Brigade lay in a "box" surrounded by mine-fields situated on the left of the 1st South African Division about twenty miles from the coast, on the right centre of the Line. The 6th Battalion had been commanded since the previous August by Lieut.-Colonel C. R. Battiscombe, a regular officer of the Regiment with twenty years' service, whose great-grandfather had fought with the 68th in the trenches before Sevastopol. He had himself shown his quality on the Dunkirk perimeter. In the 8th Lieut.-Colonel M. L. P. Jackson, Green Howards, whose blunt n111:

admirably suited the mood of the men he commanded, had recently succeeded Lieut.-Colonel C. W. Beart, appointed to an East African brigade. The 9th was still commanded by Lieut.-Colonel J. E. S. Percy, formerly a member of the 1st Battalion's polo team and possessing aptitudes which the fighting of the next few weeks were to highlight.

The battle was joined during the night of 26th /27th May. Rommel, sweeping round the left flank of the Gazala Line fifty miles in the interior, by midday on the 27th had his armour heavily engaged with our own in the rear of the 150th Brigade, which, like all formations in the Line, sat tight according to their orders. During the next few days the enemy succeeded in clearing the mine-fields on either side of the 150th's box, and on the 31st he finally broke into it from the north-east. A desperate struggle ensued, the enemy pouring in ever increasing numbers of troops until at last on 1st June the Brigade was finally overrun.

The orders of the other two brigades of the Division tied them to their positions to the north, and throughout the first phase of the battle the Durham battalions' activities were confined to vigorous patrolling and "commerce-raiding", an activity which they had pursued successfully since first entering the Desert. On 10th June, however, with the fall of Bir Hakheim, stubbornly held by the 1st Free French Brigade, the southern flank of the Line was carried, and the situation of the undefeated formations in the north, already precarious, at once became desperate.

Conventional withdrawal was impossible. The coast road was reserved for the 1st South African Division. In the immediate rear lay the main German armoured force. To the south lay more German armour. It was consequently decided to withdraw in motor transport by advancing westward against the Italian X Corps, forming "bridgeheads" through which those in rear could pass, and then turning south and making for the frontier Wire at Fort Maddalena past Bir Hakheim.

The bridgehead for the 151st Brigade was formed by the 8th Battalion, operating in two columns, at Gabr el Fakri after dark on 14th June. The right column advanced a mile and then came under fire from machine-guns, anti-tank guns and mortars; the vehicle of the column commander (Major H. S. Sell) was blown from beneath him; but after a bitter struggle the objective was reached. The left hand column (Major A. B. S. Clarke) encountered little opposition. A third column, consisting principally of the 6th Battalion and brigade headquarters, made its way into the passage, and by 2.30 a.m. on the 15th the two battalions were through. All then made hot-foot for the south-west, and then due east for Maddalena. The 6th Battalion reached the rendezvous early on the 16th without sustaining many casualties either through straggling or enemy action. The route of the 8th, following, unfortunately led through a German strong-point, which Major Sell successfully rushed, and part of Major Clarke's column ran over a mine-field. But by the night of the 16th the bulk of the 8th was assembled at Maddalena. Those who saw the battalions have commented on their high morale and the splendid fighting spirit which carried them through the maze of mine-fields in their path.

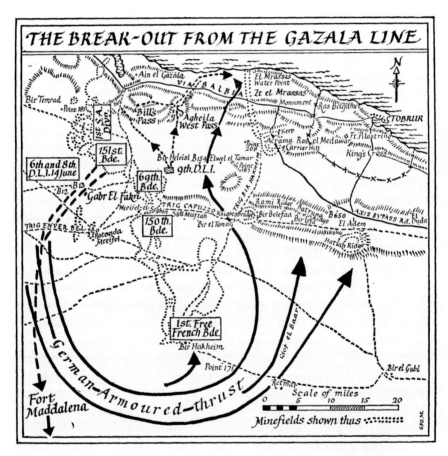

40. The Break-out from the Gazala Line, 14th—15th June, 1942

Meanwhile the 9th Battalion, which before the break-out had moved into a position to the east of the 69th Brigade, having been delayed, was given the option using either of the 8th's bridgehead or of retiring north and then east by the coast road. Neither was attractive at that hour. In their front the Italians were on the alert.

To the north-east the rearguards of the brigades of the 1st South African Division had already cleared out, presumably blowing the passes as they went. Their retreat had been temporarily secured by the fine resistance maintained throughout the 14th against the German armour by the troops posted along the Escarpment; but that protection had gone by nightfall. Nevertheless Lieut.-Colonel Percy chose that route, and moved the Battalion in two parallel columns: one under his own orders by the Agheila Pass, the other under Major J. C. Slight by Bill's Pass—where it arrived at about 6.40 a.m. on the 15th just as the South Africans were on the point of blowing the charges. Both columns reached the coast road west of the El Mrassas mine-field at about 11 to find it blocked by the enemy. The III/115th Rifle Regiment of the 15th *Panzerdivision* had moved down onto it after dark.

The confusion on the road, where all manner of miscellaneous vehicles besides those of the 9th's were fleeing east to Tobruk, was chaotic. Lieut.-Colonel Percy, seeing success only in prompt action, at once ordered an attack by such forces as he could collect from the nearest troop-carrying trucks. Led with great determination by Major Slight, whose conduct earned him the D.S.O., and assisted by a bold use of some South African field-guns and a number of carriers under Major M. R. Ferens, 6th Battalion, the attack was immediately successful. Enemy resistance crumbled under the rough onslaught, in which heavy casualties were inflicted. By 3 in the afternoon Lieut.-Colonel Percy's force was through. It went on to Tobruk, where it reported the recapture of Mrassas. It reached the Wire next day, the 16th. For a few days the two remaining brigades of the Division rested near Talata.

Mersah Matruh and Point 174, 26th-30th June

On 21st June Tobruk fell. The frontier positions in which the 151st Brigade reassembled were incapable of defence against the force Rommel could bring against them, and there was no alternative to continuing the Eighth Army's retreat to Matruh and possibly beyond. By the 25th the Brigade was in position on the side of the Escarpment south of Gerawla.

There was nothing inherently strong about Matruh, but the work devoted to the ground, where many a unit had prepared mine-fields and "boxes" in the quieter days of yore, gave promise at least of a profitable delaying action. The Eighth Army, with ample forces for an effective defence, occupied the Matruh position in a style reminiscent of Cannæ, with two very strong wings and a weak centre. Furthermore, by a curious stroke of chance, Rommel struck it in the afternoon of 26th June at its weakest point. So far, however, from intending a trap the Army commander could not decide whether or not to make a determined stand. The resemblance to Cannæ ceased at the moment when Rommel penetrated (with ease) the Matruh mine-field with his 90th Light Division, and opened the way for a deep thrust on the morrow.

Before dawn on the 27th "90 Light," pressing on vigorously, struck the 151st Brigade. The first battalion to meet its fierce onslaught was the 9th D.L.I., which, in accordance with the Eighth Army's predilection for excessive dispersion, lay well in front of the Brigade about seventeen miles south of Matruh. All three battalions were heavily engaged, but the desperate resistance offered by the 9th Battalion at Point 174, where it was almost destroyed, claims particular notice, characterised as it was by the conduct of Private A. H. Wakenshaw, of Gateshead, which was requited by a posthumous Victoria Cross. He was one of a 2-pounder anti-tank gun detachment sited on a forward slope in front of the position. Early in the action it knocked out a light gun which engaged it at close range, but another mobile gun succeeded a little later in silencing it, at the same time killing or wounding every man of the detachment. During the lull the enemy moved the mobile gun forward to 200 yards' distance to engage a company of the Battalion in rear. Wakenshaw, realising the danger to his comrades, crawled back to his gun, and although he had lost his left arm at the shoulder, with the assistance of the gun-layer he loaded and fired five more rounds, which damaged the enemy gun and set its trailer on fire. A near-miss then killed the gun-layer and wounded Wakenshaw again; but he dragged himself back, placed another round in the breech and was about to fire when a direct hit on the ammunition finally killed this brave man, whose gun now stands at the Regimental Depot as a silent reminder of his devotion.

Elsewhere on the Battalion's front the fight raged with equal ferocity. By 7.30 a.m. the three forward companies had been cut off and overrun. At 9 the rest, mostly headquarters and headquarter company, were ordered to retire to divisional headquarters to form part of its defence. Though almost annihilated, with the loss of 300 prisoners, the 9th had yet succeeded by its resistance in preventing the enemy from exploiting his advantage and falling on the exposed flank of the 8th Battalion.

Soon after dark Rommel's forces cut the coast road in rear. In other circumstances this need not have given cause for undue alarm. At night the 6th and 8th Battalions took part in a large-scale raid against the enemy communications in the interior of the desert.

Carried out in moonlight, it caused confusion among the enemy transport, but though the battalions' losses were small it had caused not much less confusion among the attackers before they were ordered back to their original positions. There the situation became more and more precarious throughout the 28th (which was a quiet day except for the 6th Battalion's successful repulse of a German column), and a break-out similar to that at Gazala was planned for the night of the 28th/29th.

The 10th Indian and 50th Divisions were ordered to break south for thirty miles and then turn east to rendezvous near Fuka. The 6th Battalion accomplished the journey without much interference. The 8th, on the other hand, ran into an ambush in a *wadi* as they climbed up the Escarpment, and succeeded in extricating itself only after a stiff fight in which a company (D) was for the most part destroyed. Fuka, moreover, was in enemy hands, and some columns that had not been diverted were captured. The rest were withdrawn, first behind the Alamein Line (1st July), and later to Mareopolis, near Alexandria (4th July), where the Division refitted and replenished its sadly depleted ranks. Except for a brief and abortive operation during 20th-23rd July, in which a composite battalion from the 6th, 8th and 9th, under Lieut.-Colonel Battiscombe, after taking its objective was largely destroyed with the capture of its commanding officer, the Durham battalions shared in no fighting until the great offensive was launched from El Alamein on 23rd October.

El Alamein, 23rd October-4th November 1942

The offensive that began in the sandhills near Alexandria and was to end triumphantly on the Gulf of Tunis was as different from light-hearted affairs like Sidi Barrani as war differs from a drive on the grouse-moors after breakfast. Carefully meditated and painstakingly planned by a master in the art of war, Alamein was the first battle the Army fought with the sole and deliberate intention of destroying the enemy's force—a grim business soberly undertaken by men who had known defeat and were determined never to taste it again.

When the Durham battalions returned to the line on 4th September, the command of the 6th Battalion had passed to Lieut.-Colonel W. I. Watson, a Territorial officer of twenty years' service whose father and great-uncle had both commanded it before him. The 8th remained under Lieut.-Colonel M. L. P. Jackson. The much reorganised 9th was commanded by Lieut.-Colonel A. B. S. Clarke, King's Own Scottish Borderers, formerly adjutant of the 8th, in succession to Lieut.-Colonel Percy, promoted to the command of the

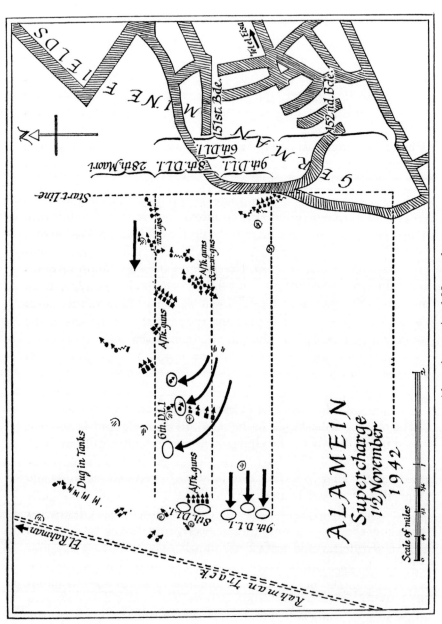

41. Alamein, 1st/2nd November, 1942

Brigade, which, with the disappearance of the 150th at Gazala, became the only survivor of the old 50th Division.

In the opening stages of the Alamein offensive, the main thrust of which was made by the XXX Corps in the north, the 50th Division played no immediate part, the role of the XIII Corps being limited primarily to misleading and containing the Italian troops in its front. It was not until the first day of November, when the Germans had moved their reserves northwards without, however, suffering a breakthrough, that the 151st and 152nd Brigades under the command of the 2nd New Zealand Division were launched at the left centre of the enemy position in the operation named *Supercharge*. Originally planned for the night of 31st October/1st November but postponed 24 hours, the operation was the culminating thrust designed to achieve the actual break-through. The objective was the Sidi Rahman Track. The attack was to be carried out under cover of darkness with the 151st on the right, its flank secured by the 28th (Maori) Battalion, across flat, almost featureless, desert, sparsely mined, against a sector held by elements of two German (90th Light and 164th) and two Italian armoured divisions (Trento and Littorio). The 8th Battalion attacked on the right, the 9th on the left. The 6th moved up in rear to mop up, and then wheeled right to face north, while the others faced west to form, as it were, the revetment of the bridgehead.

Punctually at 12.55 a.m. on the 2nd the silence of the night was shattered by the opening of the barrage, and, with visiblity of little more than fifty yards, the infantry went forward. Scattering enemy mine-laying parties, who, stunned, offered scant resistance, the leading battalions broke into and overran the main positions, his first-aid posts and headquarters, and continued through his gun lines to the intermediate objective. There they paused. The 6th Battalion, after encountering fixed-line machine-gun fire, followed on, silencing the enemy posts with the bayonet as it went, and carried out successfully the difficult manœuvre of a wheel in the dark. The pace quickened as the advance proceeded. By 4 the battalions were on the Rahman Track digging in on the margins of the corridor they had created, into which the 9th Armoured Brigade entered as day broke. Several counter-attacks by enemy tanks were delivered during the day, but were beaten off by heavy anti-tank gun fire. Early in the evening orders were received for relief, which was completed by about 3 a.m. on 3rd November, though not before the whole brigade area had been subjected to a severe shelling.

In just 24 hours these Durham battalions had carried through their task with complete success. *Supercharge* had knocked out the chock: on the 4th the enemy began his retreat. One battalion alone (the 9th) had taken over four hundred prisoners. Casualties on the other hand had not been light; they amounted to rather under 400 all ranks in the three battalions.

Mareth, 16th-23rd March 1943

The 50th took no part in the pursuit, that astonishing movement that continued for over a thousand miles, past Tobruk, past Benghazi —even past Agheila, where hopes had been twice disappointed—to Tripoli and beyond, until it confronted the Mareth Line. At the New Year the Division was at Benina, near Benghazi. It was to have taken part in the attack on Buerat (15th January 1943), had not a gale intervened to reduce the assaulting force by disrupting the Army's supply arrangements. By the time it was brought up from Benina to carry out the toughest part in the assault on the Mareth Line, the First Army was exerting a pressure on Tunisia, and the days of the Axis Armies in Africa were clearly shortening.

The Line, built before the War by the French against Italian aggression from Tripolitania, had been recognised for some time as one of the few serious geographical obstacles to be overcome. Well sited between the sea and the Matmata Hills, it ran behind the Wadi Zigzaou, a muddy stream flowing sluggishly in a valley eighty yards wide between banks averaging fifty feet in height. In addition to this, itself a formidable anti-tank obstacle, the Line consisted of a series of concrete and steel emplacements and strong-points constructed in depth, protected by anti-tank ditches and trenches and strengthened by wire and mines. It was held by a Young Fascist division, the best of the Italian troops, with the 90th Light in immediate reserve, and the 15th Panzer ready to hand. The Matmata Hills were reported as impassable by wheeled traffic. A frontal assault was obviously a costly business.

Though outflanking it by way of Foum Tataouine[8] and "Plum" Pass involved a journey of 150 miles of very rough going, Montgomery nevertheless risked the movement, at the same time combining it with a frontal attack by the 50th Division along the coastal axis. The Durham battalions were to attack on a mile-wide front between the strong-points of Ksiba Ouest and Ouerzi, the 9th Battalion taking Ksiba Ouest, the 8th Ouerzi. When they had fallen, tanks were to cross the *wadi* by causeways, followed by the 6th Battalion, which had orders to deepen the penetration. The attack was timed to take place at full moon during the night of 20th/21st March.

[8]From now on it is best to adhere to the French transliteration of Arabic place-names, *w* and *u* being replaced by *ou*, *j* by *dj*, etc.

After careful reconnaissances made under the very noses of the enemy during the night of the 18th, the Durham assault battalions advanced from the Chet Meskine at 11 p.m. on the 20th. Against a heavy but not very accurate fire of all arms C and B Companies of the 9th Battalion succeeded in crossing an anti-tank ditch and, wading across the Wadi and scrambling up the far bank by forming a human ladder, fought their way with the bayonet into the thick of the position, B Company (Captain E. W. H. Worrall) finally over-coming Ksiba Ouest. The 8th Battalion had a similar experience in overrunning Ouerzi, where the Italians fought stubbornly. Lieut.-Colonel Jackson was unfortunately killed; but by morning both battalions had reached their objectives in very severe fighting but without undue loss. On the other hand the 6th Battalion was unable to launch its attack until dark fell again, and the supply and rein-forcement of the 8th and 9th remained precarious throughout the 21st. When it did advance, however, the 6th secured its objectives, Ouerzi Ouest and Zarat Sudest, with comparative ease.

At 11 a.m. on the 22nd the 9th Battalion could clearly see the enemy tanks (from 15th Panzer) forming up opposite Ksiba Ouest for a counter-attack. To resist it only a few tanks and a very few anti-tank guns had been got across the Wadi. At the same time, by an unfortunate stroke, heavy falls of rain not only wrecked the crossing place the sappers had laboured to construct but prevented any air-strike. As it was, the 50th Division had to withstand the full weight of the counter-attack with few supporting weapons and no support from the air. The 8th had to fight hard for Ouerzi but, though surrounded, still held it at dusk. The 9th were driven out of Ouerzi Est back to the anti-tank ditch. The brunt of the attack fell on the 6th. The company in Ouerzi Ouest fought until its ammunition was exhausted; another in a post between Ouerzi Ouest and Zarat Sudest hung on also until forced back later in the afternoon; the third, under Major G. L. Wood, held fast at Zarat Sudest until 6 p.m. when it too had to fall back. The three battalions were each reduced from a strength of about 300 all ranks to 65.

Fighting continued on the north bank of the Wadi throughout most of the night. But though they managed to inflict heavy casual-ties, the outlook on the approach of daylight was black. At 4.30 a.m. on the 23rd the battalions were ordered to retire to the Wadi, and by first light all three had successfully disengaged and withdrawn to the near bank. The coastal attack was given up. It was a bitter dis-appointment to the battalions, some among whom refused to believe their orders until repeated by the commanding officers. On the other hand, the attack had drawn the German reserve to the coastal sector,

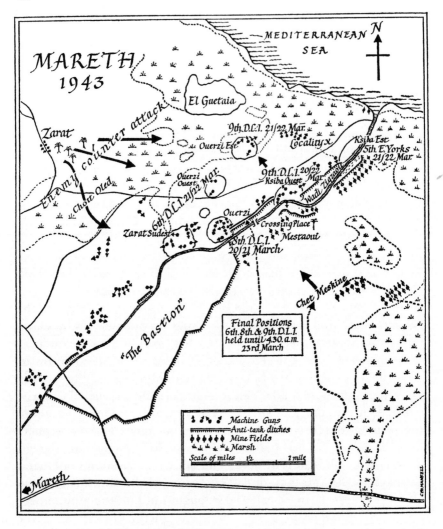

42. Mareth, 20th—23rd March, 1943

thereby easing the modified operation that followed. The flank thrust through the hills was weighted more heavily still, and when it descended on the enemy at El Hamma on 26th March it proved irresistible.

After the battle the chief-of-staff and the air-officer commanding flew over the field to study the defences. "There was no doubt," writes Sir Francis de Guingand, "about its strength, and we both felt how lucky we had been to win this battle with so little loss. The scene of the 50th Division's fighting was a nasty sight. It was sad that that gallant formation had not reaped more tangible signs of their hard fighting but in the big scheme of things they had nobly played their part."

Mareth was the last general action fought by the battalions in North Africa. The Division was at Enfidaville when on 21st April the 151st Brigade was withdrawn from the line and carried back to Alexandria.

The First Battle of Sedjenane, 28th February-4th March

Since January the Regiment had had the 16th Battalion engaged in North Africa on the First Army front.

"First Army" was a portentous title for what at first amounted to little more than two weak divisions, one of infantry (the 78th), one armoured (the 6th). Landed at Algiers on 8th November 1942, they had been rushed eastward through Sétif, Constantine and Bone. The leading groups were within sight of Tunis when on 17th November German troops, hurriedly transferred from Italy and Sicily and seizing the town under the eyes of the bewildered French authorities, just succeeded in denying the place to the Allies. The gamble had not come off. Under constant and bitter attack and counter-attack the line solidified and set fast in the hills some fifty miles west of Tunis, where it remained while each side built up its forces.

Most of Tunisia in general appearance looks not unlike southern France or Italy. It is only in the south that the country evens out to become parched desert, and even there it is not the featureless desert of Libya. The climate is European. In the north vast hills, green in winter and spring, often bald but here and there covered by thick cork-oak plantations, are tumbled in confusion as they are in the highlands of Wales or Scotland. The armies lay along an irregular range of hills through which five passes, fought for over and over again, gave access to the interior: in the north, at Sedjenane, where the metalled road from Bizerta and Tunis crossed; Hunt's Gap and Sidi Nsir; Medjaz el Bab, dominated by Longstop Hill: El Aroussa and Pont du Fahs, and in the far south, Sbeitla and Gafsa, leading west to the Kasserine Pass. On the Allied side, north and south, ran the vital lateral communication from the Tunis road at Djebel Abiod, behind Sedjenane, through Béja, Teboursoul and Thala. Any deep German penetration at the passes threatened to cut off one flank of the Army from the other, in the same way that Soult threatened Wellington's position in the Pyrenees in July 1813.

The 16th Battalion embarked at Liverpool on 25th December 1942 and, landed at Algiers on 3rd January 1943 with the 139th Brigade, the advanced brigade of the 46th Division, had occupied since 17th

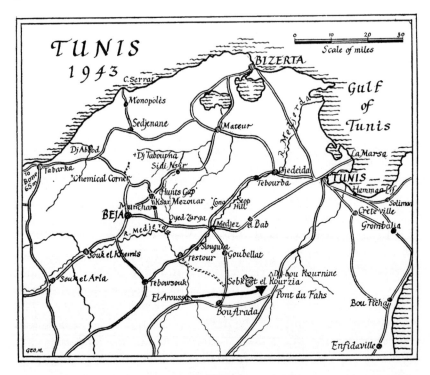

43. Tunisia

January a position at Green Hill in front of Sedjenane. Until 4th March, when the Germans aimed a powerful thrust in that direction as part of the larger policy of pinning down the First Army under continual attacks (the Nine Attacks of von Arnim, as they have been called), the front was extraordinarily quiet, offering little opportunity except for patrolling. Commanded by Lieut.-Colonel R. F. Ware, a regular officer of the Regiment who had won an M.C. in the last months of the fighting on the Western Front in 1918, the Battalion was almost entirely *Durham*, composed of excellent material, well armed, well disciplined, well behaved. Indeed, in common with the other battalions of the Brigade it lacked only one thing: its long training in England had failed to bring out the natural pugnacity of the Durham men, nor had its first quiet weeks in the line whetted its edge.

An offensive along the Sedjenane-Mateur axis was in preparation when the enemy struck. Lieut.-Colonel Ware was absent on a reconnaissance when on 1st March the Battalion was ordered north to Monopolès on the Cap Serrat road. It was still in column of threes when it encountered a strong enemy force, which scattered the leading company and caused the remainder to fall back fighting sporadically to the woods west of Sedjenane. A counter-attack organised by Lieut.-Colonel Ware on his return was only partially successful. Another counter-attack executed early on 2nd March failed with the loss of almost the whole of another company. The Battalion was compelled to fall back, first to the woods of Sedjenane, where the carrier platoons and some men under Major Ballance fought a vigorous action in conjunction with the 6th Lincoln, and, later, on 4th March, to Tabarka.

The enemy, however, was unable to penetrate to the important road junction at Djebel Abiod. The situation at Sedjenane had been narrowly saved by the stout resistance offered by the 1st Parachute Brigade and the plugging of the gap by battalion after battalion of the 46th Division, the 16th among them. It had been a rude introduction to battle for a raw battalion, whose casualties were heavy; but those who could fought well. Reorganised, reinforced and placed under the command of Lieut.-Colonel J. C. Preston, King's Own Yorkshire Light Infantry, who gave the men's pugnacious instincts full rein, the Battalion gradually recovered, as its long record of successes in Italy presently showed. For the time being the Army in Tunisia was too weak, and the situation too critical, to allow any rest to the Battalion, whose two composite companies remained in almost constant contact with the enemy under one brigade or another until it took part in the final offensive.

El Kourzia, 22nd-26th April

By the end of March Arnim's efforts at penetrating the First Army's position had been brought to a standstill, with Sedjenane, Medjez el Bab and Bou Arada still remaining in our hands. The Eighth Army had forced the Mareth Line; and on the Tunisian front a sufficient margin of superiority had been accumulated for the long delayed resumption of the offensive.

Just before the offensive opened on 22nd April the 16th Battalion was taken out of the 139th Brigade and attached to the 128th Brigade of the Division, which attacked with seven battalions upon an eight-mile front. The Brigade's objective was Bou Arada, and the Battalion's (which lay on the extreme right of the Division) the hill of Sidi Barka, held by part of the Hermann Goering Division. Under an unwontedly prodigious artillery bombardment the assault, which was carried out on a two-company front, went in at 3 a.m. Failing to reach the summit, which proved a false crest, and unable to call on the support of the tanks, which had run into a mine-field, the Battalion suffered many casualties in an exposed and difficult position. It held on obstinately, however, to its gains, and just before dawn on the 23rd it had the satisfaction of discovering the enemy had pulled out.

In the advance that ensued on this success the Battalion moved forward to Djebel Bessioud, Djebel Kournine and the Salt Lake; but though it was actively engaged in patrolling it had fought its last action in the North African campaign. At Blida during June, July and August, it underwent a period of thorough training and re-organisation.

Sicily: (i) The Landing, 9th-12th July 1943

The Regiment's honours in Sicily were won by the battalions in the 50th Division.

For the descent on the island the 151st Brigade, after undergoing a strenuous course at the Combined Training Centre at Kabrit and in the Gulf of Aqaba, was cast in the part of the divisional assault brigade. The plan of invasion practised in exercises involved the immediate occupation of the south-eastern portion of the island, the Pachino Peninsula, and demanded the capture of a sizeable port, Syracuse. The latter operation was entrusted to airborne troops and the 5th Division, whose left flank and rear were protected by the 50th Division, landing on the one beach available nearby at Ávola. The 9th Battalion (Lieut.-Colonel A. B. S. Clarke) was to land at "Jig Green" beach, a mile north of Ávola, the 6th (Lieut.-Colonel W. I. Watson) on "Jig Amber", level with the town of Ávola. Having eliminated the beach defences, both were to advance and establish themselves on the main road and at the seaward exits from the town. The 8th (since Jackson's death, under Lieut.-Colonel R. P. Lidwill, who in 1939 had been a subaltern in the King's Regiment), in reserve, was to land at one or other of the beaches as circumstances appeared to favour, pass through the other two battalions, and gain a position on the high ground beyond to deny the enemy all observation of the landing places and the maintenance area. It was an ambitious pro-gramme for two brigades, let alone one.

The battalions embarked at Port Said on 5th July. From the rendezvous at sea at 10 p.m. on the 9th, just before dark, the summit of Mount Etna could clearly be seen above the clouds "with a curious appearance of detachment from the earth". There was a considerable swell and a stronger offshore wind than was desirable; but the transfer from the ships to the landing craft was successfully accomplished. The landing craft should have touched the shore at 2.45 a.m. All of them, however, went astray through errors of navigation, and the first ashore, B Company of the 6th Battalion, was an hour and a half late in time and 3000 yards too far to the south in place. Others were even farther off-course: A Company was put ashore at Calabernardo, which was mistaken for Marina di Ávola; the 9th Battalion fared little better; and the 8th landed after daylight in the 5th Division's landing area. Nevertheless, despite the confusion caused and the extra marching involved, all the defences were neutralised at surprisingly small cost thanks largely to the feeble resistance offered by the Italian coastal divisions. "Jig Green" was reported as captured at 7.52 a.m. by the 6th Battalion, which before 9 was in occupation of Ávola railway-station; while at 10 the 9th Battalion's flag was fluttering triumphantly from the town hall. By midday all battalions were occupying the prearranged positions in the vineyards and olive-groves on the high ground, the 6th in the foothills north of Noto, the 8th overlooking Ávola, the 9th in Ávola itself and holding the line of the Mammaledi.

(ii) Solarino, 11th-13th July

The first day had been astonishingly successful. The 5th Division had captured Syracuse; the 50th were in position; and farther south the XXX Corps had landed and were in possession of all their objectives. The next day, the 11th, the Army started the advance by pressing on up the roads towards Catania.

Relieved by the 51st Division, the 50th was ordered to push through the foothills to Lentini, overlooking the Plain of Catania, and it led off with the 69th Brigade in advance. The Durham battalions were ordered forward to relieve a 5th Division brigade in the area Florídia-Solarino on the road from Syracuse to Caltagirone. The heat was intense and, little transport having been landed, the marches were fatiguing.

It was on the 12th, while the relief was still incomplete, that the first of the Italian field divisions was encountered. Flushed by a mobile column of the 69th Brigade west of Solarino, this division, the 54th (Napoli), attacked from the direction of Palazzolo, once with infantry combined with tanks and once with infantry alone. The tanks came down the road from Palazzolo towards Solarino in line ahead at full speed, and struck both the 5th East Yorkshire, who were about to move on to Sortino, and the 6th Durhams, who were relieving them in front of Solarino. Four were immediately knocked out, but a fifth, after shooting up Lieut.-Colonel Watson's jeep and wounding the medical officer, careered on to Florídia, where it ended up against a lamp-post. The infantry attack, which was launched after the 6th had taken up its new positions, was broken up by it with the timely assistance of the supporting artillery. When the advance was resumed the next day the 6th received orders to attack the enemy in his positions west of Solarino, where he lay well concealed in difficult country among boulders and olive-groves. Under a heavy artillery concentration the Battalion advanced at 4.45 a.m., and although it lost two valuable company commanders, the enemy was so demoralised by the shock that he allowed himself to be overrun in three quarters of an hour. A mobile column and the reserve company completed the rout, knocking out tanks and field-guns and capturing into the bargain the divisional commander, General Porgini, and his chief-of-staff. In a few hours at very small cost the Battalion, with the assistance of a troop of tanks, had taken 320 prisoners, 16 R35 tanks, 13 field and anti-tank guns, 6 mortars, 13 Bredas, 12 Lancia 10-tonners, 3 Fiat 15-cwts., and 13 motor-cycles, the last four items forming a useful accretion to its limited transport resources.

(iii) The Primosole Bridge, 13th-18th July

After this exhilarating episode there followed a period of the bloodiest fighting in the campaign. To accelerate the advance on Catania, the large, dirty and important town lying at the foot of Etna beyond the far bank of the Simeto, an airborne attack was staged on the Primosole Bridge spanning the river. Unknown to the Army it was defended by part of the Hermann Goering Division, fanatical Nazis, who were reinforced by a first-class regiment of parachutists from the 7th Air Division, hurriedly flown over from Tarascon in France.

The airborne operation was successfully executed during the night of 13th/14th July. The bridge was seized, the demolition charges removed and the repeated enemy counter-attacks were repelled until dusk on the 14th. The follow-up movement, however, delayed by strong rearguards at Carlentini and all over the intervening flat land, was able to reach the bridge neither before the enemy had organised a firm defence in the vineyards on the north bank of the Simeto nor before the airborne infantry had been forced from the bridge itself. The 151st Brigade, having taken over the advance from the 69th, had made a forced march of twenty-five miles and at dusk was a mile from the bridge, though too tired to undertake an attack to form a bridgehead without reconnaissance before morning.

The attack was carried out by the most forward battalion, the 9th, at 7.30 in the morning of the 15th, supported by two regiments of field artillery. The resistance they met with was unexpectedly obstinate. Some platoons managed to cross and come to grips with the bayonet in the vineyards on the other side; but after a savage struggle they were driven back. A second attempt was postponed until 10 that

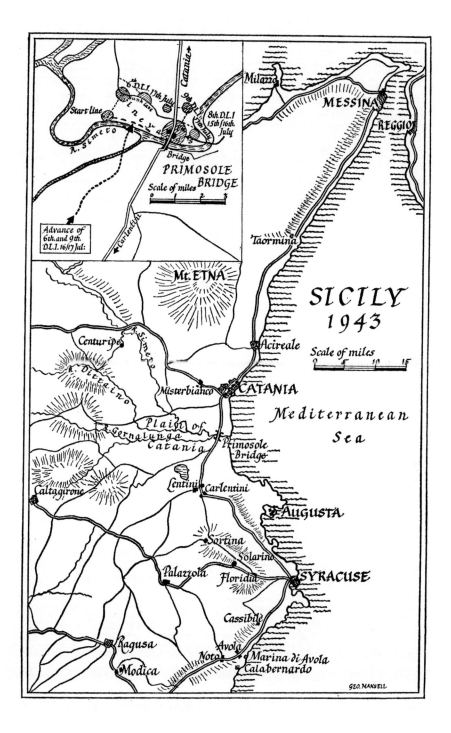

44. Sicily, with (inset) the Primosole Bridge, 15th—17th July, 1943

night, when two companies of the 8th under Lieut.-Colonel Lidwill, attacking under moonlight across a ford about 400 yards upstream, succeeded in working their way through the vines and, under a heavy artillery and machine-gun barrage, secured the head of the bridge. Owing to a breakdown in all forms of communication it was dawn before the other two companies, crossing by the bridge, were brought up. They came under a withering musketry fire from an unsuspected sunken lane which disabled all but one officer and twenty men of one company and drove a platoon of the other across the river. Further movement was rudely checked. Far from extending the bridgehead, the survivors could hold no more than a small area hardly 300 yards in depth extending 150 yards on either side of the road, all the while exchanging shots with a determined enemy repeatedly counter-attacking at ranges of twenty yards or less.

This precarious situation endured throughout the 16th. Rein-forcement by the other two battalions was difficult. Nevertheless it was attempted at 1 a.m. in the night of the 16th/17th by passing both the 6th and the 9th across by the ford used by the 8th under a heavy barrage of supporting arms. The 6th, whose objective lay on the left of the road, succeeded with praiseworthy determination in establishing themselves in a ditch on the objective, and repelled the inevitable counter-attacks in fierce close-range fighting. The 9th, which had to cross the road and press forward to their right, en-countered even stiffer resistance. But by 6.15 a.m. both battalions could report they were about a thousand yards beyond the bridge. At dawn tanks crossed by the bridge. The effect was almost immedi-ate. "A few white handkerchiefs appeared and soon everywhere the enemy was surrendering." By 10 mopping up, in which the tired men of the Durham Light Infantry assisted, had been completed; and the battle, undertaken somewhat light-heartedly but prosecuted in savage ferocity, was over.

The scene of the fight was hideous. The German battalions, who had fought to the death, left 300 of their dead on the ground. The Durham battalions between them lost 500 in killed, wounded and missing.

The fighting that followed in the advance up the coast roads (although the 9th had the misfortune to lose both its commanding officer, Lieut.-Colonel Clarke, and its second-in-command, Major W. B. Robinson) was as nothing compared with the Primosole Bridge. On 4th August the Brigade entered Catania after an ob-stinate engagement. On the 14th it reached Taormina, where it was at last able to enjoy a welcome respite of two months before receiving orders to return home.

Malta, 1942, and Cos, 1943

Malta as well as Cos, where the 1st Battalion suffered near-extinc-
tion in October 1943, are honours won by the 1st Battalion outside
the main African theatre.

If there is little to record of its service in Malta, the Battalion may
nevertheless derive some compensating satisfaction from the fact of
its being there at the most critical juncture of the island's fortunes.
Malta was a Tobruk in the grander strategical scheme of things in
the Mediterranean, as the manner of the Battalion's arrival showed.
Only 500 all ranks could be embarked at once. B Company (Major
R. F. Kirby) sailed on 24th January 1942 in the destroyer *Kingston*.
The rest, except for A Company, the carrier-platoon and some transport details, were taken on board the *Breconshire* naval storeship.
The convoy came under attack by torpedo-bombers during the 26th
but steamed unharmed into the Grand Harbour in the morning of
the 27th. Those left behind sailed from Alexandria on 12th February
in the *Clan Campbell* merchantman, in convoy M.W.9, which suffered
an attack off Tobruk the next day. The ship was so severely damaged
that she had to put in to Tobruk and eventually return to Alexandria. The detachment was unable to sail until the assembly of the
March convoy (M.W.10)—the last, as it proved, for several months
—in which it was distributed over four vessels, the *Breconshire*, *Clan
Campbell*, *Pampas* and *Talabot*. Leaving Alexandria on 20th March,
this convoy acquired fame from giving rise to the so called Second
Battle of Sirte (22nd March). The *Talabot* arrived unharmed in the
morning of the 23rd; *Pampas*, damaged, came in soon after; but the
others were not so fortunate. The *Breconshire* was hit and disabled
within eight miles of harbour, and at 10.30 a.m. the *Clan Campbell*
was hit, and sank, with twenty miles to go. Most of those aboard
were saved by destroyers. One of them, H.M.S. *Legion*, was holed as
she was picking up survivors, who were presented with the magnificent spectacle of the crew lining the decks, giving three cheers for the
King and jumping together into the water, an example of discipline
that none forgot.

Stationed in the area Verdalla/Rabat/Dingli, near the airfield at
Takali, the Battalion belonged to the Central Infantry Brigade,[9] and,
after being equipped with 400 bicycles, became the mobile reserve of
the garrison. Its routine consisted of tactical exercises and the con-

[9]Which on 14th July 1942 was redesignated 3rd (Malta) Infantry Brigade and,
on 1st April 1943, 233rd Infantry Brigade. The Battalion was transferred on 14th
May 1942 to the newly formed Western Infantry Brigade under Brigadier F. G. R.
Brittorous, which was successively redesignated 4th (Malta) Infantry Brigade and
234th Infantry Brigade.

struction of anti-blast pens for the aircraft on the airfields. Casualties from the incessant raids, which increased in intensity until they reached their peak during April and May 1942, were mercifully few. Equally mercifully, the Battalion was spared the experience of repelling the attack on the island by a German parachute division and two Italian corps which was meditated by the Axis Command from March 1942 onwards, but postponed until the successful outcome of Rommel's May offensive in the Desert.

In Cos, on the other hand, its experiences were quite otherwise. The occupation of the Ægean Islands, carried out between 15th and 18th September 1943, was part of a grander project of wide strategic implications already once tentatively planned after the Italian defeat in February 1941. Possession of the Dodecanese not only denied to the enemy airfields and bases from which he had done untold damage in the Eastern Mediterranean, but opened up the possibility of bringing Turkey into the war as an ally and, thence, the contemplation of the following fair vistas: air bases from which Greece, Romania and Bulgaria could be bombed; Allied control over the Dardanelles and the Bosphorus, and a shorter supply route for the shipments to Russia; and, finally, a threat to the enemy's most sensitive flank. Unfortunately, for a number of reasons the air support, the shipping and the troops were lacking for its execution at the right time, which was the moment Italy collapsed. Furthermore, at the critical juncture Rhodes, the most important of the islands, was taken over by a German garrison, acting with great promptitude on 11th September. Any attempt on the other islands was hazardous without the facilities Rhodes offered; yet on the other hand it did not appear that the enemy was in a position to intervene decisively if the business were put to the touch.

The troops available in September for the attempt on Rhodes were the 234th Brigade,[10] which had returned from Malta on 19th June 1943. It was entirely composed of regular battalions, but it is no disparagement of them to say that the existence they had led in Malta, a prolonged test of endurance without an opportunity of hitting back, had unfitted them to meet a sudden and unexpected onslaught. A short period of training would quickly have restored them, but that in the circumstances was impossible.

While the Brigade was still preparing for operations Rhodes fell to the Germans. A more limited operation was improvised. The battalions were distributed between descents on Cos, Leros, Samos, Simi, Stampalia and Icaria. The 1st Battalion (since August 1942 under the command of Lieut.-Colonel R. F. Kirby) was assigned to Cos, not

[10] 1st Durham Light Infantry, 2nd Royal Irish Fusiliers, 2nd Royal West Kent.

the largest but, by reasons of the airstrip at Antimachia, the most important of the islands next to Rhodes. C Company (Major E. Browne) was carried there from Ramat David in transport aircraft early on the 16th. Most of the remainder followed during the course of the next few days to relieve the 11th Parachute Battalion (which, recruited in the Middle East, contained, as it happened, several 1st Battalion men). By the end of September the garrison amounted with detachments to about 1400 men.

The Germans reacted with promptitude and vigour that came as a complete surprise. Their aircraft started bombing from the first moment, and the bombing steadily increased until the airstrip at Antimachia was neutralised. As a result, though D Company (Captain J. H. Thorpe) remained there, A and B were withdrawn to a position in some olive-groves about five miles west of Cos port, where they assisted in the preparation of a new landing ground, while C was posted in the outskirts of the town. Although the garrison had twenty-four Bofors guns, the Battalion had at its disposal only its own small arms and light mortars.

A turn of ill luck now intervened. It was known that enemy landing craft were assembling at the Piræus and in harbours in Crete, and in the evening of 2nd October a convoy was sighted by aircraft off Naxos which was assumed to be making for Rhodes. The destroyers available were forced to return to port to refuel, and two submarines ordered to intercept the convoy off Cos failed to arrive in time. The garrison commander equally assumed the convoy's destination to be Rhodes. Consequently, when the enemy seaborne assault began at 5 in the morning of 3rd October, the garrison was only conducting its ordinary routine precautions.

Landing on the north side of the island under a heavy air bombardment with about 2000 troops, the Germans rapidly advanced inland and severed the Cos/Antimachia road, while a strong force of parachutists flown in from Greece were dropped on the airstrip. D Company of the Battalion, isolated, fought hard until almost all were either killed, wounded or taken prisoner (though some managed to escape into the hills). The other companies, under Lieut.-Colonel Kirby, who had hurried from his sick-bed to take command, had been placed by Major Vaux in position astride the main road, where an obstinate pitched battle between the Battalion and the enemy raged throughout the day. Attacking frontally and feeling for the flanks, the enemy gradually made his superior strength felt. B Company, north of the road, was overrun after a stubborn resistance. C Company early lost a platoon. A (Captain J. G. G. Gray), to the south of the road, became cut off and received orders to retire to the

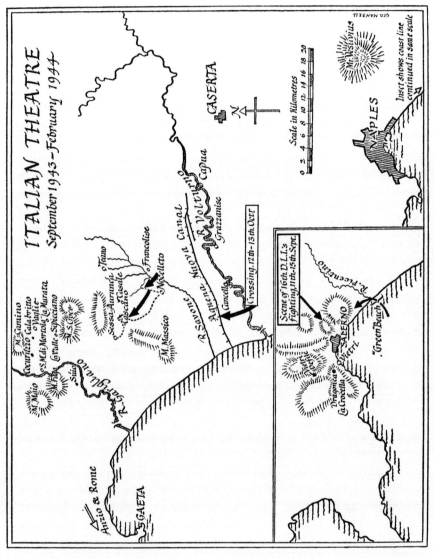

45. The Italian Theatre, September, 1943—February, 1944

outskirts of Cos. By this time the Battalion, though it had clearly inflicted heavy casualties, was reduced to less than 200 effectives, and had withdrawn to form a rough perimeter round the approaches to the town. There fighting continued into the night. An attempt was made to organise a counter-attack, but an unlucky salvo of mortar-bombs fell on the assembly-point, wounding the commanding officer, Major K. M. W. Leather (headquarter Company), Major J. E. Stafford and the Quartermaster, Captain F. H. Bush (mortally). Further organised resistance was impossible.

The orders received by Major Vaux from Force Headquarters during the night were to split the Battalion into parties of a dozen or so, who were to make their way through the hills to a rendezvous at Kargliou. About 60 managed to accomplish this successfully; but they were without food; and though the country people gave them help, after ten days the conditions of the survivors was not enviable. Most succeeded on the 13th in escaping in a caique to Casteloriso, and thence to Cyprus; and by the end of the month all that remained of the 68th, nine officers and about 120 n.c.o.s and men, were assembled at the Infantry Base Depot at Geneifa.

The Italian Campaigns, 1943-1945

With the elimination of the Axis Armies in North Africa and the occupation of Sicily, the war in Europe entered a new and encouraging phase. Military operations had long approached, and now reached, a stage in which the Allies could influence the European theatre to a degree that had been unattainable since the defeat in France. In choosing Italy as the next scene of operations they contemplated more than a convenient and obvious means of entry into *Festung Europa*. The most important consideration was to contain the maximum number of German divisions on a front whence they could be readily switched neither to Russia nor, when the invasion was launched, to France. So long, therefore, as a front was kept in being in Italy, and so long as the enemy was kept jealous, it was not essential for the Army to advance. Indeed an orderly German withdrawal, in preoccupying only a comparatively small enemy force, favoured Allied designs less than the strategy the German command in fact adopted. "Had they decided to withdraw altogether," Lord Alexander wrote in his report, "they could have defended the line of the Alps . . . with the minimum of forces and, instead of us containing them, they would be containing us." From the moment, he says, that Hitler decided to stand "the German army undertook a commitment as damaging and debilitating as Napoleon's Peninsular campaign". On the other hand, to maintain the delicate equilibrium it was essential for the Allies to keep the initiative in operations. The Italian campaigns possess as a result a peculiarly episodic character: a continual offensive on our part and a continual fighting retreat from line to line on the Germans'.

For that reason as well as the terrain the campaigns lack the broad strategical sweep that normally lends cohesion to military narrative. Moreover, the breaks in the continuity of the services of the two battalions representing the Regiment in Italy make it even harder to give an indication of their several parts in the operations. The 1st did not enter until a relatively late stage. The 16th, which was in at the beginning, was twice taken out of the theatre, once to rest (21st February to 3rd July 1944), and once to intervene in Greece (3rd December 1944 to 13th April 1945). Only once did both operate in common.

The Landing: Salerno, 9th-18th September 1943

The landing was planned as two complementary operations: a direct attack across the Straits of Messina to the Toe of Italy, and an amphibious "left hook" to secure the port of Naples. Neither was executed in ideal circumstances. General Clark, commanding the Fifth Army, which undertook the latter operation, would have preferred the Gulf of Gaeta to the beaches of Salerno: but Gaeta lay at the extreme limit of fighter cover, and recourse was had to a second best.

The 16th Battalion (139th Brigade, 46th Division) was embarked at La Pécherie near Bizerta on 5th September with a strength of 25 officers and 656 n.c.o.s and men. Though not part of the assault brigade of the Division, which, landing on 9th September on the extreme left flank of the Army, beyond the enemy's principal strong-points, made good progress against stiff opposition towards the high ground north of Picentino, two companies of the Battalion, following up over "Green Beach", joined in until united to the remainder of the Battalion on its coming ashore next day. It was not until dusk on the 11th, after relieving the 6th York and Lancaster, that the Battalion became involved in serious fighting, when it took part in an advance on the feature of Parato, which it secured and just held against counter-attack, though with some loss. It remained closely engaged throughout the 12th and 13th, during which it was forced to relinquish some of the most forward positions. The crisis in the battle occurred at dusk on the 15th, when a most determined attack of some Panzer Grenadiers was delivered on D Company (Major F. Duffy), one of a long sequence of attacks aimed by the German reserve formations along the whole Army front during the 13th,

14th and 15th. But a counter-attack, the Company's second, led by Major Duffy, restored the situation with the capture of several prisoners besides, and by midnight "Light Infantry Hill" was secure. The repulse of the German attack, the last as it proved of the many which had given rise to so much anxiety, was characteristic of the Army's "stubborn doggedness in defence" to which Lord Alexander paid tribute after the enemy had finally drawn off.

The Advance on Naples, 22nd September-1st October

The Allied offensive started on 23rd September with a struggle for the passes north of Salerno. The 16th, attached to the 138th Brigade, which had the task of forcing the exits of the Vietri defile to provide a clear passage for the armour debouching towards Naples, was given the objective of La Crocella, a hill some 1800 feet high standing on the left of the valley. The night move to Dragonea, held by our own troops, and thence up the hill by tortuous tracks and deep ravines, was an achievement in itself. But at 6.30 in the morning of the 24th the summit was gained by the two forward companies without the loss of a single casualty. A counter-attack by tanks in the afternoon was repelled with the assistance of the 70th Field Regiment, R.A., old friends of the Battalion, and the two companies, though virtually cut off, succeeded in maintaining themselves throughout the 24th and 25th until relieved. In infiltration tactics the Battalion had outplayed the enemy at his own game, and it was rewarded soon after its relief by the total collapse of the enemy's resistance, which was followed, on 1st October, by the entry into Naples. His able dispositions earned Lieut.-Colonel Preston the D.S.O.

The Crossing of the Volturno, 12th-15th October

After the fall of Naples the long slogging match began. More German divisions were employed than Allied, a state of affairs which, however satisfactory, excluded the contemplation of anything spectacular. The terrain, with its mountains, its hills and its rivers, which crossed the line of advance at right angles every ten miles or so favoured the defence. With the onset of autumn, rain at the rate of five inches in the month, and snow, which could be expected on ground above 2000 feet in December, threatened to hinder any movement. Moreover, the Germans had for some time prepared their *Winterstellung*, a position in depth of several lines running across the peninsula from Gaeta through Isernia to Vasto. By the end of the first week in October the Fifth Army was up against the first outposts of the position when it approached the Volturno, the broad and swiftly moving river on which Garibaldi's advance had been checked in 1860.

The attack across the river went in in the night of the 12th. While the X Corps made diversionary attacks at Cápua and Grazzanise, the 46th Division made the principal assault near Cancello. In view of the success at La Crocella Lieut.-Colonel Preston had asked to be allowed to make a "silent" crossing, while the 5th Foresters conducted a "noisy" attack farther upstream. A patrol, crossing first, passed a rope over the river (here a hundred yards wide), which enabled two companies under Major D. H. C. Worrall to form a small bridgehead. Casualties were only seven despite the panic of one man, whose cries attracted the fire of the enemy—fortunately firing blind—and came near to spoiling an otherwise silent and brilliantly executed operation. The two rear companies followed across on foot through cold water about 4ft. 6ins. deep, and having passed through the bridgehead swung right-handed to take up a position on the final objective, the Agnena Nuova Canal, which they occupied by dawn. Several counter-attacks were broken up during the course of the day (the 13th); and for eight days, until the Battalion was relieved on the 21st, it hung on although unsupported for some time owing to the heavy casualties sustained by its fellow battalions. Its feat of arms at the Volturno stands out as its finest achievement. If there is little to say it is because it was cleanly done.

The Forcing of the Barbara Line: Teano, 28th-31st October

After the Volturno the Fifth Army fought its way to the first line of the *Winterstellung*, the so called Barbara Line, whose southern extremity ran though Monte Santa Croce and Monte Mássico. In the attack on this sector of the position the 56th Division was to take the town of Teano and occupy the foothills of Monte Santa Croce, while the 46th Division came up from the south to open the defile at Cascano and seize the road junction near Sessa Aurunca. The 139th Brigade had orders to cross the Teano south-west of Francolise and establish itself on the Nocelleto/Sessa Aurunca road.

The crossing was slowly but successfully accomplished by two companies during the night of the 28th/29th. By daybreak despite booby-traps and machine-gun fire, the Battalion had forced a bridgehead for the tanks. The advance then continued with the tanks' assistance, and though the enemy was able from his excellent observation to bring down an accurate shell fire on all the approaches across the flat country below, the objective at the road junction was reached at dusk on the 29th. In Angelo, however, the enemy contrived to resist until the evening of the 31st, when, flanked by the advance of the 56th Division, he withdrew before an attack made by the Battalion, which on 1st November pressed on to Casale and the southern slopes of Monte Santa Croce until relieved in the night of the 1st/2nd.

The Winterstellung: Monte Camino, 1st-9th December

Between 9th September and 31st October the Battalion had lost in killed, wounded and missing 13 officers and 367 n.c.o.s and men. The figures, reminiscent of the First War, are evidence of the constant attrition taking place; and when the Battalion was withdrawn to rest it was a welcome reinforcement it received in the very good draft of junior officers, n.c.o.s and men from the 70th (Young Soldiers) Battalion, recently disbanded at Tow Law.

It returned to take part in the closing stage of the long and obstinate battle fought to breach the Bernhardt Line, the next line of the *Winterstellung*, on which the enemy counted to stand until February. The southern sector of the Bernhardt Line rested on the Monte Camino *massif*, a formidable obstacle which had already defied the first attempts made upon it by the Fifth Army early in November. The renewed attack was a deliberate operation planned in three phases. The 56th Division was to storm the steep slopes of Monte Camino on 2nd December, the day after the 46th on its left had penetrated into the Calabritto valley, seized the Cocuruzzo Spur and captured Croce and Mórtola. It was a difficult movement and, carried out as it was in full view of the enemy, all troops were stripped of their distinguishing badges.

At first the Battalion, which had moved up to Sipicciano on 21st November, remained in reserve at La Murata. But one company, B, under Major T. G. L. Ballance, was attached to the 5th Foresters, which, with the 2/5th Leicester, carried out the attack after dark on 1st December. The two battalions had almost reached their first objective when heavy fire compelled them to fall back to a position near Calabritto which, though not wholly satisfactory, yet gave some protection to the assault of the 56th Division. This began in the late afternoon of the 2nd under the heaviest artillery concentration so far fired in Italy, and met with unexpected success, enabling the 46th Division's battalions to advance again during the morning of the 3rd. On the 4th the weather changed for the worse. It was already very cold and now torrential rain came down to add acute discomfort to the heavy enemy shell fire, which was causing many casualties, among them Major Ballance. The outlook was bleak.

In fact the climax of the battle had been reached and the Army was on the verge of success. The 56th Division's continuous pressure had pushed the enemy back to the Cocuruzzo Spur, which by midday of the 5th, a fine sunny day, had become the key of the whole position. The 139th Brigade was reinforced by the 6th York and Lancaster, and the 16th Battalion was moved up to La Valle to attack the Spur from there. A co-ordinated attack went in after dark on the 5th. Working forward company by company and peak by peak during the 6th, the Battalion could report by midday of the 7th that the village of Cocuruzzo was clear of the enemy. (He had in fact abandoned his positions in a disorderly retreat, leaving a quantity of equipment at La Valle and Mórtola.) It was another forty-eight hours before the whole *massif* was clear, but the 16th's part in the operation was over with the capture of Cocuruzzo, a curious affair in which it had been able, by exploiting the success of another division, to take its own opponents in the left rear.

The Forcing of the Gustav Line: Monte Fuga,[11]
26th-30th January 1944

The Battalion's share in the fight to penetrate the last line of the *Winterstellung* was small, especially if compared with the magnitude of the undertaking, which, beset with forbidding obtacles, involved not only a frontal assault across the Garigliano and the storm of Monte Cassino but another amphibious "left hook" at Anzio. The 16th did not enter the offensive until 15th January, after the Garigliano had been crossed and the fighting had passed on into the hills beyond. Temporarily placed in the 138th Brigade, it had the task of clearing the Súio valley house by house with a view to securing the hills above. The enemy resisted strongly, and it was not until 28th January that the valley was cleared. The Battalion next approached the Colle Siola, where again, despite the enemy's stubborn resistance, it was able to make some progress during the night of the 29th with the assistance of artillery concentrations. It remained in this tiring sector until relieved on 13th February and brought back to Vaglie.

In February 1944, as part of the policy for giving battle-weary divisions a rest with opportunities of local leave and time to refit and train, the 46th Division was withdrawn from Italy to Egypt. The 16th Battalion was embarked in the M/V *Sobieski* at Naples on 21st February for Port Said, where it landed on the 27th. Before it returned to Italy in July, after spells at Qassassin, Kefar Yona near Tel-Aviv, and Er Rama near Lake Tiberias, it had undergone a thorough reorganisation and recuperation. At the same time it had lost the

[11] Of the spellings *Fuga*, *Iuga* and *Tuga*, the Battles Nomenclature Committee has adopted *Tuga*, but the inhabitants know it as Monte *Fuga*.

commanding officer who had taken it successfully through so many vicissitudes since assuming command after Sedjenane, Lieut.-Colonel Preston, appointed G.S.O.1, 78th Division, in July. His successor, Lieut.-Colonel D. H. C. Worrall, Dorset Regiment, commanded the Battalion until its disbandment at the beginning of 1946.

§

Though the scenery to which the Battalion returned differed little, the situation in Italy had altered radically. Rome had fallen and the pursuit had carried the Armies 130 miles beyond. The enemy's resistance, however, started to stiffen on the upper Tiber, and it was not until 4th August that the Allied left was able to reach the line of the Arno. From then on both the Fifth and Eighth Armies were confronted by the formidable Gothic Line.

Since May, moreover, another battalion of the Regiment had entered the theatre. The 1st Battalion after the disaster at Cos had reorganised at Mena near Cairo. It was a slow and painful business. Although there were nearly a thousand men of the Regiment extra-regimentally employed throughout the Middle East Command, some were of low medical category and many were earmarked for reinforcement of the 151st Brigade. The nucleus of two companies was obtained from a draft from the 17th Battalion. The rest were obtained from no less than twenty-nine different regiments, though a few old members of the Battalion were able to play an important part in its re-formation. Major P. H. M. May returned from the 4th Parachute Brigade in Italy as second-in-command and acting commanding officer in Lieut.-Colonel Vaux's absence; C.S.M. G. Scott returned from Malta to become R.S.M.; and Quartermaster-sergeant J. Pirie returned as R.Q.M.S. Major E. Browne and Captain G. Flannigan, formerly its R.S.M., were two of the very few remaining who had landed with the Battalion in January 1940, and Major Browne left soon after its arrival in Italy for repatriation, having served with it continuously since his enlistment in 1922. When at last brought up to establishment it was sent, before training was complete, to assist in the disarming of the mutinous Greek regiments at Amriya, and it was 30th April before it could embark for active service.

It landed at Taranto on 4th May. On the 19th it was posted as the British battalion of the 10th Indian Infantry Brigade alongside the 4/10th Baluch Regiment and the 2/4th Gurkha Rifles. The 10th Indian Division, to which the 10th Brigade belonged, was employed from the end of June in the central sector in the Tiber valley east of Lake Trasimene, and the new 1st Battalion faced the enemy for the first time a few miles north of Perugia. Its first attack, the first of many in the hard but unspectacular fighting that took it up to the Gothic Line in September, was carried out on 10th July against a feature called "Wop" north of Tréstina; in the battle for Città di Castello (16th July) it took Monte Cedrone; and similar operations occupied it in the Tiber valley and on the Pratomagno until the Division was transferred to the Adriatic sector in the first week of October.

The Gothic Line, 25th August–22nd September

The Gothic Line took brilliant advantage of the natural barrier between the Po basin and the mountains of central Italy, formed by the sudden turn north-westwards towards the Maritime Alps which the Apennines make just south of Rimini. The embellishments to what is naturally a first-class military obstacle ran along a rough line between Spezia on the Ligurian coast and Pésaro on the Adriatic. German engineers had been working at it spasmodically since July 1943. Indeed, the Germans had fought their delaying actions on the Trasimene and other lines principally to gain time in which to administer the finishing touches—which, however, were not complete when the Allied Armies breached it. Its existence had long been known to the Allied Command, but after the victories of the spring it had seemed likely to prove no more than an incident in a triumphant pursuit to the Ljubljana Gap. That dazzling prospect was dashed at the end of June. The invasions of France, to which everything was subordinate, proving as insatiable after their birth as before it, caused the withdrawal of no less than seven French and American divisions from the theatre; while at the same time Kesselring received eight divisions to reinforce an army which, earlier, had been gloomily contemplating the Brenner as the next stop.

Lord Alexander's original intention had been to attack it in the centre on a front between Pistoia to Dicomano and to debouch into the Po basin at Bologna. Both Fifth and Eighth Armies were to take part, each with their inward flanks strongly reinforced, attacking on parallel axes. On 4th August, however, the day on which it became clear for the first time since June what forces were at his disposal, he decided that the Eighth Army, instead of attacking in the centre, should advance by the east coast towards Ravenna, where, among other considerations *pro* and *con*, the terrain provided the kind of battlefield to which the Eighth Army was accustomed. The immense task then began of shifting the *Schwerpunkt* from the centre to the right (a movement which temporarily left the 10th Indian Division the sole formation responsible for the mountainous central sector), and that delayed the offensive until 25th August.

The Eighth Army's attack went in punctually an hour before midnight on 25th August. The 46th Division entered it on the right, with the objective of Monte Gridolfo. The 16th Battalion, which, refreshed by its rest, had been brought up from Naples and thence to the divisional concentration area—where it was told by the Army Commander that its ultimate objective was Vienna—first came into action at Petriano on the 28th. The enemy's resistance did not stiffen until the 31st, though by that time both the 128th and the 139th Brigades were securely in possession of Mondaino on the Monte Gridolfo ridge. An attack by the Battalion west of Mondaino encountered unexpectedly stubborn resistance; but by the morning of 2nd September it had fought its way through Saludécio into Il Poggio and up onto the ridge of Serra. Before the relief of the Division took place on the 5th it had worked its way across the Conca to Cevolabbate. Since entering the offensive it had lost nine officers and 128 n.c.o.s and men, and it had made a net advance of 25 miles into the Gothic Line.

Gemmano, 5th-15th September

By this time the German reserves had arrived in force, and a ding-dong battle developed for the Coriano ridge, the second of the Line, of which the struggle for the Gemmano ridge, though on the near bank of the Conca, formed part. Neither the 56th nor the 1st Armoured Division, which had taken the 46th's place, could make headway while under observation from Gemmano, and not only did their attacks fail but the Germans counter-attacked strongly at Croce and retook it. As a result the 46th Division was brought back to assist in a renewed assault.

The 16th Battalion re-entered the fighting in the night of 10th / 11th September when ordered to take over Point 449 from the 2 /4th K.O.Y.L.I. to favour a further advance by the 6th Lincoln. The enemy, however, contrived by infiltrating to recover Point 449 in the confusion during the night; and a bitter struggle ensued during the 11th and 12th as company after company of five or more battalions attempted in vain to retake and hold a vantage point from which the enemy could break up each attack as it formed up. For a few days the Battalion, like the rest, was called upon to endure some of the severest privations of the whole campaign. "Men lived just like rats, and the scene and smell of death were beyond description."

On the 12th the 139th Brigade was ordered to move round to the far side of the valley running north and south from the cemetery below Point 449, while the 138th Brigade cleared the Gemmano ridge itself. The move did not have the desired effect. On the other hand a brigade of the 56th Division managed on the 13th to make an impression at Croce on the other side of the Conca, which slowly affected the bloody issue on Gemmano by permitting an encirclement in place of a frontal assault. On the 14th the 139th Brigade crossed the Conca and fought their way to Monte Colombo; and when the advance was resumed on the 19th the Battalion, hitherto in brigade reserve, came to the front to take Torracia, "a nasty ridge" near Verucchio, in the republic of San Marino. The move forms a fitting conclusion to the battle for Gemmano ridge, the scene of some of the heaviest fighting experienced in the whole Italian campaign, which from first to last cost the Battalion a loss of six officers and 132 n.c.o.s and men killed or wounded.

The Battle of the Rivers: Cesena, 15th-20th October

With the crossing of the Marecchia and the capture of Rimini by the 1st Canadian Division on 21st September the penetration of the Gothic Line—at least in the Adriatic sector—may be said to have been completed. It should have led to a realisation of all the hopes entertained in the summer. Instead, for a number of reasons, it was followed by a melancholy series of operations which are popularly known as the Battle of the Rivers.

Part of the Eighth Army had at last descended into the plains. The plains, however, so far from proving a promised land for desert-minded armour, were a never-ending complex of canals and rivers swollen by heavy rains, which fell early. The enemy here was fighting for the flank on which, if forced to withdraw, he would have to swing in order to block the approaches to Austria. Taking advantage of every element in his favour he fought tenaciously to hold it. The Allied Armies, to be faithful to their strategic function of containing the maximum enemy force, had no alternative but to continue the offensive. On the eastern flank the most promising line of advance was north-westwards across the succession of rivers that flow in a north-easterly direction from the Apennines. The operations consequently developed into a succession of outflanking movements similar to Wellington's advance in southern France in February and March 1814: "as the river obstacles were reached the V Corps crossed the upper waters while the enemy was obliged to withdraw before the pressure of the Canadian Corps in the plains". It was in the crossing of the Savio at Cesena that both the Durham battalions were engaged side by side for the first and only time in the campaigns.

The 16th Battalion (46th Division, V Corps) had taken part in the stubbornly contested advance over the Marecchia (24th September), the Uso (25th) and the Fiumicino, or Rubicon[12] (9th/10th October); and by the 11th had reached a point between Balignano and Massa. The 1st Battalion, since the 12th September under the vigorous command of Lieut.-Colonel May, who by the confidence he inspired largely contributed to its re-creation, had been transferred with the rest of the 10th Indian Division from the central sector to the east in the relief of the 4th Indian Division, which took place in the first week of October. On 7th October it was at Sogliano al Rubicone, on the V Corps' left, or mountain, flank. This flank moved forward that night in an attack on Monte Farneto, which was stormed immediately. The 1st Battalion contributed to the success of the Division by clambering up the slippery slopes of Monte Spaccato during a night (9th/10th) of such torrential rain that the enemy was taken completely by surprise.

Without a pause the V Corps advanced to turn the enemy's line on the Sávio. The 46th and 10th Indian Divisions moved forward on parallel axes during the night of the 14th/15th. The 16th Battalion, its depleted ranks filled by a draft of officers and men from the 14th Foresters, came into action at Celincordia early on the 19th. After successfully seizing the monastery at Madonna del Monte, overlooking the town of Cesena, Lieut.-Colonel Worrall directed two of his companies and two squadrons of the 10th Hussars through the western suburbs to the Sávio bridge, which was still intact. Though the companies encountered some stiff resistance in the streets their progress was at first satisfactory. But the enemy continued to hold the commanding height at Abbadesse, and until that was eliminated by the 2/5th Leicester late in the afternoon, any penetration to the bridge proved impossible. At 4 a.m. on the 20th the Battalion's patrols discovered that the enemy had withdrawn across the river, blowing the bridges as they departed. The two remaining companies immediately entered and took possession of the castle. Cesena was the first large town to be captured by the Division, and the 16th Battalion received a rapturous welcome which seemed a suitable reward for almost two months of continuous and often bitter fighting.

Higher up the river the 10th Indian Division was equally successful. The 1st Battalion (temporarily under the 25th Indian Brigade, commanded by Brigadier Arderne), advancing from Monteleone, one of its earlier captures, to Sorrivoli, reached a point on the ridge near Montereale whence the spires and turrets of Cesena were plainly

[12]There was doubt as to which of the rivers was the Rubicon of the ancients until in 1933 Mussolini pronounced in favour of the Fiumicino.

visible. Indeed it begged, but in vain, to be allowed to join the 16th in the fight for the town. Both met, however, after they had been relieved, when parties from each exchanged visits, the one at Sogliano, the other at Montefiore near Gemmano.

The Gerhild Line: the Côsina Canal Crossing, 20th-23rd November

The last honour won by the 16th Battalion in its last action in Italy was the crossing of the Côsina, an essential preliminary to the capture of Faenza and the establishment of the Army on the Sénio.

The Battalion, which joined in the advance from Forlì on 15th November, had reached the east bank of the Côsina later that day. Several unsuccessful attacks having been launched during the 16th and 17th, a deliberate operation was put into execution on 20th November. Aided by air bombardment, the 2/5th Leicester seized the high ground on the near bank on the first day, and early on the 21st the 5th Foresters made encouraging progress until stopped by Brigadier Block, commanding the 139th Brigade, owing to the withdrawal of the 4th Division on its left. That afternoon, however, the 3rd Carpathian (Polish) Division, far to the left in the foothills south of the highway, advanced and took Monte Poggio di Piano and Momarte, a success which enabled the 139th Brigade to continue. The Durhams' attack went in during the night of the 21st/22nd between the Foresters and the Leicester. The enemy held on obstinately to the substantial farmhouses that lay in the river bend, but two (named "Gin" and "Beer") were taken, and by morning the Battalion had almost cleared the near bank. In a second attack delivered the next night a company which managed to get across was thrown back in a counter-attack. A third attempt was made in the morning of the 23rd. This time C Company under Major P. A. Casey successfully crossed by a passage forced by the 5th Foresters, and moving on took Corla, which it held against counter-attack. Later in the day the bridgehead was expanded and secured sufficiently to allow the 128th Brigade to pass through to the Lamone, the last river before Faenza.

It was while occupying a rest area near Forlì that the 139th Brigade was withdrawn from Italy to assist in the suppression of the rebellion in Greece. Although it returned to take part in the advance into Austria, the 16th Battalion saw no more action in a theatre in which it had lost 21 officers and 408 n.c.o.s and men in the Gothic Line and river battles alone.

The Sénio Line: Pérgola Ridge, 14th-16th December

Meanwhile the struggle for the rivers continued with the object of securing Bologna and good administrative bases for the spring offensive. On the relief of the 46th Division the 10th Indian moved up to take its place. The 1st Battalion had been heavily engaged in the crossing of the Montone (24th-25th November), the outflanking movement for Faenza; and, like most battalions, it was understrength when on 11th December the Division was moved up into the Lamone bridgehead near Pidéura to take over the slogging match.

Between the 11th and 13th the enemy had made repeated attempts to dislodge the forward brigade in the bridgehead, but all of them failed to dislocate the timing of the main V Corps' assault towards the Sénio. The 10th Brigade's attack went in at 11 p.m. on 14th December. The 1st Battalion attacked on the right from Quártolo against Pérgola. At first all went well, and the two assault companies were across the little river Canova before the enemy knew what was happening. Then the luck turned. One company, A, having reached a point little short of its objective, was stopped by mines, while the other, B, ran into an uncharted field of *schuh*-mines. C Company (Major A. M. M. Macaulay), brought up from reserve, where it had already suffered from the enemy's defensive fire intended for A and B, failed to improve the situation and lost, for the third time in two months, all its officers killed or wounded. Nevertheless, though Pérgola was beyond their grasp, the forward companies held on to their gains like grim death throughout the 15th. Air support, though difficult owing to the enemy's closeness, was twice attempted, and Major J. G. G. Gray, commanding A, refused for a time to signal for the bombers to stop because more bombs were falling on the enemy than on his company.

The Battalion was not alone in failing to reach its objectives that day: elsewhere the Division had for the first time to acknowledge failure. The advance was bitterly contested. But on the right the 2nd New Zealand Division, profiting from the pinning down of the enemy reserves, managed to break through to Celle and closed up to the Sénio, a movement which in its turn allowed the 10th Indian to advance. When A and C Companies of the Battalion moved forward in the night of the 15th they were able to top the ridge without much difficulty. Casualties had been heavy. Even after receiving reinforcements the remaining three companies were down to about 50 effectives each, and these suffered a steady drain on their strength until the Battalion was relieved on the Sénio on 2nd January.

The Final Offensive: the Síllaro Crossing,
14th-16th April 1945

After the attainment of the Sénio little was, or indeed could be, attempted by the Eighth Army during the hard winter months that followed. It was a period of rest and recuperation for formations and units that had been overtaxed and severely reduced.

When the Army resumed the offensive in the spring, however, its objective was to bring the war in Italy to an end by an attack across the Sénio and the Santerno while the Fifth Army thrust towards Bologna. It was then to drive either north-west against Budrio or north-east against Ferrara, whichever seemed the most promising direction. The offensive started on 9th April with an assault across the lower Sénio by the V Corps. This was successfully accomplished by the next day. The Santerno was reached and crossed by the evening of the 12th by the 2nd New Zealand Division, who continued their vigorous advance to the Síllaro.

It was at this juncture that the 1st Battalion entered its last battle of the campaign. Since early February it had been engaged in the snow-covered mountain sector in the upper waters of the Santerno and Síllaro in front of Castel del Rio, where it had fought a war of raids and patrols with a German parachute battalion in freezing temperatures and bleak and comfortless surroundings. Before returning to the plains on 24th March it had received some good quality reinforcements derived mainly from disbanded and anti-aircraft and coast defence units, many of them volunteers of 1939 and Durham- or Tyneside-born; and for the first time for several months it went into action with four rifle companies.

Of the battle itself there is little to say. With the rest of the 10th Brigade it was placed under the command of the New Zealand Division at Lugo with instructions to extend the breach and exploit to the utmost. In the night of 15th April it crossed the Síllaro through the front of the 5th New Zealand Brigade near Passo del Signore, cleared the west bank and pushed north next day as far as Portonovo. On the 19th, having crossed the Quaderna on the New Zealanders' right, it cleared the far bank as far as Ghiaradino. On the 20th it came up against a stubborn German rearguard fighting for the Idice before it yielded the running to the 20th Indian Brigade.

Though it remained for some time at short notice to move, its services were not called upon, and it was in comfortable billets in Ferrara when news of the Armistice reached it at 7 p.m. on 2nd May.

More fitting as a conclusion to the hard fought campaigns in Italy was the advance of the 16th Battalion, which, landed at

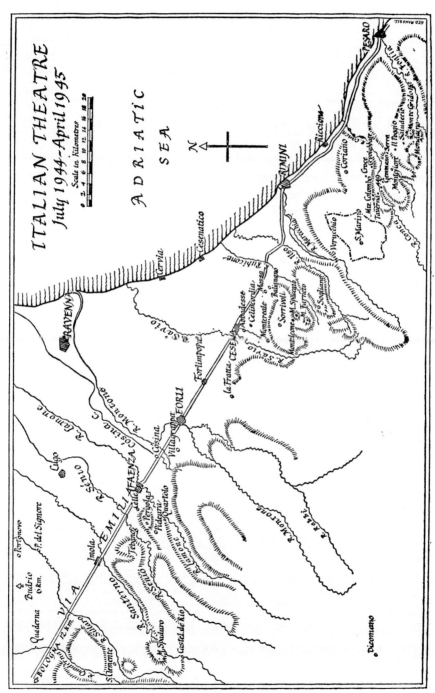

46. The Italian Theatre, July, 1944—April, 1945

Taranto on 15th April and brought up to La Fratta (where it had concentrated for the Cósina crossing), was ordered forward on 11th May by Ferrara to Padua, and thence by Caporetto into Carinthia (Unzmarkt). It was moved after a few days on 16th May to Bleiburg, to help repel some armed Croats of Tito's who were trying to make capital out of the collapse of Austria. On the withdrawal of the Russians from Styria on 23rd July it was moved east to Wildon near Graz. It had the supreme satisfaction of being the first battalion of the 46th Division to be selected for duty in Vienna (9th October to 28th November), where it was quartered in the (disused) Rudolf-Spital in the Boerhavegasse. It was still at Wildon when on 4th January it began disbanding. Eleven officers and the majority of the n.c.o.s and men went to the 1st Battalion, then in Greece. The rest went to the 2/5th Leicester or the 5th Foresters. By 24th February Lieut-Colonel Worrall's fine battalion had ceased to exist.

Greece, December 1944–April 1945

Since every Greek is himself a political party, it was hardly surprising that the Greek government on its return from exile entered upon an unenviable heritage. The two principal partisan organisations that remained after the German evacuation of the country in October 1944 were: E.D.E.S. (*Ellenikos Demokratikos Ethnikos Syndesmos*) and E.A.M./E.L.A.S. (*Ethnikon Apeleftherotikon Metopon/ Ellenikos Laikos Apeleftherotikos Stratos*), the latter a Communist-controlled organisation enjoying by far the larger share of the prestige, the men and the arms. Both had agreed to disband their forces on the arrival of the government. When, however, the time came to honour the agreement, while E.D.E.S. did so, E.L.A.S. did not. Throughout November the situation deteriorated, E.L.A.S. provoking disorders as they bullied all who were not for them; Force X under Colonel Grivas trying to snatch a quick profit from the disorder prevailing; the government powerless; the British mission attempting with the small force it had available to hold the ring until a stable government could be formed.

The 16th Battalion, flown in to Athens (Kalamaki) from Bari on 3rd December, was at first deployed in the neighbourhood of the Acropolis, one platoon being actually sited round the Parthenon. As the disorders increased it was withdrawn to Phaleron. Here, together with the 2/5th Leicester, a squadron of tanks and some R.A.F. armoured cars under the command of Brigadier A. P. Block, it formed "Blockforce", whose task was to protect the naval installations and keep open the communications between the port and the city until reinforcements could be landed. No one at that stage knew who was fighting whom, and the conflict lacked the clear-cut issues of the war in Italy.

The most critical period began about 10th December when E.L.A.S., which had in the area three "regular" divisions besides 12,000 "reserves," started attacking the Battalion's positions in the buildings along the coast road, with the obvious intention of driving it into the sea. Since the 11th, when Lord Alexander flew in (accompanied, incidentally, by his chief intelligence officer, Major-General T. S. Airey of the Regiment), E.L.A.S. controlled all but the very centre of Athens and had cut the coast road to the Piræus. Sniping exacted a steady toll, and a patrol sent out to deal with a party of snipers lost its commander. The crisis came on the 13th after the Battalion had been forced back to a position along the sea front between Lofos Kastella and Phaleron. During the day three men patrolling in carriers were wounded, and after dark every one of the company localities and battalion headquarters was subjected to a series of heavy attacks. Bitter and confused fighting continued throughout the night with dynamite, stick-grenades (left behind by the Germans by mistake on purpose) and tommy-guns. B Company lost a platoon captured when it ran out of ammunition and its commander was wounded. At dawn, however, when the attacks petered out, the Battalion was still holding all but one of its positions.

Meanwhile the 5th Brigade of the 4th Indian Division had been landed at the Piræus, and, storming Lofos Kastella under a heavy barrage on the 15th, late that day established contact with the Battalion in Phaleron. From the moment it was clear the British were not going to be beat, the attitude of the population began to change from one of veiled hostility into one of undisguised friendliness, and although it was a week before the the Piræus was cleared, the advance up the Athens road was undertaken on 22nd December in an improved atmosphere. Progress was slow and painful—house by house, block by block, each day's work marked by wire run along the whole battalion front to prevent infiltration by night. Casualties were inflicted but also suffered: B Company lost its commander, Major L. E. Stringer, wounded, on 3rd January; and it was not until 6th January 1945, after the 4th British Division had joined in too, that both Athens and the Piræus were declared free from E.L.A.S.

Athens having been cleared, the 16th Battalion and the 2/5th Leicester were embarked on 7th January for Patras, where an E.L.A.S. division had for two months been warily watching a brigade of the 4th Indian Division. Brigadier Block's first act on arriving was to issue an ultimatum to E.L.A.S. to evacuate the town by 6 a.m. next morning (10th January). Much to everyone's surprise the ultimatum was complied with, enabling the Battalion to land unopposed and advance on the 13th to secure the airfield at Araxos. Though the general truce was proclaimed next day, the Battalion remained in the area until 11th February, when it returned by road to Phaleron. It embarked at the Piræus for Taranto in the M/V *Ville d'Oran* on 13th April.

The Campaign on the Continent, 1944-1945

The opposed landings in Normandy and the defeat of the German field army in France must be regarded as the culminating act of the war in Europe. Every military activity since the summer of 1940 had led up to it and had been sacrificed for it: every step on the path to victory led from it. Since we first had a standing army it has undertaken nothing on which the existence of the nation has so intimately depended. The Regiment may therefore congratulate itself that it had no fewer than five battalions concerned in the business, three of them near the forefront of the assault.

On the other hand, in the Normandy Landings, which were the ultimate expression of the accumulated experience of opposed landings in all theatres during the past three years, the infantry no longer occupied exclusively its proud place in the foreground. This time there was no stately progress in flat-boats such as that reserved for Lambton's regiment at Cancale, nothing resembling the hair-raising assault from the *River Clyde* on the Gallipoli beaches. In the actual landing purely infantry formations made a late entry in order of appearance; their ulterior movements were even more inextricably mixed with those of the other arms than in the operations in Italy just described. Consequently, if it might seem from the account that follows that the Durham battalions played but a subordinate part, it is only because the modern battlefield recognises no aristocrats, no queens, no kings, only a combination of every weapon in the industrial armoury.

The five Durham battalions taking part were: the 6th, 8th and 9th of the 151st Brigade, and the 10th and 11th of the 70th Brigade—two brigades which, in 1940, had occupied adjacent positions on the coast in such a manner as to give the Regiment the distinction of bearing the responsibility of the defence of the realm from Plymouth to beyond Portland Bill. The 10th and 11th, after re-forming respectively under Lieut.-Colonel Marley and Lieut.-Colonel R. F. Ware during the months following Dunkirk, had both spent rather over a year (25th October 1940 to 19th December 1941) in garrison in Iceland. On its return home the 70th Brigade, which was commanded until July 1942 by Brigadier Kirkup, had been placed in the 49th Division, a division under training in Wales as one of the assault divisions. In May 1944, when the Division was brought over to Norfolk to concentrate for the invasion, the 10th Battalion was commanded by Lieut.-Colonel F. W. Sandars, the 11th by Lieut.-Colonel J. M. Hanmer, both of the Regiment. The 151st Brigade, having returned from Sicily in November 1943, had been training in Suffolk before being brought south to a concentration area near Romsey in April 1944. On 6th June the 6th Battalion was commanded by Major G. L. Wood, originally a 9th Battalion officer but now second-in-command, deputising for Lieut.-Colonel A. E. Green, Middlesex, who had to go sick with a relapse of malaria on the eve of sailing. The 8th was still commanded by Lieut.-Colonel R. P. Lidwill, who had so distinguished himself at the Primosole Bridge. The 9th was under the command of Lieut.-Colonel H. R. Woods, 60th, who had succeeded Lieut.-Colonel Clarke on his death in Sicily. The Brigade was commanded by that same Brigadier R. H. Senior who had taken it successfully through so many vicissitudes.

Both 50th and 49th Divisions belonged to the XXX Corps, (Lieut.-General G. C. Bucknall), which, with two American and one other British corps, was to punch the bridgehead in Normandy. The Corps sector ran from Port-en-Bessin on the west to La Rivière on the east, between the V American and the I British. From there it was to advance southwards along the axis Bayeux/Tilly-sur-Seulles/Villers-Bocage/Mont Pinçon to secure the Mont Pinçon *massif* and the northern slopes of the Noireau valley, which it was to reach on the line Saint-Pierre-d'Entremont/Mont de Cérisi/Condé-sur-Noireau between the twelfth and seventeenth days after landing. The initial assault of Bucknall's Corps was to be carried out by the 50th Division, which though not assigned an assault task in the original plan had been specially selected by Lord Montgomery in preference to the 49th owing to its record and experience. Reinforced for the purpose to a strength of one armoured and four infantry brigades together with a host of miscellaneous—but essential—ancillary formations and units,[13] it was to land on a two-brigade front on

[13]That the Durham battalions' part may be seen in its true perspective, the composition of the Division on 6th June 1944 is here given in full: 50th Divisional Troops; 69th Infantry Brigade; 151st Infantry Brigade; 231st Infantry Brigade; 56th Independent Infantry Brigade; 47th Royal Marine Commando; 8th Armoured Brigade; 987th Battalion, U.S. Artillery; 7th Medium Regiment, R.A.; 86th Field Regiment, R.A.; 147th Field Regiment, R.A.; 198th and 234th Anti-tank Batteries, R.A.; two squadrons Westminster Dragoons (Crabs, *i.e.* Sherman tanks with rotary flails); 6th Assault Regiment, R.E. (Avres, *i.e.* Churchill tanks with 12-in. spigot-mortars in place of the main armament); C Squadron 141st Regiment, Royal Armoured Corps (Crocodiles, *i.e.* Churchill Mark VII tanks with flame-throwers); and the 104th Beach Sub-Area.

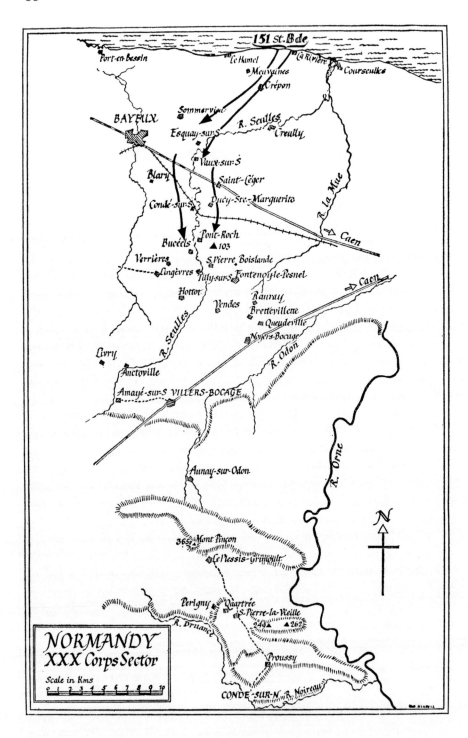

47. The Advance in Normandy, June—August, 1944

"Jig" and "King" sectors between Le Hamel and La Rivière. It was to be ready as a formation and to have cleared the Villers-Bocage area by the third day after landing, the day before the 49th Division[14] landed in its rear and started concentrating in the area of Creully.

The country in which the battalions were to operate differed markedly from anything they had known. The coastal strip behind the beaches was gently undulating pasture not unlike Salisbury Plain, though there were occasional hedges or belts of trees and the villages were usually surrounded by small orchards. South of the Bayeux/Caen road, however, they entered the *Bocage*, a very close country of small fields enclosed by hedges and banks with pollarded trees, interspersed by orchards, small copses and, occasionally, wide stretches of plantation. Aptly described as "the Cotswold country superimposed on Salisbury Plain," it was the same kind of terrain in which the Vendean peasants had so long defied the armies of the French Republic in the first years of the Revolution, admirable defensive country calling for every faculty of the human body every hour of the twenty-four. For twenty miles south of Bayeux the *Bocage* sloped gradually upwards to the Mont Pinçon hills, a "range" of rough sandstone heights rising to just over a thousand feet, covered with turf, heath and woodland. The southern slopes towards the Noireau, which are longer and gentler, revert to the usual *Bocage* pasture and orchards, but to the north and north-west of Mont Pinçon itself the woods were thick and in places almost impenetrable. The main rivers, the Aure, the Seulles and the Odon, were practically dry in summer, and the Odon alone presented much of an obstacle, and that by reason of its steep banks.

Embarked at Southampton in the evening of 5th June, the 151st Brigade was cast, with the 56th, in the role of a "reserve" brigade. It was to land in "King" sector behind the left "assault" brigade (the 69th) about two hours after the armoured assault-teams had gone in, about an hour and three-quarters after the assault-battalions and about an hour after the reserve battalions of the assault brigades. In the event, after a rough and cold crossing it arrived off the coast at about 9 a.m. on 6th June. The assault operations had progressed sufficiently satisfactorily for the Division to signal for it to land at 10.8 a.m. The first wave, carrying the Brigade's tactical headquarters, landed on "King Red" at 10.30. The 6th Battalion's first wave, in the L.C.I.(L.)s carrying 530-540 men, the bicycles and handcarts, beached at 11. By half-past the 8th Battalion was coming ashore also. The moment the 9th Battalion beached is unknown, but by 1.30 p.m.

[14]146th Infantry Brigade, 147th Infantry Brigade, 70th Infantry Brigade, 33rd Armoured Brigade.

all battalions were ashore and assembling in the prescribed concentration area on the Meuvaines ridge. Unlike the Sicily landing, each battalion was beached in exactly the right place, but all had had to wade through four feet or so of water, and most were drenched to the skin.

The enlargement of the beach-heads began about 3.30 p.m. Apart from securing a firm lodgment an essential feature of the Division's task was the capture of Villers-Bocage by the 8th Armoured Brigade if not on D-Day, at any rate on the day after. As it turned out, Villers-Bocage eluded capture for nearly two months, long after the 7th Armoured Division, landed through the 50th, was launched against it on the 13th. On the other hand the purely infantry tasks of enlarging the lodgment were carried out on the first day with fair precision. The 151st Brigade, advancing with two battalions up—the "9th D.L.I. Group" on the right, the "6th D.L.I. Group" on the left, both preceded by mobile columns on bicycles, forward observation officers and so on—advanced south-west towards the Bayeux /Caen road. By dusk the 9th's Group was on the line of the Bayeux /Saint-Léger road at Vaux-sur-Seulles, the 8th's close behind in reserve, and the 6th's at Esquay-sur-Seulles and Sommervieu. This was as far as the divisional commander wished to go before daylight. The only misfortune was the loss of the Brigadier, who was ambushed in his jeep near Crépon with all the divisional code-signs at about 4.30. Though he managed to escape next day there had been some dislocation at brigade head-quarters before Lieut.-Colonel Lidwill was appointed from the 8th Battalion to the command at 10.30 that night.

Securing the Beach-head: (i) Villers-Bocage, 8th-15th June

There followed that vital phase of the campaign in which a firm lodgment was formed behind a connected and self-supporting front in competition with the enemy effort to collect his reserves and launch a major counter-attack to thrust the Allied troops into the sea. It was essential for the Allied Command to retain the initiative by delivering a quick succession of hard blows in alternating sectors. It mattered little where. As it happened, as a result of the failure of the first attempt to take Caen, the left flank relapsed into active defence, and the main burden of the offensive was borne by the XXX Corps on the British right in a series of thrusts towards Villers-Bocage.

For the 151st Brigade as a whole the first days were relatively unspectacular. On the 7th the 9th Battalion, crossing the railway, pushed forward patrols as far as Pont-Roch, while the 6th took Ducy-Sainte-Marguerite and Condé-sur-Seulles. On the 9th both were brought to a standstill and the 6th had a stiff fight near Bucéels. On the 10th both battalions covered the advance south of the 7th Armoured Division on Villers-Bocage.

The 8th Battalion meanwhile, taken out of brigade reserve early on the 9th to join the 8th Armoured Brigade to preserve the momentum of the armoured thrust, was given the task of attacking Point 103, a height dominating the villages of Saint-Pierre and Tilly-sur-Seulles and the crossing of the Seulles. Its three assault companies were carried forward by the 24th Lancers from near Saint-Léger at 9.30 a.m. Late in the afternoon at 5.45, having taken Point 103, C and D Companies advanced under a heavy bombardment that lasted for an hour, and entered Saint-Pierre. While the reserve companies took up defensive positions the tanks of the 24th Lancers moved on. By 9, though no bridgehead over the Seulles had been formed, a salient had clearly been driven into the enemy's line.

The inevitable counter-attack began with great suddenness after stand-to at 4.45 a.m. on the 10th. The Battalion's opponents belonged to the *Panzer-Lehr-Division*, an armoured division of high quality and almost double strength, formed from demonstration units of the armoured training establishments and specially equipped for an anti-invasion role. Infiltration was not difficult, for Saint-Pierre was a picturesque little village, overgrown and threaded with narrow wooded lanes and tracks. C Company, slightly in advance in the centre, was immediately pushed back and part-overrun; A was threatened with a similar fate; and before the 24th Lancers could return to lend a hand the Battalion had been forced out of most of the village. D Company, however, on the right held fast, and by 11 a.m., with the assistance of the 24th, the attack was brought to a halt. At nightfall the three remaining companies were fairly secure in new positions overlooking the southern half of the village and Tilly. Late next day (11th) the enemy delivered a heavy attack on the 1st Dorset on Point 103 which necessarily involved the 8th in it. B Company was overrun by Tiger tanks, and by 10 p.m. the Battalion was isolated and surrounded. The remaining two companies, fighting vigorously, retired to new positions in rear, where, once again, supported by the Nottinghamshire Yeomanry and an anti-tank battery, it not only stemmed the attack but forced the enemy to withdraw. During the morning of the 12th there was no enemy activity, and after dark what was left of the Battalion was brought back under Lieut.-Colonel Lidwill (who had resumed command) to Blary, where it reverted to the 151st Brigade. In its characteristically stubborn defence it had lost 200 n.c.o.s and men and twelve officers killed or wounded, including the second-in-command, Major A. H.

Dunn, and B Company commander, Major T. L. A. Clapton, both killed.

(ii) *Tilly-sur-Seulles, 14th-19th June*

While the 8th Battalion was engaged at Saint-Pierre, the advance of the 7th Armoured Division, which the rest of the Brigade had been employed in promoting, had not progressed as favourably as had been expected. On the 11th it was disengaged to be committed to another operation designed to retain the initiative. This was a powerful right hook through Livry and Amayé on Villers-Bocage, which started on the 12th. On the 13th it suddenly encountered outside Villers a new German armoured division, the 2nd, and in a clash which was as unfortunate as it was unexpected it was roughly handled by some Tigers.

In an attempt to extricate it the 50th Division's original follow-up instructions, modified to suit the atmosphere of misplaced optimism, required the 151st Brigade to attack at 10.20 a.m. on the 14th. The 6th Battalion made some progress but was held up at Verrières for some time before it eventually entered it. The 9th experienced fierce resistance at Lingèvres, where two battalions of the 902nd Panzer Grenadiers of *Panzer-Lehr* fought stubbornly to hold it. None the less the Battalion fought its way in and by 11.30 had entered. Casualties had not been unduly heavy; but they included the 9th's commanding officer, Lieut.-Colonel Woods, killed, and all the officers of A Company from its commander, Major C. M. D'Arcy Irvine (a 1st Battalion officer), downwards.

The usual counter-attack was delivered at 4.30 in the afternoon on Lingèvres from the south-east by infantry supported by tanks. Soon the forward troops were nearly surrounded. A call for air-support was answered by Typhoons, who eased a situation which had been critical for two hours. Before he drew off the enemy had suffered 50 *per cent.* casualties, and besides discarding much equipment he left a hundred prisoners of *Panzer-Lehr* in the 9th's hands. The Brigade's total casualties were about 100.

The 15th and 16th were fairly quiet. But later on the 17th the 6th Battalion, now under Lieut.-Colonel Green again, was ordered to reinforce an attack by the 231st Brigade on Tilly. It was held up at about the same point it had reached on the 14th, though one company under Major M. J. Kirby succeeded in getting within bombing range of the objective, the Tilly-Lingèvres road. A fresh attack, however, made in conjunction with tanks under a powerful creeping barrage late in the afternoon of 18th June, proved irresistible. The enemy was blasted out of his positions. By 5 p.m., after two and a half-hours' fighting, the 6th Battalion had gained the high ground south-west of Tilly and was digging in, enabling the 56th Brigade to cap the success by taking Tilly next day.

For a month the 50th Division's front stayed almost stationary. The storm of the 19th-21st June caused a postponement of all important action, and the ensuing weeks were consumed in active patrolling and minor attacks against determined opposition.

The Battle of the Odon: the Defence of Rauray, 29th June–2nd July

The 49th Division was to have landed after the 7th Armoured Division on the fourth day as the third division of the XXX Corps, and to have been ready for action as a division on the seventh. The 70th Brigade, concentrated in East Anglia, was embarked at New-haven on 11th June, and it was landed complete by the 15th although unfavourable weather had so dislocated the beach organisation that no units landed on the right beach on the right day. It was gradually introduced to the fighting brigade by brigade. The 10th Battalion experienced its first fighting since May 1940 on 16th June near Saint-Pierre, the scene of the 8th Battalion's fine resistance; and the 11th Battalion was blooded on the 23rd in the eerie Parc de Boislonde while attached to the 147th Brigade. When on 24th June the Division assumed responsibility for the sector between the 50th on its right and the 3rd Canadian on its left, the 70th Brigade was in divisional reserve until entering the Battle of the Odon in the afternoon of the 26th.

The battle arose out of a renewed attempt on the part of 21st Army Group to capture Caen. The town was an object of jealousy alike to the Allied and the German Command, though to the British, however desirable, it was not an essential possession. Whether Lord Montgomery took it or not, by attacking it he provoked resistance and attracted enemy divisions to a flank far removed from that on which the decisive offensive was due to develop later. The attack on Caen was designed as a pincer movement, the main thrust of which was the southerly one, delivered by the VIII Corps (three divisions) through the 3rd Canadian Division across both the Odon and the Orne to gain the high ground near Bretteville-sur-Laize. The VIII Corps' right flank was to be secured by a sympathetic advance by the XXX Corps' left, formed by the 49th Division, which was to take Noyers-Bocage and exploit towards Aunay-sur-Odon. Planned to begin on 22nd June, the operation was delayed by the storms, which interfered with the landing time-table, and it was not until the 25th that it could be launched.

The 49th Division joined in at dawn on the 26th with the object of gaining the commanding terrain in the Rauray area. The 70th Brigade moved forward that afternoon from reserve to Fontenay-le-Pesnel, which had been captured the previous day; and the 11th Battalion dug in astride the road to Rauray about 800 yards farther south, where they supported the tanks of the Sherwood Rangers. After dark Lieut.-Colonel Hanmer received orders to patrol into Rauray, which, if found unoccupied, was to be seized at once. The patrol, however, which ran into the enemy and lost its officer, reported Rauray strongly held, information which determined Lieut.-Colonel Hanmer against a hurriedly improvised night attack. A fighting patrol sent forward at dawn on the 27th confirmed the prospect of a stiff enemy resistance, and Lieut.-Colonel Hanmer organised a battalion attack at midday. Both assault companies gained their objectives—though with some loss, including one company commander killed—and Rauray was carried. Next day (the 28th) the 10th Battalion attacked through the 11th to crown the success by gaining the high ground to the east and south of Rauray. Both battalions spent the following three days in close contact with the enemy under a constant fire of one sort and another.

The enemy's reaction to the offensive came in the form of a counter-attack delivered by the II SS *Panzercorps*, the most determined and the best co-ordinated armoured attack executed by the Germans in the whole campaign, which descended from the west and fell on the 70th Brigade first at 7 in the morning of 1st July. The brunt of the infantry fighting was borne by the 11th Battalion and the Tyneside Scottish at Rauray. Nine tanks were knocked out by the 24th Lancers, six by the 217th Anti-tank Battery, ten by the Tyneside Scottish, five of them by one gun with its first five rounds. Bitter fighting continued throughout the day. Four fierce attacks were delivered on Rauray, all of them unsuccessful. The last came from the direction of Queudeville early in the evening and was decisively repelled. By this time the companies were curiously mixed. The Tyneside Scottish had one company and 1½ platoons of the 11th Battalion, while Lieut.-Colonel Hanmer had three companies of the 7th Duke of Wellington's under his command—"a proper Cox and Box," as he wrote at the time. Despite the casualties suffered, however, at the end of the day C Company of the 11th and two companies of the 7th Duke of Wellington's were led by Captain W. F. McMichael, 11th, into a gallant counter-attack to straighten the line and relieve a company of the Tyneside Scottish which, though reduced to twelve men, continued to hold on. The attack was a complete success: no one had seen the enemy run so hard: and it

enabled the Brigade to claim (with justice) that it occupied the same
ground that it had when the German attack began. The 11th Battalion's casualties in this magnificent defensive action were naturally
high: two company commanders were killed and one wounded, and
casualties throughout the Battalion, particularly high in respect of
platoon commanders and n.c.o.s, amounted to some 200 all ranks.

This was the last episode in the Battle of the Odon. Caen still
defied capture, but no fewer than eight German armoured divisions,
drawn to the Allied left flank and committed, had been heavily
defeated.

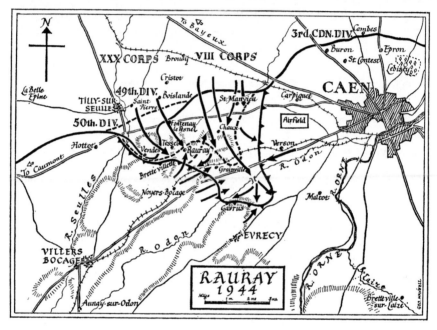

48. Rauray, June/July, 1944

It was also the last honour won for the Regiment by the 10th and
11th Battalions, though by no means their last fight. The 10th was
involved in heavy fighting at Hottot on 11th July, and the 11th
shared in the clearing of Vendes on the 18th. After the Division was
transferred to the I Corps sector east of Caen (Emiéville) on 25th
July, the two battalions took part in the great advance eastward,
which began on 15th August. On the 18th the Brigade reached
Mézidon. Beyond, the 10th Battalion, endeavouring to cross the Vie
and seize the dominating height of Montvignes, fought a fierce—and
costly—action before it won the ridge, only to be thrown off it later.
On 20th August, in order to provide reinforcements for the depleted

divisions in the Army Group, the 70th Brigade, as junior Brigade of the Division, was selected for disbandment. It was a blow particularly unwelcome to the 11th Battalion, which was at full strength and at the top of its form. Occasionally it was possible to post a rifle company complete with its officers. But all went in different directions. The 11th was mostly divided between the Green Howards, the Dorset, East Yorkshire and Devon Regiments in the 50th Division, though Lieut.-Colonel C. D. Hamilton, who had served in it since 1939 and had taken over the command from Lieut.-Colonel Hanmer on his succeeding to the 6th, went to the 7th Duke of Wellington's, which he later rose to command with distinction. Many of the 10th went to the Durham battalions of the 151st Brigade. The process of disbandment, continued throughout September, was not finally completed until 18th October.

The Break-out: Saint-Pierre-la-Vieille,
9th-16th August

Measured in purely geographical terms, the Allied advance was well behind schedule. Caen was still unwon, and in the XXX Corps' front Mont Pinçon still remained a distant objective far away beyond the horizon. The events of August were to show how deceptive gains on the map may be and how much had been accomplished by the German Command's refusal to give ground. On 25th July the American Armies which had been accumulating on the western flank began those heart-warming thrusts that were to carry their armour in a wide encircling movement from Saint-Lô, through Avranches to Alençon and Angers, and hug the German Armies in a deadly embrace in the "Falaise Pocket".

The American offensive had got well into its stride when on 30th July the VIII and XXX Corps, attacking side by side, began theirs. The 50th Division started with an advance north of Anctoville early on the 30th, but the Durham Brigade was not seriously involved until 2nd August, when in the attempt to win Villers-Bocage it reached the Amayé/Villers-Bocage road. Villers-Bocage fell at last to the 69th Brigade on the 4th, and on the 6th the 43rd Division (XXX Corps) stormed Mont Pinçon.

After that the XXX Corps, now under the dynamic command of Lieut.-General Horrocks, advanced down to the Noireau. At first the 7th Armoured Division led while the 50th followed in rear to mop up, but on 9th August, after 7th Armoured had encountered stiff resistance south of Le Plessis-Grimoult, the plan was changed to a more successful one in which the 50th did the attacking while 7th Armoured secured its left flank. For the next four days the Division pressed down the Plessis-Grimoult/Condé road against stubborn opposition.

On the 9th the 151st Brigade attacked first with the 6th and 8th Battalions up and gained its objective in a fierce hand-to-hand struggle, one of the most successful attacks in which it had taken part.

Then the 69th attacked through them but failed to gain their objective. On the 10th the 69th attacked again and got a further thousand yards, but failed to reach their objective on their left, the height immediately west of Saint-Pierre-la-Vieille. The village was strongly held by the enemy, who broke up the 69th's attacks by repeated use of self-propelled artillery in a mobile role. On the 11th the 231st Brigade attacked through the 69th, but though they advanced a further 3000 yards they failed to win their objective. On the 12th the 69th resumed the attack on Saint-Pierre, while the 231st succeeded in advancing about one thousand yards to reach their objective in the centre and on the right; and the 151st, with the 9th Battalion up under Lieut.-Colonel H. J. Mogg, Oxfordshire and Buckinghamshire Light Infantry, was brought forward to take the left-hand objectives, Points 249 and 262 to the south-east of Saint-Pierre, which were triumphantly won by 5 in the afternoon. At first light on the 13th the Division was about a mile north of Proussy when it was relieved by the 43rd.

This hard four days' slogging match carried the Durham battalions to the brink of the "Falaise Pocket", where no fewer than eighteen German divisions were caught and battered to pieces from the ground and from the air. The route of the 151st Brigade in its advance to the Seine took it across the pestilential battlefield a few days later. If such a spectacle may be called a reward, it was certainly just requital for almost three months of unremitting fighting.

The Struggle for the Albert Canal: Gheel,
8th-11th September

There followed that exhilarating advance across the Seine and through Picardy and Artois into Belgium. It was not entirely devoid of incident. A company of the 9th Battalion was attacked by a small party of the enemy on 31st August in Beauvais; and the next day the 8th had a skirmish with a rearguard at Picquigny, a village on the Somme which had been a favourite spot for an evening's recreation in the old days of 1940. The frontier was crossed early on 3rd September, and for two days the 151st Brigade had the congenial duty of garrisoning Brussels.

The first serious resistance was encountered on the general line Antwerp/Hasselt, where the enemy had assembled about three

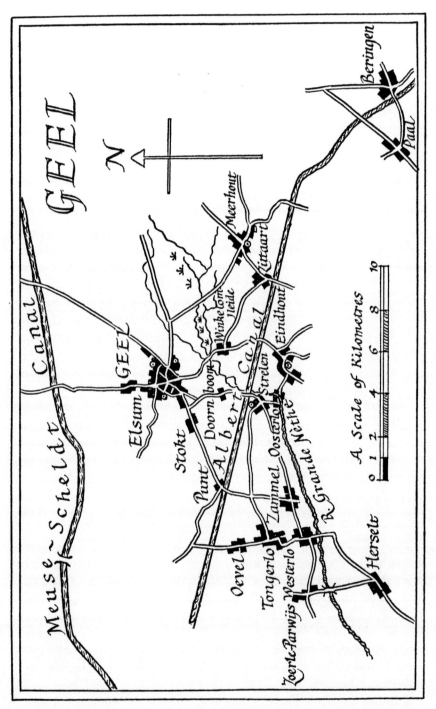

49. Gheel, 8th—11th September, 1944

divisions "bolstered up" by battle-groups from parachute formations and remnants from the 1st SS Panzer Division. The enemy front was protected by the obstacle of the Albert Canal, which runs from Antwerp to Maastricht in a flat country of sandy heath and swamp forming the western extremity of the Campine. On 8th September the Guards Armoured Division forced a crossing at Beringen, where, though heavily counter-attacked, it maintained its bridgehead. The same day the 151st Brigade reverted to the 50th Division and was moved forward to Herselt behind the 69th Brigade, which had forced a crossing near Het Punt.

A bitter struggle in heavy rain then ensued to enlarge the bridgehead. Late in the afternoon of the 8th the 8th Battalion, under the command of Lieut.-Colonel H. R. D. Oldman, Green Howards, who had succeeded Lieut.-Colonel Lidwill when he was wounded near Saint-Pierre on 9th August, received orders to make a crossing east of the 69th's in order to cover the construction of a folding-boat bridge. Covered by fire from the machine-guns and mortars of the 2nd Cheshire, A Company (Major C. L. Beattie) got across, though losing its commander, who was killed as he scrambled up the bank, as well as all its other officers; at 5.30 p.m. D followed; and by 10 the whole Battalion was across. A determined counter-attack, which was carried to within bombing range, was repelled two hours later, and early on the 9th the 61st Reconnaissance Regiment came through. Then the folding-boat bridge collapsed, isolating the 8th and delaying the crossing of the 6th until 11 a.m., when it was able to pass through and dig in in positions south of Gheel. At 2 p.m. D and C Companies of the 6th were ordered into Gheel itself, but before the attack got under way all companies but D (which successfully penetrated into the town) were subjected to a series of heavy attacks which disorganised the advance until they were beaten off to allow the Battalion to occupy Gheel. Lieut.-Colonel Green was wounded in the course of the afternoon.

The 9th Battalion meanwhile had crossed farther to the right. It was pressing forward to Winkelom when the enemy, infiltrating after dark between the companies of the 8th and 9th, delivered a whole series of heavy counter-attacks which for a time isolated the 6th in Gheel. Some of the battalions' opponents here came from the same Parachute Division they had met and defeated at the Primosole Bridge, and they fought and moved with characteristic skill. Bitter fighting continued throughout the rest of the night and the 10th. As the day wore on the situation of the 6th Battalion, short of food as well as ammunition, became precarious. Gheel was heavily shelled and countless attacks were beaten off in fierce hand-to-hand fighting

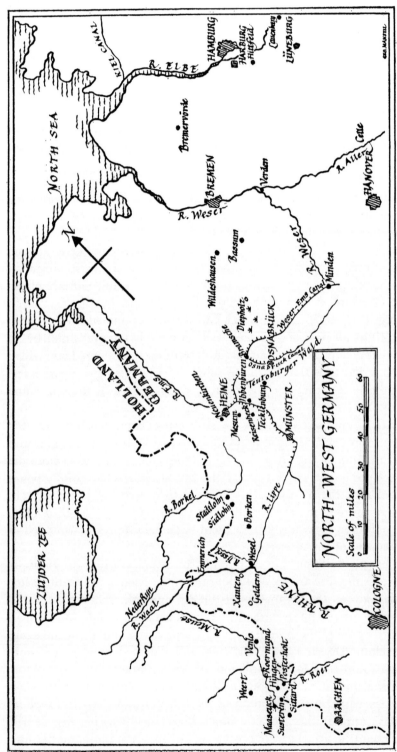

50. The Advance through Germany, January–April, 1945

in the streets until at last the depleted battalion (now under Major G. L. Wood) was forced to withdraw into the south-eastern outskirts of the town, where it was relieved by two companies of the 8th. Indeed, during the night the withdrawal of the whole brigade was contemplated.

However, as the mist cleared in the morning of the 11th the enemy himself showed signs of withdrawing. In broad daylight this was as impossible as it had been for the Durham Brigade, every movement attracting fire from our infantry and armour. He renewed his attempts to eliminate the bridgehead on the 12th, but they met with no better success. That evening the exhausted battalions were relieved by a brigade of the 15th Division. So successfully, however, had the Durham battalions fought that the next morning the enemy pulled out and retired over the Scheldt Canal without further prompting. In a fight as hard and as honourable as Alamein, Mareth and the Primosole Bridge, they had not only forced the bridgehead and held it, but also contained the troops who would otherwise have been deployed against the Guards at Beringen.

In the operation which followed the crossing of the canals, that controversial operation named *Market Garden,* which, if completely successful, would have forced the Meuse, the Waal and the Lower Rhine, the Durham battalions took little part, the 50th Division being the reserve division of the XXX Corps and the 151st Brigade remaining in divisional reserve. It reached Nijmegen on 2nd October and, crossing into the low-lying land between the Waal and the Lower Rhine known to the Division as the "Island", stayed for the remainder of its existence in uncomfortable conditions of almost stationary warfare. It was finally relieved on 29th November when the whole Division was concentrated in Belgium for dissolution.

The pitcher had been taken once too often to the well. In the thick of the fighting since the beginning, it had achieved a reputation such as only three other divisions in the whole army had acquired. Perhaps if the whole Army Group had not suffered from a lack of infantry reinforcements the Division's existence might have been prolonged. There is no denying, though, that at the end it was not what it once was. An officer present at both, comparing the invasion of Sicily with the Normandy landing, noticed that the later one was undertaken in a very different spirit, that periods of leave had reminded men of family ties which made them cast one last wistful glance backward as they embarked. The Division as a whole was brought back to England as a skeleton to act as a training division. The cadres of the 6th and 8th Battalions, containing those with the longest service, embarked at Ostend on 14th December 1944 and were soon after disbanded in Yorkshire. Many of their officers and men were posted as reinforcements to other units in 21st Army Group. The 9th, however, remained to represent the Regiment in the final defeat of the German Army.

The Roer, 16th-31st January 1945

The 9th Battalion under Lieut.-Colonel H. J. Mogg, exchanging its TT flash for the jerboa and reorganised as a lorried infantry battalion, was posted to the re-formed 131st Brigade[15] of the 7th Armoured Division, which it joined at Dilsen on 2nd December.

The first operation in which it was engaged was *Operation Blackcock*. This was an attempt to clear the country to the River Roer by driving a salient into the strongly defended enemy positions to gain the main Sittard/Roermond road, and then, by out-flanking the enemy on the left, to favour the advance of the 43rd and 52nd Divisions on the right. The object of the operation was the elimination of the awkward Heinsberg, or Roermond, Triangle at the junction of the British and American Armies, an essential preliminary to the Battle of the Rhineland. The terrain was difficult: small villages converted into strong-points lay surrounded by a maze of small streams and brooks, involving the infantry in a succession of fights from village to village and house to house. At the outset the ground was frost-bound and covered with snow, but it thawed at intervals later to render the business even more gruelling.

The operation was opened by the capture of Brakhoven on 13th January by the 1/5th Queen's, reinforced by D Company of the 9th Durhams. The Battalion's main attack, which owing to the freezing of the smoke-screen had to be postponed from the morning to the evening of the 16th, went in in 30° of frost across the Vlodbeek, and in three hours had carried the objective of Dieteren. Early next morning the 1/5th Queen's passed through to take Susteren. Supply became precarious owing partly to the heavy fire the enemy brought down on the improvised bridges and partly to the partial thaw, which bogged all wheeled traffic. Nevertheless the battalion hung on at Dieteren under the fire and beat off all attempts to throw it out.

The advance was continued in renewed frost to Echt, but at Schilberg and Hingen the column was held up and had to be reinforced by B Company of the Battalion. It was not until the afternoon of the 20th that the strong-point of Hingen fell; while farther on, St. Joost, which was defended by parachutists, stood out against a determined attack of the 1st Rifle Brigade. C Company of the Battalion (Major W. Anderson) was ordered up from Hingen to

[15] 1/5th Queen's, 2nd Devon and 9th Durham Light Infantry.

assist by seizing the bridge nearby, but it got dispersed by the heavy fire and most of it, including the commander (killed), were either captured or killed. B Company in attempting to extricate it early on the 21st was forced back. Another attempt by the three companies organised by Lieut.-Colonel Mogg later in the morning, though at first successful, equally failed with the loss of a second company commander killed (Major S. O. de B. S. Macartney). A third, however, made at dusk the same day, was rewarded by the collapse of all resistance, most of the defenders being taken in the cellars where they had been holding out. Montfort having been captured next day, the Brigade was able to advance. From 25th January to 21st February the Battalion occupied Posterholt in discomfort but comparative security.

The Pursuit: Ibbenbüren, 1st-6th April

The Battalion remained at Weert until 24th March, and it did not cross the Rhine at Xanten until the 27th, after the river had been successfully forced and the bridgehead secured. Forming part of the "5th Dragoon Guards Group" it reached Borken against slight opposition the same day. It had a very stiff fight in the streets of Stadtlohn on the 30th; but on 1st April it pressed ahead for the Ems at great speed, and that evening was in Neuenkirchen, a suburb of Rheine. The bridges having been blown and the 11th Armoured Division having forced a crossing higher up, no attack was attempted at Rheine, and the Brigade was diverted south to Mesum, where it crossed the Ems on the 2nd.

Making use of the 11th Armoured Division's bridgehead between Riesenbeck and Tecklenburg, the 7th Armoured Division intended to break through the Teutoburger Wald at Ibbenbüren and advance to the Weser south of Bremen. By the morning of the 3rd the 131st Brigade was concentrated on Riesenbeck ready to attack from the bridgehead. The first task was the capture of Ibbenbüren itself, which was not only defended by the officers and cadets of the Hanover School of Infantry but was approached through narrow wooded gorges favouring the defence.

The result was a most stubborn fight. After a successful preliminary operation had placed a battalion on the high ground, the principal attack on the town was begun, led by a squadron of the 5th Dragoon Guards and A Company of the Battalion. Against snipers, bazooka-men and numerous roving machine-gun teams progress was slow and costly, and, at nightfall, had to cease. The enemy fought desperately, some lying low while the men passed and then rising to shoot them from behind. It proved usually necessary for the tanks to demolish any buildings and bury the defenders in the rubble. One captured *feldwebel*, badly wounded and buried up to the neck, when asked when he thought the war would end replied, "When we win". The struggle continued throughout the 4th and the 5th while the rest of the 7th Armoured Division side-stepped to lead the advance over the Ems-Weser Canal. It was not until the night of the 5th that the Battalion was relieved by units of the 53rd Division, which administered the *coup-de-grâce* on the 6th April.

The Battalion's progress continued through Diepholz, Bassum (9th) and Wildeshausen (10th) until it reached Hittfeld, in the outskirts of Hamburg, on 20th April, just before the last of the Elbe bridges was blown. It was surely fitting that the preliminaries of the negotiations for the surrender of Hamburg by General Wolz on 2nd May should have been conducted through the outposts of the 9th Battalion, the personification of the old Durham Brigade, which had contributed so much to that triumphant conclusion.

The Campaigns in Burma, 1943-1945

The Regiment's battle-honours in Burma were won by the 2nd Battalion, the same battalion which had returned battered and "non-operational" from Dunkirk in May 1940. When it joined the 2nd Division's concentration area at Huddersfield there were only three combatant officers (Captain O. Pearson, the Quartermaster, and 2/Lieutenants H. O. Lyster-Todd and J. W. Rudd) and about 180 n.c.o.s and men together with the medical officer and the Battalion's much respected chaplain, the Rev. D. E. Rice, R.A.Ch.D. The reorganisation was carried out by Lieut.-Colonel G. I. Wiehe, who, the son of Colonel F. G. A. Wiehe, had won his Military Cross at Hooge when a newly joined subaltern of 19. About 500 reinforcements arrived to bring up to strength a battalion which, what with officers and men returning from hospital, soon possessed a distinct Regimental quality, with Majors G. K. Stobart and J. M. Hanmer as field officers and Captain W. B. Hutton, recovered from his wounds, as adjutant. Under Lieut.-Colonel Wiehe's strong personality and stern discipline it was not long before it resumed the appearance of a battalion, but it was not destined to be taken on service by him. Ill-health and overwork forced him to retire from the command and he died of cancer in 1941, to be succeeded by the second-in-command, Lieut.-Colonel Stobart, who took it to India in April 1942.

While stationed in this country it remained with the 6th Brigade of the 2nd Division on the Yorkshire coast near Bridlington, though from 8th September to 19th October 1941 it was moved south to Bury St. Edmunds to reorganise as a motor battalion in the 127th

Brigade of the 42nd Division. It returned, however, and embarked with the rest of the 6th Brigade at Port Glasgow in the *Empress of Canada* on 12th April 1942, sailing on the 15th. Disembarking at Bombay on 2nd June, it moved to Ahmednagar, where in country as little resembling jungle as is possible it underwent training for jungle warfare. Late in the year, the 6th Brigade having been formed into an independent infantry brigade group with four battalions and ancillary arms, the Battalion was moved to Juhu, north of Bombay, to train in combined operations; and on 17th December, under Lieut.-Colonel J. A. Theobalds, Oxfordshire and Buckinghamshire Light Infantry, who had succeeded Lieut.-Colonel Stobart in August, it entrained at Bombay for Chittagong on the Bay of Bengal to take part in the Arakan campaign with the 14th Indian Division.

The First Arakan Campaign: Donbaik, 8th January-18th March 1943

The first Arakan Campaign was undertaken to clear the enemy out of the Mayu peninsula and to take Akyab Island. It was originally intended that the latter object should have been attained by the specially trained 6th Brigade Group and the 29th, which had been employed in Madagascar. The 29th, however, was detained in South Africa with malaria, and sufficient landing craft were not available owing to operations taking place concurrently in the Mediterranean. The plan was consequently remodelled into a rapid advance down the Arakan coast by the 14th Indian Division as far as Foul Point at the tip of the Mayu Peninsula, where a short-range assault by the 6th Brigade in the few landing craft available was to be launched against Akyab. It was calculated that, though there were four Japanese divisions in Burma, only one was in the west and that there was little more than a regiment in Arakan, the principal garrisons being at Maungdaw and Buthidaung.

If a hard blow were delivered quickly there was a fair prospect of success. On the other hand the necessary speed and the rapid deployment of a large force were barely obtainable in Arakan. Down the centre of the peninsula, which is about ninety miles long and about twenty wide, runs a range of jungle-covered mountains some 2000 feet high, which fall precipitately from a razor-sharp ridge into a tangle of broken spurs which approach to within a thousand yards or so of the sea on one side and the Mayu on the other. The narrow strips of flat ground are broken into by in-numerable streams or *chaungs,* which, tidal on the sea side, are bor-derd by banks of treacherous mud at low tide, offering ideal positions for defence and effectively hampering the deployment of the attacking force. In this instance, moreover, the attacking force set out under a grave moral disadvantage. The Japanese soldier, with his ability to live hard and die hard, had as yet revealed his weaknesses to few. He was regarded as something of a superman, whom many thought it impossible to train ordinary town-bred British soldiers to match. The time was to come when the qualities of the two opponents were to be seen in a proper perspective: when it was shown that our men could dispense with an elaborate *attirail* of canteens and E.N.S.A. entertainments and stand up to a killing business in the jungle as well as the Japanese. But that time had not come in January 1943.

At first all went well. Maungdaw and Buthidaung were occupied in the middle of December 1942, and by the end of the month the 14th Indian Division had reached Indin—a patrol even rounded Foul Point to reach Magyichaung. There followed a delay, however, which the enemy used to build strong defences in the Donbaik / Laungchaung area at Rathedaung as well as at Akyab itself. An attempt was made on Donbaik on 18th January and failed. A fresh assault with tanks combined with infantry failed also in mid-February. It seemed unlikely that the Mayu peninsula could be cleared before the monsoon began to break, but another effort was enjoined by General Wavell on Lieut.-General Irwin, who was required to renew the attack on Donbaik with the 6th Independent Infantry Brigade Group, until then held at Chittagong in readiness for the attack of Akyab.

The Battalion left Chittagong on 13th February and arrived at Maungdaw two days later. After a successful amphibious raid carried out by a platoon on Myebon, well beyond Akyab, on 20th February, it began the move on Donbaik at midnight of 2nd/3rd March. The next day the advanced guard came up against the series of strong-points based on the twist in the *chaung* called Shepherd's Crook, all of which were dominated by the enemy-held Points 500 and 823. On the 6th the relief of the Indian battalions was completed.

The attack went in at 5.30 a.m. on 18th March. The 1st Royal Welch Fusiliers led, but suffered heavy casualties in storming the strong points at the east end of the *chaung*. The two assault companies of the Battalion followed into the open, over the dead bodies of their predecessors in the luckless attacks of the previous months, to seize the Elbow. D on the left reached its objective; but C (Captain W. B. Hutton, who received a wound in the same knee as he had on the Dyle) ran into difficulties despite the gallantry of the men and officers, among them Lieutenant P. F. Greenwell, one of the many Greenwells who had served in the Regiment, who led a dashing attack on one Japanese post blowing his hunting-horn. With redoubled efforts, by the end of the day most of the jungle in the Elbow was occupied, though many of the underground strong-points —horrid things requiring individual treatment with the bayonet— remained in enemy hands behind the forward troops.

The attack as a whole, however, magnificent though it was, was another costly failure. Furthermore the whole offensive was jeopardised by a bold Japanese counterthrust from the Kaladan valley. By 24th March the enemy had thrown out the troops at Rathedaung and had established a block across the Brigade's line of retreat near Indin. On the map the situation of the opposing forces began to look, as General Slim has said, like a Neapolitan ice.

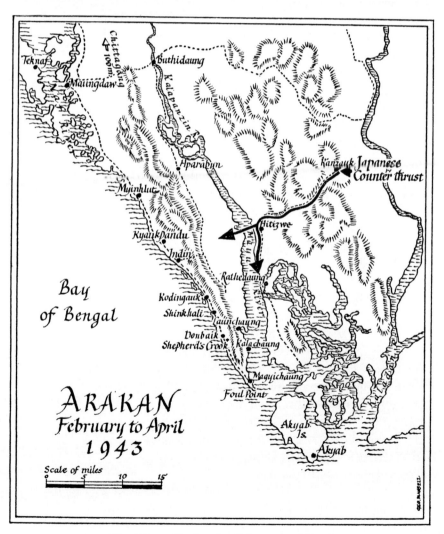

51. The Mayu Peninsula, February—March, 1943

The Battalion began its withdrawal on 4th April, and at 6 a.m. next day reached Indin none too soon. Here it took part in an attack (on Point 251) to clear the retreat. It gained its objectives with surprising ease, only to learn next day that in its absence the enemy had fallen on another battalion of the brigade at Indin. Brigade Headquarters were overrun and Brigadier Cavendish captured, but the Battalion, returning to assist, found the attack had already been repelled. Lieut.-Colonel Theobalds having temporarily succeeded to the command of the Brigade, the retreat was continued by Major G. K. C. Lyster-Todd along the beach to Kyaukpandu, after the Battalion had taken part in the bloody repulse of another enemy attack across the open. On 10th April the retreat was continued to Myinhlut, where, joining the 4th Brigade of the 26th Indian Division, the Battalion became separated from the rest of the 6th Brigade in its withdrawal to Maungdaw. After an unfortunate action in Myinhlut, in which it was fired on by Indian troops, it withdrew to Lambaguna for a month, and thence, as a result of a further Japanese thrust, through Maungdaw (which fell on 11th May) to a position near Bawli Bazar, where on 12th May it was reunited to the 6th Brigade. Within a fortnight it was back at Chittagong: within a month it was restored to the 2nd Division at Ahmednagar.

The first Arakan Campaign was a gamble which failed to come off. To the Battalion it was a miserable disappointment. Apart from the failure it had been heavily attacked by malaria, the disease which almost destroyed the Company's Army in Arakan in the First Burmese War (1824-1826), and though its sickness rate was the best in the Brigade, at one time there were over three hundred men down. On the other hand it had come face to face with the Japanese Army and it returned to India convinced it was not inferior.

Kohima, 27th March-22nd June 1944

The war had not dealt kindly with the 2nd Battalion so far, but in 1944 it was given the opportunity of sharing in one of the most glorious, though one of the bloodiest, episodes in the history of the army, and its record thereafter was one of the continuous if not uninterrupted advance.

The plan of campaign for 1944 comprised: an amphibious operation to seize the Andaman Islands: a resumption of the Arakan Campaign and the amphibious assault on Akyab; an advance across the Chindwin towards Indaw; an advance from Ledo to Myitkyina; a long range penetration by Wingate's Special Force to assist the Ledo offensive; and an advance by the Chinese from Yunnan into the Bhamo area. The 2nd Division, cast in the role of an assault division in the XXXIII Corps, was to take part in the Andaman operation, but its destination was changed after the Teheran Conference to the capture of Akyab.

Certain of these movements were already begun when on 6th March the Japanese struck. In what was intended to be a decisive blow to enter India the Japanese Command in Burma under General Kawabe concentrated all its resources on a gigantic break-through on the Assam front by the 15th Army, which was to capture Imphal and penetrate to the Brahmaputra valley. Indications of these intentions had not been wanting, and General Slim contemplated them with a fair degree of composure, intending to defeat them with equal decisiveness in the Imphal plain.

The battle did not turn out altogether as planned. The enemy closed in both on Imphal and on Kohima with astonishing speed. Kohima, and Dimapur in rear, became clearly threatened by a whole division whereas no more than a brigade group in that quarter had been anticipated. Kohima possessed only a scratch garrison, and Dimapur, our only base and railhead, had none at all. To reinforce this sector there were available the 3rd Special Service Brigade and the 5th Indian Division, both in Arakan; and at the same time the 2nd Division was released from reserve in India. It was in this manner that troops formed on an elaborate establishment and trained for combined operations in an assault role took part in a kind of enlarged Rorke's Drift, in which ordinary infantry weapons and stout hearts combined with jungle *savoir-faire* were all that was wanted.

The Battalion received its orders to move suddenly at Belgaum at 9 a.m. on 21st March. It was back in Ahmednagar on the 25th; by 3rd April it had mobilised and entrained for Calcutta; and on the 9th it was deployed around the airstrip at Dimapur under the command of Lieut.-Colonel J. H. Brown of the Regiment, who had succeeded Lieut.-Colonel Theobalds on his promotion as Brigade Second-in-Command the previous July. By that time Kohima was encircled, though not before one brigade of the 5th Indian Division had got in to reinforce the small garrison. By 15th April, when the Battalion started up the Kohima road from Dimapur, and the 17th, when it occupied reserve positions two miles from the perimeter, the place had been under constant attack for three weeks.

In peace Kohima had been the headquarters of the Naga Hills district of Assam, the seat of a district commissioner, whose bungalow, summer-house and tennis-court became three of the principal tactical points in the defence. In the war it had hitherto been an important supply depot, and other tactical features bore the names of the humdrum uses to which they had been put: F.S.D. (Field

Supply Depot) Ridge, D.I.S. (Daily Issue Store) Ridge, G.P.T. (General Purpose Transport) Ridge, and so on. In the afternoon of 19th April B Company of the Battalion (Captain R. Allen) carried out the successful attack on Terrace Hill which, though the commander was killed, secured the entry to the place, and next day the 1st Royal Berkshire effected the relief of the 4th Royal West Kent, the gaunt and haggard defenders of the heap of beastliness Kohima had become. Two days later the first two companies of the Battalion entered the perimeter and took up positions on Garrison (or Summerhouse) Hill, the last stronghold of the attenuated garrison.

The Battalion had no sooner entered before it was involved in one of the biggest night attacks the enemy ever made. C Company faced the Japanese on Kuki's Picquet, with D behind it "in nontactically sited bunkers", A and B on a plateau about one hundred feet below. The attack descended on C at about 1.30 a.m. in the morning of the 23rd. The enemy came up the slope shoulder to shoulder. They were shot down shoulder to shoulder, but as one man fell so another took his place, and by sheer weight of numbers they forced their way into the centre of the company's positions before it had time to get the wire out. However, D Company, brought up by Major W. S. Waterhouse, managed to hold the attack about C's headquarters, edging forward now and again but suffering severely from mortar fire and spring grenades. At about 5 a platoon of A led by Captain J. W. Kelley, the company commander, counter-attacked with the bayonet and succeeded in regaining some of the lost ground until it was stopped by fire from Kuki's Picquet. Day was now breaking. Neither side could do anything. For the whole of the 23rd the companies remained in their positions subjected to a heavy and constant fire from snipers who exacted a slow but steady toll. Nevertheless the Battalion had stood firm and inflicted substantial casualties. As for itself, out of the fifteen officers of the three companies involved only four remained, and A, a typical company, had only sixty men from the 136 that had gone into action in the morning.

There was another attack on the 27th, followed by a counter-attack delivered by the Battalion under a powerful barrage, which restored the situation—if "situation" is not too dignified a word for the disordered jumble of bodies, alive and dead, on Garrison Hill.

After being withdrawn for relief the Battalion came forward again on 4th May in the general assault designed to put an end to the siege and drive the Japanese down the road to Imphal. The 6th Brigade was given the task of ejecting them from the main Kohima ridge, the Battalion taking F.S.D. Ridge. The attack unfortunately miscarried with the loss, among many others, of Lieut.-Colonel Brown, killed; and although a small force remained dug in on the ridge until relieved early on the 6th, the Battalion was withdrawn to Dimapur to refit.

It returned on the 16th to a changed situation. The enemy had been driven off the nearer heights, and the Battalion, now temporarily under Major L. à B. Robinson, Royal Berkshire, shared in the long grind to clear him from the Aradura Spur, The forerunner to the monsoon, the *chota bersaht*, had begun to fall and, as one officer

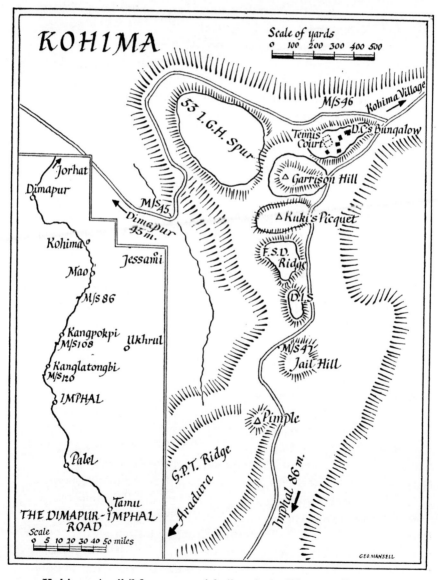

52. Kohima, April/May 1944, with (inset) the Dimapur/Imphal Road

wrote, "what with the Jap, the thick jungle, the hill and the weather, life was pretty unpleasant". The advance was none the less continued to combine with formations of the IV Corps from Imphal to cut off the Japanese line of retreat on the Chindwin, an operation in which the 2nd Division's task was to drive straight down the road to Imphal. The fighting advance, which quickened as it proceeded, began on 15th June. On the 22nd the Battalion had the honour of meeting the leading elements of the IV Corps at Milestone 108, so completing the first stage in the first major defeat inflicted on the Japanese in Burma. On 4th July the Battalion moved into camp near Milestone 86, where it remained until December.

Its losses at Kohima had been the heaviest in the Division. The names of over 150 from its ranks are inscribed on the divisional war memorial on Garrison Hill, and its sufferings and achievements in that noisome spot are deservedly remembered in the battle-honour *Kohima* which is borne upon the colours.

The Advance into Central Burma: Mandalay,
12th February-21st March 1945

Having administered a severe defeat on the Japanese 15th Army at Kohima and Imphal, General Slim retained the initiative in his plan for the 1945 campaign, which consisted of nothing less than advancing across the Chindwin, entering the Shwebo Plain and destroying the Japanese Army there, incidentally capturing Mandalay. While the 2nd Battalion was resting and refitting several bridgeheads across the Chindwin were established, namely at Sittang, Mawlaik and Kalewa. By the last-named the newly reorganised XXXIII Corps (2nd British, 20th Indian, the 268th Brigade and the 254th Tank Brigade) was to cross and then make for Shwebo from the north-west, while the IV Corps, issuing from Pakokku, approached Mandalay from the west and south, and the 19th Indian Division came down from the north.

The offensive started on 3rd December 1944. The Battalion, since July commanded by Lieut.-Colonel C. A. Southey, Essex Regiment, crossed the Chindwin River at Kalewa on the 13th and marched on to Shwegyin. Forcing its way out of the bridgehead with the 6th Brigade on the 20th, it advanced with A Company leading as far as Thetkegyin. Pinyang was passed, but the Battalion did not encounter any of the enemy until, having resumed the lead on 27th December, it reached the Sipadon Chaung. At Paga on the 28th it had a stiff fight with a detachment of the much respected Japanese 33rd Division, but the resistance was quickly overcome and the advance was continued down the Mandalay road to Kaduma, where the Battalion left the jungle for the first time in 500 miles and debouched into the plain of Central Burma on the 31st.

It resumed its advance on 15th January under Lieut.-Colonel Waterhouse, the only emergency commissioned officer to command a battalion in the Second War, marching, usually in single file, along the banks of the irrigation canals across the open rice bowl. "It must," writes Major Rissik, who served with it, "have smelt pretty opulent at this time as practically everybody was smoking the excellent Burma cheroots which were produced in the area at about three shillings a hundred." The crossing of the Irrawaddy was forced by the 5th Brigade at Ngazun in the night of 25th February. The Battalion itself crossed in *dukws* at 2.30 p.m. next day. Two sharp attacks were made by the Battalion to secure the bridgehead against an enemy who still fought to the death; but the men were old hands now and the casualties were not serious.

Meanwhile the IV Corps from the west had seized Meiktila and inflicted a decisive defeat on the Japanese Army there, while the other divisions of the XXXIII Corps were closing in on Mandalay from different directions, the 2nd being the last, as a matter of fact, to cross the Irrawaddy. Although the advance was strongly resisted the resistance was sporadic and unco-ordinated, and failed to hold up its progresss eastwards. The Battalion had several brushes with the enemy but none of them serious. Nor was it involved in the actual fighting in Mandalay itself, which was entered by the 4th and 5th Brigades.

After the fall of Mandalay, when the Battalion in its southward progress had reached Myingyan, the 2nd Division was withdrawn to India to act as a follow-up division in the amphibious assault on Rangoon. The Battalion was flown out of Burma on 7th April to Chittagong, where on the 28th, having been reorganised and re-equipped, it was embarked in the *Dilwara*. However, the convoy had got no farther than Ramree Island when it was learned that Rangoon had fallen to the first troops to land. The Battalion's disembarkation on 13th May was consequently a peaceful affair involving no more than a march through the streets to Jacob Barracks at Mingaladon.

It saw no further fighting. It was employed for two months in occupying villages down-river from Pegu, and even the attempted break out of the Japanese Army from the Pegu Yomas, the occasion of the last battle of the Burma Campaign, left it almost unaffected. On 15th August 1945 all organised resistance in Burma ceased with the surrender of Japan. By then most of the officers and men were due for repatriation. Those that remained were moved back to India in September to re-form.

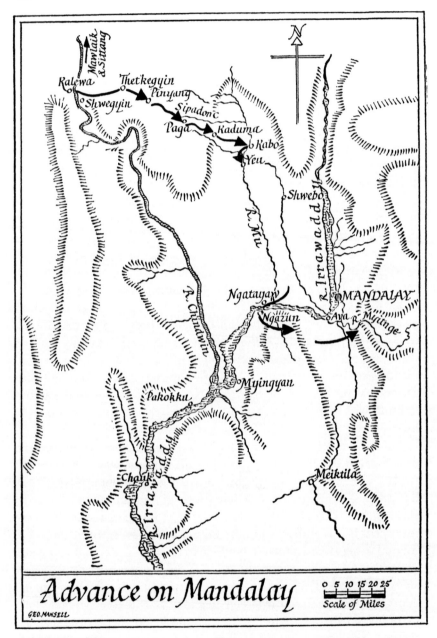

53. The Advance on Mandalay, December, 1944—February, 1945

From the Dyle to Rangoon: no other battalion suffered such vicissitudes of fortune, nor underwent so heart-searching a transformation as the 2nd. The fighting in Burma called for qualities in the individual to a degree which had not been experienced since the South African War. The extraordinary thing is that they were there. It took time to find them, as it had forty-five years before. But these men showed themselves as staunch and as adaptable as their grandfathers at Sanna's Post and Bothaville. There has yet to be found something which, given good commanders, these men cannot do.

CHAPTER XII

THE YEARS AFTER AND THE KOREAN WAR, 1945-1958

I F there is a consistent pattern in the history of British infantry after 1945 it is a pattern that is uncommonly difficult to discern. One thing is certain: the Cardwell System, on which we lived for so long, has been revealed as a luxury we can no longer afford even with conscription. At the moment armies are passing through a period of transition such as they have not experienced since the 16th and 17th Centuries. Then it lasted 150 years: what is a decade or two compared with that?

Once again the Regiment, with its quite singularly intimate connection with the County, has been spared some of the grosser changes. For the first few years after the war at any rate the pre-war routine was continued. The bare facts are these.

The 2nd Battalion remained in the Far East. Re-formed in India, it sailed on 15th November 1945 with the 2nd Division for Singapore, where the Division (less one brigade) assumed the duties of re-establishing order in Malaya. Stationed first at Singapore under Lieut.-Colonel W. Q. Findlater, Royal Irish Fusiliers, it was moved on 26th May 1946 to Seremban, where Major C. Fanning-Evans of the Regiment took over the command late in August. On 5th October it moved to Changi (the gaol on Singapore Island which acquired so baleful a reputation in the war), and on the 24th November to Majeedee Barracks at Johore Bahru. When the 2nd Division was broken up the Battalion, which had been under the command of Lieut.-Colonel F. H. Simpson since October, embarked for Burma, landing at Rangoon on 8th January 1947. In March it was moved up country to Tatkon to take part in operations against dacoits. On 12th May it went north to Maymyo. In anticipation of the independence of Burma, which was promulgated on 6th January 1948, the

Battalion was railed on 24th November 1947 to Rangoon, where it embarked for Singapore. So rapid was the turn-over of men at this period that when it landed on 30th November there were only thirty men remaining who had embarked with it at Singapore eleven months before. Since all line regiments had been reduced to a single battalion, and since the Regiment, in common with most others, had chosen the course of amalgamation rather than disband one battalion, only a cadre embarked for home on 19th January 1948, the remainder being posted to the 2nd King's Own Yorkshire Light Infantry. For six weeks after disembarkation at Liverpool on 18th February the cadre was stationed at Bicester; but on 1st April it was moved north to Brancepeth, where on 25th September, still under Lieut.-Colonel Simpson's command, it was amalgamated with the 1st Battalion.

In 1952, for three years, it enjoyed a precarious second existence. The Regiment was one of the seven[1] in the army which, containing the highest regular element, were selected to raise second battalions, and the new 2nd Durham Light Infantry was formed on 16th April 1952 at Barnard Castle from those 1st Battalion men who were in-eligible for foreign service. Commanded by Lieut.-Colonel K. M. W. Leather, whose father's services have already been mentioned as well as his own, it had attained by 8th May a strength of eight officers, twenty warrant officers and sergeants and 57 other n.c.o.s and men, which was later made up to establishment from the National Service intake. On 2nd December it left for Wuppertal, where it replaced the 1st Royal Scottish Fusiliers in the old 6th Brigade of the 2nd Division. It soon acquired a good reputation, particularly for sport, winning for the Regiment, for the first time since 1913, the Army Football Cup in 1955. But it was not destined to endure for long. Its doom foreshadowed in the Queen's Speech of 1954, it returned from Germany to Brancepeth on 7th June 1955; a solemn farewell service was held in Durham Cathedral on 10th July; and on 18th July the disbandment began by the departure of the first company to join the 1st Battalion at Barnard Castle.

The 1st Battalion is consequently the only battalion to have an unbroken history since 1945. Its last four months in Italy were spent under the command of Lieut.-Colonel May at Salsomaggiore before it embarked at Taranto on 6th January 1946 for Greece, where, landing at Salonika, it was stationed at Xanthi, at first under the command of Lieut.-Colonel R. B. Y. Simpson. Commanded temporarily from July to November by Major J. G. G. Gray and from

[1]Green Howards, Lancashire Fusiliers, Royal Welch Fusiliers, Royal Inniskilling Fusiliers, Black Watch, Sherwood Foresters and Durham Light Infantry.

November by Lieut.-Colonel R. F. Kirby, it returned to Salonika on 19th February 1947 for a year, embarking on 24th June 1948 for Liverpool, where it landed on 23rd July. After six months at Monkton Farleigh near Bath, latterly (10th October) commanded by Lieut.-Colonel F. H. Simpson (who thus shares with his brother the distinction of having commanded both battalions), it left on 6th January 1949 for Dortmund. In July that year it had a strength of 38 officers and 543 n.c.o.s and men. Lieut.-Colonel J. M. Hanmer, who succeeded to the command on 15th December 1949, took the Battalion on 4th April 1951 to Berlin, where it gained a high reputation. Losing many men to the re-formed 2nd Battalion who were replaced by men from other light infantry regiments, it returned to Brancepeth on 1st June 1952. At Bellerby, where it removed shortly after, the command was assumed by Lieut.-Colonel P. J. Jeffreys, who on 28th July 1952 embarked the Battalion for active service in Korea and commanded it throughout that very creditable episode in its history. Early in September 1953 it arrived from Korea at Moascar on the Suez Canal, where Lieut.-Colonel May took over the command on 5th November. On 26th May 1955 the Battalion embarked at Port Said for Liverpool, where it landed on 6th June. It was at Barnard Castle when the next month it amalgamated with the disbanded 2nd Battalion to form a single corps with a strength of over 1100 all ranks. The Suez Operation of the autumn of 1956 did not leave it undisturbed. Under Lieut.-Colonel R. G. Atkinson, who succeeded to the command on 5th November 1955, it was flown suddenly at 48-hours' notice on 4th November 1956 to Aden against possible employment in Kuwait. Though it had returned by mid-February 1957, a company-group under Major D. Fenner was detained in Beihan, where, dispatched to assist in repelling a Yemeni incursion in the Wadi Harib area, it contributed by its prompt and effective action towards restoring British prestige in that quarter. The Battalion remained at Barnard Castle until it left for Cyprus in August 1958.

Korea, September 1952-September 1953

When the 1st Battalion landed at Pusan under Lieut.-Colonel P. J. Jeffreys on 7th September 1952 operations in Korea had become almost completely static on the 38th Parallel. The armistice negotiations, which had been opened at Panmunjom on 10th July 1951, had been proceeding for over a year; and during its tour of duty with the Commonwealth Division—in which it relieved the 1st King's Shropshire Light Infantry in the 28th Brigade—the Battalion neither shared in any offensive nor took part in any of the famous defensive

actions. Yet, in ten months in which the usual dramatic manifesta-
tions of war were so conspicuously absent, the Battalion contrived to
win three Military Crosses and three Military Medals;[2] and it sustained a total of 148 casualties (including two company commanders
and 21 other officers, n.c.o.s and men killed, and 3 missing), losses
approaching those suffered in the whole of the Boer War.

It is only one of the apparent contradictions in one of the most
singular campaigns the Regiment has fought in. From 11th September when the Battalion first entered the line, which for tactical
reasons lay rather forward of the 38th Parallel, the Commonwealth
Division made no attempt to force the Chinese positions. On the
other hand, throughout the Panmunjom negotiations the Chinese
and North Koreans continued to direct offensives, usually synchron-
ised with the pressing of some important demand, with a view to
either a break-through or some limited tactical gain. Against any
surprise movement it was essential to keep the enemy at a distance
sufficient to enable the artillery to break up the Chinese mass attack
before it reached the line. Where a valley intervened the task was not
unduly difficult. But both at The Hook, on the extreme left of the
divisional sector, and at Point 355, on the extreme right, a ridge was
shared with the enemy, a situation of which the Chinese, indefatigable diggers, took advantage by digging farther and farther forward
until their standing patrols lay just beyond the front line of wire.
Most of the Battalion's casualties were sustained during the ceaseless patrolling activity by which it succeeded in securing such an
ascendancy in No Man's Land that it never had its positions overrun
nor suffered any major attack to be launched against it.

Just before the Battalion's arrival the enemy artillery had been
substantially augmented, and if serious losses were to be avoided
among the men in the trenches and weapon-pits on the forward slopes
of the razor-topped hills, extensive digging became as necessary as
patrolling. Traditionally a weak point of British infantry, digging was
a task at which the Durham battalion excelled. All the company
commanders had experience of war and knew its value. It was not
long before the crawl-trenches between section-posts and platoon
posts were made wide and deep enough for carrying stores and
stretchers; and shell-proof shelters were constructed to obviate the
men's retiring to their living dug-outs on the reverse slopes during a
bombardment. Some assistance in labour was obtained from the

[2]Military Crosses: 2/Lieutenant J. C. H. Cunningham (attached from the
K.O.Y.L.I.) 2/Lieutenant R. B. Macgregor-Oakford and Major R. E. Scott.
Military Medals: Lance-corporal R. A. Moore, Private D. I. Rawlings and
Corporal R. Lofthouse (attached from K.O.Y.L.I.). Lieut.-Colonel P. J. Jeffreys
received a bar to his D.S.O.

Korean porters in the Battalion, just as the Chinese relied heavily on coolie labour for the elaborate works in their own lines. It was usual also towards the end of the war for each battalion to possess some sixty "Katcoms" (or "Koreans attached Commonwealth Division") who, borne on the strength, on the whole made a useful addition to its fighting capacity.

The forward troops slept by day and worked by night. "We got up at 4.p.m.," writes a company commander, "and had a meal and then worked through until 9 the following morning. The men had breakfast at dawn, then washed and shaved, and there was an inspection at all levels within the company before they dossed down and went to bed in their dug-outs on the reverse slopes. Only the administrative element of the company (the second-in-command, the C.Q.M.S. and the platoon sergeants) were up and about during the day." The reserve companies, which found the fighting and reconnaissance patrols, could also follow a day routine, if need be studying and rehearsing their night tasks in daylight behind the forward positions.

If the Battalion's existence thus much resembled the trench life of the First War, the Chinese varied it by peculiarities of their own. While, for instance, we commonly supplemented our defences by wire and minefields (which, incidentally, required constant patrolling to maintain intact), they dispensed with minefields and relied for protection on the depth of their dug-outs and the extent of their tunnels. If attacked they retired to their holes and called down artillery and mortar fire on top. Skilled night-fighters, they were quick to detect any regular movement, and a favourite trick was to lay an ambush, say at a minefield gap, to catch a returning patrol. One of their night attacks, launched against the South Korean Division on the Battalion's immediate right, was carried out by Chinese troops who must have crossed No Man's Land the previous evening and lain up on the near side of the valley all day. To combat the enemy's skill at night-fighting the Battalion most commonly resorted to the ambush-patrol, which exploited the natural advantage the watcher has over the man that moves, besides reducing the initial disadvantage suffered by any British battalion largely composed of National Servicemen accustomed to a town life. Patrols were issued with bullet-proof vests (latterly on a scale of about thirty per company) as a protection not so much against small arms fire as against fragments from the heavy mortar-fire with which the minefield gaps were treated whenever a patrol was spotted.

The key sectors of Point 355 and The Hook were not entrusted to the Battalion until after the Division had returned from the period of rest in corps reserve, which it received in the last days of January until early April 1953. Before that it had spells on the Neachon feature and at Points 201 and 159. The latter was a sector always subjected to heavy shelling, and it was a mark of the Battalion's skill that the American unit which relieved it on the Point suffered such heavy casualties that it had to be taken out before its turn. It was here also that the Battalion had the misfortune to lose on 2nd January Major C. P. Donoghue, commanding A Company, killed on a minefield. When a young private soldier in the Battalion before the Second War he had revealed himself as a welterweight boxer of outstanding merit, and while holding a commission in the 8th Battalion he had won the Military Cross before being captured in the fighting round Matruh. He was the second company commander to go, Major J. W. Kelley, who had distinguished himself in Burma, having already been wounded during the first ten days in the line.

After the bleak discomforts of the rest camp at Camp Casey even the dug-outs and the heavy responsibilities of Point 355 came as a relief. The American unit from which the Battalion took over had allowed the Chinese to run about No Man's Land as if they owned the place, and it took some time before a proper state of affairs was re-established. Most of the patrol clashes took place at this time. In one Major J. A. Tresawna, a very capable and popular company commander attached from the Oxfordshire and Buckinghamshire Light Infantry, with whom he had won the D.S.O. at Gemmano, lost his life on 10th June 1953. A forward position in the sector, Surrey Hills, was subjected to a vigorous probe in the night of 22nd/23rd June, in the repulse of which Major R. E. Scott, commanding D Company, distinguished himself. But Point 355 was also the scene of a pleasing act of effrontery. On the occasion of the Coronation (2nd June), not only did the men give three cheers from their pits and the artillery fire red, white and blue smoke, but a platoon from Major Atkinson's (B) Company under Lieutenant W. J. Nott-Bower pegged out, during the previous night's patrol, the letters EIIR in fluorescent aircraft recognition-panels on the Chinese side of the valley.

When the armistice was signed on 27th July 1953 the Battalion was in reserve in the Hook position, which it occupied after holding a sector on the right of The Hook on Yong Dong, overlooking the River Samichon. By that time it had acquired the reputation of being perhaps the best battalion in the Division, steady and alert in the line, well disciplined and well turned out. Alongside two very good Australian battalions, in a brigade commanded and staffed—with outstanding ability—largely by Australians, it did credit to the high standards demanded of it by both the second-in-command, Major C. R. W. Norman, and its commanding officer, Lieut.-Colonel

Jeffreys, who had never spared himself from the moment he had first joined the Regiment in India twenty years before.

The Bi-Centenary, 17th May 1958

In 1958, when the Regiment celebrated the two hundredth anniversary of the day it began an independent existence as His Majesty's 68th Regiment of Foot, it consisted of three battalions. There was the lineal descendant of the 68th, the 1st Battalion, stationed at Barnard Castle under Lieut.-Colonel R. G. Atkinson. There were two battalions of Territorial infantry, the 6th and the 8th. There were, besides, two regiments of anti-aircraft artillery and a Territorial parachute battalion still mindful of their D.L.I. past. In Lambton's place there stood the Colonel, Major-General J. H. N. Poett, then Commandant of the Staff College. And, occupying a situation unknown in Lambton's day there was one of its newest members, certainly the most decorative officer ever to be gazetted to it, H.R.H. Princess Alexandra of Kent, who had been appointed Colonel-in-Chief on 24th December 1957.

It should be explained that the Territorial battalions had all been re-raised after the war. The 6th and 8th had been re-raised in March 1947 by Lieut.-Colonel Watson and Lieut.-Colonel G. L. Wood, and although recruiting was slow at first sufficiently satisfactory progress was made for the 151st Brigade to be re-formed. The 9th, which had got to Berlin before being withdrawn to Unna in the Ruhr and disbanded at Hemer on 16th October 1946, had been re-raised at the same time as the others by Lieut.-Colonel J. C. Slight, but had left the Brigade on becoming in July 1948 the 17th Parachute Battalion in the 5th (Territorial) Parachute Brigade. The former 5th and 7th Battalions, though their histories had diverged from the Regiment's on their conversion (*cf. p.* 460 *sup.*), had never severed their connections. The 1/5th, as the 54th Searchlight Regiment, R.A., had disembarked at Arromanches on 16th November 1944 and had seen active service in Belgium. The 2/5th, as the 113th Light Anti-Aircraft Regiment R.A. (D.L.I.), had served with 21st Army Group from Normandy until at the end it received the ungrateful duty of clearing up the infamous concentration-camp at Belsen. The 7th Battalion, which in 1942 became the 112th Light Anti-Aircraft Regiment, R.A., had crossed to France on 25th June 1944 and had had the distinction of being the first artillery unit to cross the Rhine on 24th March 1945. All three had been re-raised in April 1947: the 1/5th as the 589th Searchlight Regiment, R.A. (D.L.I.), the 2/5th as the 590th Light Anti-Aircraft Regiment, R.A. (D.L.I.), both being reunited in 1955 to form the 437th Light Anti-Aircraft Regi-

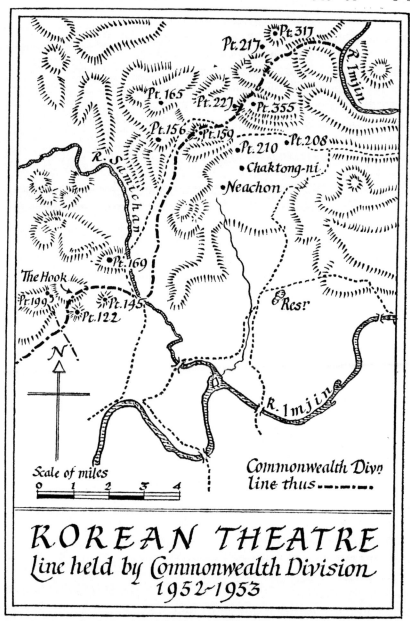

54. The Korean Theatre

ment, R.A. The 7th was re-raised first as the 582nd Light Anti-Aircraft/Searchlight Regiment, R.A. (D.L.I.), becoming later, in 1955, the 463rd (7th D.L.I.) Light Anti-Aircraft Regiment, R.A. (T.A.). The cumbersome title of the last-named conceals what in fact is an amalgamation of the descendants of the old Sunderland Volunteer Artillery and the Sunderland Volunteer Infantry.

The arrangements for the Bi-Centenary Parade were in the hands of a committee under the chairmanship of Lieut.-Colonel G. K. Stobart, himself a Durham Light Infantryman whose ancestors, long resident in the County, had given their services to the Regiment, the County Militia and the Volunteers. The affecting ceremony took place at Brancepeth Castle on Saturday, 17th May. To heighten the County quality of the occasion a new 2-6-2 V2 Type locomotive (whose driver and fireman had both served in the Regiment), which had been named *Durham Light Infantry* at Durham Station the previous 29th April, was available to draw the Princess's train when she arrived at Brancepeth that morning. She arrived at the Castle at 10.45. Parties from the 437th Regiment (5th Battalion), the 463rd Regiment (7th Battalion) and the 17th Parachute Battalion (9th Battalion) lined the road from the lodge gates to the parade ground. There, on the lawns facing the Castle the 1st, 6th and 8th Battalions, with their massed bands and bugles, were drawn up in their positions, to be reminded by words of the gracious young lady who addressed them of the dedicated services of their military forebears, which had preserved the Regiment for such a ceremony as this and for the thanksgiving service in Durham Cathedral that followed in the afternoon.

How very different from the scene at Cowes two hundred years before, when the new battalion, of awkward little "Jonases" in ill-fitting clothing and old soldiers wearing their red coats with an air, rose from its sodden tents to go on its first campaign. No massed bands then, no royal princess to grace that occasion: only some pre-occupied (and not very pretty) officers, the fifes screaming derisively the "Girl I left behind me," and, in the background, the transports at anchor, rising and falling slowly to a heavy swell.

Alas, it is the sodden tents and crowded transports that are the realities of the military life. The rest are but brief pauses in the midst of a long sequence of many episodes, at which an association of men reflects for a moment on its past and refreshes itself for the duties it must carry out on the morrow. It should not ponder too deeply. But it should remember that but for its Lambtons, its Paulets, its Freels, its Sheas, and the many other thousands who have held it dear and devoted their lives to it, there would be no morrow.

INDEX

567

574

INDEX

Waterhouse, Major W. S., 552, 555
Watson, Lieut.-Col. H. C., 262, 323, 348
Watson, Col. W. I., 263, 467, 493, 502-503, 564
Wavell, F. M. Archibald, 1st Earl, 453
Way, Lieut. A. S., 282, 303, 310, 311, 317
Wedderburn, Brigadier-General David, 46 & n.
Wesley, John, 7
Wiehe, Col. F. G. A., 335, 546
Wiehe, Lieut.-Col. G. I., 335, 356, 357, 466, 546
Wilkinson, Lieut.-Col. H. B. des V., 281, 305
Winniett, Major James, 77, 81, 102, 108, 121
Wood, Lieut.-Col. G. L., 467, 497, 529, 543, 564

Woodcock, Lieut. E. M., 229, 230, 235 240
Woodland, Col. A. L., 285-286, 298, 300, 316
Woods, Lieut.-Col. H. R., 529, 534
Worrall, Lieut.-Col. D. H. C., 514, 521, 526
Worrall, Capt. E. W. H., 497
Wynne, Major H. G., 151, 156n., 164, 166, 168, 208
Wynter, Major T. R., 217-218

Yate, Brig. V. A. C., 337n., 451, 458, 468
Youens, 2/Lieut. Frederick, 387n.
Young, Private T., 405
Ypres, 344-353, 385-391